Information Systems Project Management: A Process and Team Approach

Mark A. Fuller
Washington State University

Joseph S. Valacich
Washington State University

Joey F. George
Florida State University

PEARSON
Prentice
Hall

Upper Saddle River, NJ 07458

Library of Congress Cataloging-in-Publication Data

Fuller, Mark A.
    Information systems project management: a process and team approach/
Mark A. Fuller, Joseph S. Valacich, Joey F. George.
        p.   cm.
    ISBN-10: 0-13-145417-X (alk. paper)
    ISBN-13: 978-0-13-145417-0 (alk. paper)
    1. Project management.   2. Information resources management.   I. Valacich,
Joseph S., 1959–   II. George, Joey F.   III. Title
    HD69.P75F85 2008
    004.068′4—dc22

                                                                            2006102281

AVP/Executive Editor: Bob Horan
VP/Editorial Director: Jeff Shelstad
Manager, Product Development:
    Pamela Hersperger
Assistant Editor: Ana Jankowski
Editorial Assistant: Kristen Varina
Product Development Manager,
    Media: Nancy Welcher
Marketing Assistant: Laura Cirigliano
Associate Director, Production
    Editorial: Judy Leale
Senior Managing Editor:
    Cynthia Zonneveld
Senior Production Editor: Carol Samet
Permissions Coordinator:
    Charles Morris
Associate Director, Manufacturing:
    Vinnie Scelta

Manufacturing Buyer: Diane Peirano
Cover Design: Bruce Kenselaar
Cover Illustration/Photo:
    Getty Images.com
Director, Image Resource Center:
    Melinda Patelli
Manager, Rights and Permissions:
    Zina Arabia
Manager, Visual Research: Beth Brenzel
Image Permission Coordinator:
    Kathy Gavilanes
Photo Researcher: Teri Stratford
Composition: Integra Software Services
Full-Service Project Management:
    Elaine Lattanzi, BookMasters Inc.
Printer/Binder: Von Hoffman Graphics,
    Owensville
Typeface: Palatino 10/12

Credits and acknowledgments borrowed from other sources and reproduced, with
permission, in this textbook appear on appropriate page within text.

Microsoft® and Windows® are registered trademarks of the Microsoft Corporation
in the U.S.A. and other countries. Screen shots and icons reprinted with permission
from the Microsoft Corporation. This book is not sponsored or endorsed by or affili-
ated with the Microsoft Corporation.

Pearson Education LTD.
Pearson Education Singapore, Pte. Ltd
Pearson Education, Canada, Ltd
Pearson Education–Japan

Pearson Education Australia PTY, Limited
Pearson Education North Asia Ltd
Pearson Educación de Mexico, S.A. de C.V.
Pearson Education Malaysia, Pte. Ltd.

10 9 8 7 6 5 4 3 2 1
ISBN-13: 978-0-13-145417-0
ISBN-10:   0-13-145417-X

DEDICATION

To my wonderful wife Tanya, whose love steadies me during life's ups and downs, and to my daughters Emma and Grace, who constantly remind me of what life is about.

Mark Fuller

To Jackie, Jordan, James, and the rest of my family. Your love and support are my greatest inspiration.

Joe Valacich

To my family: Karen, Evan, and Caitlin

Joey George

PHOTO CREDITS

Chapter 1: page 3, NASA/Johnson Space Center; page 4, Jeff Greenberg/Omni-Photo Communications, Inc.; page 8, John Huseby/District 4 Photography/California Department of Transportation–Photography Department; page 19, Dorling Kindersley Media Library; page 20 (top), Bureau of Reclamation; page 20 (bottom), National Atomic Museum Foundation.

Chapter 2: page 75, Hong Kong Airport Authority/AP Wide World Photos.

Chapter 3: page 78, Canadian Space Agency.

Chapter 4: page 138, Steve Niedorf Photography/Getty Images Inc.–Image Bank; page 140 (top), Polycom Inc.; page 140 (bottom), Logitech Inc.; page 141, Microsoft Corporation; page 144, Groupsystems.com.

Chapter 5: page 156, Leif Skoogfors/CORBIS-NY.

Chapter 7: page 242, Sonda Dawes/The Image Works.

Chapter 8: page 283, TRONIC'S Microsystems; page 284, NASA Headquarters; page 286, The W. Edwards Deming Institute.

Chapter 9: page 316, David McNew/Getty Images; page 320 (left) Sergei Karpukhin/AP Wide World Photos; page 320 (right) Jorge Uzon/AFP/Getty Images, Inc.–Agence France Presse; page 331, Cathy Spann/Groupsystems.com.

Chapter 10: page 349, Colin Hawkins/Getty Images Inc.–Stone Allstock.

Chapter 11: page 384, John P. Kelly/Getty Images Inc.–Image Bank.

BRIEF CONTENTS

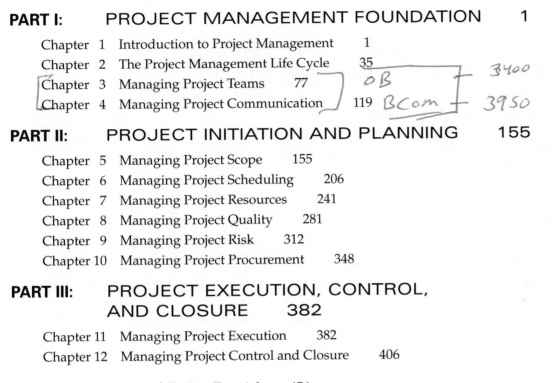

CONTENTS

PREFACE

Projects involving information systems are prevalent in virtually all organizations and are frequently a key determinant of an organization's competitiveness. The ability to manage these projects is thus a critical skill that can help drive organizational success. Projects in today's business environment are typically addressed by teams of skilled personnel whose activities are coordinated by a project manager. Further, these projects may involve significant global components, either in terms of the resultant system's intended users or in terms of the team members engaged in accomplishing the project itself.

Based on nearly 40 years of combining teaching experience plus extensive experience in the high-technology sector, the authors provide the knowledge and skills necessary to successfully manage information systems projects in the modern organization. This book takes an active learning approach to project management, where the focus is on the process of project management rather than simply on a series of topical discussions about the components of project management. It operates on the assumption that project management in the modern organization is a complex, team-based process which relies on software that supports both project management and collaboration activities. Further this book assumes that, in many cases, project teams may be operating in a virtual context, where team members are at different locations—sometimes across the world. Our approach to project management thus tries to encompass the new working arrangements in our technology-driven global economy. Finally, the content of this book is firmly grounded on the Project Management Body of Knowledge as provided by the Project Management Institute, which provides training and certifications to project managers world wide. Our approach to learning project management thus emphasizes five key focal areas: process focus, team focus, technology focus, global focus, and Project Management Body of Knowledge focus.

Process Focus

Unlike the more common approach to learning project management that exposes the student to a variety of project management subtopics, this book employs a *learn-by-doing* approach that actively engages the student in *managing a real information systems project* as part of the class. After presenting foundational material in the first four chapters, we take you step-by-step through the stages of project management, with assignments corresponding to deliverables that typically would be required in an organization as employees tackle real information systems projects. While still covering the essential information associated with project management, this book also helps you actively learn project management by applying typical project management activities—such as the development of project charters, work breakdown structures, and project schedules—to an ongoing class project. This contextual treatment of information systems project management topics not only solidifies your understanding of various project management techniques, but also creates an immediate understanding of why these techniques are critical to effective project management.

Team Focus

Project management is largely a team sport, not an individual one. This book is unique in its focus on team-based project management. Although an individual working alone can gain some knowledge, the reality is that few organizational projects are done this way; thus, knowledge acquired without consideration of the team is largely incomplete. This book covers the types of groups in organizations, the types of tasks those groups work on, the advantages gained by working in groups, and the problems (and solutions) that groups will encounter. Topics addressed include group processes, leadership, communication, group conflict, cross-cultural issues, and so on.

Technology Focus

To successfully manage projects in today's complex business environments requires project teams to employ technologies such as project management software, group support technology, and organizational memory systems that capture project knowledge. The advantages of project planning software are discussed, and you will be given hands-on experience using common project planning software. You will then use this same project planning software to support your course project. Group support technologies include the various communication and planning tools that project teams can use. In addition to discussing such tools throughout the text, we pay particular attention to this topic in Chapter 4 which focuses on managing project communications. These collaborative technologies enable groups to communicate effectively across distance and time, reduce the losses associated with working in groups, and enhance the group's decision-making. Finally, organizational memory systems help project teams to capture and recall knowledge accumulated from previous project teams and to update such knowledge management systems with current project experiences.

Global Focus

Project management in today's organizations is global. In addition to the inherent difficulties of working in teams, workers in today's organizations may no longer work in the same office, building, or even country as other project team members. The global virtual project team is a common organizational entity, and managing teams in this type of environment is even more complex. We address the unique advantages of virtual teams, the difficulties they encounter, and solutions to those difficulties. Project management is global in another sense as well. We live in a global economy, and outputs created by project teams may be intended for a global audience. As a result, project teams need to be sensitive to cultural differences when developing information systems applications.

Project Management Body of Knowledge Focus

One critical purpose of this textbook is to provide you with a high level of competency in all key areas of project management. The Project Management Institute (PMI)—a professional organization focused on meeting the needs of project managers—has encapsulated the key knowledge areas of project management into its Project Management Body of Knowledge (PMBOK). This text prepares you to master these knowledge areas and provides information consistent with PMI's professional project management certification exam. To facilitate your use of this book as a study guide, the end of each chapter also provides a table identifying the elements of the PMBOK that each chapter has covered. By the conclusion of the textbook, you will have been exposed in detail to all the knowledge areas identified by the PMBOK.

AUDIENCE

While *project management* is a general term and can be applied in many fields, this text is written specifically to address information systems projects. This textbook is targeted primarily at upper-division undergraduate students pursuing a management information systems or related degree. The treatment of project management material is also detailed enough for this book to be useful for graduate courses as well. Finally, this text, because of its close ties to the Project Management Body of Knowledge, can also serve as useful study guide in preparation for PMI certification.

COMMON CHAPTER ELEMENTS

Each chapter has an opening case, learning objectives, and a roadmap—in Gantt chart form—that illustrates where the chapter fits in the book's overall framework. Following this, an introduction briefly reviews previously covered material and provides an overview of what the current chapter covers. The main chapter contents are then presented, followed by an illustration of which PMBOK topics were covered, a running case illustrating the conversations and activities a typical project team might have during the relevant project management phase, a chapter summary, key terms, review questions, chapter exercises, an ongoing real business case (focused on the Sedona Management Group and the Seattle Seahawks) appropriate to the relevant chapter, and an ongoing information systems project that allows student teams to reinforce newly acquired project management techniques. This latter project is intended to give you hands-on experience managing all phases of the project life cycle.

KEY FEATURES

In addition to the standard elements, each chapter includes highlighted elements entitled Tips from the Pros, Ethical Dilemmas, Common Problems, and Global Implications. The composition of each element reflects the current chapter content, and helps you prepare for the intricacies of managing information systems projects.

Tips from the Pros

Tips from the Pros contain tips or information used by real project managers that describe what they do to make their projects successful and the pitfalls that experience has taught them to avoid.

Ethical Dilemmas

Ethical Dilemmas discuss some of the ethical questions faced by project managers or members of project teams as they try to achieve their goals.

Common Problems

Common Problems discuss barriers that project team members will frequently face and how to overcome them.

Global Implications

Global Implications address how project characteristics and management techniques vary as project teams cope with global outsourcing, off-shoring, and international project teams.

SUPPLEMENTS

The following support materials are available on the Web and on the Instructor's Resource CD-ROM.

- *Instructor's Manual.* The Instructor's Manual features not only answers to review, discussion, case study, and group project questions but also in-depth lecture outlines, teaching objectives, key terms, teaching suggestions, and Internet resources.
- *Test Item File and TestGen.* The Test Item File is a collection of true–false, multiple-choice, fill-in-the-blank, and essay questions.
- *PowerPoint Slides.* The slides build on key concepts in the text.
- *Image Library.* The Image Library is a resource that helps instructors create vibrant lectures. The images and lecture notes can be easily imported into Microsoft PowerPoint to create new presentations or to add to existing ones.
- *Project Management Templates.* These online templates help the students structure the various project management deliverables needed throughout the project lifecycle.

Microsoft Project 2003 is available separately as a value-pack option with this text. Please contact your sales representative for ordering information.

ORGANIZATION

This book is divided into three major parts. Part I, "Project Management Foundations," includes chapters introducing the discipline of project management, the project management life cycle, the management of project teams, and finally how to manage project communications with all project stakeholders. Part II, "Project Initiation and Planning," includes chapters on managing various critical project activities such as project scope, activity scheduling, resource assignment and project duration implications, project quality, project risk, and project procurement. Part III, "Project Execution, Control, and Closure," includes chapters on managing project execution, as well as on managing project control and closure processes.

Part I: Project Management Foundations

The purpose of Part I is to help you understand the foundations of information systems project management.

In Chapter 1, "Introduction to Project Management," we discuss the defining characteristics of projects. We then discuss the significance and meaning of project

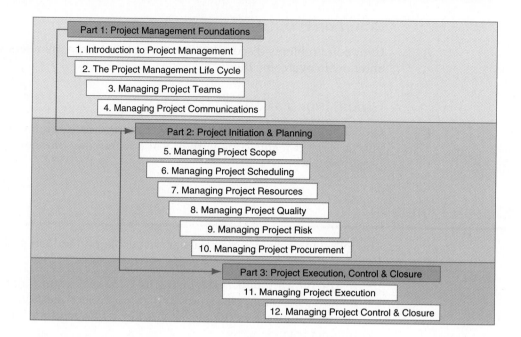

failure, and we detail what helps make projects a success. Next, we explain what differentiates information systems (IS) projects from non-IS projects and describe the history of modern project management, as well as some of the key terminology, techniques, and tools used in project management today. Finally, we discuss how this book applies a multi-faceted approach to the topic of information systems project management through its consideration of process, team, technology, global, and PMBOK perspectives to managing such projects.

In Chapter 2, "The Project Management Life Cycle," we define the project management life cycle and compare it with the information systems development life cycle. We also explore the business context in which project management occurs. We also introduce Gantt charts and project network diagrams and discuss the various types of project management software that can benefit project managers. Finally, we discuss project management processes and describe the various activities that occur in each.

In Chapter 3, "Managing Project Teams," we discuss the distinctive nature of team-based project management. Topics such as motivation, leadership, power, and conflict management in project teams are all explored. Finally, we discuss the concept of global project teams and the unique characteristics of such teams and how to manage them.

Chapter 4, "Managing Project Communication," describes the various types of project communications, including communication planning, information distribution, performance reporting, and administrative closure. In addition, we discuss various methods for enhancing team communication and explain how to run an effective meeting, deliver effective presentations, become a better listener, utilize communication templates, and make walk-through presentations. Finally, we describe the various collaboration technologies that can enhance team communications.

The four chapters in Part I explain the key foundational knowledge areas necessary to better manage information systems projects in team environments. All subsequent chapters in this book will rely heavily on this material.

Part II: Project Initiation and Planning

The purpose of Part II is to help you understand how project managers initiate projects, schedule projects, and manage project resources while paying attention of risk and quality issues.

In Chapter 5, "Managing Project Scope," we discuss organizational processes for identifying and selecting new projects. The process of project selection does not focus on one specific project but, rather, on choosing from a variety of project opportunities available to the organization. We discuss the project initiation process, including how to identify, rank, and select information systems projects. In addition, we introduce the concept of the project charter and the role that the project charter serves in an organization. Next we explain project-scope planning, which includes information on how to develop the project workbook and scope statement, as well as the baseline project plan. We end with a discussion of scope definition and verification and introduce the concept of change control.

In Chapter 6, "Managing Project Scheduling," we discuss the project management processes related to scheduling project activities. Project scheduling is one of the project manager's most critical activities. The project schedule enables project managers to determine how long each task will take, the critical path for the project, and consequently, how long completing the project will take. In this chapter we discuss the fundamentals, characteristics, and challenges related to project scheduling. We also identify the various phases of project schedule development, as well as the various techniques and tools used to develop project schedules.

In Chapter 7, "Managing Project Resources," we discuss the various techniques that project managers use to assign and manage resources, and the implications of such resource assignments on project schedules and overall project duration. We define the concept of project resources, discuss the various major types of project resources, and give examples of resources used during actual projects. In addition, we discuss why project resource management is critical for establishing project duration. Finally, we discuss the various techniques and tools that project managers can use to manage project resources.

In Chapter 8, "Managing Project Quality," we discuss the tools and techniques that project teams use to manage project quality across the entire project management life cycle. We define project quality, explain why it is important, and recount its history. We also discuss various quality management certifications and standards and the implications of poor quality management. Finally, we discuss the tools and techniques that allow project managers to manage project quality.

In Chapter 9, "Managing Project Risk," we discuss how project managers deal with the issue of project risk, something organizations deal with every day. Choices about which products to develop, which investments to make, which employees to hire, and which projects to undertake are all examples of organizational activities that involve risk. We discuss what risk is, how it can affect projects, and the techniques and tools project managers can use to address it.

In Chapter 10, "Managing Project Procurement," we discuss many choices currently available for systems development, including the use of information technology services firms, packaged software providers, vendors of enterprise-wide solution software, on-demand computing providers, and open-source software. We also discuss the very timely topic of outsourcing. We then detail the procurement process itself and the various steps it comprises.

The six chapters in Part II explain the key techniques that project managers need to know in order to choose projects, plan projects, and manage project issues such as resources, quality, risk, and procurement. These six chapters are the heart of the book.

Part III: Project Execution, Control, and Closure

The purpose of Part III is to help you understand how project managers execute, control, and close projects after the extensive planning that was covered in Part II.

In Chapter 11, "Managing Project Execution," we discuss the processes that organizations follow for executing projects after their extensive planning. We present the different project management processes that make up project execution in the PMBOK. The inputs, tools and techniques, and outputs of project execution are all discussed. We then cover the project manager's key duties during execution, namely monitoring progress and managing change (covered more thoroughly in Chapter 12). We discuss tools such as the kickoff meeting, as well as problems that are common to the execution of IT projects. We also cover two areas central to successful project execution: managing communication and documentation.

In Chapter 12, "Managing Project Control and Closure," we discuss possibly the most important issue for ensuring project management success, project control. How successful can your project be if after the planning is finished, you simply sit back and wait for the tasks to get completed? What happens if a critical task takes two weeks longer to complete than planned? How do you know if costs are running unexpectedly high? Could issues arise that affect the quality of your product or the project's risks? Are you even aware of these potential problems? Project control allows managers to identify and deal with the inevitable problems and promotes flexibility within the plan to allow for them. We discuss tools for controlling projects across the major project-management core areas already covered in Part II. We end this chapter by discussing another important, but often overlooked, aspect of project management, project closure. We cover the appropriate techniques for handing off projects, as well as the critical process for documenting project outcomes so that future project teams will have a better idea of what to expect.

The two chapters in Part III explain the key knowledge necessary to help project managers control projects for successful outcomes and then close out those projects in a way that benefits the clients and the project team. These final two chapters are where it all comes together. The techniques they cover are extremely useful in managing projects.

Appendix: Microsoft Project

The Microsoft Project appendix provides a tutorial on using Microsoft Project, showing how to use this technology to create many of the deliverables detailed in this textbook.

SUMMARY

Our approach is to teach project management by having you work on a project, creating not only the project itself but also the various project management deliverables associated with the typical stages of a project. We have stressed a team-based approach, paying attention to today's global project environment and the current body of knowledge associated with modern project management. We hope you find this book both interesting and useful.

Chapter

1

Introduction to Project Management

Opening Case: Bell Identifies a Potential Project for Phoenix Technologies

In 2002, Cliff Bell, Phoenix Technologies, Ltd. chief information officer, identified the need to improve the functionality of the company's intranet. During a routine perusal of the company's Taiwan office Web pages (see Figure 1.1), Bell noticed that the pages had last been modified sometime during the year 2000. He also noticed that the site, written in a traditional idiom used only on the Chinese mainland, did not include the dialect used by some of the company's Taiwanese office employees. Because Bell recognized this potential issue, a new project was eventually launched to address changes needed in the company's intranet.

Using project management techniques gained through a partnership with Allin Consulting, Phoenix Technologies, Ltd. completed a project that greatly improved the usability of the company's intranet. The site is now available in five languages, including both the mainland China and Taiwanese dialects. Additionally, the site was upgraded so that intranet users can now update Web pages themselves. This latter capability is a marked improvement over the previous process of having to put in a request for information technology personnel to make changes.

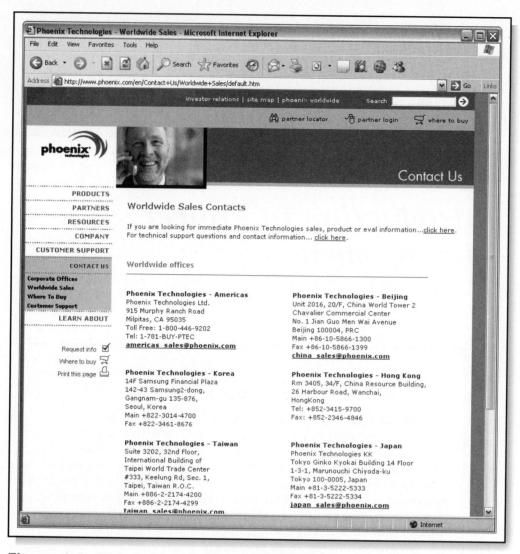

Figure 1.1 Web site for Phoenix Technologies, Ltd.

Source: Reproduced with permission from Phoenix Technologies, Ltd. www.phoenix.com

LEARNING OBJECTIVES

After reading this introductory chapter, you will be able to:

➤ Differentiate between projects and nonprojects, as well as understand the defining characteristics of a project.

➤ Understand reasons for both project failure and project success.

➤ Explain what differentiates IS projects from non-IS projects.

➤ Define key terms in project management and describe some of the tools and techniques used in project management.

➤ Understand the history of project management.

Designing the space shuttle (see Figure 1.2). Building the Golden Gate Bridge. Developing the Social Security Administration's national database on benefits. Planning a trip to the Rocky Mountains. Studying for your accounting final. All of these activities have something in common, and that something is that they are all projects. They all require a decision regarding their priority versus other potential projects. They all require a plan, the execution of that plan, and on completion, an assessment of how well the group or person doing the project followed the plan. All of these projects also eventually come to an end.

Projects can be extensive undertakings combining the resources of thousands of people (see Figure 1.3 for an example of such a project), or they can be simple endeavors requiring the attention of only one individual. They can last anywhere from several days to many years. Although most of us do not follow a specific methodology to do all of the things that might be classified as projects in our everyday lives, as projects grow in importance, complexity, and length, it becomes increasingly important for organizations to have systematic processes for managing them. This book is about how organizations and the people within them can effectively manage information systems projects.

In this chapter, you will learn what projects are and, conversely, what they are not. You will learn why the study of project management is important by examining some statistics regarding project failures, some specific examples of project failures, and finally, some possible causes of project failures. You will also gain a basic understanding of what can be done to help ensure project success. You will also learn about the specific nature of information systems projects, how all types of projects share many common elements but also how they all present unique challenges. We will then describe project management itself, as well as its history. You will also learn how technology can be used

Figure 1.2
Photo of Space
Shuttle

Figure 1.3
Photo of building
construction

to help manage projects and how technology can be classified. Finally, we will discuss the unique nature of this textbook and why we believe our method of studying project management will provide an extremely rich exposure to the topic (see Figure 1.4).

Figure 1.4   Information systems project management focusing on introduction to project management

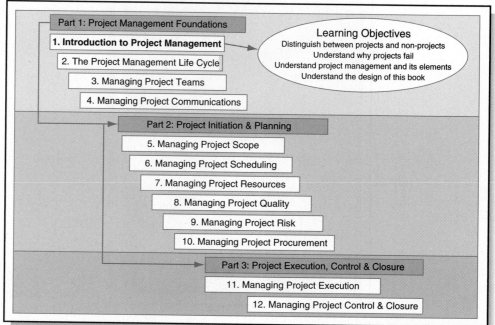

Depending upon the source, the definition of the term *project* may vary. As an example, the *New Oxford American Dictionary* defines a project as "an individual or collaborative enterprise that is carefully planned and designed to achieve a particular aim." Each project has a goal or specific purpose, a duration, and resource requirements such as money, people, infrastructure, and technology. The **Project Management Institute** (PMI), an association designed to bring together project management professionals and systematically capture project management knowledge, describes projects as unique, temporary endeavors designed to meet the specific needs of the project's stakeholders. For the purpose of this book, we've chosen a definition that incorporates dimensions of all of these descriptions, defining a **project** as "a planned undertaking of related activities to reach an objective that has a beginning and an end."

Projects are executed to meet a specific need for a stakeholder or group of stakeholders. **Stakeholders** are those entities that have a vested interest in a project, including project team members, project sponsors, stockholders, employees, and the community.

Projects are also temporary in that they begin and end on specific predetermined dates. Project teams are often formed at the beginning of a project and then disbanded at its completion, with team members being reassigned to new projects. As a result, project team dynamics are often different from the dynamics of other, more permanent teams such as those used in a production environment. Finally, projects need support from senior-level executives. A **project sponsor** is a member of the organization who is responsible for the high-level support of the project. The project sponsor has the responsibility of making sure the project is given the resources necessary to its successful completion. Resources can include personnel and facilities, as well as any other needs the project personnel may have.

In the 1980s, for example, the Social Security Administration created a plan for a national database (see Figure 1.5), a project focused on creating a completely new centralized database that would allow any U.S. citizen to call a 1–800 telephone number and talk with a representative. This representative could immediately access information on how much the caller had contributed toward their social security benefits and when they would be eligible for those benefits, as well as a host of other topics. This project was to be developed over 5 years at the cost of nearly $500 million. This effort had a goal, a proposed timeline for completion, project sponsors, and project stakeholders—including project team members, citizens, legislators, and Social Security employees. The development of the Social Security Administration's centralized database clearly meets the criteria of a project as defined above.

Business projects frequently have an assigned project manager. In information systems projects, the **project manager** needs a diverse set of skills—general management, leadership, technical, conflict management, and customer relationship management—and is responsible for initiating, planning, executing, and closing a project. A project manager's environment is one of continual change and problem solving. In some organizations, the project manager is a very experienced systems analyst, whereas in others, both junior and senior analysts are expected to take on this role, managing parts of a project, with the more junior member supporting and learning from a more senior colleague. Understanding the project management process is a critical skill for your future success. A project manager is often referred to

Project Management Institute
An association designed to bring together project management professionals and systematically capture project management knowledge.

Project
A planned undertaking of related activities to reach an objective that has a beginning and an end.

Stakeholder
A person who has an interest in a new or existing project.

Project sponsor
A member of the organization who is responsible for the high-level support of the project.

Project manager
A person with a diverse set of skills— general management, leadership, technical, conflict management, and customer relationship management— who is responsible for initiating, planning, executing, controlling and monitoring, and closing down a project.

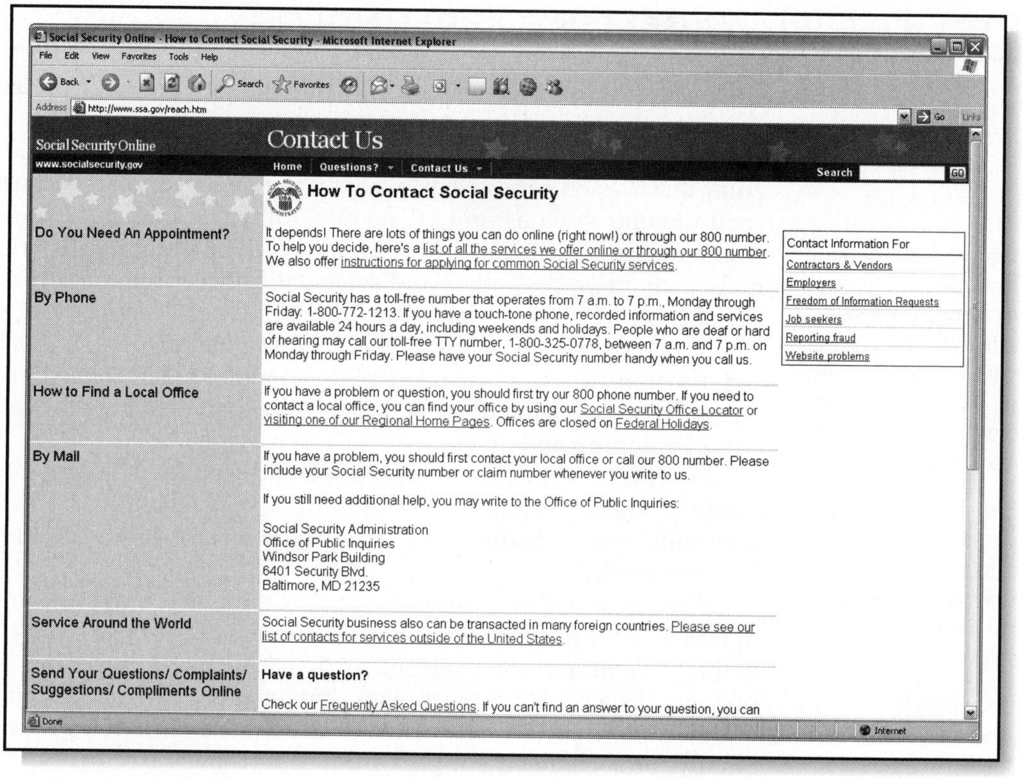

Figure 1.5 Screen shot of Social Security Administration contact page

as a juggler keeping aloft many balls that reflect the various aspects of a project's development. The project manager is instrumental to the successful completion of any project.

Information systems projects are undertaken for two primary reasons: to take advantage of business opportunities and to solve business problems. Taking advantage of an opportunity might mean providing an innovative service to customers through the creation of a new system. For example, a professional sports franchise may want to create a Web site so that customers can easily access its catalog of sports apparel and place orders at any time or purchase tickets for an upcoming sporting event online. Solving a business problem could involve modifying how an existing system processes data to provide users more accurate or timely information. For example, in order to reduce the number of telephone calls received by their sales staff this same professional sports franchise may want to provide ways for the potential customers to see exactly what seats are available in a stadium before they purchase tickets .

Once a potential project has been identified, a feasibility study may need to be conducted. This involves determining the resources required for the project's completion. To determine necessary resources, the scope of the project is analyzed and the probability of successful completion is determined. The organization can then use this information to decide whether taking advantage of an opportunity or solving a particular problem is feasible within time and resource constraints. If deemed feasible, a more detailed project analysis is then conducted. As you will see, the ability to determine the size, scope, and resource requirements of a project is just one of the many skills that a project manager must possess. All of these skills and related techniques will be covered in subsequent chapters.

Global Implications: U.S. Business Firms Look Overseas for IT Help

The growing demand for inexpensive yet competent programming talent is encouraging U.S. IT service providers to increase their use of overseas workers for certain types of tasks. "The technology skills needed to program in languages, such as C++, COBOL, and even Java, are available in China, the Philippines, Russia, and other countries, but offshore outsourcing is most mature in India. The Indian government has been supportive of IT for decades and has continued to improve on the solid educational systems built by the British," says Mukesh Mehta, VP of corporate systems for Metropolitan Life Insurance Company, which has an offshore-outsourcing contract with Cognizant Technology Solutions Corp. For instance, the Indian Parliament granted the Indian Institute of Technology its charter in 1961, and the school has evolved into a center for teaching, research, and industrial consulting.

Although India is the primary resource for offshore programmers and project managers, it is predicted that the demand for offshore workforce will soon outstrip the country's supply. A recent survey by India's National Association of Software and Services Companies (NASSCOM) has predicted that by 2008, 1 million IT workers will be needed in India, whereas India's IT workforce will grow to only 885,000 people. "A 25% cost savings on an outsourcing contract is a realistic goal when working with an offshore provider," according to Forrester analyst Christine Overby. Given this demand, as the labor costs in India continue to rise, companies might look to countries such as China, when thinking about offshoring their work.

To reduce the risk of outsourcing and to attract new clients, many offshore companies have management personnel in the United States who act as liaisons with overseas staff. The continued reliance on offshore talent by well-known service providers, such as Accenture, EDS, and IBM Global Services, also lends credence to the offshore model. In fact, a recent study by the Information Technology Association of America and Global Insight has estimated that in 2008 U.S. companies will spend $31 billion for global outsourcing of software and services, up from $10 billion in 2003. This translates into an increase from 2.3 percent to 6.2 percent of total corporate spending for software and services. According to the study, by 2008 the cost savings enabled by global outsourcing will add over $120 billion to the U.S. real gross domestic product.

What began more than a decade ago as an inexpensive way to supplement overworked internal application developers with workers from India has grown into a worldwide search for the right mixture of talent, resources, and cost savings to create and manage today's most complex IT environments. (Sources: Global Insight [2003], Chai [2003], Greenemeier [2002], Yamamoto [2004])

PROJECT FAILURES AND PROJECT SUCCESS

Did you know that the number of information technology project failures reported by U.S. businesses continues to outweigh those reported as successful? According to research conducted by the Standish Group (1994), companies report project failures at an alarming rate. The following statistics are based on five years' worth of data collected from a cross-section of large, medium, and small businesses and were reported as part of the Standish Group's findings (Booth, 2000).

- Roughly 40 percent of all IT projects fail to meet business requirements.
- The average cancelled IT project is scheduled to last 27 weeks and is cancelled on week 14, which results in at least $1 million spent each year on IT work that does not lead to successful business outcomes.
- The average IT organization annually ties up 10 percent of its IT staff on work that contributes no value to the business.
- Project team members are keenly aware of a project's doom a full 6 weeks before it is finally cancelled by management, who fail to recognize problems as quickly.
- When projects are failing, an average of 11 IT professionals end up coming to work and contributing nothing of value to the organization for those 6 weeks.

Examples of Project Failure

Project failures can take many forms. Project failures can be defined in terms of projects that finish over budget, projects that are not completed on time, and projects that may have been finished on time and on budget but failed to deliver a system that met stakeholder expectations. The following projects are among those that failed in at least one of these areas:

- Original project cost and time estimates for building the East Span of the San Francisco Bay Bridge (see Figure 1.6) proved to vastly underestimate actual figures. Originally planned for completion by 2007 at a cost of $780,000,000, this project is now expected to cost nearly $6.3 billion and be open to traffic in the year 2013. Further, project estimates continue to rise as material costs have continued to increase (ConstraCostaTimes.com, March 29, 2006).
- A $185 billion magnetic train project designed to connect Berlin and Hamburg was canceled due to environmental concerns, *after* millions had already been spent on the project (Ingbretsen, 2003).
- Sobeys Inc. (see Figure 1.7), Canada's second-largest grocery chain, abandoned attempts to implement a SAP designed **enterprise system** after a 5-day shutdown that affected the company's business operations for almost a month. The damage? An after-tax write-off of nearly $49 million (Mearian, 2001).
- FedEx began an ambitious business-to-business (B2B) project designed to integrate its massive supply chain. Two years later, the project broke ground;

Enterprise system
A comprehensive system designed to integrate systems from diverse parts of a business (also called an enterprise resource planning system, or ERP).

Figure 1.6
Photo of East Span San Francisco Bay Bridge

Figure 1.7 Sobey's Web site

however, after only another two years, the project was cancelled. The damage? $15 million and four years' time (*CIO*, 2001).

- Nash Finch Inc., a food wholesaler and supermarket operator, cancelled most of its ERP implementation and instead was forced to rely on a crash program allocating additional resources to fix the company's mainframe system. The damage? $50 million (Stedman, 1998).

- The failure of a data storage project so painful that the advisory project manager asked that the name of the organization be withheld was also reported in the *CIO* magazine article "The Secret to Software Success." The damage? Eight years, tens of millions of dollars, and the loss of 35 programmers.

Having established that projects in modern organizations still fail often, our next step is to attempt to identify why this happens.

Causes of Project Failure

Why do some IT projects succeed while many others fail? BULL, a French computer manufacturer, requested an independent research company to conduct a survey to identify the causes of IT project failures in the UK. The company surveyed 203 managers who were charged with taking a lead role in integrating large information

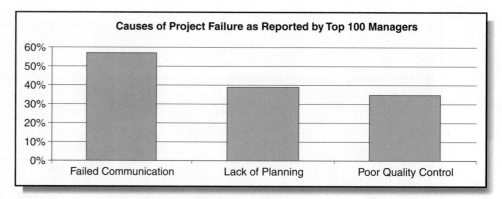

Figure 1.8 Project failure statistics

technology systems by companies listed in the *Times* 100 (see Figure 1.8). This survey identified the main causes of project failure as failed communication among parties (57%), lack of planning (39%), and poor quality control (35%) (IT Cortex, 2003).

Other surveys, such as the KPMG Canada survey, the CHAOS report, and the 1995 OASIG study (a special interest group in the UK concerned with the social and organizational aspects of information technology), have also reported findings associated with project failure. For example, in the OASIG study, 45 project management experts reported on what they perceived as the top five causes of project failure, none of which focus on technology issues, but rather focus on a number of social and organization issues (see Figure 1.9).

Failures can take place during any of the project management processes. For example, during the initiation phase, managers may select the wrong project by failing to establish a clear connection between a given project and the company's business strategy. During the planning process of project management, problems can occur due to failure to correctly estimate the cost, time, or complexity of the project. During the execution process, personnel carrying out the actual project activities can make mistakes that may also result in project failure. During the control process, managers can make errors when estimating either the expected or actual performance of the project. These incorrect estimations might result in an inaccurate picture of the project status. Finally, failures during closure can include closing down the project before the agreed-upon final deliverables have been handed over.

Project Success

What can be done to make a project a success? Although the answer to this question will be addressed throughout this textbook, simply put, good project management practices can enable companies to reduce both the causes of project failures and, ultimately, the

OASIG Report
Top five reasons for project failure

- Lack of attention to human and organizational factors
- Poor project management
- Poor articulation of user requirements
- Inadequate attention to business needs and goals
- Failure to involve users appropriately

Figure 1.9
Top five causes of project failure

It is a challenge for software developers to deliver projects on time and within budget (Wallace and Keil, 2004). The Standish Group, an IT consulting firm, provides statistics of both successful and unsuccessful technology projects. This firm conducted a seven-year study (1994–2000), to determine project success rates and time and cost overruns by analyzing a sample of 280,000 projects. The results indicated that 137,000 projects were late, over budget, or both, while another 65,000 failed. Clearly, the failure rate for software development projects is of significant concern. Wallace and Keil (2004) have identified 53 items that reflect the range of likely software project risks. While these risks will be delineated more thoroughly in Chapter 9, "Managing Project Risk," we summarize them here, grouped within ten broad categories:

1. *Lack of executive support*. Lack of top management support and organizational commitment for the project.

2. *Lack of user input*. Lack of user participation, users resistant to change, lack of user cooperation, and lack of user commitment to the project.

3. *Inexperienced project manager*. Lack of leadership skills, project progress not monitored closely, and ineffective communication.

4. *Inexperienced team members*. Inadequately trained team members, lack of team members' commitment to project, and frequent turnover within the project team.

5. *Unclear business objectives*. Ill-defined project goals, conflicting systems requirements, continually changing project objectives, and undefined project success criteria.

6. *Unreliable estimates*. Inadequate estimation of project schedule, budget, and required resources and unclear project milestones.

7. *Lack of an effective project management methodology.*

8. *New software infrastructure*. Use of new technology that has not been used in prior projects and use of immature and highly complex technology.

9. *Unstable organizational environment*. Changes in organizational management during the project, corporate politics impeding the project, and restructuring organization during the project.

10. *Unreliable outside suppliers*. Dependence on unreliable suppliers and involvement of many external suppliers.

failures themselves. Following are some examples of how project management techniques can lead to project success:

- The Ford Motor Company Customer Service Division faced on-time delivery of ordered parts as low as 30 percent. By teaming with Cap, Gemini Ernst & Young and using project management techniques, the Customer Service Department successfully integrated legacy systems using distribution resource planning tools. The result? An order fill-rate between 93 to 98 percent (Hoffman, 2003).

- The OMEGA facility of Medco Health was finished in October 2001, 11 weeks ahead of schedule and 2 percent under budget, through the use of project management techniques embedded within the company's Change Management and Implementation (CMI) program. The result? A facility that exceeded goals in the areas of quality, service, productivity, and safety (see Figure 1.10) (Foti, 2003).

- After adopting the PMI guidebook to develop project management standards, New York's Thruway Authority completed a Human Resources Management Services initiative on time and under budget (Jaques, 2003).

- Copa Airlines in Panama City, Panama, worked through their project management office to ensure that project stakeholders and sponsors stayed on track in

Pillars of Performance		
The Medco Health team exceeded the project's goals:		
Pillar	**Goal**	**Actual**
Quality (Dispensing Action)	Six Sigma Quality (3.4 Errors per Million)	No dispensing errors
Service (Dispensing Timeliness)	92% of Prescriptions Dispensed in One Day	98.9% of Prescriptions Dispensed in One Day
Productivity (Labor Efficiency)	2.8 Prescriptions per Labor Hour	10.5 Prescriptions Per Labor Hour
Safety (Lost Time Rate)	≤13.9 Days	≤0.5 Days

Figure 1.10 OMEGA project chart

terms of project objectives. The result? Annual benefits between $1 and $2 million in additional revenues (Foti, 2003).

- TA Orange asked its technology department to install a $5.6 million packet-over-sonet network in the 8 weeks prior to entering the Thai mobile commercial service market. Through the use of established project management techniques, the tech department was able to complete the project even before the entrance initiative was finished (Parkes, 2002).

UNIQUE FEATURES OF IS PROJECTS

This book is focused on information systems project management. It is, thus, important for us to answer the question, What characteristics of information systems projects make them different from non-IS projects? There are many unique aspects, but here are just a few.

First, the technological context in which companies operate today is in constant flux. As new technologies are introduced, firms must quickly decide whether to invest in them or risk losing a potential competitive advantage or simply whether to match the capabilities of competitors who already have adopted a new technology. For example, Barnes and Noble, a well-known book retailer, was forced to establish a Web presence in order to offset the competitive advantage gained by Amazon.com's online presence. The number of new technologies also means that firms may find themselves juggling the resources required to manage not just one but many projects focused on technological innovations. These factors create an exciting, yet stressful, environment both for the businesses involved and the project teams that do the work.

A second unique aspect of IT projects is the difficulty of hiring and retaining experienced IT project employees. In other words, not only may technologies change during projects, but a project team may also experience turnover as valued employees seek new opportunities. This is made even more challenging by the fact that the demand for employees with good IT project experience may be particularly high; thus, companies may need to design lucrative compensation packages to prevent other organizations from recruiting these employees. This, of course, assumes that the company can recruit personnel with IT project experience to begin with.

A third unique aspect of IT projects is the need to manage the extensive user involvement necessary in information technology projects. Unlike many other types of projects, an information system might be replicated across different parts of an organization, possibly in different parts of the world. As a result, project teams need to focus particular attention on each subset of potential users as the system is built, and be aware that an information system is likely to be used by people with very different levels of technical proficiency. As a result, many different types of users need to be involved in the development process to ensure system success. Systems designers charged with the development of an IT system must ensure that the system's end users are involved throughout the project—not only during planning but also during both implementation and maintenance.

Ethical Dilemma: Protecting the Existing Structures—An Ethical Dilemma in ISD

User input is one of the most important factors of successful information systems development; end users often have a good insight regarding what a new system should look like. Having worked extensively with existing systems, end users can point to features they would like to see added, changed, or dropped from a new system. For these reasons, the systems analyst usually seeks user input at different stages of the systems development life cycle.

Frequently, different stakeholders in an information systems development have divergent goals, especially in cases where existing business processes are radically changed. Consider Dave, the human resources manager of ACME Inc., a company that is about to introduce a new payroll processing system. As a human resources manager, Dave is able to provide extensive input during the analysis and design process for a new system. The systems analyst has indicated adding certain modules to the system would make several jobs redundant, possibly making some employees unnecessary. While Dave is supportive of creating a more efficient system, he also does not want to disrupt the excellent work climate at his organization. Which direction is more beneficial to the company? Should Dave support the creation of the new modules even if it changes the workplace dynamics?

Discussion Questions
1. What are the relative advantages and disadvantages of each strategy, that is, creating a system to automate certain jobs or maintaining the existent jobs in the company?
2. Under what conditions would it be more important to forego the creation of a system that would automate jobs?
3. What should Dave do?

Systems development life cycle
A structured approach to systems development.

A fourth unique aspect of IT projects is the need to understand established systems development methodologies and how these can be integrated into a project management framework. Literally dozens of published methodologies for developing and maintaining systems are available to organizations and project teams. These methodologies may be similar to the traditional **systems development life cycle** (SDLC) or closely aligned with **rapid application development** (RAD) or prototyping. In any event, understanding how they relate to the standard project management techniques is a unique aspect of managing information-technology related development efforts.

A fifth unique aspect differentiating IT project from many other types of projects is that the attempted solutions may never have been tried before. Whereas building a new house is certainly a project, it is a project that is likely very similar to past projects your general contractor has attempted. IT projects, however, may focus on building a system that has an entirely new functionality. In such a case, the project team may have few guidelines or past lessons learned to rely on.

A sixth unique aspect of IT projects that creates a level of complexity beyond non-IT projects is related to managing project scope. Project scope, which involves the planned definition and size of a project, is likely to change in many projects; however, progressive, uncontrolled increases in project scope (see the discussion of scope creep in Chapter 5) are commonplace in IT projects. In many instances, this again might relate to the fact that the end product has never been developed before. In such a situation, users may be less definite about what characteristics they want in the final project output. In addition, users may naively believe that software projects are easily modified even after they have begun—after all, it is just changing a few lines of code. It is up to the project team to manage these perceptions.

Finally, the seventh unique feature of IT projects is that the technologies involved in projects may change during the course of the project, presenting a moving target for the project team. As an example, a company may be involved in the deployment of an enterprise system, such as **SAP**, for the purpose of connecting various functional areas of the business, such as production, sales, and accounting. During the middle of such a project, a new version of the system may be released, and the company may find itself faced with a decision regarding whether to continue with the original product or adopt the new technology. Such changes in technology are commonplace, adding to the complexity of managing projects of this nature. In some cases, the technology might become obsolete before the project is even finished (see Figure 1.11 for IT project complexities).

Although projects may take many forms, one common factor most often leads to project success. This common factor is project management.

Figure 1.11   IS project complexities

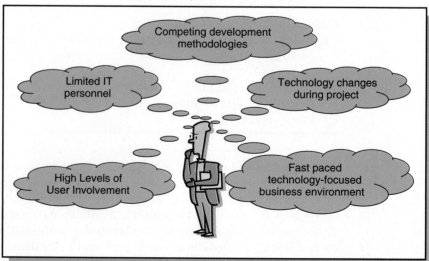

WHAT IS PROJECT MANAGEMENT?

Project management
The application of knowledge, skills, tools, and techniques to project activities to meet project requirements.

Project management process groups
Major project phases, such as initiating, planning, executing, controlling, and closing a project.

Project management life cycle
The phases a project goes through from concept to completion.

Microsoft Project
Software designed by Microsoft to help people manage projects.

Work breakdown structure
A listing of the activities necessary for the completion of a project.

Gantt chart
A bar chart showing the start and end dates for the activities of a project.

Network diagram
A schematic display that illustrates the various tasks in a project as well as their sequential relationship.

The Project Management Institute defines **project management** as "the application of knowledge, skills, tools, and techniques to project activities in order to meet project requirements." **Project management process groups** are major project phases, such as initiating, planning, executing, controlling, and closing a project (see Figure 1.12). All of these process groups together are known as the **project management life cycle**, thus, a project's the life cycle illustrates all the phases a project goes through from concept to completion. Each of these major process groups may include many subprocesses or activities. While the groups and their subprocesses will be covered in greater detail in Chapter 2, it will be useful to discuss the major groups briefly here.

The initiating process identifies potential projects and then evaluates their importance to the organization. The need for IT projects can be discovered in many ways, including recognition by managers and end users. Once these needs have been identified, key management can evaluate the potential projects' alignment with company strategies and goals.

The planning process considers crucial aspects of the project such as scope, time, cost, and risk planning. In this phase, project management tools (such as **Microsoft Project**) may be used to create **work breakdown structures** (WBS) (see Figure 1.13), **Gantt charts**, and **network diagrams** (see Figure 1.14).

During execution, the actual project deliverables are completed. A large portion of project control also occurs during this phase when performance is measured and then compared against planned performance. If problem areas are found, steps are taken to correct them.

Finally, during closeout, all paper work is finalized and the responsible parties sign off on the project.

Understanding how to manage these process groups is so important to project success that the Project Management Institute (PMI) was formed in 1969 to provide information and training on these topics. As of 2006, PMI has a membership of nearly 214,000 people representing 159 countries worldwide. PMI delivers educational services to project managers and offers certification as a project management professional (PMP) for those with extensive project management experience. Additionally, PMI publishes three periodicals, *PM Network*, the *Project Management Journal*, and *PM Today*. The ever-increasing popularity of PMI underscores the growing importance of project management techniques in today's organizations. Information about the organization is available on their Web site at www.pmi.org (see Figure 1.15).

In addition to the processes of initiation, planning, execution, control, and closure, the Project Management Institute maintains a repository on the core project

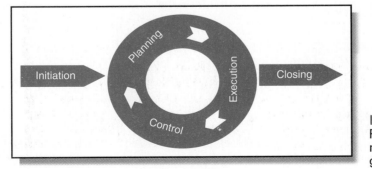

Figure 1.12
Project management process groups

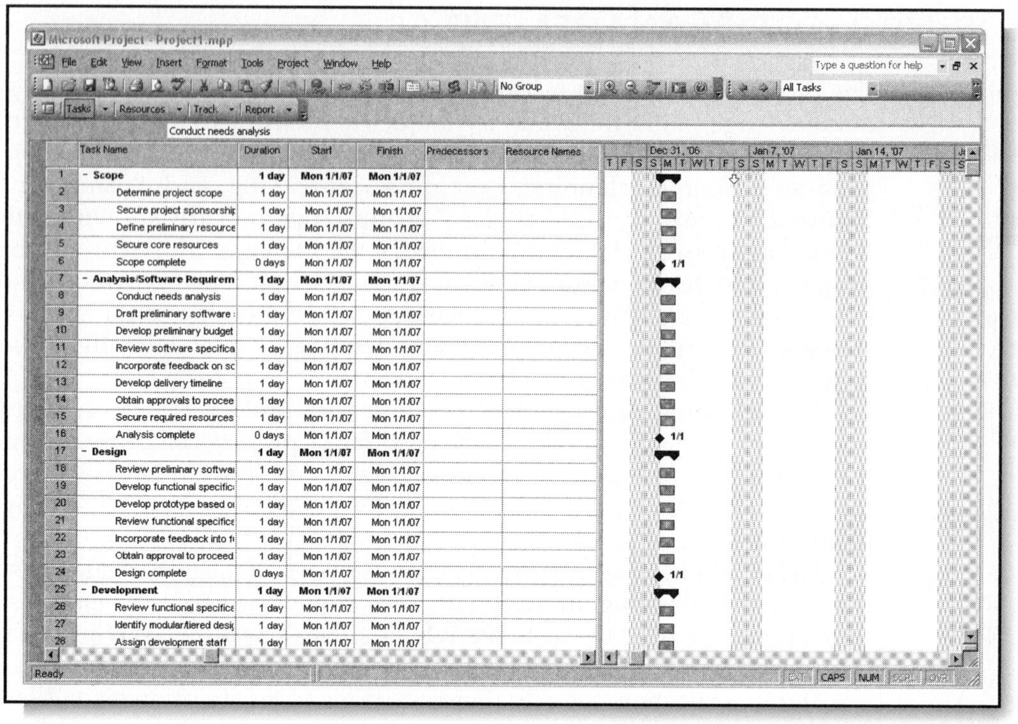

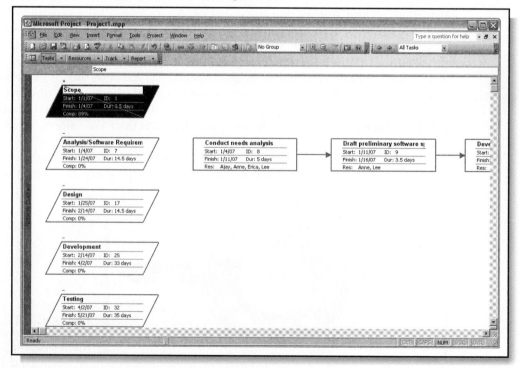

Figure 1.13 Sample work breakdown structure (WBS)

Figure 1.14 Sample network diagram

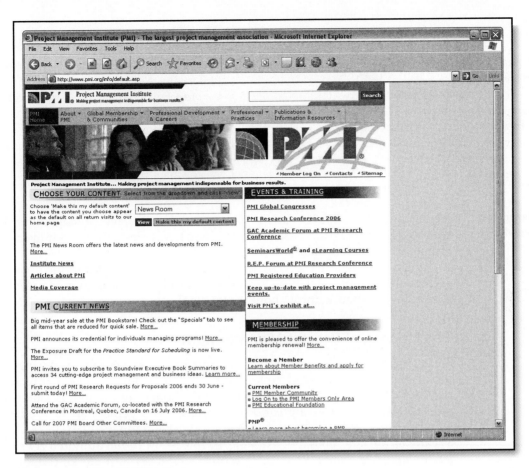

Figure 1.15   PMI Web site screen shot

TIPS FROM THE PROS
Project Management Institute

Established in 1969, the Project Management Institute (PMI) is an international society that focuses on the needs of project professionals around the world. It includes over 100,000 members from 125 countries; they come from various industries, such as aerospace, automotive, business management, construction, engineering, financial services, healthcare, information technology, pharmaceuticals, and telecommunications. Due to the complexity of information systems projects, the CEO of Knowledge Movers Inc., Jack Davis, has recommended that to increase the success rate of IT projects, more project managers should work toward earning PMI's Project Management Professional certification (Davis, 2002). Why should a project manager be a PMI member? The reasons include (www.pmi.org):

- *Education and Training.* Through seminars, PMI members can improve their knowledge and skills in project management.
- *Knowledge Acquisition.* Members have access to research results so that they can stay up-to-date with any changes or developments in the project management field.
- *Professional Development.* Project managers can attend educational events where they can learn about international and regional concerns of other project managers through case studies and simulations.
- *Networking.* PMI members have the opportunity to interact with members from different organizations to develop relationships and work

(*continued*)

on advancing the project management profession.
- *Career Advancement.* PMI offers Project Management Professional (PMP) certification to those individuals who have sufficient project experience and have passed a rigorous comprehensive examination in project management.

- *Professional Awards.* Annual awards are presented to PMI members who bring honor and recognition to the project management profession and PMI.
- *Career Services.* PMI also offers career services to project management professionals.
- *Publications.* Along with its three periodicals, PMI publishes project management books, training tools, and other learning products.

Project Management Body of Knowledge (PMBOK)
A repository of the key project management knowledge areas.

management knowledge areas known as the **Project Management Body of Knowledge (PMBOK)**. These nine core knowledge areas, along with their associated activities, are listed in Table 1.1.

When looking at these knowledge areas, their ties to each of the project process groups of initiation, planning, execution, control, and closeout are evident. We will revisit this association throughout the textbook.

The History of Project Management

Some argue that project management originated in ancient Egypt during the building of the great pyramids (see Figure 1.16). Huge stone blocks that were formed, carved, and moved into place all without the benefit of modern machinery would, indeed, seem to require a great deal of project management skills. Modern project management, however, is often argued to have begun in the early 1900s or, perhaps, as early as the late 1800s. For example, in 1857, T. D. Judah authored *A Practical Plan for Building the Pacific Railroad* in which engineers and clerks prepared formal

Table 1.1 Project Management Core Areas of Knowledge

PROJECT INTEGRATION MANAGEMENT	PROJECT SCOPE MANAGEMENT	PROJECT TIME MANAGEMENT
• Project plan development • Project plan execution • Integrated change control	• Initiation • Scope planning • Scope definition • Scope verification • Scope change control	• Activity definition • Activity sequencing • Activity duration estimating • Schedule development • Schedule control
PROJECT COST MANAGEMENT	PROJECT QUALITY MANAGEMENT	PROJECT HUMAN RESOURCE MANAGEMENT
• Resource planning • Cost estimating • Cost budgeting • Cost control	• Quality planning • Quality assurance • Quality control	• Organizational planning • Staff acquisition • Team development
PROJECT COMMUNICATIONS MANAGEMENT	PROJECT RISK MANAGEMENT	PROJECT PROCUREMENT MANAGEMENT
• Communications planning • Information distribution • Performance reporting • Administrative closure	• Risk management planning • Risk identification • Qualitative risk analysis • Quantitative risk analysis • Risk response planning • Risk monitoring and control	• Procurement planning • Solicitation planning • Solicitation • Source selection • Contract administration • Contract closeout

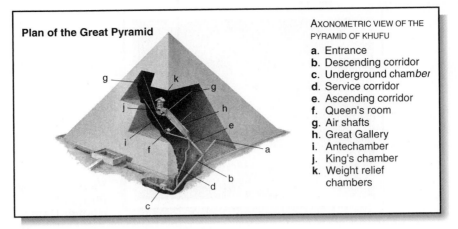

Figure 1.16   Great Pyramids

reports at the project office as survey information arrived from field managers. The information was then analyzed, updated, and forwarded to field managers and engineers. The project office was also responsible for relationships with investors, cost estimation, feasibility studies, and field surveys (Kwak, 2003).

Henry Lawrence Gantt (1861–1919) was a mechanical engineer and management consultant who in 1917 developed what is now known as the Gantt chart, a tool used to plan and track project activities that is still in use today. Gantt charts allowed for the visual display of project planning and status information. An overview of the history of Gantt charts is provided at www.ganttcharts.com/index.html. A sample Gantt chart is shown in Figure 1.17. We will discuss the Gantt chart in more detail in Chapter 6, "Managing Project Scheduling."

Figure 1.17   Sample Gantt chart

Figure 1.18
Photo of
Hoover Dam

In 1931, the development and use of project management techniques similar to those in use today was necessary for the construction of the Hoover Dam (see Figure 1.18). This massive project required the extensive use of both materials and human resources. Because the project involved six companies integrated together as one general contractor, it was crucial for the companies to use project planning and control techniques. Although these project management techniques were then in their infancy, the Hoover Dam was not only successfully completed but completed ahead of time and under budget.

The modern concept of project management originated in 1942 during the well-known Manhattan Project (see Figure 1.19), which was the code name for the United States' effort to develop an atomic bomb during World War II. This project provided some of the first evidence of the potential of modern project management techniques. It lasted from 1942 to 1946, involved hundreds of scientists, and was accomplished at a cost of approximately $1.8 billion, which in today's dollars would be well over $20 billion. The necessary planning and security were so extensive that three secret cities were built to support the Manhattan Project's activities. Coordinating the huge amount of tasks necessary for this undertaking was a huge endeavor, and the project management tools developed to do so are still in use today.

Between 1958 and 1979, additional project management tools were introduced. These tools included both the **critical path method** (CPM) shown in Figure 1.20 and the **program evaluation and review technique** (PERT). Both the critical path method and

Critical path method
A method used for determining the sequence of task activities that directly affect the completion of a project.

Program evaluation and review technique
A technique that uses optimistic, pessimistic, and realistic time to calculate the expected time for a particular task.

Figure 1.19
Photo of
Manhattan Project
in Los Alamos

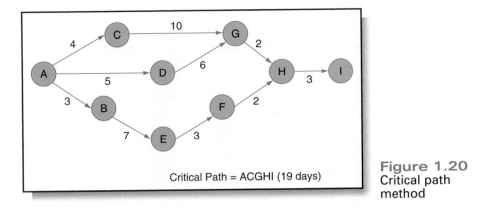

Critical Path = ACGHI (19 days)

Figure 1.20
Critical path
method

PERT are used in different ways to estimate project durations. Project management processes continued to evolve through the 1980s as the ability of project managers to exert local control over projects increased, due in part to the shift from mainframe computing to personal computing technology.

In the last 10 years, both the people involved in project management and the technology used to support project management activities have become more diverse. Exemplifying this diversity, while 72 percent of PMI members were from North America (the United States and Canada), nearly 60,000 members were from regions in Asia Pacific, Europe, Latin America, and the Caribbean. Industry representation is equally varied. Although the top industry area represented in membership is focused on information technology, more than 30 special interest groups are dedicated to industries such as aerospace, education, financial services, government, and manufacturing. Other interest groups focus on growing membership groups, such as Women in Project Management. The capabilities of project management software—such as Microsoft Project (see Figure 1.21)—has facilitated the ascent of

Figure 1.21   Microsoft project screen shot

![Microsoft Project screen shot showing a Gantt chart with task list including Scope, Analysis/Software Requirements, Design, and Development phases]

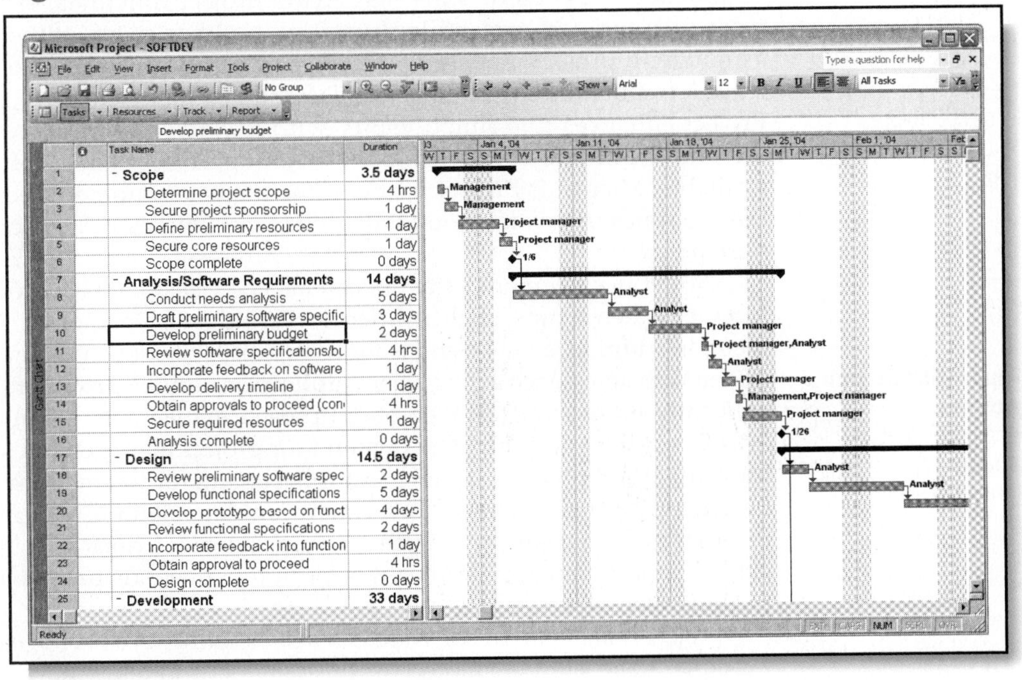

this profession by aiding in the management of increasingly complex projects in a wide variety of industries and in companies that have global stakeholders.

Student chapters are also a growing segment of PMI as more and more educational institutions are integrating project management training in their curriculum. While students are not likely to leave school and immediately become project managers (given the difficulty of the role), introducing project management in school can help students understand the exciting opportunities that await them in this field. For students interested in project management as a career, it is critical to gain not only technical expertise but also to develop their ability to successfully interact in team settings, motivating and supporting team members. Good leadership skills are a key ingredient for successful project management, and organizations look for people who can facilitate team performance and grow into these challenging roles. Joining organizations like PMI can help students gain such skills by connecting with others in the industry and learning from them. Eventually, through continuing education and workplace experience, the new project manager can gain PMI certification as a Project Management Professional (PMP).

Technology for Project Management

A variety of project management software tools can help in planning and visualizing project tasks and activities. Some types of project management software can allow two or more project team members using different computers to work together on various project activities. Such collaboration is necessary for very large projects and when project members are not in the same location. Because IT projects frequently include project members in dispersed locations (in many instances team members may even be located in other countries), project management software that supports collaboration gives project members up-to-date information on the status of various project tasks.

Nearly all project management software contains tools that support activities across the planning, execution, and control phases of the project life cycle. Automated versions of tools that create project timelines, estimate costs, assign resources, and perform similar functions, build on many of the manual techniques available to project managers in the past. As an example, tools to create a Gantt chart are commonplace in most project management software, although Microsoft Project enhances this functionality with features like resource assignments that are built right into the Gantt chart. Although many good software packages are available, Microsoft Project is one of the most common and accessible. Therefore, the examples in this textbook will all be from Microsoft Project 2003 unless otherwise noted.

Project management software can also be classified based on the software platform on which it runs, such as Microsoft Windows, Unix, or the Macintosh environment. In addition, a new trend is for companies to host project management software on the Web, in essence acting as an **application service provider** (ASP) environment. Currently more than 130 Web-based project management providers are available. This trend illustrates the great demand for project management software and shows how important project management is becoming for the modern organization. Web-based software eliminates deployment problems, and a user requires only a Web browser to use the software. Such software, however, does not eliminate the need for skilled project managers; rather, it is just a tool that aids project managers in accomplishing their objectives.

Project management software can also be industry specific (see Figure 1.22). For example, AbacusPM is tailored for the detailers and fabricators. Similarly, SYMPAQ

Application service provider
A company that provides application software hosting.

Industry	Software Package
General Purpose	Microsoft Project
Detailers and Fabricators	AbacusPM
Audio/Visual/Multimedia Production	AlterMedia
Construction	Hard Hat Manager
Small Business	4aBetterBusiness
Software Development	DOVICO Track-IT
Manufacturing and Mining	Crest Soft

Figure 1.22 Project management software by industry

SQL (from Alebaron Inc.) is geared toward project-oriented cost accounting for government contractors. On the information systems front, CS/10,000 (from Client/Server Connection Ltd.) helps in client–server development projects by generating client-server and logical network architectures in addition to its more traditional project management tools. Teamwork, from Teamwork.com, can compare a current project to a baseline project that was done earlier in the organization's history. This software package can be used in industries where projects that are reasonably similar to each other are repeated. Software specific to a particular industry may have built-in templates for activities that are common for that environment. These templates may help reduce the time required for a user to input and generate a project plan and the associated project activities. It may also guide the user to better practices in that specific industry.

An additional classification of project management software is based upon the target market and price of the product (see Figure 1.23). Products range from low-end software packages targeted at small companies to high-end, multiuser-licensed packages targeted at enterprise organizations. An example of a low-end system is Copper 2004. Small companies can purchase the Copper 2004 software package either by buying the license outright for $199 or by using the hosting service (this is an example of an ASP) offered by the company for a per-user fee (Element Software, 2004). Representing a slightly more expensive product, Primavera currently offers its SureTrak project management software package for $499 (Primavera, 2003). The

Figure 1.23 Project Management Software by Price

Software Package	Price*
ProjectCompanion 2003	Free
4aBetterBusiness: Single user license	$125
5 user license	$495
10 user license	$895
Palo Alto Business Plan: Single user license	$200
Microsoft Project 2003 Standard: Single user license	$360
Small Business 3 user license	$1045
Primavera SureTrak Project Manager 3.0: 10 user license	$3900
20 user license	$7120
25 user license	$8370

* Prices subject to change depending on retailer/market conditions
* Prices in U.S. Dollars

SureTrak product is designed to run on stand-alone PC systems. Probably the most well-known project management software package is MS Project. Perhaps its most attractive feature is its ability to be used by one user on a stand-alone PC or by more than 1,000 users in a network setting. EF Development offers eFPro Manager, an enterprise Web-based system that enables team collaboration and client interaction. To price this high-end system, prospective buyers must contact the company (eFDev, 2003).

Doing Projects in Business Environments

Although projects can be carried out by individuals, most organizational projects use teams. What does that mean in terms of project management? Simply, team dynamics must be taken into consideration during the project. As early as the planning phase, human resource managers must decide which employees will have the greatest chance for success when working as part of a team. Additionally, human resource managers must determine which employees may be available for a given project. For large organizations, enterprise-wide human resource systems may be used to help identify available employees who possess the skills needed for a given project.

Successful IT projects require that various types of personnel work together. Specific groups of employees needed can include project managers, systems analysts, programmers, and end users. When teams are formed from such diverse groups of individuals, group dynamics are often of special concern. Considerable research has been conducted in this area, and we will have much more to say about this subject in later chapters. For now, suffice it to say that communication among team members is of major concern due to the unique jargons often used by individual groups.

OVERVIEW OF THIS BOOK'S APPROACH

This book is designed to walk you through the experience of project management. It is process focused, team focused, technology focused, globally focused, and project-management-professional focused (see Figure 1.24). Let's examine each of these principles in turn.

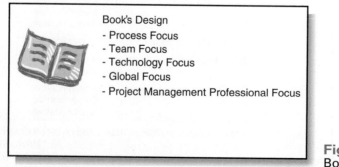

Figure 1.24
Book design

Process Focus

As opposed to the more common buffet of project management subtopics, this book focuses on *learning by doing* by actively engaging students in *managing a real information systems project*. After a small amount of introductory material, the book quickly transitions to taking the student step-by-step through the stages of project management, with assignments corresponding to the deliverables that an organization typically would require as employees tackle real information systems projects. While covering the essential material included in other project management texts, this book helps you actively learn project management by walking you through issues like project charters or work breakdown structures as you encounter them in the course of your class projects. This contextual treatment of information systems project management topics will not only solidify your understanding of various project management techniques, but it also will create an immediate understanding of why these techniques are critical to effective project management.

Each section briefly reviews material previously covered, previews what is covered in the current chapter as well as where this material falls in the overall project life cycle, sets the stage with a miniature case, discusses the content, and wraps up with a chapter summary and lessons learned. Assignments at the end of each chapter focus on an integrative, team-based information systems project that continues throughout the semester. This project is intended to give you hands-on experience in managing all phases of the project life cycle. Although a variety of projects can be done in conjunction with the book, we outline a suggested Web-based development project and also include optional project idea.

Team Focus

Project management is largely a team sport, not an individual one. This book is unique in its focus on team-based project management. Unless you experience project management in a group setting, your project management knowledge will be largely incomplete. This book covers the types of groups in organizations, the types of tasks they work on, the advantages of working in groups, and the problems that groups will encounter and the solutions to those problems. Topics addressed include group processes, leadership, group conflict, and so on.

In addition to the inherent difficulties of working in teams, workers in today's organization also face the fact that they may no longer work in the same office, building, or even country with their fellow project team members. The virtual project team is a common organizational entity, and managing teams in this type of environment creates even more complexity. We address the unique advantages of virtual teams, the difficulties they encounter, and solutions to those difficulties. We pay particular attention to the effects of collaborative technology and groupware on project team productivity.

Technology Focus

This book focuses not only on technology projects but also on the ability of technology to *enable* projects. A list of a few of the technologies that we will discuss follows.

Project Management Software

A variety of technologies are available to support the project management process. The advantages of project planning software are discussed, and you are given hands-on experience using a common project-planning-software environment. You will subsequently use this same project-planning software to support your course project.

Group Support Technologies

In addition to project management software, a variety of types of group support systems can be used to support project teams. These technologies enable groups to communicate effectively across distances and time, reduce the losses that can be associated with working in groups, and enhance the group's decision-making.

Knowledge Management and Organizational Memory Systems

A common problem for organizations is how to capture the project knowledge that previous project teams have accumulated. This text also addresses the important topic of knowledge-management systems and organizational memory and how they can be used to house project lessons learned for future project teams.

Global Focus

This book illustrates the changing nature of projects in the modern world, particularly as it relates to global project management. Many of the chapters in this book, for example those on teams, project communication, and outsourcing, focus on the changing face of project teams. Organizations involved in IT projects may span global boundaries either in the focus of the project itself or in the composition of its teams. Virtual team-work, as an example, is commonplace as organizations put together resources to deliver an IT project. Outsourcing beyond one's home country is also commonplace. This book attempts to address these issues throughout its various chapters.

Project Management Professional Focus

One critical element of this textbook is focused on preparing the student to show a high level of competency over all key areas of project management. The Project Management Institute (PMI)—a professional organization focused on meeting the needs of project managers—has encapsulated the key knowledge areas of project management into their Project Management Body of Knowledge (PMBOK). This text prepares the student to master these knowledge areas, and provides the necessary knowledge for passing PMI's professional project management certification exam. By the conclusion of the textbook, the student will have been exposed in detail to all the knowledge areas identified by the PMBOK. This will help the student to prepare for certifications in project management (such as PMI's Project Management Professional). In addition to our alignment with the PMBOK, we also provide other practical guidance gleaned from practicing project managers. Included in this book you'll find elements such as Tips from the Pros, Ethical Dilemmas, Common Problems, and Global Implications. These elements contain useful information that can be applied to future projects.

INTRODUCTION TO PROJECT MANAGEMENT AND THE PMBOK

As mentioned earlier, PMI's *PMBOK* (2004) is an excellent guide to measuring your mastery of project-management-related knowledge areas. This textbook includes a table at the end of each chapter that will help you keep track of what portion of the PMBOK has been covered in the current chapter, as well as show you what we have covered to that point and what we will cover in future chapters. The table can also serve as a useful reference for guiding your study for taking PMI's certification exam for a Project Management Professional. This table will show the PMBOK knowledge areas—as established by PMI—in its left column. This textbook's chapter numbers are shown horizontally along the top of the table. An empty circle designates where the particular PMBOK knowledge area is covered in the textbook. A filled in circle designates coverage in the current chapter.

For this chapter—Introduction to Project Management—we have introduced the PMBOK knowledge areas defining a project and describing the field of project management as well as its relationship with other disciplines. We have also discussed the distinction between project phases, the project life cycle, project processes, and project groups. Figure 1.25 identifies this coverage and illustrates the coverage in upcoming chapters as well.

Figure 1.25 Chapter 1 and PMBOK coverage

Textbook Chapters ➝		1	2	3	4	5	6	7	8	9	10	11	12
PMBOK Knowledge Area													
1	**Introduction to Project Management**												
1.1	What is a Project?	✓											
1.2	What is Project Management?	✓											
1.3	Areas of Expertise		○										
1.4	Project Management Context	✓											
2	**Project Life Cycle and Organization**												
2.1	The Project Life Cycle	✓	○										
2.2	Project Stakeholders	✓	○										
2.3	Organizational Influences		○	○	○			○					
3	**Project Management Processes for a Project**												
3.1	Project Management Processes	✓	○										
3.2	PM Process Groups	✓	○										
3.3	Process Interactions		○										
3.4	Project Management Process Mapping		○										
4	**Project Integration Management**												
4.1	Develop Project Charter					○							
4.2	Develop Preliminary Project Scope Statement					○	○						
4.3	Develop Project Management Plan					○							
4.4	Direct and Manage Project Execution										○		
4.5	Monitor and Control Project Work												○
4.6	Integrated Change Control												○
4.7	Close Project												○
5	**Project Scope Management**												
5.1	Scope Planning					○							
5.2	Scope Definition					○							
5.3	Create WBS					○	○						
5.4	Scope Verification					○							
5.5	Scope Control					○							○
6	**Project Time Management**												
6.1	Activity Definition						○						
6.2	Activity Sequencing						○						

(continued)

Figure 1.25 (continued)

	Textbook Chapters →	1	2	3	4	5	6	7	8	9	10	11	12
	PMBOK Knowledge Area												
6.3	Activity Resource Estimating							o					
6.4	Activity Duration Estimating							o					
6.5	Schedule Development							o					
6.6	Schedule Control							o					o
7	**Project Cost Management**												
7.1	Cost Estimating							o					
7.2	Cost Budgeting							o					
7.3	Cost Control							o					o
8	**Project Quality Management**												
8.1	Quality Planning								o				
8.2	Perform Quality Assurance								o				
8.3	Perform Quality Control								o				o
9	**Project Human Resource Management**												
9.1	Human Resource Planning			o				o					
9.2	Acquire Project Team			o				o					
9.3	Develop Project Team			o				o					
9.4	Manage Project Team			o				o					
10	**Project Communications Management**												
10.1	Communications Planning				o							o	
10.2	Information Distribution				o							o	
10.3	Performance Reporting				o								o
10.4	Manage Stakeholders				o								o
11	**Project Risk Management**												
11.1	Risk Management Planning									o			
11.2	Risk Identification									o	o		
11.3	Qualitative Risk Analysis									o			
11.4	Quantitative Risk Analysis									o			
11.5	Risk Response Planning									o			
11.6	Risk Monitoring and Control									o			o
12	**Project Procurement Management**												
12.1	Plan Purchases and Acquisitions										o		
12.2	Plan Contracting										o		
12.3	Request Seller Responses										o		
12.4	Select Sellers										o		
12.5	Contract Administration										o		
12.6	Contract Closure										o		o

Key: ●-where material is covered in past chapters; ✓-current chapter coverage;
O-where material is covered in future chapters

CHAPTER SUMMARY

Explain why projects fail. Projects fail for many reasons. Project failures can be defined in terms of finishing over budget, not being completed on time, or failing to deliver a system that meets stakeholder expectations.

Define IT projects. IT projects differ from more traditional projects in at least four ways. The rapid change of information technology is the basis for the first of these differences. The ever-changing nature of information technology means that new developments are constantly being introduced. As these technologies are introduced, firms must quickly decide whether to invest in them or risk losing a potential competitive advantage. Additionally, many companies find they are forced to adopt a new technology to match the capabilities of competitors. A second difference is the difficulty associated with hiring experienced IT personnel. As personnel gain IT-specific project experience, they are quickly recruited by other organizations. Thus, retaining these individuals becomes a challenge for human resources staff. A third difference involves managing the end user's involvement during the requirements-analysis phase of systems development. A project development team must be aware that people with widely varied levels of technical proficiency are likely to use an information system. As a result, many different types of users need to be involved in the development process to ensure system success. Designers charged with developing an IT system must ensure that the system's end users are involved throughout the project. A final difference is the need for IT project team members to be aware of the many different development methodologies. These methodologies include the systems development life cycle (SDLC) and rapid application development (RAD).

Define project management. Project management is defined as "the application of knowledge, skills, tools, and techniques to project activities in order to meet project requirements." Many organizations use some form of the project management life cycle to better manage organizational initiatives. In addition to the phases associated with the project management life cycle, the Project Management Institute has published nine key knowledge areas.

Understand the project management life cycle. The project management life cycle is a generic term describing a set of procedures used to manage organizational initiatives. While there may be some variation among organizations, the project management life cycle generally consists of initiation, planning, executing, controlling, and closing phases.

Discuss the history of project management. The history of project management can be traced as far back as the building of the great pyramids. Over time, as projects have increased in complexity and become more formalized within organizations, new project management tools have been developed. These tools include the Gantt chart, the critical path method, and the program and evaluation review technique.

Identify project management technologies. Project management software such as Microsoft Project is commonly used by organizations for managing information system projects. Project management technology can be classified in terms of the operating platform, the industry in which it is used, and by its cost.

Projects are an integral part of organizational life. Projects can be simple and of relatively short duration, complex and quite lengthy, or somewhere in between. They can be initiated for something as simple as the collection of information, a task that may take only a couple of days, or for something as complex as implementing an enterprise-wide information system that could take several years. Both simple and complex projects will be discussed as we progress through the chapters that follow, and both will be used to help explain the concepts outlined in this chapter. Take your time, complete the Chapter 1 review exercises, and then let's get started on the Chapter 2!

KEY TERMS REVIEW

- Application service provider
- Critical path method
- Enterprise system
- Gantt chart
- Microsoft project
- Network diagram
- Program evaluation and review technique
- Project
- Project management
- Project Management Body of Knowledge

- Project Management Institute
- Project management life cycle
- Project management process groups
- Project manager
- Project sponsor
- Rapid application development
- Systems development life cycle
- SAP
- Stakeholder
- Work breakdown structure

Match each of the key terms with the definition that best fits it.

1. _____ An association designed to bring together project management professionals and systematically capture project management knowledge.

2. _____ A planned undertaking of related activities to reach an objective that has a beginning and an end.

3. _____ A person who has an interest in a new or existing project.

4. _____ A member of the organization who is responsible for the high level support of the project.

5. _____ A person with a diverse set of skills—management, leadership, technical, conflict management, and customer relationship—who is responsible for initiating, planning, executing, controlling and monitoring, and closing down a project.

6. _____ A comprehensive system designed to integrate systems from diverse parts of a business (also called an enterprise resource planning system, or ERP).

7. _____ A structured approach to systems development.

8. _____ An expedited approach to systems development.

9. _____ A particular brand of enterprise systems.

10. _____ The application of knowledge, skills, tools, and techniques to project activities to meet project requirements.

11. _____ Major project phases, such as initiating, planning, executing, controlling, and closing a project.

12. _____ The phases a project goes through from concept to completion.

13. _____ Software designed by Microsoft to help people manage projects.

14. _____ A listing of the activities necessary for the completion of a project.

15. _____ A bar chart showing the start and end dates for the activities of a project.

16. _____ A schematic display that illustrates the various tasks in a project as well as their sequential relationship.

17. _____ A repository on the key project management knowledge areas.

18. _____ A method used for determining the sequence of task activities that directly affect the completion of a project.

19. _____ A technique that uses optimistic, pessimistic, and realistic time to calculate the expected time for a particular task.

20. _____ A company that provides application software hosting.

REVIEW QUESTIONS

1. What is the definition of a project?
2. What are some examples of projects, and how do they differ from nonprojects?
3. What does it mean for a project to fail, and how often does this occur?
4. What are some common reasons for project failure?
5. List five unique characteristics of IT projects.
6. What is project management? What are five stages of project management?

7. How does a project management life cycle differ from the systems development life cycle?
8. Are all project management life cycles the same? Explain your answer.
9. What are three potential classifications of project management technology? Explain each one.
10. List three major historical projects that used project management processes.

CHAPTER EXERCISES

1. Log on to the Internet and access the PMI site at www.pmi.org. What are some of the services provided by the PMI? In one or two paragraphs describe some of the services offered by the institute. Find the "Knowledge and Wisdom Center" page, and find the Knowledgebase. Using the Knowledge and Wisdom Center Knowledgebase key-word search function, perform a search for common terms such as *project*, *project management*, and *project management life cycle*. Write a one-page summary of the information available for these topics and how managers might use this information to better manage projects.

2. What problems can occur if a project does not have support from senior level executives?

3. The project manager has a diverse set of skills. List some of these skills and describe a situation where each skill would be useful.

4. Explain the two main reasons for undertaking information systems projects.

5. Describe five reasons why IS projects fail, and what can be done to avoid such failures.

6. Using the Internet, find examples of IS projects that have failed. Were these easy to find? If not, explain some of the reasons why organizations do not publicize project failures.

7. This chapter provides several examples of how project management techniques can lead to project success. Using the Internet, find at least three other examples of project success that can be attributed to good project management techniques and describe what the managers of those projects did well.

8. Describe the unique features that make IT projects so difficult to manage.

9. What are the project management process groups? Describe each in reference to a project that you have recently worked on.

10. Several historically significant projects were mentioned in the chapter. Using the Internet or any other resource, find at least three other historical projects that used project management processes. Write one paragraph for each project describing the project management processes that were used and how they were applied.

11. Using the Internet or any other resource, perform a search for "project management life cycle." Find at least three different project management life cycles that are not information-systems related. Write a one-page summary explaining the differences and similarities of the life cycles that you find.

12. Using the Internet or any other resource, perform a search for "systems development life cycle." Write a one-page summary that outlines the similarities and differences between the systems development life cycle (SDLC) and each of the project management life cycles you summarized in exercise three.

CHAPTER CASE

Seattle Seahawks and the Internet

The Seattle Seahawks are a professional football team that joined the National Football League (NFL) in 1976. With their home offices and training center in Kirkland, a suburb of Seattle, the Seahawks were founded when the league granted an expansion team franchise to John Nordstrom, a department store owner in Seattle. During the Seahawks' first season, quarterback Jim Zorn passed for over 2,500 yards and was named the league's top offensive rookie. Jack Patera was named coach of the year in 1978 after he led the Seahawks to their first winning season. The club played in Seattle's Kingdome from 1976 to 1999. Following the demolition of the Kingdome in 2000, the club played temporarily in the Husky Stadium at the University of Washington until construction of their new stadium, Quest Field, was completed in 2002.

From their inception until the present, the Seahawks have had many notable coaches and players. Well-known coaches include Chuck Knox and Mike Holmgren, with eminent players such as Steve Largent, Jim Zorn, Dave Brown, Curt Warner, Jacob Green, Kenny Easley, Dave Kreig, Walter Jones, Matt Hasselbeck, and Shaun Alexander. With top-ranked personnel, the Seattle Seahawks are consistently positioned for a run at the championship. Following an outstanding 2005 season, the Seahawks played the Pittsburgh Steelers in Super Bowl XL in February 2006.

Figure 1.26
Seahawks Web site screen shot

While the Seahawks were concentrating on football, the early 1990s saw the development of the World Wide Web and the Internet tools created for that environment. The Web provided tremendous opportunities for many businesses to more effectively disseminate information about their products and services. Eventually, the Web helped to facilitate the creation of new products, as well as to enable consumers to buy those products online. Sports teams were not immune to these trends. Web sites devoted to sports franchises now provide for fan discussion forums, purchasing event tickets and sports apparel online, and the distribution of information on the team and players. A modern Web presence that facilitates all of these activities and more is as critical for a professional sports team as it is for any other business.

In 1997, the Seattle Seahawks put out a request for proposals related to the development of a comprehensive Web presence. The Seahawks Web site would eventually include over 100 menu options, including such functionalities as detailed team information, tickets and seating options, luxury suite information, links to local hotel accommodations, an online pro shop, detailed press releases, photographs, transportation options, and even games. While the Seahawks could have tried to develop this system in-house, they elected to outsource it because it was not their core competency. The case study following each chapter of this textbook discusses how the development company Sedona Management Group (SMG) was eventually chosen and how Sedona proceeded to develop the system using modern project management techniques and tools.

Following each Chapter Case, we'll also have a Chapter Project that allows you and your team members to apply the materials from each chapter in the development of an entertainment Web site similar to the one created by SMG for the Seattle Seahawks.

CHAPTER 1 PROJECT ASSIGNMENT

1. Go to the Web site www.seahawks.com and familiarize yourself with the Seattle Seahawks Web site.
   a. What types of features does it have?
   b. How is the Web site organized?
   c. Could you find everything you were looking for?
   d. How many times did you look in the wrong place for something?
   e. Does the Web site look like it will work well on monitors of different resolutions?
2. Next, go to www.nfl.com and randomly select two other Web sites to view.
   a. How do their features and layout compare to the Seahawks' Website?
   b. Write up your rough impressions of all three sites in three different paragraphs.
3. Conclude by describing which site you believe is best and why.

REFERENCES

Adamick, M. (2003, March 29). Bridge Costs Soar. Retrieved September 21, 2006, from ContraCostaTimes.com Web site: http://www.contracostatimes.com/mld/cctimes/14211865.htm.

Booth, R. (2000). IT Project Failures Costly, TechRepublic/Gartner Study Finds. Retrieved February 27, 2005, from Tech Republic Web site: techrepublic.com.com/5100-22-1062043.html?tag=search.

Chai, W. (2003, February 19). India Could Face IT Staff Drought. Retrieved February 27, 2005, from CNet News.com Web site: news.com.com/2100-1001-985118. html?tag=nl.

CIO Magazine (2001). The Secret to Software Success. Retrieved February 27, 2005, from CIO Magazine Web site: www.cio.com/archive/070101/secret_sidebar_2.html.

Davis, J. (2002, August 5). Not So Extreme. ComputerWorld. Retrieved February 27, 2005, from ComputerWorld's Web site: www.computerworld.com/managementtopics/management/story/0,10801,73184,00.html.

eFDev (2003). eFPro Manager Software. Retrieved February 27, 2005, from eF Development Corporation Web site: www.efdev.com/products/efpromanager/default.asp.

Element Software. Retrieved February 27, 2005, from Copper 2004 Software Web site: www.copperproject.com.

Foti, Ross (2003). Destination: Competitive Advantage. PM Network 17(8), 28–36.

Foti, Ross (2003). What the Doctor Ordered. PM Network 17(9), 26–32.

Global Insight (2004, March). Executive Summary: The Comprehensive Impact of Offshore IT Software and Services Outsourcing on the U.S. Economy and the IT Industry. Retrieved February 27, 2005, from Information Technology Association of America Web site: www.itaa.org/itserv/docs/execsumm.pdf.

Greenemeier, L. (2002, February 11). Offshore Outsourcing Grows to Global Proportions. InformationWeek. Retrieved February 27, 2005, from the InformationWeek Web site: www.informationweek.com/showArticle.jhtml?articleID=6501137.

Hoffman, William (2003). Missing Links. PM Network 17(6), 50–54.

IT Cortex. (2003). Failure Causes. Retrieved February 27, 2005, from IT Cortex Web site: www.it-cortex.com/Stat_Failure_Cause.htm#The%20Bull% 20 Survey%20.

Jaques, Timothy. (2003). A New York State of Mind. *PM Network* 17(1), 28–33.

Kwak, Y. (2003). Brief History of Project Management. In Carayannis, Kwak, and Anbari (eds.), *The Story of Managing Projects*, Quorum Books.

Mearian, L. (2001, February 2). Canadian Supermarket Chain Abandons SAP's Retail Software. *ComputerWorld.* Retrieved February 27, 2005, from *Computerworld* Web site: www.computerworld.com/softwaretopics/software/story/0,10801,57293,00.html.

Microsoft. (2003, August). Content Management Solution Streamlines Software Providers Web Site Production, Boosts IT Staff Credibility. Retrieved February 27, 2005, from Microsoft Web site: members.microsoft.com/CustomerEvidence/Search/EvidenceDetails.aspx?EvidenceID=1773&LanguageID=1.

Parkes, Sarah (2002). Strong Project Skills Prove Key to Thai Mobile Success. *PM Network* 16(8), 28–33.

PMBOK (2004). *A Guide to the Project Management Body of Knowledge* (3rd ed.). Newtown Square, PA: Project Management Institute.

Primavera Software. Retrieved February 27, 2005, from Primavera Web site: https://www.primavera.com/orders/st3fullorder.html.

Project Management Institute. Retrieved February 27, 2005, from the Project Management Institute Web site: www.pmi.org.

Standish Group (1994). The CHAOS Report (1994), Retrieved February 27, 2005, from the Standish Group Web site: www.standishgroup.com/sample_research/chaos_1994_1.php.

Stedman, C. (1998, November 1). Big Retail SAP Project Put on Ice. ComputerWorld.

Wallace, L. and Keil, M. (2004). Software Project Risks and Their Effect on Outcomes. *Communications of the ACM* 47(4), 68–73.

Yamamoto, M. (2004, March 29). Will India Price Itself Out of Offshore Market? Retrieved February 27, 2005, from CNet News.com Web site: news.com.com/2100–1022_3–5180589.html.

Chapter

2

The Project Management Life Cycle

Opening Case: EDS Follows a Spiral Project Life Cycle to Develop an Inventory System

Electronic Data Systems (EDS), a worldwide leader in IT project outsourcing, was called upon by a company within the manufacturing sector to assist in developing a company-wide inventory system (see Figure 2.1). Given a 6-month time frame, EDS was asked to develop a system that would allow company managers access to timely, accurate, interdepartmental inventory information. The new system was designed to replace a series of previously developed departmental databases that did not allow sharing of data across departmental boundaries.

To develop the new inventory system, EDS followed a customized project life cycle consisting of four linear phases—identification, design, construction, and evaluation. The project life cycle followed a spiral pattern in which the four phases were repeated cyclically. Similar to the prototyping approach generally used within a rapid application development (RAD) life cycle, a preliminary version of the system was delivered at the end of each iteration through the project phases. At the conclusion of the first iteration, EDS delivered what they termed an alpha system, and at the conclusion of the second iteration a beta system. At the end of the third iteration, the final system was delivered to the customer.

Using this spiral model project life cycle, EDS was able to deliver a system that not only met the requirements of the customer but also was completed on time and on budget (Source: Miller [2000]).

Figure 2.1 Web site for EDS

LEARNING OBJECTIVES

After reading this chapter, you will be able to:

➤ Describe the project management life cycle.
➤ Explain the five parts of the information systems development life cycle.
➤ Understand the project management context.
➤ Read Gantt charts and project network diagrams.
➤ Understand the basics of software that supports project management.
➤ Comprehend project management processes.

INTRODUCTION

Projects start. Projects end. That seems like a simple enough idea, but between the start and the end of any given project, a lot happens. As you read in Chapter 1, any project that is worthy of the management processes and techniques you will learn about in this book involves many people, substantial resources, and moderate to long periods of time. For example, the median project budget in the United States is $2 million, meaning half of all projects have budgets below $2 million and

Figure 2.2
Information systems project management focusing on the project management life cycle

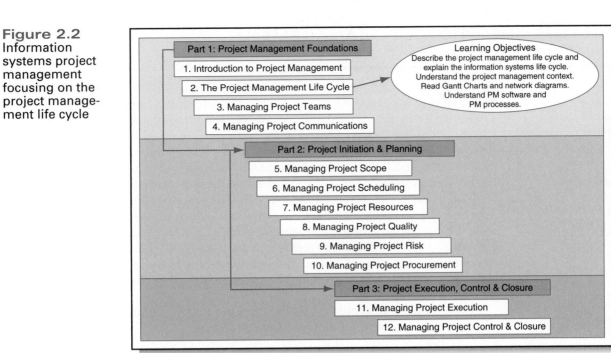

half have budgets greater than $2 million. The average U.S. project budget is $55 million (PMI, 2001). All of these resources and people need to be closely managed for the duration of the project. Nothing can be overlooked if the primary goals of meeting deadlines and budgets and providing the requested functionality are to be met. The duration of a project is captured in the concept of a project life cycle, essentially what goes on between the start of the project and its end. Although the idea of a life cycle is not new—it has been applied to fields such as marketing and manufacturing and engineering—it is very useful. Thinking of a project as having a "life" reinforces the idea that it has a beginning and an ending and that what happens in between requires close and careful management (see Figure 2.2).

In this chapter, you will learn about project management life cycles, and you will learn about a particular type of project life cycle, the information systems development life cycle. The information systems life cycle typically has five phases: 1) planning and selection, 2) analysis, 3) design, 4) implementation, and 5) maintenance, but it can have from four to nine or even more phases. Next you will learn about the context in which projects exist. This larger context includes stakeholders (people who have a vested interest in the project), organizational culture and structure, and social, economic, and environmental influences. You will also read about general management skills that are useful for project managers to master. The next section in the chapter introduces you to tools and techniques that have been developed to help with the project management life cycle, including Gantt charts and network diagrams. You will also be introduced to software for project management, Microsoft's Project. A more complete treatment of Microsoft Project is included in Appendix A. Finally, you will read about the five different project management process groups—Initiating, Planning, Executing, Controlling, and Closing—and 44 different project management processes that can be mapped to these five groups.

WHAT IS THE PROJECT MANAGEMENT LIFE CYCLE?

Phase
A smaller part of a project.

Phase exits
Review of the deliverables at the end of a phase of the project.

As discussed in Chapter 1, projects are divided into smaller parts called **phases**. Breaking down all of the work required in a project into smaller parts makes the project easier to understand and to manage. All of the phases considered together are known as the project life cycle. Each phase is marked by the completion and review of its deliverables, all of which have been defined in the project's early phases. The end of a phase is marked by a review of the deliverables. These review points are sometimes called **phase exits**, stage gates, or kill points.

Project life cycles vary by industry and organization. They determine the beginning and end of a project and define what work is done in each phase, as well as who should be involved in doing it. The sequencing of phases generally involves technology transfer or other handoffs from one phase to the next, such as handing off system requirements to design. Generally, the deliverables from one phase are approved before the next phase starts. Although phases are thought of as separate and distinct, they often overlap.

Even though project life cycles vary from industry to industry and organization to organization, most share common characteristics:

- Cost and staffing levels are low at the start, higher at the end, and drop rapidly as the project nears completion (see Figure 2.3).
- The probability of successfully completing the project is lowest at the beginning, so risk and uncertainty are also the highest at that point.
- The stakeholders' ability to influence the project product's final characteristics is highest at the beginning and lowest at the end.

Although project life cycles have similar phase names with similar deliverables, few are identical. Some life cycles have relatively few phases, from four to five. Others have as many as nine or even more. Depending on its size and complexity, a given project may be divided into subprojects, each of which has its own distinct project life cycle. In the next section, you'll read about a generic life cycle for information systems development with five phases. This life cycle illustrates the activities and their sequence in a typical information systems development project.

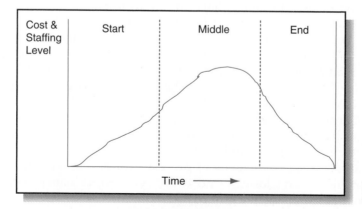

Figure 2.3
Generic life cycle

Ethical Dilemma: Dual Use Information Technologies

Information technology (IT) is malleable. Regardless of the original intentions of the designers and developers, almost all IT can be used for other purposes. Supercomputers used to predict hurricane trajectories can also be used for military purposes. Encryption software designed to help ordinary people keep their e-mails and files private can also be used by terrorists, drug dealers, and mobsters to keep their criminal dealings secret. The data-mining software that can be used to help retailers determine the best product mix for individual sales regions can also enable governments to spy on their citizens by searching and correlating data on individual purchases. Because of these multiple uses of IT, some governments have forbidden the export of so-called dual use technologies to other countries.

As an IT developer and member of an IT project team, you may be called on to work on systems designed for a particular purpose that can also be used for other functions. Many of the codes of ethics developed by professional IT associations call for developers to be wary of how systems might be used. For example, the very first section of the code of ethics of the Association for Computing Machinery says, "An essential aim of computing professionals is to minimize negative consequences of computing systems, including threats to health and safety. When designing or implementing systems, computing professionals must attempt to ensure that the products of their efforts will be used in socially responsible ways, will meet social needs, and will avoid harmful effects to health and welfare" (Source: Association for Computing Machinery).

Discussion Questions:

1. As an IT professional, how can you determine if a particular IT system has the potential to be used for purposes other than those for which it has been designed?
2. If you are called on by your employer to work on a system that has clear dual-use potential, how should you react? What should you do?

PROJECT MANAGEMENT AND SYSTEMS DEVELOPMENT OR ACQUISITION

Systems development life cycle (SDLC) A common methodology for systems development that marks the phases or steps of information systems development.

The **systems development life cycle (SDLC)** is a common methodology for systems development in many organizations. It marks the phases or steps of information systems development: Someone has an idea for an information system and what it should do. The organization that will use the system decides to devote the necessary resources to acquiring it. A careful study is done of how the organization currently handles the work the system will support. Professionals develop a strategy for designing the new system, which is then either built or purchased. Once complete, the system is installed in the organization, and after proper training, the users begin to incorporate the new system into their daily work. Every organization uses a slightly different life cycle model for these steps, with anywhere from three to almost twenty identifiable phases. A generic SDLC might include these five steps (see Figure 2.4):

1. Planning
2. Analysis
3. Design

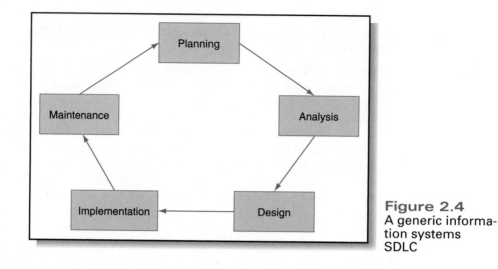

Figure 2.4
A generic information systems SDLC

4. Implementation

5. Maintenance

Sometimes the life cycle is iterative; that is, phases are repeated as required until an acceptable system is found. Some systems analysts consider the life cycle to be a spiral in which we constantly cycle through the phases at different levels of detail, as illustrated in Figure 2.5. The figure illustrates how the end of one system's useful life leads to the beginning of another project that will replace the existing system altogether. However conceived, the systems development life cycle is an orderly set of activities conducted and planned for each development project. The skills required of a systems analyst apply to all life cycle models.

In an SDLC, each phase has specific outcomes and deliverables that feed important information to other phases. At the end of each phase (and sometimes at intermediate steps within phases), a systems development project reaches a milestone. Then, as deliverables are produced, they are often reviewed by parties outside the project team including managers and executives.

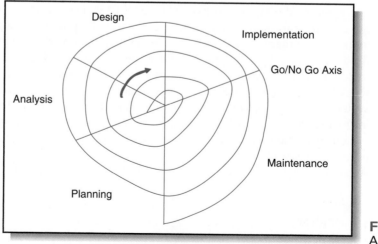

Figure 2.5
A spiral IS SDLC

Phase 1: Systems Planning

The first phase in the SDLC, **systems planning**, involves two primary activities. First, someone identifies the need for a new or enhanced system. The organization's information needs are examined, and projects to meet these needs are identified. Information system needs may result from:

- Requests to deal with problems in current procedures
- The desire to perform additional tasks
- The realization that information technology could be used to capitalize on an existing opportunity

The systems analyst prioritizes and translates the needs into a written plan for the IS department, including a schedule for developing new major systems. Requests for new systems spring from users who need new or enhanced systems. During the systems planning phase, an organization determines whether or not it should devote resources to the development or enhancement of each information system under consideration. A feasibility study is conducted before the second phase of the SDLC to determine the system's economic and organizational impact.

The second task in the systems planning phase is to investigate the system and determine the proposed system's scope. The team of systems analysts then produces a specific plan for developing the proposed project. This baseline project plan customizes the standardized SDLC and specifies the time and resources needed for its execution. The formal definition of a project is based on the likelihood that the organization's IS department can develop a system that will solve the problem or exploit the opportunity and determine whether the costs of developing the system outweigh the possible benefits. The final presentation of the plan and its subsequent project phases is usually made to the organization's management by the project leader and other team members.

Phase 2: Systems Analysis

The second phase of the systems development life cycle is **systems analysis**. During this phase, the analysts thoroughly study the organization's current procedures and the information systems used to perform tasks such as general ledger, shipping, order entry, machine scheduling, and payroll. Analysis includes several subphases. The first subphase involves determining the requirements of the system. In this subphase, analysts work with users to determine exactly what the users will want from a proposed system. This requires a careful study of any current systems, either manual or computerized, that might be replaced or enhanced as part of this project. Next, the analysts study the requirements and structure them according to their interrelationships, eliminating any redundancies. Third, the analysts generate alternative initial designs to meet the requirements. Then they compare these alternatives to determine which one best meets the requirements given the cost, labor, and technical resources the organization is willing to commit to the development process. The output of the analysis phase is a description of the solution finally recommended by the analysis team. Once the organization accepts the recommendation, analysts can make plans to acquire any hardware and system software necessary to build or operate the system as proposed.

Phase 3: Systems Design

Systems design
The third phase in the SDLC, where the descriptions of the recommended alternative are converted into a logical description and then into physical system specifications.

Logical design
Specifications that focus on the origin, flow, and processing of data in a system but are not tied to any specific hardware and systems software platform.

Physical design
Structured systems design that can be broken down into smaller and smaller units for conversion into instructions written in a programming language.

The third phase of the SDLC is called **systems design**. During systems design, analysts convert the description of the recommended alternative solution into a logical description and then into physical system specifications. Analysts must design all aspects of the system, from input and output screens to reports, databases, and computer processes.

Logical design is not tied to any specific hardware or systems software platform. Theoretically, the system being designed could be implemented using any hardware and systems software. Logical design concentrates on the business aspects of the system; that is, how the system will impact the functional units within the organization. The **physical design** converts the logical design into physical, or technical, specifications. For example, analysts must convert diagrams that map the origin, flow, and processing of data in a system into a structured systems design that can then be broken down into smaller and smaller units for conversion to instructions written in a programming language. During physical design, the analyst team decides which programming languages will be used to write the computer instructions; which database systems and file structures will be used to manage the data; and which hardware platform, operating system, and network environment will be used to run the system. These decisions finalize the hardware and software plans initiated at the end of the analysis phase. The final product of the design phase is the physical system specifications, presented in a form such as a diagram or written report that is ready to be turned over to programmers and other system builders for construction.

Phase 4: Systems Implementation

During the fourth phase of the SDLC, **systems implementation**, system specifications are turned into a working system that is tested and then put into use. Implementation

Figure 2.6 Products of the information system SDLC phases

Products of the SDLC Phases	
Phase	**Products, Outputs, or Deliverables**
Systems planning and selection	Priorities for systems and projects
	Architecture for data, networks, hardware, and IS management
	Detailed work plan for selected project
	Specification of system scope
	System justification or business case
System analysis	Description of current system
	General recommendation on how to fix, enhance, or replace current system
	Explanation of alternative systems and justification for chosen alternative
System design	Detailed specifications of all system elements
	Acquisition plan for new technology
Systems implementation	Code
	Documentation
	Training procedures and support capabilities
Systems maintenance	New versions or releases of software with associated updates to documentation, training, and support

Systems implementation
The fourth phase in the SDLC, where the system specifications are turned into a working system that is tested and then put into use.

includes coding, testing, and installation. During coding, programmers write the programs that make up the system. During testing, programmers and analysts test individual programs and the entire system in order to find and correct errors. During installation, the new system becomes a part of the daily activities of the organization. Application software is installed, or loaded, on existing or new hardware; then users are introduced to the new system and trained. Planning for both testing and installation should begin as early as the project planning and selection phase because both require extensive analysis to develop exactly the right approach.

Phase 5: Systems Maintenance

Systems maintenance
The final phase in the SDLC, where programmers make the changes that users ask for and modify the system to reflect changing business conditions.

The fifth and final phase of the SDLC is **systems maintenance**. While a system is operating, users sometimes find problems with how it works and often think of improvements. During maintenance, programmers make the changes that users ask for and modify the system to reflect changing business conditions. These changes are necessary to keep the system running and useful. The amount of time and effort devoted to system enhancements during the maintenance phase depends a great deal on how well the previous phases of the life cycle were completed. There inevitably comes a time, however, when an information system no longer performs as desired, when the costs of keeping it running become prohibitive, or when the organization's needs have changed substantially. Such problems indicate that it is time to begin designing the system's replacement, thereby completing the loop and starting the life cycle over again.

The SDLC is a linked set of phases in which products developed in one phase feed the activities in subsequent phases. Figure 2.6 summarizes the outputs or products of each phase based on the previous descriptions.

Global Implications: Adding More People to a Project Does Not Always Work

Thirty years ago, Frederick P. Brooks, Jr., published *The Mythical Man-Month*, one of the most influential books ever in the software development field. The book's main point is that it is a mistake to add more people to a software project that is running late. Compressing the time needed to complete a software project by adding more people to the team just doesn't work. In fact, adding more people can make progress even slower because coordinating and managing more people takes more time and effort.

Today, according to Tom Bigelow, CEO of Performance Software Corp., project managers have to relearn the lessons Brooks taught as they add more and more low-cost programmers from India and elsewhere to their projects. Faced with cuts in their project budgets, managers have turned to offshore programmers as a way to increase their workforces and save money at the same time. The results, according to Bigelow, are often "late projects, bad projects, and dead projects." Controlling and coordinating overseas workgroups is much more difficult than many people may realize. Offshore workers tend to be better used for certain parts of a software project, such as testing and verification.

(continued)

According to Bigelow, the best approach to outsourcing in software project management is something he calls tri-partnering. The three partners in such an effort are the organization itself, the offshore partners, and other U.S.-based firms. The ideal scenario, says Bigelow, is for 60% of the work to be done in-house, 30% sent offshore, and the remaining 10% outsourced to other U.S.-based firms. Such an arrangement helps to achieve a balance between the number of workers, the tasks they perform, and their coordination by project management (*Source:* Hall [2004]).

THE PROJECT MANAGEMENT CONTEXT

Whether their purpose is information systems development or something else, projects do not exist in a vacuum. They are part of their broader environment. Project managers have to be attuned to overseeing the day-to-day activities of their projects, but they ignore the context in which those projects exist at their peril. In the next sections, you will read about some of the aspects of the organizational environment that can affect projects and their successful management: project stakeholders, organizational structure, and socioeconomic and environmental influences. You will also read about the general management skills that are useful for project managers.

Project Stakeholders

A project exists because someone saw a need or had a desire and was willing to pay for that need or desire to be met. The individuals who cause a project to be initiated and those who are most directly affected by the project's completion are called stakeholders. Stakeholders are individuals and groups and organizations that are actively involved in the project, who have a vested interest in its success, or who have influence over the project and its results.

The project management team must identify the project stakeholders in order to manage their expectations. If stakeholders expect too much from a project or if their expectations are not realistic, then they are unlikely to be satisfied with the project's progress or its end product. Failure to identify a key stakeholder can cause major problems for a project.

Many different individuals can be stakeholders for a particular project. Key stakeholders include:

- Project manager
- Customer
- Performing organization: those doing the work of the project
- Project team members
- Influencers: those who may not buy or use the project's product but who can have a positive or negative influence on the project due to their organizational position
- Project management office
- Sponsor

The sponsor is the individual in the organization who has ultimate responsibility for the project and its success and who may also have financial responsibility for it. Many others both inside and outside the project organization may be stakeholders. These include sellers, owners, government agencies, media, lobbying organizations, and so on. Many different individuals and groups with a stake in a project can contribute to different and conflicting expectations. The more expectations, and the more they contradict each other, the more difficult it will be to manage them. How does a project manager decide whom to try to keep happy? This is a big challenge. One rule of thumb is to try to meet the customer's requirements, but that does not mean everyone else can be safely ignored.

Organizational Influences

Projects typically exist within a larger organization, and that organizational context can influence the project. Three different elements of an organization that can affect a project are the organization's culture, its structure, and the role of its project management office (if it has one).

Organizational Culture

Organizations develop their own unique cultures over time. An organization's culture reflects what those who work there hold to be most important. Some organizations are known for their aggressive cultures, such as brokerage firms and financial institutions that handle mergers and acquisitions. Other organizations have cultures that are relaxed, where rules are not as important as the quality of the final product. Some software development firms, especially during the Internet boom, were known for being relatively relaxed. Still other organizations are like families, and many other types of cultures have emerged at different organizations. It is also important to note that cultures are not static—they change over time. For instance, the Ford Motor Company is different now than it was when it was founded over 100 years ago.

An organization's culture in its current manifestation often influences the projects it undertakes. For example, a software development project that originated in a brokerage firm in 1997 would be more likely to resemble the aggressive characteristics of a brokerage firm than to take on the relaxed characteristics of an Internet company at the height of the Internet boom.

Organizational Structure

If you have taken a course on management or organizational design, or if you have worked for more than one company, you know that organizational structures can differ dramatically from one company to another. Organizational structure can also affect projects and how they are managed. One key area of a project that structure affects is the availability and allocation of resources.

Organizations may or may not be project based. Those that are not project based typically lack the management systems necessary for efficient and effective project management. Organizations that are project based typically are either those that get most of their revenue from projects, such as IT consulting firms or that have adopted a philosophy of management by projects. Project-based organizations have systems in place to support project management. There are many ways to categorize organizational structures. The Project Management Institute (2000) categorizes them as spanning a spectrum that ranges from functional to matrix to projectized.

Figure 2.7
A functional
organization
structure

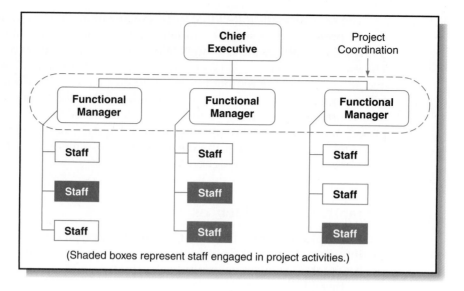

Chief
Executive

Project
Coordination

Functional
Manager

Functional
Manager

Functional
Manager

Staff

Staff

Staff

Staff

Staff

Staff

Staff

Staff

Staff

(Shaded boxes represent staff engaged in project activities.)

Functional organization structure
A traditional hierarchical organization, sometimes thought of as resembling a pyramid, with top management at the fulcrum, direct workers at the bottom, and middle managers in between.

Projectized organization structure
A type of organization structure where people from different functional backgrounds work with each other throughout the lifetime of the project.

Matrix organization structure
A type of organization structure that typically crosses functional design (on one axis) with some other design characteristic (on the other axis).

A **functional organization structure** is a traditional hierarchical organization, sometimes thought of as resembling a pyramid, with top management at the fulcrum, direct workers at the bottom, and middle managers in between (see Figure 2.7). Each employee has one clearly designated supervisor, and employees are grouped by specialization into accounting, marketing, information systems, manufacturing, and other functional groups. In such organizations, the scope of a project is limited to functional boundaries. People within different functional areas work separately on different parts of a project. For example, marketing determines what will sell, engineering designs the product based on what they learned from marketing, and engineering passes its specifications on to manufacturing, which separately determines how to build the product. Many times, engineering has to make product changes that marketing doesn't like, simply because they cannot develop a design that satisfies all of marketing's desires, and manufacturing has to make changes engineering doesn't like in order to build a working product based on the manufacturing technologies in place. This process is often called the over the wall problem—one group takes their part of the project and throws it "over the wall" to the next group. The result is often more work for everybody involved and a product that is less than what it could have been.

At the other extreme of the organizational structure spectrum is the **projectized organization structure** (see Figure 2.8). The project scope and team members cross organizational boundaries, with people from different functional backgrounds working with each other throughout the project's lifetime. Team members are all part of the same organizational unit instead of belonging to different functional areas. The organizational structure is designed to provide the necessary resources for project work. Project managers have the authority and independence necessary to carry the project through to successful completion because they report directly to the organization's chief executive.

In the middle of the spectrum of organizational structures are **matrix organization structures**. Matrix organizations are so named because they typically cross functional design (on one axis) with some other design characteristic (on the other axis), in this case project management. There are several ways to organize matrix organizations;

Figure 2.8
A projectized
organization
structure

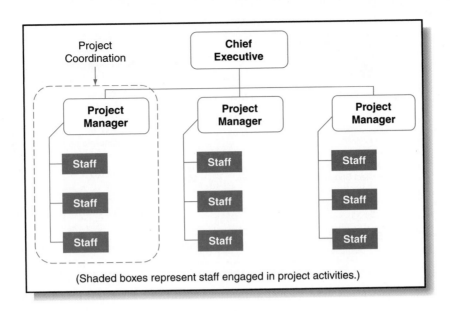

(Shaded boxes represent staff engaged in project activities.)

Figure 2.9 shows a strong matrix structure. A strong matrix has many of the characteristics of a projectized organization, with full-time project managers who have authority and full-time project administrative staff. Project staff report to project managers as well as to the heads of their functional areas. A weak matrix structure would more closely resemble a functional organization, with project managers acting more as coordinators than as independent managers.

Figure 2.10 compares the features of functional, matrix, and projectized organizational structures. The figure features three types of matrix designs, namely weak,

Figure 2.9 A strong matrix organization structure

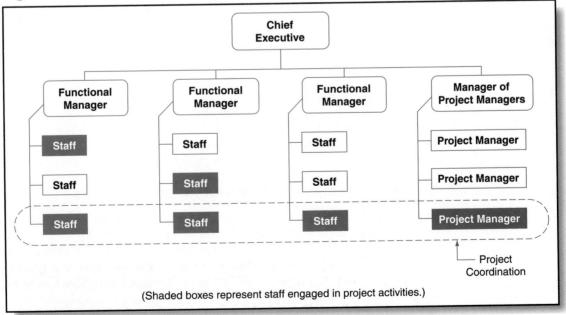

(Shaded boxes represent staff engaged in project activities.)

Project Characteristics \ Organization Structure	Functional	Matrix			Projectized
		Weak Matrix	Balanced Matrix	Strong Matrix	
Project Manager's Authority	Little or None	Limited	Low to Moderate	Moderate to High	High to Almost Total
Resource Availability	Little or None	Limited	Low to Moderate	Moderate to High	High to Almost Total
Who Controls the Project Budget	Functional Manager	Functional Manager	Mixed	Project Manager	Project Manager
Project Manager's Role	Part-time	Part-time	Full-time	Full-time	Full-time
Project Management Administrative Staff	Part-time	Part-time	Part-time	Full-time	Full-time

Figure 2.10 Comparing organizational structure influences on projects

balanced, and strong. It shows how different aspects of project management differ from one organizational structure to the next. It is especially revealing to look at how differences in organizational structure affect the project manager's role.

Project Management Office

Project management office (PMO)
An organizational unit created to centralize and coordinate the projects within an organization.

A **project management office (PMO)** is an organizational unit created to centralize and coordinate the projects within an organization. A project management office oversees the management of projects, programs, or both. Not all organizations have project management offices. Matrix organizations often have a project management office, and organizations with projectized organizational structures will almost always have one. What a project office does is not standard across organizations. In some organizations, the project office may provide support for projects, whereas in others, the office may actually be responsible for all project results. In such cases, the project management office will delegate authority to the project manager and provide him or her with administrative support. Between these two extremes are many different sets of responsibilities and functions for the project office. The existence of a project office and its organizational role can have an impact on individual projects in a given organization.

Social, Economic, and Environmental Influences

Just as a project exists within a wider organizational context, it also exists within a context that extends beyond the organization. Elements of this still broader extra-organizational context can and will affect any given individual project. It has become something of a cliché, but business is increasingly dynamic and global, and these aspects of the larger business environment also affect individual projects. Although there are many different ways to think about the larger environment in which projects exist, here we will look at the four areas of social, economic, and environmental influences identified in the Project Management Institute's Project Management Body of Knowledge (PMBOK):

1. Standards and regulations
2. Internationalization
3. Culture
4. Social-economic-environmental sustainability

These topics are important for the project managers' understanding of how trends in the business world may affect their projects.

Standards and Regulations

Standard
A document approved by a recognized body that provides, for common and repeated use, rules, guidelines, or characteristics for products, processes, or services with which compliance is not mandatory.

Regulation
A document that specifies product, process, or service characteristics, including the applicable administrative provisions, with which compliance is mandatory.

The International Organization for Standardization defines a **standard** as a "document approved by a recognized body, that provides, for common and repeated use, rules, guidelines, or characteristics for products, processes, or services with which compliance is not mandatory" (ISO, 1994). Similarly, a **regulation** is defined as a "document, which lays down product, process, or service characteristics, including the applicable administrative provisions, with which compliance is mandatory" (ISO, 1994). Standards may eventually become de facto regulations driven by market pressures or by habit. Compliance with standards and regulations can be mandated at different levels. The project manager may determine which standards need to be applied; the organization may have certain expectations for its projects or their products; the government, at whatever jurisdictional level, may impose regulations in the name of safety or other public goods.

Standards and regulations can have substantial impacts on a project. They may dictate the inclusion of additional design elements in a product, which increases project time and effort, or they may dictate the inclusion of additional processes in the project itself, such as safety testing. Sometimes these impacts are well known, sometimes not. Where the potential impacts are not well understood, the effects of standards and regulations need to be considered under project risk management. A regulatory law enacted in the United States in 2002 is the Sarbanes-Oxley Act (sometimes called SARBOX or SOX; Fleming and Koppelman, 2005). The act was passed in the wake of several high-profile corporate fraud cases and bankruptcies, such as Enron and MCI. The focus of the act is to put more overt responsibility on executives to be aware of their companies' true financial situation. The outcomes of certain organizational projects, especially large multiyear projects, have impacts on corporate profitability and finances, so an accurate assessment of project status and the costs of completing them becomes doubly important under Sarbanes-Oxley reporting requirements.

Internationalization

Work in many industries today is becoming more and more global, with project and team members spread across many countries and time zones. Work that is global means projects that are global, too. For example, in software development, it is increasingly common for many project members to be located in southern Asia, where skill levels are high but pay is relatively low. Managers and team members for global projects need to take into account the effects of time zone differences, which affect the logistics of teleconferencing, as well as keep track of such things as national and regional holidays and political differences.

Cultural Influences

Where projects are global, cultural issues obviously exist that potentially can affect the project. However, even when a project exists entirely within national boundaries, culture can be an issue. In a heterogeneous population, such as exists in the United States, project members may have very different backgrounds and views in such areas as politics, economics, ethnic origins, demographics, and religion. Project managers need to try to understand how these differences might affect project members and, hence, the project.

Social-Economic-Environmental Sustainability

All projects are planned and implemented within a larger social, economic, and environmental context that extends beyond the project, the organization, and even the nation where the project work was completed. As is the case with many human endeavors, projects have intended and unintended consequences. While one would hope that the intended consequences are all positive, the unintended consequences may be both positive and negative. Organizations are increasingly accountable for the project's results and its effects long after it has been completed, whether those effects were intended or not. Although it is, by definition, impossible to identify unintended consequences beforehand, thinking in terms of the project's larger social, economic, and environmental context may help alleviate some of the worst possible outcomes.

Key General Management Skills

General management is a broad subject that deals with all aspects of managing an organization. It includes skills related to different functional areas of an organization, such as finance and accounting, purchasing, marketing, contracts and commercial law, and manufacturing. It also includes high-level organization-wide skills, such as logistics and supply chain, strategic, tactical, and operational planning; understanding organizational structure and behavior; health and safety practices; and information technology. Project management, though highly specialized, is still a form of management. General management skills apply much as they would to any other form of management, and these general skills provide a strong foundation for project managers. In fact, general management skills are often essential for successful project management. Project management also calls for keen interpersonal skills, such as being able to act as a leader, to communicate effectively, to negotiate and manage conflict, to solve problems, to influence the organization, and to motivate people. Each of these is explored in more detail in the following sections.

Leading

Leadership is a broad term encompassing many areas related to working with others. To lead means, among other things, to establish direction, align people with that direction, motivate them to work hard and do their best, and inspire them to succeed, often by example. A project manager is sometimes expected to be the project leader. On large projects, however, the project manager and the project leader may not be the same person.

TIPS FROM THE PROS
How to Avoid Wasting Time on Projects

Time is a major resource in project management, and it always seems to be in short supply. Many information technology (IT) projects are late, despite recent advances in project management techniques and in software designed to improve the overall project management process. Here is a list of nine things known for wasting project time, along with suggestions from several project managers on how to deal with them (Source: Mearian [2004]):

1. *Rushing in.* There has always been a temptation in IT projects to skip analysis and design and go right to coding. If business requirements have not been adequately addressed upfront, however, there will be problems later, especially in testing, when it's discovered that business needs were not well defined. Lois Zells, a project management consultant in Redondo Beach, California, recommends resisting this temptation. A basic rule of thumb is that every hour of planning saves three hours of work.

2. *The life cycle rut.* Johanna Rothman, president of Rothman Consulting Group Inc., says that some traditional life cycles that are designed to yield fewer defects actually draw out project time. One solution is to look for alternative life cycles that reduce defects but do not slow projects down. Managers shouldn't use a life cycle just because it is familiar.

3. *Poor communication.* Mark Brooks, a project team leader at a large financial services firm, says lack of communication is often the cause of project slowdowns. To avoid poor communication, Brooks sets up a telephone bridge that is open all day. A telephone bridge is an electronic system that links multiple telephone lines. The bridge functions like a conference calling line but is much less expensive. On one recent project, the bridge worked to avoid a project shutdown due to the impending failure of a key server. Using the bridge, project members were able to find an alternative solution and keep the project going.

4. *Excessive research.* Project team members can waste weeks of time combing through industry white papers on products, and much of what they find is more hype than reality. Kevin Gungiah, director of systems administration for The Weather Channel Interactive Inc., instead recommends calling customer references to ask what their experiences have been with a product.

5. *Untamed e-mail.* Sometimes important e-mail can get lost among spam and all the other e-mail people receive. Mark Brooks recommends setting up project standards for e-mail early in the project. For example, Brooks establishes a six-letter acronym for the project that is put in every e-mail subject line. This makes it easier to identify and file project-related e-mail. He also recommends that action items in e-mail be put in the first couple of lines of text so that the work needed can be seen in the e-mail preview page.

6. *Indecision.* Business stakeholders waste project time when they cannot decide on issues, such as technical standards, that are key to the project. Larry Sisemore, an international manager of systems development at FedEx Corp., recommends that project managers be assertive with stakeholders, explaining how their lack of a decision is affecting the project.

7. *Obsessing.* IT workers sometimes get so focused on a problem they lose track of time. Catherine Tomczyk, a project manager at First Data Corporation, says that she establishes project rules dictating that if someone is stuck on a problem for more than eight hours, the problem gets escalated and a buddy is assigned to help with it.

8. *Between-meeting paralysis.* If review meetings are held weekly, a problem that pops up just after a meeting may go a week without resolution. Catherine Tomczyk recommends short daily meetings to make sure problems are addressed as soon as they are discovered.

9. *Embellishment.* Johanna Rothman observes that many IT developers add features and embellish systems if they think they have the time to do so. Rothman uses release criteria that define what "done" means so that developers know when to stop.

Communicating

Communicating—exchanging information—is something we all do every day, but it is also something most of us don't do well. Communication has many dimensions. It can be written or oral, involve speaking and listening, be internal or external, formal or informal, vertical or horizontal. Furthermore, it involves choosing the appropriate media, establishing a clear and precise writing style, developing good presentation techniques, and learning how to successfully run and manage a meeting.

Negotiating

Negotiation involves coming to terms and reaching an agreement. Negotiating is a constant part of project management. The three key elements of any project—scope, cost, and schedule—are subject to continual negotiation, as are contracts, personnel assignments, and resource allocation.

Problem Solving

Solving problems has two aspects: problem definition and decision making. Defining a problem sounds trivial and obvious, but correctly defining a problem means the difference between solving the real problem or solving something else. Defining a problem correctly means distinguishing between causes and symptoms, and it involves gathering information and problem finding.

Decision making involves analysis of the problem, which leads to possible solutions and choosing from among them. It is important to note that all decisions have time restrictions, so that it is rarely possible to find and collect all relevant information. Decision making rarely results in optimal decisions. Instead, due to time limitations and limits to human processing, decision making often results in "satisficing"—choosing the best alternative available as soon as it is found.

Influencing the Organization

Because a project exists within an organizational context, its successful completion is intertwined with the organization and its operation. Project managers must not only understand the organizational context; they must also be able to influence the context in the project's favor. Influencing the organization gives managers the ability to get things done. It requires understanding the formal and informal organizational structures involved, which typically also requires understanding the organization's politics and power distribution.

Motivating People

Project managers need to determine how to get other people to do project tasks and to do them well. Motivating team members to succeed means energizing them to achieve at high levels and to overcome obstacles to change. Project managers have many motivational tools at their disposal, including many types of rewards and sanctions.

COMMON PROBLEMS
Where Do You Go for Help?

Project management is challenging. It is a complex activity that requires a good balance of managerial and technical skills. Any given project offers many opportunities but also presents its share of problems. As you gain experience working on projects and managing them, you will accumulate a set of effective solutions for many common problems. You will learn which solutions work best for which problems. Sometimes,

(continued)

TECHNOLOGY AND TECHNIQUES TO SUPPORT THE PROJECT MANAGEMENT LIFE CYCLE

A project manager can utilize a wide variety of techniques for depicting and documenting project plans. These planning documents can take the form of graphical or textual reports, although graphical reports have become more popular. The most commonly used are Gantt charts and network diagrams. While both of these will be covered in greater detail later in the book, we will introduce them here. Because Gantt charts are not intended to indicate how tasks must be ordered (precedence) but simply show when a task should begin and when it should end, they are often more useful for depicting relatively simple projects or subparts of a larger project, for showing the activities of a single worker, or for monitoring the progress of activities compared to the scheduled completion dates (see Figure 2.11a). Gantt charts can be very helpful for complex projects, nonetheless. See the special case at the end of the chapter, "Making It Work: Hong Kong's New International Airport at Chek Lap Kok." A network diagram illustrates how activities can be ordered by connecting a task to its predecessor and successor tasks (see Figure 2.11b). Sometimes a network diagram is preferable; other times a Gantt chart more clearly shows certain aspects of a project. The key differences between these two representations are:

- A Gantt chart depicts the duration of tasks, whereas a network diagram depicts the sequence dependencies between tasks.

- A Gantt chart depicts the time overlap of tasks, whereas a network diagram does not show time overlap but does show which tasks can be done in parallel.

- Some forms of Gantt charts can depict slack time available within an earliest start and latest finish duration. A network diagram shows this by the data contained within activity rectangles.

Project managers also use textual reports that depict resource utilization by tasks, complexity of the project, and cost distributions to control activities. For example, Figure 2.12 shows a screen from Microsoft Project for Windows that summarizes all project activities, their durations in weeks, and their scheduled starting and ending dates. Most project managers use computer-based systems to help develop their graphical and textual reports.

A project manager will periodically review the status of all ongoing project task activities to assess whether they will be completed early, on time, or late. If early or late, the duration of the activity, depicted in column 2 of Figure 2.11a, can be updated. Once changed, the scheduled start and finish times of all subsequent tasks will also change. Making such a change will also alter any Gantt chart or

Figure 2.11
Graphical diagrams that depict project plans
(a) a Gantt chart
(b) a network diagram

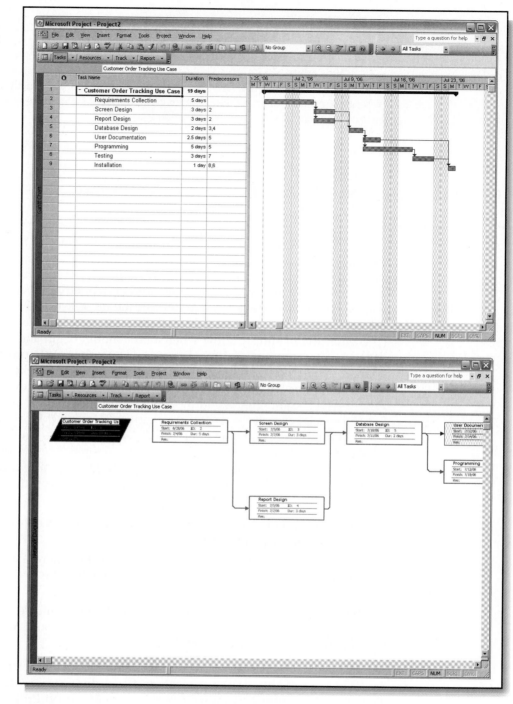

network diagram used to represent the project tasks. The ability to easily make changes to a project is a very powerful feature of most project management environments. It enables the project manager to determine easily how changes in task duration will impact the project completion date. It is also useful for examining the impact of what-if scenarios of adding or reducing resources, such as personnel, for an activity.

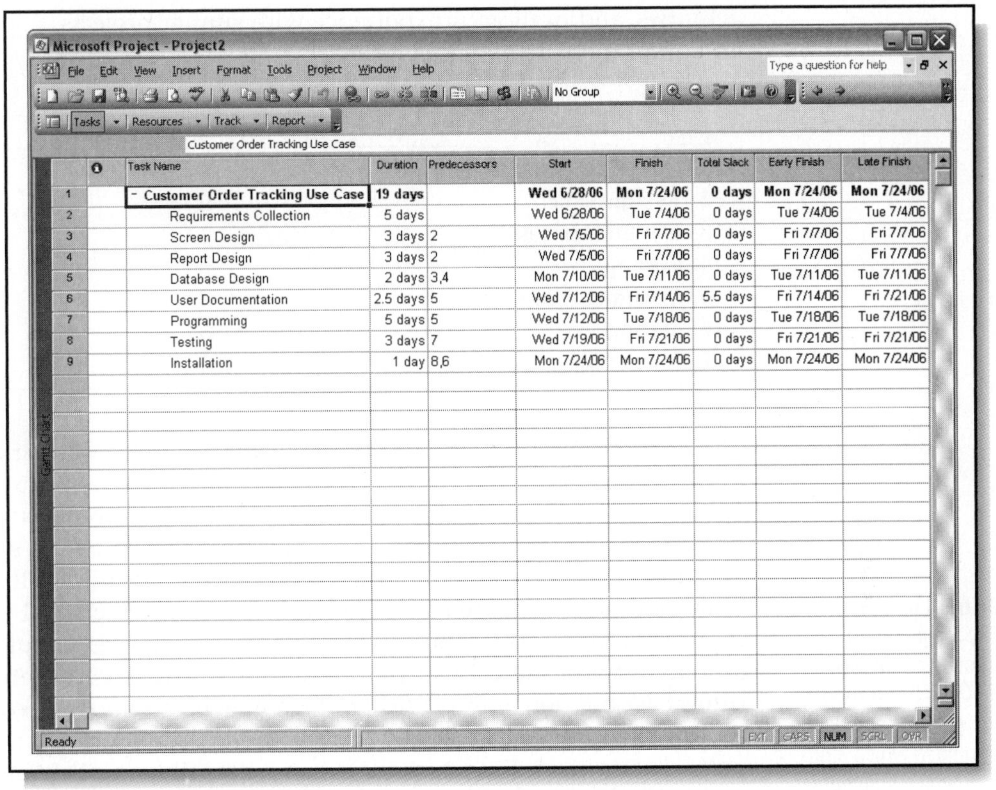
Microsoft Project - Project2
File Edit View Insert Format Tools Project Window Help
Type a question for help
No Group
Tasks Resources Track Report
Customer Order Tracking Use Case
Task Name | Duration | Predecessors | Start | Finish | Total Slack | Early Finish | Late Finish
1 Customer Order Tracking Use Case | 19 days | | Wed 6/28/06 | Mon 7/24/06 | 0 days | Mon 7/24/06 | Mon 7/24/06
2 Requirements Collection | 5 days | | Wed 6/28/06 | Tue 7/4/06 | 0 days | Tue 7/4/06 | Tue 7/4/06
3 Screen Design | 3 days | 2 | Wed 7/5/06 | Fri 7/7/06 | 0 days | Fri 7/7/06 | Fri 7/7/06
4 Report Design | 3 days | 2 | Wed 7/5/06 | Fri 7/7/06 | 0 days | Fri 7/7/06 | Fri 7/7/06
5 Database Design | 2 days | 3,4 | Mon 7/10/06 | Tue 7/11/06 | 0 days | Tue 7/11/06 | Tue 7/11/06
6 User Documentation | 2.5 days | 5 | Wed 7/12/06 | Fri 7/14/06 | 5.5 days | Fri 7/14/06 | Fri 7/21/06
7 Programming | 5 days | 5 | Wed 7/12/06 | Tue 7/18/06 | 0 days | Tue 7/18/06 | Tue 7/18/06
8 Testing | 3 days | 7 | Wed 7/19/06 | Fri 7/21/06 | 0 days | Fri 7/21/06 | Fri 7/21/06
9 Installation | 1 day | 8,6 | Mon 7/24/06 | Mon 7/24/06 | 0 days | Mon 7/24/06 | Mon 7/24/06
Gantt Chart
Ready
EXT CAPS NUM SCRL OVR

Figure 2.12 A screen from Microsoft project that summarizes all project activities, their durations in weeks, and their scheduled starting and ending dates

Network Diagrams and Project Life Cycles

Project scheduling and management requires that time, costs, and resources be controlled. While the concepts of resources, critical path analysis, and slack are covered in greater detail later in this text, we briefly introduce these concepts at this time to illustrate how information systems projects are managed, and how we get estimates regarding project durations. Resources are any person, group of people, piece of equipment, hardware, software, or material used in accomplishing an activity. Network diagramming is a scheduling technique used for controlling resources. A network diagram is one of the most widely used and best-known scheduling methods. A major strength of network diagramming is its ability to show how changes to completion times impact the overall schedule. Because of this, it is used more often than Gantt charts to manage projects such as information systems development, where variability in the duration of activities is the norm. You would use a network diagram when tasks:

- Are well-defined and have a clear beginning and endpoint
- Can be worked on independently of other tasks
- Are ordered

To better understand project resource scheduling (again, covered more thoroughly in Chapter 7), we also need to briefly introduce the concept of a critical path. To illustrate this concept, assume that you have been assigned to work on a small project defining the major steps for a key feature within a larger system. We will call this the *Key Feature Project*. For this particular project, you identify seven major activities, and from your experience with similar projects, you make time estimates and order these activities as follows:

Activity	Time Estimate (In Days)	Preceding Activity
1. Collect Requirements	1	—
2. Design Screens	2	1
3. Design Database	2	1
4. Coding	3	2, 3
5. Documentation	2	4
6. Testing	3	4
7. Integration	1	5, 6

With this information, you are now able to draw a network diagram. Recall that network diagrams are composed of circles or rectangles representing activities and connecting arrows showing required work flows as illustrated in Figure 2.13. The critical path of a network diagram is represented by the sequence of connected activities that produce the longest overall time period. All nodes and activities within this sequence are referred to as being "on" the **critical path**. The critical path represents the shortest time in which a project can be completed. In other words, any activity on the critical path that is delayed in completion delays the entire project. Nodes not on the critical path, however, can be delayed (for some amount of time) without delaying the final completion of the project. Nodes not on the critical path contain **slack time** and allow some flexibility in scheduling. Slack (addressed more thoroughly in Chapter 7) indicates the amount of time an activity can be delayed without delaying the project.

To determine the critical path and the expected completion time for the *Key Feature Project* you must calculate the earliest and latest expected completion time for each activity (see Figure 2.14). To do this, you must first calculate the earliest expected completion time (T_E) for each activity by summing the estimated time (ET) for each activity from left to right (i.e., in precedence order), starting at activity 1 and working toward activity 7. For example, to get T_E for activity 2, take the ET for activity 1, which is 1, and add the ET for activity 2, which is 2, giving a T_E of 3 for activity 2. In this case, T_E for activity 7 is equal to 10 days. If two or more activities precede an activity, the longest expected completion time of these activities is used in calculating the new activity's expected completion time. For example, because activity 7 is preceded by both activities 5 and 6, the longest expected completion time between 5 and 6 is 9, so T_E for activity 7 is 9 + 1, or 10. The earliest expected completion time for the last activity of the project represents the amount of time the project should take to complete. Because the time of each activity can vary, however, the projected completion

Critical path
The longest path through a network diagram illustrating the shortest amount of time in which a project can be completed.

Slack time
The amount of time that an activity can be delayed without delaying the project.

Figure 2.13
A network diagram for the *Key Feature Project* showing activities (represented by circles) and sequences of those activities (represented by arrows)

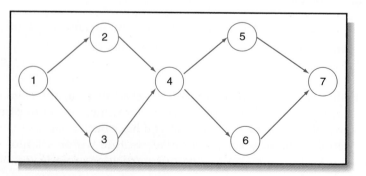

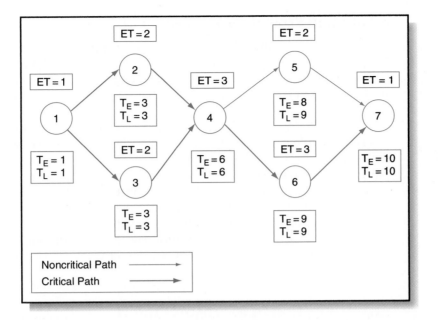

Figure 2.14
A network diagram for the *Key Feature Project* showing estimated times for each activity and the earliest and latest expected completion time for each activity

time represents only an estimate. The project may, in fact, require more or less time for completion.

The latest expected completion time (T_L) refers to the time in which an activity can be completed without delaying the project. To find the values for each activity's T_L, start with activity 7 and set T_L equal to the final T_E (10 days). Next, work from right to left toward activity 1 and subtract the expected time for each activity. For example, this would give you a total T_L of 9 for both activities 5 and 6, because you subtract the ET of activity 7, or 1, from its T_L of 10. The slack time for each activity is equal to the difference between its latest and earliest expected completion times $(T_L - T_E)$. The slack time calculations for all activities of the *Key Feature Project* are as follows:

Activity	T_E	T_L	Slack: $T_L - T_E$	On Critical Path?
1	1	1	0	Yes
2	3	3	0	Yes
3	3	3	0	Yes
4	6	6	0	Yes
5	8	9	1	No
6	9	9	0	Yes
7	10	10	0	Yes

Note that all activities with a slack time equal to zero are on the critical path. Thus, all activities except 5 are on the critical path. Also, the diagram in Figure 2.14 shows two critical paths between activities 1–2–4 and 1–3–4 because both of these parallel activities have zero slack. In addition to the possibility of having multiple critical paths, there are two possible types of slack. *Free slack* refers to the amount of time a task can be delayed without delaying the early start of any task immediately following. *Total slack* refers to the amount of time a task can be delayed without delaying the completion of the project. Understanding free slack and total slack allows the project manager to better identify where tradeoffs can be made if changes to the project schedule are needed. For more information on slack and how it can be used to manage tasks, see *Project Management for Business and Technology: Principles and Practice* (Nicholas, 2001).

Estimating Project Times Using PERT

Program Evaluation Review Technique (PERT)
A technique that uses optimistic, pessimistic, and realistic time estimates to calculate the expected time for a particular task.

Another technique that can be used to support project scheduling is the **Program Evaluation Review Technique (PERT).** While PERT will be covered more comprehensively in Chapter 7 where we address managing project resources and duration, we introduce PERT here since it is another technique that helps us manage the project life cycle.

One of the most difficult and most error-prone activities in constructing a project schedule is the determination of each task's duration within a work breakdown structure (see Chapter 5 for more on work breakdown structures). It is particularly problematic to make these estimates when a task involves a high degree of complexity and uncertainty. PERT uses optimistic, pessimistic, and realistic time estimates to calculate the *expected time* for a particular task. This technique helps you obtain a better estimate when there is some uncertainty as to how much time a task will require. PERT thus helps us understand the durations of tasks, which have implications on project life cycle times. The term "PERT Chart" is also used sometimes to refer to a network diagram.

An Introduction to Microsoft Project

A wide variety of automated project management tools are available to help manage development projects. New versions of these tools are continuously being developed and released by software vendors. Most of the available tools share a common set of features that include the ability to define and order tasks, assign resources to tasks, and easily modify tasks and resources. These systems vary in the number of task activities supported, the complexity of relationships, system processing and storage requirements, and of course, cost. Prices can range from a few hundred dollars for personal-computer–based systems to more than $100,000 for large-scale multiproject systems. Yet a lot can be done with systems like Microsoft Project as well as public domain and shareware systems. For example, numerous shareware project management programs (e.g., MinuteMan, Delegator, or Project KickStart) can be downloaded from the World Wide Web (e.g., at www.download.com).

We will now illustrate the types of activities you would perform when using project management software. Because it is widely used and has had consistently high marks in computer publication reviews, we will base our discussion on the Microsoft Project for Windows project management system. While more information on Microsoft Project is covered in later chapters, as well as in Appendix A, we briefly illustrate the use of this technology to show how it can be used to support the software development process. When using this system to manage a project, you need to perform at least the following activities:

- Establish a project starting or ending date
- Enter tasks and assign task relationships
- Select a scheduling method to review project reports

Establishing a Project Starting Date

Assume you have been assigned to design, develop, and implement a new corporate intranet site for your company's personnel director. You have been given 12 weeks to complete this system, called *InfoNet*. The vision for *InfoNet* is to create a Web portal for employees, providing information on corporate performance, news, benefits plans, training programs, job postings, corporate policies, and so on. The personnel director

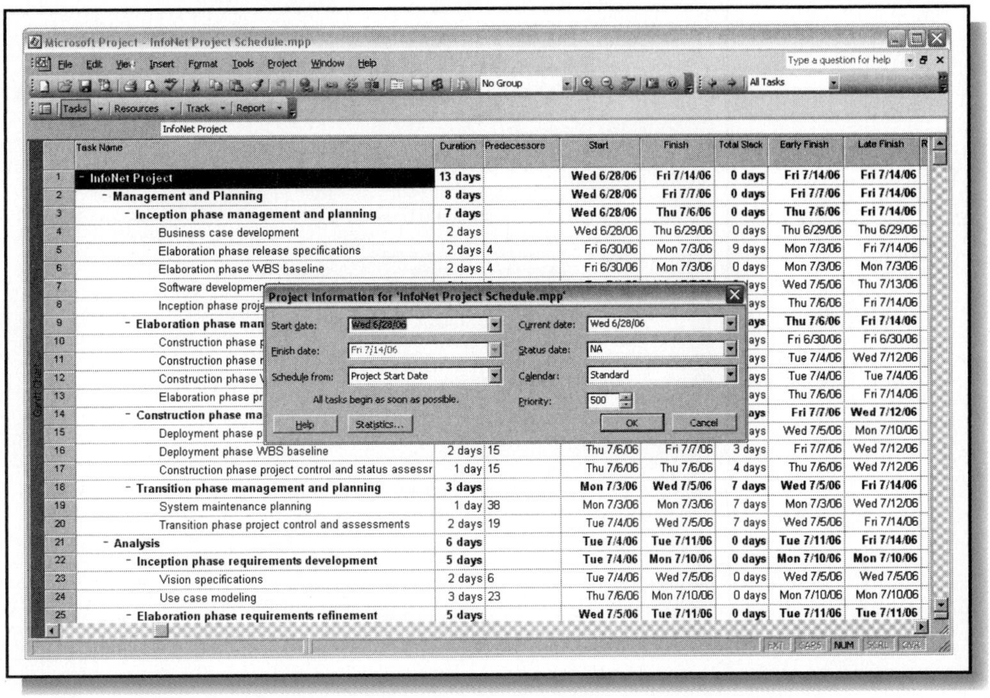

Figure 2.15   Establishing a project starting date in Microsoft Project for
the *InfoNet* project

also would like *InfoNet* to be interactive so that employees could, for example, change insurance plans or register for training courses using an online interface.

A preliminary step in using Microsoft Project to represent a project schedule is to enter the project starting date into the system. Starting (or ending) dates are used to schedule future activities or backdate others based upon their duration and relationships to other activities. Figure 2.15 illustrates how to set a starting date of November 3, 2003, for the *InfoNet* project.

Entering Tasks and Assigning Task Relationships

The next step in defining a project is to establish project tasks, their duration, and sequence. Once you have done this, you can begin entering the tasks into Microsoft Project. The task entry screen, shown in Figure 2.16, is similar to a spreadsheet program. The user moves the cursor to a cell and then simply enters a textual name, a numeric duration for each activity, and task predecessors. Scheduled start and scheduled finish are automatically entered based upon the project start date and duration entered previously. To set a task-precedent relationship, the task number (or numbers) that must be completed before the start of the current task is entered into the predecessors column. The project management software uses this information to construct Gantt charts, network diagrams, and other project-related reports.

Selecting a Scheduling Method to Review Project Reports

As you enter more and more task information into Microsoft Project, it is very easy to review the information in a variety of graphical and textual formats. For example, Figure 2.17 shows the current project information in a Gantt chart format and

Figure 2.16 Entering tasks and assigning task relationships in Microsoft Project for the *InfoNet* project

Figure 2.17 Gantt chart of the *InfoNet* project

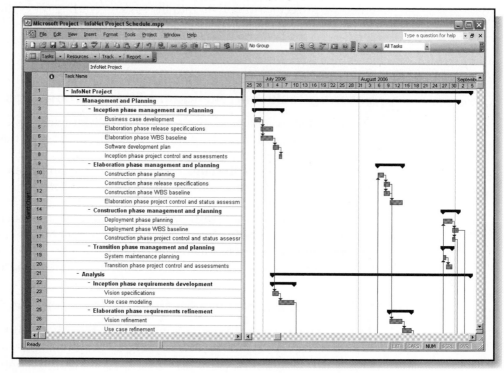

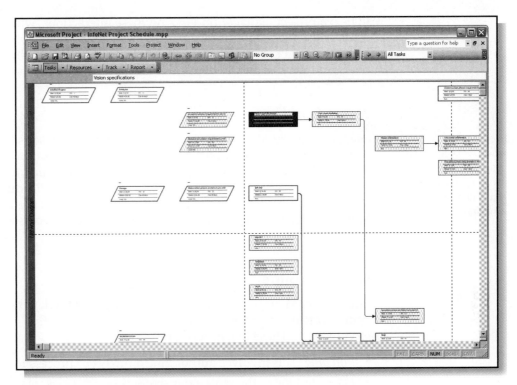

Figure 2.18 Network diagram of the *InfoNet* project

Figure 2.18 shows a network diagram. You can easily change how you view the information by making a selection from menu options on the left side of the screen.

This brief introduction to project management software only scratches the surface of these systems' power and features. Other widely available and especially useful features for multiperson projects relate to resource usage and utilization. Resource-related features allow you to define characteristics such as standard costing rates and daily availability via a calendar that records holidays, working hours, and vacations. These features are particularly useful for billing and estimating project costs. Often, resources are shared across multiple projects, which could significantly affect a project's schedule. Depending upon how projects are billed within an organization, assigning and billing resources to tasks is very time-consuming for most project managers. The tools provided in these powerful systems can greatly ease project planning and management and enhance the effective use of the resources committed to those jobs.

PROJECT MANAGEMENT PROCESSES

Projects tend to be complex, involving many resources, including people, money, and equipment, and they tend to span several months if not years. If projects did not tend to be complex, we would not need powerful techniques or software packages to manage them successfully. Because projects are complex, however, managing them tends to be integrative. What happens in one part of a project affects other parts, so it is important for a project manager to understand all of the different project management processes and their interactions. Project management techniques and software can help a project manager understand these interactions, which often require trade-offs among project objectives. The next sections of the chapter, will discuss project processes, project process groups, and process interactions, all of which will help you understand the complexity of projects and how to manage that complexity.

Project Processes

Funk and Wagnall's Standard Desk Dictionary defines **process** as "a series of continuous actions that bring about a particular result, end, or condition." A project is a set of processes. Project management processes describe, organize, and complete the work of the project, and they are applicable to most projects. Product-oriented processes specify and create the project's product. These processes are defined by the project life cycle. Project management and product-oriented processes overlap and interact throughout a project.

Process Groups

In the Project Management Body of Knowledge (PMBOK), the Project Management Institute organizes project management processes into five groups of two or more processes each. These five groups are:

- *Initiating.* This involves authorizing a project or process to begin.
- *Planning.* One of the most extensive sets of processes, planning involves defining goals and selecting the best way to achieve them. Many of the activities that require management techniques and project management software involve planning processes.
- *Executing.* Once the project is planned, the next step is carrying out the plan. Executing processes involve coordinating people and other resources to carry out the plan.
- *Monitoring and Controlling.* Controlling processes are designed to regularly monitor and measure progress during execution in order to identify variances from the plan and to take corrective action when necessary.
- *Closing.* The counterpart to the initiating process, closing processes occur when a project is formally accepted and brought to an end.

Process groups are linked by the results they produce. The output from one process group often becomes the input for another. The relationships among the process groups are illustrated in Figure 2.19. Note that while this figure differs from Figure 1.15 introduced last chapter (which also depicted process groups and their relationships) neither depiction is necessarily inaccurate, but rather simply reflect different visualizations of the same concept.

Process groups overlap and vary within a phase (see Figure 2.20). Although projects are conceived and described as discrete phases and processes, in reality there are many overlaps. Planning is an ongoing and iterative process.

Involving stakeholders in project phases can increase their satisfaction with the project's outcome. As noted earlier, one of the project manager's key tasks is to successfully manage stakeholders' expectations. Involving them in project processes encourages ownership and buy-in, partly through allowing stakeholders to modify their expectations as they experience firsthand the progress of the project and its products. Ownership on the part of stakeholders is often critical to project success. One of the key factors for the success of information systems development projects is

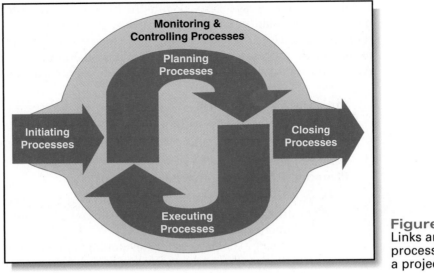

Figure 2.19
Links among process groups in a project phase

the participation of users, who are key stakeholders, in the analysis and design process. Involvement has to be real, however. Stakeholders have to believe that their participation makes a difference and that they are being taken seriously if they are to buy in.

Process Interactions

Within each of the five process groups, individual processes are linked by their inputs and outputs. By focusing on these links, each process can be described in terms of its inputs and outputs and the methods and procedures for converting inputs to outputs. PMI (2004) has identified 44 project management processes

Figure 2.20 Overlap of process groups in a project phase

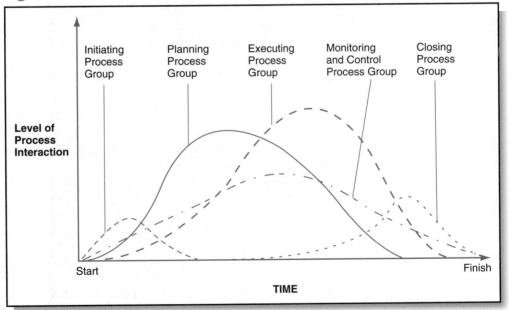

within the five process groups. While the interactions between these processes will be covered in detail in later chapters, we will introduce these process groups, and their sub-processes, here. Initiating and closing each include two processes. The remaining 40 processes are distributed among the remaining three process groups. All 44 processes, with their official PMBOK definitions, are as follows:

Initiating. Two processes:

- *Develop project charter*. Authorize the project or phase.
- *Develop preliminary project scope statement*. Produce high level definition of the project using the Project Charter and other inputs.

Planning. Twenty-one separate processes:

- *Develop project management plan*. The process for defining, preparing, integrating, and coordinating all subsidiary plans into a project management plan.
- *Scope planning*. The process for developing a project scope management plan.
- *Scope definition*. The process necessary for developing a detailed project scope statement.
- *Create WBS*. The process for subdividing major project deliverables into smaller more manageable components, called the work breakdown structure (WBS).
- *Activity definition*. The process of identifying the specific activities that must be performed to produce the various project deliverables.
- *Activity sequencing*. The process for identifying and documenting interactivity dependencies.
- *Activity resource estimating*. The process for estimating the type and quantities required to perform each schedule activity.
- *Activity duration estimating*. The process for estimating the number of work periods that will be needed to complete individual activities.
- *Schedule development*. The process for analyzing activity sequences, activity durations, and resource requirements to create the project schedule.
- *Cost estimating*. The process for developing an approximation (estimate) of the costs of the resources required to complete project activities.
- *Cost budgeting*. The process for aggregating the estimated costs of individual activities to establish a cost baseline.
- *Quality planning*. The process for identifying which quality standards are relevant to the project and determining how to satisfy them.
- *Human resource planning*. The process necessary for identifying project roles, responsibilities, and reporting relationships.
- *Communications planning*. The process for determining the information and communications needs of the stakeholders.
- *Risk management planning*. The process for deciding how to approach and plan for risk management in a project.
- *Risk identification*. The process for determining which risks might affect the project and documenting their characteristics.
- *Qualitative risk analysis*. The process for prioritizing risks for subsequent further analysis or action by assessing and combining their probability of occurrence and impact.
- *Quantitative risk analysis*. The process for numerically analyzing the effect on overall project objectives of identified risks.
- *Risk response planning*. The process for developing options and actions to enhance opportunities and to reduce threats to the project's objectives.

- *Plan purchases and acquisitions*. The process for determining what to purchase or acquire, and determining when and how.
- *Plan contracting*. The process for documenting products, services, and results requirements and identifying potential sellers.

Executing. Seven processes:

- *Direct and manage project execution*. The process for directing the various technical and organizational interfaces that exist in the project to execute the work defined in the project management plan.
- *Perform quality assurance*. The process for applying the planned, systematic quality activities to ensure that the project employs all processes needed to meet requirements.
- *Acquire project team*. The process for obtaining the human resources necessary for completing the project.
- *Develop project team*. The process for improving the competencies and interaction of team members to enhance project performance.
- *Information distribution*. The process for making information available to project stakeholders in a timely manner.
- *Request seller responses*. The process for obtaining information, quotations, bids, offers, or proposals.
- *Select sellers*. The process for reviewing offers, choosing from among potential sellers, and negotiating a written contract with the seller.

Controlling. Twelve processes:

- *Monitor and control project work*. The process for collecting, measuring, and disseminating performance information. One key part of the process is to use performance information to improve process.
- *Integrated change control*. The process for controlling factors that create changes to make sure the changes are beneficial, determining when a change has occurred, and managing the approved changes, when they occur.
- *Scope verification*. The process for formalizing acceptance of the completed project deliverables.
- *Scope control*. The process for controlling changes to project scope.
- *Schedule control*. The process for controlling changes to the project schedule.
- *Cost control*. The process of influencing the factors that create variances, and controlling changes to the project budget.
- *Perform quality control*. The process for monitoring specific project results to determine whether they comply with relevant quality standards and identifying ways to eliminate causes of unsatisfactory performance.
- *Manage project team*. The process for tracking team member performance and includes providing feedback, resolving issues, and making changes that lead to team performance.
- *Performance reporting*. The process for collecting and distributing performance information.
- *Manage stakeholders*. The process for communicating with stakeholders in order to satisfy their requirements and resolve any issues they might have.
- *Risk monitoring and control*. The process for keeping track of identified risks, monitoring residual risks, executing risk response plans, and evaluating their effectiveness throughout the project life cycle.
- *Contract administration*. The process for managing contracts between buyers and vendors, including the monitoring of vendor performance.

Closing. Two processes:

- *Close project.* The process to finalize all activities across all of the process groups to formally close the project or a project phase.
- *Contract closure.* The process for completing and settling each contract, including resolution of any open items, and closing each contract applicable to the project or a project phase.

Mapping Project Management Processes

Forty-four processes are a lot to keep track of, which again shows the usefulness of project management techniques and software. But not all processes are needed on all projects, and not all interactions will apply to all projects. Experienced project managers have a good feel for which processes apply to projects in their industries and their organizations or to projects of particular scopes and durations. An overview mapping the 44 project management processes into the five process groups is provided in Figure 2.21.

Figure 2.21 Mapping project management processes to process groups

Knowledge Area Processes	Project Management Process Groups				
	Initiating Process Group	**Planning Process Group**	**Executing Process Group**	**Monitoring & Controlling Process Group**	**Closing Process Group**
4. Project Management Integration	Develop Project Chapter 3.2.1.1 (4.1) Develop Preliminary Project Scope Statement 3.2.1.2 (4.2)	Develop Project Management Plan 3.2.2.1 (4.3)	Direct and Manage Project Execution 3.2.3.1 (4.4)	Monitor and Control Project Work 3.2.4.1 (4.5) Integrated Change Control 3.2.4.2 (4.6)	Close Project 3.2.5.1 (4.7)
5. Project Scope Management		Scope Planning 3.2.2.2 (5.1) Scope Definition 3.2.2.3 (5.2) Create WBS 3.2.2.4 (5.3)		Scope Verification 3.2.4.3 (5.4) Scope Control 3.2.4.4 (5.5)	
6. Project Time Management		Activity Definition 3.2.2.5 (6.1) Activity Sequencing 3.2.2.6 (6.2) Activity Resource Estimating 3.2.2.7 (6.3) Activity Duration Estimating 3.2.2.8 (6.4) Schedule Development 3.2.2.9 (6.5)		Schedule Control 3.2.4.5 (6.6)	

Figure 2.21 (continued)

7. Project Cost Management		Cost Estimating 3.2.2.10 (7.1) Cost Budgeting 3.2.2.11 (7.2)		Cost Control 3.2.4.6 (7.3)	
8. Project Quality Management		Quality Planning 3.2.2.12 (8.1)	Perform Quality Assurance 3.2.3.2 (8.2)	Perform Quality Control 3.2.4.7 (8.3)	
9. Project Human Resource Management		Human Resource Planning 3.2.2.13 (9.1)	Acquire Project Team 3.2.3.3 (9.2) Develop Project Team 3.2.3.4 (9.3)	Manage Project Team 3.2.4.8 (9.4)	
10. Project Communications Management		Communications Planning 3.2.2.14 (10.1)	Information Distribution 3.2.3.5 (10.2)	Performance Reporting 3.2.4.9 (10.3) Manage Stakeholders 3.2.4.10 (10.4)	
11. Project Risk Management		Risk Management Planning 3.2.2.15 (11.1) Risk Identification 3.2.2.16 (11.2) Qualitative Risk Analysis 3.2.2.17 (11.3) Quantitative Risk Analysis 3.2.2.18 (11.4) Risk Responce Planning 3.2.2.19 (11.5)		Risk Monitoring and Control 3.2.4.11 (11.6)	
12. Project Procurement Management		Plan Purchases and Acquisitions 3.2.2.20 (12.1) Plan Contracting 3.2.2.21 (12.2)	Request Seller Responses 3.2.3.6 (12.3) Select Sellers 3.2.3.7 (12.4)	Contract Administration 3.2.4.12 (12.5)	Contract Closure 3.2.5.2 (12.6)

THE PROJECT MANAGEMENT LIFE CYCLE AND THE PMBOK

For this chapter—The Project Management Life Cycle—we have discussed the project management context and the project management processes. Specifically we have talked about project phases and the project life cycle, project stakeholders, organizational influences, key management skills, and environmental influences. In addition, we have talked about the distinctions between project processes and process groups and how the processes interact with one another. Figure 2.22 identifies this coverage and illustrates the coverage of upcoming chapters as well.

Figure 2.22 Chapter 2 and PMBOK coverage

	Textbook Chapters →	1	2	3	4	5	6	7	8	9	10	11	12
	PMBOK Knowledge Area												
1	**Introduction to Project Management**												
1.1	What is a Project?	●											
1.2	What is Project Management?	●											
1.3	Areas of Expertise		✓										
1.4	Project Management Context	●											
2	**Project Life Cycle and Organization**												
2.1	The Project Life Cycle	●	✓										
2.2	Project Stakeholders	●	✓										
2.3	Organizational Influences		✓	○	○			○					
3	**Project Management Processes for a Project**												
3.1	Project Management Processes	●	✓										
3.2	PM Process Groups	●	✓										
3.3	Process Interactions		✓										
3.4	Project Management Process Mapping		✓										
4	**Project Integration Management**												
4.1	Develop Project Charter					○							
4.2	Develop Preliminary Project Scope Statement					○	○						
4.3	Develop Project Management Plan					○							
4.4	Direct and Manage Project Execution										○		
4.5	Monitor and Control Project Work												○
4.6	Integrated Change Control												○
4.7	Close Project												○
5	**Project Scope Management**												
5.1	Scope Planning					○							
5.2	Scope Definition					○							
5.3	Create WBS					○	○						
5.4	Scope Verification					○							
5.5	Scope Control					○							
6	**Project Time Management**												
6.1	Activity Definition						○						
6.2	Activity Sequencing						○						
6.3	Activity Resource Estimating							○					
6.4	Activity Duration Estimating							○					
6.5	Schedule Development							○					
6.6	Schedule Control							○					○

(continued)

Figure 2.22 (continued)

	Textbook Chapters →	1	2	3	4	5	6	7	8	9	10	11	12
	PMBOK Knowledge Area												
7	**Project Cost Management**												
7.1	Cost Estimating							o					
7.2	Cost Budgeting							o					
7.3	Cost Control							o					o
8	**Project Quality Management**												
8.1	Quality Planning								o				
8.2	Perform Quality Assurance								o				
8.3	Perform Quality Control								o				o
9	**Project Human Resource Management**												
9.1	Human Resource Planning			o				o					
9.2	Acquire Project Team			o				o					
9.3	Develop Project Team			o				o					
9.4	Manage Project Team			o				o					
10	**Project Communications Management**												
10.1	Communications Planning				o							o	
10.2	Information Distribution				o							o	
10.3	Performance Reporting				o								o
10.4	Manage Stakeholders				o								o
11	**Project Risk Management**												
11.1	Risk Management Planning									o			
11.2	Risk Identification									o	o		
11.3	Qualitative Risk Analysis									o			
11.4	Quantitative Risk Analysis									o			
11.5	Risk Response Planning									o			
11.6	Risk Monitoring and Control									o			o
12	**Project Procurement Management**												
12.1	Plan Purchases and Acquisitions										o		
12.2	Plan Contracting										o		
12.3	Request Seller Responses										o		
12.4	Select Sellers										o		
12.5	Contract Administration										o		
12.6	Contract Closure										o		o

Key: ●-where material is covered in past chapters; ✓-current chapter coverage;
o-where material is covered in future chapters

Jim Woo looked around his new office. He couldn't believe that he was the assistant director of information technology at Petrie's Electronics, his favorite consumer electronics retail store. He always bought new DVDs and video games for his Xbox at Petrie's. In fact, he had bought his DVD player and his Xbox at Petrie's, along with his surround-sound system and his 42 inch flat-screen HD plasma TV. Now he worked there, too. The employee discount was a nice perk of his new job, but he was also glad that his technical and people skills were finally recognized by the people at Petrie's. He had worked for five years at Pine Valley Furniture as a senior systems analyst, and it was clear that he was not going to be promoted there. He was really glad he had put his resume up on Monster.com and that now he had a bigger salary and a great job with more responsibility at Petrie's.

Petrie's Electronics had started as a single electronics store in 1984 in San Diego, California. The store was started by Jacob Rosenstein in a strip mall. It was named after Rob Petrie, the TV writer played by Dick Van Dyke in the TV show of the same name. Rosenstein always liked that show. When he had grown the operation to a chain of 13 stores in the Southern California area, it was too much for Rosenstein to handle. He sold out in 1992, for a handsome profit, to the Matsutoya Corporation, a huge Japanese conglomerate that saw the chain of stores as a place to sell its many consumer electronics goods in the United States.

Matsutoya had aggressively expanded the chain to 218 stores nationwide by the time they sold it in 2002, for a handsome profit, to Sam and Harry's, a maker and seller of ice cream. Sam and Harry's was looking for a way to diversify and invest the considerable cash they had made creating and selling ice cream, with flavors named after actors and actresses, like their best selling Lime Neeson and Jim Carreymel. Sam and Harry's had brought in professional management to run the chain and had added 15 more stores, including one in Mexico and three in Canada. Even though they originally wanted to move the headquarters to their base state of Delaware, Sam and Harry decided to keep Petrie's headquartered in San Diego.

The company had made some smart moves and had done well, Jim knew, but he also knew that competition was fierce. Petrie's competitors included big electronics retail chains like BestBuy, Circuit City, and CompUSA, as well as the electronics departments of huge chains like Wal-Mart and Target. In California, Fry's was a ferocious competitor. Jim knew that part of his job in IT was to help the company grow and prosper and beat the competition—or at least survive.

Just then, as Jim was trying to decide if he needed a bigger TV, Ella Whinston, the chief operations officer at Petrie's, walked into his office. "How's it going, Jim? Joe keeping you busy?" Joe was Joe Swanson, Jim's boss, the director of IT. Joe was away for the week, at a meeting in Pullman, Washington. Jim quickly pulled his feet off his desk.

"Hi, Ella. Oh, yeah, Joe keeps me busy. I've got to get through the entire corporate strategic IT plan before he gets back—he's going to quiz me—and then there's the new help desk training we are going to start next week."

"I didn't know we had a strategic IT plan," Ella teased. "Anyway, what I came in here for is to give you some good news. I have decided to make you the project manager for a project that is crucial to our corporate survival."

"Me?" Jim said. "But I just got here."

"Who better than you? You have a different perspective, new ideas. You aren't chained down by the past and by the Petrie's way of doing things like the rest of us. Not that it matters, because you don't have a choice. Joe and I both agree that you are the best person for the job."

"So," Jim asked, "What's the project about?"

"Well," Ella began, "the executive team has decided that the number-one priority we have right now is to not only survive but to thrive and to prosper, and the way to do that is to develop closer relationships with our customers. The other person on the executive team who is even more excited about this than me is John (John Smith, the head of marketing). We want to attract new customers, like all of our competitors. But also like our competitors, we want to keep our customers for life, kind of like a frequent flier program, but better. Better for us and for our loyal customers. And we want to reward most the customers who spend the most. We are calling the project 'No Customer Escapes.'"

"I hope that's only an internal name," Jim joked. "Seriously, I can see how something like this would be good for Petrie's, and I can see how IT would play an important, no, crucial role in making something like this happen. OK, then, let's get started."

CHAPTER SUMMARY

Describe the project management life cycle. The project management life cycle differs in its form and content from industry to industry and project to project, but the basic idea is the same: Projects are broken down into smaller pieces called phases. Output from one phase becomes input for the next. Phases end when they produce approved deliverables that were defined earlier in the project.

Explain the five parts of the information systems development life cycle. The information systems development life cycle has five phases: 1) systems planning, 2) systems analysis, 3) systems design, 4) systems implementation, and 5) systems maintenance. Planning involves identifying the need for a new system; analysis involves determining the requirements for the new system; design deals with creating the system's technical specifications; implementation involves building and installing the system; and maintenance involves operating and improving the system during its lifetime.

Understand the project management context. Projects exist within organizations, which exist within larger industrial, economic, and societal contexts. The organizational context for projects includes the stakeholders, organizational culture, and organizational structure. The broader context includes standards and regulations, internationalization, culture, and social-economic-environmental sustainability.

Read Gantt charts and project network diagrams. A Gantt chart shows project activities and when they should begin and end but not how tasks must be ordered (precedence). Gantt charts, therefore, are often more useful for depicting relatively simple projects or subparts of a larger project, the activities of a single worker, or for monitoring the progress of activities compared to scheduled completion dates. A network diagram shows project activities and when they should begin and end, but it also shows the ordering of activities by connecting a task to its predecessor and successor tasks.

Understand the basics of software that supports project management. Software that supports project management allows a project manager to enter information about project activities, their start and end times, and their precedence relationships. The software can display project life cycles as Gantt charts or as network diagrams, and it can automatically calculate critical paths and slack times. Project management software also includes features for better managing human and material resources.

Comprehend project management processes. The Project Management Body of Knowledge lists 44 different project management processes that are categorized into five process groups: initiating, planning, executing, monitoring and controlling, and closing. Initiating and closing include the fewest processes, with two each. Planning, on the other hand, includes 21 different processes, underscoring the centrality of planning to project management.

KEY TERMS REVIEW

- Critical path
- Functional organization structure
- Logical design
- Matrix organization structure
- Phase
- Phase exits
- Physical design

- Process
- Project management office (PMO)
- Projectized organization structure
- Regulation
- Slack time
- Standard
- Systems analysis

- Systems design
- Systems development life cycle (SDLC)
- Systems implementation
- Systems maintenance
- Systems planning

Match each of the key terms with the definition that best fits it.

1. _____ A smaller part of a project.

2. _____ Review of the deliverables at the end of a phase of the project.

3. _____ A common methodology for systems development that marks the phases or steps of information systems development.

4. _____ The first phase of the SDLC, where the need for a new or enhanced system is identified and the proposed system's scope is determined.

5. _____ The second phase in the SDLC, where the systems requirements are determined, alternative solutions are developed, and one is chosen that best meets those requirements given the cost, labor, and technical resources the organization is willing to commit.

6. _____ The third phase in the SDLC, where the descriptions of the recommended alternative are converted into logical and then physical system specifications.

7. _____ Specifications that focus on the origin, flow, and processing of data in a system but are not tied to any specific hardware and systems software platform.

8. _____ Structured systems design that can be broken down into smaller and smaller units for conversion into instructions written in a programming language.

9. _____ The fourth phase in the SDLC, where system specifications are turned into a working system that is tested and then put into use.

10. _____ The final phase in the SDLC, where programmers make the changes that users ask for and modify the system to reflect changing business conditions.

11. _____ A traditional hierarchical organization, sometimes thought of as resembling a pyramid, with top management at the fulcrum, direct workers at the bottom, and middle managers in between.

12. _____ A type of organization structure where people from different functional backgrounds work with each other throughout the lifetime of the project.

13. _____ A type of organization structure that typically crosses functional design (on one axis) with some other design characteristic (on the other axis).

14. _____ An organizational unit created to centralize and coordinate the projects within an organization.

15. _____ A document approved by a recognized body that provides, for common and repeated use, rules, guidelines, or characteristics for products, processes, or services with which compliance is not mandatory.

16. _____ A document that specifies product, process, or service characteristics, including the applicable administrative provisions, with which compliance is mandatory.

17. _____ The longest path through a network diagram illustrating the shortest amount of time in which a project can be completed.

18. _____ The amount of time that an activity can be delayed without delaying the project.

19. _____ A series of continuous actions that bring about a particular result, end, or condition.

REVIEW QUESTIONS

1. What is the project management life cycle?
2. List and explain the five phases of the information systems development life cycle.
3. Are all project management life cycles the same? Explain your answer.
4. What is the organizational context in which projects exist? Why should project managers be aware of this organizational context?
5. Name three types of organizational structures and how they affect project management.
6. What is the broader extra-organizational context in which projects exist? Why should project managers be aware of this extra-organizational context?
7. What is the difference between a standard and a regulation?
8. What general management skill sets are useful for project managers? Why?
9. What is the key difference between a Gantt chart and a network diagram? When should a Gantt chart be used? When should a network diagram be used?
10. What is a critical path on a network diagram?
11. What are the benefits of using project management software?
12. What is a project management process?
13. Name and define the five project management process groups.
14. How many project management processes are associated with planning? Why?

1. A project has been defined to contain the following list of activities along with their required times for completion.

Activity No.	Activity	Time (Weeks)	Immediate Predecessors
1	Collect requirements	2	—
2	Analyze processes	3	1
3	Analyze data	3	2
4	Design processes	7	2
5	Design data	6	2
6	Design screens	1	3,4
7	Design reports	5	4,5
8	Program	4	6,7
9	Test and document	8	7
10	Install	2	8,9

   a. Draw a network diagram for the activities.
   b. Calculate the earliest expected completion time.
   c. Show the critical path.
   d. What would happen if activity 6 were revised to take 6 weeks instead of 1 week?

2. Construct a Gantt chart for the project defined in Problem 1.

3. Look again at the activities outlined in Problem 1. Assume that your team is in its first week of the project and has discovered that each of the activity duration estimates is wrong. Activity 2 will take only two weeks to complete. Activities 4 and 7 will each take three times longer than anticipated. All other activities will take twice as long to complete as previously estimated. In addition, a new activity, number 11, has been added. It will take one week to complete, and its immediate predecessors are activities 10 and 9. Adjust the network diagram and recalculate the earliest expected completion times.

4. Various vendors make add-in programs for Microsoft Project. One such vendor is called Critical Tools Inc. (www.criticaltools.com/). One of their add-ins for Microsoft Project is called PERT Chart EXPERT. One of the features of PERT Chart EXPERT is that it enables the user to create timescaled PERT charts. For this exercise, go to the Web site for PERT Chart EXPERT (www.criticaltools.com/pertmain.htm) and investigate what a timescaled PERT chart would look like. As you investigate the Web site, you'll find a page that compares timescaled to non-timescaled charts. Explain what a timescaled PERT chart is and how it compares to regular PERT charts in Microsoft Project. Why would a project manager want to use timescaled charts? Continue to explore the Web site and report on the other features of PERT Chart EXPERT, as well as its price, compatibility, and system requirements. Your instructor may also want you to download the demo and report about it as well.

6. Write a research paper on the Sarbanes-Oxley Act of 2002 and its potential effects on project management.

CHAPTER CASES

Sedona Management Group and the Project Management Life Cycle

Sedona Management Group (SMG) is a small company situated in Bellevue, Washington. It specializes in developing custom software for Web sites, intranet, extranet, and electronic commerce applications using Windows 2000/XP, .Net, ASP.Net, Visual Basic, SQL Server databases, XML, Flash, Premier, and After Effects technologies. SMG's mission has been to develop high-quality and robust state-of-the-art Internet-centric software as well as commercial software products and components for clients. At the same time, the team at Sedona strives to achieve consumer satisfaction through the products and services they deliver to their clients.

Over the last 10 years, the Sedona team has developed Web sites for many organizations, including the Seattle Seahawks, the Portland Trail Blazers, the Golden Baseball League, and Alliance Builder. These clients typically provide very good reviews of the products and services they receive from SMG. One positive review was from Mike Flood, vice president of community relations with the Seattle Seahawks. Flood not only praised SMG on the timely development of a high-quality Web site for the Seahawks but has also noted that since Sedona's development of an additional e-mail–based permission marketing system, membership in the Hawk Mail Club has doubled and continues to grow. Other clients have indicated increases in revenues and improved customer service brought about by the improved quality and maintainability of their Web sites.

How does the Sedona team achieve customer satisfaction? Tim Turnpaugh, the founder of SMG, attributes this achievement to the core competency of his team, which is great project management. One of the reasons Turnpaugh stresses good project management at SMG is that project failure results in business failure. He explains this relationship by making the important distinction between commercial and corporate software development. Turnpaugh defines commercial development as the development of software products for other commercial enterprises, where the software is the primary output from the organization. He distinguishes commercial development from corporate development, where software is developed in-house by an IT group that builds applications for the business as a whole. According to Turnpaugh, the risk associated with project failure in the

commercial development market is simple to understand: Do a bad job and you go out of business. In contrast, in corporate application development, the financial resources available to the IT group allow them to mitigate the risks associated with any one project running over time or over budget. Commercial development environments, such as SMG's, require very different project selection and management processes.

SMG spends a great deal of time on the project initiation phase to ensure the right types of projects are selected. A primary characteristic of the projects that SMG chooses to pursue is based on project scope, both in terms of the initial size of the project and whether the group has experience and expertise in such projects. In terms of project management techniques associated with planning and execution, SMG follows a standardized project management life cycle, allowing it to approach every project in a very consistent manner. This maximizes Sedona's ability to anticipate and deal with problems they may encounter during the development process. As an example, after mapping out a project, one of the first execution processes SMG performs is to develop the back-end database associated with the Web site. They then turn to the administration aspect of the Web site, which involves updating its content, and defining security. In parallel with the development of the database, the team also develops the presentation layer, or the user interface, of the Web site. SMG strives to exploit high-quality project management techniques in all phases of the project management life cycle, which include initiation, planning, execution, control, and closure. Further, SMG is very attentive to using the latest advances in technology, including the reuse of code if a project permits it, as well as using the latest in development environments, such as Microsoft's .NET environment. The team believes that leveraging technology has allowed them to double their work speed. All of these aspects help SMG ensure the timely and successful completion of the projects they undertake.

Chapter 2 Project Assignment

The Seattle Seahawks needed a Web site to allow fan discussion forums, the purchase of event tickets, and the provision of information on the team and players.

Similarly, an entertainer, whether a singer, a musician, or a comedian, needs a Web site that contains information about the artist, any forthcoming events, and any products fans can purchase online. Moreover, from an entertainment standpoint, the Internet is an invaluable tool to connect with fans and establish a fan base.

The project you will be doing for this course is the development of an entertainment Web site. At this point, the project involves uncertainty, and consequently it is a good practice to divide it into several phases. The project life cycle is a collection of these different phases. The assignment for this chapter requires you to develop a project life cycle for the Web site development project. For this assignment, provide responses to the following questions:

1. What are the five different phases of the information systems development life cycle?
2. Describe each of the phases briefly.
3. Provide a description of which activities you will perform in each individual phase of the Web site development project.
4. Compare your answers to those of your other team members.
5. Create a master document for the team that is a compilation of your individual work.

Special Case: Making It Work—Hong Kong's New International Airport at Chek Lap Kok

Few projects are as large and as successful as Hong Kong's International Airport at Chek Lap Kok (see Figure 2.23). The need for a new airport to replace aging Kai Tak airport became apparent in the 1960s, and planning and financial planning were conducted in 1982. The project itself, which was really a series of 10 projects called the Airport Core Programme (ACP), was announced in 1989, and work began in 1992 (see Figure 2.24). In addition to reclaiming the land needed to build the airport, the ACP also involved building the necessary road and rail connections to get from Hong Kong Island to the new airport. Among the many tasks necessary to build the route from the island to the airport were reclaiming land adjacent to Hong Kong Island and building a new railway station there, building a new tunnel between Hong Kong Island and Kowloon, and constructing the Lantau Link, a 3.5 kilometer artery, consisting of two suspension bridges and a viaduct, between Kowloon and Lantau Island. The Lantau Link has two levels, with the top built for 6 lanes of road traffic and the bottom level built for two railroad tracks. The total length of the link between Hong Kong Island and the airport is 34 kilometers. In addition to the engineering challenges, the project was completed against the backdrop of the handover of the Hong Kong territory from the United Kingdom to the People's Republic of China on June 30, 1997.

Seven of the 10 projects were completed on time and within budget in 1997. The railway built to serve the airport opened in June 1998. The second runway opened in May 1999, and an extension to the north-south concourse was completed in January 2000. The ACP involved hundreds of contracts and 21,000 workers from hundreds of countries. The total cost of the ACP was $20.6 billion (Source: Hong Kong Airport Core Programme, Hong Kong Highways Department, and Major Projects Association).

Figure 2.23
Photo of Hong Kong's new airport under construction

Source:
www.hyd.gov.hk/airport

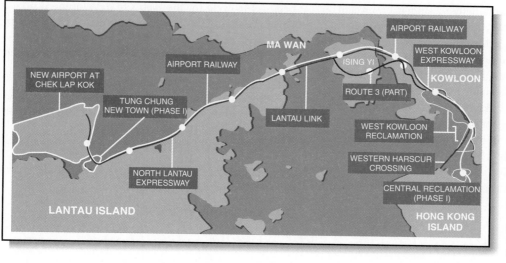

Figure 2.24
The 10 projects that made up Hong Kong's Airport Core Program

Source:
www.info.gov.hk/napko/index-e.html

REFERENCES

Association for Computing Machinery. "ACM Code of Ethics and Professional Conduct." Adapted 10/16/92. Available at www.acm.org/constitution/code.html.

Fleming, Q. W. and Koppelman, J. M. (2005). "Sarbanes-Oxley: Does Compliance Require Earned Value Management on Projects?" Available at chiefprojectofficer.comwww.chiefprojectofficer.com/article_index.php). Accessed 6/29/2005.

Funk and Wagnall's Standard Desk Dictionary. Vol. 2, 1979.

George, J. F., Batra, D., Valacich, J. S., and Hoffer, J. A. (2004). *Object-Oriented Systems Analysis and Design.* Prentice Hall: Upper Saddle River, NJ.

Hall, M. (2004). "Offshoring Revives Man-Month Myth . . ." 11/15/2004. www.computerworld.com/softwaretopics/software/appdev/story/0,10801,97508,00.html. Accessed 12/20/2004.

Hoffer, J. A., George, J. F. and Valacich, J. S. (2002). *Modern Systems Analysis and Design.* 3rd ed. Prentice Hall: Upper Saddle River, NJ.

Hong Kong Airport Core Programme. www.info.gov.hk/napko/index-e.html. Accessed 7/2/2003.

Hong Kong Highways Department. Airport Core Programme Highways Project. www.hyd.gov.hk/airport. Accessed 7/2/2003.

International Organization for Standardization. (1994). *Code of Good Practice for Standardization (Draft International Standard).* Geneva, Switzerland: ISO Press.

Major Projects Association. (2001). Hong Kong International Airport. www.majorprojects.org. Accessed 7/2/2003.

Mearian, L. (2004). Killing Time on IT Projects. *ComputerWorld.* May 31. www.computerworld.com/developmenttopics/development/story/0,10801,93470,00.html.

Nicholas, J. (2001). *Project Management for Business and Technology: Principles and Practice.* Prentice Hall: Upper Saddle River, NJ.

Project Management Institute. (2001). *Project Management Fact Book.* 2nd ed. Newton Square, PA: PMI.

Project Management Institute. (2004). *A Guide to the Project Management Body of Knowledge.* 3rd ed. Newton Square, PA: PMI.

Chapter 3

Managing Project Teams

Opening Case: Flexible Project Teams Deliver Project on Time

Consider the difficulty of a project undertaken by MD Robotics to develop a special purpose dexterous manipulator (SPDM) for the Canadian Space Agency. The SPDM, a specially developed robotic arm (see Figure 3.1), was to be developed for use on NASA's international space station. To encourage freedom of communication as well as timely problem solving, the executive project team decided to co-locate project staff on a single floor of the MD Robotics facility. The SPDM project group was divided into smaller subproject teams which in the spirit of true co-location and collaboration, worked in an open office environment designed to promote communication. Project managers were able to freely interact with engineers, and project teams were able to communicate with each other under a "no-surprises rule" implemented by senior management. The no-surprises rule specified that project teams should communicate any needed SPDM design changes to other project teams as soon as they were identified. Although the senior management team was made aware of any design changes, it did not have to sign off before teams were allowed to implement the changes.

Using this team-based project structure, combined with the policy of allowing teams the autonomy to make developmental changes, MD Robotics was able to deliver the SPDM to the Canadian Space Agency both on budget and on time (Sources: Canadian Space Agency [2003]; Carey [2005]).

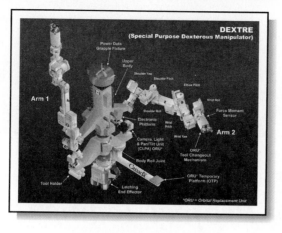

Figure 3.1
MD Robotics
special purpose
dexterous manip-
ulator (SPDM)

LEARNING OBJECTIVES

After reading this chapter, you will be able to:

➤ Describe the characteristics of a project team and the factors that influence team performance.

➤ Explain what is meant by need and process theories of motivation.

➤ Contrast trait, behavioral, and contingency theories of leadership.

➤ Explain the sources of power and how these sources can be used to influence people.

➤ Contrast functional versus dysfunctional conflict and explain how conflict can be beneficial to a project team.

➤ Explain why global project teams are increasing and describe the challenges of managing these teams.

INTRODUCTION

People are the most important and expensive part of an information systems project. Project time estimates for task completion and overall system quality are significantly influenced by the effectiveness of the project team. Unfortunately, good information systems personnel are in short supply. In fact, the U.S. Department of Commerce is predicting huge labor shortages over the next decade for people with skills in using, developing, and managing information systems (Kaihla, 2003). Nearly every industry, not just computer hardware and software companies, relies heavily on information systems professionals; therefore, the shortage in skilled technology workers could have a big impact on the economy.

The U.S. Bureau of Labor Statistics has reported that high demand for technology-related workers and escalating salaries could lead to inflation and lower corporate profits as companies scramble to offer competitive salaries to the best and brightest people in this industry. Additionally, labor shortages will lead to increased use of global project teams, making effective projects more complex and more difficult to manage. Given the competitiveness of this labor pool, retaining the best personnel is

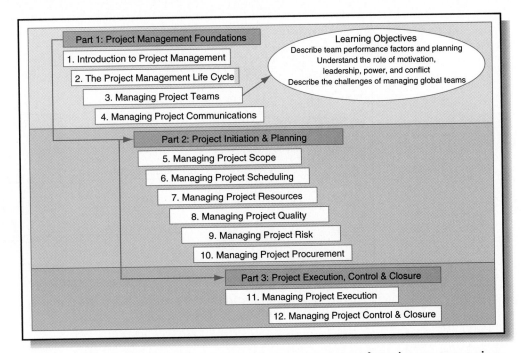

Figure 3.2 Information systems project management focusing on managing project teams

also a critical issue for many organizations. Therefore, finding ways not only to reward people adequately but also to create a positive work experience through well-managed projects, meaningful team assignments, and good interpersonal relationships not only can enhance project effectiveness but also can help to retain employees within the organization. Understanding the issues related to effectively managing project teams is the next step in gaining a comprehensive understanding of information systems project management, as shown in Figure 3.2.

In the next section, we begin by discussing what a project team is, how teams evolve, and the various factors that influence project team performance. This is followed by a discussion of several motivation theories that will help you better understand how team members can be influenced to have high work productivity and job satisfaction. Next, we discuss the roles of leadership, power, and conflict within project teams. Finally, we examine several issues related to the management of global project teams.

WHAT IS A PROJECT TEAM?

Project team
Two or more people who share the same goals, are interdependent, have complementary skills, and are mutually accountable to the organization and to each member of the team.

In the context of organizational work, groups and teams are not necessarily the same thing. A group consists of two or more people who work together to achieve a common objective (Robbins and Judge, 2007). Yet a group may be formed for a temporary purpose, and its members may not necessarily share the same goals. A project team, however, is much more than a group. A **project team** is mutually accountable to the organization and to its own individual team members; the team members are also highly interdependent, having both shared goals and complementary skills (see Figure 3.3). When project teams are formed, the group of people typically takes some time to evolve into a high-performing project team. This evolution is discussed next.

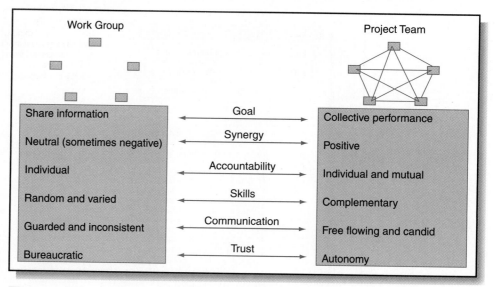

Figure 3.3   Comparing work groups and project teams (adapted from Robbins and Judge, 2007)

Project Team Development

Project team development

Five stages—forming, storming, norming, performing, and adjourning—through which a team evolves in order to reach optimal performance.

Teams do not automatically become highly interdependent and productive. Researchers have found that teams develop and evolve through various stages as they work together over time (Robbins and Judge, 2007). During **project team development**, five stages—forming, storming, norming, performing, and adjourning. To reach optimal performance, the project team moves through each phase.

During *forming*, team members get to know each other and establish team goals and work assignments. This stage is completed when a majority of the members feel that they are part of the team. During *storming*, team members struggle to establish goals, power, and leadership roles. This stage is completed when a majority of the members have a relatively clear understanding of each member's role within the team. During *norming*, teams develop a sense of common purpose and specify normal operating procedures. Additionally during this stage, high levels of team collegiality are typically present, and close friendships are formed. This stage ends with members having a strong sense of proper team behavior. During *performing*, the team undertakes the actual project work. This stage ends with the completion of the project. For permanent, ongoing project teams, performing is the last stage in their evolution. For temporary teams established to complete a single project, there is also an adjourning stage. During *adjourning*, team members wrap up the project's final activities and engage in activities related to subsequent team assignments or jobs. During this stage, individuals often respond differently to adjournment—some members will delight in the team's accomplishments, whereas others will feel a sense of sadness or loss. As a project manager, you need to understand where your team is in regard to its development in order to better understand its challenges and its potential.

Factors That Influence Project Team Performance

Researchers have focused a great deal of effort on identifying factors that lead to effective teams (Robbins and Judge, 2007). These factors can be categorized into four types: work design, composition, context, and process (see Figure 3.4). Unfortunately, even if

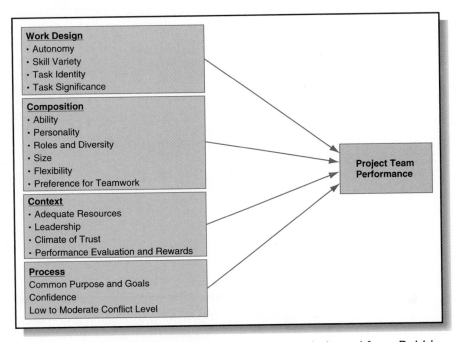

Work Design
- Autonomy
- Skill Variety
- Task Identity
- Task Significance

Composition
- Ability
- Personality
- Roles and Diversity
- Size
- Flexibility
- Preference for Teamwork

Context
- Adequate Resources
- Leadership
- Climate of Trust
- Performance Evaluation and Rewards

Process
Common Purpose and Goals
Confidence
Low to Moderate Conflict Level

Project Team Performance

Figure 3.4 Project team performance factors (adapted from Robbins and Judge, 2007)

numerous effectiveness factors are present, they do not guarantee a productive project team. However, when these factors are present, higher performance is much more likely.

Numerous *work design* factors can be configured to influence team member performance. For instance, work design that provides team members with autonomy, skill variety, task identity, and significance has been found to be highly motivating. Likewise, *team composition* can also play a major role in project team performance. Factors that have been found to be important include member ability, personality, role diversity, size, flexibility, and preference for teamwork. Of these, personality and team size have been found to play a significant role in many project teams. For example, research has found that it can be very difficult to blend some personality types into an effective team. Because of this, many organizations give potential team members personality tests like the **Myers-Briggs Type Indicator (MBTI)** to more effectively match team members and to help them learn more about each other. The MBTI is the most widely used personality test; its advocates feel that it can help to improve work and personal relationships, increase productivity, and identify leadership and interpersonal communication preferences of team members. Nonetheless, there is no universal agreement that such personality tests are accurate or even helpful. (To learn more about the MBTI, see www.cpp.db.com.)

Likewise, team size can also significantly influence team performance. As the size of the team increases, it becomes increasingly difficult to effectively communicate and coordinate project activities. The rule of thumb is to use the fewest people possible; the most effective teams rarely have more than ten members (see Figure 3.5). If more than ten members are needed for a very large project, smaller subteams should be used to minimize communication and coordination problems. Getting the right people, and the right number of people, on your project team can make it easier for the group to perform.

All good sports teams have players with clearly defined roles and abilities. Likewise, a good project team needs members with a diversity of skills and abilities. It is also important to select members who are flexible—in regard to task activities and roles—and who clearly want to belong to the team. To be effective, project teams

Myers-Briggs Type Indicator (MBTI)
A widely used personality test that can be used to improve work and personal relationships, increase productivity, and identify leadership and interpersonal communication preferences of team members.

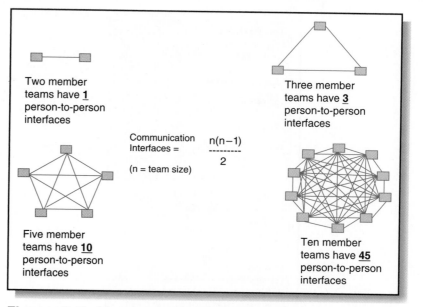

Figure 3.5 Team communication and management complexity increase rapidly with group size

must agree on a broad range of member roles and must design work processes that ensure that all members contribute equally to the team performance. An experienced project manager has a deep understanding of the variety of roles and skills needed to build a successful team. Researchers have found that people can also have different types of work personalities within software development teams, including the following (Howard, 2001; see Figure 3.6):

1. *Deliverer.* A person who is good at getting things done quickly and is good in emergency situations such as repairing a system failure.

Figure 3.6 Information systems project teams need members with differing work personalities

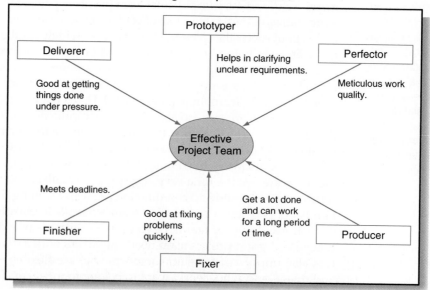

2. *Prototyper*. A person who is useful for projects where the system requirements are initially unclear or in situations where building the right system is more important than building something quickly.

3. *Perfector*. A person whose work is meticulous and who is useful when everything must be done correctly, such as a system that could impact human safety.

4. *Producer*. A person who is good at getting a lot of work accomplished but often ignores standard conventions such as structured methods and documentation.

5. *Fixer*. A person who has a deep understanding of a system and can quickly examine a problem and make a needed repair.

6. *Finisher*. A person who is good at meeting deadlines but may often ignore rules or procedures in order to do so.

Just like successful sports teams, successful project teams repeatedly have been found to have members who play different roles.

Four *contextual factors*—adequate resources, leadership, trust, and performance evaluation and rewards—have also been found to be important for achieving high team performance. It is obvious that teams must have adequate resources or will feel it is impossible to succeed. High-performing project teams must also have clear leadership and structure so that members will know who is responsible for completing various tasks, as well as how schedules, tasks, and roles will be assigned. High-performing teams must also trust each other because doing so allows members to work independently and cooperatively. Lastly, a team-oriented performance evaluation and reward system is needed to achieve maximum team effort, commitment, and performance.

Finally, three *process factors* also have been found to significantly shape the performance of project teams. Teams that share a common purpose and goals, have confidence in their ability to be successful, and have low-to-moderate levels of conflict, typically perform better than teams that don't. In sum, many factors influence a team's performance. Understanding how various factors shape team performance will help you design a more effective team and achieve higher performance.

TIPS FROM THE PROS
How to Pick a Project Team

Experienced project managers have become experts in how to best select the right members for a team. According to Bill Hagerup, a project management specialist at Ouellette & Associates Inc., a consulting firm in Bedford, New Hampshire, building a successful team takes the right mix of "soft" skills, personalities, and attitudes. Picking people exclusively for their technical skills is often a mistake. Some other tips include (Source: Melymuka [2004]):

- *Keep teams small and manageable*. You often have to balance departmental representation with overall team effectiveness, but teams bigger than five members are frequently difficult to manage.
- *Get the right personalities*. Look for people with strong work ethics and positive, upbeat personalities. One cynic can spoil the entire team's outlook, whereas positive upbeat personalities can lift the team's spirit.
- *Embrace diversity*. Because technology professions tend to attract similar types of people, work hard to build diversity on your teams so that they will not be as susceptible to groupthink and narrow solutions.
- *Reuse successful teams*. It takes a lot of work to build and nurture a successful team, so reuse successful teams when you can.
- *Plan ahead to get the right people*. The best people for a team are often very busy, so it is important to plan ahead to line up key people well in advance.
- *Use your network*. Getting the best people to join a team often requires that you convince their boss or others that it is in the organization's best interest for this person to be on your team. Use your friends and close colleagues to identify and recruit the right people.

MOTIVATING TEAM MEMBERS

Motivation
An individual's intensity, direction, and persistence of effort toward attaining a goal.

One of the keys to project success is having a project team with motivated members. **Motivation** refers to an individual's intensity, direction, and persistence of effort toward attaining a goal (Robbins and Judge, 2007). *Intensity* refers to how hard someone tries to attain the goal. However, intensity alone may not result in favorable results, unless the *Direction* of that intensity is channeled toward attaining the appropriate goal. Direction thus is focused on the quality of the effort. *Persistence* refers to how long someone maintains an effort toward the goal. To be ultimately successful, a person needs all three traits. For example, a person can work hard, but if this effort is not directed correctly or is not sustained, success may not be possible. Motivating team members is, therefore, critical to gaining optimum team performance.

Job satisfaction
The general attitude a person has toward his or her job.

Absenteeism
The failure to report to work.

Turnover
The rate at which people voluntarily or involuntarily leave an organization.

Over the years, a lot of research has been conducted to identify why and how people are motivated. From this research, it has been found that different people are motivated by different things and in different ways. For example, some people are primarily motivated by external factors such as financial rewards while others are motivated by internal factors such as a sense of accomplishment. Also, the researchers have put forth and tested different theories of motivation that have been useful for understanding work productivity as well as job satisfaction, absenteeism, and turnover. **Job satisfaction** refers to the general attitude a person has toward his or her job; **absenteeism** refers to the failure to report to work; and **turnover** refers to the rate at which people voluntarily or involuntarily leave an organization. Some theories have been good for understanding job satisfaction, whereas others have been useful for understanding work productivity. In sum, understanding why and how people are motivated to be satisfied, to come to work, to stay with the organization, or to work hard is important for all project managers. Consequently, we briefly review various motivational theories to help you better understand motivation. More in-depth discussions of motivation can be found in Robbins and Judge (2007) or Verma (1996).

Need Theories of Motivation

For more than 50 years, researchers have examined various theories of how different personal factors can shape a person's motivation. Although support for these theories has been mixed when examined in controlled research settings, they are nonetheless widely used within organizations when designing work practices and reward systems. In this section, we briefly examine the most popular need theories of motivation.

Hierarchy of Needs

Hierarchy of needs
A hierarchy of needs—physiological, safety, social, esteem, and self-actualization—where as each need is met, the next higher-level need becomes the motivating focus.

One of the most famous motivational theories is Maslow's **hierarchy of needs** (Maslow, 1954). This theory states that within every person, there exists a hierarchy of five needs: physiological, safety, social, esteem, and self-actualization (see Figure 3.7). This theory states that as each lower-level need is met (or substantially met), the next higher-level need becomes the individual's motivating focus. This means that if you want to motivate people, you need to understand where they are in this hierarchy and use mechanisms to help them satisfy needs at the next higher level. Although Maslow's hierarchy of needs is easy to understand and is widely recognized by many project managers, research has not found it valid for consistently explaining motivation. Basically, research has found that unsatisfied needs do not necessarily motivate, that satisfied needs do not always activate movement to higher levels in the hierarchy, and that more than one need from different levels may be desired

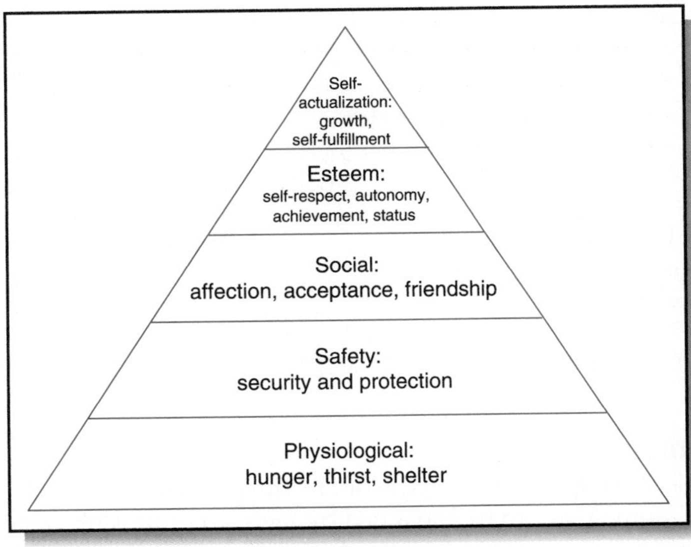
Self-
actualization:
growth,
self-fulfillment
Esteem:
self-respect, autonomy,
achievement, status
Social:
affection, acceptance, friendship
Safety:
security and protection
Physiological:
hunger, thirst, shelter

Figure 3.7 Maslow's hierarchy of needs

simultaneously. As a result, researchers have continued to look for a more sophisticated understanding of motivation.

ERG Theory

ERG theory
Three core needs—Existence, Relatedness, and Growth—of which more than one may be operative at the same time; if the fulfillment of a higher-level need is unrealized, the desire to satisfy a lower-level need becomes the motivating focus.

A related theory, **ERG theory**, refined the hierarchy of needs theory to more closely match the research findings in this area. In particular, ERG theory argues that there are three core needs—Existence, Relatedness, and Growth—of which more than one may be operating at the same time. Additionally, if the fulfillment of a higher-level need is unrealized, the desire to satisfy a lower-level need increases (Alderfer, 1969). Within ERG theory, existence focuses on satisfying our basic material needs and most closely relates to Maslow's physiological and safety needs. Relatedness focuses on maintaining interpersonal relationships and most closely relates to Maslow's social needs. Lastly, growth focuses on personal development and most closely relates to Maslow's esteem and self-actualization categories. Researchers have found ERG theory to be more valid than Maslow's hierarchy of needs because it more closely reflects our knowledge of how the importance of various factors can simultaneously motivate an individual.

Two-Factor Theory

Two-factor theory
Intrinsic factors—*motivational factors*—such as achievement, recognition, advancement, and responsibility are related to job satisfaction, whereas extrinsic factors—*hygiene factors*—such as salary, relationships with colleagues, and work conditions are associated with job dissatisfaction.

Another need theory, the motivational-hygiene theory, or simply the **two-factor theory**, was proposed by Frederick Herzberg (Herzberg, Mausner, and Snyderman, 1959). This theory predicts that intrinsic factors—*motivational factors*—like achievement, recognition, advancement, and responsibility, are related to job satisfaction, while extrinsic factors—*hygiene factors*—like salary, relationships with colleagues, and work conditions, are associated with job dissatisfaction (see Table 3.1). This theory predicts that the factors that lead to job satisfaction are separate and distinct from those that lead to dissatisfaction (see Figure 3.8). In other words, people will not be dissatisfied if extrinsic factors are adequate, but they won't necessarily be satisfied either. For a person to be satisfied, intrinsic factors must also be adequately met. As with Maslow's hierarchy of needs, the two-factor theory is not universally accepted. Nonetheless, many managers and organizations have accepted its concepts, and it has been instrumental in the development of programs that allow workers greater control over their day-to-day activities.

Table 3.1 Common Hygiene and Motivational Factors

HYGIENE FACTORS	MOTIVATIONAL FACTORS
• Company policies and administration	• Opportunity for achievement
• Relationship with supervisor, peers, and subordinates	• Opportunity for recognition
• Working conditions	• Challenges and variety of the work itself
• Salary and benefits	• Sense of responsibility
• Status	• Opportunity for advancement
• Security	• Opportunity for personal growth

Theory of Needs

Theory of needs
Individuals' motivation can be explained by their need for achievement, power, and affiliation.

One last needs theory is McClelland's **theory of needs**, which proposes that individuals' motivation can be explained by their need for achievement, power, and affiliation (McClelland, 1961). The need for achievement refers to having a drive to excel beyond a set of standards. The need for power refers to having a drive to control the behavior of others. The need for affiliation refers to having the desire for close and friendly interpersonal relationships. Researchers have developed questionnaires that can be used to help rate people on various dimensions. High achievers are not necessarily good managers, whereas good managers have a high need for power and a low need for affiliation. Of all need theories, McClellan's has been found to best predict work productivity, whereas the others have had the most success in explaining a person's job satisfaction.

Process Theories of Motivation

Process theories attempt to understand a person's behavior based on intrinsic or personal factors used to motivate specific behavior. In general, this perspective on motivation suggests that project managers need to create a proper environment, work processes, and rewards to create the greatest motivation in people. Several of the most notable process theories of motivation are described next.

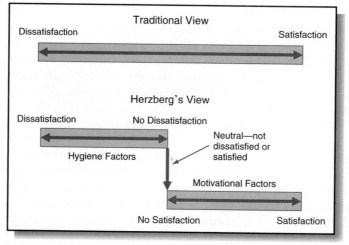

Figure 3.8
Contrasting views of job satisfaction in Herzberg's two-factor theory (adapted from Verma, 1995)

Theory X and Theory Y

In the early 1960s, Douglas McGregor proposed Theory X and Theory Y to reflect contrasting views of human behavior, management, and motivation (McGregor, 1960). **Theory X** assumes that people dislike work, are lazy, dislike responsibility, and must be coerced to work hard. Alternatively, **Theory Y** assumes that people like work, are creative, like autonomy, and seek responsibility. A project manager who believes Theory X is the right approach for motivating individuals will typically be autocratic, leave no doubt with others about who is in charge, and have little concern about the feelings of others. A Theory Y manager will be participative and encourage a high level of involvement by team members in their assignments, work processes, and decisions. Theory Y has been found to be a much better management philosophy for motivating professionals and highly educated individuals.

Theory Z

In the 1980s, William Ouchi proposed an extension to Theory X and Theory Y, which he called **Theory Z** (Ouchi, 1981). This theory reflects the Japanese work philosophy that includes a belief in lifetime employment, strong company loyalty, and group consensus. A Theory Z management philosophy views workers as long-term partners who are capable of working without close supervision; decisions are made by the entire team with high levels of group consensus. Project managers who believe Theory X, Theory Y, or Theory Z will treat team members differently and design vastly different work processes and rewards (or punishments).

Goal-Setting Theory

Goal-setting theory offers another perspective on understanding a person's motivation (Locke, 1968). This theory suggests that specific and difficult goals, with clear feedback on how well a person is meeting them, can enhance a person's work productivity. This means that telling someone to "do their best" will likely result in their not doing their best! However, giving people higher, specific job performance goals ("Please complete the new user interface by Friday noon") will most often lead to higher levels of performance, especially when clear feedback is given.

Equity Theory

Equity theory suggests that individuals compare their work inputs and outcomes with those of others and then respond to eliminate inequities (Adams, 1965). For example, if individuals feel they are not being treated fairly, they will work less, reduce their outputs, change their perceptions, or quit. Alternatively, individuals who believe they are being treated fairly will remain relatively satisfied and motivated to perform. Although equity theory has demonstrated that making relative comparisons to others influences motivation, it is most powerful in predicting absenteeism and turnover, not levels of work productivity (Robbins and Judge, 2007).

Reinforcement Theory

Reinforcement theory argues that both positive and negative feedback, or reinforcement, conditions behavior (Komaki, Coombs, and Schepman, 1996). In other words, reinforcement theory proposes that if desirable behavior is rewarded—with

---

Theory X
Motivational theory that assumes people dislike work, are lazy, dislike responsibility, and must be coerced to work hard.

Theory Y
Motivational theory that assumes people like work, are creative, like autonomy, and seek responsibility.

Theory Z
Management theory reflecting the Japanese work philosophy that includes a belief in lifetime employment, strong company loyalty, and group consensus.

Goal-setting theory
Specific and difficult goal, with clear feedback on how well a person is meeting that goal, can enhance a person's work productivity.

Equity theory
Individuals compare their work inputs and outcomes with those of others and then respond to eliminate any inequities.

Reinforcement theory
A motivation theory that argues that both positive and negative feedback condition behavior.

pay increases, incentives, or other valued items—it will be repeated. Likewise, undesirable behavior can be discouraged by punishment. This theory has a very broad following and has become the basis of the reward systems within many modern organizations.

Expectancy Theory

Lastly, **expectancy theory**, one of the most widely accepted and supported motivational theories, predicts that people will be motivated to exert a high level of effort when they believe that (Vroom, 1964):

1. Effort will lead to a good performance appraisal.
2. A good appraisal will lead to rewards.
3. These rewards will satisfy their needs.

Figure 3.9 shows each of these three relationships. The effort-performance relationship reflects the belief that increased individual effort leads to higher work performance. The performance-rewards relationship reflects the belief that work performance at a particular level will lead to specific outcomes such as a bonus, a salary increase, or promotion. Finally, the rewards-personal goals relationship reflects the belief that organizational rewards will satisfy a person's goals or needs. Expectancy theory has been very useful for understanding why many workers are, or are not, motivated to do their jobs well. To adequately motivate employees to perform their best, the organization must design job evaluation and reward systems that accurately measure effort and performance, and it must design reward systems that meet each employee's specific needs. If employees believe that effort will lead to the rewards that meet their personal needs, then optimal work performance can be achieved.

General Guidelines for Motivating Team Members

As can be seen from this discussion of employee motivation, there is no single approach to optimally motivating an individual. Over the years, researchers have examined many approaches for enhancing motivation (see Table 3.2). From this work, several general recommendations can be made for managing your project team (Robbins and Judge, 2007):

1. *Recognize individual differences.* Because your team members will have different needs and goals, it is essential that you learn what is important to each person.

Figure 3.9 Expectancy theory links a person's effort to their performance, their performance to rewards, and their rewards to goals

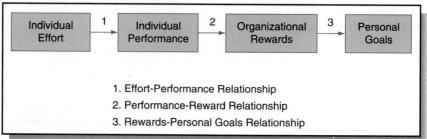

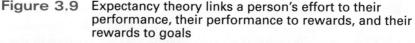

Table 3.2 Various Theories That Have Been Developed to Explain Motivation

NEED THEORIES OF MOTIVATION

Hierarchy of Needs	A hierarchy of needs—physiological, safety, social, esteem, and self-actualization—in which as each need is met the next-higher-level need becomes the motivating focus.
ERG Theory	Three core needs—Existence, Relatedness, and Growth—in which more than one need may be operative at the same time; if the fulfillment of a higher-level need is unrealized, the desire to satisfy a lower-level need becomes the motivating focus.
Two-Factor Theory	Intrinsic factors—*motivational factors*—such as achievement, recognition, advancement, and responsibility are related to job satisfaction, whereas extrinsic factors—*hygiene factors*—such as salary, relationships with colleagues, and work conditions are associated with dissatisfaction.
Theory of Needs	Individuals' motivation can be explained by their need for achievement, power, and affiliation.

PROCESS THEORIES OF MOTIVATION

Theory X	Assumes that people dislike work, are lazy, dislike responsibilities, and must be coerced to work hard.
Theory Y	Assumes that people like work, are creative, like autonomy, and seek responsibility
Theory Z	Reflects the Japanese work philosophy that includes a belief in lifetime employment, strong company loyalty, and group consensus.
Goal-Setting Theory	A specific and difficult goal, with clear feedback related to how well a person is meeting that goal, can be used to understand a person's work productivity.
Equity Theory	Individuals compare their work inputs and outcomes with those of others and then respond to eliminate any inequities.
Reinforcement Theory	Both positive and negative feedback condition behavior.
Expectancy Theory	People's effort leads to their performance; their performance leads to rewards; and their rewards lead to the fulfillment of personal goals.

2. *Use specific goals and feedback.* Teams should set specific goals, with specific feedback on how each member is doing, in order to achieve optimal performance.

3. *Allow team members to participate in decisions that affect them.* Team members should be allowed to participate in most decisions that affect them in order to increase productivity, commitment, motivation, and job satisfaction.

4. *Link rewards to performance.* Rewards should be clearly tied to performance in order to optimally motivate team members.

5. *Check the system for equity.* Monitor team members for perceptions of inequality to make sure that any differences in experiences, skills, abilities, and effort lead to clear differences in pay, job assignments, and other rewards.

Understanding why and how people are motivated is an important skill for all project managers. Subtle changes in work processes, evaluation systems, and rewards can have a tremendous influence on a person's motivation. Next, we examine how leadership and power can also be used to influence the performance of project teams.

COMMON PROBLEMS
Managing Einsteins

An "Einstein" is an intelligent, curious, and technologically proficient knowledge worker who has the know-how to keep everything operating without costly delays, breakdowns, and crashes—and the individual to drive managers insane.

Information systems project teams often consist of extremely intelligent individuals who possess extraordinary skills but also sometimes abhor management authority. Researchers have recently identified six types of Einsteins that are common on technical project teams (see Ivancevich and Duening, 2002):

1. Arrogant Einsteins
2. Know-It-All Einsteins

3. Impatient Einsteins
4. Eccentric Einsteins
5. Disorganized Einsteins
6. Withdrawn Einsteins

Researchers point out how every type of Einstein can be troublesome to a project team in one way or another. However, with careful management each can be nurtured to perform their best. To be successful, project managers must be skilled at profiling, recruiting, rewarding, leading, and even disciplining Einsteins.

LEADERSHIP, POWER, AND CONFLICT IN PROJECT TEAMS

The exercise of leadership and power is a natural part of project teams. Over the life of a project, project managers and team members will interact with a broad range of people both from within the team and from outside. Some of these people may hold a higher rank within the organization, whereas others may be customers or contractors outside the organization. How you use your leadership abilities and power to influence the behavior of others can have a tremendous impact on the success or failure of a project.

Leadership and Project Team Effectiveness

The terms *management* and *leadership* are often used interchangeably but are really quite different. A **manager** is typically someone who has a formal position of authority and is responsible for planning, organizing, directing, monitoring, and controlling project activities. A **leader** is someone, who, by virtue of his or her personal attributes, can influence others. Therefore, **leadership** is defined as the ability to influence people toward the achievement of goals. Note that leaders may or may not be managers. Likewise, some managers may not be effective leaders. Effective project managers have the right mix of both management and leadership abilities (see Table 3.3). Experience has shown that successful project teams have great management and great leadership. Managers are essential for keeping the team on track. Leaders are critical for inspiring the team to define its vision and the steps needed to reach success. It has been said that good managers focus on "doing things right," whereas good leaders focus on "doing the right things." Successful projects need both!

Manager
A formal position of authority in an organization that is responsible for planning, organizing, directing, monitoring, and controlling the activities of others.

Leader
A person, who, by virtue of his or her personal attributes, can exert influence on others.

Leadership
The ability to influence people toward the achievement of goals.

Table 3.3   Characteristics of Managers versus Leaders

MANAGERS FOCUS ON:	LEADERS FOCUS ON:
• Objectives	• Vision
• Telling how and when	• Selling what and why
• Shorter range	• Longer range
• Organization and structure	• People
• Autocracy	• Democracy
• Restraining	• Enabling
• Maintaining	• Developing
• Conforming	• Challenging
• Imitating	• Originating
• Administrating	• Innovating
• Controlling	• Directing
• Procedures	• Policy
• Consistency	• Flexibility
• Risk avoidance	• Risk opportunity
• Bottom line	• Top line

Source: Adapted from Verma, 1996.

Trait Theories of Leadership

Trait theories of leadership
A set of leadership theories that argue personality, appearance, competency, and other personal characteristics differentiate leaders from nonleaders.

As you might expect, there are different views on what makes a good leader and whether people are "born leaders" or can be "made" leaders through training and education. One body of research focused on identifying the traits, or personal attributes, of leaders. These **trait theories of leadership** argue that personality, appearance, competency, and other personal characteristics differentiate leaders from nonleaders. This research has found that successful leaders often share some similar personal attributes, including:

- Intelligence and competency in task and organizational activities
- Maturity and a broad range of interests
- Considerate interpersonal skills and respect for the needs and differences of others
- Goal-oriented focus and a strong motivation to achieve success

Although trait-focused research has been useful for identifying characteristics of leaders, it has failed to determine why people become leaders or how people can be better leaders. Additionally, it has been found that people can possess the traits of leaders, but this alone does not guarantee success. Nonetheless, what can be concluded from this research is that people who emerge as leaders are much more likely to possess intelligence, maturity, consideration for others, and a goal-orientated focus.

Behavioral Theories of Leadership

Behavioral theories of leadership
A set of leadership theories that suggest people's actions determine their potential to be successful leaders.

A second view of leadership can be found in the **behavioral theories of leadership**. Although there are several different behavioral theories of leadership, all share a common view that people's actions, rather than personal traits, determine their potential to be successful leaders. In this work, two general types of leaders—task-oriented and relationship-oriented—have been identified. On the one hand, leaders who are relationship-oriented emphasize interpersonal relationships with team members in order to gain the greatest influence. For example, relationship-oriented leaders take a personal interest in team members and accept individual differences among them as being a positive team characteristic. On the other hand, task-oriented leaders use their influence to get tasks completed as effectively as possible, with much less concern for the relationships among team members. There is no consensus on which type of leader is most effective. In some situations, task-oriented leaders have been most effective, whereas in others relationship-oriented leaders have been most effective.

Contingency Theories of Leadership

A third and final general group of leadership theories referred to as **contingency theories of leadership** consider the *situation* the most critical element for identifying leadership success. Specifically, these theories suggest the most effective leadership behavior depends upon the situation, suggesting that no particular leadership style or approach is always best. For example, the Fiedler Contingency Model examined the contexts in which task-oriented versus relationship-oriented leaders would be most successful (Fiedler, 1967). This research found that the interplay of the leader-member relationships, the task structure, and the amount of power the leader possesses determines whether a task- or relationship-oriented leader would be most successful in a given situation. Figure 3.10 shows that both task- and relationship-oriented leaders can be successful, depending upon the leader-member

Figure 3.10 The influence of leader-member relations, task structure, and power on leadership performance (adapted from Robbins and Judge, 2007)

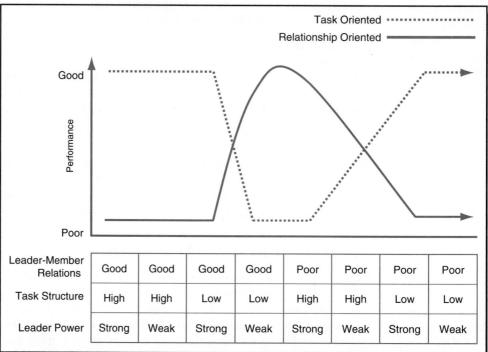

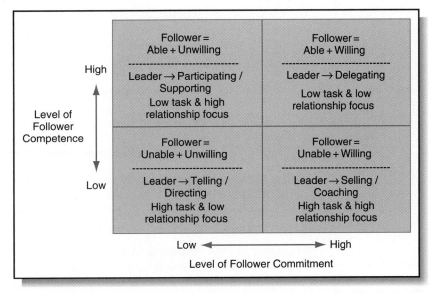

Figure 3.11 How the commitment and competency of a follower influences leadership style

relationship (good versus poor), the task structure (high versus low), and the power of the leader (strong versus weak).

Similar to Fiedler's Contingency Model, Blanchard and colleagues' (2005) Situational Leadership Model (SLM) focuses on characteristics of *followers* to determine the best leadership style. Specifically, followers can be competent (able) and agreeable (willing) to perform a task or can be incompetent and/or reluctant. Depending on a follower's willingness and ability, the leader should choose a different approach, focusing more on task completion (e.g., guiding a follower who lacks ability) or emotional-relationship activities (e.g., coaching the unwilling) (see Figure 3.11). Although the SLM is widely used in management training, research efforts to test its predictive power have been disappointing. Nevertheless, it remains a popular leadership approach for many organizations.

There are several other contingency-based models of leadership, each with its own strengths and weaknesses. Each variation attempts to refine certain aspects of the context to better explain how leaders emerge and when they will be successful. Clearly, there is the potential for many types of successful leaders.

General Leadership Guidelines

Today, most leadership researchers believe that effective leadership can be taught and that the key to effective leadership can be summarized in five essential practices (Tucker, McCarthy, and Benton, 2002):

1. *Challenging the process.* Effective leaders search for opportunities to change the status quo and, by doing so, experiment and take risks.
2. *Inspiring a shared vision.* Effective leaders passionately believe they can make a difference and envision the future, enlisting other team members to see the same future.
3. *Enabling others to act.* Effective leaders cultivate collaboration and build spirited teams, strengthening others in the process by creating trust and fostering human dignity.

Table 3.4 Guidelines for Effective Leadership

- Challenge the process.
- Inspire a shared vision.
- Enable others to act.
- Model the way.
- Encourage the heart.

4. *Modeling the way.* Effective leaders create standards of excellence, set an example for others, and help others achieve success.
5. *Encouraging the heart.* Effective leaders recognize the contributions of others and celebrate their accomplishments, making team members feel like heroes.

With organizations becoming increasingly global and with the increasing use of global project teams within information systems projects, effective leadership has never been more important for achieving project team success. Achieving the right balance between manager and leader is a significant challenge; however, reaching the proper balance will help your project team reach its greatest potential (see Table 3.4).

Power Within Project Teams

Power
The absolute capacity of a person to influence the behavior or attitudes of one or more target persons at a given point in time.

Closely related to leadership is power. **Power** refers to the absolute capacity of a person to influence the behavior or attitudes of one or more target persons at a given point in time (Yukl, 2006). Leaders use power to influence team members to achieve the team's goals. Power can be thought of as the ability to *force* people to do something they would not normally do. This makes power seem like a bad thing, but it isn't necessarily; the use of power to influence the behavior of others is a natural part of all project teams and organizations. Researchers have identified two different types of power, positional (sometimes referred to as formal) power and personal power (French and Raven, 1959; Robbins and Judge, 2007). **Positional power** is based on an individual's position in an organization and can be one of five types.

Positional power
Power derived from an individual's position in an organization.

1. *Legitimate power.* Influencing people based on being in a position of authority.
2. *Reward power.* Influencing people based on being in a position to distribute rewards.
3. *Coercive power.* Influencing people based on being in a position to punish.
4. *Information power.* Influencing people based on their dependency on controlled information.
5. *Ecological power.* Influencing people based on controlling physical resources such as equipment and space.

Personal power
Power derived from an individual's unique characteristics.

Alternatively, **personal power** is an outcome of an individual's unique characteristics and can be one of three types.

1. *Expert power.* Influencing people based on having expertise, special skills, or knowledge (e.g., financial guru Warren Buffett).
2. *Referent power.* Influencing people based on their strong affection, admiration, or loyalty (e.g., former U.S. Secretary of State Colin Powell).
3. *Charismatic power.* Influencing people based on having a favorable personality and interpersonal style (e.g., entertainment mogul Oprah Winfrey).

In sum, each individual on a project team will possess different amounts of power, and this power will be derived from various sources, both positional and personal.

Table 3.5 Sources of Positional and Personal Power

SOURCES OF POSITIONAL POWER	SOURCES OF PERSONAL POWER
• Legitimate power • Reward power • Coercive power • Information power • Ecological power	• Expert power • Referent power • Charismatic power

Conflict
The opposition of people in an organization arising from incompatible or opposing needs, drives, wishes, or external or internal demands.

Functional conflict
Conflict that supports the goals of the team and improves its performance.

Dysfunctional conflict
Conflict that hinders group performance and interferes with team performance.

Understanding what power is, where it comes from, and why people possess it in differing amounts helps us to better understand various team roles and why and how some teams perform better than others (see Table 3.5). Of course, when power is exercised to influence people, it sometimes causes conflict. This topic is discussed next.

Managing and Resolving Project Team Conflict

Conflict is the opposition of people in an organization who have incompatible or opposing needs, drives, wishes, or external or internal demands (Verma, 1996). Like leadership and power, conflict is a natural part of project teams and organizations. Years ago, any conflict within a project team was viewed as a very serious problem that had to be eliminated. Today, however, researchers believe that some *functional* conflict is absolutely necessary for a team to perform effectively. **Functional conflict** helps to support the goals of the team and improve its performance. Alternatively, **dysfunctional conflict** hinders group performance and interferes with team performance. So when we say that some conflict is good, we mean that some *functional* conflict is good (see Figure 3.12).

Figure 3.12 Conflict and team performance (adapted from Robbins and Judge, 2007)

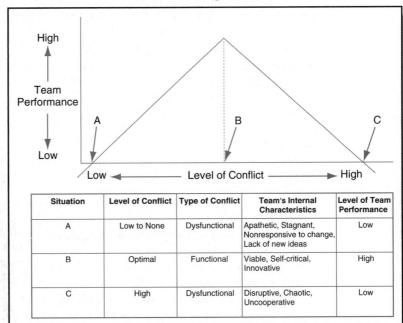

Situation	Level of Conflict	Type of Conflict	Team's Internal Characteristics	Level of Team Performance
A	Low to None	Dysfunctional	Apathetic, Stagnant, Nonresponsive to change, Lack of new ideas	Low
B	Optimal	Functional	Viable, Self-critical, Innovative	High
C	High	Dysfunctional	Disruptive, Chaotic, Uncooperative	Low

Table 3.6 Conditions That Can Lead to Project Conflict

Condition	Description
Ambiguous roles, work boundaries, responsibility, and authority	Project teams often have members with different reporting structures and overlapping or conflicting responsibilities that can lead to conflict.
Inconsistent or incompatible goals	Team members may perceive others to have different or conflicting goals that can lead to conflict.
Communication problems	Task, process, or relationship ambiguity can result in reduced or ineffective communication that can lead to conflict.
Dependence on another party	Team members depend on others to complete tasks or provide resources; delays or work quality issues can lead to conflict.
Specialization or differentiation	Team members from different professional backgrounds often have different viewpoints, languages, and goals that can lead to conflict.
Need for joint decision making and consensus	Teams with a diverse mix of members may feel pressure to conform to the majority opinion, which can lead to conflict.
Behavior regulations	Project teams have norms for working together that may conflict with an individual's preferred work processes.
Unresolved prior conflicts	Past unresolved issues between team members can lead to conflict.

Source: Adapted from Verma, 1995.

Among project teams, conflict can arise from tasks, work processes, or relationships (see Table 3.6). *Task conflict* relates to the content and goals of the work itself. *Relationship conflict* relates to interpersonal relationships among team members. *Process conflict* relates to how the work gets done within a team. Research has found that low-to-moderate levels of task conflict, as well as low levels of process conflict, can help a team's performance. High levels of task conflict—not agreeing on what should be done and what the objective is—will never lead to enhanced performance. Likewise, moderate-to-high levels of process conflict—not agreeing on how work will be performed or who will do it—does not lead to enhanced performance. Additionally, this research has found that relationship conflicts—personality conflicts and relationship problems—will always hinder team performance (Robbins and Judge, 2007). This means that functional conflict is always related to task and process issues, whereas dysfunctional conflict can be rooted in tasks, processes, or relationships, depending upon its intensity. In sum, conflict can be thought of as varying in intensity from none to extreme (see Figure 3.13). Functional conflict is typically at the lower end of this continuum, whereas dysfunctional conflict can span its entire range.

Within project teams, researchers have identified the primary causes of conflict to be (Thamhain and Wilemon, 1975):

1. *Schedule.* Disagreements on task duration and sequencing.
2. *Project priorities.* Disagreements on project vision and scope.
3. *Manpower.* Disagreements on the utilization of people, especially those simultaneously involved in multiple projects.
4. *Technical.* Disagreements over system design elegance and resource limitations.
5. *Administration.* Disagreements due to authority over key resources.
6. *Personality.* Disagreements due to dysfunctional interpersonal interactions.
7. *Cost.* Disagreements arising from increasing resource constraints as a project evolves.

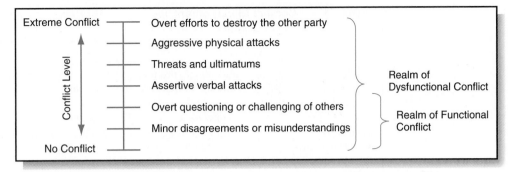

Figure 3.13 Conflict intensity can range from no conflict to extreme (adapted from Robbins and Judge, 2007)

In most cases, effective project management can minimize these causes of conflict. For example, an incomplete work breakdown schedule can lead to conflict related to the project schedule, or a vague project scope statement can lead to conflict related to project priorities. Additionally, as a project evolves, different sources of conflict may be more likely (e.g., project priorities will likely occur early within the project). In addition to effective project management techniques, many good conflict management approaches can be utilized. These are discussed next.

Although there is no single best way to manage all types of conflict, some approaches have been found to be better than others. Approaches for resolving conflict can range from completely autocratic to more cooperative. Situational factors, such as time pressure, the intensity of the conflict, the importance of the problem, and the level of cooperation among parties, can influence which approach is most appropriate. Likewise, because low-to-moderate levels of conflict have been found to benefit team performance, some techniques can be used to purposefully *stimulate* functional conflict within a team. **Conflict management**, the use of resolution and stimulation techniques to achieve a desired level of team conflict, is a valuable skill for all project managers. Table 3.7 summarizes many of the most widely used techniques. By using these techniques, you should be able to better sustain the desired level of conflict within your team.

Conflict management The use of resolution and stimulation techniques to achieve a desired level of team conflict.

Managing Project Politics

Politics are a natural part of all organizations and reflect the use of covert mechanisms to obtain power and control. Within the context of information systems projects, politics are the art of getting things done. Although some view politics as a somewhat evil or distasteful part of organizational life, they are not necessarily a bad thing or something to avoid. There are, of course, good and bad politicians; the good politicians look for win–win opportunities, while the bad look for opportunities to win at any cost. Being a successful project manager in modern organizations requires that you also become a savvy politician. Some advice for improving your political skills includes (Choo, 2003):

1. *Understand what your organization values.* To be a good organizational politician, you need to understand what the organization values (e.g., its mission, goals, and strategy) and align your personal goals and behavior to best help the organization achieve its objectives. By aligning your objectives with those of the organization, you are more likely to gain the support of powerful decision makers within the organization.

Table 3.7 Conflict Management Techniques for Resolving and Stimulating Team Conflict

CONFLICT RESOLUTION TECHNIQUES	
Problem solving	Face-to-face meetings can be used to identify and resolve conflicts through open and candid discussions.
Shared goals	Create shared goals that can only be achieved through the cooperation of the conflicting parties.
Resource expansion	When conflict is caused by resource scarcity—say, money, opportunities, space, equipment—additional resources can be used to resolve discrepancies.
Avoidance	Withdrawal from, or suppression of, the conflict.
Smoothing	Playing down differences while emphasizing common interests between the conflicting parties.
Compromise	Each party to the conflict gives up something of value.
Authoritative command	A person of power mandates an outcome and communicates it to the conflicting parties.
Altering team member behavior	Use some type of training or intervention to alter the attitudes or behaviors that are causing conflict.
Altering the team structure	Change the formal team structure so that conflicting members limit their interaction; a more extreme solution is to remove members from the team.
CONFLICT STIMULATION TECHNIQUES	
Communication	Using ambiguous or threatening messages to increase conflict levels
Bringing in outsiders	Adding new members to the team who have different backgrounds, attitudes, values, or managerial styles
Restructuring the team	Realigning the tasks, work or communication processes to disrupt the status quo
Appointing a devil's advocate	Have an assigned critic to argue against the team's majority position

Source: Adapted from Robbins and Judge, 2007.

2. *Understand how decisions are made in your organization.* In most organizations, decisions are not necessarily made based on the formal organizational structure chart. Understanding how decisions are made and who truly has influence on those decisions is necessary for building successful alliances.

3. *Expand and strengthen your network.* To get complex development projects completed on time often requires that you are able to gain access to scarce resources and expertise. These valuable resources are often controlled by other managers who may or may not want to help you to be successful. Being a valued colleague to others by giving your time, expertise, and support, is a great way to get a favor returned when one is critically needed.

4. *Develop a clear and easy-to-communicate story.* Being a successful politician requires having the right story, for the right audience, at the right time. Hearing the right story motivates team members, sponsors, and other critical stakeholders. Much like a successful coach, you must inspire confidence to get the most from you team.

5. *Lead by example.* If you are to be a great leader, your team must respect your values, judgment, work ethic, and competency to deliver a successful project. Successful project managers understand that leading by example is a great way to inspire others to go beyond the call of duty to make the project a success.

In sum, project politics is not about winning at any cost. It is about finding common ground and building alliances to achieve organizational objectives. Being a successful project manager requires that you also be a skilled organizational politician.

MANAGING GLOBAL PROJECT TEAMS

Global project team
A project team whose members are located throughout the world.

One important trend that most organizations are facing in the development of information systems is the increased use of **global project teams**, often referred to as *virtual teams*, with members located throughout the world. In this section, we first examine several catalysts for this trend. Next, we examine various challenges related to managing these teams. The section concludes with advice for developing stronger global information systems project teams.

Growing Numbers of Global Information Systems Projects

The use of global teams for information systems projects has become extremely popular. This growth can be attributed to three primary factors (see Figure 3.14):

1. Advances in telecommunications
2. Increased globalization
3. Increased outsourcing

All of these factors are related. For example, advances in telecommunications have enabled organizations to more easily outsource part of their information systems operations, such as data entry, user support, or application programming to locations that offer cheaper labor. Yet without a high-quality network connection between sites, this would be much more difficult. In the remainder of this section, we briefly examine each of these factors.

Figure 3.14 Factors that affected the growth in international information systems projects

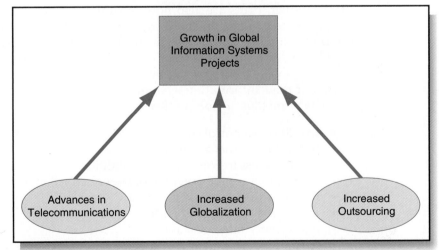

Advances in Telecommunications

In recent years, there have been tremendous advances in telecommunications. The proliferation of the Internet and the World Wide Web is the most significant example of how the connectivity across the globe has increased. Today more than 200 countries and over a billion people have access to the Internet. Advances in telecommunications—for example, 24-hour global news, the Internet, "world" phones, instant messaging, and Web logs (blogs)—have led to vast increases in globalization and have also spurred the use of global project teams.

Increased Globalization

Globalization refers to the compression of the world and the increased awareness that no country or individual can shut itself off from others (Robertson, 1992; Walsham, 2001). Today, organizations are increasingly moving away from focusing exclusively on local markets. For example, Asian businesses, such as Mitac and Creative Technologies, are focusing on global markets by attempting to become serious competitors in the PC, telecommunications equipment, computer parts, and digital services industries. The Thai subsidiary of Texas Instruments is also increasing its global customer base, becoming one of the world's largest producers of microchips. Price Waterhouse LLP is focusing on forming overseas partnerships to increase its client base and better serve regions away from its U.S. home. Today, more and more organizations are operating throughout the world; this, too, has led to an increased use of global project teams.

Changes in political systems have also opened new markets, most notably in Asia and Latin America. For instance, Hong Kong, with its sophisticated fiber-optic–based telecommunications infrastructure and multinational banks, has become a center for organizations focusing on Internet-enabled business. Many Latin American countries have also liberalized and expanded their global trade, most notably Brazil, which is home to more than half of the Internet users in Latin America. Additionally, many economies in former Soviet-bloc and eastern European countries are rapidly evolving. In sum, the globalization of the world's markets is another important factor contributing to the growth of global information-systems project teams.

Increased Outsourcing

The advances in telecommunications and increased globalization have enabled organizations to seek partners with cheap, yet high-quality, labor (see Table 3.8). Much like a firm would outsource the manufacturing of some component of a physical product, firms are also now outsourcing information system development, support, and management. Today the global outsourcing market exceeds $500 billion annually and is predicted to rapidly increase over the next decade. Additionally, nearly 90 percent of all large organizations are expected to use some form of global IT outsourcing by 2006. Companies are choosing to outsource some or all of their information systems development, support, or management for a variety of reasons, including (King, 2003):

- To reduce or control costs
- To free up internal resources
- To gain access to world-class capabilities
- To increase revenue potential of the organization
- To reduce time to market
- To increase process efficiencies
- To outsource noncore activities
- To compensate for a lack of specific capabilities or skills

Table 3.8   Salary Differences Have Helped to Make Global Outsourcing Popular

COUNTRY	AVERAGE ANNUAL SALARY FOR EXPERIENCED SYSTEMS PROGRAMMER
Poland and Hungary	$4,800 to $8,000
India	$5,880
Philippines	$6,564
Malaysia	$7,200
Russian Federation	$5,000 to $7,500
China	$8,952
Canada	$28,174
Ireland	$23,000 to $34,000
Israel	$15,000 to $38,000
United States	$63,331

Source: Hoffman and Thibodeau, 2003.

Ethical Dilemma: Implications of Global Outsourcing

"It's considered a crime against humanity today, where for the last 15 years, it was a sound business move." IBM spokesman John Bukovinsky recently stated what many companies think about global outsourcing. From software development to call centers, many companies have used outsourcing to get access to highly skilled but inexpensive labor in foreign countries, mainly India and China. Often, companies choose to outsource certain jobs because they have a hard time finding the right workers in the United States; in many cases, however, outsourcing is done to decrease costs, which increases a company's bottom line.

Although outsourcing can be beneficial for companies, it often results in domestic job cuts. For the displaced worker, the outsourcing is not beneficial. Recent studies claim that offshore outsourcing is not a zero-sum game; companies often use the cost reductions from outsourcing to move into new business segments or to invest in new products, thereby creating new jobs in the United States.

Nevertheless, in the short run, moving a job to India can roughly be translated into laying-off a domestic employee. Should this be viewed as a sound business move or a crime against humanity? (Sources: Cringely [2003], Lopez [2004], Morphy [2004])

Discussion Questions
1. Should there be limits on the extent to which organizations can outsource work to other countries? Explain.
2. If you were a project manager who oversaw a global project team with outsourced members, what benefits and challenges would you envision?

In addition to these factors, a "buy-versus-build" mentality is becoming more pervasive as higher quality and more sophisticated off-the-shelf applications become available from a broader range of vendors. Additionally, with better low-level support and more programming tasks being outsourced, organizational IT groups increasingly are being used to integrate off-the-shelf modules with applications developed by outsourcing partners. Increased system integration and the use of global outsourcing providers make effective project planning and management extremely important; "It is one thing to have cheap labor available to perform routine development tasks, it is another to ensure that the software is being effectively designed and projects are effectively managed." Next, we will examine some of the challenges associated with managing global information systems project teams.

Challenges for Managing Global Information Systems Project Teams

Whether or not a firm is trying to integrate information systems across countries, develop a system in one country for use in another, or outsource parts of its systems development abroad, it faces many challenges when it seeks to operate across national boundaries. Challenges for managing global information systems project teams can be categorized into four broad categories (see Figure 3.15):

1. Technology-related challenges
2. Cultural challenges
3. Human-resource challenges
4. Environmental challenges

Technology-Related Challenges
The primary technological challenge faced by organizations operating across national boundaries is related to the telecommunications infrastructure. The price, quality, and speed of telecommunications can vary from country to country. For

Figure 3.15   Challenges of managing global information systems project teams

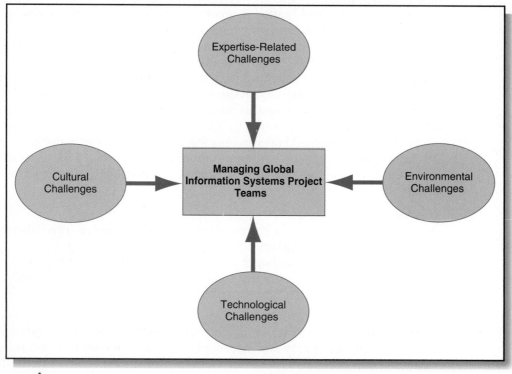

example, the price of an Internet connection in Europe can be more than double the price of a similar connection in the United States. Such price differences can be even greater when contrasting developed and less-developed countries. Additionally, the quality of the telecommunications infrastructure can vary significantly, causing problems in data transfer and connectivity. For instance, in Greece, only half of the telecommunications network is digital, making it much slower and less reliable than the network in say, Finland, which is 100 percent digital. Likewise, the sophistication and geographic coverage of a country's telecommunications infrastructure can also vary. In less developed countries, such as those in Asia or Africa, large areas can exist where no network access is available. Such gaps act as a significant barrier to developing global partnerships. For example, a Hong Kong-based company recently opened operations in Thailand, only to realize that no common telecommunications connections were available, limiting its ability to interact with its headquarters (Sarker and Sarker, 2000).

Apart from the price, the quality, and the pervasiveness of the infrastructure, telecommunications standards can also vary throughout the world. In addition to infrastructure challenges, the hardware and software environments can also be different, causing serious communication and integration problems. Whereas the United States has seen a predominance of the use of IBM mainframes or network servers with Windows-based clients, Unix-based workstations have been an extremely popular hardware platform in Europe. Software preferences can also be different; most European nations prefer to use PDF files when exchanging documents; U.S.-based organizations prefer Microsoft Office-based document sharing. Such hardware and software differences can cause serious problems in data sharing, data transfer, and overall project communication, adding to the complexity of managing global projects and teams.

Cultural Challenges

Culture
The collective programming of the mind that distinguishes the members of one group or category of people from another.

Hofstede (2001) defines **culture** as the "collective programming of the mind that distinguishes the members of one group or category of people from another" (p. 9). Culture is manifested in how individuals view a variety of cultural dimensions, such as power distance, uncertainty avoidance, individualism/collectivism, masculinity/femininity, time, and life focus (see Table 3.9). In essence, each nation has its own culture, which can often have important implications for managing global project teams.

Power distance
A cultural characteristic that describes how different societies handle the issue of human inequality.

Power distance refers to how different societies handle the issue of human inequality and sheds light on the inherent power structure within organizations and teams. Some cultures are higher in power distance, preferring autocracy, whereas other cultures are lower in power distance, fostering more collaborative teamwork and less hierarchical structures. Consequently, differences in power distance can pose serious challenges for managing global project teams.

For instance, an information systems development project was undertaken by a Jamaican insurance company to improve its claim processing (Walsham, 2001). For this project, Indian software developers were hired to jointly develop the new information system with their Jamaican counterparts. In the initial project stages, the group worked effectively together. Over time, however, there was significant and ongoing conflict between the two groups. One of the major causes of this conflict related to differences in power distance between the Indian and Jamaican cultures. The Indian software developers, originating from a country with a relatively high power-distance culture, were viewed as being highly autocratic and were not used to being contradicted or questioned. In contrast, the Jamaican developers came from a relatively low power-distance culture, believing in consensual and democratic management styles. For

Table 3.9 Critical Cultural Dimensions for Various Countries

Critical Cultural Dimensions	Group 1: USA, Canada, Australia	Group 2: Germany, Austria, Switzerland	Group 3: Mexico, Venezuela, Peru	Group 4: Japan	Group 5: India, Hong Kong, Singapore
Power Distance	Moderately Low	Moderately Low	Moderately High	Moderately High	High
Individualism/ Collectivism	Highly Individualistic	Moderately Individualistic	Highly to Moderately Collectivistic	Moderately Collectivistic	Highly to Collectivistic
Masculinity/ Femininity	Moderately Masculine	Moderately Masculine	Moderately to Highly Masculine	High Masculinity	Masculine
Uncertainty Avoidance	Moderately Weak	Moderately Strong	Moderately Weak	Strong	Moderately Weak
Concept of Time	Long Term	Long Term	Short Term	Long Term	Short Term
Life Focus	Quantity	Quantity	Quality	More on Quality than Quantity	Changing from Quality to Quantity

Source: Verma 1997, adapted from Owens and McLaurin, 1993.

Uncertainty avoidance
A cultural characteristic that helps in understanding the risk-taking nature of a culture.

Individualism/ collectivism
A cultural characteristic that reflects the extent to which a society values the position of an individual versus the position of a group.

Masculinity/femininity
A cultural characteristic that refers to the degree to which a society is characterized by masculine or feminine qualities.

Concept of time
A cultural characteristic that reflects the extent to which a culture has a longer- or shorter-term orientation.

Life focus
A cultural characteristic that contrasts the extent to which a culture focuses on quantity of life versus quality of life.

them, it was most natural to sit down as a group and talk through issues when making decisions. The difference in power distance for these teams led to extensive clashes, delaying the actual development process and hurting the overall project quality.

The degree of **uncertainty avoidance** helps in understanding the risk-taking nature of a culture. From a project team perspective, this might result in team members from some cultures being more cautious; this can be particularly troublesome when they are reluctant to adopt new technologies or techniques. A related dimension, **individualism/collectivism**, reflects the extent to which a society values the position of an individual versus the position of a group. In collectivist societies, peer pressure often plays an important role in shaping group interaction and decision-making. Mixing individually and collectively oriented individuals on a team can often cause excessive conflict if not carefully managed. Additionally, **masculinity/femininity** refers to the degree to which a society is characterized by masculine qualities, such as assertiveness, or by feminine characteristics, such as nurturance, which can have important implications in terms of user preferences for technology, how user requirements are collected, or how teams assign roles and collaborate.

The **concept of time** can also differ across cultures, with some cultures having a relatively longer-term orientation, reflecting an appreciation for future rewards, perseverance, and long-term planning. Conversely, cultures with shorter-term orientation focus on the past and the current situation. Clearly, time orientation differences can greatly influence project planning, task assignments, and overall team performance. A last cultural dimension, **life focus**, contrasts the extent to which a culture focuses on *quantity* of life versus *quality* of life. A quantity-of-life orientation reflects a more competitive culture that values achievements and the acquisition of material goods. A quality-of-life orientation values relationships, interdependence, and concern for others. Life focus differences can influence group development, task and role assignments, and reward preferences among team members. In sum, global project teams composed of people with differing cultural values will be much more difficult to manage. Effective project teams will require members who are sensitive and respectful to the differences of others; it is crucial that project managers employ differing and flexible management techniques in order to help a team reach its optimal performance.

In addition to cultural barriers, many other barriers can hinder global project team interaction and performance, including:

- Language—for example, communication language and norms
- Work culture—for example, work skills, habits, and attitudes toward work
- Aesthetics—for example, art, music, and culture
- Education—for example, attitudes toward education and literacy
- Religion, beliefs, and attitudes—for example, spiritual institutions and values
- Social organizations—for example, family and social cohesiveness
- Political life—for example, political stability

Each of these cultural elements can greatly influence project team interaction and performance, as outlined in Table 3.10. For example, the lack of a common language can often lead to disastrous results when communicating technical information such as user requirements or design specifications. Likewise, differences in work culture can influence project team interaction and effectiveness. For instance, Europeans typically approach a project by focusing on its beginning and incrementally moving forward until the project is concluded. Americans, in contrast, typically look at the end first, and work backward to the start (Heichler, 2000). In sum, differences in language, work culture, and other cultural elements can have serious implications for managing cross-cultural information-systems project teams.

Expertise Related Challenges

Apart from the cultural issues, the nature of the IS workforce can also pose significant challenges for global project teams. Different countries have different concentrations of skilled workers and, as previously discussed, differing costs for those workers. For example, most industrial nations have made significant investments in building a large base of skilled information systems personnel. However, these workers will

Table 3.10 How Various Cultural Elements Can Affect Project Team Interaction and Performance

Cultural Element	How It Can Impact the Project
Language	Communication problems can influence project team efficiency, understanding, and performance.
Work Culture	Different skills, work habits and attitudes can influence project performance and manpower constraints.
Aesthetics	Art, music, and dance reflect nonwork interests that can be used to enrich team communication and cohesiveness.
Education	Education level limits skill levels, technological sophistication, and infrastructure.
Religion, Beliefs, and Attitudes	Basic values and beliefs can influence attitudes toward work, promptness, punctuality, mutual trust, respect, and cooperation.
Social Organization	Social norms can influence formal and informal communication, including negotiations and job assignments.
Political Life	Differing political systems can influence the delivery of supplies and equipment, human rights, the legal system, and overall stability.

Source: Adapted from Verma, 1997.

typically also be much more costly to employ than those from less developed countries. The types of skills prevalent in different countries may also vary. For instance, a cross-cultural software development project involving analysts and developers from both Norway and the United States led to conflict regarding the preferred development methodology and programming environment (Sarker and Sahay, 2004). This conflict hindered workload sharing and team cohesiveness.

Environmental Challenges

Environmental issues can also pose significant challenges for managing global IS projects and teams due to differing rules and regulations. One example is the European Union Data Protection Directive of 1998, which controls transborder data flow between nations. Contrary to many of the regulations in the United States, this directive states that personal data collected in Europe can only be used for the purposes for which it has been collected and cannot be transferred across national borders. This has caused significant challenges for U.S. organizations that employ European project team members.

Legal policies can also differ, which is often an outgrowth of the inherent culture of the country. For example, the copyright laws in China are fairly relaxed because copying is seen as a compliment to the originator of the work. The concept of ownership of intellectual property goes against the Chinese' notion that the value of the society is greater than the value of the individual. The political environment can also play an important role in global project team management. A stable, political government that is keen on investing in information systems infrastructure is always more attractive to potential partners. Likewise, currency fluctuations can have significant implications for global operations and teams where changes in the exchange rate can quickly transform a low-cost geographical area to a high-cost area and vice versa. In sum, many challenges related to technology, culture, expertise, and environment can influence the difficulty of managing global project teams. In addition to these challenges, relatively minor issues such as differences in time zones or how intellectual property is viewed can pose formidable challenges to global project teams.

Developing Global Information Systems Project Teams

One of the keys to creating successful global project teams is to have members who can work together effectively. This means that effective project team members will not only have strong technical skills but will also be effective at working in cross-cultural teams. Unfortunately, people with good cross-cultural team training are in short supply. Nevertheless, there are several effective strategies for developing stronger global project teams, and these are discussed next (see Figure 3.16).

Hire Individuals Experienced in Working Across Cultures

The first strategy is very straightforward. Simply put, hiring individuals who are experienced in working on cross-cultural project teams and possess the necessary cultural sensitivity to empathize with other cultures will greatly enhance global project team performance. Pat Zilvitis, the CIO of Gillette, has repeatedly found that people who have "technical astuteness, business understanding, cultural sensitivity, and ability to communicate well" are perfect candidates for global project team assignments (Heichler, 2000). Given that it is often difficult to find people with global project team experience, another strategy is to develop the skills of existing

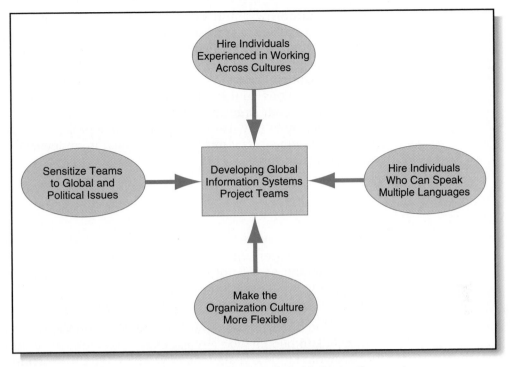

Figure 3.16 Strategies for developing global information systems project teams

employees. For example, many companies are rotating staff into global project teams or assigning staff to locations throughout the world.

Hire Individuals Who Can Speak Multiple Languages

A second strategy is to hire individuals who can speak different languages. Language problems within global project teams are often hidden beneath the surface. Many people are embarrassed to admit when they don't completely understand a foreign colleague. Unfortunately, the miscommunication of important design information can have disastrous effects on a project. Having at least one person at each remote location who is fluent in the host country's language can help to alleviate this problem.

Make the Organizational Culture More Flexible

A third strategy is to design a flexible organizational culture that best reflects the cultural values of the local employees. For example, Fujitsu has been making strong gains in its international markets, especially in Internet and multimedia products, after years of overseas failure. To gain flexibility, Fujitsu changed its culture significantly to fit the needs of local environments, such as the relaxation of strict Japanese standards of dress and the introduction of flexible working hours. This flexibility has led to enhanced organizational and project team performance.

Sensitize Teams to Global Cultural and Political Issues

A fourth strategy focuses on the development of mechanisms to help global project teams be more sensitive to the various cultural and political differences of their members. Such sensitivity and awareness can be developed through careful and in-depth training and by having a diverse mix of employees representing different cultures within the organization and team. Project team members who understand current events and the political climate of a global project team member's country will enhance project communication, team cohesiveness, and performance.

Globalization is a reality within the information systems departments of most large organizations. In the not too distant future, it will be a reality in virtually all organizations, both large and small. For better or worse, it appears that global outsourcing is here to stay. Thus, to be an effective project manager in this increasingly global environment, you must become skilled in understanding and working with cross-cultural teams.

Global Implications: Managing International Projects

Project managers who are successful in managing projects within their home countries are not always successful when assigned to manage a project in an international location. To increase your chances of success, prior to your assignment do the following:

1. Read books, newspapers, magazines, and Web sites about the country.
2. Talk to people who already know the country and its culture.
3. Avoid literal translations of work materials, brochures, memos, and other important documents.
4. Watch locally produced television and monitor the local news through international news stations and Web sites.
5. After arriving in the new country, take time to tour local parks, monuments, museums, entertainment locations, and other cultural venues.
6. Share meals and breaks with local workers and discuss more than just work-related issues, such as current local events and topics.
7. Learn several words and phrases in the local language.

To create a successful project team environment, you need to build trust. Trust is built by showing sensitivity to and awareness of local issues, language, and culture. By following these steps, you will not only increase the project's likelihood of success; you will also make your project experience much more enjoyable (Source: Treitel [2000]).

MANAGING PROJECT TEAMS AND THE PMBOK

In this chapter, we have focused primarily on Knowledge Area 9, Project Human Resource Management, of the Project Management Institute Body of Knowledge (*PMBOK*, 2004) (see Figure 3.17). Specifically, three key processes—organizational planning, staff acquisition and team development—have been discussed. Additionally, we have also discussed issues related to Knowledge Area 2, the Project Management Context, by examining various organizational influences on projects and project managers, as well as several key general management skills for project managers. Together, this information provides a solid foundation for managing project teams.

Figure 3.17 Chapter 3 and PMBOK coverage

	Textbook Chapters ➞	1	2	3	4	5	6	7	8	9	10	11	12
	PMBOK Knowledge Area												
1	**Introduction to Project Management**												
1.1	What Is a Project?	●											
1.2	What Is Project Management?	●											
1.3	Areas of Expertise		●										
1.4	Project Management Context	●											
2	**Project Life Cycle and Organization**												
2.1	The Project Life Cycle	●	●										
2.2	Project Stakeholders	●	●										
2.3	Organizational Influences		●	✓	○		○						
3	**Project Management Processes for a Project**												
3.1	Project Management Processes	●	●										
3.2	PM Process Groups	●	●										
3.3	Process Interactions		●										
3.4	Project Management Process Mapping		●										
4	**Project Integration Management**												
4.1	Develop Project Charter					○							
4.2	Develop Preliminary Project Scope Statement					○	○						
4.3	Develop Project Management Plan					○							
4.4	Direct and Manage Project Execution										○		
4.5	Monitor and Control Project Work												○
4.6	Integrated Change Control												○
4.7	Close Project												○
5	**Project Scope Management**												
5.1	Scope Planning					○							
5.2	Scope Definition					○							
5.3	Create WBS					○	○						
5.4	Scope Verification					○							
5.5	Scope Control					○							○
6	**Project Time Management**												
6.1	Activity Definition						○						
6.2	Activity Sequencing						○						
6.3	Activity Resource Estimating							○					
6.4	Activity Duration Estimating							○					
6.5	Schedule Development							○					
6.6	Schedule Control							○					○

(continued)

Figure 3.17 (continued)

Textbook Chapters ➞	1	2	3	4	5	6	7	8	9	10	11	12
PMBOK Knowledge Area												
7 Project Cost Management												
7.1 Cost Estimating							o					
7.2 Cost Budgeting							o					
7.3 Cost Control							o					o
8 Project Quality Management												
8.1 Quality Planning								o				
8.2 Quality Assurance								o				
8.3 Quality Control								o				o
9 Project Human Resource Management												
9.1 Human Resource Planning			✓				o					
9.2 Acquire Project Team			✓				o					
9.3 Develop Project Team			✓				o					
9.4 Manage Project Team			✓				o					
10 Project Communications Management												
10.1 Communications Planning				o							o	
10.2 Information Distribution				o							o	
10.3 Performance Reporting				o								o
10.4 Administrative Closure				o								o
11 Project Risk Management												
11.1 Risk Management Planning									o			
11.2 Risk Identification									o	o		
11.3 Qualitative Risk Analysis									o			
11.4 Quantitative Risk Analysis									o			
11.5 Risk Response Planning									o			
11.6 Risk Monitoring and Control									o			o
12 Project Procurement Management												
12.1 Plan Purchases and Acquisitions										o		
12.2 Plan Contracting										o		
12.3 Request Seller Responses										o		
12.4 Select Sellers										o		
12.5 Contract Administration										o		
12.6 Contract Closure										o		o

Key: ●-where material is covered in past chapters; ✓-current chapter coverage;
o-where material is covered in future chapters

Jim Woo, the assistant director of information technology at Petrie's, a Southern California-based electronics retail store, walked into his building's conference room. It was early in the morning for Jim, but the meeting was important to him. He was going to put together his team for the customer-relationship project he had just been named to manage. It was Jim's first big project to manage at Petrie's, and he was excited about getting started.

"Hi, Jim," said Ella Whinston, the chief operation officer. With Ella was a guy Jim did not know. "This is Bob Petroski, Jim. I've asked that he be on your project team to represent me."

Jim and Bob shook hands. "Nice to meet you, Jim. I'm looking forward to working with you on this project."

"Bob knows how important this project is to me," Ella said, "so I expect him to keep me informed about your progress." Ella smiled.

Great, Jim thought, more pressure. That's all I need.

Just then, John Smith, the head of marketing walked into the conference room. With him was a young woman Jim recognized, but he wasn't sure where he had seen her.

"Jim," John said, "let me introduce you to Sally Fukuyama. She is the assistant director of marketing. She will be representing marketing and me on your No Customer Escapes project."

"Hi, Jim," Sally said, "I have a lot of ideas about what we can do. Even though I still have my regular job to worry about, I'm excited about working on this project."

"Who else will be on your team?" Ella asked.

"I am bringing Sanjay Agarwal from IT," Jim said. "He is in charge of systems integration in the IT department and reports to me. In addition to me and Sanjay and Sally and Bob, we will also have a store manager on the team. I'm trying to get Juanita Lopez, the manager of the store in Riverside. Like the rest of us, she is really busy, but I think we have to have a store manager on the team."

"Riverside?" Ella asked. "That's one of our top stores. Juanita should have a lot of insight into the issues related to keeping customers if she is managing the Riverside store. And you are right, she is going to be very busy."

"So," John asked, "when is your first meeting?"

CHAPTER SUMMARY

Describe the characteristics of a project team and the factors that influence team performance. A project team consists of two or more people who are mutually accountable to the organization and to each member of the team; they are also highly interdependent, having both shared goals and complementary skills. Project teams do not automatically become highly interdependent and productive but must develop and evolve through various stages as they work together over time. When teams develop, they pass through five stages: forming, storming, norming, performing, and adjourning. Work design, composition, context, and process factors are just some of the many factors that influence team performance.

Explain what is meant by need and process theories of motivation. Motivation refers to an individual's intensity, direction, and persistence of effort toward attaining a goal. There have been contrasting views of how, why, and when people are motivated. Need theories of motivation deal with factors within a person that act to energize, direct, or stop various behaviors. For example, good working conditions may energize a person to work hard on a project. Process theories of motivation attempt to understand a person's behavior based on intrinsic or personal factors that are used to motivate specific behavior. In general, this perspective suggests that project managers need to create a proper environment, work processes, and rewards to achieve the greatest motivation from people.

Contrast trait, behavioral, and contingency theories of leadership. Leadership is the ability to influence people toward the achievement of goals. There are three primary schools of thought regarding why certain people are great leaders. The first, trait theories of leadership, believes that personality, appearance, competency, and other personal characteristics differentiate leaders from nonleaders. The second, behavioral theories of leadership, proposes that people's actions, rather than personal traits, determine their potential to be successful leaders. The third, contingency theories of leadership, proposes that the situation is the most critical element for successful leadership. Today, researchers believe that effective leadership can be taught and that the behavioral and contingency theories of leadership most accurately predict leadership success.

Explain the sources of power and how these sources can be used to influence people. Power refers to the absolute capacity of a person to influence the behavior or attitudes of one or more target persons at a given point in time. Researchers have identified two general types of power that can be used to influence the behavior and attitudes of others: positional power and personal power. Positional power is based on an individual's position in an organization and can be one of five types: legitimate, reward, coercive, informational, and ecological. Personal power is an outcome of an individual's unique characteristics and can be one of three types: expert, referent, and charismatic. Understanding what power is, where it comes from, and why people possess it in differing amounts helps us to better understand various team roles and why and how some teams perform better than others.

Contrast functional versus dysfunctional conflict and explain how conflict can be beneficial to a project team. Conflict is the opposition of people in an organization arising from incompatible or opposing needs, drives, wishes, or external or internal demands. There are two general types of conflict within project teams: functional and dysfunctional. Functional conflict helps to support the goals of the team and improve its performance, whereas dysfunctional conflict hinders group performance and is destructive to team performance. Today, researchers believe that conflict is a natural part of a project team and that some functional conflict—centered on task and work processes—is absolutely necessary for a team to perform effectively; conflict centered on personal relationships is never good for team performance.

Explain why global project teams are increasing and describe the challenges of managing these teams. The use of global teams for information systems projects has become increasingly popular due to three primary factors: 1) advances in telecommunications, 2) increased globalization, and 3) increased outsourcing. Although global project teams are becoming widespread, there are many challenges for managing these teams, including: 1) technology-related challenges, 2) cultural challenges, 3) human-resource challenges, and 4) environmental challenges. Because of this, you must become skilled in understanding and working with cross-cultural teams to be an effective project manager.

KEY TERMS REVIEW

- Absenteeism
- Behavioral theories of leadership
- Concept of time
- Conflict
- Conflict management
- Contingency theories of leadership
- Culture
- Dysfunctional conflict
- ERG theory
- Equity theory
- Expectancy theory
- Functional conflict
- Global project team

- Globalization
- Goal setting theory
- Hierarchy of needs
- Individualism/ collectivism
- Job satisfaction
- Leader
- Leadership
- Life focus
- Manager
- Masculinity/ femininity
- Motivation
- Myers-Briggs Type Indicator (MBTI)
- Personal power

- Positional power
- Power
- Power distance
- Project team
- Project team development
- Reinforcement theory
- Theory of needs
- Theory X
- Theory Y
- Theory Z
- Trait theories of leadership
- Turnover
- Two-factor theory
- Uncertainty avoidance

Match each of the key terms above with the definition that best fits it.

1. _____ Two or more people who share the same goals, are interdependent, have complementary skills, and are mutually accountable to the organization and to each member of the team.

2. _____ Five stages—forming, storming, norming, performing, and adjourning—through which a team evolves in order to reach optimal performance.

3. _____ A widely used personality test that can be used to improve work and personal relationships, increase productivity, and identify leadership and interpersonal communication preferences of team members.

4. _____ An individual's intensity, direction, and persistence of effort toward attaining a goal.

5. _____ The general attitude a person has toward his or her job.

6. _____ The failure to report to work.

7. _____ The rate at which people voluntarily or involuntarily leave an organization.

8. _____ A hierarchy of needs—physiological, safety, social, esteem, and self-actualization—where as each need is met, the next higher-level need becomes the motivating focus.

9. _____ Three core needs—Existence, Relatedness, and Growth—of which more than one need may be operative at the same time; if the fulfillment of a higher-level need is unrealized, the desire to satisfy a lower-level need becomes the motivating focus.

10. _____ Intrinsic factors—*motivational factors*—such as achievement, recognition, advancement, and responsibility are related to job satisfaction, whereas extrinsic factors—*hygiene factors*—such as salary, relationships with colleagues, and work conditions are associated with dissatisfaction.

11. _____ Individuals' motivation can be explained by their need for achievement, power, and affiliation.

12. _____ Motivational theory that assumes people dislike work, are lazy, dislike responsibilities, and must be coerced to work hard.

13. _____ Motivational theory that assumes people like work, are creative, like autonomy, and seek responsibility.

14. _____ Management theory reflecting the Japanese work philosophy that includes a belief in lifetime employment, strong company loyalty, and group consensus.

15. _____ Specific and difficult goal, with clear feedback on how well a person is meeting that goal, can enhance a person's work productivity.

16. _____ Individuals compare their work inputs and outcomes with those of others and then respond to eliminate any inequities.

17. _____ A motivation theory that argues that both positive and negative feedback condition behavior.

18. _____ People exert a high level of effort when they believe that 1) effort will lead to a good performance appraisal, 2) a good appraisal will lead to rewards, and 3) these rewards will satisfy their needs.

19. _____ A formal position of authority in an organization that is responsible for planning, organizing, directing, monitoring, and controlling the activities of others.

20. _____ A person, who, by virtue of his or her personal attributes, can exert influence on others.

21. _____ The ability to influence people toward the achievement of goals.

22. _____ A set of leadership theories that suggest personality, appearance, competency, and other personal characteristics differentiate leaders from nonleaders.

23. _____ A set of leadership theories that argue people's actions determine their potential to be successful leaders.

24. _____ A set of leadership theories that suggest that the situation is most critical for identifying leadership success.

25. _____ The absolute capacity of a person to influence the behavior or attitudes of one or more target persons at a given point in time.

26. _____ Power derived from an individual's position in an organization.

27. _____ Power derived from an individual's unique characteristics.

28. _____ The opposition of people in an organization arising from incompatible or opposing needs, drives, wishes, or external or internal demands.

29. _____ Conflict that supports the goals of the team and improves its performance.

30. _____ Conflict that hinders group performance and interferes with team performance.

31. _____ The use of resolution and stimulation techniques to achieve a desired level of team conflict.

32. _____ A project team whose members are located throughout the world.

33. _____ The compression of the world and the increased awareness that no country or individual can shut itself off from others.

34. _____ The collective programming of the mind that distinguishes the members of one group or category of people from another.

35. _____ A cultural characteristic that describes how different societies handle the issue of human inequality.

36. _____ A cultural characteristic that helps in understanding the risk-taking nature of a culture.

37. _____ A cultural characteristic that reflects the extent to which a society values the position of an individual versus the position of a group.

38. _____ A cultural characteristic that refers to the degree to which a society is characterized by masculine or feminine qualities.

39. _____ A cultural characteristic that reflects the extent to which a culture has a longer- or shorter-term orientation.

40. _____ A cultural characteristic that contrasts the extent to which a culture focuses on quantity of life versus quality of life.

REVIEW QUESTIONS

1. What are the major processes involved in project team management?
2. How is a project team different from a group?
3. Describe the five stages of project team development.
4. Discuss how work design, composition, context, and process influence project team performance.
5. What is motivation and why is it important for project managers to understand why and how people are motivated?
6. Describe and contrast the hierarchy of needs, the ERG theory, and the two-factor theory.
7. What are process theories of motivation?
8. Contrast what is meant by hygiene factors versus motivational factors in the two-factor theory of motivation. Which is more important? Why?
9. Describe how leadership and power can be used to influence project team members.
10. Explain and contrast trait, behavioral, and contingency theories of leadership.
11. Describe various types of positional power and personal power.
12. Describe and contrast functional versus dysfunctional conflict and how conflict management techniques can be used to manage conflict within a team.
13. What factors have led to the increased use of global project teams?
14. Explain and contrast various technological, cultural, human-resource, and environmental challenges of managing global project teams.

1. Do you prefer to work as part of a team or alone? Why? How do you think your answer compares with others in your class? Does this preference depend on what type of task you are working on?

2. What types of problems might occur at each stage in the five-stage team development model?

3. Can a person be too motivated? Why or why not?

4. What motivates professional employees? What motivates hourly workers?

5. Do you think you have the traits and skills to be a leader? Why or why not?

6. Distinguish between leadership and management. Do you think you would be a better leader or a better manager? Why?

7. What type of power—positional or personal—has the greatest influence on other team members within an information systems project team? Why?

8. Some conflict is good for a project team, whereas other types of conflict are bad. What type of conflict causes the greatest problems in project teams? Why?

9. Global outsourcing appears to be here to stay. Use the Web to identify a company that is providing low-cost labor from some less-developed part of the world. Provide a short report that explains who they are, where they are located, who their customers are, what services and capabilities they provide, how long they have been in business, and any other interesting information you can find in your research.

10. Examine Table 3.9 and rate yourself for each of the critical cultural dimensions. Do your ratings match those of your country in every instance? If they do, why do you think this is so? If not, why not?

11. Contrast the pros and cons of managing diverse project teams.

12. What are the implications of new forms of technology-mediated communication for managing project teams?

13. Leaders can come from all backgrounds, genders, and races. Meet with a team of three to five students and identify what makes the following individuals more effective (or less effective) leaders: President George W. Bush, Microsoft's Bill Gates, Senator Hillary Clinton, and entertainer Oprah Winfrey. Write a one-page summary of your results.

14. Throughout your life—at school, work, or socially—you have undoubtedly participated on a team. Meet with a team of three to five students and identify, without naming names, the "worst team member I have ever worked with." During this discussion, identify the key factors as to why each nominated worst team member was chosen and summarize this in a one-page report to your instructor.

CHAPTER CASE

Sedona Management Group and Managing Project Teams

The Sedona Management Group (SMG) recognizes the importance of teamwork in the successful completion of projects. Tim Turnpaugh also believes in building a project team based on both the skills and diversity in background of the project team members. To Turnpaugh, diversity in background adds fresh ideas that can enhance the quality of SMG's products. As an example, the chief programmer at SMG not only has the expected skills in ASP.Net, VB, and SQL Server, but he is also a professional jazz musician. Another member of SMG's team, a graphic designer, was a physical therapist and an artist prior to joining the team. Turnpaugh believes that such diverse backgrounds allow people to approach problems differently, see issues from different perspectives, and in many ways, enhance the quality of the work environment. All of these factors not only result in enhanced project quality but also help the team learn to "think out of the box" and build new products and services that enhance customer satisfaction and loyalty.

What does it take to be an employee at SMG? The Sedona team looks for intrinsically motivated individuals, people who enjoy their work, whether it be building applications or interacting with SMG's diverse client base. While these individuals should have the necessary technical expertise, such as skills in ASP.Net, VB, and SQL Server, their ability to work as members of the Sedona team and create a fun work environment are also highly valued. SMG looks for people who strive for perfection in what they do. Turnpaugh believes that these characteristics—while they can be developed to some extent—are highly dependent on the person's basic personality and attitudes. Individuals who enjoy their work and pay attention to details make great employees for a self-managed work team environment, such as that at SMG. While compensation and other forms of extrinsic motivation are always important for any work environment, Turnpaugh seeks employees who are self-motivated to succeed and have fun while doing it.

In several situations, Turnpaugh has trained unskilled employees—what he calls rookies. He emphasizes that if an individual comes from a different background, the focus is not on stripping the employee's knowledge and starting over again but rather on finding ways to complement that existing knowledge with the knowledge that will be gained working with the team. In the case of the graphic designer turned Web interface designer, the employee's knowledge as an artist augments his ability in designing the interface for the system. As these skills are merged, Turnpaugh calls these people Ninjas, in that they become experts in their areas—beyond the normal black belt. He adds that he would rather have a few Ninjas on his team than a bunch of non-Ninjas. Central to SMG's personnel philosophy is that recruitment is key. A smart, personable, hard-working individual can, in many instances, acquire the appropriate skills for his position. The reverse, however, is not true. While skilled, a person who isn't motivated to work hard and cannot enjoy the work environment may never acquire these attributes.

SMG's reward and recognition system is set up to reward both individual behavior and teamwork. While Turnpaugh recognizes individual members of the Sedona team who have done something extra to ensure customer satisfaction, rewards are also given for group-level performance to ensure people are pulling together as a team. To further enhance the social fabric and teamwork aspects of his organization, social events are frequently planned after the team has successfully completed a project. Many members of the Sedona team genuinely like each other and share common hobbies and time together after work.

Finally, Turnpaugh stresses the importance of smaller teams with three to seven members. Larger teams frequently suffer from problems associated with managing schedules and interteam communication. The Sedona team has found that communication is vital to the management and success of any project and that members of a smaller team tend to be in constant communication with each other. Consequently, these smaller teams can work more effectively toward fulfilling the customer's needs.

CHAPTER 3 PROJECT ASSIGNMENT

As you have learned from this chapter, it takes teamwork to successfully complete most projects. The members of your entertainment Web site development team must work together to achieve the project objectives. For this assignment, you will find out what you need to work as a successful team.

1. As an individual-level assignment, determine at least five things that really work well, and five that do not, when managing teams.
2. Get together with your team members and discuss what each of you has written in response to Question 1.
3. Establish a set of ground rules that you will use during the project to manage team interactions.
4. Also determine a responsibility assignment matrix that defines who will perform what work at a very general level.
5. Identify the skills that are most important for the project manager.

REFERENCES

Adams, J. S. (1965). Inequity in Social Exchanges. In L. Berkowitz (ed.), *Advances in Experimental Social Psychology*, New York: Academic Press, pp. 267–300.

Alderfer, C. P. (1969). An Empirical Test of a New Theory of Human Needs. *Organizational Behavior and Human Performance*, May, 142–175.

Blanchard, K., Fowler, S., and Hawkins, L. (2005). *Self Leadership and the One Minute Manager: Increasing Effectiveness Through Situational Self Leadership*. New York: William Morrow.

Canadian Space Agency. (2003). Evaluation of the Major Crown Project: The Canadian Space Station Program (MCP-CSSP). Retrieved March 5, 2006, from the Canadian Space Agency Web site: www.space.gc.ca/asc/eng/resources/publications/report_mcp-2003.asp.

Carey, B. (2005). Remote Access: Canadarm 2 Gets a Hand from Group Control. space.com, May 4, www.space.com/businesstechnology/technology/050504_canadarm2_access.html. Accessed March 5, 2006.

Choo, G. (2003). The Politics of Projects. Gantthead.com, January 13, www.gantthead.com/articlesPrint.cfm?ID=157963.

Cringely, R. X. (2003). Body Count: Why Moving to India Won't Really Help. PBS, August 7, www.pbs.org/cringely/pulpit/pulpit20030807.html.

Fiedler, F. E. (1968). *A Theory of Leadership Effectiveness*. New York: McGraw-Hill.

French, J. R. P., Jr., and Raven, B. (1959). The Bases of Social Power. In D. Cartwright (ed.), *Studies in Social Power*, Ann Arbor: University of Michigan, Institute for Social Research, pp. 150–167.

Heichler, E. (2000). A Head for the Business. Information from www.cio.com, June 15. Information verified March 5, 2006.

Herzberg, F., Mausner, B, and Snyderman, B. (1959). *The Motivation to Work*. New York: Wiley.

Hoffman, T., and Thibodeau, P. (2003). Exporting IT Jobs. Information from www.cio.com, April 28. Information verified March 5, 2006.

Hofstede, G. (2001). *Cultures Consequences: Comparing Values, Behaviors, Institutions, and Organizations Across Nations* (2nd ed.), Thousand Oaks: Sage Publications.

Howard, A. (2001). Software Engineering Project Management. *Communications of the ACM* 44(5), 23–24.

Ivancevich, J. M., and Duening, T. N. (2002). *Managing Einsteins: Leading High-Tech Workers in the Digital Age*. New York: McGraw Hill.

Kaihla, P. (2003). The Coming Job Boom. *Business 2.0*, September, 97–104.

King, J. (2003). "IT's Global Itinerary: Offshore Outsourcing is Inevitable." Information from www.cio.com, September 15. Information verified March 5, 2006.

Komaki, J. L., Coombs, T., and Schepman, S. (1996). Motivational Implications of Reinforcement Theory. In R. M. Steers, L. W. Porter, and G. Bigley (eds.), *Motivation and Work Behavior* (6th ed.), New York: McGraw-Hill, pp. 87–107.

Locke, E. A. (1968). Towards a Theory of Task Motivation and Incentives. *Organizational Behavior and Human Performance*, May, pp. 157–189.

Lopez, Jason (2004). IBM Calls Daksh Buy Strategic Move. *Contact Center Today*, April 9, http://www.enterprise-security-today.com/story.xhtml?story_id=23647.

Maslow, A. (1954). *Motivation and Personality*. New York: Harper & Row.

McClelland, D. C. (1961). *The Achieving Society*. New York: Van Nostrand Reinhold.

McGregor, D. (1960). *The Human Side of Enterprise*. New York: McGraw-Hill.

Melymuka, K. (2004). How to Pick a Project Team. *ComputerWorld*, April 12. www.computerworld.com/managementtopics/management/story/0,10801,92031,00.html.

Morphy, Erika (2004). "Research: Outsourcing Risks and Rewards." *CRM Daily*, April 2, crm-daily.newsfactor.com/story.xhtml?story_id=23600.

Ouchi, W. G. (1981). *Theory Z: How American Business Can Meet the Japanese Challenge*. Reading, MA: Addison-Wesley.

Owens, S. D., and McLaurin, J. R. (1993). Cultural Diversity and Projects: What the Project Manager Needs to Know. *Proceedings of the 1993 Seminars and Symposium*. Upper Darby, PA: Project Management Institute.

PMBOK (2004). *A Guide to the Project Management Body of Knowledge* (3rd ed.). Newtown Square, PA: Project Management Institute.

Robertson, R. (1992). *Globalization: Social Theory and Global Culture*. London: Sage.

Robbins, S. P., and Judge, T. A. (2007). *Organizational Behavior* (12th ed.). Upper Saddle River, NJ: Prentice Hall.

Sarker, S., and Sahay, S. (2004). Implications of Space and Time for Distributed Work: An Interpretive Study of US-Norwegian Systems Development Teams. *European Journal of Information Systems* 13(1), 3–20.

Sarker, S., and Sarker, S. (2000). Implementation Failure of an Integrated Software Package: A Case Study from the Far East. *Annals of Cases on Information Technology Applications and Management in Organizations* 2, 169–186.

Thamhain, H., and Wilemon, D. L. (1975). Conflict Management in Project Life Cycles. *Sloan Management Review* 17(3), 21–50.

Treitel, R. (2000). Global Success. www.gantthead.com, October 9, www.gantthead.com/articles/articlesPrint. cfm?ID=12706.

Tucker, M. L., McCarthy, A. M., and Benton, D. A. (2002). *The Human Challenge: Managing Yourself and Others in Organizations* (7th ed.). Upper Saddle River, NJ: Prentice Hall.

Verma, V. K. (1996). *Human Resource Skills for the Project Manager*. Newtown Square, PA: Project Management Institute.

Verma, V. K. (1997). *Managing the Project Team*. PA: Project Management Institute.

Vroom, V. H. (1964). *Work and Motivation*. New York: Wiley.

Walsham, G. (2001). *Making a World of Difference: IS in a Global Context*. Chichester: John Wiley & Sons, Ltd.

Yukl, G. (2006). *Leadership in Organizations* (6th ed.). Upper Saddle River, NJ: Prentice Hall.

Chapter 4

Managing Project Communication

Opening Case: Microsoft Broadcasts Channel 9 to Enhance Developer Communication

In an attempt to improve communication within its developer community, Microsoft launched Channel 9, a Web site promoting dialogue between internal software evangelists—Microsoft programming and application experts—with its external developer community (see Figure 4.1). Channel 9 provides up-to-date collections of video interviews with members of various Microsoft product groups so that the developer community can be the first to learn of changing plans, new developments, or potential problems. The site provides an online forum, allowing developers to create profiles for themselves and to post comments and questions about videos and other content. Channel 9 also incorporates Web logs, mobile blogs, wikis, and user-editable Web pages to better reach out to its developer community. Visitors can gain an insider's view of current and future developments. The site was named after the United Airlines in-flight audio channel that broadcasts cockpit communications. In a similar way, Microsoft envisions that allowing developers to listen in on internal Microsoft communication will not only enhance communication but also enable the organization to learn how to best serve its developer community. The welcome page on the site makes this point by stating, "We think developers need their own Channel 9, a way to listen in to the cockpit at Microsoft, an opportunity to learn how we fly, a chance to get to know our pilots." Microsoft is convinced that better communication is fundamental to better serving its customers through dialogue and learning (Sources: Bishop, 2004; Evers, 2004).

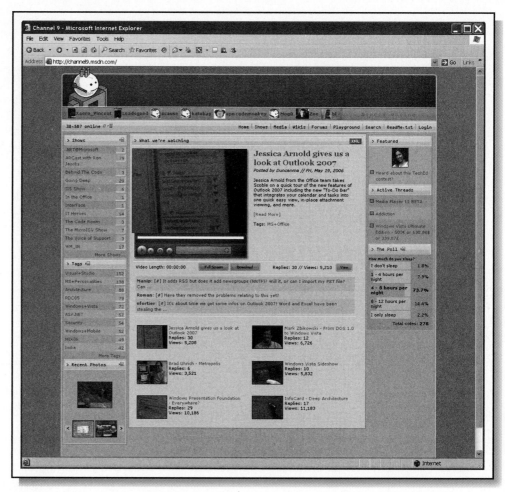

Figure 4.1   Channel 9 is improving Microsoft's communication with its developer community

LEARNING OBJECTIVES

After reading this chapter, you will be able to:

➤ Describe how communication planning, information distribution, performance reporting, and administrative closure are used to enhance project success.

➤ Understand various methods for enhancing project communication including how to run an effective meeting, deliver an effective presentation, be a better listener, utilize communication templates, and make a walk-through presentation.

➤ Describe various collaboration technologies and how they can be utilized to enhance project communication.

INTRODUCTION

In the previous chapter, we discussed how critical people are to the success of a project. We examined various aspects of project team composition and management, including motivation, leadership, power, conflict, and a variety of other issues. One factor that we did not discuss is the role of effective communication in project team success. Effective communication is particularly important within information systems projects because there is often a broad communication gap between technical development team members and nontechnical individuals, both inside and outside the team. This gap is the result of at least two factors. First, some individuals with technical training often do not have adequate communication skills. Second, the nature of information technology is in constant change, with new devices and jargon. Together these factors can create formidable communication barriers between technical and nontechnical people. Examining project team communication is the next step in gaining a comprehensive understanding of information systems project management, as shown in Figure 4.2. In this chapter, therefore, we focus on project team communication. In the next section, we examine four key communication processes for project teams—communication planning, information distribution, performance reporting, and administrative closure. Next, we examine several methods or techniques for enhancing project communication. We conclude by describing various collaboration technologies that project teams can utilize to enhance communication.

Figure 4.2 Information systems project management focusing on managing project communication

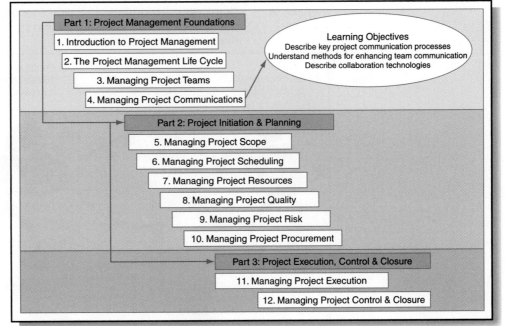

MANAGING PROJECT COMMUNICATION

Communication—a process by which information is exchanged between individuals through a common system of symbols, signs, or behavior (Verma, 1997)—is the lifeblood of a project team. Without effective communication, a team cannot be successful. For communication to be successful, the communication receiver must understand the message that the communication sender *intended* to send, and *both* the sender and receiver must *agree* that the receiver has understood the message (see Figure 4.3). After sending a message, the sender actively seeks confirmation from the receiver through **feedback** to assure that the message was delivered and understood. Within the communication process, **noise** can affect the transmission and reception of the message, either consciously or unconsciously, through audio, visual, or environmental interference. Communication noise can be as simple as an open window with a warm breeze, the smell of food when hungry, or the sight or sounds of people outside an open office door. Given communication's importance to project success, the Project Management Institute has identified four key project communication processes (PMBOK, 2004):

1. *Communication Planning.* A process for developing a comprehensive communication plan that identifies project stakeholders, the information they need, when they need it, and the format in which it should be delivered.
2. *Information Distribution.* The processes involved in providing project information to all relevant stakeholders in a timely manner.
3. *Performance Reporting.* The processes for collecting and distributing project status information.
4. *Administrative Closure.* The processes for careful and detailed documentation of a project or project phase at its termination.

In the remainder of this section, we examine each of these four key communication processes.

Figure 4.3 Successful communication requires that both the sender and receiver agree that the receiver has understood the message

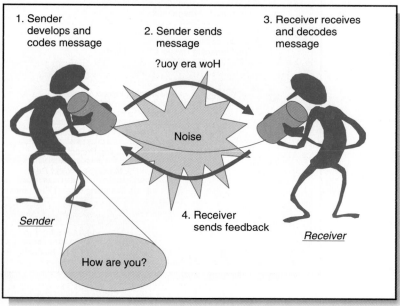

Misuse of corporate e-mail, instant messaging, and other communication resources has become a source of substantial liability in many organizations. Because of this, many organizations are defining policies to better ensure that government regulations are met, sensitive data are secure, and customer privacy is protected. Ken Beer, product line manager of Tumbleweed Communications, outlined 10 steps to gaining a secure e-mail policy (Source: Beer, 2003).

1. *Clearly outline all personal use restrictions.* Make sure employees understand whether personal use is permitted, and if so, what types of correspondence and content are acceptable and unacceptable.

2. *Unauthorized transmission of company trade secrets, confidential information, or privileged communication is strictly prohibited.* Because the majority of a company's intellectual capital is now stored digitally, it is crucial that employees not transmit these valuable assets without consent.

3. *Be aware of industry-specific government regulations.* Various industries such as health care and financial services have differing standards for privacy of information; policies should reflect each industry's unique restrictions.

4. *Inform employees that their e-mail and other computing activities may be monitored.* It is the organization's right to monitor electronic transmission, but employees should be notified and asked to sign a waiver acknowledging the acceptance of this policy.

5. *Implement tools to enforce polices.* Firewalls, spam filters, virtual private networks (VPNs) and other emerging tools should be utilized by the organization to better implement policy.

6. *Carefully define what content can and cannot leave your organization.* To limit corporate liability firewall filters should look for profane, sexually explicit, racist, or other potentially litigious content, as well as keywords that might refer to confidential product or customer information.

7. *Employ "intelligent" policy enforcement.* Not everyone in the organization should be treated equally. Different job functions and seniority may require different levels of restrictiveness.

8. *Protect sensitive business data from the vulnerability of plain-text e-mail.* Use VPN, encryption, passwords, and other data securing technologies when transmitting sensitive information on public networks.

9. *Establish a secure public network.* Use capabilities of existing messaging infrastructure to create secure and trusted communications channels between key members of the organization (e.g., CEO and CFO).

10. *Ensure the privacy of your customers' data.* Secure customer data as if it were critical organizational intellectual property.

Communication Planning

Communication planning
The process of developing a comprehensive plan for informing project stakeholders of all relevant information on a timely basis.

For a project to run smoothly, all project stakeholders need various types of information throughout the life of the project. **Communication planning** is the process of developing a comprehensive plan for informing project stakeholders of all relevant information on a timely basis. In short, this process focuses on identifying what information each stakeholder needs, when it is needed, and in what format it needs to be provided. The goal of this activity is to outline the communication procedures among external management, project members, customers, and other relevant stakeholders. The communication plan includes:

- When and how written and oral reports will be provided by the team
- How team members will coordinate work
- What messages will be sent to announce project milestones
- What kinds of information will be shared with vendors and external contractors involved in the project

It is also important that free and open communication occur among all parties with respect for proprietary information and confidentiality with the customer.

Because effective communication is fundamental to project success, communication planning is done very early in the life of the project. When developing a communication plan, numerous questions must be answered in order to assure that the plan is comprehensive and complete, including:

- Who are the stakeholders for this project?
- What information does each stakeholder need?
- When does this information need to be produced, and at what intervals?
- What sources will be used to gather and generate this information?
- Who will collect, store, and verify the accuracy of this information?
- Who will organize and package this information into a document?
- Who will be the contact person for each stakeholder should any questions arise?
- What format will be used to package this information?
- What communication medium will be most effective for delivering this information to the stakeholder?

Once these questions are answered for each stakeholder, a comprehensive communication plan can be developed. This plan will outline a summary of communication documents, work assignments, schedules, and distribution methods. Additionally, a project communication matrix that provides a summary of the overall communication plan can be developed (see Figure 4.4). This matrix can be shared easily among team members, and stakeholders outside the project team to ensure that the right people are getting the right information in the right format at the right time.

Information Distribution

Information distribution
The execution of the project communication plan and the response to any ad hoc information requests by stakeholders.

Information distribution focuses on getting needed project information to project stakeholders in a timely manner. In other words, information distribution is the *execution* of the project communication plan and the response to any ad hoc information requests by stakeholders. A broad variety of methods can be used to distribute information, each with its own strengths and weaknesses. Some methods are easier for the information sender but more difficult or less convenient for the receiver. With the maturing of digital networks and the Internet, more and more digital information is

Figure 4.4   The project communication matrix provides a high-level summary of the communication plan

Stakeholder	Document	Format	Team Contact	Date Due
Team Members	Project Status Report	Project Intranet	Juan Kim	First Monday of Month
Management Supervisor	Project Status Report	Hard Copy	Juan Kim	First Monday of Month
User Group	Project Status Report	Hard Copy	James Kim	First Monday of Month
Internal IT Staff	Project Status Report	Email	Jackie James	First Monday of Month
IT Manager	Project Status Report	Hard Copy	Juan Jeremy	First Monday of Month
Contract Programmers	Software Specifications	Email / Project Intranet	Jordan Kim	October 4, 2005
Training Subcontractor	Implementation and Training Plan	Hard Copy	Jordan James	January 10, 2006

COMMON PROBLEMS
Communication in Emergency Situations

Organizations face a variety of emergency situations where clear communication policies are necessary, including:

- *Natural disasters.* Fires, blizzards, hurricanes, and earthquakes
- *Man-made disasters.* Oil and chemical leaks, transportation incidents, threats of violence, hoaxes and pranks, food-borne illness, and bioterrorism
- *Technology disasters.* Network downtime, service interruptions, power outages, computer viruses, and security breaches

Given the current speed of today's business and the global nature of the economy, organizations must be increasingly prepared for communication disruptions. Beyond natural and man-made disasters, organizations are increasingly being hit with technology-related disasters, such as security breaches and computer viruses. Given increasing dependency on global communication networks, emergency plans of the past are not comprehensive enough to address the broad range of threats facing today's organizations. To evaluate your situation and plan for the future, experts suggest you ask the following questions:

1. Can you communicate to remote personnel on a variety of devices?
2. Can you immediately reach a cross-departmental crisis team for each threatening event?
3. Do you have a mechanism by which executives can collaborate during a crisis to make critical decisions?
4. Can you account for employees' whereabouts at any time?
5. Do you have the ability to notify constituents if a segment of your business becomes unavailable?
6. Do your constituents know when to resume normal activity following an emergency?

When you can positively answer each of these questions, you may be ready for the next communication emergency (Source: Levitan, 2003).

---

being exchanged. Two types of information are routinely exchanged throughout the project: *work results*—the outcomes of the various tasks and activities that are performed to complete the project—and the *project plan*—the formal comprehensive document that is used to execute the project. The project plan includes numerous items, such as the project charter, project schedule, budgets, risk plan, and others. All of these documents are discussed in more detail in later chapters. Project teams communicate in a variety of ways: written versus oral versus nonverbal, informal versus formal, vertical versus horizontal, or internal versus external to the team. Next, we briefly review the strengths and weaknesses of these various communication options.

Written, Oral, and Nonverbal Communication

Written communication—the exchange of memos, reports, letters, e-mail, instant messaging, and so on through the use of standard symbols—provides a record of the communication and is particularly useful for formal and complex communication. Of course, written communication is relatively time consuming to produce. **Oral communication**—the exchange of spoken words—is fast, requires little effort to produce, and is less formal than written communication. One major drawback of oral communication is the ease with which messages can be distorted as they are passed along to others. Oral communication, especially presentations, can often be enhanced, however, through the use of visual aids, such as overhead transparencies, flip charts, handouts, or computer-aided slide shows (we will examine the factors that influence the quality of a presentation later in the chapter).

Nonverbal communication—information that is conveyed by body language through our posture, hands, facial expressions, eye contact, and personal space—can

Written communication
The exchange of memos, reports, letters, e-mail, instant messaging, and so on through the use of standard symbols.

Oral communication
The exchange of spoken words.

Nonverbal communication
Information that is conveyed by body language through our posture, hands, facial expressions, eye contact, and personal space.

Table 4.1   How and When to Use Oral and Written Communication

PURPOSE OF COMMUNICATION	COMMUNICATION METHOD (LEVEL OF EFFECTIVENESS)		
	ORAL	WRITTEN	ORAL + WRITTEN
General overview	Medium	Medium	High
Immediate action required	Medium	Low	High
Future action required	Low	High	Medium
Directive, order, or policy change	Low	Medium	High
Progress report to supervisor	Low	Medium	High
Awareness campaign	Low	Low	High
Commendation for quality work	Low	Low	High
Reprimand a team member	High	Low	Medium
Settle a dispute	High	Low	Medium

Source: Verma, 1996.

play an important role in transmitting and decoding oral communication. Research studies have found that up to 70 percent of what is *really* being communicated between individuals is done nonverbally (Barnum and Wolniansky, 1989). Table 4.1 summarizes whether oral or written communication is more effective for different types of project-related communication (see also Robbins and Judge, 2007, or Verma, 1996).

Informal Versus Formal Communication

Informal communication grows out of people's social interactions and is bound by convention, custom, and culture (Tucker, McCarthy, and Benton, 2003). Every project team has one or more informal communication methods, whether it is hallway conversations or instant messaging over the Internet. Different people with different relationships will have different ways for exchanging informal information. Sometimes informal information is very accurate, and sometimes it is not. It is often used to exchange rumors or gossip, but also serves some important uses for a project team. For example, informal communication is useful for having personal and collegial conversations, and it can be used to quickly exchange information when clarifying communications related to work activities.

Alternatively, **formal communication** comprises the routine methods for communicating within organizations. Formal communication often follows customs and norms with regard to authority, rank, and the type of information. Formal communication is typically in writing and often follows a standard format so that formal documents can be easily identified and stored. Project teams use a variety of settings and communication technologies when exchanging formal versus informal communication, as shown in Figure 4.5.

Vertical Versus Horizontal Communication.

Vertical communication refers to communication that flows between higher and lower levels within an organization. Upward communication typically flows to a single individual such as a superior, while downward communication can flow to one or many individuals. Of course, there are exceptions, but vertical communication tends to be more formal.

Alternatively, **horizontal communication** refers to communication that flows among team members or across functional areas within the same level of an organization. Within-team communication is typically viewed as horizontal

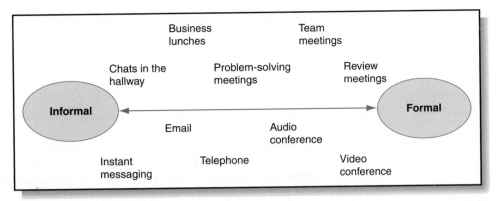

Figure 4.5 How project teams exchange formal and informal communication

communication—even when cross-functional—and is typically less formal. External team communication is often viewed as being vertical and is more formal (see Figure 4.6).

In sum, information distribution is a significant part of an effective communication strategy for project teams. With the advent of the Internet and other digital technologies, there are a broad range of options to choose from. However, each communication method has strengths and weaknesses for exchanging different types of information. In the past, the general rule for communication was that formal communication was written and informal was oral. However, given the need for having an effective team memory and the desire to efficiently utilize the sophisticated networking environment provided by the Internet, more and more information

Figure 4.6 Horizontal communication is typically less formal than vertical communication

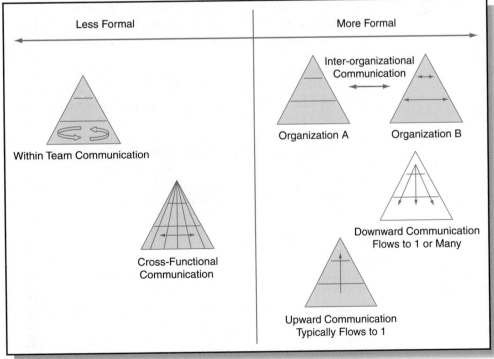

is being distributed on digital media. In Chapter 5, "Managing Project Scope," we discuss the development of a project workbook, a repository that contains all project-related documents, both paper and electronic.

Performance Reporting

Performance reporting
The collection and distribution of project performance information to stakeholders so that they understand the status of the project at any given time.

Performance reporting involves the collection and distribution of project performance information to stakeholders so that they understand the status of the project at any given time. Performance reporting involves three general types of reports: status, progress, and forecasting. **Status reports** describe current information about the project, such as project schedule or budget information. **Progress reports** describe what the project team has accomplished. Finally, **forecasting reports** make predictions about future status and progress. In general, performance reporting should provide information on project scope, schedule, cost, and quality (PMBOK, 2004). Numerous standard tools and techniques for performance reporting will be described throughout the remainder of this book, including variance analysis, trend analysis, and earned value analysis. Additionally, when projects conclude, there is closure reporting to complete.

Status reports
Reports designed to describe current information about the project.

Progress reports
Reports designed to describe what the project team has accomplished.

Forecasting reports
Reports designed to make predictions about future status and progress.

Administrative closure
The careful and detailed documentation of a project or project phase at its termination.

Administrative Closure

Administrative closure occurs at the termination of a project or project phase and consists of careful and detailed documentation of the project's results so that all related information reflects the most accurate account of the success or failure of the project. Projects and project activities can conclude with a natural or unnatural termination. A *natural termination* occurs when the requirements of the project or phase have been met—the project or phase has been completed and is a success. An *unnatural termination* occurs when the project is stopped before completion. Several events can cause unnatural termination of a project or phase. For instance, it may be learned that some assumptions that were used to guide the project proved false, that the performance of the system or the development team was somehow inadequate, or that the project requirements are no longer relevant or valid in the current business environment. The most likely reasons for unnatural termination of a project relate to running out of time or money, or both. In order for future teams to learn from past projects, accurate and complete documentation is required. It is important to note that project closure activities occur throughout the duration of the project. Failure to comprehensively close each phase as it concludes will likely result in the loss of important information. In short, a project or project phase is not complete until it is closed.

In this section, we discussed a variety of processes and techniques for better managing communication with project stakeholders. By actively managing the communication with stakeholders, you will more likely keep the project on track and head off problems due to ineffective communication. Making sure that all stakeholders clearly understand the project status as well as all outstanding issues that might impact the project is fundamental to success. Next, we examine several ways to enhance project communication.

ENHANCING PROJECT COMMUNICATION

Although many people are natural communicators, nearly everyone can improve their communication skills. Being an effective communicator is likely the single biggest factor in determining how successful you will become in your career. In other words, if you cannot effectively use oral and written communication, the likelihood of great career

Table 4.2 Problems That Make Meetings Less Effective Than They Could Be

- Lack of adequate notification and preparation
- No agenda
- Wrong people or too many people in attendance
- Lack of control
- Political pressure and hidden agendas
- No conclusions or follow-up

success is quite low. Fortunately, there are many options for helping you improve your communication skills. For example, some organizations provide training seminars within the human resource management department to help employees develop these valuable skills. Another option that many students pursue is to join Toastmasters International (www.toastmasters.org), a worldwide organization dedicated to helping people become better communicators. In the remainder of this section, we examine several techniques for improving your project communication skills.

Running Effective Project Meetings

Meetings are an important part of project team interaction. They are used for a broad variety of purposes, including planning actions, reviewing status, providing briefings and presentations, solving problems, and negotiating contracts. Unfortunately, most meetings are not as effective as they could be. Researchers have identified numerous potential problems that make meetings less effective than they could be. For example, meetings that have no agenda or that include the "wrong people" (i.e., people who don't have the needed information or are not empowered to make relevant decisions) tend to be very ineffective. Table 4.2 summarizes these problems. Nonetheless, meetings have to occur and can provide many benefits to the team (see Table 4.3).

Meetings that are well planned and executed can have a big positive impact on the team's performance. To run an effective meeting, you need to do several activities before, during, and after the meeting. For instance, prior to the meeting, you must

Table 4.3 Meeting Benefits to Project Teams

- Define the project, team members, and key stakeholders.
- Provide a forum for revising, updating, modifying, and clarifying key aspects of the project.
- Provide an opportunity for team members to better understand how their contribution fits within the scope of the overall project.
- Increase team member commitment to the project and the team through shared decision making and collaboration.
- Increase work productivity and job satisfaction by clarifying task assignments and other project details.
- Provide an opportunity for the project manager to demonstrate leadership and vision.
- Provide an opportunity for project members to demonstrate their creativity, skills, and commitment to the project and team.

Source: Adapted from Verma, 1996.

carefully plan; during the meeting, you must carefully control the agenda; and after the meeting, you must carefully document its outcomes and communicate them to all relevant parties. Table 4.4 provides clear pre-, during, and postmeeting guidelines. Given that meetings are so valuable and important to project success, all project managers need to be skilled at running an effective meeting. In fact, to enable more effective meetings, many organizations develop a set of ground rules that are widely distributed to and agreed on by all organizational members (see Table 4.5).

Making Effective Presentations

Presentations are used throughout the duration of the project for briefing team members and external stakeholders. Like meetings, presentations can provide many benefits to the team. Also like meetings, presentations are often not well done. With the proliferation of computer technology and the availability of powerful software to assist in designing and delivering presentations, making an effective presentation has never been easier. Microsoft's PowerPoint has emerged as the de facto standard for creating computer-based presentations. Although this program is relatively easy to use, it can also be misused such that the "bells and whistles" added to a computer-based presentation actually detract from the presentation. To be effective, a presentation must be planned, designed, and delivered. Planning and designing your presentation

Table 4.4   Guidelines for Running an Effective Project Meeting

Before the meeting:
- Define the meeting purpose.
- Set the ground rules for discussion.
- Identify and invite only those people who need to attend.
- Notify people in advance of the meeting's purpose, location, and time.
- Distribute agenda in advance.
- Prepare any presentation, handouts, or other materials.

During the meeting:
- Start and end the meeting on time.
- Begin by specifying the purpose of the meeting.
- Gather information from all participants using good listening skills.
- Take good notes or have someone assigned to record the meeting minutes.
- Keep things moving and stay on topic.
- Use visual aids to enhance the sharing of information.
- Periodically summarize the results of the discussion in terms of consensuses achieved or disagreements to be resolved.
- Assign action items to participants with clear deadlines if possible.

After the meeting:
- Review and professionally prepare the minutes. Minutes should include at least the following information:
  - Time and place of the meeting.
  - List of attendees with their project role.
  - Agenda items discussed.
  - Decisions reached or held for further study.
  - Action items—include who is responsible and timelines for completion.
  - Time and place of the next meeting, if necessary.
- Review and circulate the minutes among all attendees. Request clarifications and corrections with a deadline.
- Circulate the finalized minutes to all attendees and relevant nonattending members.

Source: Adapted from Verma, 1996.

Table 4.5 Meeting Ground Rules for XYZ Corporation

MEETING GROUND RULES

1. All team meetings will start and end on time.
2. All team members will arrive on time and be prepared to actively participate.
3. All team meetings will have an agenda, and team members will respect the agenda unless a majority of the members choose to deviate.
4. Any team members who have a meeting conflict will notify the meeting leader prior to the meeting if they will be absent, late, or have to leave early.
5. All team members will actively participate, listen carefully, and respect the opinions of others.
6. No one-to-one or side meetings will occur during a team meeting.
7. Team members will work hard to reach consensus on decisions using agreed upon methods for resolving disagreements (e.g., majority vote).
8. All team members are responsible for keeping the team on the agenda.
9. Breaks will be included in all meetings that last longer than one hour or when a member requests a short break.

_____   _____
Signed   Date

are equally important to delivering it. Effective delivery will include the good use of eye contact, body language, information pacing, and other factors that help the audience focus on the presentation's content, not on how the information is being delivered. Likewise, if your slides are poorly laid out, hard to read, or inconsistent, it won't matter how good your delivery is; your audience will think more about the poor quality of the slides than about what you are saying. Fortunately, with a little work it is easy to design a high-quality presentation if you follow the few simple steps outlined in Table 4.6.

Being a Better Listener

Listening
An active activity that consists of hearing, understanding, remembering, and acting.

Most people believe that they are good listeners; however, research has repeatedly shown that most people are relatively poor listeners (Kramer, 2001). **Listening** is an *active* activity that consists of hearing, understanding, remembering, and acting. Most people speak at a rate of around 120–140 words per minute, whereas people can listen at up to 600 words per minute. This gap between the speeds at which people talk and listen will sometimes allow our minds to wander to a point where we fail to *listen*—hear, understand, remember, and act on what is being said. The difference between a good and bad listener is usually easy to spot (see Table 4.7). Fortunately, a few simple rules can help you to be a better listener (Tucker, McCarthy, and Benton, 2002):

1. *Listen without evaluating.* Don't judge or guess what is being said.
2. *Do not anticipate.* Don't assume you know what someone is going to say.
3. *Note taking.* Take detailed notes because we forget one-third to one-half of what we hear within 8 hours.
4. *Listen for themes and facts.* Try to organize what is being said into larger concepts.
5. *Do not fake attention.* Really paying attention is actually easier than faking it.
6. *Review.* Review what is being said and restate it back to the speaker as you understand it.

Being a better listener can pay numerous dividends when working with stakeholders and your team members. You will not only have better job performance, you will also improve your personal relationships with others.

Table 4.6 Guidelines for Making an Effective Presentation

PRESENTATION PLANNING	
Who is the audience?	To design the most effective presentation, you need to consider the audience (e.g., What do they know about your topic? What is their education level?).
What is the message?	Your presentation should be designed with a particular objective in mind.
What is the presentation environment?	Knowledge of the room size, shape, and lighting is valuable for designing an optimal presentation.
PRESENTATION DESIGN	
Organize the sequence	Organize your presentation so that like elements or topics are found in one place instead of randomly scattered throughout the material.
Keep it simple	Make sure that you don't pack too much information onto a slide so that it is difficult to read. Also, work to have as few slides as possible; in other words, only include information that you absolutely need.
Be consistent	Make sure that you use consistent types of fonts, font sizes, colors, design approach, and backgrounds.
Use variety	Use both textual and graphical slides to convey information in the most meaningful format.
Don't rely on the spell-checker alone	Make sure you carefully review your presentation for typographical and wording errors.
Use bells and whistles sparingly	Make sure that you use familiar graphical icons to guide and enhance slides; don't lose sight of your message as you add bells and whistles. Also, take great care when making transitions between slides and elements so that special effects don't take away from your message.
Supplemental materials	Take care when using supplemental materials so that they don't distract the audience. For example, don't provide handouts until you want the audience to actually read them.
Have a clear beginning and end	At the beginning, introduce yourself and your teammates (if any), thank your audience for being there, and provide a clear outline of what will be covered during the presentation. At the conclusion, have an ending slide so that the audience clearly sees that the presentation is over.
PRESENTATION DELIVERY	
Practice	Make sure that you thoroughly test your completed work on yourself and others to be certain it covers your points and presents them in an effective manner within the time allowed.
Arrive early and cue up your presentation	It is good practice when feasible to have your presentation ready to go before the arrival of the audience.
Learn to use the special software keys	Using special keys to navigate the presentation will allow you to focus on your message and not on the software.
Have a backup plan	Have a backup plan in case technology fails or your presentation is lost when traveling.
Delivery	To make an effective presentation, you must become an effective public speaker through practice.
Personal appearance	Your appearance and demeanor can greatly enhance how the audience receives your presentation.

Table 4.7 What Makes a Good Listener?

THE POOR LISTENER . . .	THE GOOD LISTENER . . .
Always interrupts	Does not interrupt
Is impatient	Waits until the end, then asks questions
Makes hasty judgments	Asks for clarification
Shows disinterest (poor posture, wandering eyes)	Pays close attention
Doesn't try to understand	Verifies understanding by repeating what was said
Doesn't respond	Gives feedback: smiles, nods, or frowns
Mentally prepares an argument to "win"	Avoids arguing and its negative effects on a relationship
Reacts to people and loses temper	Responds to the idea, not to the person
Fidgets with pen, paper clips	Gets rid of distractions
Goes off the subject	Concentrates on both the words and feelings behind them; stays on track

Source: Verma, 1996.

Using Communication Templates

Communication templates
Specifications that enforce standards for the appearance and content of formal project documents.

Virtually all successful organizations have standard templates for most formal communications. **Communication templates** assure that all formal documents follow a standard layout and contain all required information. These templates are similar to those that are provided with popular software productivity tools, such as Microsoft Word, that include templates for formatting a résumé and countless other documents. With the use of the Web, communication templates can be further enhanced. For example, organizations can quickly create online templates for most project-related documents in which project members only have to fill in the blanks to create a report; once the report is created, other team members can be automatically notified, or online documents can be automatically routed to other team members or stakeholders. Thus, not only does the use of templates enhance team productivity, it also assures that all related documents follow a standard format and include all required information. Given these benefits, there are countless possibilities for using predefined templates within project teams (see Figure 4.7).

Making a Walk-Through Presentation

Walk-through
A peer-group review of any product created during the systems development process.

Users, management, developers, and other stakeholders attend numerous formal meetings to review various aspects of the project throughout its life. These meetings are called **walk-throughs** and are widely used by most professional development organizations. Walk-throughs have two primary objectives (Hoffer, George, and Valacich, 2007). First, walk-throughs are used to ensure that a deliverable being reviewed at the meeting conforms to organizational standards and project specifications. Second, walk-throughs are used to ensure that all relevant stakeholders understand and agree with the correctness and completeness of the deliverable. Experience has shown that walk-throughs are a very effective way to ensure the quality of an information system, and they have become a common day-to-day activity for many project managers. Walk-throughs have been used to review virtually all aspects of projects, including:

- Project scope statements
- Budget and schedule reviews
- System specifications

Change Request		
To be completed by the requestor.		
CHANGE REQUEST NUMBER:	DATE SUBMITTED:	PRIORITY (H/M/L):
Requestor Name:		Project/Application Name:
Description of Request:		
Reason for Request		
To be completed by the project manager.		
Assigned To:		Date Assigned:
Skills Needed for Task:		
Estimated Effort Hours, Cost, and Duration:		
Comments:		
Customer Section		
Approval to Begin Work:		DATE:
Approval to Move Work to Production Status:		DATE:
Approval That Work Has Been Successfully Completed:		DATE:

Figure 4.7 A project template for requesting a design change

- Logical and physical designs
- Code or program segments
- Test procedures and results
- Documentation and user training materials

Most walk-throughs are not rigidly formal or exceedingly long. It is important, however, to establish a specific agenda for the walk-through so that all attendees will understand what is to be covered and the expected completion time. At walk-through meetings, individuals should play the following specific roles (Yourdon, 1989):

- *Coordinator.* This person plans the meeting and facilitates a smooth meeting process. The coordinator may be the project leader or a lead analyst responsible for the current life-cycle step.
- *Presenter.* This person describes the work product to the group. The presenter is usually an analyst who has done all or some of the work being presented.
- *User.* This person (or group) makes sure that the work product meets the needs of the project's customers. The user would usually be someone not on the project team.
- *Secretary.* This person takes notes and records decisions or recommendations made by the group. The secretary may be a clerk assigned to the project team or may be one of the analysts on the team.
- *Standards bearer.* The role of this person is to ensure that the work product adheres to organizational technical standards. Many larger organizations have staff groups within the unit who are responsible for establishing standard procedures, methods, and documentation formats. These standards bearers validate the work so that it can be used by others in the development organization.
- *Maintenance oracle.* This person reviews the work product in terms of future maintenance activities. The goal is to make the system and its documentation easy to maintain.

When scheduling a walk-through meeting, most organizations use a *walk-through review form* to ensure that a qualified individual is assigned to each walk-through role, that each member has been given a copy of the review materials, and that each member knows the agenda, date, time, and location of the meeting (see Figure 4.8). At the conclusion of the walk-through, the coordinator can poll each representative for his or

Walk-Through Review Form

Session Coordinator: _____

Project/Segment: _____

Coordinator's Checklist:

1. Confirmation with producer(s) that material is ready and stable: _____
2. Issue invitations, assign responsibilities, distribute materials: [ ] Y   [ ] N
3. Set date, time, and location for meeting:

    Date:____ / ____ / ____   Time: _____ A.M. / P.M. (circle one)

    Location:_____

Responsibilities	Participants	Can Attend	Received Materials
Coordinator	_____	[ ] Y [ ] N	[ ] Y [ ] N
Presenter	_____	[ ] Y [ ] N	[ ] Y [ ] N
User	_____	[ ] Y [ ] N	[ ] Y [ ] N
Standards	_____	[ ] Y [ ] N	[ ] Y [ ] N
Secretary	_____	[ ] Y [ ] N	[ ] Y [ ] N
Maintenance	_____	[ ] Y [ ] N	[ ] Y [ ] N

Agenda:

_____ 1. All participants agreed to follow Rules of a walk-through

_____ 2. New material: walk-through of all material

_____ 3. Old material: item by item check of all previous action list

_____ 4. Creation of new action list contribution by each participant

_____ 5. Group decision (see below)

_____ 6. Deliver copy of this form to the project control manager

Group Decision:

_____ Accept product as-is

_____ Revise (no further walk-throughs)

_____ Review and schedule another walk-through

Signatures		

Figure 4.8 Walk-through review form

her recommendations concerning the work product. The results of this voting may result in validation of the work product, validation pending changes suggested during the meeting, or a suggestion that the work product requires major revision before being presented for approval. In this last case, substantial changes to the work product are usually requested, after which another walk-through must be scheduled before the work product can be approved. Suggested changes are recorded by the walk-through secretary on a walk-through action list (see Figure 4.9) and given to the project manager to be incorporated into a final version of the work product.

One of the key advantages to using a structured review process like a walk-through is to ensure that formal review points occur during the project. At each subsequent phase of the project, a formal review should be conducted (and shown on the project schedule) to make sure that all aspects of the project are satisfactorily accomplished before assigning additional resources to it. This conservative approach of reviewing each major project activity with continuation contingent on successful completion of the prior phase is called *incremental commitment*. It is much easier to stop or redirect a project at any point when using this approach.

Walk-Through Action List

Session Coordinator

Project/Segment:

Date and Time of Walk-Through:

Date: ___ / ___ / ___   Time: _____

Fixed [✓]	Issues raised in review:

Figure 4.9   Walk-through action list

USING COLLABORATION TECHNOLOGIES TO ENHANCE PROJECT COMMUNICATION

With the advent of the Internet and other advanced communication technologies, teams have many options to choose from when deciding how to communicate. Traditional office technologies, such as telephones, fax machines, and pagers, are useful but are not well suited to supporting all types of collaboration, especially when team members are spread across multiple locations and possibly across multiple time zones. Telephones, fax machines, and pagers also are not useful for rich, rapid, multiperson team collaboration but are best suited for person-to-person communication. E-mail is a very useful tool for exchanging information and documents, but it does not provide the structure needed for effective multiperson interactive problem solving. Next, we discuss how various communication methods differ in a number of important dimensions.

Ethical Dilemma: Is Big Brother Watching You?

If you think you're the only one reading your private e-mail, we have some bad news for you. Ever since the inception of employer-employee relationships, employers have been trying to control whether employees are doing their jobs. Traditionally, offices have been equipped with surveillance equipment, which was mostly used for security purposes. Information technology, however, has taken employee monitoring to a whole new level. Using the right software, your employer can read your e-mails, monitor your Web surfing, and even log the keystrokes on your computer.

In addition to this, technologies like radio-frequency ID (RFID) tags can be used to track employee movements throughout the company's buildings. Global positioning system (GPS) technology could track your location virtually anywhere in the world if you were using your company's vehicle. In the current legal environment, your company has the right to collect almost any information about what you do. Often, companies use this freedom to collect sensitive data under the disguise of attempting to safeguard their data or equipment. While this certainly can help to avoid the potential wrongdoings of a few malicious employees, many privacy rights groups complain about the intrusion on the employees' privacy.

You might think that you're not affected by this. If you're using a computer in your university's library for private activities that are not directly related to your studies, you might already be violating your university's appropriate use policies. And because you are using your university's (organization's) resources, they have complete rights to monitor what you're doing (Source: James, 2004).

Discussion Questions:

1. Do you believe that organizations have the right to monitor employees? Explain.
2. What communication monitoring policy should organizations use to best manage project teams?

How Communication Methods Differ

All communication methods have strengths and weaknesses for supporting different types of project team communication (see Table 4.8). Likewise, collaboration technologies vary in their ability to structure the team-communication and problem-solving process. Electronic meeting software (discussed later) provides rigid

Table 4.8 Different Communication Methods and Technologies Can Be Configured to a Situation and Have Strengths and Weakness for Different Types of Information

COMMUNICATION METHOD	STRUCTURE	INTERACTION	RICHNESS	NUMBER OF PEOPLE
Face-to-face	Low-high	Synchronous	High	Low-high
Video conference	Medium-high	Synchronous	Medium-high	Low-medium
Telephone	Low-medium	Synchronous	Medium	Low
Instant Messenger	Low	Synchronous	Medium	Low
Synchronous groupware	Medium-high	Synchronous	Medium	Low-medium
Asynchronous groupware	Low-high	Asynchronous	Low-medium	Low-high
Electronic mail	Low-medium	Asynchronous	Low-medium	Low-high
Written mail	Medium-high	Asynchronous	Low	Low-high

Session: Risk Assessment

GroupSystems

Activity: Which of risks are most important to address?

Vote	Results	Report	Transfer Data	Delete Votes
New Item	New Criteria	Edit	Delete	Outdent	Indent
Cast Vote	Save	Abstain

| | Criteria=> | Likelihood | Impact |
Ballot Items	Vote Method=>	SlidingScale	HighMedLow
1. A new product line means new competitors	0 (0)	1 8 10	(H) M L
2. Our current customers could become confused about our focus	0 (0)	1 10 10	H (M) L
3. Other companies are already successful and entrenched in this market	0 (0)	1 6 10	H M (L)
4. Increased spending on R&D could cause a cash crunch	0 (0)	1 4 10	(H) M L
5. Without a creative marketing strategy, we won't succeed	0 (0)	1 2 10	H M (L)
6. Loss of existing market share to other soft drink categories	0 (0)	1 7 10	H (M) L
7. Increased sales of sports drink could cannibalize our soft drink	0 (0)	1 8 10	H (M) L

Figure 4.10 Electronic meeting software provides highly structured communication and voting templates

Source: Reproduced with permission from Group Systems. www.groupsystems.com.

Synchronous communication
A form of communication where all parties involved are present at the same time but not necessarily in the same place.

Asynchronous communication
A form of communication where all parties involved need not be available or present at the same time or the same place.

Information richness
The extent to which a communication environment allows the exchange of verbal and nonverbal cues, supports interaction and feedback, and can be personalized to the communicator.

communication and voting templates that highly structure the team's interaction (see Figure 4.10). Some technologies allow simultaneous, **synchronous communication**, whereas others support **asynchronous communication**. For example, video conferencing supports synchronous communication, and voice mail and e-mail are examples of asynchronous technologies (see Figure 4.11).

Communication technologies also vary in their ability to exchange rich information. **Information richness** is the extent to which a communication environment allows the exchange of verbal and nonverbal cues, supports interaction and feedback, and can be personalized to the communicator (Daft and Lengel, 1986). *Rich* environments support the exchange of verbal and nonverbal cues and rapid feedback and are highly personal. Face-to-face communication is considered the richest environment. *Lean* environments allow a limited range of cues to be exchanged and

Figure 4.11 Video conferencing has become a standard way of communicating within many project teams

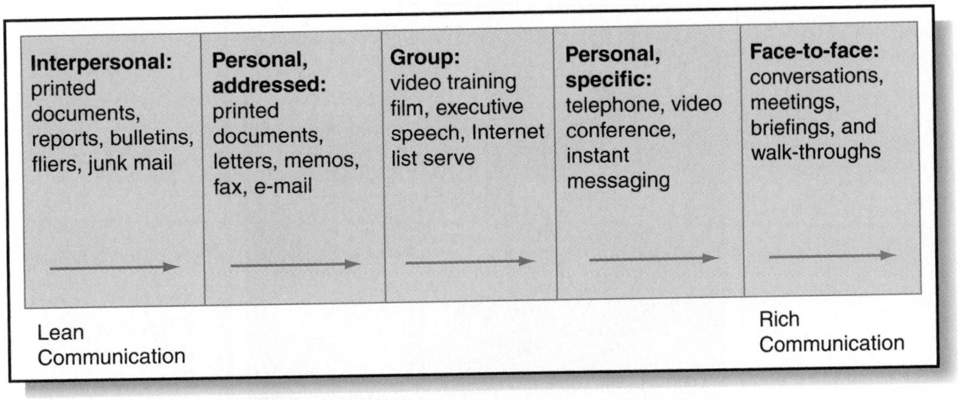

Interpersonal: printed documents, reports, bulletins, fliers, junk mail	Personal, addressed: printed documents, letters, memos, fax, e-mail	Group: video training film, executive speech, Internet list serve	Personal, specific: telephone, video conference, instant messaging	Face-to-face: conversations, meetings, briefings, and walk-throughs
→	→	→	→	→

Lean Communication   Rich Communication

Figure 4.12   Communication can range from relatively lean to relatively rich (Adapted from Kramer, 2001)

limited or delayed feedback and are relatively impersonal. Because of their potential for information richness, various types of collaboration technologies are more appropriate for some communication than for others (see Figure 4.12). For example, when your communication is complex, difficult to accept, or involves a nonroutine problem, it may need a richer environment that provides a broad variety of cues, rapid feedback, and a personal orientation. However, for simple, routine, or impersonal communication, a relatively lean environment may be adequate.

Communications methods also differ in the number of people who can effectively participate for a specific communication event. For example, telephone communication is most effective with a low number of participants, whereas e-mail can be used to communicate effectively with a large number of participants. The quality, variety, and sophistication of communication methods will continue to improve. Likewise, the role of these technologies within project teams, especially within information systems project teams, will continue to expand. To be a more effective communicator, you need to understand the strengths and weaknesses of the various methods available and select those that are most appropriate for the message and the audience. Next we examine various collaboration technologies that are being utilized by project teams and conclude with a description of enterprise-wide project management environments.

Collaboration Technologies

To build the best project teams, organizations constantly need to bring together the right combinations of people who as a group have the appropriate set of knowledge, skills, information, and authority to solve problems quickly and easily. Often, teams can consist of members from different locations or from around the world. Consequently, organizations need technologies that enable team members to interact either at the same place and time or at different times and in different locations, with structure to aid in interactive problem solving and access to software tools and information. A number of technologies, described in the following sections, fit the bill.

Videoconferencing

Videoconferencing
The use of integrated telephone, video recording, and playback technologies by two or more people to interact with each other from remote sites.

In the 1960s at Disneyland and other theme parks and special events, the picture-phone was first demonstrated to large audiences. The phone company estimated that we would be able to see a live picture with our phone calls in the near future. It took another 30 years, but that prediction has come true within many organizations. Some of these organizations are conducting **videoconferencing**, and the

Figure 4.13
Polycom's
Executive
Collection video-
conferencing unit
with dual 50-inch
displays

demand for videoconferencing equipment is growing quickly. For example, sales for Polycom, a leading videoconferencing company, grew from $39 million in total revenue in 1996 to over $580 million in 2005. Dedicated videoconferencing systems can cost from a few thousand dollars to more than $60,000—Polycom's top-of-the-line Executive Collection video conferencing unit comes with dual 50-inch plasma displays and has video quality similar to that of broadcast television (see Figure 4.13).

Desktop Videoconferencing

Desktop videoconferencing represents a second generation of video communication that has been made possible by the growing power of processors running personal computers. A desktop system is usually comprised of a fast personal computer; a small camera (often with fixed focus, though zooming and panning features are available); a speaker telephone or separate microphone; videoconferencing software (e.g., Skype, Yahoo! Messenger, or Windows Live Messenger); and a high-speed Internet connection. Using the Internet or a high-speed phone line, desktop videoconferencing is a less expensive option than stand-alone videoconferencing, but the quality of the video and audio is not as good. For example, for under $100, you can purchase one of a number of cameras, such as a Logitech QuickCam (see Figure 4.14), which plugs directly into the

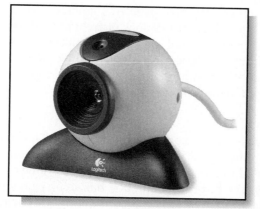

Figure 4.14
Logitech's popular
QuickCam

USB port on your personal computer. You can then use desktop videoconferencing software, such as Microsoft's NetMeeting or Yahoo! Messenger.

The Future of Desktop Videoconferencing

As computer components and fast connections to the Internet become less and less expensive, you can expect to see more desktop videoconferencing using personal computers. In fact, some notebook computers are now manufactured and sold with video cameras built in. However, one of the most intriguing new technologies for desktop videoconferencing is Microsoft Office Roundtable 2007, a communications device that incorporates a 360-degree camera and unified communications software with a built-in microphone (see Figure 4.15). This system allows all meeting content to be recorded, indexed, and stored for later playback. When combined with Microsoft Office Communications Server 2007, Roundtable provides meeting participants from remote locations a panoramic view of everyone in the conference room plus close-up views triggered by voice activation. Originally developed as a prototype in Microsoft Research, Roundtable is now being further developed for commercialization by Microsoft Corp.'s Unified Group.

Groupware

Groupware
Software that enables people to work together more effectively.

The term **groupware** refers to a class of software that enables people to work together more effectively. As mentioned earlier, groupware and other collaboration technologies are often distinguished along two dimensions:

1. If the system supports groups working together at the same time (synchronous groupware) or at different times (asynchronous groupware).
2. If the system supports groups working together face-to-face or at different locations.

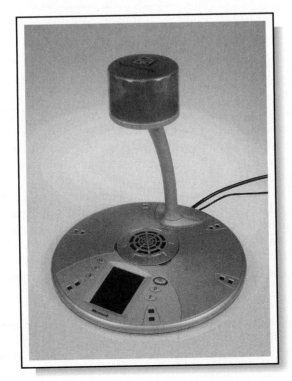

Figure 4.15
Microsoft Office Roundtable 2007

(*Source:* Microsoft Office Roundtable Fact Sheet – June 2006, http://download. microsoft.com/ download/2/E/2/ 2E252D1C-7C69– 424B-A492- A8CF4EDAB60D/ RoundTableFS.doc)

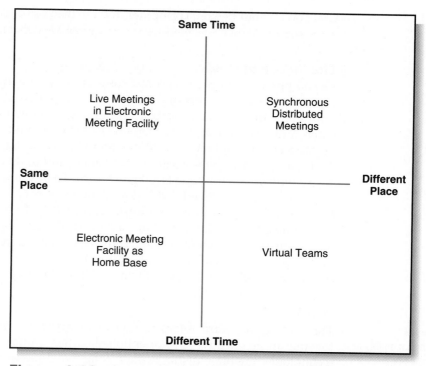

Same Time

Live Meetings
in Electronic
Meeting Facility

Synchronous
Distributed
Meetings

**Same
Place**

**Different
Place**

Electronic Meeting
Facility as
Home Base

Virtual Teams

Different Time

Figure 4.16 Groupware supports same and different time, as well as same and different place group interaction

Using these two dimensions, groupware systems can be categorized according to their ability to support four types of group interaction methods, as shown in Figure 4.16. With the increased use of group-based problem solving and virtual teams, there are many potential benefits from utilizing groupware systems. These benefits are summarized in Table 4.9.

Asynchronous Groupware

A large number of asynchronous groupware tools are becoming commonplace in organizations, including e-mail, newsgroups and mailing lists, workflow automation systems, intranets, group calendars, and collaborative writing tools. One of the most popular groupware systems, and arguably the system that put groupware into the mainstream, entered the market in 1989 when Lotus Development released its Notes software product (today, Lotus is owned by IBM). In recent years, many new groupware products have emerged, most of which work through or with the Internet. Even with all these alternative asynchronous groupware systems available, Notes continues to be an industry leader and is widely deployed throughout the world (see Figure 4.17). In addition to enterprise type solutions like Lotus Notes, many organizations encourage project teams to utilize free and easy-to-access Web environments like Yahoo! Groups. In such environments, project teams can create a secure Web site that provides messaging, file sharing, chatting, voting tools, calendaring, databases, and member distribution lists.

Synchronous Groupware

Like asynchronous groupware, many forms of synchronous groupware also are available to support a wide variety of activities, including shared whiteboards, online chat, electronic meeting support systems, and of course, video communication systems (discussed previously). Although many forms of groupware can help groups work

Table 4.9 The Benefits of Groupware

BENEFITS	EXAMPLES
Process structuring	Keeps teams on track and helps them avoid costly diversions (e.g., doesn't allow people to get off topic or the agenda)
Parallelism	Enables many people to speak and listen at the same time (e.g., everyone has an equal opportunity to participate)
Group size	Enables members in larger teams to participate (e.g., brings together broader perspectives, expertise, and participation)
Group memory	Automatically records member ideas, comments, votes (e.g., allows members to focus on content of discussions rather than on recording comments)
Access to external information	Can easily incorporate external electronic data and files (e.g., plans and proposal documents can be collected and easily distributed to all members)
Spanning time and space	Enables members to collaborate from different places at different times (e.g., reduces travel costs or allows people from remote locations to participate)
Anonymity	Member ideas, comments, and votes not identified to others (if desired) (e.g., can make it easier to discuss controversial or sensitive topics without fear of identification or retribution)

more effectively, one category of groupware focuses on helping groups have better meetings. These systems are commonly referred to as **electronic meeting systems (EMSs)**. An EMS is essentially a collection of personal computers networked with sophisticated software tools to help group members solve problems and make decisions through interactive electronic idea generation, evaluation, and voting. Some

Figure 4.17 Lotus Notes is an award-winning groupware application with an installed base of millions of users worldwide

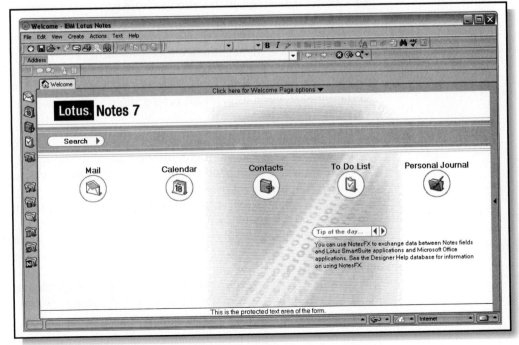

Figure 4.18
An electronic meeting facility at the University of Arizona, complete with networked PCs and electronic meeting systems software

Electronic meeting system
A collection of personal computers networked with sophisticated software tools to help group members solve problems and make decisions through inter-active electronic idea generation, evaluation, and voting.

typical uses for an EMS include strategic planning sessions, marketing focus groups, brainstorming sessions for system requirements definition, business process reengi-neering, and quality improvement. EMSs have traditionally been housed within dedicated meeting facilities, as shown in Figure 4.18. However, EMSs are also being implemented with notebook computers so that the system can be taken on the road. Additionally, Web-based implementations are supporting distributed meetings for which group members access the EMS software from their computers in their offices or from home. While EMSs and related software have been around for quite some time, organizations are now beginning to discover how useful these tools can be to support e-meetings and other forms of teamwork. Evidence that groupware has become main-stream is the recent media blitz for Microsoft LiveMeeting and WebEx online meeting software (Lilly Tomlin says, "We have to start meeting this way!").

Enterprise Project Management Environments

In addition to utilizing collaboration technologies to improve project team communica-tion, many organizations are deploying enterprise-wide project management environments. These environments, such as Microsoft's Enterprise Project Management or eProject's Project Management Office, provide a variety of capabilities to enhance the management of a portfolio of projects, especially when project teams are composed of members who are geographically dispersed. These environments provide a Web-based interface for accessing all relevant project information and provide numerous capabili-ties, including the abilities to:

• Manage multiple projects as an overall portfolio for better decision making in regard to resource assignment, problem identification, and trend and risk analysis
• More closely track resource usage and workload as well as plan better for short- and long-term resource assignments
• Manage stakeholders' expectations by effectively reporting project status in regard to time and resources
• Enforce organizational best practices of project methodologies and processes
• Support improved participation by enabling team members to easily manage, track, and report project updates
• Better manage project-related deliverables through the use of a central document repository with versioning and editing control

Given these capabilities, enterprise project management environments have become a powerful tool for enhancing project team communication and collaboration, especially for complex project environments where members are dispersed (potentially across the globe) and multiple projects are utilizing shared resources.

MANAGING PROJECT COMMUNICATION AND THE PMBOK

In this chapter, we have focused primarily on Knowledge Area 10, Project Communication Management, within the Project Management Institute Body of Knowledge (PMBOK, 2004) (see Figure 4.19). Specifically, four key processes—communication planning, information distribution, performance reporting, and administrative closure—for managing the communication needs of projects stakeholders have been discussed. Additionally, we have also discussed issues related to Knowledge Area 2, the Project Life Cycle and Organization, by examining the communication needs of stakeholders and various organizational influences on projects and project managers. Together, this information provides a solid foundation for managing project communication.

Figure 4.19   Chapter 4 and PMBOK coverage

	Textbook Chapters ⟶	1	2	3	4	5	6	7	8	9	10	11	12
	PMBOK Knowledge Area												
1	**Introduction to Project Management**												
1.1	What Is a Project?	●											
1.2	What Is Project Management?	●											
1.3	Areas of Expertise		●										
1.4	Project Management Context	●											
2	**Project Life Cycle and Organization**												
2.1	The Project Life Cycle	●	●										
2.2	Project Stakeholders	●	●										
2.3	Organizational Influences		●	●	✓			○					
3	**Project Management Processes for a Project**												
3.1	Project Management Processes	●	●										
3.2	PM Process Groups	●	●										
3.3	Process Interactions		●										
3.4	Project Management Process Mapping		●										
4	**Project Integration Management**												
4.1	Develop Project Charter					○							
4.2	Develop Preliminary Project Scope Statement					○	○						
4.3	Develop Project Management Plan					○							
4.4	Direct and Manage Project Execution										○		
4.5	Monitor and Control Project Work												○
4.6	Integrated Change Control												○
4.7	Close Project												○
5	**Project Scope Management**												
5.1	Scope Planning					○							
5.2	Scope Definition					○							
5.3	Create WBS					○	○						
5.4	Scope Verification					○							
5.5	Scope Control					○							○
6	**Project Time Management**												
6.1	Activity Definition						○						
6.2	Activity Sequencing						○						
6.3	Activity Resource Estimating							○					
6.4	Activity Duration Estimating							○					
6.5	Schedule Development							○					
6.6	Schedule Control							○					○

(continued)

Figure 4.19 (continued)

Textbook Chapters →	1	2	3	4	5	6	7	8	9	10	11	12
PMBOK Knowledge Area												
7 Project Cost Management												
7.1 Cost Estimating							○					
7.2 Cost Budgeting							○					
7.3 Cost Control							○					○
8 Project Quality Management												
8.1 Quality Planning								○				
8.2 Quality Assurance								○				
8.3 Quality Control								○				○
9 Project Human Resource Management												
9.1 Human Resource Planning			●				○					
9.2 Acquire Project Team			●				○					
9.3 Develop Project Team			●				○					
9.4 Manage Project Team			●				○					
10 Project Communications Management												
10.1 Communications Planning				✓							○	
10.2 Information Distribution				✓							○	
10.3 Performance Reporting				✓								○
10.4 Administrative Closure				✓								○
11 Project Risk Management												
11.1 Risk Management Planning									○			
11.2 Risk Identification									○	○		
11.3 Qualitative Risk Analysis									○			
11.4 Quantitative Risk Analysis									○			
11.5 Risk Response Planning									○			
11.6 Risk Monitoring and Control									○			○
12 Project Procurement Management												
12.1 Plan Purchases and Acquisitions										○		
12.2 Plan Contracting										○		
12.3 Request Seller Responses										○		
12.4 Select Sellers										○		
12.5 Contract Administration										○		
12.6 Contract Closure										○		○

Key: ● -where material is covered in past chapters; ✓ -current chapter coverage;
○ -where material is covered in future chapters

It was the big project kickoff meeting. Jim and three other members of his team—Sanjay, Bob, and Sally—were all in the conference room down the hall from Jim's office in IT. Also meeting with them was Ella Whinston, Petrie's COO. Ella was now the official executive sponsor of the project. She would not meet with the team on a regular basis—in fact, she would hardly meet with them at all—but she would be a key stakeholder for the project, and she would be their main link to the executive team at Petrie's. She had already convinced John Smith, the head of marketing, to free up Sally from many of her daily duties as assistant director of marketing so Sally could concentrate on the project. Ella would be able to help the team in other ways as the project progressed. Ella had just finished her "official" kickoff remarks to the team.

Jim had been successful in getting Juanita Lopez, the manager of the Riverside store, to be on the team. Due to work pressures, though, Juanita was not able to be in San Diego for the meeting, and she was also late joining the meeting by speakerphone.

Just then, Juanita called in to the meeting. "Hello? This is Juanita."

"Juanita," Jim said, "I just wanted to say how glad I am that you can join us today and that you can be on the team."

"Can you hear me okay?" Juanita asked. "Is that good? I can hear you, Jim."

"I can hear you fine," Jim replied.

"This is Sally."

"And this is Bob."

"Sanjay here."

"And this is Ella, Juanita. Can you hear us all okay?"

"Bob, you might want to move closer to the speaker," Juanita said. "Well, I'm glad to be on the team. I think this is going to be a really fun project. I just hope I have the time that I want to devote to it. Oh, and for future reference, Monday afternoon is a really bad time for me to meet."

"Why's that?" Jim asked.

"Tuesday is the release day for most new DVDs. Monday is the day we get most of the DVDs in, and we have to get ready to set up the new displays for what we expect to be the big sellers. And we have to move lots of other stuff around to get ready."

"Of course," Sally said. "I should have known that."

"Me too," Jim said. "I'll try to be better about that kind of thing. Which brings up a new topic—when can we meet? I need everyone to make sure I have access to their calendars so I can set up a regular weekly meeting. That is part of the agenda I have for today's meeting—communication planning, which includes meetings, and information distribution."

"I need to leave," Ella said, getting up from the conference table. "Once again, I wish you all a lot of success with this." Ella walked toward the door.

"Thanks, Ella," Jim said. "And now about communication."

"I think we should set up some space on the Petrie-net for the project," Sanjay said. The Petrie-net was Petrie's intranet.

"That is such an awful name," Sally said. "Can't we change that name?"

"Using the intranet for the team is a great idea," Juanita said, "since I am out here in Riverside and you guys are all in San Diego."

"I'm going to be traveling a lot this quarter," Bob said, "so that works for me."

"And distribution?" Jim asked.

"Let's figure out who outside the team needs to know about what we are doing, and what they need to know and when," Sanjay suggested.

"Good plan," Sally said.

"Well, we know that Ella is first on that list," Jim said. "But we also know that Bob will keep her informed." Everyone laughed. "But seriously . . . "

The team worked together through the rest of the meeting to list the project's key stakeholders and to determine an information distribution plan for them.

CHAPTER SUMMARY

Describe how communication planning, information distribution, performance reporting, and administrative closure are used to enhance project success. Communication is the process by which information is exchanged between individuals through a common system of symbols, signs, or behavior. Effective communication is fundamental to project team success. Throughout a project, four key communication processes are performed: communication planning, information distribution, performance reporting, and administrative closure. Communication planning refers to the process for developing a comprehensive communication plan that identifies project stakeholders, the information they need, when they need it, and in what format it should be delivered. Information distribution includes the processes involved in providing project information to all relevant stakeholders in a timely manner. In other words, it is the execution of the communication plan. Performance reporting refers to the processes for collecting and distributing project status information to project stakeholders using status, progress, and forecasting reports. Administrative closure refers to the careful and detailed documentation of a project or project phase at its termination.

Describe various methods for enhancing team communication including how to run an effective meeting, deliver an effective presentation, be a better listener, utilize communication templates, and make a walk-through presentation. There are a variety of methods for enhancing project team communication. Meetings can be more effective if they are carefully planned and executed. Additionally, to get the most out of a meeting, you must carefully document the meeting outcomes and communicate them to all relevant parties. Like meetings, presenta-

tions are much more effective if they are carefully planned, designed, and delivered. Because most people are relatively poor listeners, improving team members' listening to customers and other team members can enhance project team communication and overall project performance. Project team communication can also be enhanced through the use of communication templates by helping to assure that many important documents follow a standard layout and contain all required information. Walk-throughs are a special type of team meeting that utilizes both presentations and templates to assess a broad variety of project team deliverables. During walk-throughs, team members play various important roles to assure project quality and meeting effectiveness.

Describe various collaboration technologies and how they can be utilized to enhance team communication. With the advent of the Internet and other advanced communication technologies, project teams have many options to choose from when deciding how to communicate. All communication methods have strengths and weaknesses; not all methods are effective for all types of communication. Communication methods differ in how much structure they impose on the communication, how information richness can be conveyed, whether they allow synchronous or asynchronous exchanges, and how many team members can effectively communicate. A variety of collaboration technologies has become commonplace in organizations for supporting project teams, including videoconferencing, desktop videoconferencing, asynchronous groupware, and synchronous groupware. The quality, variety, and sophistication of collaboration technologies will continue to improve and further enhance project team communication.

KEY TERMS REVIEW

- Administrative closure
- Asynchronous communication
- Communication
- Communication planning

- Communication templates
- Desktop videoconferencing
- Electronic meeting system (EMS)
- Feedback

- Forecasting reports
- Formal communication
- Groupware
- Horizontal communication

- Informal communication
- Information distribution
- Information richness
- Listening
- Noise

- Nonverbal communication
- Oral communication
- Performance reporting
- Progress reports
- Status reports

- Synchronous communication
- Vertical communication
- Videoconferencing
- Walk-throughs
- Written communication

Match each of the key terms with the definition that best fits it.

1. _____ A process by which information is exchanged between individuals through a common system of symbols, signs, or behavior.

2. _____ The response process by a receiver to a sender within the communication process.

3. _____ Audio, visual, or environmental interference within the communication process.

4. _____ The process of developing a comprehensive plan for informing project stakeholders of all relevant information on a timely basis.

5. _____ The execution of the project communication plan and the response to any ad hoc information requests by stakeholders.

6. _____ The exchange of memos, reports, letters, e-mail, instant messaging, and so on through the use of standard symbols.

7. _____ The exchange of spoken words.

8. _____ Information that is conveyed by body language through our posture, hands, facial expressions, eye contact, and personal space.

9. _____ Ad hoc methods of communication within organizations.

10. _____ Routine methods for communication within organizations.

11. _____ Communication that flows between higher and lower levels within an organization.

12. _____ Communication that flows among team members or across functional areas within the same level of an organization.

13. _____ The collection and distribution of project performance information to stakeholders so that they understand the status of the project at any given time.

14. _____ Reports designed to describe current information about the project.

15. _____ Reports designed to describe what the project team has accomplished.

16. _____ Reports designed to make predictions about future status and progress.

17. _____ The careful and detailed documentation of a project or project phase at its termination.

18. _____ An *active* activity that consists of hearing, understanding, remembering, and acting.

19. _____ Specifications that enforce standards for the appearance and content of formal project documents.

20. _____ A peer-group review of any product created during the systems development process.

21. _____ A form of communication where all parties involved are present at the same time but not necessarily at the same place.

22. _____ A form of communication where all parties involved need not be available or present at the same time or the same place.

23. _____ The extent to which a communication environment allows the exchange of verbal and nonverbal cues, supports interaction and feedback, and can be personalized to the communicator.

24. _____ The use of integrated telephone, video recording, and playback technologies by two or more people to interact with each other from remote sites.

25. _____ The use of integrated computer, telephone, video recording, and playback technologies—typically by two people—to interact with each other using their desktop computers from remote sites.

26. _____ Software that enables people to work together more effectively.

27. _____ A collection of personal computers networked with sophisticated software tools to help group members solve problems and make decisions through interactive electronic idea generation, evaluation, and voting.

REVIEW QUESTIONS

1. What are the major processes involved in managing project communication?
2. What information do you need in order to develop a communication plan?
3. Describe a project communication matrix.
4. Describe and contrast written versus oral versus non-verbal, informal versus formal, and vertical versus horizontal communication in a project team setting.
5. What is project performance reporting, and what reports are typically contained in a performance report?
6. Describe and contrast two ways in which projects can conclude within administrative closure.
7. Why are many project meetings less effective than they could be?
8. What benefits can meetings bring to project teams?
9. Describe how to run an effective meeting.
10. Describe how to make an effective presentation.
11. What steps can you take to be a better listener?
12. What is a communication template, and why does it enhance project team communication?
13. Describe the walk-through process. What roles need to be performed during a walk-through?
14. Describe various communication methods and how they differ.

CHAPTER EXERCISES

1. "Ineffective communication is the fault of the sender." Do you agree or disagree? Why?
2. Construct a communication matrix for a project you have previously worked on or are currently working on.
3. What is nonverbal communication? Does it aid or hinder verbal communication?
4. Why do project teams need a broad variety of methods for distributing information?
5. Describe and contrast three different types of performance reports.
6. Describe and contrast different types of administrative closure communication for a project that was successfully completed versus one that was stopped due to unnatural termination.
7. Plan a project team meeting and write a memo that clearly defines the purpose of the meeting, identifies participants, and outlines the meeting agenda.
8. What problems can occur if a project team's members fail to effectively listen to one another?
9. Design a project communication template for sharing some type of project information with a project team.
10. Using the concept of information richness, give examples of project-related messages best conveyed face-to-face or using telephone, instant messaging, and e-mail.
11. In what project situations would the richness of face-to-face communication be a drawback rather than advantage? Which communication method would be preferable in those situations, and why?
12. Design a template that allows you to collect answers to at least 10 different questions regarding a particular type of collaboration technology (e.g., e-mail, instant messaging, video conferencing, and so on) from family members, friends, or work colleagues who are not in your class and are regular users of this technology. Your goal is to find out how they use the technology, what they feel it is useful for, their likes, dislikes, and so on. Using e-mail, send your template to these people and have them reply via e-mail. Once you have your results, write a memo to your instructor reporting your findings; make sure you include your survey template.

13. Collect the same type of information requested in Exercise 12 from at least six people using interviews rather than an e-mail survey. Once you have your results, write a memo reporting them to your instructor; make sure you include your interview questions.

14. Using the findings from your survey or interviews on collaboration technologies from Exercise 12 or 13, prepare a 3-minute briefing for your class. Make sure you follow the guidelines presented in the chapter on making effective presentations.

15. Attend a staff meeting of an organization on your campus. Obtain permission first if the meeting is not open to the public, explaining that your purpose for attending the meeting is to study meeting dynamics for a class project. Evaluate the meeting according to the guidelines presented in the chapter. Specifically, identify any problems that made the meeting less effective than it could have been; also identify things that were done well. Prepare an evaluation of the meeting in the form of a memo to your instructor.

16. Most organizations, including universities, have policies concerning acceptable computer/network use (see infotech.wsu.edu/itroot/Services/computeruse.html for an example). Assume you work for a for-profit organization and are assigned by your boss to develop a policy statement regarding acceptable use of instant messaging. Make sure your policy differentiates between internal and external use, work-related and personal use, and so on.

CHAPTER CASE

Sedona Management Group and Managing Project Communication

Communication is one of the more important factors for success in project management, and the team at Sedona Management Group (SMG) recognizes this. Traditionally, computer professionals have been viewed as people who like to work in isolation. Communication between these IT professionals and the users for whom systems are being developed has typically been difficult. IT professionals have been viewed as individuals who can only communicate things in technical terms, frequently beyond the understanding of the everyday system user. Fortunately, this state of affairs has changed over the years, and now computer professionals need a combination of both strong technical and "soft" skills. These soft skills include interpersonal abilities—such as those required to lead teams, understand user needs, and educate users—and overall the ability to communicate effectively with all project stakeholders.

Two-way communication is critical to the Sedona team's business model. At the start of any project at SMG, communication between the customer and the team is very crucial. Tim Turnpaugh indicates that most of the time the customers do not have a clear idea of what they want in the initiation phase of a project. Therefore, it is important for the team to spend time with customers to

determine their needs. For such meetings, the Sedona team usually favors face-to-face meetings, not only because of the importance and sensitivity of the information being shared, but also because face-to-face meetings often provide a richer context for interactions when people are unfamiliar with each other. These early meetings are important for helping develop and nurture the relationship between the customer and the Sedona team.

Over the lifecycle of the project, the predominant form of communication the Sedona team uses to communicate with the customer is verbal communication. This does not necessarily mean that face-to-face meetings are used all of the time. Instead, phone conversations are used occasionally for updates and any inquiries that the Sedona team or the customer may have when working on the project. Interestingly, Turnpaugh prefers that members of his team do not use voice mail for communication because he believes it creates a bad impression of inaccessibility to the customer. Answering the phone and being accessible during business hours are critical components of SMG's customer service and image management.

The company also makes extensive use of e-mail to communicate with customers. Turnpaugh was a codeveloper of Continental Bank's initial e-mail system and has been an advocate of e-mail use for over 33 years. Although it may not be a good medium for early meetings employed to assess user needs, e-mail, according to Turnpaugh, is very helpful for disseminating status reports to the customer, as well as to other uses. Over time, the Sedona team has become sensitive to the communication preferences of their regular customers. For example, no one on the project team has ever personally seen one of SMG's long-term customers, but instead phone conversations and e-mail have been the predominant modes of communicating with her.

In addition to SMG's need to communicate effectively with customers and other external stakeholders, the members of the Sedona team also must communicate with each other. Several forms of communication are used for this purpose. During a typical working day, Turnpaugh has formal and informal face-to-face meetings with co-workers to determine progress on various projects. For example, team members may update each other on the status of a project during a coffee break. In addition, it is typical for a project status meeting to occur at the start of every business day. During the planning phase of the projects undertaken at SMG, milestones are established, and through frequent informal and formal meetings, team members and Turnpaugh can make sure that these milestones are being met. SMG strives to complete projects in a timely fashion—in many instances around 3–6 weeks—and frequent team communication is essential to keep projects on track and decrease the risk of project failure. In addition to these face-to-face meetings, SMG also uses e-mail and instant messaging to facilitate team communication. The popularity of instant messaging as a form of communication has rapidly been increasing, and the Sedona team considers it a great way to keep each other updated on the status of a project and to collaborate. While such online communication is useful, Turnpaugh recognizes that it is not a replacement for face-to-face meetings or phone conversations.

CHAPTER 4 PROJECT ASSIGNMENT

During the life cycle of the entertainment Web site development project, you will need to communicate with other project team members as well as various other stakeholders. The purpose of this assignment is to create a communication plan. You will need to determine who the project stakeholders are, what type of communications they need to receive and how often, and the most effective media necessary for those communications.

1. Identify the stakeholders of your project.
2. Create a stakeholder analysis that documents information such as key stakeholders' names and organizations, their roles on the project, and their influence on the project.
3. Identify the different types of information needed by stakeholders throughout the project.
4. Indicate when you will use each type of communication.
5. Create a communication plan, which is a document that guides communication throughout the lifecycle of the project. This communication plan will be a table with columns identifying stakeholders, type of information to provide to stakeholders, communication frequency, and communication media.

REFERENCES

Barnum, C., and Wolniansky, N. (1989). Taking Cues from Body Language. *Management Review*, June 1, 1989, 59–60.

Beer, K. (2003). Top 10 Tips for Setting a Secure Communications Policy. *Computerworld*, January 22, www.computerworld.com/printthis/2003/0,4814,77786,00.html.

Bishop, T. (2004). Microsoft Notebook. This Just In: Channel 9 Adds New Way to Get Message Out. *Seattle Post-Intelligencer*, April 26, seattlepi.nwsource.com/business/170561_msftnotebook26.html?searchpagefrom=1&searchdiff=150.

Daft, R. L., and Lengel, R. H. (1986). Organizational Information Requirements, Media Richness, and Structural Design. *Management Science* 32, 554–571.

Evers, J. (2004). Microsoft's Channel 9 Gets Social with Developers. *Computerworld*, April 6, www.computerworld.com/developmenttopics/development/story/0,10801,91979,00.html.

Gilhooly, K. (2001). "The Staff That Never Sleeps." *ComputerWorld*, June 25, www.computerworld.com/careertopics/careers/story/0,10801,61588,00.html.

Hoffer, J. A., George, J. F., and Valacich, J. S. (2007). *Modern Systems Analysis and Design* (5th ed.). Upper Saddle River, NJ: Prentice Hall.

James, Geoffrey (2004). "Can't Hide Your Prying Eyes: New Technologies Can Monitor Employee Whereabouts 24/7, but CIOs Must Be Prepared for the Backlash." *Computerworld*, March 1, www.computerworld.com/securitytopics/security/privacy/story/0,10801,90518,00.html.

Kramer, M. (2001). *Business Communication in Context*. Upper Saddle River, NJ: Prentice Hall.

Levitan, B. (2003). Emergency Redefined: Why Communication Is Critical. *Computerworld*, May 21, www.computerworld.com/printthis/2003/0,4814,81405,00.html.

PMBOK (2004). *A Guide to the Project Management Body of Knowledge* (3rd ed.). Newtown Square, PA: Project Management Institute.

Robbins, S. P., and Judge, T. A. (2007).*Organizational Behavior* (12th ed.). Upper Saddle River, NJ: Prentice Hall.

Tucker, M. L., McCarthy, A. M., and Benton, D. A. (2002). *The Human Challenge: Managing Yourself and Others in Organizations* (7th ed.). Upper Saddle River, NJ: Prentice Hall.

Verma, V. K. (1996). *Managing the Project Team.* Newtown Square, PA: Project Management Institute.

Verma, V. K. (1997). *Human Resource Skills for the Project Manager.* Newtown Square, PA: Project Management Institute.

Yourdon, E. (1989). *Structured Walkthroughs* (4th ed.). Upper Saddle River, NJ: Prentice Hall.

Chapter

5

Managing Project Scope

Opening Case: Betting on the Value of
Information Systems at Harrah's

Founded in 1937, Harrah's Entertainment Inc. is one of the largest casinos in the United States, with nearly 30 locations that operate under the brand names of Harrah's, Rio, Showboat, Horseshoe, and Harveys (see Figure 5.1). Harrah's objective is to provide great customer service and build customer loyalty in the very competitive world of casino entertainment. Information systems and technology investments have become a cornerstone of Harrah's strategy for improved customer service and loyalty. To get the most from its technology-related investments, Harrah's has developed very robust financial projection monitoring, measuring, and tracking capabilities for accurately estimating the cost and benefits of all information systems and technology projects. As projects progress, all costs and benefits are carefully tracked and updated so that executives can "raise the bets" on promising projects and revamp or "fold" those that are underperforming. Evidence that Harrah's is on a "winning streak" in managing its technology investment portfolio is its recent number-one ranking (of 130 *Fortune* 1,000 companies) by researchers at Northwestern University in best practices for technology portfolio management. The "payout" for its improved portfolio management has been substantial; project throughput has nearly tripled from 112 projects in 2001 to 324 in 2003, and over 77 percent of all projects have been completed on time, on budget, and on target. Through careful planning and management, information systems and technology have become a "sure thing" at Harrah's (Source: Melymuka, 2004).

Figure 5.1
Harrah's has a sophisticated process for tracking the payback of information systems development projects

LEARNING OBJECTIVES

After reading this chapter, you will be able to:

➤ Describe the project initiation process, including how to identify, rank, and select information systems projects, as well as establish a project charter.

➤ Explain project scope planning, including how to develop the project workbook, scope statement, and baseline project plan (BPP).

➤ Describe project scope definition, verification, and change control.

INTRODUCTION

The acquisition, development, and maintenance of information systems consume substantial resources for most organizations. This suggests that organizations can benefit from following a formal process for identifying and selecting projects. Project identification and selection focuses on the activities during which the need for a new or enhanced system is recognized. This activity does not deal with a specific project but, rather, identifies the portfolio of projects to be undertaken by the organization. Thus, project identification and selection is often thought of as a preproject step to an overall project. This recognition of potential projects may come as part of a larger planning process, or information systems planning, or from requests from managers and business units. Regardless of how a project is identified and selected, the next step is to conduct a more detailed assessment during project initiation. This assessment does not focus on how the proposed system will operate but, rather, on understanding the scope of a proposed project and the feasibility of its completion given the available resources. It is crucial that organizations understand whether resources should be devoted to a project; otherwise, very expensive mistakes can be made (DeGiglio, 2002). Therefore, the focus of this chapter is on those processes necessary for better managing project identification and selection (see Figure 5.2).

In the next section, the project initiation process is described. You will learn about a general method for identifying and selecting projects, and the deliverables and outcomes from this process. This includes brief descriptions of corporate strategic planning and information systems planning, two activities that can greatly improve the project identification and selection process. In addition, numerous techniques for assessing

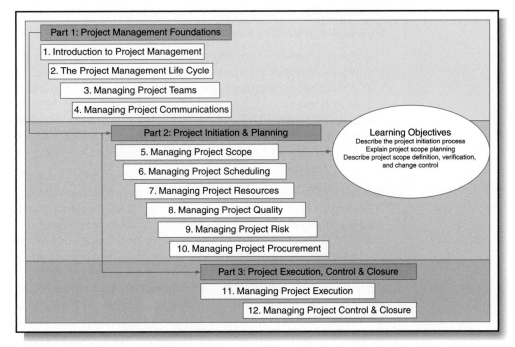

Part 1: Project Management Foundations
1. Introduction to Project Management
2. The Project Management Life Cycle
3. Managing Project Teams
4. Managing Project Communications

Part 2: Project Initiation & Planning
5. Managing Project Scope
6. Managing Project Scheduling
7. Managing Project Resources
8. Managing Project Quality
9. Managing Project Risk
10. Managing Project Procurement

Learning Objectives
Describe the project initiation process
Explain project scope planning
Describe project scope definition, verification,
and change control

Part 3: Project Execution, Control & Closure
11. Managing Project Execution
12. Managing Project Control & Closure

Figure 5.2 Information systems project management focusing on managing project scope

project feasibility are presented. We then discuss project scope planning, focusing specifically on developing the project workbook, project scope statement, and baseline project plan, which organizes the information uncovered during project initiation. Once this plan is developed, the scope definition, verification, and change control processes can be formalized and developed. Together, these topics will provide you with a clear understanding of how projects are identified, selected, and documented so that all stakeholders have a clear understanding of the project's scope.

PROJECT INITIATION

Project initiation
The process of authorizing a new project or continuing an existing project.

Project initiation is the process of authorizing a new project or of continuing an existing project. Although how project initiation is performed varies somewhat among organizations, it generally involves four distinct activities:

1. Identifying information systems development projects
2. Classifying and ranking information systems development projects
3. Selecting information systems development projects
4. Establishing the project charter

In the remainder of this section, we will provide an overview of each of these key activities.

Identifying Information Systems Projects

There is no single method by which organizations identify information systems projects. Some organizations use very careful planning processes to identify projects, whereas others use more ad hoc methods. Organizations also vary as to who within the organization is responsible for identifying information systems projects. For example, this process might be performed by:

- A key member of top management, either the CEO of a small- or medium-sized organization or a senior executive in a larger organization
- A steering committee composed of a cross-section of managers with an interest in systems
- User departments, in which either the head of the requesting unit or a committee from the requesting department decides which projects to perform
- The development group or a senior information systems manager

All methods of project identification have strengths and weaknesses. Research has found, for instance, that projects identified by top management more often have a strategic organizational focus. Alternatively, projects identified by steering committees more often reflect the diversity of the committee and, therefore, have a cross-functional focus. Projects identified by individual departments or business units most often have a narrow tactical focus. Finally, a dominant characteristic of projects identified by the development group is the ease with which existing hardware and systems will integrate with the proposed project. Other factors, such as project cost, duration, complexity, and risk, are also influenced by the source of a given project. Characteristics of each project initiation method are briefly summarized in Table 5.1. In addition to who proposes the project, characteristics specific to the organization—such as the level of firm diversification, level of vertical integration, or extent of growth opportunities—can also influence any investment or project identification decision (Dewan et al., 1998; Luftman, 2004).

Although there are numerous motivations for carefully planning the project identification process (see Atkinson, 1990; Ross and Feeny, 2000; Luftman, 2004), many organizations have not traditionally used a systematic planning process when determining how to allocate information systems resources. Instead, projects often have resulted from attempts to solve isolated organizational problems. In effect, organizations have asked the question, "What procedure (application program) is required to solve this particular problem as it exists today?" The difficulty with this approach is that the required organizational procedures are likely to change over

Table 5.1 Characteristics of Alternative Methods for Making Information Systems Initiation Decisions

SELECTION METHOD	CHARACTERISTIC
Top management	Greater strategic focus Largest project size Longest project duration
Steering committee	Cross-functional focus Great organizational change Formal cost-benefit analysis Larger and riskier projects
User department	Narrow, nonstrategic focus Faster development Fewer users, management layers, and business functions
Development group	Integration with existing systems focus Fewer development delays Less concern with cost-benefit analysis

Source: Adapted from McKeen, Guimaraes, and Wetherbe, 1994.

time as the environment changes. For example, if a company decides to change its method of billing customers or a university changes its procedure for registering students, it usually will be necessary to modify existing information systems.

In contrast, planning-based approaches to identifying new potential information systems projects essentially ask the question, "What information (or data) requirements will satisfy the decision-making needs or business processes of the enterprise today and well into the future?" A major advantage of this approach is that an organization's informational needs are less likely to change (or will change more slowly) than its business processes. For example, unless an organization fundamentally changes its business, its underlying *data* structures may remain reasonably stable for more than 10 years. However, the *procedures* used to access and process the data may change many times during that same period. Therefore, the challenge of most organizations is to design comprehensive information models containing data that are relatively independent from the languages and programs used to access, create, and update them.

To benefit from a planning-based approach for identifying projects, an organization must analyze its information needs and select its projects carefully. Without careful planning, organizations may construct databases and systems that support individual processes but cannot be easily shared throughout the organization. Further, as business processes change, lack of data and systems integration will hamper the speed at which the organization can effectively make business strategy or process changes. Therefore, a disciplined approach driven by top management is a prerequisite to most effectively applying information systems toward organizational objectives.

To help you better understand the planning-based approach to project identification, we briefly describe corporate strategic planning and information systems planning. Together, these two planning processes can significantly improve the quality of project identification decisions.

Corporate Strategic Planning

A prerequisite to making effective project selection decisions is to gain a clear idea of where an organization is, its vision of where it wants to be in the future, and how to make the transition to that desired future state. Figure 5.3 represents this as a three-step process. The first step focuses on gaining an understanding of the current enterprise. In other words, if you don't know where you are, it is impossible to tell where you are going. Next, top management must determine where it wants the enterprise to be in the future. Finally, after planners gain an understanding of the current and future enterprise, they can develop a strategic plan to guide this transition. The process of developing and refining models of the current and future enterprise as well as a transition strategy is often referred to as **corporate strategic planning**.

Corporate strategic planning
An ongoing process that defines the mission, objectives, and strategies of an organization.

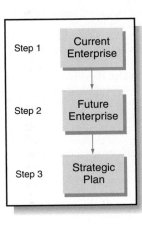

Figure 5.3 Corporate strategic planning is a three-step process

Source: Hoffer, George & Valacich (2007). *Modern Systems Analysis and Design.* Upper Saddle River, NJ: Prentice Hall.

During corporate strategic planning, executives typically develop a mission statement, statements of future corporate objectives, and strategies designed to help the organization reach its objectives.

All successful organizations have a mission. The **mission statement** of a company typically states in very simple terms what business the company is in. For instance, the mission statement for Microsoft is shown in Figure 5.4. Closely linked to their mission, organizations also define several **objective statements** that refer to broad and timeless goals for the organization. These goals can be expressed as a series of statements that are either qualitative or quantitative but typically do not contain details that are likely to change substantially over time. Objectives are often referred to as *critical success factors* or *corporate values*. Here, we will simply use the term *objectives*. The objectives for Microsoft are listed in Figure 5.4, with most relating to some aspect of the organizational mission. For example, the second objective relates to how Microsoft views its role as a global organization from both a customer and employee perspective.

A **competitive strategy** is the method by which an organization attempts to achieve its mission and objectives. In essence, the strategy is an organization's game plan for playing in the competitive business world. In his classic book on competitive strategy, Michael Porter (1980) defined three generic strategies—low-cost producer,

Mission statement
A statement that defines what business the company is in.

Objective statements
A series of statements that express an organization's qualitative and quantitative goals for reaching a desired future position.

Competitive strategy
The method by which an organization attempts to achieve its mission and objectives.

Figure 5.4 Microsoft's corporate mission statement and objectives
Source: www.microsoft.com.

Microsoft's Mission Statement:

To enable people and businesses throughout the world to realize their full potential.

Microsoft's Objective Statements:

- **Broad Customer Connection:** Connecting with customers, understanding their needs and how they use technology, and providing value through information and support to help them realize their potential.

- **A Global, Inclusive Approach:** Thinking and acting globally, enabling a diverse workforce that generates innovative decision-making for a broad spectrum of customers and partners, innovating to lower the costs of technology, and showing leadership in supporting the communities in which we work and live.

- **Excellence:** In everything we do.

- **Trustworthy Computing:** Deepening customer trust through the quality of our products and services, our responsiveness and accountability, and our predictability in everything we do.

- **Great People with Great Values:** Delivering on our mission requires great people who are bright, creative, and energetic, and who share the following values:
  - Integrity and honesty.
  - Passion for customers, partners, and technology.
  - Open and respectful with others and dedicated to making them better.
  - Willingness to take on big challenges and see them through.
  - Self-critical, questioning, and committed to personal excellence and self-improvement.
  - Accountable for commitments, results, and quality to customers, shareholders, partners, and employees.

- **Innovative and Responsible Platform Leadership:** Expanding platform innovation, benefits, and opportunities for customers and partners; openness in discussing our future directions; getting feedback; and working with others to ensure that their products and our platforms work well together.

- **Enabling People to Do New Things:** Broadening choices for customers by identifying new areas of business; incubating new products; integrating new customer scenarios into existing businesses; exploring acquisitions of key talent and experience; and integrating more deeply with new and existing partners.

At Microsoft, we're committed to our mission of helping our customers scale new heights and achieve goals they never thought possible.

Table 5.2 Generic Competitive Strategies

STRATEGY	DESCRIPTION
Low-Cost Producer	This strategy reflects competing in an industry on the basis of product or service cost to the consumer. For example, in the automobile industry, the South Korea-produced Kia is a product line that competes on the basis of low cost.
Product Differentiation	This strategy reflects capitalizing on a key product criterion requested by the market (e.g., high quality, style, performance, roominess). In the automobile industry, many manufacturers are trying to differentiate their products on the basis of quality (e.g., "At Ford, quality is job one.").
Product Focus or Niche	This strategy is similar to both the low-cost and differentiation strategies but with a much narrower market focus. For example, a niche market in the automobile industry is the convertible sports car market. Within this market, some manufacturers may employ a low-cost strategy, whereas others may employ a differentiation strategy based on performance or style.

Source: Adapted with permission of The Free Press, A Division of Simon & Schuster Adult Publishing Group, from *Competitive Advantage: Creating and Sustaining Superior Performance* by Michael E. Porter. Copyright ©1985, 1998 by Michael E. Porter. All Rights Reserved.

product differentiation, and product focus or niche—for achieving corporate objectives (see Table 5.2). These generic strategies allow you to more easily compare two companies in the same industry that may not employ the same competitive strategy. In addition, organizations employing different competitive strategies often have different informational needs to aid decision making. For example, Rolls Royce and Kia Motors are two car lines with different strategies. One is a high-prestige line in the ultraluxury niche, whereas the other produces a relatively low-priced line for the general automobile market. Rolls Royce may build information systems to collect and analyze information on customer satisfaction to help manage a key company objective, while Kia may build systems to track plant and material utilization in order to manage activities related to its low-cost strategy.

To effectively deploy resources, such as the creation of a marketing and sales organization, or to build the most effective information systems, an organization must clearly understand its mission, objectives, and strategy. Otherwise it will be impossible to know which activities are essential to achieving business objectives. From an information systems development perspective, by understanding which activities are most critical for achieving business objectives, an organization has a much greater chance to identify those activities that need to be supported by information systems. In other words, *only through the clear understanding of the organizational mission, objectives, and strategies should information systems development projects be identified and selected.* The process of planning how information systems can be employed to help organizations reach their objectives is the focus of the next section.

Information Systems Planning

Information systems planning
An orderly means of assessing the information needs of an organization and defining the systems, databases, and technologies that will best satisfy those needs.

The second planning process that can play a significant role in the quality of project identification decisions is called **information systems planning (ISP)**. ISP is an orderly means of assessing the information needs of an organization and defining the information systems, databases, and technologies that will best satisfy those needs (Carlson, Gardner, and Ruth, 1989; Parker and Benson, 1989; Segars and Grover, 1999; Luftman, 2004). This means that during ISP, you (or, more likely, senior information systems managers responsible for the ISP) must model current and future organization informational needs and develop strategies and project plans to

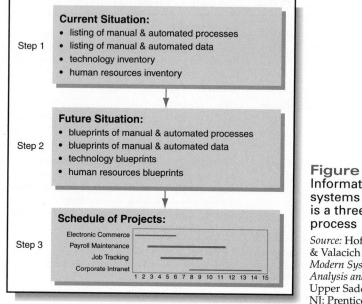

Figure 5.5
Information systems planning is a three-step process

Source: Hoffer, George & Valacich (2007). *Modern Systems Analysis and Design.* Upper Saddle River, NJ: Prentice Hall.

migrate the current information systems and technologies to their desired future state. ISP is a top-down process that takes into account the outside forces—industry, economy, relative size, geographic region, and so on—that are critical to the success of the firm. This means that ISP must look at information systems and technologies in terms of how they help the business achieve its objectives as defined during corporate strategic planning.

The three key activities of this modeling process are represented in Figure 5.5. Like corporate strategic planning, ISP is a three-step process in which the first step is to assess current information systems-related assets—human resources, data, processes, and technologies. Next, target blueprints of these resources are developed. These blueprints reflect the desired future state of resources needed by the organization to reach its objectives as defined during strategic planning. Finally, a series of scheduled projects is defined to help move the organization from its current state to its future desired state. Of course, scheduled projects from the ISP process are just one source for projects. Others include bottom-up requests from managers and business units, such as the **system service request** (SSR) in Figure 5.6 (also commonly referred to as a change request). An SSR is a form used in many organizations to request new development, to report problems, or to request new features within an existing system.

For example, a project may focus on the reconfiguration of a telecommunications network to speed data communications, or it may restructure work and data flows between business areas. Projects can include not only the development of new information systems or the modification of existing ones but also the acquisition and management of new systems, technologies, and platforms. These three activities parallel those of corporate strategic planning, as shown in Figure 5.7. Numerous methodologies, such as business systems planning (BSP) and information engineering (IE), have been developed to support the ISP process (see Segars and Grover, 1999). Most contain these three key activities:

1. *Describe the current situation.* The most widely used approach for describing the current organizational situation is generically referred to as top-down planning.

System service request

A form used in most organizations to request new development, to report problems, or to request new features within an existing system.

```
Pine Valley Furniture
System Service Request

REQUESTED BY ____Jackie Judson_____    DATE: __August 1, 2007_____

DEPARTMENT    __Marketing_____

LOCATION      __Headquarters, 570c_____

CONTACT       __Tel: 4-3290    FAX: 4-3270    e-mail: jjudson_____

TYPE OF REQUEST                   URGENCY
  [ X ] New System                  [   ] Immediate – Operations are impaired or opportunity lost
  [   ] System Enhancement          [   ] Problems exist, but can be worked around
  [   ] System Error Correction     [ X ] Business losses can be tolerated until new system installed

PROBLEM STATEMENT

Sales growth at PVF has caused a greater volume of work for the marketing department.This
volume of work has greatly increased the volume and complexity of the data we need to deal
with and understand. We are currently using manual methods and a complex PC-based
electronic spreadsheet to track and forecast customer buying patterns.This method of analysis
has many problems:(1) we are slow to catch buying trends as there is often a week or more
delay before data can be taken from point of sales system and be manually entered it into our
spreadsheet; ( 2) the process of manual data entry is prone to errors (which makes the results
of our subsequent analysis suspect); and (3) the volume of data and the complexity of
analyses conducted in the system seem to be overwhelming our current system—sometimes
the program starts recalculating and never returns while for others it returns information that
we know cannot be correct.

SERVICE REQUEST

I request a thorough analysis of our current method of tracking and analysis of customer
purchasing activity with the intent to design and build a completely new information system.
This system should handle all customer purchasing activity, support display and reporting of
critical sales information, and assist marketing personnel in understanding the increasingly
complex and competitive business environment. I feel that such a system will improve the
competitiveness of PVF, particularly in our ability to better serve our customers.


IS LIAISON    Jim Woo,    4-6207    FAX:4-6200    e- mail: jwoo_____

SPONSOR       Jackie Judson, Vice-President, Marketing_____

. . . . . . . . . . . . . . . TO BE COMPLETED BY SYSTEMS PRIORITY BOARD . . . . . . . . . . . . .

  [  ] Request approved        Assigned to _____
                               Start date _____
  [  ] Recommend revision
  [  ] Suggest user development
  [  ] Reject for reason _____
```

Figure 5.6   System service request (SSR)

Source: Hoffer, George & Valacich (2007). *Modern Systems Analysis and Design.* Upper Saddle River, NJ: Prentice Hall.

Top-down planning
A generic information systems planning methodology that attempts to gain a broad understanding of the information system needs of the entire organization.

Top-down planning attempts to gain a broad understanding of the informational needs of the entire organization. This approach begins with conducting an extensive analysis of the organization's mission, objectives, and strategy and determining the information requirements needed to meet each objective. As its name implies, it takes a high-level organizational perspective with active

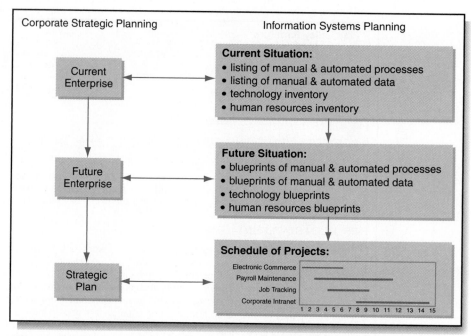

Figure 5.7 Parallel activities of corporate strategic planning and information systems planning

Source: Hoffer, George & Valacich (2007). *Modern Systems Analysis and Design.* Upper Saddle River, NJ: Prentice Hall.

involvement of top-level management. The top-down approach to ISP has several advantages over other planning approaches, which are summarized in Table 5.3.

In contrast to the top-down planning approach, a **bottom-up planning** approach requires planners to identify problems and opportunities that are then used to define projects. Using the bottom-up approach for creating ISPs can be faster and less costly than using the top-down approach and also has the advantage of identifying pressing organizational problems. Yet the bottom-up approach often fails to view the informational needs of the *entire* organization.

Bottom-up planning
A generic information systems planning methodology that identifies and defines information systems development projects based upon solving operational business problems or taking advantage of business opportunities.

Table 5.3 Advantages of the Top-Down Planning Approach

ADVANTAGE	WHY IMPORTANT
Broader Perspective	If not viewed from the top, information systems may be implemented without first understanding the business from general management's viewpoint.
Improved Integration	If not viewed from the top, totally new management information systems may be implemented rather than planning how to evolve existing systems.
Improved Management Support	If not viewed from the top, planners may lack sufficient management acceptance of the role of information systems in helping them achieve business objectives.
Better Understanding	If not viewed from the top, planners may lack the understanding necessary to implement information systems across the entire business rather than simply to individual operating units.

Source: Daniel J. Couger, Mel A. Colter and Robert W. Knapp, "Business Systems Planning," from *Advanced Systems Development/Feasibility Techniques*, pp. 236–237. © 1982 John Wiley & Sons, Inc.

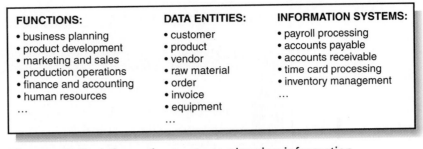

Figure 5.8 Information systems planning information

Source: Hoffer, George & Valacich (2007). *Modern Systems Analysis and Design.*
Upper Saddle River, NJ: Prentice Hall.

This can result in the creation of disparate information systems and databases that are redundant or not easily integrated without substantial reworking.

The process of describing the current situation begins with selecting a planning team that includes executives chartered to model the existing situation. To gain this understanding, the team needs to review corporate documents; interview managers, executives, and customers; and conduct detailed reviews of competitors, markets, products, and finances. The type of information that must be collected to represent the current situation includes all organizational locations, units, functions, processes, data (or data entities), and information systems (see Figure 5.8). Once high-level information is collected, each item typically can be broken into smaller units as more detailed planning is performed (see Figure 5.9). After creating these lists, the team can develop a series of matrices to cross-reference various parts of the organization. For example, Figure 5.10 shows a portion of a data entity-to-business function matrix where the X in various cells indicates which business functions utilize which data entities (for more information on planning matrices, see Hoffer, George, and Valacich, 2005).

2. *Describe the target situation, trends, and constraints.* After describing the current situation, the next step in the ISP process is to define the target situation that reflects the desired future state of the organization. This means that the target situation consists of the desired state of the locations, units, functions, processes, data, and information systems (see Figure 5.5). For example, if the desired future state of the organization includes several new branch offices or a new product line that requires several new employee positions, functions, processes, and data, then most lists and matrices will need to be updated to reflect this vision. The target situation must be developed in light of technology and business trends, in addition to organizational constraints. This means that lists of business trends and constraints should also be constructed to help ensure that the target situation reflects these issues.

3. *Develop a transition strategy and plan.* Once the creation of the current and target situations is complete, a detailed transition strategy and plan are developed. This plan should be very comprehensive, reflecting broad, long-range issues and providing sufficient detail to guide all levels of management concerning what needs to be done, how and when it needs to done, and who in the organization will be doing it. The components of a typical information systems plan are outlined in Figure 5.11.

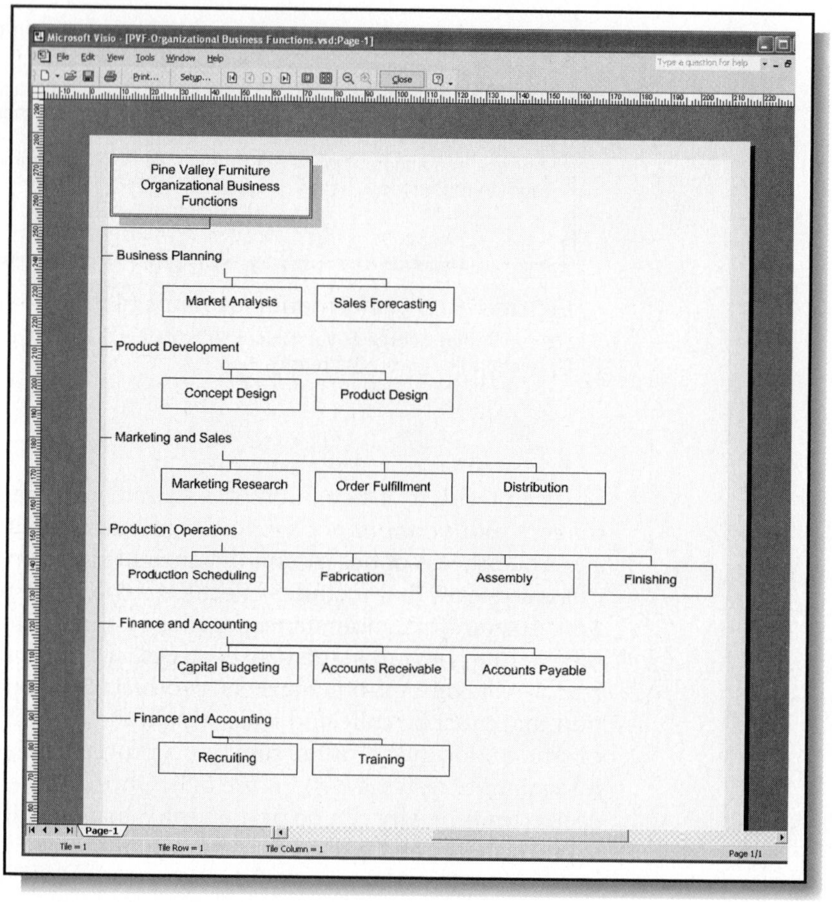

Figure 5.9 Functional decomposition of information systems planning information

Figure 5.10 Data entity-to-business function matrix

	Customer	Product	Vendor	Raw Material	Order	Work Center	Equipment	Employees	Invoice	Work Order	...
Marketing and Sales											
Marketing Research	X	X									
Order Fulfillment	X	X			X				X		
Distribution	X	X									
Production Operation											
Production Scheduling						X	X	X		X	
Fabrication						X	X	X		X	
Assembly						X	X	X		X	
Finishing						X	X	X		X	
Finance and Accounting											
Capital Budgeting					X	X	X				
Accounts Receivable	X	X	X	X	X				X		
Accounts Payable											
...											

I. Organizational Mission, Objectives, and Strategy
Briefly describes the mission, objectives, and strategy of the organization. The current and future views of the company are also briefly presented (i.e., where are we now, where do we want to be in the future).

II. Informational Inventory
This section provides a summary of the various business processes, functions, data entities, and information needs of the enterprise. This inventory will view both current and future needs.

III. Mission and Objectives of Information Systems
Description of the primary role IS will play in the organization to transform the enterprise from its current to future state. While it may later be revised, it represents the current best estimate of the overall role for IS within the organization. This role may be as a necessary cost, an investment, or a strategic advantage, for example.

IV. Constraints on IS Development
Briefly describes limitations imposed by technology and current level of resources within the company—financial, technological, and personnel.

V. Overall Systems Needs and Long-Range IS Strategies
Presents a summary of the overall systems needed within the company and the set of long-range (2–5 years) strategies chosen by the IS department to fill the needs.

VI. The Short-Term Plan
Shows a detailed inventory of present projects and systems and a detailed plan of projects to be developed or advanced during the current year. These projects may be the result of the long-range IS strategies or of requests from managers that have already been approved and are in some stage of the life cycle.

VII. Conclusions
Contains likely but not-yet-certain events that may affect the plan, an inventory of business change elements as presently known, and a description of their estimated impact on the plan.

Figure 5.11 Outline of an information systems plan

Source: Hoffer, George & Valacich (2007). *Modern Systems Analysis and Design.* Upper Saddle River, NJ: Prentice Hall.

The information systems plan is typically a very comprehensive document that looks at both short- and long-term organizational development needs. The short- and long-term developmental needs it identifies are typically expressed as a series of projects (see Figure 5.12). Projects from the long-term plan tend to build a foundation for later projects (such as transforming databases from old technology to newer technology). Projects from the short-term plan consist of specific steps to fill the gap between current and desired systems or respond to dynamic business conditions. The top-down (or plan-driven) projects join a set of bottom-up (or needs-driven) projects submitted as systems service requests (SSRs) from managers to form the short-term systems development plan. Collectively, the short- and long-term projects set clear directions for project selection. The short-term plan includes not only those

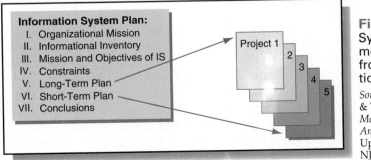

Figure 5.12 Systems development projects flow from the information systems plan

Source: Hoffer, George & Valacich (2007). *Modern Systems Analysis and Design.* Upper Saddle River, NJ: Prentice Hall.

projects identified from the planning process but also those selected from bottom-up requests. The overall information systems plan may also influence all development projects. For example, the information systems mission and constraints may require certain technologies to be chosen for some projects or certain application features to be emphasized as systems are designed.

In this section, we outlined a general process for developing an information systems plan. ISP is a detailed process and an integral part of deciding how to best deploy information systems and technologies to help reach organizational goals. Although it is beyond the scope of this chapter to extensively discuss ISP, it should be clear from our discussion that planning-based project identification will yield substantial benefits. It is probably also clear that, as a project manager, you are not usually involved in high-level information systems planning because this process requires senior information systems and corporate management participation. On the other hand, the results of information systems planning can be a source of very valuable information as you classify and rank a potential project.

Ethical Dilemma: Intelligent Disobedience for Bad Project Ideas

Intelligent disobedience often refers to the behavior of guide dogs when working with the blind. For instance, at a busy intersection, if the blind person initiates a movement to cross the street at an unsafe time, the guide dog will *intelligently* disobey this command. The blind person learns to trust the guide dog to their mutual benefit. Within organizations, experienced project managers are often the guide dogs who must resist doing what they are told to do by managers and customers with half-baked or harebrained project ideas. Intelligent disobedience for project managers is, therefore, the ability to say no to the demands of powerful managers and customers that will put the project, and hence the organization, in harm's way. As with guide dogs, intelligent disobedience requires empowerment and trust. If a project manager does not feel that he or she will be supported when refusing an ill-conceived "command" by a powerful manager or customer, it is likely that many projects will be doomed to failure (Source: Kapur, 2004).

Discussion Questions
1. What steps can an organization take to encourage intelligent disobedience?
2. If you were a project manager facing a bad idea from a powerful customer or manager, how would you say no?

Classifying and Ranking Information Systems Development Projects

The second major activity in the project initiation process focuses on assessing the relative merit of potential projects. As with the project identification process, classifying and ranking projects can be performed by top managers, a steering committee, business units, or the information systems development group. Additionally, the criteria for assigning the relative merit of a given project can vary. Commonly used criteria for assessing projects are summarized in Table 5.4. In any given organization, one or several criteria might be used during the classifying and ranking process.

The actual criteria used to assess projects will vary by organization. If, for example, an organization uses a steering committee, it may choose to meet

Table 5.4 Possible Evaluation Criteria when Classifying and Ranking Projects

EVALUATION CRITERIA	DESCRIPTION
Value chain analysis	Extent to which activities add value and costs when developing products and/or services
Strategic alignment	Extent to which the project is viewed as helping the organization achieve its strategic objectives and long-term goals
Potential benefits	Extent to which the project is viewed as improving profits, customer service, and so forth and the duration of these benefits
Resource availability	Amount and type of resources the project requires and their availability
Project size/duration	Number of individuals and the length of time needed to complete the project
Technical difficulty/risks	Level of technical difficulty to successfully complete the project within given time and resource constraints

monthly or quarterly to review projects and use a wide variety of evaluation criteria. At these meetings, new project requests will be reviewed relative to projects already identified, and ongoing projects are monitored. The relative ratings of projects are used to guide the final stage of this identification process—project selection.

All projects are feasible given unlimited resources and infinite time (Pressman, 2005). Unfortunately, most projects must be developed within tight budgetary and time constraints. This means that assessing project feasibility is required for all information systems projects and is a potentially large undertaking. It demands that you, as a project manager, evaluate a wide range of factors. Typically, some of these factors will be more important for some projects and relatively unimportant for others. Although the specifics of a given project will dictate which factors are most important, most feasibility factors are represented by the following categories:

- Economic
- Technical
- Operational
- Schedule
- Legal and contractual
- Political

Business case
The justification that presents the economic, technical, operational, schedule, legal and contractual, and political factors influencing a proposed information systems project.

Economic feasibility
A comparison of the financial benefits and costs associated with a development project.

Together, the culmination of these feasibility analyses forms the **business case** that justifies the expenditure of resources on the project. In the remainder of this section, we will examine various feasibility issues.

Assessing Economic Feasibility

The purpose of assessing **economic feasibility** is to identify the financial benefits and costs of the development project. Economic feasibility is often referred to as *cost-benefit analysis*. During project initiation and planning, it will be impossible to precisely define all benefits and costs related to a particular project. Yet it is important to spend adequate time identifying and quantifying these items, or it will be impossible to conduct an adequate economic analysis and make meaningful comparisons between rival projects. When conducting an economic analysis, you need to estimate the project's potential benefits and costs. Once these benefits and costs are estimated, various analyses can be conducted to better evaluate the project. Economic analyses are typically done throughout the project's life to decide whether to continue, redirect, or kill it.

Determining Project Benefits. An information system can provide many benefits to an organization. For example, a new or renovated information system can automate monotonous jobs, reduce errors, provide innovative services to customers and suppliers, and improve organizational efficiency, speed, flexibility, and morale. In general, the benefits can be viewed as being both tangible and intangible.

Tangible benefit
A benefit that can be measured in dollars and with certainty.

Tangible benefits can be measured in dollars and with certainty. For example, a tangible benefit might allow a company to perform a task with fewer employees, thus providing cost reduction through reduced employee salaries and benefits. Most tangible benefits fit in one or more of the following categories:

- Cost reduction and avoidance
- Error reduction
- Increased flexibility
- Increased speed of activity
- Improvement of management planning and control
- Opening new markets and increasing sales opportunities

The tangible benefits for a proposed information system are summarized in a worksheet in Figure 5.13.

Intangible benefit
A benefit that cannot be easily measured in dollars or with certainty.

Alternatively, **intangible benefits** *cannot* be easily measured in dollars or with certainty. Intangible benefits may have direct organizational benefits, such as the improvement of employee morale, or they may have broader societal implications, such as the reduction of waste creation or resource consumption. Potential tangible benefits may have to be considered intangible during project initiation because you may not be able to quantify them in dollars or with certainty at this stage in the project. During later stages, such intangibles can become tangible benefits as you better understand the ramifications of the system you are designing. When this occurs, planning documents and budgets can be updated for ongoing evaluation of the project. Intangible benefits include:

- Competitive necessity to stay on par with competitors
- Increased organizational flexibility
- Increased employee morale
- Promotion of organizational learning and understanding
- More timely information

After determining project benefits, project costs must be identified.

TANGIBLE BENEFITS WORKSHEET
Customer Tracking System Project

	Year 1 through 5
A. Cost reduction or avoidance	$ 4,500
B. Error reduction	2,500
C. Increased flexibility	7,500
D. Increased speed of activity	10,500
E. Improvement in management planning or control	25,000
F. Other _____	0
TOTAL tangible benefits	**$50,000**

Figure 5.13
Tangible benefits for a proposed system

Source: Hoffer, George & Valacich (2007). *Modern Systems Analysis and Design.* Upper Saddle River, NJ: Prentice Hall.

Tangible cost
A cost that can be measured in dollars and with certainty.

Intangible cost
A cost that cannot be easily measured in terms of dollars or with certainty.

Determining Project Costs. Similar to benefits, an information system can have both tangible and intangible costs. **Tangible costs** are those that you can easily measure in dollars and with certainty. From an information systems development perspective, tangible costs include items such as hardware costs and labor costs, and operational costs, such as employee training and building renovations. Alternatively, **intangible costs** are those items that you cannot easily measure in terms of dollars or with certainty. Intangible costs can include loss of customer goodwill, employee morale, or operational inefficiency. Table 5.5 provides a summary of common costs associated with the development and operation of an information system. Predicting the costs associated with the development of an information system is an inexact science. Information systems researchers, however, have identified several guidelines for improving the cost-estimating process (see Table 5.6). Both underestimating and overestimating costs are problems you must avoid (Lederer and Prasad, 1992). Underestimation results in cost overruns, whereas overestimation results in unnecessary allocation of resources that might be better utilized.

Beside tangible and intangible costs, you can distinguish information-systems–related development costs as either being one-time or recurring costs (the

Table 5.5 Possible Information Systems Costs

TYPES OF COSTS	EXAMPLES	TYPES OF COSTS	EXAMPLES
Procurement	• Consulting costs • Equipment purchase or lease • Equipment installation costs • Site preparation and modifications • Capital costs • Management and staff time	Project-related	• Application software • Software modifications to fit local systems • Personnel, overhead, etc., from in-house development • Training users in application use • Collecting and analyzing data • Preparing documentation • Managing development
Start-up	• Operating system software • Communications equipment installation • Start-up personnel • Personnel searches and hiring activities • Disruption to the rest of the organization • Management to direct start-up activity	Operating	• System maintenance costs (hardware, software, and facilities) • Rental of space and equipment • Asset depreciation • Management, operation, and planning personnel

Source: Adapted from King and Schrems, 1978, with the permission of the Association for Computing Machinery. Copyright © 1978 J. L. King and E. Schrems.

Table 5.6 Guidelines for Better Cost Estimating

- Assign the initial estimating task to the final developers.
- Delay finalizing the initial estimate until the end of a thorough study.
- Anticipate and control user changes.
- Monitor the progress of the proposed project.
- Elevate proposed project progress by using independent auditors.
- Use the estimate to evaluate project personnel.
- Study the cost estimate carefully before approving it.
- Rely on documented facts, standards, and simple arithmetic formulas rather than guessing, intuition, personal memory, and complex formulas.
- Don't rely on cost-estimating software alone for an accurate estimate.

Source: Adapted from Lederer and Prasad, 1992, with the permission of the Association for Computing Machinery. Copyright © 1992 A. L. Lederer and J. Prasad.

One-time cost
A cost associated with project start-up and development or system start-up.

Recurring cost
A cost resulting from the ongoing evolution and use of a system.

same is true for benefits, although we do not discuss this difference for benefits). **One-time costs** are those associated with project initiation and development and the start-up of the system. These costs typically encompass activities such as systems development, new hardware, and software purchases, user training, site preparation, and data or system conversion (see Figure 5.14). When conducting an economic cost-benefit analysis, a worksheet should be created for capturing these expenses. For very large projects, one-time costs may be staged over one or more years. In these cases, a separate one-time cost worksheet should be created each year. This separation will make it easier to perform present value calculations (described later). **Recurring costs** are those costs resulting from the ongoing evolution and use of the system. Examples of these costs typically include:

- Application software maintenance
- Incremental data storage expenses
- Incremental communications
- New software and hardware leases
- Supplies and other expenses (e.g., paper, forms, data center personnel)

Recurring costs for a proposed information systems project are summarized in a worksheet in Figure 5.15.

ONE-TIME COSTS WORKSHEET
Customer Tracking System Project

	Year 0
A. Development costs	$20,000
B. New hardware	15,000
C. New (purchased) software, if any	
1. Packaged applications software	5,000
2. Other _____	0
D. User training	2,500
E. Site preparation	0
F. Other _____	0
TOTAL one-time cost	**$42,500**

Figure 5.14
One-time costs for a proposed system

Source: Hoffer, George & Valacich (2007). *Modern Systems Analysis and Design.* Upper Saddle River, NJ: Prentice Hall.

RECURRING COSTS WORKSHEET
Customer Tracking System Project

	Year 1 through 5
A. Application software maintenance	$25,000
B. Incremental data storage required: 20 MB × $50. (estimated cost/MB = $50)	1,000
C. Incremental communications (lines, messages....)	2,000
D. New software or hardware leases	0
E. Supplies	500
F. Other _____	0
TOTAL recurring costs	**$28,500**

Figure 5.15
Recurring costs for a proposed system
Source: Hoffer, George & Valacich (2007). *Modern Systems Analysis and Design.* Upper Saddle River, NJ: Prentice Hall.

Both one-time and recurring costs can consist of items that are fixed or variable. Fixed costs are costs that are billed or incurred at a regular interval and usually at a fixed rate, such as a facility lease payment. Variable costs are costs that vary in relation to usage, such as long-distance phone charges.

Cost-Benefit Analysis. It should be clear that many potential benefits and costs are associated with any given project. Additionally, because the development and useful life of a system may span several years, these benefits and costs must be normalized into present-day values in order to perform meaningful cost-benefit comparisons. To do this, organizations use a variety of **cost-benefit analysis** techniques for determining the financial feasibility of a project. Most cost-benefit analysis techniques encompass the concept of the *time value of money* (TVM), where present cash outlays are compared to future expected returns. As previously discussed, the development of an information system has both one-time and recurring costs. Furthermore, benefits from systems development will likely occur sometime in the future. Because many projects may be competing for the same investment dollars and may have different useful life expectancies, all costs and benefits must be viewed in relation to their present value when comparing investment options.

A simple example will help explain the TVM. Suppose you want to buy a used car from an acquaintance, and she asks that you make three payments of $1,500 for 3 years, beginning next year, for a total of $4,500. If she would agree to a single lump sum payment at the time of sale, what amount do you think she would agree to? Should the single payment be $4,500? Should it be more or less? To answer this question, we must consider the time value of money. Most of us would gladly accept $4,500 today rather than three payments of $1,500, because a dollar today (or $4,500 for that matter) is worth more than a dollar tomorrow or next year, because money can be invested. The rate at which money can be borrowed or invested is called the cost of capital or, for TVM calculations, the **discount rate**. Let's suppose that the seller could put the money received for the sale of the car in the bank and receive a 10 percent return on her investment. A simple formula can be used when figuring the **present value** of the three $1,500 payments:

$$PV_n = Y \times \frac{1}{(1 + i)^n}$$

where PV_n is the present value of Y dollars n years from now when i is the discount rate.

Cost-benefit analysis
The use of a variety of analysis techniques for determining the financial feasibility of a project.

Discount rate
The rate of return used to compute the present value of future cash flows.

Present value
The current value of a future cash flow.

From our example, the present value of the three payments of $1,500 can be calculated as

$$PV_1 = 1{,}500 \times \frac{1}{(1 + .10)^1} = 1{,}500 \times .9091 = 1{,}363.65$$

$$PV_2 = 1{,}500 \times \frac{1}{(1 + .10)^2} = 1{,}500 \times .8264 = 1{,}239.60$$

$$PV_3 = 1{,}500 \times \frac{1}{(1 + .10)^3} = 1{,}500 \times .7513 = 1{,}126.95$$

where PV_1, PV_2, and PV_3 reflect the present value of each $1,500 payment in years 1, 2, and 3, respectively.

To calculate the *net present value (NPV)* of the three $1,500 payments, simply add the present values calculated above ($NPV = PV_1 + PV_2 + PV_3 = 1{,}363.65 + 1{,}239.60 + 1{,}126.95 = \$3{,}730.20$). In other words, the seller could accept a lump sum payment of $3,730.20 as equivalent to the three payments of $1,500, given a discount rate of 10 percent.

When performing an economic analysis, project managers typically create a summary worksheet reflecting the present values of all benefits and costs, as well as all pertinent analyses (see Figure 5.16). To perform these analyses, the useful life of the project, as well as the cost of capital (discount rate), must be determined.

Figure 5.16 Summary spreadsheet reflecting the present-value calculations of all benefits and costs for a proposed information systems project

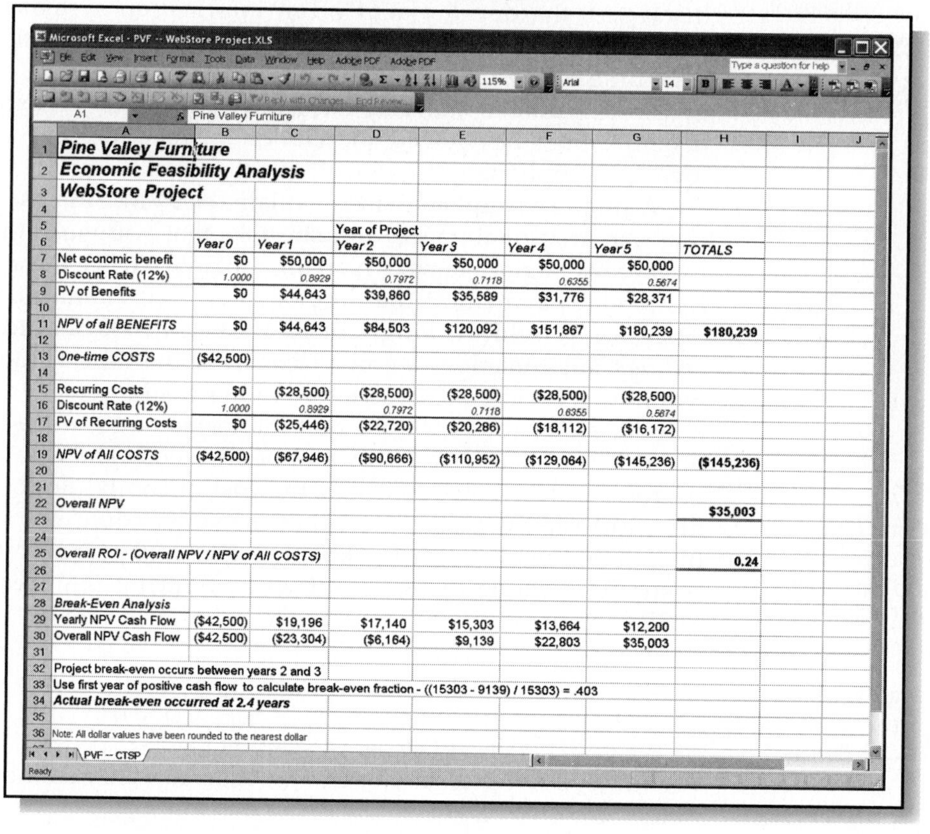

Pine Valley Furniture							
Economic Feasibility Analysis							
WebStore Project							
			Year of Project				
	Year 0	*Year 1*	*Year 2*	*Year 3*	*Year 4*	*Year 5*	*TOTALS*
Net economic benefit	$0	$50,000	$50,000	$50,000	$50,000	$50,000	
Discount Rate (12%)	1.0000	0.8929	0.7972	0.7118	0.6355	0.5674	
PV of Benefits	$0	$44,643	$39,860	$35,589	$31,776	$28,371	
NPV of all BENEFITS	$0	$44,643	$84,503	$120,092	$151,867	$180,239	**$180,239**
One-time COSTS	($42,500)						
Recurring Costs	$0	($28,500)	($28,500)	($28,500)	($28,500)	($28,500)	
Discount Rate (12%)	1.0000	0.8929	0.7972	0.7118	0.6355	0.5674	
PV of Recurring Costs	$0	($25,446)	($22,720)	($20,286)	($18,112)	($16,172)	
NPV of All COSTS	($42,500)	($67,946)	($90,666)	($110,952)	($129,064)	($145,236)	**($145,236)**
Overall NPV							**$35,003**
Overall ROI - (Overall NPV / NPV of All COSTS)							**0.24**
Break-Even Analysis							
Yearly NPV Cash Flow	($42,500)	$19,196	$17,140	$15,303	$13,664	$12,200	
Overall NPV Cash Flow	($42,500)	($23,304)	($6,164)	$9,139	$22,803	$35,003	
Project break-even occurs between years 2 and 3							
Use first year of positive cash flow to calculate break-even fraction - ((15303 - 9139) / 15303) = .403							
Actual break-even occurred at 2.4 years							
Note: All dollar values have been rounded to the nearest dollar							

Table 5.7 Commonly Used Economic Cost-Benefit Analysis Techniques

ANALYSIS TECHNIQUE	DESCRIPTION
Net Present Value (NPV)	NPV uses a discount rate determined from the company's cost of capital to establish the present value of the project. The discount rate is used to determine the present value of both cash receipts and outlays.
Return on Investment (ROI)	ROI is the ratio of the net cash receipts of the project divided by the cash outlays of the project. Trade-off analysis can be made among projects competing for investment by comparing representative ROI ratios.
Break-Even Analysis (BEA)	BEA finds the amount of time required for the cumulative cash from a project to equal its initial and ongoing investment.

For example, for the summary spreadsheet in Figure 5.16, the useful life was determined to be five years and the cost of capital to be 12 percent. Additionally, Cell H11 of the worksheet summarizes the NPV of the total tangible benefits from the project. Cell H19 summarizes the NPV of the total costs from the project. The NPV for the project shown in cell H22 ($35,003) indicates that overall benefits from the project exceed costs.

The overall return on investment (ROI) (defined in Table 5.7) for the project is also shown on the worksheet in cell H25. Because alternative projects will likely have different benefit and cost values and, possibly, different life expectancies, the overall ROI value is very useful for comparing projects on an economic basis. Of course, this example shows ROI for the overall project. An ROI analysis could be calculated for each year of the project.

Break-even analysis
A type of cost-benefit analysis used to identify when (if ever) benefits will equal costs.

The last analysis shown in Figure 5.16 is a **break-even analysis**. The objective of the break-even analysis is to discover at what point (if ever) benefits will equal costs. To conduct this analysis, the NPVs of the yearly cash flows are determined. Here, the yearly cash flows are calculated by subtracting both the one-time costs and the present values of the recurring costs from the present value of the yearly benefits. The overall NPV of the cash flow reflects the total cash flows for all preceding years. Line 30 of the worksheet shows that breakeven occurs between years 2 and 3. Because year 3 is the first in which the overall NPV cash-flow figure is nonnegative, the identification of when breakeven occurs during the year can be derived as follows:

$$\text{Break-Even Ratio} = \frac{\text{Yearly NPV Cash Flow} - \text{Overall NPV Cash Flow}}{\text{Yearly NPV Cash Flow}}$$

Using data from Figure 5.16,

$$\text{Break-Even Ratio} = \frac{15{,}303 - 9{,}139}{15{,}303} = .403$$

Therefore, project breakeven occurs at approximately 2.4 years. Using the information from the economic analysis, a project review board is able to better understand the potential economic impact of a project. Without such information, it would be virtually impossible to know the cost-benefits of a proposed system and to make an informed decision regarding approval or rejection of a project. There are many techniques to compute a project's economic feasibility. Because most information systems have a useful life of more than 1 year and will provide benefits and incur expenses for more than 1 year, most techniques for analyzing economic feasibility employ the concept of the TVM (see Table 5.7). For a more detailed discussion of TVM or cost-benefit analysis techniques in general, review an introductory finance or managerial accounting textbook.

A systems project to be approved for continuation may not have to achieve breakeven or have an ROI above some organizational threshold as estimated during project initiation and planning. Because you may not be able to quantify many benefits or costs at this point in a project, such financial hurdles for the project may be unattainable. In this case, as thorough an economic analysis as possible, including producing a long list of intangibles, may provide sufficient justification for the project to progress. One other option is to run the type of economic analysis shown in Table 5.7 using pessimistic, optimistic, and expected benefit and cost estimates during project initiation and planning. This range of possible outcomes, along with the list of intangible benefits and the support of the requesting business unit, will often be enough to justify allowing the project to continue to the analysis phase. Your economic analysis, however, must be as precise as possible, especially when investment capital is scarce. In this case, it may be necessary to conduct some typical analysis phase activities during project initiation and planning in order to clearly identify inefficiencies and shortcomings with the existing system and to explain how a new system will overcome these problems. Thus, building the economic case for a systems project is an open-ended activity; how much analysis is needed depends on the particular project, stakeholders, and

COMMON PROBLEMS
Reducing Information Systems Development Costs

When performing financial feasibility analyses, project managers identify potential benefits and costs. For a project to be selected for development, its benefits typically need to exceed its costs. Therefore, one way to increase the potential value of a project to the organization is by reducing information systems development costs. Development costs can be controlled and reduced by following a few strategies, including:

1. *Standardizing hardware platforms.* Standardizing server and storage platforms can significantly reduce recurring costs; quantity purchases can reduce one-time costs.

2. *Standardizing application infrastructure.* Common application environments reduce recurring costs by reducing system and data integration as well as ongoing maintenance.

3. *Improving security.* Standardizing on a single operating system and automating updates can reduce the need for individual desktop repair and upgrades, as well as increase overall system security and simplify administration; together, these steps reduce one-time and recurring system costs.

4. *Managing operations.* By carefully monitoring and proactively administering system updates and security repairs, operational problems can be dramatically reduced or eliminated, thus reducing recurring system costs.

As the amount of work reacting to system differences, security breaches, and update administration is reduced, organizational resources can be focused on providing organizational benefits. Looking for opportunities to better control one-time and recurring costs will enhance both project and organizational performance (Source: Burry, 2003).

business conditions. Also, conducting economic feasibility analyses for new types of information systems can be very difficult.

Assessing Technical Feasibility

Technical feasibility
An assessment of the development organization's ability to construct a proposed system.

The purpose of assessing **technical feasibility** is to gain an understanding of the organization's ability to construct the proposed system. This analysis should include an assessment of the development group's understanding of the possible target hardware, software, and operating environments to be used, as well as system size and complexity and the group's experience with similar systems. In this section, we will discuss a framework for assessing the technical feasibility of a project in which the level of technical project risk can be determined after answering a few fundamental questions.

It is important to note that all projects have risk and that risk is not necessarily something to avoid (see Chapter 9, *Managing Project Risk*). Yet it is also true that, because organizations typically expect a greater return on their investment for riskier projects, understanding the sources and types of technical risks is a valuable tool when you assess a project. Also, risks need to be managed in order to be minimized; you should, therefore, identify potential risks as early as possible in a project. The potential consequences of not assessing and managing risks can include the following:

- Failure to attain expected benefits from the project
- Inaccurate project cost estimates
- Inaccurate project duration estimates
- Failure to achieve adequate system performance levels
- Failure to adequately integrate the new system with existing hardware, software, or organizational procedures

You can manage risk on a project by changing the project plan to avoid risky factors, assigning project team members to carefully manage the risky aspects, and setting up monitoring methods to determine whether potential risk is, in fact, materializing.

The amount of technical risk associated with a given project is contingent on four primary factors: project size, project structure, the development group's experience with the application and technology area, and the user group's experience with systems development projects and the application area (see also Kirsch, 2000). Aspects of each of these risk areas are summarized in Table 5.8. Using these factors for conducting a technical risk assessment, four general rules emerge:

1. *Large projects are riskier than small projects.* Project size, of course, relates to the relative project size with which the development group is familiar. A small project for one development group may be relatively large for another. The types of factors that influence project size are listed in Table 5.8.
2. *A system in which the requirements are easily obtained and highly structured will be less risky than one in which requirements are messy, ill-structured, ill-defined, or subject to the judgment of an individual.* For example, the development of a payroll system has requirements that may be easy to determine due to legal reporting requirements and standard accounting procedures. On the other hand, the development of an executive support system would need to be customized to the particular executive decision style and critical success factors of the organization, thus making its development more risky (see Table 5.8).

Table 5.8 Technical Project Risk Assessment Factors

RISK FACTOR	EXAMPLES
Project size	• Number of members on the project team • Project duration time • Number of organizational departments involved in the project • Size of programming effort (e.g., hours, function points)
Project structure	• New system or renovation of existing system(s) • Organizational, procedural, structural, or personnel changes resulting from system • User perceptions and willingness to participate in effort • Management commitment to system • Amount of user information in system development effort
Development group	• Familiarity with target hardware, software development environment, tools, and operating system • Familiarity with proposed application area • Familiarity with building similar systems of similar size
User group	• Familiarity with information systems development process • Familiarity with proposed application area • Familiarity with using similar systems

Source: Adapted from Applegate, Austin, and McFarlan, 2007.

3. *The development of a system employing commonly used or standard technology will be less risky than one employing novel or nonstandard technology.* A project has a greater likelihood of experiencing unforeseen technical problems when the development group lacks knowledge related to some aspect of the technology environment. A less risky approach is to use standard development tools and hardware environments. It is not uncommon for experienced system developers to talk of the difficulty of using leading-edge (or in their words, bleeding-edge) technology (see Table 5.8).

4. *A project is less risky when the user group is familiar with the systems development process and application area.* Successful information systems projects require active involvement and cooperation between user and development groups. Users familiar with the application area and the systems development process are more likely to understand the need for their involvement and how this involvement can influence the success of the project (see Table 5.8).

A project with high technical risk may still be conducted. Many organizations look at risk as a portfolio issue: considering all projects, it is acceptable to have a reasonable percentage of high-, medium-, and low-risk projects. Given that some high-risk projects will get into trouble, an organization cannot afford to have too many of them. Alternatively, having too many low-risk projects may not be aggressive enough to make major breakthroughs in innovative uses of systems. Each organization must decide on its acceptable mix of projects of varying risk. A matrix for assessing the relative risks related to the general rules just described is shown in Figure 5.17.

		Low Structure	High Structure
High Familiarity with Technology or Application Area	Large Project	(1) Low risk (very susceptible to mismanagement)	(2) Low risk
	Small Project	(3) Very low risk (very susceptible to mismanagement)	(4) very low risk
Low Familiarity with Technology or Application Area	Large Project	(5) Very high risk	(6) Medium risk
	Small Project	(7) High risk	(8) Medium-low risk

Figure 5.17 Effects of degree of project structure, project size, and familiarity with application area on project implementation risk.

Source: Adapted from Applegate, Austin, and McFarlan, 2007, with the Permission of The McGraw-Hill Companies. Copyright © 2007 L. M. Applegate, R. D. Austin, and F. W. McFarlan.

Global Implications: Deciding When to Offshore

Most economists and business leaders believe that offshore outsourcing is here to stay. As businesses work hard to remain competitive, most are examining what types of projects should or should not be sent offshore. To be successful, identifying the right projects is crucial. The rule of thumb for choosing which projects to choose and which not to choose for offshoring is not always clear. Nevertheless, organizations with long-term success in utilizing offshoring typically do not offshore the following types of projects:

- Complex projects that involve multiple coordinated teams
- Core-competency or core intellectual property related projects
- "Crash" projects to return another project back onto schedule
- New product development projects
- Projects initiated to produce immediate cost savings (because it typically takes time to realize project benefits)

Alternatively, projects that have been identified as good candidates for offshoring include those for the maintenance, support, or extension of legacy systems, as well as non–mission-critical systems that do not involve key intellectual property or processes. Even though organizations may choose the "right" type of projects for offshoring, there is still a great risk of failure if the project is not carefully managed. Key management issues include having a local project manager who is experienced and skilled in managing an offshore team, good communication plans, and frequent

(continued)

(*continued*)

milestones to ensure that problems are quickly identified. Organizations can realize many benefits from offshoring, however, as with all types of systems development projects, good project execution is essential to realizing the optimal benefits (Sources: Printer, 2004; Thibodeau, 2004).

Assessing Other Feasibility Concerns

In this section, we will briefly conclude our discussion of project feasibility issues by reviewing other forms of feasibility that should be considered when formulating the business case for a system during project initiation. The first relates to examining the likelihood that the project will attain its desired objectives, called **operational feasibility**. Its purpose is to gain an understanding of the degree to which the proposed system will likely solve the business problems or take advantage of the opportunities outlined in the systems service request (SSR) or project identification study. For a project arising from information systems planning, operational feasibility includes justifying the project on the basis of being consistent with, or necessary for accomplishing the information systems plan. In fact, the business case for any project can be enhanced by showing a link to the business or information systems plan. Your assessment of operational feasibility should also include an analysis of how the proposed system will affect organizational structures and procedures. Systems that have substantial and widespread impact on an organization's structure or procedures are typically riskier projects to undertake. In other words, it is important for you to have a clear understanding of how an information system will fit into the organization's current day-to-day operation.

Another feasibility concern relates to project duration and is referred to as **schedule feasibility**. The project manager's purpose in assessing schedule feasibility is to gain an understanding of the likelihood that all potential time frames and completion date schedules can be met and that meeting these dates will be sufficient for dealing with the organization's needs. For instance, a system may have to be operational by a government-imposed deadline, by a particular point in the business cycle (such as the beginning of the season when new products are introduced), or at least by the time a competitor is expected to introduce a similar system. Further, detailed activities may only be feasible if resources are available when called for in the schedule. For example, the schedule should not call for system testing during rushed business periods or for key project meetings during annual vacation or holiday periods. Also, near-term activities will be planned more carefully than long-term ones. This means that assessing schedule feasibility during project initiation is more of a "rough-cut" analysis of whether the system can be completed within the constraints of the business opportunity or the desires of the users. While assessing schedule feasibility, you should also evaluate scheduling trade-offs; factors such as project team size, availability of key personnel, subcontracting or outsourcing activities, and changes in development environments may all be considered as having a possible impact on the eventual schedule. As with all forms of feasibility, schedule feasibility will be reassessed as the project proceeds.

A third concern relates to assessing **legal and contractual feasibility** issues. In this area, you need to determine any potential legal ramifications due to the construction of the system. Possible considerations might include copyright or nondisclosure infringements, labor laws, antitrust legislation (which might limit the creation of systems to share data with other organizations), foreign trade regulations (e.g., some countries limit access to employee data by foreign corporations), and financial reporting standards, as well as current or pending contractual obligations. Contractual obligations may involve ownership of software used in joint ventures,

---

Operational feasibility
The degree to which a proposed system will solve business problems or take advantage of business opportunities.

Schedule feasibility
The degree to which the potential time frame and completion dates for all major activities within a project meet organizational deadlines and constraints for affecting change.

Legal and contractual feasibility
The potential legal and contractual ramifications due to the construction of a system.

license agreements for use of hardware or software, nondisclosure agreements with partners, or elements of a labor agreement (e.g., a union agreement may preclude certain compensation or work-monitoring capabilities a user may want in a system). A common situation is that development of a new application system for use on new computers may require new or expanded, and more costly, system software licenses. Typically, legal and contractual feasibility is a greater consideration if your organization has historically used an outside organization for specific systems or services that you are now considering handling yourself. In this case, ownership of program source code by another party may make it difficult to extend an existing system or link a new system with an existing purchased system.

A final feasibility concern focuses on assessing **political feasibility**—how key stakeholders within the organization view the proposed system. Because an information system may affect the distribution of information within the organization and, thus, the distribution of power, the construction of an information system can have political ramifications. Those stakeholders not supporting the project may take steps to block, disrupt, or change the intended focus of the project.

In summary, depending upon the given situation, numerous feasibility issues must be considered when initiating a project. This analysis should consider economic, technical, operational, schedule, legal and contractual, and political issues related to the project. In addition to these considerations, project selection by an organization may be influenced by issues beyond those discussed here. For example, a project may be selected for construction even given high project costs and high technical risk if the system is viewed as a strategic necessity; that is, the organization views the project as being critical to the organization's survival. Alternatively, projects may be selected because they are deemed to require few resources and have little risk. Projects may also be selected due to the power or persuasiveness of the manager proposing the system. This means that project selection may be influenced by factors beyond those discussed here and beyond items that can be analyzed. Understanding the reality that projects may be selected based on factors beyond analysis, your role as a project manager is to provide a thorough examination of the items that can be assessed. Your analysis will ensure that a project review committee has as much information as possible when making project approval decisions. In the next section, we discuss how project plans are typically reviewed and selected.

Selecting Information Systems Development Projects

The third activity in the project initiation process is the actual selection of projects for further development. Project selection is a process of considering both short- and long-term projects and selecting those most likely to achieve business objectives. Additionally, as business conditions change over time, the relative importance of any single project may substantially change. Thus, the identification and selection of projects is a very important and ongoing activity.

Numerous factors must be considered when selecting projects. Figure 5.18 shows that a selection decision must consider the perceived needs of the organization, existing systems and ongoing projects, resource availability, evaluation criteria, current business conditions, and perspectives of the decision makers. Numerous outcomes can result from this decision process. Of course, projects can be accepted or rejected. Acceptance of a project usually means that funding to conduct the next project phase has been approved. Rejection means that the project will no longer be considered for development. However, projects may also be conditionally accepted; they may be accepted pending the approval or availability of needed resources or dependent upon the demonstration that a particularly difficult aspect of the system can be developed.

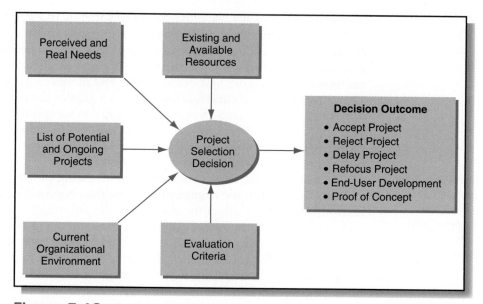

Figure 5.18 Project selection decisions must consider numerous factors and can have numerous outcomes

Source: Hoffer, George & Valacich (2007). *Modern Systems Analysis and Design.* Upper Saddle River, NJ: Prentice Hall.

Projects may also be returned to the original requesters with instructions to develop or purchase the requested system themselves. Finally, the requesters of a project may be asked to resubmit their request after making suggested changes or clarifications.

Value Chain Analysis

Value chain analysis
The process of analyzing an organization's activities to determine where value is added to products and/or services and the costs incurred for doing so.

One important project evaluation method that is widely used for assessing information systems development projects is called value chain analysis (Porter, 1985; Shank and Govindarajan, 1993). **Value chain analysis** is the process of analyzing an organization's activities for making products and/or services to determine where value is added and costs are incurred. Once an organization gains a clear understanding of its value chain, it can improve its operations and performance. Information systems projects providing the greatest benefit to the value chain will be given priority over those with fewer benefits.

As you might have guessed, information systems have become one of the primary ways for organizations to make changes and improvements in their value chains. Many organizations, for example, are using the Internet to exchange important business information such as orders, invoices, and receipts with suppliers and customers. To conduct a value chain analysis for an organization, think about the organization as a big input/output process (see Figure 5.19). At one end are the inputs to the organization, supplies that are purchased. Within the organizations, those supplies and resources are integrated in some way to produce products and services. At the other end are the outputs, which represent the products and services that are marketed, sold, and then distributed to customers. In value chain analysis, you must first understand each activity, function, and process where value is or should be added. Next, you determine the costs (and the factors that drive costs or cause them to fluctuate) within each of the areas. After understanding your value chain and costs, you can benchmark (compare) your value chain and associated costs with those of other organizations, preferably your competitors. By making these comparisons, you can identify priorities for applying information systems projects.

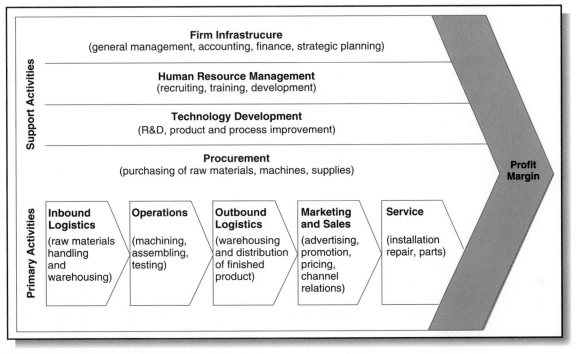

Figure 5.19   Organizational value chain

Source: Porter, M. [1985]. Reprinted with the Permission of The Free Press, a Division of Simon & Schuster, Inc. Copyright © 1985 M. Porter.

Multicriteria analysis
A project selection method that uses weighted scoring for a variety of criteria to contrast alternative projects or system features.

Multicriteria Analysis

Another method for deciding among different projects or among alternative designs for a given system is called multicriteria analysis (see Figure 5.20). **Multicriteria analysis** uses a weighted scoring method for a variety of criteria to contrast alternative projects or system features. For example, suppose that for a given system that has been identified and selected, three alternative designs could be pursued—A, B, or C. Let's also suppose that early planning meetings identified

Figure 5.20   Alternative projects and system design decisions can be assisted using weighted multicriteria analysis

Source: Hoffer, George & Valacich (2007). *Modern Systems Analysis and Design.* Upper Saddle River, NJ: Prentice Hall.

Criteria	Weight	Alternative A		Alternative B		Alternative C	
		Rating	Score	Rating	Score	Rating	Score
Requirements							
Real-time data entry	18	5	90	5	90	5	90
Automatic reorder	18	1	18	5	90	5	90
Real-time data query	14	1	14	5	70	5	70
	50		122		250		250
Constraints							
Developer costs	15	4	60	5	75	3	45
Hardware costs	15	4	60	4	60	3	45
Operating costs	15	5	75	1	15	5	75
Ease of training	5	5	25	3	15	3	15
	50		220		165		180
Total	100		342		415		430

three key system requirements and four key constraints that could be used to help make a decision on which alternative to pursue. The left column of Figure 5.20 lists three system requirements and four constraints. Because not all requirements and constraints are of equal importance, they are weighted based on their relative importance. In other words, you do not have to weight requirements and constraints equally; it is certainly possible to make requirements more or less important than constraints. Weights are arrived at in discussions among the analysis team, users, and sometimes, managers. Weights tend to be fairly subjective and, for that reason, should be determined through a process of open discussion to reveal underlying assumptions followed by an attempt to reach consensus among stakeholders. Notice that the total of the weights for both the requirements and constraints is 100 (percent).

Next, each requirement and constraint is rated on a scale of 1 to 5. A rating of 1 indicates that the alternative does not meet the requirement very well or violates the constraint. A rating of 5 indicates that the alternative meets or exceeds the requirement or clearly abides by the constraint. Ratings are even more subjective than weights and should also be determined through open discussion among users, analysts, and managers. A score is calculated for each requirement and constraint by multiplying its rating by its weight. The final step is to total the weighted scores for each alternative. Notice that we have included three sets of totals: one for requirements, one for constraints, and one overall. If you look at the totals for requirements, alternative B or C is the best choice, because both meet or exceed all requirements. However, if you look only at constraints, alternative A is the best choice because it does not violate any constraints. When we combine the totals for requirements and constraints, we see that the best choice is alternative C. Whether alternative C is actually chosen for development, however, is another issue. The decision makers may choose alternative A, knowing that it does not meet two key requirements, because it has the lowest cost. In short, what may appear to be the best choice for a systems development project may not always be the one that ends up being developed. By conducting a thorough analysis, organizations can greatly improve their decision-making performance.

Developing the Project Charter

Once a project has been identified and selected, the project charter can be developed. The **project charter** is a short (typically one page), high-level document prepared for the customer that describes what the project will deliver and outlines many of its key elements. A project charter can vary in the amount of detail it contains but often includes the following elements:

- Project title and date of authorization
- Project manager name and contact information
- Customer name and contact information
- Projected start and completion dates
- Key stakeholders, project role, and responsibilities
- Project objectives and description
- Key assumptions or approach
- Signature section for key stakeholders

The project charter ensures that both you and your customer gain a common understanding of the project. It is also a very useful communication tool; it helps to announce to the organization that a particular project has been chosen for development. A sample project charter is shown in Figure 5.21.

Project charter
A short document prepared for the customer during project initiation that describes what the project will deliver and outlines generally at a high level all work required to complete the project.

Project Name:	Customer Tracking System
Project Manager:	Jim Woo (jwoo@pvf.com)
Customer:	Marketing
Project Sponsor:	Jackie Judson (jjudson@pvf.com)
Project Start/End (projected):	8/1/07—2/1/08

Project Overview:

This project will implement a customer tracking system for the marketing department. The purpose of this system is to automate the . . . to save employee time, reduce errors, have more timely information . . .

Objectives:
- Minimize data entry errors
- Provide more timely information
- . . .

Key Assumptions:
- System will be built in-house
- Interface will be a Web browser
- System will access customer database
- . . .

Stakeholders and Responsibilities

Stakeholder	Role	Responsibility	Signatures
Jackie Judson	VP Marketing	Project Vision, Resources	*Jackie Judson*
Alex Datta	CIO	Monitoring, Resources	*Alex Datta*
Jim Woo	Project Manager	Plan, Monitor, Execute Project	*Jim Woo*
James Jordan	Director of Sales	System Functionality	*James Jordan*
Mary Shide	VP Human Resources	Staff Assignments	*Mary Shide*

Figure 5.21 A project charter for a proposed information systems project

PROJECT SCOPE PLANNING

Project scope planning
The process of progressively elaborating and documenting the project work plan in order to effectively manage a project.

Once a project has been identified and formally selected, project scope planning can begin. **Project scope planning** is the process of progressively elaborating and documenting the project work plan in order to effectively manage a project. During project scope planning, three major activities occur. First, the project workbook is created. The project workbook is a repository of all project-related documents and information—both paper and electronic. Second, the project scope statement is developed. This short document briefly outlines all work that will be done and clearly describes what the project will deliver and helps to make sure that you, the customer, and other project team members have a clear and common understanding of the project. Third, once all the project scope definition activities have been completed, you are able to develop the baseline project plan. This baseline plan provides an estimate of the project's tasks and resource requirements and is used to guide the next project phase. As new information is acquired throughout the project, the baseline plan will continue to be updated. Each of these activities is described next.

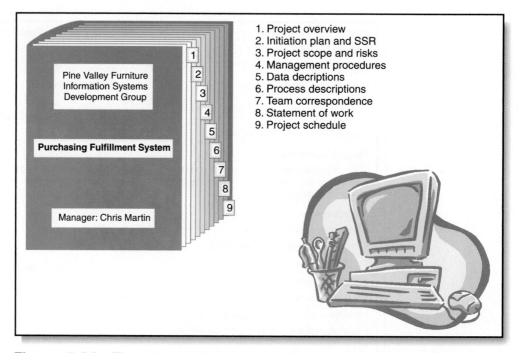

Figure 5.22 The project workbook can be a hard-copy or an electronic document

Source: Hoffer, George & Valacich (2007). *Modern Systems Analysis and Design.* Upper Saddle River, NJ: Prentice Hall.

Establishing the Project Workbook

Project workbook
An on-line or hard-copy repository for all project correspondence, inputs, outputs, deliverables, procedures, and standards established by the project team.

The focus of this activity is to collect and organize the tools that you will use while managing the project and to construct the project workbook. Diagrams, charts, and system descriptions provide much of the project workbook contents. Thus, the **project workbook** serves as a central repository for all project correspondence, inputs, outputs, deliverables, procedures, and standards established by the project team. The baseline project plan (BPP) described later is a key piece of the project workbook. The project workbook contains both paper and electronic documents and can be stored in a large three-ring binder or more typically as a project Web site (see Figure 5.22). The project workbook is used by all team members and is useful for project audits, orientation of new team members, communication with management and customers, identifying future projects, and performing postproject reviews. Establishing and diligently recording all project information in the workbook are two of the most important activities you will perform as project manager. Today, most project teams keep their project workbooks on the Web. A Web site can be created so that all project members can easily access all project documents. This Web site can be a simple repository of documents or an elaborate site with password protection and security levels. The best feature of using a Web-based repository is that it enables project members and customers to continually review a project's status and all related information.

Defining the Project Scope Statement

The purpose of the project scope statement is to clearly define and articulate the content and complexity of the project. During this activity, the project manager will work with the customer to reach agreement on the following questions:

- What problem or opportunity does the project address?
- What quantifiable results are to be achieved?
- What needs to be done?
- How will success be measured?
- How will we know when we are finished?

Project scope statement
A document prepared for the customer that describes what the project will deliver and outlines generally at a high level all work required to complete the project.

Once this information is clearly understood, the **project scope statement** is created. This short document is prepared primarily for the customer to clearly describe what the project will deliver and outline all the work required for completing the project. It is, therefore, a very useful communication tool. The project scope statement ensures that both you and your customer gain a common understanding of project size, duration, and outcomes. The project scope statement is a very easy document to create because it typically consists of a high-level summary of the baseline project plan (BPP) information (described next). A sample project scope statement is shown in Figure 5.23.

Figure 5.23 A project scope statement for a proposed information systems project

Source: Hoffer, George & Valacich (2007). *Modern Systems Analysis and Design.* Upper Saddle River, NJ: Prentice Hall.

Pine Valley Furniture
Statement of Project Scope

Prepared by: Jim Woo
Date: August 7, 2007

General Project Information
 Project Name: Customer Tracking System
 Sponsor: Jackie Judson, VP Marketing
 Project Manager: Jim Woo

Problem/Opportunity Statement:
 Sales growth has outpaced the marketing department's ability to accurately track and forecast customer buying trends. An improved method for performing this process must be found in order to reach company objectives.

Project Objectives:
 To enable the marketing departments to accurately track and forecast customer buying patterns in order to better serve customers with the best mix of products. This will also enable PVF to identify the proper application of production and material resources.

Project Description:
 A new information system will be constructed that will collect all customer purchasing activity, support display and reporting of sales information, aggregate data, and show trends in order to assist marketing personnel in understanding dynamic market conditions. The project will follow PVF's systems development life cycle.

Business Benefits:
 Improved understanding of customer buying patterns
 Improved utilization of marketing and sales personnel
 Improved utilization of production and materials

Project Deliverables:
 Customer tracking system analysis and design
 Customer tracking system programs
 Customer tracking documentation
 Training procedures

Estimated Project Duration:
 5 months

Depending upon your relationship with your customer, the role of the project scope statement may vary. At one extreme, the project scope statement can be used as the basis for a formal contractual agreement outlining firm deadlines, costs, and specifications. At the other extreme, it can simply be used as a communication vehicle to outline the current best estimates of what the project will deliver, when it will be completed, and what resources it may consume. A contract programming or consulting firm, for example, may establish a very formal relationship with a customer and use a project charter that is more extensive and formal. Alternatively, an internal development group may develop a project scope statement that is shorter and less formal because it will be intended to inform customers rather than to set contractual obligations and deadlines.

Developing the Baseline Project Plan

Baseline project plan
A major outcome and deliverable from the project scope definition process that contains the best estimate of a project's scope, benefits, costs, risks, and resource requirements.

The final activity within project scope definition is the development of the project's baseline project plan. The **baseline project plan (BPP)**, referred to as the Project Management Plan within the PMBOK (2004), contains all information collected and analyzed during project initiation and scope definition. The plan reflects the best estimate of the project's scope, benefits, costs, risks, and resource requirements given the current understanding. The BPP specifies detailed project activities for the next project phases and some details for subsequent project phases. Because subsequent phases depend on the results of preceding phases, limited information is available at this time. Similarly, benefits, costs, risks, and resource requirements will become more specific and quantifiable as the project progresses. The organization's project review committee uses the BPP to help decide whether the project should be continued, redirected, or canceled. As the project evolves, the BPP is the foundation document for all subsequent project activities and is continuously updated. In other words, as more is learned during subsequent project phases, the baseline plan will be updated.

The project size and organizational standards will dictate the comprehensiveness of the project scope definition process as well as the BPP. Yet most experienced project managers have found careful project planning to be invaluable to overall project success. The outline provided in Figure 5.24 shows that a baseline project plan contains four major sections:

1. Introduction
2. System description
3. Feasibility assessment
4. Management issues

Next, we briefly describe each of these sections.

The Introduction Section of the Baseline Project Plan

The purpose of the introduction is to provide a brief overview of the entire document and outline a recommended course of action (see Figure 5.24). The entire introduction is often limited to only a few pages. Although it is sequenced as the first section of the BPP, it is often the final section to be written. Only after performing most of the project planning activities can a clear overview and recommendation be created.

The System Description Section of the Baseline Project Plan

The second section of the BPP is the system description, which outlines possible alternatives to the solution deemed most appropriate for the given situation (see Figure 5.24). Note that this description is at a very high level, mostly narrative in form. For example, alternatives may be stated as simply as this:

BASELINE PROJECT PLAN REPORT

1.0 Introduction
    A. Project Overview—Provides an executive summary that specifies the project's scope, feasibility, justification, resource requirements, and schedules. Additionally, a brief statement of the problem, the environment in which the system is to be implemented, and constraints that affect the project are provided.
    B. Recommendation—Provides a summary of important findings from the planning process and recommendations for subsequent activities.

2.0 System Description
    A. Alternatives—Provides a brief presentation of alternative system configurations.
    B. System Description—Provides a description of the selected configuration and a narrative of input information, tasks performed, and resultant information.

3.0 Feasibility Assessment
    A. Economic Analysis—Provides an economic justification for the system using cost-benefit analysis.
    B. Technical Analysis—Provides a discussion of relevant technical risk factors and an overall risk rating of the project.
    C. Operational Analysis—Provides an analysis of how the proposed system solves business problems or takes advantage of business opportunities in addition to an assessment of how current day-to-day activities will be changed by the system.
    D. Legal and Contractual Analysis—Provides description of any legal or contractual risks related to the project (e.g., copyright or nondisclosure issues, data capture or transferring, and so on).
    E. Political Analysis—Provides a description of how key stakeholders within the organization view the proposed system.
    F. Schedules, Timeline, and Resource Analysis—Provides a description of potential time frame and completion data scenarios using various resource allocation schemes.

4.0 Management Issues
    A. Team Configuration and Management—Provides a description of team member roles and reporting relationships.
    B. Communication Plan—Provides a description of the communication procedures to be followed by management, team members, and the customer.
    C. Project Standards and Procedures—Provides a description of how deliverables will be evaluated and accepted by the customer.
    D. Other Project-Specific Topics—Provides a description of any other relevant issues related to the project uncovered during planning.

Figure 5.24 Outline of a baseline project plan

Source: Hoffer, George & Valacich (2007). *Modern Systems Analysis and Design.* Upper Saddle River, NJ: Prentice Hall.

1. Web-based online system
2. Mainframe with central database
3. Local area network with decentralized databases
4. Batch data input with online retrieval
5. Purchasing of a prewritten package

If the project is approved for construction or purchase, you will need to collect and structure information in a more detailed and rigorous manner during subsequent project activities and evaluate in greater depth these and other alternatives for the system. At this point in the project, however, your objective is only to identify the most obvious alternative solutions.

The Feasibility Assessment Section of the Baseline Project Plan

The feasibility assessment outlines issues related to project costs and benefits, technical difficulties, and other such concerns (see Figure 5.24). This is also the section where high-level project schedules are specified using network diagrams and Gantt charts (see Chapter 6, "Managing Project Scheduling"). Recall that this process is referred to as a work-breakdown structure. During project initiation and planning, task and activity estimates are not generally detailed. An accurate work breakdown can only be done for the next one or two project activities. After defining the primary tasks for the project, an estimate of the resource requirements can be made. As with defining tasks and activities, this activity is primarily concerned with gaining rough estimates of the human resource requirements, because people are the most expensive resource element. Once you define the major tasks and resource requirements, a preliminary schedule can be developed. Defining an acceptable schedule may require that you find additional resources or different resources, or change the scope of the project. The greatest amount of project planning effort is typically expended on these feasibility assessment activities.

The Management Issues Section of the Baseline Project Plan

The final section, management issues, outlines a number of managerial concerns related to the project (see Figure 5.24). Items commonly addressed in this section of the BPP include:

- Team configuration and management
- Communication plan
- Project standards and procedures
- Other project-specific topics

This will be a very short section if the proposed project is going to be conducted exactly as prescribed by the organization's standard systems development methodology. Most projects, however, have some unique characteristics that require minor to major deviation from the standard methodology. In the team configuration and management portion, for example, you identify the types of people to work on the project, who will be responsible for which tasks, and how work will be supervised and reviewed (see Figure 5.25). Likewise, in the communications plan portion, you explain how the user will be kept informed of project progress (e.g., periodic review meetings or even a newsletter) and what mechanisms will be used to foster sharing of ideas among team members (e.g., some form of computer-based conference facility)

Figure 5.25 Task-responsibility matrix

Project: Web Store		Prepared by: Juan Gonzales			Legend: P = Primary S = Support		
Manager: Juan Gonzales		**Page:** 1 of 1					
		Responsibility Matrix					
Task ID	**Task**	**Jordan**	**James**	**Jackie**	**Jeremy**	**Kim**	**Juan**
A	Collect Requirements	P	S				S
B	Develop Data Model			P		S	S
C	Program Interface		P		S		S
D	Build Database			S		P	S
E	Design Test Scenarios	S	S	S	P	S	S
F	Run Test Scenarios	S	S	S	S	S	P
G	User Documentation	P	S				S
H	Install System	S	P			S	S
I	Customer Support	S	P			S	S

Stakeholder	Document	Format	Team Contact	Date Due
Team Members	Project Status Report	Project Intranet	Juan Kim	First Monday of Month
Management Supervisor	Project Status Report	Hard Copy	Juan Kim	First Monday of Month
User Group	Project Status Report	Hard Copy	James Kim	First Monday of Month
Internal IT Staff	Project Status Report	Email	Jackie James	First Monday of Month
IT Manager	Project Status Report	Hard Copy	Juan Jeremy	First Monday of Month
Contract Programmers	Software Specifications	Email / Project Intranet	Jordan Kim	October 4, 2007
Training Subcontractor	Implementation and Training Plan	Hard Copy	Jordan James	January 10, 2008

Figure 5.26 Project communication matrix

(see Figure 5.26). An example of the type of information contained in the project standards and procedures portion would be the standard operating procedures for submitting and approving project change requests and any other issues deemed important for the project's success (see Chapter 12, "Managing Project Control and Closure").

You should now have a feel for how a BPP is constructed and the types of information it contains. Its creation is not meant to be a project in and of itself but, rather, a step in the overall systems development process. Developing the BPP has three primary objectives. First, it helps to ensure that the customer and development group share a common understanding of the project. Second, it helps to provide the sponsoring organization with a clear idea of the scope, benefits, and duration of the project. Third, it is actively used to manage the project.

PROJECT SCOPE DEFINITION, VERIFICATION, AND CHANGE CONTROL

Project scope definition
The process of subdividing the major project deliverables—as identified in the project scope statement—into smaller, more manageable activities in order to make more accurate cost, task duration, and resource estimates.

The remaining activities of the project scope management process focus on scope definition, verification, and change control. Scope definition focuses on developing a work breakdown structure (WBS) and updates to the project scope statement. Scope verification focuses on gaining formal acceptance of the project scope by the stakeholders—sponsor, customer, and other project team members. Finally, scope change control focuses on formal procedures for managing proposed changes to the project scope. Each of these activities is briefly described next.

Project Scope Definition

Project scope definition focuses on subdividing the major project deliverables—as identified in the project scope statement—into smaller, more manageable activities (PMBOK, 2004). When major project deliverables are broken into smaller parts, accurate cost, task duration, and resource estimates can be made. During scope definition, you will also establish a baseline for performance estimates and project control. Also, as the project is divided into smaller and more manageable pieces, it becomes much easier to clearly assign tasks and responsibilities to various team members. The process of dividing the entire project into manageable tasks and then logically ordering them to ensure their smooth evolution is referred to as creating the work breakdown structure (WBS). This process is described in Chapter 6, "Managing Project Scheduling."

Project Scope Verification

Project scope verification is the process of obtaining the project stakeholders' formal acceptance of a project's scope. During this process, users, management, developers, and other project stakeholders have a formal walk-through meeting to ensure that the proposed system conforms to organizational standards and to make sure that all relevant parties understand and agree with the information in the scope statement and baseline plan (see Chapter 4, "Managing Project Communication," for more information on walk-throughs).

Project scope verification
The process of obtaining the project stakeholders' formal acceptance of a project's scope.

Project Scope Change Control

A final project scope management activity is the project scope change control process. **Project scope change control** is a formal process for assuring that only agreed-upon changes are made to the project's scope. Throughout the life of a project, various types of change requests can be made—from correcting minor or severe design defects to improving or extending system functionality and features. Requests are typically made using a system service request, as discussed previously and shown in Figure 5.6. Over the life of a project (or of a system), a log of all service requests is kept so that the status of any request can be immediately known. Many organizations have created Web-based forms for submitting service requests and for keeping service logs (see Figure 5.27).

Project scope change control
A formal process for assuring that only agreed-upon changes are made to the project's scope.

From a management perspective, as service requests are made, deciding which requests to accept and which to reject is a key issue. Because some requests will be more critical than others, a method of assessing and prioritizing the relative value of scope change requests must be established. In Chapter 12, "Managing Project Control and Closure," we outline a formal process for managing the change control process.

Figure 5.27 A system service request log

No.	Short Request Description	Requestor's Name	Request Date	Request Type	Urgency	Assigned To	Assigned Date	Status	Close Date
1									
2									
3									
4									
5									
6									
7									
8									
9									
10									

This controlled process should be applied when handling project scope change requests as well as any other relevant project change request items, including:

- Project specifications
- Project schedules
- Budgets
- Resources

It is critical that the project scope change control process be completely integrated in the overall project control process so that any accepted changes are reflected in updated schedules, resource requirements, risks, and other relevant items.

The primary reason that strict scope change control is necessary is that many projects suffer from **scope creep**—a progressive, uncontrolled increase in project scope. Scope creep is typically a result of a poorly designed scope change control or a poorly defined project scope statement, or both. When either condition exists, small incremental features are often added to the system as it evolves, without careful evaluation or formal approval from all relevant stakeholders. As this continues, the project moves away from its original design, resulting in negative consequences for its schedule and budget. Consequently, without formal approval of scope changes, the project very likely will overrun its original budget and schedules because more is expected to be done without formal updating and approval. Left unchecked, scope creep can lead to a runaway project of constantly changing specifications, uncontrolled budgets, and abandoned schedules. Experienced project managers have found scope creep to be the single biggest reason for project failure or missed targets.

Scope creep
A progressive, uncontrolled increase in project scope.

TIPS FROM THE PROS
Outsmarting Scope Creep

Because scope creep is the greatest threat to project success, all successful project managers know how to manage it effectively. Mark Robinson, vice president for information technology at Saia Motor Freight, outlined 10 steps for outsmarting scope creep (Source: Ruriani, 2003):

1. *Educate your staff.* Make sure all project members understand the dangers of scope creep.

2. *Clearly define the project.* A poorly defined project is one of the leading causes of scope creep.

3. *Gather all relevant information.* Talk to all relevant parties to make sure the scope of the project is complete and is understood by all stakeholders very early in the life of the project.

4. *Define the objectives and deliverables.* Write a clear project scope statement that includes project objectives and deliverables.

5. *Assign a project sponsor.* Have a project sponsor at the beginning; changing team composition often leads to project scope changes.

6. *Create an approval process.* A clear project scope change control process is necessary to limit changes to only those that have been formally approved.

7. *Stay on track.* Use comprehensive project management techniques to keep the project on schedule, on budget, and on track.

8. *Create a good communication process.* Keep all project team members and stakeholders informed of project status and changes.

9. *Understand when change is necessary.* Sometimes it is necessary to make project changes; update all project materials—schedules, budgets, resources, etc.—when changes occur.

10. *Schedule regular meetings.* Regular meetings help to keep everyone informed of the project's status and are useful for resolving any disagreements or misunderstandings.

MANAGING PROJECT SCOPE AND THE PMBOK

In this chapter, we have focused primarily on Knowledge Areas 4 and 5, Project Integration Management and Project Scope Management, respectively, within the Project Management Body of Knowledge (PMBOK, 2004) (see Figure 5.28). Specifically, eight key

Figure 5.28 Chapter 5 and PMBOK coverage

Textbook Chapters →	1	2	3	4	5	6	7	8	9	10	11	12
PMBOK Knowledge Area												
1 Introduction to Project Management												
1.1 What is a Project?	●											
1.2 What is Project Management?	●											
1.3 Areas of Expertise		●										
1.4 Project Management Context	●											
2 Project Life Cycle and Organization												
2.1 The Project Life Cycle	●	●										
2.2 Project Stakeholders	●	●										
2.3 Organizational Influences		●	●	●			○					
3 Project Management Processes for a Project												
3.1 Project Management Processes	●	●										
3.2 PM Process Groups	●	●										
3.3 Process Interactions		●										
3.4 Project Management Process Mapping		●										
4 Project Integration Management												
4.1 Develop Project Charter					✓							
4.2 Develop Preliminary Project Scope Statement					✓	○						
4.3 Develop Project Management Plan					✓							
4.4 Direct and Manage Project Execution										○		
4.5 Monitor and Control Project Work												○
4.6 Integrated Change Control												○
4.7 Close Project												○
5 Project Scope Management												
5.1 Scope Planning					✓							
5.2 Scope Definition					✓							
5.3 Create WBS					✓	○						
5.4 Scope Verification					✓							
5.5 Scope Control					✓							○
6 Project Time Management												
6.1 Activity Definition						○						
6.2 Activity Sequencing						○						
6.3 Activity Resource Estimating							○					
6.4 Activity Duration Estimating							○					
6.5 Schedule Development							○					
6.6 Schedule Control							○					○

(continued)

Figure 5.28   (continued)

	Textbook Chapters → / PMBOK Knowledge Area	1	2	3	4	5	6	7	8	9	10	11	12
7	**Project Cost Management**												
7.1	Cost Estimating							○					
7.2	Cost Budgeting							○					
7.3	Cost Control							○					○
8	**Project Quality Management**												
8.1	Quality Planning								○				
8.2	Perform Quality Assurance								○				
8.3	Perform Quality Control								○				○
9	**Project Human Resource Management**												
9.1	Human Resource Planning			●				○					
9.2	Acquire Project Team			●				○					
9.3	Develop Project Team			●				○					
9.4	Manage Project Team			●				○					
10	**Project Communications Management**												
10.1	Communications Planning				●							○	
10.2	Information Distribution				●							○	
10.3	Performance Reporting				●								○
10.4	Manage Stakeholders				●								○
11	**Project Risk Management**												
11.1	Risk Management Planning									○			
11.2	Risk Identification									○	○		
11.3	Qualitative Risk Analysis									○			
11.4	Quantitative Risk Analysis									○			
11.5	Risk Response Planning									○			
11.6	Risk Monitoring and Control									○			○
12	**Project Procurement Management**												
12.1	Plan Purchases and Acquisitions										○		
12.2	Plan Contracting										○		
12.3	Request Seller Responses										○		
12.4	Select Sellers										○		
12.5	Contract Administration										○		
12.6	Contract Closure										○		○

Key: ● -where material is covered in past chapters; ✓-current chapter coverage;
○ -where material is covered in future chapters

processes—develop project charter, develop preliminary project scope statement, develop project management plan (baseline project plan), scope planning, scope definition, create WBS, scope verification, and scope change control—have been discussed. Additionally, we have also reviewed issues related to Knowledge Area 3, Project Management Processes, as we've discussed how aspects of initiating projects and managing project scope fit within the broader context of project management. Together, this information provides a solid foundation for understanding project scope management.

Now that the "No Customer Escapes" project team has been formed and a plan has been developed for distributing project information, Jim has begun working on the project's charter, scope statement, workbook, and baseline project plan. He first drafted the project's charter and posted it on the project's intranet (see Figure 5.29). He then sent a short e-mail message to all team members requesting feedback.

Minutes after Jim posted the project charter, his office phone rang.

"Jim, it's Sally. I just looked over the project charter and have a few comments."

Figure 5.29 A project charter for Petrie's customer relationship management system

Petrie's Electronics	Prepared: February 5, 2007
Project Charter	

Project Name:	No Customer Escapes
Project Manager:	Jim Woo (jwoo@petries.com)
Customer:	Operations
Project Sponsor:	Ella Whinston (ewhinston@petries.com)
Project Start/End (projected):	2/5/07—7/30/07

Project Overview:

This project will design and implement a customer relationship management system in order to provide superior customer service by rewarding our most loyal customers. Specifically, the system will track customer purchases, assign points for cumulative purchases, and allow points to be redeemed for "rewards" at local stores. The goal of this system is to provide an incentive to customers to choose Petrie's Electronics as their first and only choice for making electronic purchases. The system will provide Petrie's management with improved information on the purchase behavior of our most loyal customers.

Objectives:

• Track customer purchases
• Accumulate redeemable points
• Reward customer loyalty and provide loyalty incentives
• Provide improved management information

Key Assumptions:

• System development will be outsourced
• Interface will be a Web browser
• System will access existing customer sales databases

Stakeholders and Responsibilities:

Stakeholder	Role	Responsibility	Signatures
Ella Whinston	Chief Operating Officer	Project Vision, Executive Sponsor	*Ella Whinston*
Bob Petroski	Senior Operations Manager	Monitoring, Resources	*Bob Petroski*
Jim Woo	Project Manager	Plan, Monitor, Execute Project	*Jim Woo*
Sally Fukuyama	Assistant Director, Marketing	System Functionality	*Sally Fukuyama*
Sanjay Agarwal	Lead Analyst	Technical Architect	*Sanjay Agarwal*

"Great," replied Jim, "It's just a draft. What do you think?"

"Well, I think that we need to explain more about how the system will work and why we think this new system will more than pay for itself."

"Those are good suggestions; I am sure many others will also want to know that information. However, the project charter is a pretty high-level document and doesn't get into too much detail. Basically, its purpose is to just formally announce the project, providing a very high-level description, as well as to briefly list the objectives, key assumptions, and stakeholders. The other documents that I am working on, the baseline project plan and scope statement, are intended to provide more details on specific deliverables, costs, benefits, and so on. So, anyway, that type of more detailed information will be coming next."

"Oh, OK, that makes sense. I have never been on a project like this, so this is all new to me," said Sally.

"Don't worry," replied Jim, "Getting that kind of feedback from you and the rest of the team will be key for us doing a thorough feasibility analysis. I am going to need a lot of your help in identifying possible costs and benefits of the system. When we develop the baseline project plan, we do a very thorough feasibility analysis—we examine financial, technical, operational, schedule, and legal and contractual feasibility, as well as potential political issues arising through the development of the system."

"Wow, we have to do all that? Why can't we just build the system? I think we all know what we want," replied Sally.

"That is another great question," replied Jim. "I used to think exactly the same way, but what I learned in my last job was that there are great benefits to following a fairly formal project management process when designing a new system. By moving forward with care, we are much more likely to build the right system, on time and on budget."

"So," asked Sally, "What is the next step?"

"Well, we need to do the feasibility analysis I just mentioned, which becomes part of the project's baseline project plan. A high-level summary of this information is put into the project scope statement. Once this is completed, we will have a walk-through presentation to management to make sure they agree with and understand the scope, risks, and costs associated with making 'No Customer Escapes' a reality," said Jim.

"This is going to be a lot of work, but I am sure I am going to learn a lot," replied Sally.

"So, let me get to work on the feasibility analysis," said Jim. "I will be sending requests out to all the team members to get their ideas. I should have this e-mail ready within an hour or so."

"Great. I will look for it and will reply as soon as I can," answered Sally.

"Thanks. The faster we get this background work done, the sooner we will be able to move on to what the system will do," replied Jim.

"Sounds good. Talk to you later. Bye," Sally said.

"Bye, Sally, and thanks for your quick feedback," answered Jim.

CHAPTER SUMMARY

Describe the project initiation process, including how to identify, rank, and select information systems projects, as well as establish a project charter. Project initiation is the process of authorizing a new project or continuing an existing project. It generally includes four distinct activities: identifying, ranking, and selecting information systems projects, as well as establishing the project charter. Different organizational members or units can be assigned to perform this process, including top management, a diverse steering committee, business units and functional managers, the development group, or the most senior information systems executive. Potential projects can be evaluated and selected using a broad range of criteria, such as value chain analysis or multicriteria analysis. The quality of the process can be improved if decisions are guided by corporate strategic planning and information systems planning. Selected projects will be those considered most important in supporting the organizational strategy. A key activity in project initiation is the assessment of numerous feasibility issues associated with the project, including economic, technical, operational, schedule, legal and contractual, and political feasibility. All of these feasibility factors are influenced by the project size, the type of system proposed, and the collective experience of the development group and customers of the system. Once a project has been identified and selected, the project charter can be developed. The project charter is a short (typically one page), high-level document prepared for the customer that describes what the project will deliver and outlines many of the key elements of the project. Its development helps to assure that both you and your customer gain a common understanding of the project, and it also helps to announce to the organization that a particular project has been chosen for development.

Explain project scope planning, including how to develop the project workbook, scope statement, and baseline project plan (BPP). Project scope planning is the process of progressively elaborating and documenting the project work plan in order to effectively manage a project. The project workbook is an online or hard-copy repository for all project correspondence, inputs, outputs, deliverables, procedures, and standards; it is used for performing project audits, orienting new team members, communicating with management and customers, identifying future projects, and performing postproject reviews. The project scope statement is a short document that briefly outlines all work that will be done and clearly describes what the project will deliver. It is used to assure that the customer and other team members have a clear and common understanding of the project. The baseline project plan (BPP) includes a high-level description of the proposed system or system change, an outline of the various feasibilities, and an overview of the management issues specific to the project.

Describe project scope definition, verification, and change control. Project scope definition focuses on subdividing the major project deliverables into smaller, more manageable activities. Once it is completed, making accurate cost, task duration, and resource estimates is much easier. Scope verification refers to the process of reviewing and agreeing upon the project's scope definition by users, management, and the development group using a walkthrough. Project scope change control refers to a formal process for assuring that only agreed-upon changes are made to the project's scope in order to reduce or eliminate scope creep and for assuring that all scope changes are incorporated into all planning documents as well as communicated to all project stakeholders.

KEY TERMS REVIEW

- Baseline project plan
- Bottom-up planning
- Break-even analysis
- Business case
- Competitive strategy
- Corporate strategic planning
- Cost-benefit analysis
- Discount rate
- Economic feasibility
- Information systems planning
- Intangible benefit
- Intangible cost
- Legal and contractual feasibility

- Mission statement
- Multicriteria analysis
- Objective statements
- One-time cost
- Operational feasibility
- Political feasibility
- Present value
- Project charter
- Project initiation
- Project scope change control
- Project scope definition
- Project scope planning
- Project scope statement

- Project scope verification
- Project workbook
- Recurring cost
- Schedule feasibility
- Scope creep
- System service request
- Tangible benefit
- Tangible cost
- Technical feasibility
- Top-down planning
- Value chain analysis

Match each of the key terms with the definition that best fits it.

1. _____ The process of authorizing a new project or continuing an existing project.

2. _____ An ongoing process that defines the mission, objectives, and strategies of an organization.

3. _____ A statement that defines what business a company is in.

4. _____ A series of statements that express an organization's qualitative and quantitative goals for reaching a desired future position.

5. _____ The method by which an organization attempts to achieve its mission and objectives.

6. _____ An orderly means of assessing the information needs of an organization and defining the systems, databases, and technologies that will best satisfy those needs.

7. _____ A form used in most organizations to request new development, to report problems, or to request new features within an existing system.

8. _____ A generic information systems planning methodology that attempts to gain a broad understanding of the information system needs of the entire organization.

9. _____ A generic information systems planning methodology that identifies and defines information systems development projects based upon solving operational business problems or taking advantage of business opportunities.

10. _____ The justification that presents the economic, technical, operational, schedule, legal and contractual, and political factors influencing a proposed information systems project.

11. _____ A comparison of the financial benefits and costs associated with a development project.

12. _____ A benefit that can be measured in dollars and with certainty.

13. _____ A benefit that cannot be easily measured in dollars or with certainty.

14. _____ A cost that can be measured in dollars and with certainty.

15. _____ A cost that cannot be easily measured in terms of dollars or with certainty.

16. _____ A cost associated with project start-up and development or system start-up.

17. _____ A cost resulting from the ongoing evolution and use of a system.

18. _____ The use of a variety of analysis techniques for determining the financial feasibility of a project.

19. _____ The rate of return used to compute the present value of future cash flows.

20. _____ The current value of a future cash flow.

21. _____ A type of cost-benefit analysis used to identify when (if ever) benefits will equal costs.

22. _____ An assessment of the development organization's ability to construct a proposed system.

23. _____ The degree to which a proposed system will solve business problems or take advantage of business opportunities.

24. _____ The degree to which the potential time frame and completion dates for all major activities within a project meet organizational deadlines and constraints for affecting change.

25. _____ The potential legal and contractual ramifications due to the construction of a system.

26. _____ An evaluation of how key stakeholders within the organization view the proposed system.

27. _____ The process of analyzing an organization's activities to determine where value is added to products and/or services and the costs incurred for doing so.

28. _____ A project-selection method that uses weighted scoring for a variety of criteria to contrast alternative projects or system features.

29. _____ A short document prepared for the customer during project initiation that describes what the project will deliver and outlines generally at a high level all work required to complete the project.

30. _____ The process of progressively elaborating and documenting the project work plan in order to effectively manage a project.

31. _____ An online or hard-copy repository for all project correspondence, inputs, outputs, deliverables, procedures, and standards established by the project team.

32. _____ A document prepared for the customer that describes what the project will deliver and outlines generally at a high level all work required to complete the project.

33. _____ A major outcome and deliverable from the project scope definition process that contains the best estimate of a project's scope, benefits, costs, risks, and resource requirements.

34. _____ The process of subdividing the major project deliverables—as identified in the project scope statement—into smaller, more manageable activities in order to make more accurate cost, task duration, and resource estimates.

35. _____ The process of obtaining the project stakeholders' formal acceptance of a project's scope.

36. _____ A formal process for assuring that only agreed-upon changes are made to the project's scope

37. _____ A progressive, uncontrolled increase in project scope.

REVIEW QUESTIONS

1. Contrast the following terms:
   a. Mission, objective statements, competitive strategy
   b. Corporate strategic planning, information systems planning
   c. Top-down planning, bottom-up planning
   d. Low-cost producer, product differentiation, product focus or niche
   e. Break-even analysis, net present value, return on investment
   f. Economic feasibility, legal and contractual feasibility, operational feasibility, political feasibility, schedule feasibility
   g. Intangible benefit, tangible benefit
   h. Intangible cost, tangible cost

2. Describe and contrast the characteristics of alternative methods for making information systems identification decisions.

3. Describe the steps involved in corporate strategic planning.

4. What are three generic competitive strategies?

5. Describe what is meant by information systems planning and the steps involved in the process.

6. List and describe the advantages of top-down planning over other planning approaches.

7. Describe several project evaluation criteria.

8. What are the types, or categories, of benefits from an information systems project? What intangible benefits might an organization obtain from the development of an information systems project?

9. Describe three commonly used methods for performing economic cost-benefit analyses.

10. What are the potential consequences of not assessing the technical risks associated with an information systems development project? In what ways could you identify an information systems project that was technically riskier than another?

11. List and discuss the different types of project feasibility factors. Is any factor most important? Why or why not?

12. Describe and contrast value chain versus multicriteria analysis.

13. What is a project charter, and what information does it typically contain?

14. What is the project workbook, and what information does it contain?

15. What is the project scope statement, and what information does it contain?

16. What is contained in a baseline project plan? Are the content and format of all baseline plans the same? Why or why not?

17. Describe what occurs during project scope definition and verification.

18. What is scope creep, and why do organizations need to effectively manage changes to a project's scope?

EXERCISES

1. Write a mission statement for a business that you would like to start. The mission statement should state the area of business you will be in and the aspect of the business you value highly. When you are happy with the mission statement, describe the objectives and competitive strategy for achieving that mission.

2. Consider an organization that you believe does not conduct adequate strategic information systems planning. List at least six reasons why this type of planning is not done

appropriately (or is not done at all). Are these reasons justifiable? What are the implications of this inadequate strategic information systems planning? What limits, problems, weaknesses, and barriers might this present?

3. Information systems planning, as depicted in this chapter, is highly related to corporate strategic planning. What might those responsible for information systems planning have to do if they operate in an organization without a formal corporate planning process?

4. The economic analysis carried out during the project initiation is rather cursory. Why is this? Consequently, what factors do you think tend to be most important for a potential project to survive this first phase of the life cycle?

5. In those organizations that do an excellent job of information systems planning, why might projects identified from a bottom-up process still find their way into the project initiation process?

6. Consider, as an example, buying a network of PCs for a department at your workplace, or alternatively, consider outfitting a laboratory of PCs for students at a university. For your example, estimate the one-time and recurring costs outlined in Table 5.5.

7. For the situation you chose in Exercise 6, either buying a network of PCs for a department at your workplace or outfitting a laboratory of PCs for students at a university, estimate the costs and benefits of your system. Then calculate the net present value (NPV) and return on investment (ROI) and present a break-even analysis (BEA). Assume a discount rate of 12 percent and a 5-year time horizon.

8. Assuming monetary benefits of an information system at $85,000 per year, one-time costs of $75,000, recurring costs of $35,000 per year, a discount rate of 12 percent, and a 5-year time horizon, calculate the net present value (NPV) of an information system's costs and benefits. Also calculate the overall return on investment (ROI) of the project and then present a break-even analysis (BEA). At what point does break-even occur?

9. Change the discount rate for Exercise 8 to 10 percent and redo the analysis.

10. Change the recurring costs in Exercise 8 to $40,000 and redo the analysis.

11. Change the time horizon in Exercise 8 to 3 years and redo the analysis.

12. For the situation you chose in Exercise 6, either buying a network of PCs for a department at your workplace or outfitting a laboratory of PCs for students at a university, conduct a multicriteria analysis that contrasts at least three alternative configurations with at least three different requirements and three different constraint criteria.

13. For the situation you chose in Exercise 6, either buying a network of PCs for a department at your workplace or outfitting a laboratory of PCs for students at a university, write a project charter. List your assumptions on a separate page.

14. For the situation you chose in Exercise 6, either buying a network of PCs for a department at your workplace or outfitting a laboratory of PCs for students at a university, write a project scope statement. List your assumptions on a separate page.

15. For the situation you chose in Exercise 6, either buying a network of PCs for a department at your workplace or outfitting a laboratory of PCs for students at a university, use the outline for the baseline project plan provided in Figure 5.24 to complete section 1.0 A, Project Overview, of the baseline project plan report. How important is it that this initial section of the baseline project plan report is done well? What could go wrong if this section is incomplete or incorrect? List your assumptions on a separate page.

16. For the situation you chose in Exercise 6, either buying a network of PCs for a department at your workplace or outfitting a laboratory of PCs for students at a university, use the outline for the baseline project plan provided in Figure 5.24 to complete section 2.0 A, Alternatives, of the baseline project plan report. Without conducting a full-blown feasibility analysis, what is your gut feeling as to the feasibility of this system? List your assumptions on a separate page.

17. For the situation you chose in Exercise 6, either buying a network of PCs for a department at your workplace or outfitting a laboratory of PCs for students at a university, use the outline for the baseline project plan provided in Figure 5.24 to complete section 2.0 B, System Description, of the baseline project plan report. List your assumptions on a separate page.

18. For the situation you chose in Exercise 6 above, either buying a network of PCs for a department at your workplace or outfitting a laboratory of PCs for students at a university, use the outline for the baseline project plan provided in Figure 5.24 to complete Section 3.0, Feasibility Assessment, of the baseline project plan report. How does this feasibility analysis compare with your gut feeling from Exercise 16? What might go wrong if you relied on your gut feeling in determining system feasibility? List your assumptions on a separate page.

19. For the situation you chose in Exercise 6, either buying a network of PCs for a department at your workplace or outfitting a laboratory of PCs for students at a university, use the outline for the baseline project plan provided in Figure 5.24 to complete Items A–C of Section 4.0, Management Issues, of the baseline project plan report. Why might people sometimes feel that these additional steps in the project plan are a waste of time? What would you say to them to convince them that these steps are important? List your assumptions on a separate page.

20. Different organizations use different formats for defining a project's charter. Search the Web (e.g., search using the keywords *project charter template*) and contrast at least four different templates. What is similar? What is unique? Is there one best way to define a project's charter?

21. Using the information you gathered in Exercise 20, develop your own best-practices project charter template.

22. Different organizations use different formats for defining a project's scope statement. Search the Web (e.g., search using the keywords *project scope statement template*) and contrast at least four different templates. What is similar? What is unique? Is there one best way to define a project's scope statement?

23. Using the information you gathered in Exercise 22, develop your own best-practices project scope statement template.

24. In what ways is a request to change the scope of an information system handled differently from a request for a new information system? In what ways are they the same?

25. Describe a personal situation in which you experienced scope creep. Your example does not have to be a technology-oriented project.

CHAPTER CASE

Sedona Management Group and Managing Project Scope

Over the last ten years, Sedona Management Group (SMG) has not missed an agreed-to deadline on any contract related to a development project they've undertaken. Given the statistics on project failures we have discussed so far in this book, this is rather astounding. Tim Turnpaugh attributes this success to the company's core competency, great project management. He recognizes that one of the most important and difficult aspects of project management is scope management, which involves defining and controlling what is or is not included in the project. For that reason, Turnpaugh dedicates a great deal of time to project initiation, which includes deciding what projects to pursue and then defining their scope.

At SMG, primary goals of scope management are to ensure that the project team and the customer have the same understanding of the project deliverables and that the deliverables are reasonable given budget and time constraints. The first step in managing scope is deciding what projects to pursue. What does the Sedona team look for in potential clients? Turnpaugh prefers to work for customers who come at a project with an aggressive attitude—where the company is willing to think outside the box and not be constrained by what has been accomplished in the past. In addition, over the last 10 years SMG has built a solid reputation through word-of-mouth, and Turnpaugh avoids projects that might detract from that reputation. First, SMG stays away from projects in certain industries—for example, the adult entertainment industry. Second, the team prefers not to develop systems for customers who can't develop a clear vision of what they want to accomplish but rather want a system simply because everyone else has one. Third, Turnpaugh avoids customers that have low interest and motivation in the project because this may lead to downstream problems related to Web site maintenance—which ultimately may reflect poorly on the Sedona team. Finally, the team will not undertake a project for a customer who is not willing to be highly accessible during the various project phases because SMG feels such communication is critical to project success.

Turnpaugh states that in the project initiation phase, it is not uncommon for the customer to be somewhat vague in terms of what they're trying to achieve from the systems development effort. For this reason, it is essential to spend sufficient time with the customer on needs analysis. Using his personal knowledge and guided by a set of standard questions, Turnpaugh helped the Seattle Seahawks identify their needs, determine the market they are trying to tap, and in some cases, expand on that vision with new possibilities. One past client approached SMG with the idea of promoting a fitness chain. In the past, the target market for this industry may have involved males interested in weight training, but this firm wanted to target average individuals—particularly women—who wanted a place to exercise with a wide range of aerobic and strength-training options. Given this potential audience, the resultant Web site needed to include attributes that would appeal to women and entire families rather than just men. Not only does the content in such a site differ—for example, the Web site might need to include information on such amenities as daycare—but the physical design of the site also might need to be substantially different.

Another central aspect of project selection involves understanding the customer's budget for the project.

Based on past experience, Turnpaugh knows how to price projects to be both profitable and attractive to the customer. In many cases, SMG likes to take a phased approach—that is, work on a simple Web site for a customer initially and then eventually make improvements to that existing Web site as the relationship with the customer develops over time. Turnpaugh refers to these kinds of projects as multiphase projects.

If necessary, the Sedona team will go through several iterations to make sure the customer's needs are understood. To accurately determine the duration and the cost of the project, Turnpaugh says that a tight scope is needed. In all instances, SMG likes to take projects one step at a time. Turnpaugh likens this to flying an airplane. A pilot can't worry about every event that might go wrong during a flight, but rather needs to focus on doing the current task correctly. Similarly, in the initiation phase of the project, the focus is on understanding the customer's needs.

Once a clear understanding of the project scope is gained, a project scope statement is developed. The scope statement forms part of the contract that will be drafted for the customer and ensures that both the Sedona team and the customer have a common understanding of project scope. The scope statement includes a detailed description of the project's product, a summary of all project deliverables (e.g., database and codes), and a statement of what determines project success. Anything beyond what is mentioned in the scope statement is a change order, which would entail longer project duration and an additional charge.

Through Sedona's interactions with the Seattle Seahawks, Turnpaugh determined that the organization met all of his requirements for potential clients. In interacting with Seahawks representative Mike Flood, Turnpaugh was immediately impressed with Flood's desire to not simply duplicate what other NFL teams were doing but to think about the purpose and opportunities that a Web site could provide. The Seahawks' Web site goes beyond providing simple information about the team but, rather, attempts to engage fans in a variety of interactive capabilities that continue to be enhanced. Despite this ongoing development, the original system was carefully scoped to meet the Seahawks organization's needs, as well as be achievable within Sedona's typical project lifecycle.

CHAPTER 5 PROJECT ASSIGNMENT

An entertainment Web site should present value to fans through its contents and features. Therefore, these features must be developed properly to assure that the consumer is satisfied with the experience. The first step in the design process of your entertainment Web site is to examine several existing entertainers' Web sites. This is an important stage of this project to get a feel for the best practices. This analysis also shows common trends in entertainment sites. It can be used to determine the types of materials and features that users come to expect from sites such as the one to be designed.

This activity requires you to do an inventory of existing entertainment Web sites.

1. Find and examine four different entertainment Web sites (these could include sports personalities, musicians, actors/actresses, sports teams).
2. For each Web site, create a bulleted list of features or characteristics that it employs (e.g., biographical data, interaction with other users, media clips, merchandise access, access to entertainment, technolo-gies used, etc.). Also include a short definition of the feature. Note: You should easily compile 20 or more features.
3. Indicate the relative importance of the criteria by assigning a weight to each. Please note that the weights should sum to 1.0 or 100%.
4. Determine how well each site used each of its features (i.e., through a critical examination of each site, decide what scores you give each entertainment/entertainer site on the features you came up with).
5. Following the example shown, create a weighted scoring table by multiplying each of the entertainment scores by the weight and determining an analysis score.

Criteria	Weight	Web Site 1	Web Site 2	. . .	Web Site n
Criteria 1 (e.g., Ease of use)	0.20	5	2	. . .	2
Criteria 2 (e.g., Merchandise availability)	0.10	1	4	. . .	4
Feature 3 (e.g., Entertainer bio availability)	0	1	2	. . .	
. . . .	. . .	. . .	. . .	. . .	. . .
Feature n (e.g., Interaction with entertainer)	0.5	5	5	. . .	5
Analysis Score	Should add to 1.0	$(0.2\times5)+(0.1\times1)$ $+(0\times1)+(0.5\times5)$ $= 3.6$	$(0.2\times2)+(0.1\times4)$ $+(0\times2)+(0.5\times5)$ $= 3.3$	. . .	ditto

6. Choose an entertainer for whom you would like to design a site. You can redesign a bad entertainment site you reviewed, or you can develop an entirely new site.
7. Develop your project charter. Typical parts of a project charter might include:
   - Project name
   - Project sponsor
   - Assigned project manager
   - Project team members and their role in the project
   - Statement of purpose (i.e., overarching goals, including what entertainer you are focusing on)
   - Statement of features, including
     - What features seem to be important for entertainment Web sites?
     - What features seem to be less important?
     - Do certain features seem to be more appropriate for different types of celebrities?
     - Are some features incompatible (e.g., if you do one thing, should you not do another)?
   - Statement of objectives (i.e., specific high-level project deliverables)
   - Stakeholders
   - A basic statement of how the team will approach the work
   - Authorized project resources (i.e., people, budget—for your case the budget may be based on hours, and you can assign a base rate to all of your work)
   - Technology you are going to use for the Web site
   - Site map, describing the various pages your site will contain and how they are related (This is a nested list showing the layout of the pages, that is, the main pages and subpages.)
   - Screen mock-ups (essentially, samples of what your screens will look like, easily done in Microsoft PowerPoint)
   - Basic project timeline (which can be substantially refined in the project plan to follow)

REFERENCES

Applegate, L. M., Austin, R. D., and McFarlan, F. W. (2007). *Corporate Information Strategy and Management: The Challenges of Managing in a Network Economy* (7th ed.). Boston: Irwin/McGraw-Hill.

Atkinson, R. A. (1990). "The Motivations for Strategic Planning." *Journal of Information Systems Management* 7(4), 53–56.

Burry, C. (2003). Increasing Value from Fixed IT Costs. *Computerworld*, March 4, www.computerworld.com/managementtopics/roi/story/0,10801,78025,00.html.

Carlson, C. K., Gardner, E. P., and Ruth, S. R. (1989). Technology-Driven Long-Range Planning. *Journal of Information Systems Management* 6(3), 24–29.

DeGiglio, M. (2002). Measure for Measure: The Value of IT. www.cio.com, June 17, information verified April 2, 2006.

Dewan, S., Michael, S. C., and Min, C. K. (1998). Firm Characteristics and Investments in Information Technology: Scale and Scope Effects." *Information Systems Research* 9(3), 219–232.

Hoffer, J. A., George, J. F., and Valacich, J. S. (2007). *Modern Systems Analysis and Design* (5th ed.). Upper Saddle River, NJ: Prentice Hall.

IBM. (1982). Business Systems Planning. In *Advanced System Development/Feasibility Techniques*, Couger, J. D., Colter, M. A., and Knapp, R. W. (eds.). New York: Wiley, 236–314.

Kapur, G. K. (2004). Intelligent Disobedience. *Computerworld*, March 30, www.computerworld.com/careertopics/careers/story/0,10801,95504,00.html.

King, J. L., and Schrems, E. (1978). Cost Benefit Analysis in Information Systems Development and Operation. *ACM Computing Surveys* 10(1), 19–34.

Kirsch, L. J. (2000). Software Project Management: An Integrated Perspective for an Emerging Paradigm. In *Framing the Domains of IT Management: Projecting the Future from the Past*, Zmud, R. W. (ed.). Cincinnati: Pinnaflex Educational Resources, 285–304.

Lederer, A. L., and Prasad, J. (1992). Nine Management Guidelines for Better Cost Estimating. *Communications of the ACM* 35(2), 51–59.

Luftman, J. N. (2004). *Managing the Information Technology Resource*. With Bullen, C. V., Liao, D., Nash, E., and Neumann, C. Upper Saddle River, NJ: Prentice Hall.

McKeen, J. D., Guimaraes, T., and Wetherbe, J. C. (1994). A Comparative Analysis of MIS Project Selection Mechanisms. *Data Base* 25 (February), 43–59.

Melymuka, K. (2004). Harrah's: Betting on IT Value. *ComputerWorld*, May 3. www.computerworld.com/managementtopics/roi/story/0,10801,92759,00.html.

Parker, M. M., and Benson, R. J. (1989). Enterprisewide Information Management: State-of-the-Art Strategic Planning." *Journal of Information Systems Management* 6 (Summer), 14–23.

PMBOK (2004). *A Guide to the Project Management Body of Knowledge* (3rd ed.). Newtown Square, PA: Project Management Institute.

Porter, M. (1980). *Competitive Strategy: Techniques for Analyzing Industries and Competitors*. New York: Free Press.

Porter, M. (1985). *Competitive Advantage*. New York: Free Press.

Pressman, R. S. (2005). *Software Engineering* (6th ed.). New York: McGraw-Hill.

Printer, H. (2004). When—and When Not—to Offshore. *ComputerWorld*, November 8, www.computerworld.com/developmenttopics/development/story/0,10801,97273,00.html.

Ross, J., and Feeny, D. (2000). The Evolving Role of the CIO. In *Framing the Domains of IT Management: Projecting the Future from the Past*, Zmud, R. W. (ed.). Cincinnati, OH: Pinnaflex Educational Resources, 385–402.

Ruriani, D. C. (2003). Outsmarting Scope Creep. Inboundlogistics.com, May, www.inboundlogistics.com/articles/10tips/10tips0503.shtml.

Segars, A. H., and Grover, V. (1999). Profiles of Strategic Information Systems Planning. *Information Systems Planning* 10(3), 199–232.

Shank, J. K., and Govindarajan, V. (1993). *Strategic Cost Management*. New York: Free Press.

Thibodeau, P. (2004). Internal Resistance Can Doom Offshore Projects. *ComputerWorld*, January 26, www.computerworld.com/careertopics/careers/story/0,10801,89364,00.html.

Chapter

Managing Project Scheduling

Opening Case: Dan McDonald

Consider the plight of Dan McDonald. Dan was called upon by management to lead a new project to develop an inventory control system (see Figure 6.1). Although a 20-year veteran of the company's information technology department, he had no formal training in project management. As a further complication, the system had to be developed in time for next year's holiday season. How was Dan to define the activities associated with the development of the new system? What about the sequence of the activities? How was he to know how long each activity should take? In addition, what resources would he need, and how could he assign those resources to each activity?

LEARNING OBJECTIVES

After reading this chapter, you will be able to:

➤ Provide an overview of project scheduling, including its importance and the challenges associated with it.
➤ Describe project scheduling techniques, such as the Work Breakdown Structure, Activity Definition, and Activity Sequencing.
➤ Describe how project management software packages can help with project scheduling.

206

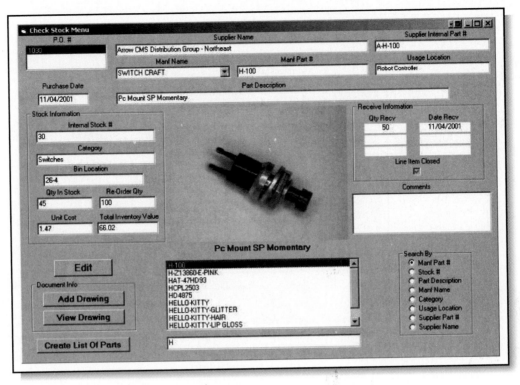

Figure 6.1 Inventory control system

Source: Reproduced with permission from www.DynamicControlSoftware.com

INTRODUCTION

Project scheduling
The process of defining project activities, determining their sequence, and estimating their duration.

In the planning phase of any project, scheduling is a crucial activity. **Project scheduling** is the process of defining project activities, determining their sequence, and estimating their duration (see Figure 6.2). To successfully complete a project, the project manager must be aware of all the activities the project entails. The project management team manages and tracks these activities through a process of decomposition, meaning that the entire project is broken down into more manageable and controllable parts. This decomposition is captured in the work breakdown structure (briefly introduced in the last chapter). Thus, a project manager follows a "divide and conquer" strategy of breaking down a project into components that can be managed and controlled more easily than the project in its entirety.

Once the project's components are determined, the project management team establishes a sequence for doing the work associated with them. To help determine how to sequence these activities, the project manager considers technical constraints, safety or efficiency concerns, policies, the availability of resources, and the need to begin some tasks only after others are completed. Scheduling tools, such as network diagrams, help the project manager visualize the result of this planning process; project management software packages assist by offering powerful tools to create, maintain, and update these charts.

In addition to defining and sequencing activities, another important facet of project scheduling is assigning resources to those activities. In most cases, resource availability plays a major role in determining the duration of a project. This chapter focuses on how to define and sequence project activities. The aspects of project time

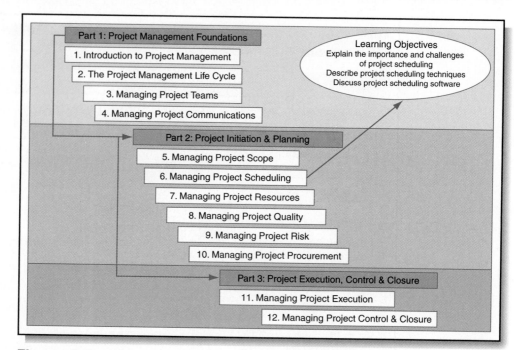

Figure 6.2 Information systems project management focusing on managing project scheduling

management involving resource estimation and allocation, as well as the management of those resources, are discussed in Chapter 7.

This chapter's opening section provides a brief overview of the importance and challenges associated with project scheduling. The subsequent section discusses specific techniques for breaking down a complex project into more manageable components and then determining the sequence of activities for accomplishing those components. The first step in this process is the creation of a work breakdown structure (WBS), a chart detailing the project's specific components. The second step is determining what activities are needed to complete those project components. The third step is to determine how to sequence these activities. Throughout this discussion we will highlight the different types of diagrams used to graphically represent project schedules, their benefits and drawbacks, and how project management software can help with the different project scheduling activities.

THE IMPORTANCE AND CHALLENGES OF PROJECT SCHEDULING

A project schedule is generally created early in the project, specifically during the initiation and planning phases. However, schedules are used in the execution phase to offer guidance to the project team and, further, are often updated to incorporate project changes. Schedules are also important in the control phase, when they are often used for project tracking (see Figure 6.3). Although scheduling may seem mundane, its importance to the success of the project cannot be overstated. Without a clearly established project schedule, managers cannot accurately plan activities or,

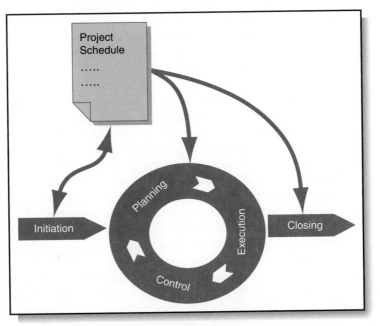

Figure 6.3 Project scheduling and the project management processes

for that matter, track those activities to determine if the project is proceeding as planned—an aspect of project control.

In a recent survey, project managers were asked to identify the top five challenges of project management (see Table 6.1). The top challenge mentioned was lack of clarity about the scope of the project (BIA, 2005). This challenge is directly related to project scheduling. When project managers, in close cooperation with project team members and the project sponsor, create schedules that clearly characterize project activities, they are better prepared to define accurately the project's scope.

Schedules are rarely perfect because of the very difficult task of accounting for all potential problems. Project managers often find themselves in the unenviable position of having to modify project schedules on the fly to address circumstances that were unforeseen during the original schedule development. This is particularly problematic in organizations that compete in rapidly changing business environments. As business conditions or technology change, the project manager is frequently faced with new and unanticipated challenges. Although a project schedule should serve as the fundamental guide to successfully completing a project, project managers must also realize that these schedules may frequently need to be updated as the project progresses. For example, the loss of a talented systems developer after the project has already started

Table 6.1 Top Five Project Management Challenges

1. Lack of clarity in scope of the project
2. Shifting organizational priorities
3. Project changes not well managed
4. A lack of project management skills
5. Training of project sponsors

may require an adjustment of the project schedule. It is also important to realize that project schedules may be created for different purposes (for internal management of project effort or for communicating with other stakeholders). Internal schedules may contain greater details on tasks and assignments. External schedules may be more general and may even have buffers built in to account for unexpected delays.

The PMBOK highlights the importance of project scheduling as part of Project Time Management. **Project Time Management** (see Figure 6.4) includes the processes of activity definition and activity sequencing (which we discuss in this chapter), as well as the processes of activity resource estimating, activity duration estimating, schedule development (all discussed in Chapter 7), and schedule control (discussed in Chapter 12). Project Time Management is seen as a series of processes that interact not only with each other but also with other key knowledge areas and the overall project management life cycle.

As a project moves forward, estimations of the time needed to accomplish project components become progressively more accurate. Along with describing the WBS, which serves as the basis for Project Time Management processes, this chapter will focus on the processes of activity definition and activity sequencing.

This process of gradually moving toward more accurate estimates was originally reported by Barry Boehm (1981) and is referred to as a **cone of uncertainty.** The cone of uncertainty graphically represents the uncertainty of early project time estimations, as well as the growing accuracy of these estimations as the project moves farther along (see Figure 6.5). The PMI presents a similar view of the progressive accuracy of project estimates, which it discusses in terms of decreasing variability in estimates. According to the PMI, projects progress through different estimation phases, including *order of magnitude estimates*—important but inexact estimates occurring very early in a project's life cycle—that may be used to justify a project's consideration. These early estimates may vary by as much as +75 percent to –25 percent. *Budgetary estimates*, which occur later as the various project components are specified in greater detail, may vary only from +25 percent to –10 percent. Finally, *definitive estimates* for a project, developed when the project's resources and activities are highly detailed, may vary only from +10 percent to –5 percent. In both the cone of uncertainty and PMI's progressive estimates, greater knowledge about project costs and schedules is represented as project plans become more detailed.

Technological advances and specific types of scheduling software have had an enormous impact on the ability of managers to handle increasingly complex projects. For example, Web-based network technology now allows project managers to manage schedules across time and space with considerably less effort than would have been required 10 years ago. Using Web-based technology, managers can post a schedule that can be viewed by others involved in the project, and problem areas can quickly be identified and addressed. As remote activities are completed, remote managers can enter that information into the Web-based schedule, providing a vehicle for almost real-time feedback to senior project managers. Complementing Web-based network infrastructures or providing stand-alone project scheduling functionality, scheduling software increases the project managers' ability to manage complex projects.

Scheduling also involves the consideration of team resources, another major focus of this textbook. For instance, when developing project schedules and eventually determining project duration, the assignment of various types of resources (discussed further in Chapter 7) is critical to successful project management processes. One type of resource is personnel, both the project team and human resources external to the team. All of the team management techniques discussed in Chapter 3 are, thus, very important considerations during project scheduling.

Project time management
The reiteration of the processes of activity definition, sequencing, and duration estimation as part of schedule development.

Cone of uncertainty
A progressively more detailed and accurate projection of the project schedule and duration as the project manager or project team specifies project deliverables and activities in more detail.

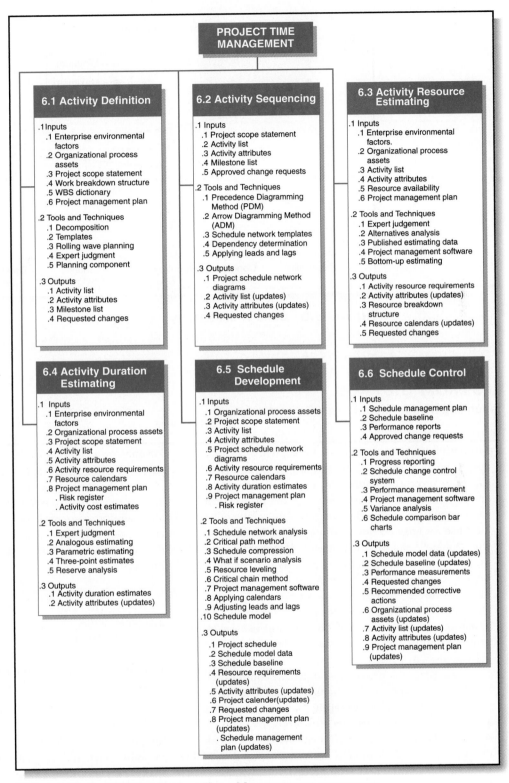

PROJECT TIME MANAGEMENT

6.1 Activity Definition

.1 Inputs
  .1 Enterprise environmental factors
  .2 Organizational process assets
  .3 Project scope statement
  .4 Work breakdown structure
  .5 WBS dictionary
  .6 Project management plan

.2 Tools and Techniques
  .1 Decomposition
  .2 Templates
  .3 Rolling wave planning
  .4 Expert judgment
  .5 Planning component

.3 Outputs
  .1 Activity list
  .2 Activity attributes
  .3 Milestone list
  .4 Requested changes

6.2 Activity Sequencing

.1 Inputs
  .1 Project scope statement
  .2 Activity list
  .3 Activity attributes
  .4 Milestone list
  .5 Approved change requests

.2 Tools and Techniques
  .1 Precedence Diagramming Method (PDM)
  .2 Arrow Diagramming Method (ADM)
  .3 Schedule network templates
  .4 Dependency determination
  .5 Applying leads and lags

.3 Outputs
  .1 Project schedule network diagrams
  .2 Activity list (updates)
  .3 Activity attributes (updates)
  .4 Requested changes

6.3 Activity Resource Estimating

.1 Inputs
  .1 Enterprise environmental factors.
  .2 Organizational process assets
  .3 Activity list
  .4 Activity attributes
  .5 Resource availability
  .6 Project management plan

.2 Tools and Techniques
  .1 Expert judgement
  .2 Alternatives analysis
  .3 Published estimating data
  .4 Project management software
  .5 Bottom-up estimating

.3 Outputs
  .1 Activity resource requirements
  .2 Activity attributes (updates)
  .3 Resource breakdown structure
  .4 Resource calendars (updates)
  .5 Requested changes

6.4 Activity Duration Estimating

.1 Inputs
  .1 Enterprise environmental factors
  .2 Organizational process assets
  .3 Project scope statement
  .4 Activity list
  .5 Activity attributes
  .6 Activity resource requirements
  .7 Resource calendars
  .8 Project management plan
    . Risk register
    . Activity cost estimates

.2 Tools and Techniques
  .1 Expert judgment
  .2 Analogous estimating
  .3 Parametric estimating
  .4 Three-point estimates
  .5 Reserve analysis

.3 Outputs
  .1 Activity duration estimates
  .2 Activity attributes (updates)

6.5 Schedule Development

.1 Inputs
  .1 Organizational process assets
  .2 Project scope statement
  .3 Activity list
  .4 Activity attributes
  .5 Project schedule network diagrams
  .6 Activity resource requirements
  .7 Resource calendars
  .8 Activity duration estimates
  .9 Project management plan
    . Risk register

.2 Tools and Techniques
  .1 Schedule network analysis
  .2 Critical path method
  .3 Schedule compression
  .4 What if scenario analysis
  .5 Resource leveling
  .6 Critical chain method
  .7 Project management software
  .8 Applying calendars
  .9 Adjusting leads and lags
  .10 Schedule model

.3 Outputs
  .1 Project schedule
  .2 Schedule model data
  .3 Schedule baseline
  .4 Resource requirements (updates)
  .5 Activity attributes (updates)
  .6 Project calender(updates)
  .7 Requested changes
  .8 Project management plan (updates)
    . Schedule management plan (updates)

6.6 Schedule Control

.1 Inputs
  .1 Schedule management plan
  .2 Schedule baseline
  .3 Performance reports
  .4 Approved change requests

.2 Tools and Techniques
  .1 Progress reporting
  .2 Schedule change control system
  .3 Performance measurement
  .4 Project management software
  .5 Variance analysis
  .6 Schedule comparison bar charts

.3 Outputs
  .1 Schedule model data (updates)
  .2 Schedule baseline (updates)
  .3 Performance measurements
  .4 Requested changes
  .5 Recommended corrective actions
  .6 Organizational process assets (updates)
  .7 Activity list (updates)
  .8 Activity attributes (updates)
  .9 Project management plan (updates)

Figure 6.4 PMBOK Project Time Management processes

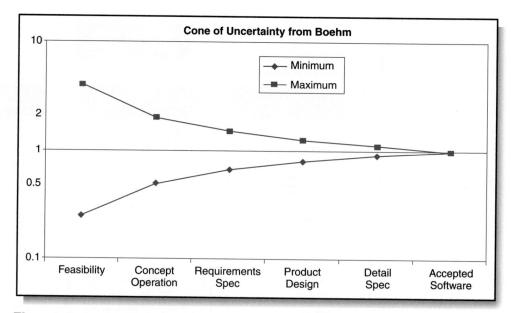

Figure 6.5 Cone of uncertainty

TIPS FROM THE PROS
Debunking Myths About Project Estimation

Estimating the time necessary to complete a project, despite being an imperfect science, is still an important aspect of project management. Project stakeholders are always concerned about whether the project will come in on time (and under budget), and usually have little use for answers such as "maybe" or "probably". Unfortunately, stakeholders usually demand accurate estimates precisely at the time (e.g., early in the project life cycle) when such estimates are likely to be the most inaccurate. After all, it would be nearly impossible to obtain support for a project without some sort of estimation as to time and budget, and useless to provide highly accurate estimates when all project deliverables have been completed.

Over time, the project management community has developed some assumptions believed to increase the quality of estimates. Recently, these project management practices were reconsidered by Phillip Armour (2002) in an article entitled "Ten Unmyths of Project Estimation." Armour described an unmyth as a commonly held truth that is simply not true. Armour's ten unmyths of project estimation are:

1. *We can have accurate estimates.* The "accuracy" assumption should be tempered by what we know of the cone of uncertainty, but we should also be aware that an estimate is still an estimate, and therefore contains an assumption of possible error. Logically, this makes little sense because this would indicate that we're committing to a probability.

2. *The job of estimating is to come up with a date for completion.* The "end date" assumption assumes that when we estimate a time frame, we're estimating the date that the project will be finished. This is problematic because we're not predicting a specific time frame; we're predicting the *probability* that we'll complete the project within a certain time frame.

3. *The estimate and the commitment are the same.* The "end date" assumption leads to the "commitment" assumption where people confuse the estimate of an end date and commitment to the estimate.

4. *A project estimate is dependent on the size of the final system.* The assumption that the estimate is dependent on the size of the final system is partly true: On average, larger systems take longer to complete than smaller ones. However, some large projects may not take very long if the system is similar to another that the project manager or organization has completed in the past.

5. *Historical data is an accurate indicator of productivity.* The historical data assumption is partly true in that previous experience from previous projects provides information about how long activities will take. However, the current project is not the same as the previous project no matter how much it appears to be so, and in fact, most companies hope past experience may speed things up for future projects.

6. *Productivity is an accurate indicator of project duration.* Productivity as an indicator of project duration is also problematic, since in many cases productivity might be measured by the speed with which we can build something, without accounting for the quality or what we're building.

7. *Lines of code count is a good way to size a system.* Lines of code (LOC) may not provide a good metric for sizing a system because the quantity of lines may not represent the complexity of a system. For estimation purposes, the size of the system should be related to the amount of knowledge that must be obtained and the difficulty of obtaining such knowledge. We wouldn't measure how much knowledge is in a book by weighing it, so why do we assume that several million lines of code *couldn't* be written to accomplish simple tasks?

8. *Function points are a good way to size a system.* Similar to the logic use in LOC estimations, the use of function points—a popular method used to gauge the size and complexity of a system based on quantifying the functionality provided by a user—suffers similarly. This may be particularly true in modern development environments making greater use of code reuse from past applications. In this case, great functionality may exist but the application may be less complex to build.

9. *We can get the system faster by assigning more resources.* Adding people to hasten project completion is still one of the most common mistakes project teams make. While it would seem that the resources assigned to a project should have a direct bearing on the speed at which project tasks are completed, the relationship is actually more complicated than this. Different skill sets among participants, the ability to have a common understanding of both the problem and the solution, and the overhead of managing more resources may all contribute to delaying project completion rather than hastening it. This idea was ably captured in *The Mythical Man-Month: Essays on Software Engineering*, in which author Fred Brooks posited that adding manpower to a late software project simply makes it later (Brooks, 1995).

10. *Given enough time, we can create a defect-free system.* The assumption that we can create defect-free systems is also problematic. While we may strive for a defect-free end product, this may be an unreachable goal. Humans have a finite capacity for knowledge, and it is impossible for a project team to anticipate every conceivable variable that might affect the system.

Recognizing these assumptions is the first step toward overcoming them. Armour (2002) provides some tips regarding the issues raised previously:

- *Accuracy.* Strive for estimates that are accurate enough to not make bad decisions.
- *End-date.* Define estimate outputs as a range of probabilities for given dates.
- *Commitment.* Establish processes with discrete estimate and commitment stages.
- *History.* Recognize that historical data may not be relevant. Think of it as an indicator, rather than as a predictor.
- *Productivity.* Recognize this assumption. Think of it as an indicator rather than a predictor.
- *Lines of Code.* Recognize this assumption, and try to find a better metric that represents knowledge.
- *Function Points.* Recognize this assumption. As above, try to determine a better method for measuring knowledge.
- *More People.* Be attentive to a critical mass of people and that adding more can hinder productivity.
- *Defect Free.* Set goals for quality, develop estimates that will allow achievement of quality goals realistically, realizing the goal is to satisfy the customer, not necessarily achieve perfection.

While the creation of the project schedule generally occurs early in the project—specifically during the initiation and planning phases—schedules are used during the execution phase to offer guidance to the project team and are often updated to incorporate project changes. Schedules are also important in the control phase, where they are used for project tracking and managing project changes. They are further used to determine whether the project is progressing successfully. We now discuss some specific techniques for managing project schedules.

TECHNIQUES FOR MANAGING PROJECT SCHEDULES

Quite often, a complex task might seem overwhelming. A common analogy used in project management is, "How does one eat an elephant?" The answer is, "One bite at a time." For example, professors often assign term papers that might be 25 to 50 pages long. A student might make this task less daunting by dividing it into smaller parts, such as doing background reading, writing an outline, adding the details to the individual sections, and finally, proofreading and editing the paper (see Figure 6.6). Each of those tasks is much more specific and easier to accomplish than the overall project of writing a term paper.

Similarly, project managers will divide an entire project into discrete activities in order to set up a schedule. Representing a project as discrete activities allows them to more easily allocate time and resources, and thus better estimate how long each of the activities will take. This process of breaking up work tasks or components to make them more easily manageable is termed **decomposition**. Decomposition is used at various stages of project scheduling. For example, decomposition is used to create the work breakdown structure (discussed later), which results in defining the various components that make up the entire project. Further, the decomposition

Decomposition
The process of subdividing tasks to make them more easily manageable.

Figure 6.6 One way to make a term paper more manageable

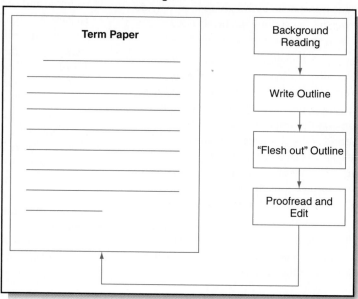

process is also used to break down these components into the activities necessary to complete them. The next sections discuss the work breakdown structure, describing its inputs, tools and techniques, and outputs in detail.

Creating a Work Breakdown Structure (WBS)

A complex product, like almost anything else, can be divided into smaller, less complex parts. Consider a personal computer, which can be decomposed into a large number of small, distinct components, such as a motherboard, a power supply and fans, the central processing unit, storage devices, and ports for plugging in peripheral devices. These major components can be further broken down into distinct subcomponents. One component, the computer's storage, can be further decomposed into primary and secondary storage. Primary storage can be broken down into RAM (volatile) and ROM (nonvolatile). Similarly, secondary storage can be decomposed into magnetic and optical storage. Magnetic storage can be broken down into hard drives and floppy disk drives; optical storage can be decomposed into CD or DVD drives. The list of components that make up a larger product is sometimes referred to as a **product breakdown structure** (PBS). A PBS shows a product's components in a hierarchical fashion, comparable to an organizational chart or a family tree (see Figure 6.7). The PMBOK refers to the PBS as the bill of materials (BOM).

A **work breakdown structure** (WBS) is based on a similar concept. Like the product breakdown structure, a work breakdown structure describes the components needed to create the overall project. Unlike the product breakdown structure, a work breakdown structure's purpose is not to provide a bill of materials but, rather, to serve as an aid in illustrating the project's scope and as a launching point for describing the activities necessary for creating the various subcomponents of the project. To distinguish between a PBS and a WBS, the latter might include a system requirements

Product breakdown structure (PBS)
The output from the process of dividing a product into its individual components.

Work breakdown structure (WBS)
The output that results from the process of dividing the entire project into manageable tasks (usually presented as a hierarchical chart or in tabular form).

Figure 6.7 Product breakdown structure for a personal computer

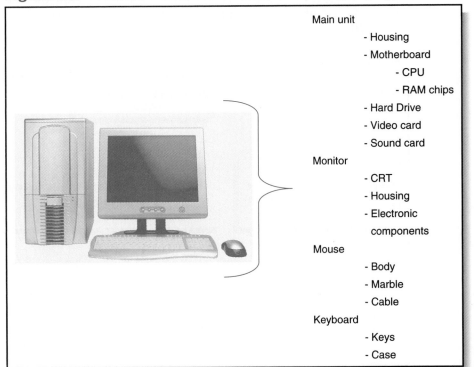

Main unit
- Housing
- Motherboard
    - CPU
    - RAM chips
- Hard Drive
- Video card
- Sound card

Monitor
- CRT
- Housing
- Electronic
  components

Mouse
- Body
- Marble
- Cable

Keyboard
- Keys
- Case

analysis which documents the desired functionality of a system. This would fall outside the scope of a sub-component of the product itself that might be documented in a PBS. The WBS is used in a variety of project activities that we'll discuss in more detail in other chapters, including scope definition, costing, estimating, budgeting, and scheduling. The WBS plays a central role in the overall success of a project. Work breakdown structures can be presented in both hierarchical fashion and tabular form.

This process of identifying all of the deliverables necessary to complete the project is the first step in project scheduling. These deliverables are then decomposed into smaller and smaller deliverables. As an example, think for a moment about what it would take to build a custom home and its relationship to the concept of the WBS. There are many steps in building a home, including pouring the foundation, erecting and insulating the walls, installing electrical and plumbing components, putting on the roof, putting shingles on the roof, finishing all wall surfaces both inside and out, and inspecting the final product. A WBS representing the creation of a home (the overall project outcome or goal) would thus involve major deliverables such as the foundation, the walls, the plumbing and electrical systems, the roof, and so forth. Obviously all of these major deliverables could also be further decomposed as well. For example, the foundation might include wood framing, smoothed cement, conduits for plumbing and electrical systems, and other components. The WBS is thus a technique for iteratively decomposing a project into subcomponents, which eventually (when at a sufficiently decomposed level) can be used to specify the individual activities necessary to produce the project outcome.

Many project managers regard a WBS as being oriented toward deliverables; as a result, they see all of the WBS components as objects (e.g., wood framing for a house's foundation). These objects are then created through activities, such as buying wood, measuring wood, cutting wood, laying out the frame, and the like (see this chapter's section on Activity Definition). Such activities usually have verb phrase labels (e.g., *cut* wood for framing), so they are often not considered to be part of the WBS. In contrast, other project managers view the WBS as composed not of objects, but of the activities themselves, always referring to the components of the WBS as tasks (e.g., creating a program module, as opposed to the program module

Figure 6.8 Work breakdown structure

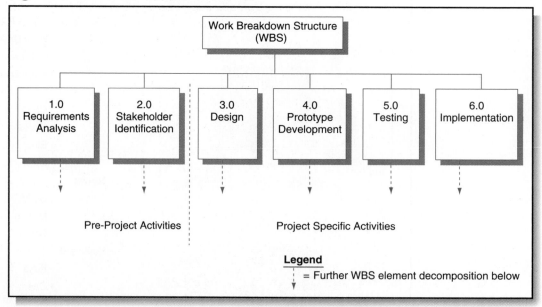

itself). While opinions vary, one argument for separating the deliverables (as objects) from the activities needed to produce them is that such a method gives the "doers" more freedom about how to produce the deliverable (Berg and Colenso, 2000), which may have positive organizational effects. This book, therefore, treats the components of the WBS as deliverable-oriented and then examines the work necessary to create the deliverable in the activity definition phase. Keep in mind, however, that the WBS is a tool that should serve *you*; thus, if your project (or organization) prefers a work-oriented WBS, then you should take that approach.

WBS Inputs

Project managers creating a WBS rely on a variety of sources to determine how to decompose the entire project. In addition to the project scope management plan, the primary input of this process is the project scope statement (see Chapter 5). This statement covers the essence of the project by specifying the nature of the final deliverable as well as the broad steps necessary to complete the project. Other inputs can be the project manager's experiences with similar projects, organizational process assets (such as internal policies, procedures, or guidelines), or approved changes to the project scope statement.

WBS Tools and Techniques

The primary technique for building a WBS is the process of decomposition. This decomposition process of breaking up a large project into smaller parts can proceed until the desired level of detail is reached. Typically, the entire project (level 0) is broken down into its major deliverables, which are then further decomposed until the work packages are reached at the lowest level of each branch of the WBS. Whereas some components need to be decomposed only into one or two levels, others might need more levels; thus, depending on the complexity of the major objectives, there might be several levels before the work package level is reached. During the planning stage, especially in projects of longer duration, a project management team might not be able to decompose some of the project's later components. In this case, the team defers breaking down these components until the components are further clarified, and the decomposition takes place as the project progresses, a process called **rolling wave planning**. Usually, the project team and the customer are involved in creating the WBS to arrive at a clear understanding of what must be done to finish the project. Further, it often helps to use the expertise of the "doers," that is, the people executing the different activities, because these people have a good understanding of what needs to be done at a more detailed level. During decomposition, an owner should be assigned to each component of the WBS; the owner will be ultimately responsible for completing the deliverable.

After the major deliverables are identified, they should be structured and organized in the WBS. Following that, major deliverables (which correspond to the higher levels of the WBS) need to be further decomposed into lower-level deliverables. Once the individual components have been assigned unique codes (usually in an outline number format, which clearly shows the component's level and which branch of the "tree" it belongs to), the project manager has to assess whether or not the components have been sufficiently broken down to provide enough detail at the lower levels. Care has to be taken that each higher-level deliverable is the sum of all the lower-level deliverables on the same branch, so that each higher-level component contains only the lower-level components needed to complete it, nothing more and nothing less. The following paragraphs describe decomposing a project in more detail.

Different strategies for determining the higher-level deliverables in the WBS can be employed. For example, the entire project can be broken down according to the major deliverables, phases of the project life cycle, functional areas, or a combination

Rolling wave planning
A scheduling technique in which the team defers breaking down components until they are further clarified, and the decomposition takes place as the project progresses.

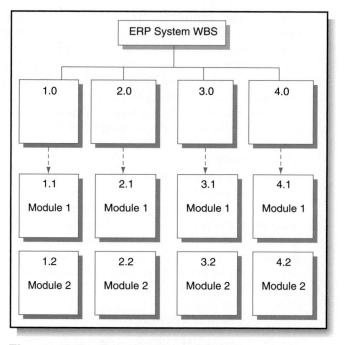

Figure 6.9 Sample work breakdown structure for an ERP system

of these. As an example, Figure 6.9 can be used to represent the WBS for an enterprise resource planning (ERP) system, where the entire project is represented at level 0. Level 1 would then represent the different modules (such as accounting, finance, human resources, and so on) in the ERP. These level 1 modules could then be further broken down to include the subdeliverables needed for their completion.

Another method is to use the phases of the systems development life cycle (SDLC) or project life cycle as level 1 deliverables. This method has the advantage of assisting in sequencing the different activities in later phases of the planning stage. An example of a WBS oriented around a modified SDLC for an ERP system is illustrated in Figure 6.10. Once the major deliverables have been identified, they should be represented in the WBS in a logical order to make interpreting the final WBS easier.

At the next level (level 2 in Figure 6.10), the deliverables identified in the previous step would be decomposed into individual components, which are "verifiable products, services, or results" (PMBOK, p. 115). The level of detail needed here depends on the complexity of the major deliverables. As mentioned earlier, depending on the complexity of the first level, several levels of decomposition might be needed to reach the lowest level of each branch.

Work packages
The lowest-level units illustrated in the WBS, used to estimate project schedule and budget.

The lowest-level deliverables, **work packages**, are used to estimate the project's schedule and budget. Although the work packages should be detailed enough to allow for planning, managing, and control, too much detail can actually hinder the progress of the project by leading to micromanagement. What is a sufficient level of detail? Deciding on the size of a work package comes down to a tradeoff: If the work packages are too detailed, the project will have to be micromanaged, but if the work packages are too complex and have too long a duration, the project manager can lose control over the progress of the project. In general, and dependent upon the size of the project, a work package should be relatively short in duration; that is, the deliverable should be finishable within one or two weeks. Another recommendation for the size of the work packages is that they should all be about the same size or

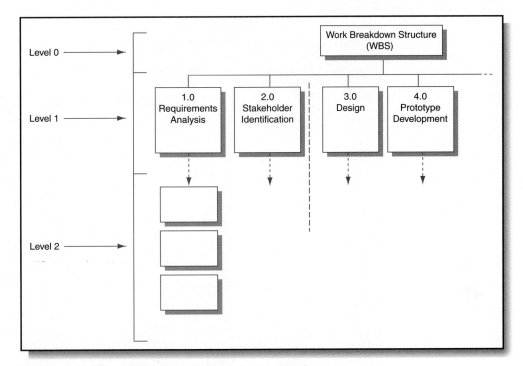

Figure 6.10 ERP WBS oriented on the SDLC

should require about the same effort to produce. Finally, a work package should be specific enough to be completed by one person or a small, well-defined group.

Assigning numeric codes to the different deliverables, summary tasks, and activities will help to develop the activity list from the finished WBS. Again, these numeric codes should follow a simple outline number format that represents both the level of the deliverable and the branch it belongs to. As a final step in creating the WBS, the project management team should further verify that the decomposition is at the right level of detail for each branch.

The most common process of decomposing a project into different components normally follows a top-down approach, from higher-level to lower-level components. Sometimes, especially for particular types of projects, a bottom-up approach might be useful; in this approach, all team members try to determine as many of the tasks necessary to complete the project as possible. Then, they group those different tasks in some logical way to finally plan the entire project. This way of building a WBS can be useful for novel projects; further, it helps to get the buy-in of all project team members. A bottom-up approach, however, can be time consuming.

Templates
Lists of activities from previous projects.

Another method of determining the deliverables and individual work packages needed to complete the project is the use of **templates**. Templates are lists of activities established during earlier projects. A project manager working on similar projects does not have to reinvent the wheel every time a new project is planned but, rather, can adapt and use the WBSs generated for earlier projects. Oftentimes, project managers have a repository of standard WBS templates to facilitate project planning. Experienced project managers can build a WBS based on their recollection of prior projects, but to avoid overlooking important deliverables, it is generally recommended to use documentation rather than to rely on recollection.

Most project scheduling processes, including the inputs, tools and techniques, and outputs already discussed, can be specified within Microsoft Project. Often, project

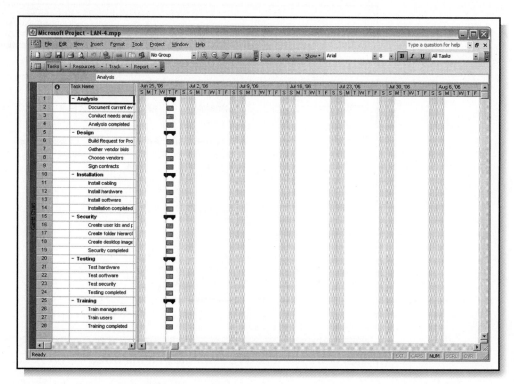

Figure 6.11 WBS in Microsoft Project

Gantt chart
A bar chart showing the start and end dates for the activities of a project.

WBS dictionary
A document that accompanies the WBS and provides additional information about the individual components of the WBS.

Milestones
Important dates with a project schedule that are meaningful in terms of the completion of specific sets of project events.

managers create WBSs using diagramming tools such as Microsoft Visio. In Microsoft Visio, the WBS is represented in the form of an organizational chart. Alternatively, the objects or activities associated with the WBS can be entered in the Task Name column within the **Gantt chart** view of Microsoft Project (see Figure 6.11). As you will recall from Chapter 1, a Gantt chart is a bar chart showing the start and end dates for the activities of a project. The Gantt charts lists activity names on the vertical axis and durations on the horizontal axis (Gantt charts are covered in more detail in Chapter 7). Although Figure 6.11 does not yet incorporate the time dimension of the various project tasks (note the absence of time illustrated on the horizontal), this Gantt chart view can be used early on to illustrate the WBS. As relationships and, later, task resource assignments and durations are defined (see Chapter 7), this task list depicting the WBS in Microsoft Project will start to look like a more formal Gantt chart.

If you have both Project and Visio installed on your computer, you can easily transform the tabular structure presented in Project into an organizational chart by using the Visio WBS Chart Wizard in the analysis toolbar of Microsoft Project. Once you have entered the tasks, as well as additional information for each task, in Project, you can easily create a WBS dictionary by creating a report displaying the pertinent information for each task.

WBS Outputs

Outputs of this step include the WBS itself, as well as a WBS dictionary. A **WBS dictionary** provides details about the individual components of the WBS, such as a description of each component, who is responsible for its completion, a statement of work, critical **milestones**, and preliminary estimates of costs or resources required. The creation of the WBS might lead to change requests if the project management team identifies additional work needed to complete the project. Finally, the project scope statement and the project scope management plan might be updated to reflect the components identified during the WBS creation. The project scope statement, the WBS, and the WBS dictionary together form the **scope baseline**.

Activity Definition

Activity definition is the next step in scheduling a project. In this stage, the different work packages of the WBS are broken down into discrete activities, and the attributes of these activities are defined, including a description, resource requirements, logical predecessor or successor activities, and the like. Clearly defining the different activities as well as their attributes greatly aids in determining the sequence of the activities. The inputs, tools and techniques, and outputs of the activity definition process will be discussed in the following sections.

Activity Definition Inputs

During activity definition, the **schedule activities** (or, simply, activities) within a given project are identified. These activities are needed to produce the lowest-level deliverables of the WBS, namely, the work packages, and usually have verb labels (such as "pour cement"). Schedule activities are used to guide the planning, scheduling, and execution of the project work, as well as to monitor and control progress. The preliminary WBS and the WBS dictionary, the project scope statement, the project management plan (which is also called the baseline project plan and was defined in Chapter 5), organizational process assets (such as historical information, procedures, and policies), and enterprise environmental factors (such as availability of tools and resources) all serve as inputs during the activity definition process. The scope statement—covered in more detail in Chapter 5—is a document that contains both the project justification and the project objectives. The project management plan contains all pertinent information about the project. Project managers may use historical information, specifically information about similar projects in the past, to develop a more accurate project schedule. Figure 6.12 summarizes the required inputs, the resulting outputs, and the tools and techniques used during activity definition.

Activity Definition Tools and Techniques

Defining project activities usually entails determining all the tasks needed to produce the WBS work packages. Similar to our conversation about work packages, a

Scope baseline
A document containing the WBS and the WBS dictionary; the scope baseline specifies the deliveries and components of a project and serves to measure any deviations from that baseline during project execution.

Activity definition
The process of identifying and defining activities that must be performed to produce project deliverables.

Schedule activity (activity)
Small components used to plan, schedule, execute, monitor, and control the project.

Figure 6.12 PMBOK required inputs, tools and techniques used, and resulting outputs during activity definition

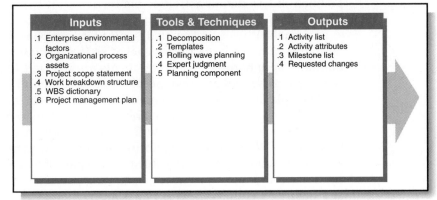

Inputs	Tools & Techniques	Outputs
.1 Enterprise environmental factors .2 Organizational process assets .3 Project scope statement .4 Work breakdown structure .5 WBS dictionary .6 Project management plan	.1 Decomposition .2 Templates .3 Rolling wave planning .4 Expert judgment .5 Planning component	.1 Activity list .2 Activity attributes .3 Milestone list .4 Requested changes

central question in determining activities is, when is a sufficient level of detail reached? While there are no hard-and-fast rules for when to stop decomposition, there are a few guidelines. Typically, an activity

- Can be performed by one person or a well-defined group
- Has a single, clearly identifiable deliverable
- Has a known method or technique
- Has well-defined predecessor and successor steps
- Is measurable so that the level of completion can be determined

Another guideline for determining the level of detail needed is the duration of the activity. Usually, a project manager cannot oversee the task while it is being completed and will not be able to know the status of the activity during that time. Thus, if a task takes longer than a few days, a project manager will not know if everything is working out as planned while the person or group assigned to it is working on it. If something does not work according to plan, valuable time will be lost before the project manager will know about the problem. Limiting the duration of an activity to several hours or a few days, therefore, helps to limit the negative impact of any potential delays.

Templates, as part of an organization's process assets that illustrate generic activity lists generated from information about similar projects in the past, can be used in scheduling other projects. For example, generating a report or a user interface almost always entails essentially the same activities, so information from prior projects can reliably be used to accomplish this task.

Expert judgment may be used to better define project activities based on the recollection of a project expert. However, as the PMBOK guide acknowledges, this method may be less reliable than using documentation from prior projects. In addition to the experience of a project manager, the experience of "doers"—that is, the people executing the activities—is a valuable input in the activity definition phase. For instance, a database manager knows the detailed steps to be performed in setting up certain database queries.

Often, only the activities to be accomplished in the project's next few steps can be planned at a sufficient level of detail. In this case, project managers use a technique called rolling wave planning, introduced earlier. Whereas the closest activities are planned at a detailed level, activities farther in the future are planned only at a general level. During execution of the project, these activities are planned in more detail. Thus, as discussed earlier, there is a cone of uncertainty in which activities are planned in more detail as the project progresses. Because near-term activities are planned in great detail and future activities are planned in less detail, activities planned with different levels of detail can exist during any phase of a project.

When the WBS is first created, some of its components might not have been fully decomposed to the work package level, so they cannot yet be used for detailed estimation. These higher-level components are referred to as planning components, which are to be broken down at later stages. If the individual work packages have not been planned, a control account (or cost account) is established for future planning. These control accounts describe what work is to be performed in the future, who will perform it, and who will pay for it. They are, in a sense, an intersection between the WBS and the organizational breakdown structure (which describes the area of an organization responsible for each part of a project). Subcomponents of the control accounts are referred to as planning packages. These planning packages are at a higher level than the work packages; when using rolling wave planning, the

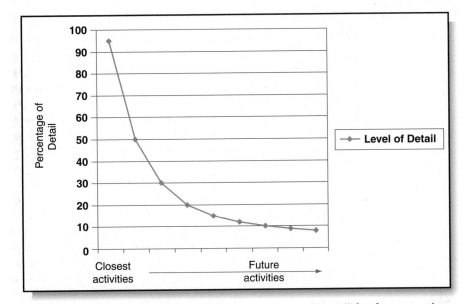

Figure 6.13 Rolling wave planning—level of detail for future tasks

planning packages are broken down into work packages and schedule activities sometime before the execution of their corresponding components (see Figure 6.13).

Activity Definition Outputs

Outputs from the activity definition process include an activity list, supporting detail (such as activity attributes and milestones), and any requested changes to the project scope statement and the WBS. The activity list, an extension of the WBS, is a complete listing of all the schedule activities that make up the project. As an extension to the WBS, the activity list can be used to ensure that all project activities are also part of the current WBS. *Supporting detail* can be seen as a general term encompassing any information that can further define work packages. However, although the activity list is based on—and can be seen as an extension of—the WBS, the PMBOK does not consider the schedule activities as part of the WBS. Rather, it sees them as components of the project schedule (although, depending on your needs and your software's capabilities, you might choose to include the activities in the WBS).

The activity attributes include all pertinent attributes of a schedule activity, including description, constraints and assumptions, leads and lags (discussed later in this chapter), logical relationships, and predecessor and successor activities. These attributes help later in the activity sequencing process. Finally during activity definition, a list of milestones is generated to aid in the execution of the project.

Activity sequencing
The process of developing a network diagram and updating the activity list from the activity definition phase.

Network diagram
A schematic display that illustrates the various tasks in a project as well as their sequential relationship.

Activity Sequencing

Activity sequencing is the next process within the PMBOK's Project Time Management knowledge area. It is designed to develop a **network diagram** and update the activity list from the activity definition phase. A network diagram is a schematic display that illustrates the various activities (or tasks) in a project as well as their sequential relationships.

The outputs of the activity definition stage guide this step in developing the project schedule, which involves determining the necessary order of the schedule activities identified in the previous step. This is typically referred to as determining the precedence—or order—of the tasks. As noted earlier, in some instances, one task must precede another. As an example, in home construction, a cement foundation is typically laid before the walls are built, which in turn are typically built before the roof is put on. This sequence of activities is no different from that which might occur in an information systems development project where, for example, the requirements for the system must be identified before system development can begin.

Based on the previous definition, project scheduling involves defining project activities, determining their sequence within a project schedule, estimating the resources needed, and estimating the activities' durations. Managers must clearly define project activities before the duration of each can be accurately estimated. Following the definition of each activity, project managers can begin to determine their sequence and to estimate the resources and time needed to complete each specific activity. The estimation of each activity needs to be as accurate as possible because its length, in combination with the sequencing of all activities, leads to an overall estimation of the project's completion date. If the project must be completed to meet a specific date—say, to meet a corporate mandate—estimating the activities' time to completion can be especially crucial. The following sections discuss activity sequencing; Chapter 7 discusses estimating each activity's resources and duration.

When determining the sequencing of activities, it may be important in some instances for activities that can be performed in parallel to be scheduled simultaneously in order to speed project completion. This is particularly applicable when considering activities that affect the overall time required to complete the project (see the discussion of the critical path in Chapter 7). When determining the sequence of the project's activities, the project team should take into account certain constraints, which fall into one or more of these broad categories:

- Technical requirements and specifications
- Safety and efficiency
- Preferences and policies
- Resource availability

Technical requirements and specifications clearly dictate the sequence of some activities. It only makes sense that requirements collection must precede screen design in an information systems project. Sometimes, safety and efficiency should be considered. For example, important data should be backed up before installing new hardware or software; similarly, a system should be beta tested before the final version is launched. Whereas technical requirements, specifications, and safety concerns often require a certain sequence, efficiency concerns are not mandatory; in other words, a project manager can choose to use a different (and potentially suboptimal) sequence if other concerns (such as safety) override the efficiency criterion.

Company policies and preferences also influence the sequence of activities. In some companies, the marketing efforts start a long time before final product launch; for example, Microsoft typically announces new versions of its operating systems long before they are actually launched. When a project has been behind schedule, these marketing efforts might have been more appropriately scheduled later in the project but were not because of corporate policies. Finally, the availability of

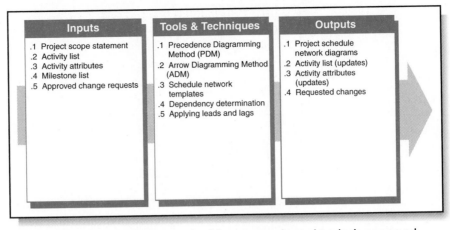

Inputs	Tools & Techniques	Outputs
.1 Project scope statement .2 Activity list .3 Activity attributes .4 Milestone list .5 Approved change requests	.1 Precedence Diagramming Method (PDM) .2 Arrow Diagramming Method (ADM) .3 Schedule network templates .4 Dependency determination .5 Applying leads and lags	.1 Project schedule network diagrams .2 Activity list (updates) .3 Activity attributes (updates) .4 Requested changes

Figure 6.14 PMBOK required inputs, tools and techniques used, and resulting outputs during activity sequencing

resources can significantly influence the sequence of activities. If funding is tight at a certain stage of the project, some activities requiring more funds might have to be delayed until later stages while other activities take precedence.

Activity Sequencing Inputs

The schedule activities defined in the previous stage are the most important input into the process of activity sequencing. The activities' attributes (such as logical predecessor or successor activities) also serve to determine the project's best possible sequence. Further, the project scope statement, the milestone list, and the approved change requests serve as inputs to activity sequencing. In many instances, the product description—which is simply a description of the product being constructed—or the product breakdown structure are also included as inputs to this process because developing the project schedule often depends on the product characteristics. In IS terms, the product description is the system being developed. The various inputs to activity sequencing are illustrated in Figure 6.14.

Activity Sequencing Tools and Techniques

A variety of tools and techniques specified by the PMBOK guide can be used to illustrate the activity sequencing process. These include the precedence diagramming method, the arrow diagramming method, conditional diagramming methods, and network templates. The following paragraphs discuss the more commonly used methods of precedence diagramming and arrow diagramming, as well as the use of network templates.

Precedence diagramming method
A network diagramming technique that uses boxes and rectangles connected by arrows to represent activities and their precedence relationships.

The **precedence diagramming method (PDM)** is a network diagramming technique that uses boxes and rectangles connected by arrows to show the order and precedence (or dependency) of activities within the project (see Figure 6.15). The boxes represent project activities, and the arrows represent the relationships among these activities or tasks. Key to PDM is its ability to illustrate four types of task dependencies among activities—that is, four ways that tasks exist in relation to other tasks. The first of these is finish-to-start, which is probably the most common of the task dependency types. Finish-to-start indicates that one activity

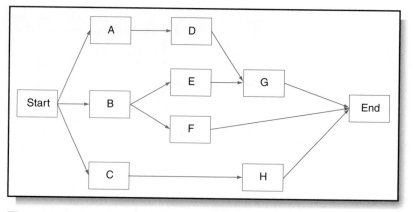

Figure 6.15 Precedence diagramming method

cannot be started until another has been completed. For example, in an information systems development project, the programmer cannot begin actual programming until the programming language has been chosen. The second type of task dependency is start-to-start. In this situation, the start of the successor depends on the start of the predecessor. Again using our information systems example, programming cannot begin until some portion of the program design is decided on (e.g., 75% of the design activities might be completed). The third type of task dependency is finish-to-finish, meaning that the completion of the successor activity depends on the completion of the predecessor. In our information systems example, testing a system cannot be finished until the programming is completed. Finally, a fourth type of dependency is start-to-finish, in which the completion of the successor depends on the beginning of the predecessor. In our information systems example, a copy of the program—even if incomplete—cannot be saved until programming begins. Figure 6.16 illustrates all four of these types of dependencies.

Figure 6.16 Four types of task dependencies in order of decreasing frequency of occurrence

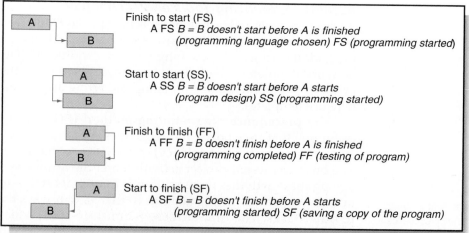

Global Implications: Managing Activities Across the Globe

With the increasing tendency of organizations to conduct business across the globe—undertaking IT projects that involve team members from different company offices, possibly in different countries, and quite likely in different time zones—time is an important variable that cannot be overlooked. A project manager overseeing a globally distributed team must be aware of the impact of time on every aspect of the project from planning to closure. Some of these issues are noted in the following quote:

> Time is all-pervasive as it constantly helps to provide the organizing frame of reference for work groups through agendas, meeting schedules, videoconference sessions, and *strategizing about "our time" and "their time" and about synchronizing activities.* Further, the success or failure of IT projects is heavily dependent on time. Project outcomes are often judged based on whether time deadlines are met, *which in turn depends on issues such as effective coordination of work.* (Sarker and Sahay 2004, p. 5, emphasis added)

Sarker and Sahay studied virtual team formation in U.S. college students who had to complete an information systems development project with a group of team members from Norway. During the study, the authors uncovered four major time-related general principles with which globally distributed virtual teams must deal to effectively manage time over the course of a project.

1. Team members in different time zones likely have different cultural and social attitudes and different physiological cycles with respect to time. These attitudes and cycles are difficult to change, and perceived lack of sympathy to these differences can cause problems in developing relationships.
2. With differences in time zones and possible differences with respect to daylight savings or standard time, seemingly simple clock-time differences become increasingly difficult to accommodate. Mistakes regarding clock time can cause groups to miss important meetings and deadlines.
3. Being able to work simultaneously with team members who could be as many as 12 to 16 hours behind or ahead becomes almost impossible. Because some tasks require responses from the distributed team members, groups can have long unproductive lapses while they wait for the other team members to respond.
4. Such lapses, even if only due to the time difference, can be interpreted by the waiting team members as incompetence or lack of commitment. (Sarker and Sahay, 2004)

Given these issues, time management becomes increasingly critical, especially with globally distributed teams. A project manager must be aware of cultural differences with respect to the perception of time and different national holiday and vacation rules and must actively manage the effects of time-related problems on team performance.

A PDM diagram—which represents activities on nodes—is created based on the activity list as well as the activity attributes (specifically, the predecessor information) identified in the previous step (see Figure 6.15). First, a start node is created, indicating the beginning of the project. Then, based on the inputs, all activities with no predecessors are drawn as nodes (boxes) to the right of the start node (these will be the first activities of different sequences of activities because they have no predecessors) and connected with arrows to the start node. Then, the predecessor information is analyzed to determine what activities must follow, and these new activities are drawn to the right of those drawn in the previous step. Boxes are connected with arrows, taking into account the precedence relationships. This step is repeated until all activities are represented in the diagram. Finally, all nodes with no successor are connected to a dummy end node. Note that a dummy node—or **dummy activity**—is an activity of zero duration that is used to show a logical relationship or dependency in a network diagram.

Microsoft Project greatly facilitates the creation of a network diagram. While creating the WBS and the activity definition, you have learned how to enter deliverables, activities, and predecessors in Microsoft Project's Gantt chart view. Switching to the Network diagram view renders the display of a PDM diagram. Note that Microsoft Project's network diagram presents information such as start and finish dates, as well as task durations. These are, strictly speaking, not part of a PDM diagram and will be discussed in Chapter 7.

The **arrow diagramming method (ADM)**—also called the activity on arrow (AOA) method—is a network diagramming technique that shows the project tasks or activities as the arrows in the diagram—as opposed to the nodes described in a PDM. The nodes in an ADM diagram can be conveniently used as milestones for the project (see Figure 6.17). Although this type of network diagramming method is sometimes easier to understand than a PDM diagram, one downside is that sometimes dummy nodes are needed to represent the different types of task dependencies mentioned above. The widespread use of ADM diagrams has declined somewhat because most commercial software packages (including Microsoft Project) support PDM rather than ADM. This type of diagram is a useful tool, however, for teaching concepts such as the critical path, introduced in Chapter 2 and discussed in more detail in Chapter 7.

Similar to the creation of the work breakdown structure and activity definition, project managers can use organizational assets such as information about prior projects to facilitate the activity sequencing process. Such schedule **network templates** usually apply to the entire project. Templates used for only parts of a project are referred to as subnetwork templates; such templates can exist for different parts of a project, such as interface or database design.

Dummy activity
An activity of zero duration that is used to show a logical relationship or dependency in a network diagram.

Arrow diagramming method
A network diagram consisting of arrows to represent activities and their precedence relationships and nodes to represent project milestones.

Network template
A template developed from previous projects used to shorten the development time of network diagrams.

Figure 6.17 Arrow diagramming method

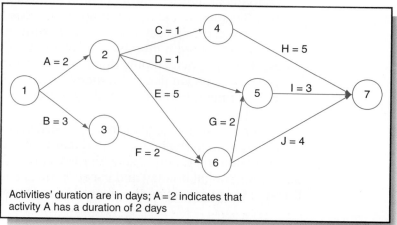

Activities' duration are in days; A = 2 indicates that activity A has a duration of 2 days

Ethical Dilemma: Adherence to the WBS at All Costs

Work breakdown structures (WBS) have been used by organizations for some time. Consider the case of a large computer manufacturer (the Company). In the mid-1980s, because of several factors, including changes in upper management, the Company began using WBSs to streamline its various projects. On the surface, this seemed like an excellent idea because projects now had specific deliverables that were sufficiently decomposed to be manageable by one person or a small group of people. This ideally allowed managers to concentrate less on micromanaging every task. All the advantages of using WBS that we have presented were realized, but problems arose as well.

The Company had support for using WBSs—in fact, a directive from the highest-level executives that they were important and needed. But at the same time, the CEO was experimenting with round-the-clock staffing and flex-time, causing some unintended scheduling problems. Because of these experiments, mid- and lower-level managers failed to consider the non–work-related consequences of strictly adhering to the new WBS-driven schedule. For example, if the start of Task C depended on the completion of Task B and had a 4-hour duration and Task B was scheduled to be completed at 10:00 P.M. on a Tuesday, managers would schedule Task C to begin at 10:00 P.M. Tuesday and Task D to begin at 2:00 A.M. Wednesday. Given the differential skills of the project team members, in many cases employees were working different, and sometimes consecutive, shifts.

While seemingly efficient on the surface, employee feedback indicated the system occasionally failed because factors like family or personal obligations—for example, after-school events—made adhering to such a schedule difficult, if not impossible. The resultant conflict caused a breech between employees and management. In response, some managers started to use the WBS as a tool for punishment, justifying scheduling people to work at unreasonable times.

Although WBSs and the diagramming tools presented here have clear advantages, sometimes such systems can also have unintended consequences. The Company rectified these situations by setting up specific schedules for all of the team members, then assigning people to tasks, then going back to fill in the gaps. This resulted in projects' lasting longer than they might have, but now they place more reasonable requirements on team members' time. Unfortunately, these countermeasures were not instituted in time to keep several talented people from leaving the Company or to keep some managers from using the WBS as leverage to make life unpleasant for certain employees.

Despite the vast array of project management tools and techniques available to control project schedules, it is important to realize that a) schedules are not set in stone, b) rigid adherence to a schedule may have significant organizational consequences outside of the project itself, and c) almost any tool can be misused. Organizations and managers need to constantly monitor for these unintended effects.

Discussion Questions

1. What steps can an organization take to diminish the misuse of project management tools, as in the above example?
2. If you were a project manager in charge of employees affected by the situation above, what approach might you use to discuss the issue with upper management?

Mandatory dependencies
The relationship of activities that cannot be performed in parallel.

Discretionary dependencies
The relationship of activities based on the preferences of project managers; often based on best-practices procedures.

External dependencies
The relationship of project activities and external events, such as the delivery of project components.

Lead time
The time required by one task before another task can begin.

Lag time
The time delay between the completion of one task and the start of the successor.

Conditional diagramming
A network logic method that allows managers to depict nonsequential activities.

The relationships between different activities can take several forms. **Mandatory dependencies** represent the relationship between project activities that cannot be performed in parallel. In the construction example introduced earlier, the walls of a house cannot be erected before the foundation is built. In an information systems development project, a system cannot be built before the user requirements are determined.

Discretionary dependencies are those dependencies that are based on the preferences of project managers and are generally based on some type of best-practices procedures. An example might be the selection of a development language after doing a requirements analysis on what a system is supposed to do. Although it is certainly possible to choose the language first (for a variety of reasons, such as the skill set of those doing the development), it may make sense to make this choice after defining what the system is to do. Concerns for efficiency or decisions based on company policies or resource availability can result in the creation of discretionary dependencies.

External dependencies represent the relationships between project activities and external events such as the delivery of an important project component. In an information systems development project, creating a new human resource intranet may require the installation of new hardware supplied by a vendor outside the control of the project team.

As a last step in activity sequencing, the leads and lags associated with the different activities should be determined. **Lead time** is the time required by one task before another task can begin. As an example, in a start-to-start relationship, activity A may need to be worked on for a certain amount of time before activity B can commence. As a specific information systems example, ongoing quality control inspections (activity B) may not begin until a sufficient amount of progress (e.g., some threshold number of lines of code) has been made on developing a particular aspect of the information system (activity A). **Lag time** is a similar concept; it refers to the amount of time delay between the completion of one task and the start of the successor. A familiar example is the drying time for paint. While the task of painting a wall might take 1 hour, it might require an additional 4 hours of lag time before the next task—putting on the second coat of paint—can begin. An information systems example might include the time required to compile a program before testing it for errors.

Although we have presented several tools and techniques for activity sequencing, other tools and techniques are available to assist the project manager in accomplishing the activity sequencing process. As an example, **conditional diagramming** methods allow managers to depict nonsequential activities, as well as activities that may have loops or conditional branches. Other charts, such as Gantt charts, that display both activity sequences and durations will be discussed in Chapter 7.

Activity Sequencing Outputs

Outputs from the activity sequencing process include project network diagrams and updates to the activity list and the activity attributes discussed earlier. In some cases, the creation of the network diagrams reveals the need for further change requests, which are also considered an output of the activity sequencing process in the PMBOK. Project network diagrams can be any of the previously mentioned types, as well as others not listed here. Regardless of the type, the importance of a network diagram lies in its ability to graphically render the

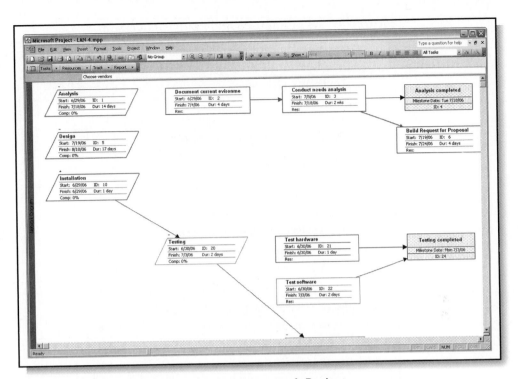

Figure 6.18 Network diagram in Microsoft Project

sequence of activities in the project schedule. Microsoft Project includes a built-in tool that automatically renders network diagrams based on the WBS entered by the user (see Figure 6.18). Updates to the project activity list are another important output and are generally used to identify any problems among the previously defined activities. Figure 6.14, discussed earlier, provides a summary of the required inputs, the resulting outputs, and the tools and techniques used during activity sequencing.

MANAGING PROJECT SCHEDULING AND THE PMBOK

This chapter has discussed the fundamentals, characteristics, and challenges of developing a project schedule, focusing primarily on Knowledge Areas 5 and 6, Project Scope Management and Project Time Management. Continuing our conversation of project scope from Chapter 5, in this chapter we discussed the development of the WBS, which outlines the major deliverables associated with a project. After the development of the WBS, we then turned our attention to two processes associated with Project Time Management, Activity Definition and Activity Sequencing. These two processes involve, respectively, the identification of activities needed to produce the WBS deliverables, and then the sequencing of these activities. We also discussed the various tools and techniques available to address common project scheduling problems. Figure 6.19 summarizes this coverage and illustrates what will be discussed in upcoming chapters as well.

Figure 6.19 Chapter 6 and PMBOK coverage

Textbook Chapters →	1	2	3	4	5	6	7	8	9	10	11	12
PMBOK Knowledge Area												
1 Introduction to Project Management												
1.1 What is a Project?	●											
1.2 What is Project Management?	●											
1.3 Areas of Expertise		●										
1.4 Project Management Context	●											
2 Project Life Cycle and Organization												
2.1 The Project Life Cycle	●	●										
2.2 Project Stakeholders	●	●										
2.3 Organizational Influences		●	●	●			○					
3 Project Management Processes for a Project												
3.1 Project Management Processes	●	●										
3.2 PM Process Groups	●	●										
3.3 Process Interactions		●										
3.4 Project Management Process Mapping		●										
4 Project Integration Management												
4.1 Develop Project Charter					●							
4.2 Develop Preliminary Project Scope Statement					●	✓						
4.3 Develop Project Management Plan					●							
4.4 Direct and Manage Project Execution										○		
4.5 Monitor and Control Project Work												○
4.6 Integrated Change Control												○
4.7 Close Project												○
5 Project Scope Management												
5.1 Scope Planning					●							
5.2 Scope Definition					●							
5.3 Create WBS					●	✓						
5.4 Scope Verification					●							
5.5 Scope Control					●							○
6 Project Time Management												
6.1 Activity Definition						✓						
6.2 Activity Sequencing						✓						
6.3 Activity Resource Estimating							○					
6.4 Activity Duration Estimating							○					
6.5 Schedule Development							○					
6.6 Schedule Control							○					○

(continued)

Figure 6.19   (continued)

Textbook Chapters ⟶	1	2	3	4	5	6	7	8	9	10	11	12
PMBOK Knowledge Area												
7 Project Cost Management												
7.1 Cost Estimating							○					
7.2 Cost Budgeting							○					
7.3 Cost Control							○					○
8 Project Quality Management												
8.1 Quality Planning								○				
8.2 Perform Quality Assurance								○				
8.3 Perform Quality Control								○				○
9 Project Human Resource Management												
9.1 Human Resource Planning			●				○					
9.2 Acquire Project Team			●				○					
9.3 Develop Project Team			●				○					
9.4 Manage Project Team			●				○					
10 Project Communications Management												
10.1 Communications Planning				●							○	
10.2 Information Distribution				●							○	
10.3 Performance Reporting				●								○
10.4 Manage Stakeholders				●								○
11 Project Risk Management												
11.1 Risk Management Planning									○			
11.2 Risk Identification									○	○		
11.3 Qualitative Risk Analysis									○			
11.4 Quantitative Risk Analysis									○			
11.5 Risk Response Planning									○			
11.6 Risk Monitoring and Control									○			○
12 Project Procurement Management												
12.1 Plan Purchases and Acquisitions										○		
12.2 Plan Contracting										○		
12.3 Request Seller Responses										○		
12.4 Select Sellers										○		
12.5 Contract Administration										○		
12.6 Contract Closure										○		○

Key: ●-where material is covered in past chapters; ✓-current chapter coverage;
○-where material is covered in future chapters

Jim Woo walked into the conference room to find everyone on his team in their seats, sharing with each other the scheduling information they had developed for the project. As usual, Juanita was on speakerphone with Riverside. She had faxed over a couple of pages of information. Jim had stopped by the fax machine nearest his desk on his way to the meeting.

Jim plugged the projector into his laptop and adjusted the setting so that he could display the work on his laptop on the screen (see Table 6.2). "Here is the list of tasks that I have compiled, based on what you guys sent me. You'll see it is pretty high-level stuff at this point. I tried to order these in some kind of temporal sequence, but it's only an approximation at this point. As of right now, I have 21 different tasks."

"You're right," Sanjay said, "These are pretty high level. Each one of these tasks is going to have to be broken down into subtasks."

"That's OK," Bob said. "I think this gives us a good place to start. And we can get a good first approximation of how long the entire project will take, and whether we can finish what needs to be done in the time given to us by Ella and the rest of the executive team."

"Like we have a choice," Sally replied.

"Clearly the kickoff meeting and going live are the bookends of the project," Juanita added. "What can be done in parallel? Let's set up the basic schedule structure first, and then we can come back and refine the duration of each task."

"Sounds good," Jim said, switching to Microsoft Project (see Figure 6.20). "I've already given that some thought. Here is what I came up with."

"You can see that, for simplicity, I have collapsed all four of the customer loyalty research tasks into one and all three of the IT research tasks into one. But all seven of these tasks can be done in parallel," Jim explained.

Table 6.2 Running Case: Key High-Level Project Tasks

KEY HIGH LEVEL TASKS
Project kickoff meeting
Establish project charter, objectives, etc.
Create schedule
Create resource allocations
Research executive management ideas about encouraging customer loyalty
Research store management ideas about encouraging customer loyalty
Research customer ideas about customer loyalty
Research competitor methods for encouraging customer loyalty
Research existing IT for supporting customer loyalty programs
Research customer relationship management software
Research data warehousing systems
Perform risk analysis
Write call for proposals
Receive bids
Evaluate bids from vendors
Choose winning bid
Work with Legal to write contract
Implement system
Prepare training program
Prepare advertising campaign
Go live

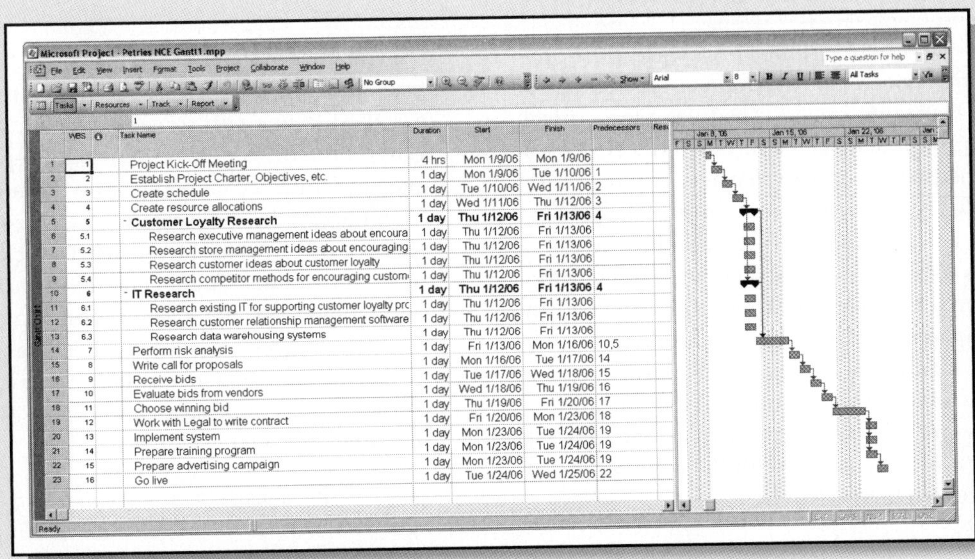

Figure 6.20 Initial Gantt chart for the Petrie project

"And implementation, preparation of the training program, and preparation of the advertising program can all be done in parallel too," Sally pointed out.

"But some of these really depend on the others," Bob said.

The team spent the next hour trying to determine their best estimates for how the various tasks should be sequenced and making some rough estimates of their duration. The results of this discussion are shown in Figure 6.21.

"This is pretty good," Jim said, "but it's going to need some refining. Let me work on it. One thing I can see right now, though, is that we are going to need some additional resources to pull this off. We all need to think about what it is going to take to finish this project in the time we have and just how much each of us can contribute."

"You know," Sanjay offered, "this is a pretty ambitious project."

Figure 6.21 Gantt chart for the Petrie project, with the team's revised estimated durations

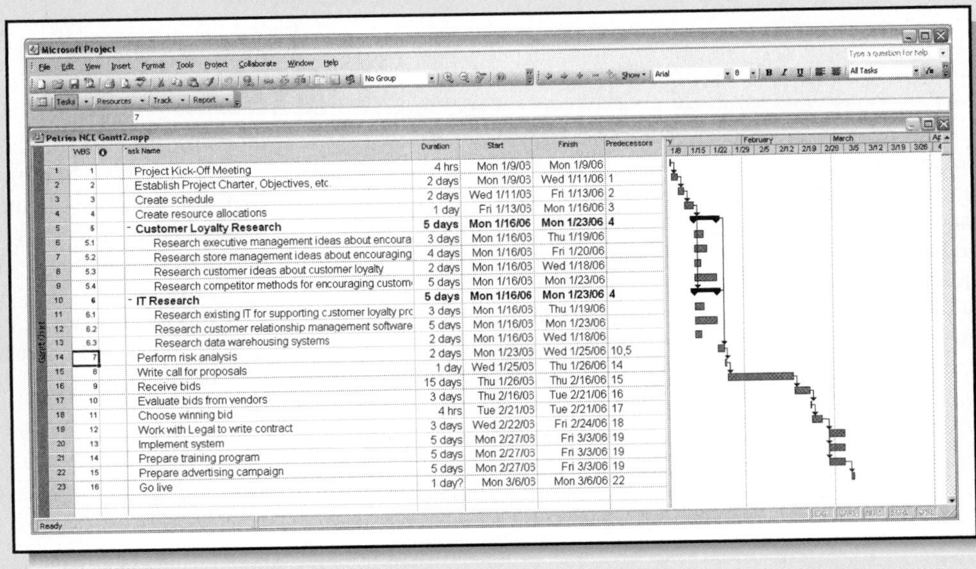

CHAPTER SUMMARY

Provide an overview of project scheduling, including its importance and the challenges associated with it. Managing project schedules are a critical aspect of project management. When developing a project schedule, the project manager together with relevant team members and other stakeholders develops an accurate and acceptable schedule. Schedules are rarely perfect, because everything about a project is seldom known in advance. In addition, information systems related projects may introduce additional issues, such as technology upgrades, which create additional complications. Schedules are frequently refined as the project moves forward, consistent with the cone of uncertainty discussed in the chapter.

Describe project scheduling techniques, such as the Work Breakdown Structure, Activity Definition, and Activity Sequencing. When developing a project schedule, the project manager together with relevant team members develops a work breakdown structure (WBS) by decomposing the entire project into smaller, more manageable parts, which in turn, can be further decomposed. Mapping out this decomposition process results in a WBS that allows project managers to determine smaller specific deliverables that, when aggregated over the lifespan of the project, will result in the completion of the macrolevel project deliverable. Once the initial WBS has been developed, project managers then define

the activities outlined in the WBS to a level of detail fine enough to allow specific activities to be assigned to one person or to a small, well-defined group but still general enough to keep micromanagement from becoming an issue. Taking the output from the activity definition phase, project managers sequence the activities to optimize efficiency given a set of constraints. These constraints include technical requirements and specifications, safety and efficiency, preferences and policies, and resource availability. Precedence relationships need to be considered, as do lead and lag times as the project schedule is created.

Describe how project management software packages can help with project scheduling. Several project scheduling tools have been presented in this chapter. These software tools can assist in software decomposition, activity definition, and also activity sequencing. In many cases, these tools have the advantage of transferring information from one type of schematic to another. For example, Microsoft Project allows the creation of a WBS, which (after additional information is added) allows the user to display the same information in Gantt charts or precedence diagrams. Further, successful project managers use templates, which may come from previous projects they have worked on or from documentation from previous projects within the organization.

KEY TERMS REVIEW

- Activity definition
- Activity sequencing
- Arrow diagramming method
- Conditional diagramming
- Project scheduling
- Cone of uncertainty
- Decomposition
- Discretionary dependencies
- Dummy activity

- External dependencies
- Gantt chart
- Lag time
- Lead time
- Mandatory dependencies
- Milestones
- Network diagram
- Network template
- Precedence diagramming method

- Product breakdown structure
- Project Time Management
- Rolling wave planning
- Schedule activities
- Scope baseline
- Templates
- WBS dictionary
- Work breakdown structure
- Work packages

Match each of the key terms with the definition that best fits it.

1. _____ The process of defining project activities, determining their sequence, and estimating their duration.

2. _____ The reiteration of the processes of activity definition, sequencing, and duration estimation as part of schedule development.

3. _____ A progressively more detailed and accurate projection of the project schedule and duration as the project deliverables and activities are specified in more detail by the project manager or project team.

4. _____ The process of subdividing tasks to make them more easily manageable.

5. _____ The output from the process of dividing a product into its individual components.

6. _____ The output that results from the process of dividing the entire project into manageable tasks (usually presented as a hierarchical chart or in tabular form).

7. _____ Lists of activities from previous projects.

8. _____ The lowest level units illustrated in the WBS, which are used to estimate project schedule and budget.

9. _____ A document that accompanies the WBS and provides additional information about the individual components of the WBS.

10. _____ A document containing the WBS and the WBS dictionary; it specifies the deliveries and components of a project and serves to measure any deviations from that baseline during project execution.

11. _____ The time required by one task before another task can begin.

12. _____ The process of identifying and defining activities that must be performed to produce project deliverables.

13. _____ Small components used to plan, schedule, execute, monitor, and control the project.

14. _____ The process of developing a network diagram and updating the activity list from the activity definition phase.

15. _____ A schematic display that illustrates the various tasks in a project as well as the sequential relationship among those tasks.

16. _____ The time delay between the completion of one task and the start of the successor.

17. _____ A network diagramming technique that uses boxes and rectangles connected by arrows to represent activities and their precedence relationships.

18. _____ A network diagram consisting of arrows to represent activities and their precedence relationships and nodes to represent project milestones.

19. _____ A template developed from previous projects used to shorten the development time of network diagrams.

20. _____ The relationship of activities that cannot be performed in parallel.

21. _____ The relationship of activities based on the preferences of project managers; often based on best-practices procedures.

22. _____ The relationship of project activities and external events, such as the delivery of project components.

23. _____ A scheduling technique in which the team defers breaking down components until they are further clarified, and the decomposition takes place as the project progresses.

24. _____ A network logic method that allows managers to depict nonsequential activities.

25. _____ Important dates with a project schedule that are meaningful in terms of the completion of specific sets of project events.

26. _____ A bar chart showing the start and end dates for the activities of a project, where activity names are listed on the vertical axis and durations on the horizontal axis.

27. _____ An activity of zero duration that is used to show a logical relationship or dependency in a network diagram.

1. Compare and contrast a product breakdown structure (PBS) and a work breakdown structure (WBS).
2. Define *decomposition*.
3. Discuss why a WBS has different levels and what each level represents.
4. What is the difference between decomposing levels using a top-down approach and a bottom-up approach, and what types of projects are best suited to each approach?
5. Why are templates useful for developing project schedules?
6. What is a scope baseline, what are its components, and why is it important?
7. To what level of detail should activities be decomposed? Why?
8. Define a work package and describe its characteristics.
9. Describe strategies that project managers might use to define activities.
10. Describe the differences and similarities between the cone of uncertainty and rolling wave planning.
11. List and briefly describe the classes of constraints on determining the activity sequence.
12. Give an example of each class of constraint on determining the activity sequence.
13. From a precedence diagramming method perspective, list and briefly discuss each type of task dependency.
14. From an arrow diagramming method perspective, list and briefly discuss each type of task dependency.

1. Fully decompose a project you've done in another course (e.g., a semester project or term paper). Discuss the level of detail where you stopped decomposing and explain why.
2. Create a WBS based on the decomposition you carried out for the previous question.
3. You have just been selected as the manager for a project to automate the distribution center at XYZ Co. This project has significant executive support and an engaged executive sponsor. The executive you report to asks you if you will be able to complete the project in less than 6 months. Describe to the executive sponsor what you must do from a project scheduling perspective before you can give her an answer. Based on what has been presented in this chapter, can you give her an answer? Why or why not?
4. After determining that there is a relatively high probability that the project can be completed within 6 months, the executive you report to wonders if she can trust your determination. After all, she has heard all the reports about IT projects going over budget and past their deadlines. Address these concerns. That is, how would you reassure her that your estimation is good?
5. Working in a small group, pick a project (it could be anything, such as planning a party, writing a group term paper, developing a database application, etc.) and then write the various tasks that need to be done to accomplish the project on Post-Its (one task per Post-It). Then, use the Post-Its to create the WBS from the project. Was it complete? Add missing tasks if necessary. Were some tasks at a lower level in the WBS than others? What was the most difficult part of doing this?
6. Create a precedence diagram based on the following information:
   a. There are 10 total tasks named A–J.
   b. Tasks A, B, and H have durations of 2 days.
   c. Tasks C, E, I, and J have durations of 3 days.
   d. Tasks D, F, and G have durations of 1 day.
   e. Tasks A, B, and D can be conducted in parallel.
   f. Task C must precede task B.
   g. Tasks A and F must precede Task E.

h. Task E must precede Task G.

i. Tasks B and D must precede Tasks H and I, respectively.

j. Tasks G, H, and I may be conducted in parallel.

k. Tasks G, H, and I precede Task J.

7. Create an arrow diagram with the information from Exercise 6.

8. Create a precedence diagram for your project from Exercise 2.

9. Which diagramming method do you prefer? Why?

CHAPTER CASE

Sedona Management Group and Managing Project Scheduling

Time is the least flexible factor during the life cycle of a project. No matter what else happens during the project, time continues to pass. Tim Turnpaugh recognizes that managing time through good project scheduling is integral to project success. As mentioned earlier, project schedules are managed so well at SMG that the team has not missed a deadline in the last ten years, and this includes SMG's projects for the Seattle Seahawks.

For any project, and in particular for the Seattle Seahawks' Web site, SMG's first step—as mentioned in Chapter 5—is to determine customer needs and project scope with a great deal of certainty. Once these two elements are established, determining the end date of a project is greatly facilitated. If customers are uncertain about their needs, the Sedona team understands that more time should be spent on needs analysis. Usually, the project team will start working on the project the next business day after the customer signs the contract with SMG. In the case of the initial Seattle Seahawks project, the primary focus was to provide information to customers interested in learning about the Seahawks organization. This included information about upcoming events, information about the team, and information about the overall organization. Given SMG's past experiences and leveraging the newest technologies to enhance development speed, Turnpaugh was able to provide very accurate estimates regarding the time required for the Seahawks project.

The first step in time management is activity definition, which involves identifying the various activities that need to be performed for project completion. Turnpaugh indicates that most projects SMG takes on have some fundamental reoccurring components. These include designing the database, working on the Web site content, working on the Web site presentation, connecting the presentation layer to the database, implementing the system, training users, and if necessary, maintaining the system. These components serve as the top level of the project work breakdown structure (WBS) and help define the various work packages associated with the project.

After establishing the WBS and subtasks, the focus is on developing the project schedule. Project scheduling, as discussed in this chapter, is concerned with establishing the order and duration of the tasks required to complete the project. Although some mandatory dependencies certainly occur when designing the project, in many cases, tasks in a project schedule can occur in parallel rather than in a strict sequence. This was exactly the case with the Seahawks project, where the database design and Web-site-presentation-layer development occurred in parallel. In other instances, a sequence of activities is required, as with the tasks related to connecting the database to the presentation layer (what Turnpaugh refers to as wiring up). In this instance, wiring up cannot be performed until the first three activities have been completed.

The next step in managing the project schedule involves estimating the duration of each activity; that is, estimating the time it will take to complete the different activities. Through experience, Turnpaugh and other members of his team have become very good estimators of the time and resources it takes to complete various project tasks. In an iterative process, project resources, time estimates, and task sequencing requirements are manipulated until a completed project schedule is developed.

The Sedona team also takes several steps to control changes to the project schedule. To begin with, the project team always tries to develop a very realistic project schedule that is based on past experiences with other customers. The project team also has regular progress meetings, where they update each other on the status of their assigned work and adjust the schedule if needed. Through these meetings, activities that are not on track can be identified, and any actions needed (e.g., assigning more resources to a project task or, perhaps, doing the task in parallel with some other task) can be taken to ensure the timely completion of the project.

CHAPTER 6 PROJECT ASSIGNMENT

In this assignment, you will work on developing a schedule for your entertainment Web site project. The project end date needs to be consistent with the course duration. The project schedule will be developed using a Gantt chart in Microsoft Project.

1. Create a work breakdown structure (WBS) for your project. This involves developing a detailed list of tasks and subtasks, which should be accomplished to complete the project.
2. Create the schedule by assigning durations to the tasks identified, as well as sequencing them.
3. Show the major deliverables as milestones.
4. Identify some challenges that you and your team members will face in following this schedule.
5. Identify and explain different techniques you will use during the life cycle of the project to manage project time.

REFERENCES

Armour, P. (2002). Ten Unmyths of Project Estimation: Reconsidering Some Commonly Accepted Project Management Practices. *Communications of the ACM* 45(11), 15–18.

Berg, C., and Colenso, K. (2000). Work Breakdown Structure Practice Standard Project: WBS vs. Activities. *PM Network*.

BIA (2005). The Top Project Management Challenges. Retrieved October 11, 2005, from www.bia.ca/articles/TheTopProjectManagementChallenges.htm.

Boehm, B. W. (1981). *Software Engineering Economics.* Upper Saddle River, NJ: Prentice Hall.

Brooks, F. P. (1995). *The Mythical Man-Month: Essays on Software Engineering.* 2nd ed. Reading, MA: Addison-Wesley.

Sarker, S., and Sahay, S. (2004). Implications of Space and Time for Distributed Work: An Interpretive Study of U.S.-Norwegian Systems Development Teams. *European Journal of Information Systems* 13(1), 3–20.

Chapter 7

Managing Project Resources

Opening Case: The FBI's "Trilogy" Project

At the turn of the 21st Century, the FBI began a major overhaul of its IT infrastructure and case file software applications. As the name implies, this project had three parts: upgrading the desktop hardware and software for the entire enterprise; deploying a modern network infrastructure; and creating a Virtual Case File (VCF) system allowing for improved information sharing and analysis of case information. Started before the September 11, 2001, terror attacks, the Trilogy project ran both over budget and over time. While phases 1 and 2 were completed, the VCF system may prove to be one of the most extreme examples of scope creep in IT history. In the face of several reports suggesting that the project would go over budget and beyond the deadline, the FBI insisted that it could meet the original December 2003 deadline. In March 2004, FBI Director Robert Mueller assured the Senate Appropriations Committee that the project would be completed by December 2004. In April 2004, the FBI completed the infrastructure enhancements of the Trilogy project; however, there were still major problems with the Virtual Case File (VCF) system. In May 2004, Mueller again insisted that the December 2004 deadline would be met. However, in Senate testimony in February 2005, Mueller stated that the VCF system was only 10 percent complete (Charette, 2005).

While a host of project management deficiencies and political pressures can be cited for the failure of the VCF system project, schedule management issues clearly played a part in problems related to the system. It seems likely the project team had not instituted appropriate schedule control mechanisms to help manage project task durations. Given that the project experienced 1.3 change requests per day, control over the schedule was critical to project success (Charette, 2005).

Figure 7.1
Photo of the
J. Edgar Hoover
FBI Building
entrance sign

LEARNING OBJECTIVES

After reading this chapter, you will be able to:

➤ Understand what resources are, and the types of resources that are typically available.
➤ Appreciate the importance of managing project resources, and their effect on project duration.
➤ Apply project resource management tools and techniques for managing project time.

INTRODUCTION

Like any well-run organization—or even a well-run household—a project needs to use resources efficiently. Chapter 6 discussed the first part of Project Time Management, which we termed project scheduling. This included developing the WBS, activity definition, and activity sequencing. Chapter 6 thus included discussions on how a project can be divided into deliverables and activities and how these activities are ordered. However, an additional aspect of Project Time Management is an understanding of how project task durations are determined. This involves assessing the resources needed for each task. This chapter explores the concepts of activity resource estimating, activity duration estimating, and schedule development. We will also discuss what resources are, why it is important to manage them, and what techniques and tools project managers have at their disposal to manage resources, to develop project schedules based on resources, and to avoid resource related problems that may influence project completion (see Figure 7.2).

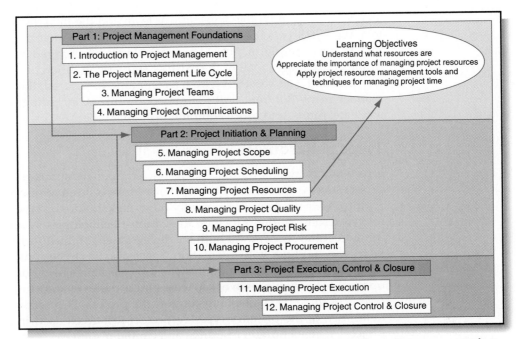

Figure 7.2   Information systems project management focusing on managing project resources

WHAT ARE RESOURCES?

Resource
A source of supply or support, such as money, people, materials, technology, and space.

Resources are commonly thought of as "sources of supply or support," a description that holds true in the case of project management resources, which include money, people, materials, technology, and space (see Figure 7.3). For information systems projects, a more specific listing of resources might include systems developers, project managers, systems analysts, stakeholders, development environments, facilities, and information

Figure 7.3   Some examples of project resources

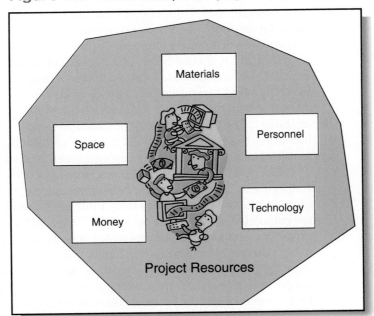

architectures for both the development team and the final implementation of the system. We will discuss these various types of resources in more detail later in this chapter.

As an example, a project manager may be charged with leading a project designed to integrate all of the existing software in different functional areas (financial, human resources, etc.) within a company. To succeed, the project manager must manage many different types of project resources, including people, hardware and software, funds, and office equipment, among others.

Types of Resources

Effectively managing human resources, equipment, space, and money is critical to project success. For information systems projects, human resources include not only the project team itself but possibly other stakeholders in the process. Equipment-related resources might include the various technologies—hardware, software, and infrastructure—needed for both the development of the information systems and for its testing and final implementation. Space also has to be considered because people interact with the organization for which the system is being designed and the development team occupies workspaces. Finally, and related to all of these, financial resources must be available to support the project. This section discusses in greater detail two of the primary types of project resources used in information systems projects, namely human resources and capital resources.

Human Resources

Developing an information system involves using people with different skills. The project manager plays a key role in determining the human resources necessary for a project. **Human resources** include all project stakeholders, such as customers, project team members, support staff, project suppliers, and end users. The job of systems analysts, for example, may be to elicit requirements from the customer, then determine the design of the system. Typically these analysts not only understand the intricacies of systems development but are also knowledgeable about business processes. Their role is to extract customer needs and convey them in a meaningful way to the personnel doing the actual systems development.

The systems developers, alternatively, depend less on business knowledge and more on in-depth technical knowledge of the hardware and software platforms necessary to optimize system performance. Certain project personnel may also be involved in acquiring both new personnel and necessary materials and technologies. Other human resources related to a project would also include stakeholders from the client's organization as well as stakeholders (such as upper management) from the firm undertaking the systems development project (such as top level management). The project manager, therefore, must have skills in a variety of areas, including the projects technical domain and the business context, as well as excellent leadership, planning, and communication skills (see Chapters 3 and 4).

Effectively managing these resources is critical to the success of any project. Neglecting to properly manage human resources dramatically increases the likelihood of project failure. Project personnel must be monitored to ensure that necessary tasks are completed on time and on budget. Relationships with the customer must also be properly managed to ensure open and honest communication. Relationships with end-users, who are often also the customer, must be managed to ensure an easy transition once the project is complete and ready to implement. Managing relationships with suppliers is also critical in ensuring that the necessary resources are available for use when needed. For all of these reasons, it is imperative that project managers develop and maintain good communication networks among all project stakeholders.

Human resources
All project stakeholders, including customers, project team members, support staff, project suppliers, and end users.

To estimate the human resources needed for a project, the tasks associated with the project are first defined as explained in Chapter 6, then the personnel needs for each task are evaluated. The selection of personnel may be influenced by the availability, cost, and skills of the project manager's resource pool. After determining the appropriate human resources to accomplish a given activity as well as other resource requirements, the project manager can begin to estimate the duration of project tasks and develop the project schedule.

Global Implications: Human Resource Management as an Advantage to Offshoring

The types of projects that are most likely to be offshored were discussed in Chapter 5's Global Implications: Deciding when to Offshore. With respect to managing human resources on a project, one other reason companies might choose to offshore is to "follow the sun" in an attempt to maintain a 24-hour software development cycle (Edwards and Swidhar, 2005). In 2001, Motorola revealed several techniques that it used to manage human resources across the globe during a critical project (Battin, Crocker, Kreidler, and Subramanian, 2001). Anticipating potential problems with globally distributed teams, the Motorola team identified 10 problems likely to emerge and developed 12 techniques to alleviate them (see Figure 7.4).

As can be seen from the figure, many of these problems are resource management issues, including how to manage capital resources (e.g., choosing and managing the types of technology used by the project team to communicate, coordinate, and execute project activities across time and space) as well as human resources (developing a sense of "teamness" and managing cultural differences). Motorola's example shows that global resources can be used to the project's advantage if properly managed.

Figure 7.4 Global project teams: problems and solutions

Source: Battin, Crocker, Kreidler, and Subramanian, 2001.

Global Development Issues and Solution Strategies

Category name	issue	Liaisons	Communication	Architectural principles	Incremental integration	Rational task assignment	Common tools	Common work products	Contracts	Centralized bug reporting	Experience	Don't impose process	Complete life cycle
Loss of communication richness	Physical distance	X	X			X	X						
	Time zone disparity	X	X	X	X	X	X						
	Domain expertise	X	X	X		X					X		
Coordination break down	Architecture	X	X	X	X	X							X
	Software integration	X	X	X	X	X							X
	Software conf. mngt.						X	X					
Geographical dispersion	Vendor support		X						X	X	X		
	Governmental issues										X		
Loss of "teamness"	Development process	X	X		X		X	X			X	X	X
Cultural differences	Local impression of remote terms	X	X								X		

Capital Resources

Capital resources
The tools and infrastructure used to produce other goods and services.

Capital resources can be thought of as the tools and infrastructure used to produce other goods and services. Therefore, for the purposes of this section, we will group infrastructure and materials into the broader category of capital resources. In information systems development projects, both the development software and the technological platform on which the software resides are capital resources. As an example, if a project required Microsoft's Visual Studio development environment to develop .NET applications, that software would be considered a capital resource. Similarly, if that software resided on a Dell workstation, the workstation also would be a capital resource. Even the software specifically used to organize project activities—such as Microsoft Project—might be regarded as a capital resource. Notably, in some instances technology related capital resources might be located outside the company itself, supplied through third-party providers. Acquiring necessary project materials or services from outside the company is the focus of Chapter 10, which deals with managing project procurement. Other types of capital resources more traditionally associated with non-IS projects, such as team meeting facilities, could also be part of the IS project environment.

Of specific interest for project teams is the growing use of a formal project management office (PMO)—also called the IT war room (Johnson and Horsey, 2001). As defined in Chapter 2, a PMO is a dedicated part of the organization—frequently consisting of support personnel and a physical facility—whose purpose is to focus on various aspects of project management. The PMO serves as a center of excellence that fosters good project management practices. The PMO may provide a variety of benefits to project teams working on projects at any one time in the organization, including help with methodologies for planning or controlling project activities. In some instances, project managers are members of the PMO and are then assigned to new projects as they are launched.

Opportunity cost
The measure of the alternative opportunities forgone in the choice of one good or activity over others.

The management of capital resources is particularly important when considering opportunity costs. **Opportunity costs** are a measure of the alternative opportunities forgone in the choice of one good or activity over others. Because organizations are typically involved in multiple projects and because buildings, technology, and other available infrastructure may sometimes be used by only one project at a time, organizations must decide how to use these limited available capital resources (see Figure 7.5). During project initiation—and specifically the selection process—project managers must clearly identify their capital resource needs to facilitate project selection decisions.

Figure 7.5
Managing information systems capital resources

So far this discussion of capital resources has focused on how best to *use* capital resources to facilitate project completion and on the role of capital resource needs during project selection. However, capital resources can also be the goal of projects. Questions about the organization's focus must be carefully considered for projects designed to update technology. Potential questions include: How best can we improve our technology to support our business objectives? What changes to our existing infrastructure will we need to make in order to install the new technology? How much risk will the organization be taking in changing the capital resources? The organization and its leadership need to consider these questions and many others before making changes to the existing infrastructure.

AN OVERVIEW OF MANAGING PROJECT RESOURCES

The efficient and effective use of resources can often make or break a project. Because resources are limited, some might be hard to obtain (such as a systems analyst with specialized knowledge about a particular industry), expensive (such as a supercomputer with customized processors necessary for studying genetic diseases), or both (such as highly skilled programmers). Consequently, managing project resources is an important part of the planning and execution stages of any project. In the following sections, you will learn more about the importance of managing resources, as well as the implications of failures and successes.

The Importance of Managing Resources

The efficient use of project resources should be a primary goal for every project manager because the allocation of resources can have a major influence on project schedules. Of specific concern are scarce resources because their allocation can easily scuttle the project schedule. For example, if a scarce resource, such as a limited number of experienced programmers, is not carefully allocated, critical project activities might be delayed.

Project resources can influence many of the key knowledge areas, such as project time, cost, quality, and risk management. In terms of Project Time Management, discussed both in Chapter 6 and the current chapter, resource allocation plays a large role in determining activity duration. For example, a particular task in a project—say, requirements gathering—could have a number of different durations depending on the number of people allocated to the task and their skills. Project resources also influence project cost management. Resources obviously have costs, and how they are allocated impacts the project's budget. The resources used to complete tasks may also influence the quality of project deliverables. Finally, if specific resources to be used during the project are new, project risk may be increased.

Resource Management Statistics
With the clear connection between resource allocation, activity duration, and costs, we can see how developing project management skills related to these areas can improve the likelihood that projects will be successfully completed on time and at or under budget. According to the Standish Group's *Extreme Chaos* report (2001), several key statistics regarding the success and failure of projects improved from 1994 to 2000 (see Table 7.1). From a resource allocation standpoint, the most impressive statistics are the percentages of time overruns and cost overruns from 1994 to 2000. As Table 7.1 shows, time overruns fell from 222 percent in 1994 to 63 percent in 2000, and cost overruns fell from 189 percent to 45 percent.

Table 7.1 *Extreme Chaos* Report Statistics Improving from 1994 to 2000

PERCENTAGE OF	1994	1996	1998	2000
Project success	16%	27%	26%	28%
Project failure	31%	40%	28%	23%
Time overrun	222%			63%
Cost overrun	189%			45%
Required features included in final product	61%			67%

The Standish Group reports that the key reasons for these declines were newer, better tools for monitoring and controlling progress and that "better skilled project managers with better management processes are being used." Later in this chapter we present several tools that will allow you as a project manager to better estimate activity durations and, as a result, project duration, and to better assign resources to optimize efficiency over the course of a project. Given the importance of resource allocation to managing project cost and time, developing the skills to efficiently allocate resources will boost your success rate in managing projects.

Implications of Failure

Resources affect both the time to complete a project and its cost. If, because of poor planning, any necessary resources are unavailable for a task on a project's critical path, the entire project may be delayed. To correct the error, the project manager may assign additional resources to a task to try to get back on schedule—this is known as crashing and will be discussed later. However, even if the project's schedule gets back on track, crashing may well result in higher costs because the project manager must now cover the expenses of recruiting more people or paying overtime. Because poor resource planning is seldom an isolated incident, the likely result is a project that will run over budget and take longer than anticipated to complete.

One clear example of poor resource planning is illustrated by a recent project undertaken by the United Kingdom's government in conjunction with Electronic Data Systems (EDS). The new system was intended to create a child-support case-management and telephony system at a cost of more than $800 million over 10 years. This system, designed to replace older, paper-based systems, was in jeopardy with complaints about delayed rollout, inability to transfer all data into the new system, and an increasing backlog in entering new data. As in many projects that are faced with great difficulties, the project managers for this project had to make difficult resource decisions in order to salvage the situation (Songini, 2004).

Success Story

Successful projects are usually defined by the fact that they come in at or under budget, meet their deadlines, and provide the needed functionality for the stakeholders. An example of an organization that has repeatedly completed successful projects is Bekins, the moving and storage company.

In 1999, Bekins entered the business to consumer (B2C) e-commerce market by developing and implementing a shipping and tracking system for its customers. The successful implementation of this project in large part was the result of good schedule management practices. One resource management technique used by Bekins was to break this e-commerce initiative into modules (see the discussion of decomposition mentioned in Chapter 6) that could each be completed within 90 to 120 days. According to Bekins' director of data management and e-business architecture,

Randall Mowen, "To keep on task and put a deliverable out every quarter has been a valuable thing for us. When things go longer than that, the expectations are so different from what they were in the beginning, the deliverable might not represent what the business was looking for" (Harreld, 2001).

To keep to such a demanding deployment schedule, Bekins ensures they have spent adequate time up front planning and designing the system, devoting as much as 30 to 40 percent of the project's life cycle to these phases. This heavy reliance on project planning, during which time resources are estimated and schedules created, is the key to Bekins' IT project success.

Managing Resources and the Project Life Cycle

When planning a project, project managers first decide on the deliverables of the project and the activities needed to produce them. Once they have determined the best sequence for the activities, they estimate the resources needed. The combination of resource needs and resource availability helps to determine the time needed to complete the individual activities, as well as the entire project. Although the sequence of activities can be determined without considering the resources, the time needed to complete these activities, as well as the entire project, depends on the resources' availability. To address this need, project management software can be used to track and allocate resources.

Managing resources should be considered during the initiation, planning, execution, control, and close-out phases of a project. Some examples of activities in each of these phases follow. During initiation, for instance, resources critical to the project should be considered when deciding which type of project to pursue. One selection criterion might be the availability of new technologies. During the planning phase, schedules should be developed with specific resources in mind, and scarce resources must be carefully allocated. During a project's execution phase, resource reallocation may become necessary as the project unfolds to protect the project schedule. During project control, managers need to constantly monitor the allocation and use of resources to facilitate any approved project changes. Finally, during project close-out, purchased resources and any outstanding contracts must be settled. Any discrepancies between purchased materials and delivered materials must be identified, and steps must be taken to settle those discrepancies.

Duration versus Effort

Effort
Actual time spent working on an activity.

Duration
Elapsed time between the start and finish of an activity.

Before jumping into the discussion of techniques for resource and duration estimating, we need to clarify the distinction between duration and effort. When completing an activity, the "doers" expend a certain amount of effort. **Effort** is the actual time required to perform an activity, not accounting for any breaks, meetings, and the like. For example, designing an interface might take eight hours of effort, so a programmer could finish the activity in one day. If, however, the programmer has to attend meetings during the day, she might need two or three days to complete the task. Although the effort would still be eight hours, the duration from start to finish for that task would be two or three days. Thus, **duration** is the time that elapses between the start and the finish of an activity, including any interruptions. When planning a project, managers have to take into account the number of people working on a task, potential interruptions, and the like to estimate the duration for each individual activity. In the next section, we examine several specific techniques for managing project resources.

When scheduling a project, managers can employ a wide variety of tools and techniques to facilitate resource management. These techniques are primarily associated with estimating the resource needs associated with project activities, estimating the duration of the activities, and finally, developing the schedule. These sections will finish our discussion of how to plan a project. In Chapter 6, you learned how to define the project's deliverables and the associated activities, as well as how to define the sequence of these activities. Now you will learn how to estimate the resources and time needed, as well as how to tie everything together in order to create the project schedule.

Activity Resource Estimating

The goal of activity resource estimating, an aspect of the PMBOK's Project Time Management knowledge area, is to estimate the resources needed for each activity so they can be deployed in the most effective manner. In some instances, assigning more resources can speed the completion of activities, but in others, assigning more resources will actually hinder progress because of increased communication and coordination efforts. The following sections discuss how to estimate the resources needed and how to estimate the project's duration based on these estimates.

As Figure 7.6 shows, project managers rely on a wide variety of different inputs during activity resource estimating. As in most stages of project scheduling, managers use enterprise environmental factors (such as scheduling tools and software) and organizational process assets (such as historical information from prior projects) to establish initial activity sequences and assign and manage resources. In addition, they use outputs from prior stages of project planning. For example, the activity list and activity attributes identified during the activity definition phase help to estimate the resources needed. As Figure 7.7 shows, resource needs have to be matched with resource availability. In other words, a project manager has to know which resources she can draw upon before deciding on which resources to use. Finally, the project management plan is used as an input to activity resource estimating. Specifically, the schedule management

Figure 7.6 PMBOK required inputs, tools and techniques used, and resulting outputs during activity resource estimating

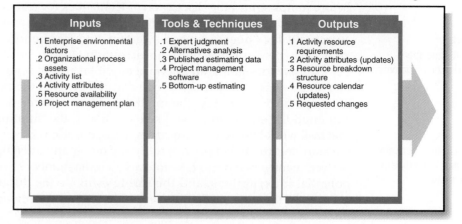

Inputs	Tools & Techniques	Outputs
.1 Enterprise environmental factors .2 Organizational process assets .3 Activity list .4 Activity attributes .5 Resource availability .6 Project management plan	.1 Expert judgment .2 Alternatives analysis .3 Published estimating data .4 Project management software .5 Bottom-up estimating	.1 Activity resource requirements .2 Activity attributes (updates) .3 Resource breakdown structure .4 Resource calendar (updates) .5 Requested changes

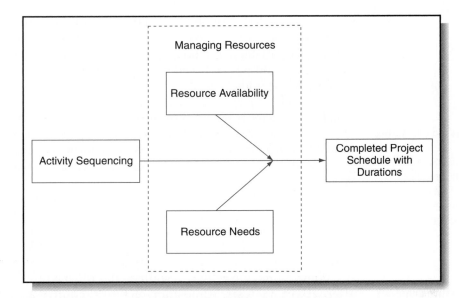

Figure 7.7 Project scheduling and managing resources

plan is used, primarily in determining how to manage changes in a project's schedule. The different tools and techniques used for resource estimating, as well as the outputs, will be covered in the following sections.

Resource Estimation Techniques

Although project managers can choose from among a variety of tools and techniques, they should never depend solely on the results of just one technique for estimating project resources. Rather, they should use a combination of estimation techniques (see Figure 7.8). If the results of these techniques converge, the project manager can be fairly confident about the accuracy of the resource estimates. Whether using one or several techniques to estimate resource needs, the project manager should avoid having to give quick estimates based on a gut feeling. Because such estimates will most likely be inaccurate, the project manager should always employ the techniques described below before providing any estimate.

One of the primary tools of project resource estimating is **expert judgment**. Usually, experts can give valuable inputs into estimating resource needs. In most cases, the "doers" can give very precise estimates about the resources needed. In an

Expert judgment
Estimation based on the experience of one or more experts on the particular activity or project.

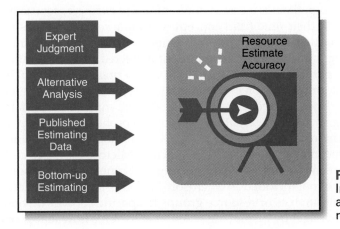

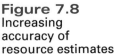
Figure 7.8
Increasing accuracy of resource estimates

information systems project, the database administrator can give good estimates about how long it takes to create certain database queries, and a programmer can give good estimates about how long it takes to code common modules. However, the estimates should not be based solely on recollections of prior projects or activities, which will most likely lead to biased estimates because people often have a hard time remembering exact details. Rather, a combination of expert judgment and hard data (e.g., data recorded from prior projects) is preferable.

Published estimating data
Hard data from specific activities carried out on previous projects that may be used to more accurately estimate resource needs.

Another source of hard data about resource needs is **published estimating data** available from market research companies, a form of benchmarking. These companies gather and analyze research needs for a variety of projects in a variety of industries. When planning to implement a new ERP system, for example, you can obtain benchmarking data both from ERP vendors and from independent organizations to help prepare estimates of resources needed. Usually, these data are based on a number of different companies, so you can get a good overview of average, minimum, or maximum resource needs. These data also help to benchmark one's resource needs against those of direct competitors or industry leaders.

Alternatives analysis
An estimating technique in which trade-offs between the time needed, the resources invested, and the desired quality of the final deliverable are examined.

When estimating activity resources, it is often advisable to conduct some form of **alternatives analysis**. Almost any activity requires a trade-off between the time needed, the resources invested, and the desired quality of the final deliverable. For example, assigning more human resources to a project might speed completion time but at tremendously higher costs; further, quality might be inconsistent across the people working on the activity. On the other hand, fewer people might still be able to complete the activity within the desired time frame but might introduce more errors because of time pressure. Other times, a project manager might realize that outsourcing the activity is the most efficient solution. Carefully analyzing alternatives helps a project manager make optimal choices, given the available resources and desired outcomes.

Bottom-up estimating
An estimating technique in which complex activities are further decomposed to a point where more accurate estimates can be made.

Bottom-up estimating is a technique applied when the resource needs of an activity cannot be easily estimated. This is often the case if the work package itself is fairly complex. In this instance, the activity should be decomposed further until a level is reached where reasonable estimates can be provided. If a work package for an ERP system consists of, say, the user interface for the payroll module, it might be hard to estimate the resources needed to complete this deliverable; if so, the deliverable can be further decomposed into the individual screens, for which it is easier to estimate the resources needed. These lower-level estimates can then be combined into an estimate for the activity itself.

While these are the four techniques listed by the PMBOK, it should be noted that companies will use a variety of techniques to arrive at their estimations. Benchmarking against competitors is a common practice. For example, competing automakers might benchmark their time from conception to market. Techniques utilizing project team members, such as brainstorming sessions or mind mapping, might also be useful in gathering valuable information about expected project duration. In brainstorming sessions, participants are charged with generating ideas without fear of group censure. A brainstorming session on estimating a project's duration, or possible problems that might be encountered, can serve as valuable input in the final estimation. In mind mapping, visual representation of tasks and problems may help the project team come up with more accurate project representations and associated durations.

Project management software, such as Microsoft Project, can greatly help in estimating resource needs and matching those needs with resource availability and costs. One tool included in Microsoft Project is a resource calendar that can be used to assign resources or resource groups to specific activities. These calendars help the project manager by displaying whether a resource is available or might be tied up by a different activity. Further, costs can be assigned to the different resources, which helps in conducting alternative analyses. To specify the details about the different resources, a Resource Sheet view lets you specify a name for each resource, as well as attributes such as type, standard and overtime rate, cost/use, and the like. Other views such as Resource Usage display the resource allocation in an easy-to-use way.

All of these techniques, however, are only as good as the inputs into the resource estimating process. In other words, if the activities are not clearly defined, the resource estimates will most likely be inaccurate, leading to frustrated clients and project managers. There has to be a clear, mutual understanding of project scope, the work packages that make up that scope, and the activities that are required for each work package before an accurate duration estimate can be made.

Resource Estimation Outputs

The primary output of the activity resource estimating process (see Figure 7.6) is a detailed listing of the resource requirements (both types and quantities needed) for the individual activities. Often, the resource needs for different activities are combined to represent the resource needs for each WBS work package. The **activity resource requirements** can be very detailed and should include any assumptions made during the estimation process. That way, if a certain assumption does not hold, the project manager immediately knows that the schedule has to be adjusted accordingly. These resource requirements will be an important input into the schedule development process discussed later.

To represent the resources in an easy-to-use format, a **resource breakdown structure** (RBS) is created. Analogous to a product breakdown structure or a work breakdown structure, an RBS presents all needed resources hierarchically, usually ordered by type or category. An RBS helps to visualize the different types of resources needed for a project. The RBS is useful in roll-up reporting, for instance, where the project manager wants to show all of the resources (both human and capital) necessary for accomplishing various components of a project. As an example, level 0 of a WBS represents the entire scope of a project. The equivalent level in an RBS would then list all resources necessary for the entire project. At a lower level of the WBS, the corresponding RBS might illustrate those resources necessary to complete the particular work package(s) associated with a major component of the project (e.g., development of the user interface for a new system).

Another output of the resource estimating process is the updated **resource calendar**, which displays the availability of the different resources. For human resources, a resource calendar specifies working and nonworking days, such as weekends or holidays. A project manager can use resource calendars to quickly identify whether specific resources are idle (and available) or occupied by another task. Every work resource should have its own calendar, which can be specified in many types of project management software

The activity definition process (remember, that means defining all the activities necessary to create a particular project deliverable) entails providing preliminary activity attributes, such as predecessors, successors, and constraints. The resources needed to accomplish the activities estimated in the present stage also become part of a more refined set of activity attributes that can now be used to create more accurate schedules. Further, in case the process of estimating resources yields additional changes to the activities (e.g., the realization that additional resources may be necessary to accomplish an activity), such changes will be incorporated into updated activity attributes. Needless to say, all changes must be approved following the project's change control guidelines.

Activity resource requirements
A very detailed listing of the resource requirements for the individual activities.

Resource breakdown structure
A hierarchical, graphical representation of all needed resources ordered by type or category.

Resource calendar
A specific type of project calendar that is used to track the hours when certain resources are available.

Activity Duration Estimating

Activity duration estimation
The process of estimating the duration of the project activities using both project scope and resource information.

The next phase in PMBOK's Project Time Management knowledge area is **activity duration estimation** (see Figure 7.9). This phase generally involves using both project scope and resource information to estimate the duration of the project activities. The people with the greatest knowledge of the specific activity are most often called on to approve the estimation. The duration estimates will then be combined with the activity sequencing to determine the duration of the entire project, as well as to identify the critical path. As with all project planning activities, activity duration estimations become more precise as the project progresses (recall the cone of uncertainty discussed in Chapter 6) because more detailed information is usually available during later stages of the project.

As Figure 7.9 shows, inputs for this phase include the activity list, attributes, resource requirements, and the resource calendar, in addition to the project scope statement, enterprise environmental factors (such as project management software), and organizational process assets (such as historical information). Finally, the risk register (a formal listing of identified risks) and the activity cost estimates (both part of the project management plan) serve as inputs to the activity duration estimation. Some of the inputs for the activity duration estimation were also inputs for or outputs from other phases. In those cases, we will only briefly mention their characteristics.

The primary inputs in this phase, then, are the activity list, associated attributes, and activity resource requirements produced as an output from the last phase. An initial estimate of these resource requirements has been determined during the process of resource estimation. The resource calendar (produced during the activity resource estimation) specifies the availability of the different resources; that is, it specifies the times when the resources are available for a certain task. The scope of the project is captured in the project scope statement and is used as an input to keep the focus on the project's activities. Enterprise environmental factors (such as estimating databases) assist in the duration estimation, as do organizational process assets. These can be used to better estimate activity durations and may consist of company historical documents as well as project team members' knowledge gained during previous projects. The risk register (described in Chapter 9) captures the different activities' risks, taking into consideration those that have a high probability of impacting the project schedule. Finally, the activity

Figure 7.9 PMBOK required inputs, tools and techniques used, and resulting outputs during activity duration estimating

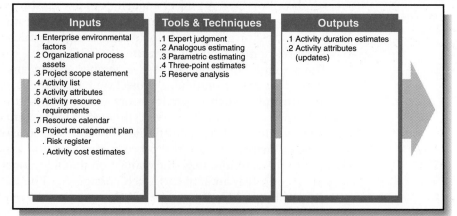

cost estimates help identify to what degree resource allocations impact the costs for completing the activities.

Reassessments related to calculating activity duration can also occur at this point. For instance, if it appears that an activity's duration is going to be too long, more resources could be assigned. As an example, the time needed to code an initial prototype can be greatly reduced by the number of programmers assigned to the task. This might require adding new resources to the project, the creation of a new resource calendar, or some similar measure. The caveat, of course, is that at some point, merely adding programmers will not shorten the task duration because the number of programming assignments is limited. The point is clear, however, that the amount of resources allocated to a given task will surely influence its duration.

Duration Estimating Techniques

Tools and techniques used during the activity duration estimation process include expert judgment, analogous estimating, quantitatively based duration estimating (such as parametric estimating or three-point estimating), and reserve analysis (see Figure 7.10). As with resource estimating, using several techniques to estimate activity duration, as opposed to relying on only one, can increase the overall accuracy of any estimates. Next, each of these and techniques is discussed in more detail.

Expert judgment, previously mentioned under the activity definition process, can be used as a means to better estimate activities' durations and their need for specific resources. As with its use during activity definition, care should be taken, for expert judgment can rely on the subjective opinion of project participants. While programmers might be able to give a fairly accurate estimate of how long it takes to write a certain number of lines of code, they might not be able to give accurate estimates of less common tasks.

Analogous estimating is simply using the duration of a similar activity as a basis for estimating the current activity. For information systems development projects, analogous estimating can be used for standard tasks such as building interfaces. Historical

Analogous estimating
The estimation of activities' durations based upon the duration of similar activities.

Figure 7.10 Activity duration estimation techniques

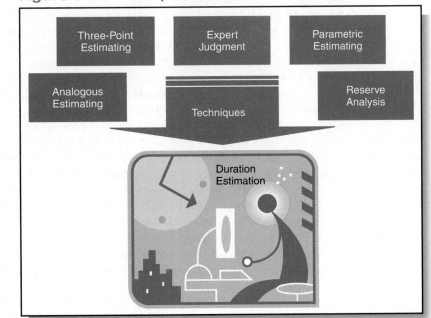

data or expert judgment can be used to estimate the duration of these activities because components like these are often fairly standardized and thus take the same amounts of time to complete. In addition to company historical data, published data (from past projects done in the company) about durations of similar activities can be used.

Parametric estimating is a quantitatively based duration estimation technique that uses some type of mathematical process to determine the activity's duration. In some cases, the number of lines of code a programmer generates in a normal workday can be used in conjunction with the number of lines of code estimated for a given activity to determine that activity's duration.

Three-point estimates can increase accuracy by accounting for optimistic, pessimistic, and most likely estimates. To arrive at an accurate estimate, these three estimates are averaged, taking into consideration the risk involved in completing the activities. If a high risk is associated with the activity, the estimate will lean toward the pessimistic end. PERT analysis is a specific form of three-point estimate, where specific weights are applied to the optimistic, pessimistic, and most likely estimates. This is explained in more detail later in our discussion of PERT analyses in the schedule development section.

Reserve analysis considers the different activities to establish reserve times (basically, time set aside as a reserve in case activity durations don't match the plan) within a project schedule for the purpose of guarding against potential risks to the schedule. In the case of reserve time, any buffer in the project schedule should be documented and accounted for.

Duration Estimating Outputs

The outputs of the activity duration estimation process are updated activity attributes, as well as activity duration estimates (refer back to Figure 7.9). A Gantt chart is one such representation of project duration. As introduced in Chapter 2 and defined in Chapter 6, a Gantt chart is a bar chart that employs time lines and other types of symbols to illustrate the project schedule. Activity or task names are usually listed along the vertical axis. Activity durations are listed on the horizontal access. A sample Gantt chart is illustrated in Figure 7.11 (in this instance, a column that shows activity durations is highlighted). A Gantt chart traditionally doesn't capture all aspects of a network diagram (such as the precedence relationships discussed in Chapter 6), but it does convey information about the duration of the various activities, and by capturing the various anticipated start and stop dates of those activities, it also illustrates the duration of the overall project.

As mentioned above, what this type of bar chart typically does not represent is the complex nature of the relationships between the various activities—relationships that are typically illustrated by a network diagram (e.g., see our discussion of precedence in the prior chapter). Interestingly, project management software has evolved, combining both network diagram and bar chart functionality in Gantt chart representations. The arrows connecting the various duration bars associated with tasks in Figure 7.11 capture the relationship information that is more commonly available only in network diagrams.

Duration estimates associated with activities can be either fixed-point or range estimates. Often, customers desire a very precise, fixed-point estimate of the time needed to complete an activity. However, especially during the early stages of a project, it is frequently very difficult to give precise estimates unless the project team has done very similar projects in the past. The prudent project manager should try to provide range rather than point estimates. Further, the estimates should be precise only to the degree possible. In other words, if a project manager can give an estimate only within ±50 percent, she should not try to provide a ±10 percent estimate because this

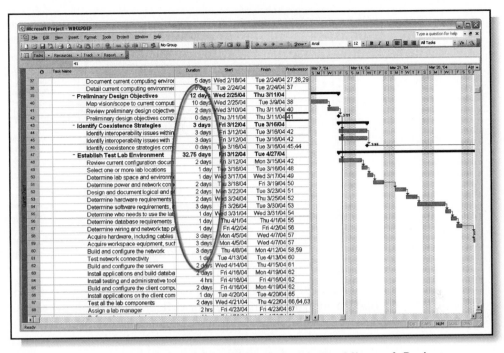

Figure 7.11 Screenshot of a Gantt chart created in Microsoft Project

will lead to dissatisfaction (as well as other complications) if the actual time falls outside the range of the estimate (especially at the upper end). Usually, range estimates are expressed as time periods needed to complete the task, such as 6 months ±2 weeks.

Providing optimistic, pessimistic, and most likely estimates will give the customer a good picture of the different scenarios. These different estimates can be further supported by the likelihood of finishing the activity in the different times; for example, the project manager can say that there is a 50 percent chance of finishing the activity in 10 days, a 30 percent chance of finishing in 8 days, and a 20 percent chance of finishing in 12 days. As estimates become more precise during the course of the project (recall the cone of uncertainty), the customer can be provided with updated information. No matter how precise the estimates are, the project manager should take great care to continually provide the customer with the refined estimates; this way, the customer is in the loop and aware of any factors affecting the project's schedule.

Schedule Development

Schedule development
The process of determining start and finish dates for project activities.

Schedule development is an iterative process designed to determine start and finish dates for project activities. Whereas activity sequencing was the topic of Chapter 6, activity durations are necessary to determine the final project schedule. During the process of schedule development, the activity duration estimates, in combination with the activity sequences, are used to establish the final project schedule, a critical component of the baseline project plan used to track the project's progress.

Inputs to schedule development include organizational process assets, the project scope statement, project network diagrams, the activity list, activity attributes, activity duration estimates, resource requirements, resource calendars, and the risk register of the project management plan (see Figure 7.12). Most of these inputs have been discussed in prior sections and will thus be mentioned only briefly.

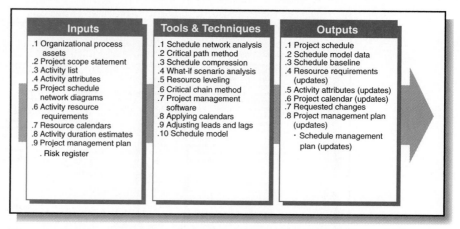

Inputs	Tools & Techniques	Outputs
.1 Organizational process assets	.1 Schedule network analysis	.1 Project schedule
.2 Project scope statement	.2 Critical path method	.2 Schedule model data
.3 Activity list	.3 Schedule compression	.3 Schedule baseline
.4 Activity attributes	.4 What-if scenario analysis	.4 Resource requirements (updates)
.5 Project schedule network diagrams	.5 Resource leveling	.5 Activity attributes (updates)
.6 Activity resource requirements	.6 Critical chain method	.6 Project calendar (updates)
.7 Resource calendars	.7 Project management software	.7 Requested changes
.8 Activity duration estimates	.8 Applying calendars	.8 Project management plan (updates)
.9 Project management plan	.9 Adjusting leads and lags	· Schedule management plan (updates)
. Risk register	.10 Schedule model	

Figure 7.12 PMBOK required inputs, tools and techniques used, and resulting outputs during schedule development

Organizational process assets can be as simple as a project calendar. Often developed using Microsoft Project or collaboration tools such as Outlook or SharePoint, such a calendar specifies working and nonworking days. Calendars are necessary to show what hours and time periods are available for work scheduling. For example, is the project based on an 8-hour-a-day, 40-hour workweek or on a 10-hour-a-day, 4-day workweek? Is overtime available, and if so, how much and how will it be allocated? Most software makes these working-time decisions easy to implement by allowing broad level changes to organizational asset availability (i.e., put in holidays, personal time off, overtime, standard working time, and specified work weeks). Software such as Microsoft Project can be used to record and display resource availability information (see Figure 7.13).

Figure 7.13 Changing working time in Microsoft Project

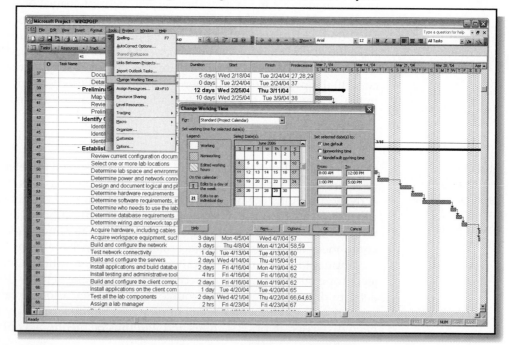

Imposed Dates
Dates imposed to meet some type of development deadline.

The project scope statement (introduced in Chapter 5) presents the scope of the entire project and also details any constraints or assumptions that can affect the project's schedule. In terms of schedule development, constraints are usually of two types, imposed dates and milestones. **Imposed dates** are dates that are imposed to meet some type of development deadline. For example, a new information systems rollout may need to be in effect by a certain date for the company to keep its first-mover strategic advantage. Another example would be a date imposed by an environmental agency that the company must meet in order to remain in business. The most common types of such constraints are "start no earlier than" and "finish no later than" (see precedence relationships in Chapter 6 for a more comprehensive explanation). These and other constraint types are available in Microsoft Project (see Figure 7.14), which has a dropdown box containing all available constraint types. As defined in Chapter 6, milestones are dates in the schedule that are meaningful for the completion of specific sets of project events. Milestones are often set by senior management and usually cannot be changed. In many types of project management software, a milestone is represented by entering a task with a duration of zero.

The next inputs, including the activity list (which also includes activity attributes), activity duration estimates, project schedule network diagrams, activity resource requirements, and the resource calendar were discussed earlier. The risk register (as part of the project management plan) specifies how control measures will be implemented to identify potential risks to the project schedule. For example, if the risk is high that a new mainframe computer will not be installed on time, this might influence the project schedule, and more contingency reserve (discussed earlier in this chapter) should be planned for this activity.

Schedule Development Techniques

Some of the primary tools and techniques for the schedule development process include schedule network analysis, critical path analysis, schedule compression, what-if-scenario analyses, resource leveling heuristics, and the critical chain method

Figure 7.14 Choosing constraint types in Microsoft Project

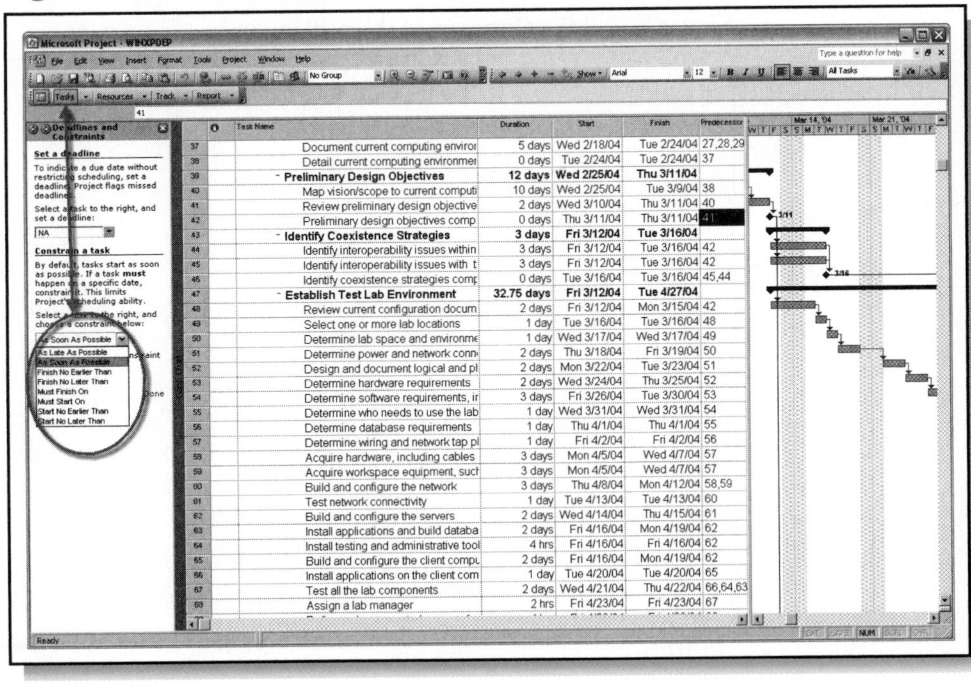

(refer back to Figure 7.12). Dealing with the time component of project scheduling—calculating the expected start and finish dates, as well as early or late start and finish dates of project activities—is referred to as **schedule network analysis**. The schedule network analysis aids managers in determining when activities can be performed given resources and constraints. Some techniques require certain adjustments to the network diagrams. Specifically, the network diagrams have to be analyzed for any errors in the network, such as network loops (paths that follow through the same node more than once) or open ends (activities that do not have a successor). The following sections discuss the different techniques, as well as the use of project management software for schedule development.

One often-used technique is the **critical path method** (CPM), a network analysis technique that determines the sequence of task activities that directly affect the completion of a project. Introduced in Chapter 2, a project's critical path is the longest path through a network diagram that illustrates the shortest amount of time in which a project can be completed. While this definition may sound confusing, just remember that the purpose of the critical path is to establish how quickly a project can be completed given the tasks, durations, and dependencies illustrated in the networking diagram.

Figure 7.15 illustrates the concept of the **critical path**. In the figure, the critical path includes the activities A, E, G, and I. Therefore, if any of these activities (termed **critical activities**) is delayed, the completion of the entire project will be delayed because the overall time of the critical path increases. Activities not on the critical path can be delayed (to some extent) without affecting the duration of the entire project. Accordingly, these activities contain slack time (often referred to as float). In this figure, Path 4 has 1 day's slack time; Path 5 has 2 days' slack time, Path 6 has 3 days' slack time; Path 1 has 4 days' slack time; and Path 2 has 6 days' slack time; thus, the activities on Path 2 can be delayed by a maximum of 6 days before the overall project schedule is affected. To determine a project's critical path, the durations of all activities on each individual path have to be added; the path with the longest overall duration is the critical path (note that there can be multiple critical paths). In Microsoft Project, the

Schedule network analysis
The process of calculating expected, early, and late start and finish dates of a project.

Critical path method
A technique used for determining the sequence of task activities that directly affect the completion of a project, accomplished by determining the longest path through a network diagram that illustrates the shortest amount of time in which a project can be completed.

Critical path
The longest path through a network diagram illustrating the shortest amount of time in which a project can be completed.

Critical activity
Any activity on the critical path.

Figure 7.15 Concept of the critical path

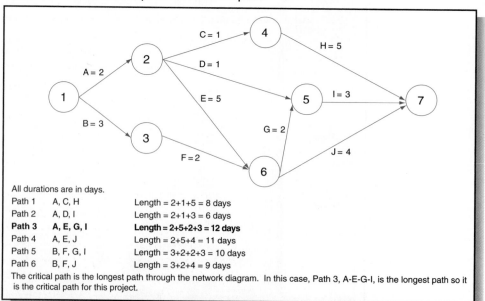

All durations are in days.

Path 1	A, C, H	Length = 2+1+5 = 8 days
Path 2	A, D, I	Length = 2+1+3 = 6 days
Path 3	**A, E, G, I**	**Length = 2+5+2+3 = 12 days**
Path 4	A, E, J	Length = 2+5+4 = 11 days
Path 5	B, F, G, I	Length = 3+2+2+3 = 10 days
Path 6	B, F, J	Length = 3+2+4 = 9 days

The critical path is the longest path through the network diagram. In this case, Path 3, A-E-G-I, is the longest path so it is the critical path for this project.

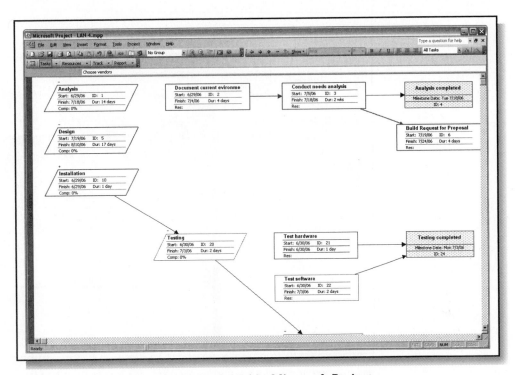

Figure 7.16 Critical path displayed in Microsoft Project

critical path is highlighted in red in the Network Diagram view (see Figure 7.16). Using project management software, the project team members do not have to do tedious calculations to determine the critical path, but it is critical that they understand the concept. Any changes in durations of critical activities will be reflected in the critical path.

The critical path method uses the concepts of **free float** (free slack) and **total float** (total slack) to determine the late and early completion times of a project. Described briefly in Chapter 2, free float is the time an activity can be delayed without affecting the immediately following activity; total float, in contrast, is the time an activity can be delayed without affecting the overall completion date of a project. Free float is always found in noncritical paths because any increase in duration of the activities in the critical path directly affects a project's schedule. The critical path is thus a path that has zero or negative total float. If a network path is not a critical path, it can have positive float; a delay in completion of one activity does not necessarily affect the completion date of the entire project. The existence of positive total float implies that somewhere in the project there is free float; that is, at least one activity can be delayed without affecting the early start date of its immediate successor.

Although the slack times can be calculated by doing a forward pass (to determine the early start and early finish dates) and a backward pass (to determine the late start and late finish dates) through a network diagram, doing so is tedious. Consequently, most project managers use project management software such as Microsoft Project for this process; in addition to greater ease of use, the software can provide real-time updates to any changes in the project schedule. In the Gantt chart view of Microsoft Project, slack can be presented, including task names, early and late start and finish dates, and free and total slack for the individual tasks (see Figure 7.17). An update to the duration of any task immediately updates the start and finish dates, as well as the slack times.

Figure 7.17 Free slack and total slack displayed in Microsoft Project

Program evaluation and review technique (PERT)

A technique that uses optimistic, pessimistic, and realistic time estimates to calculate the expected time for a particular task.

A similar but nowadays less commonly used method to estimate project duration when individual activity duration estimates are uncertain is the **program evaluation and review technique (PERT)**, which was defined and briefly described in Chapter 2. To compensate for this uncertainty, PERT applies probabilistic time estimates for optimistic, most likely, and pessimistic estimates for activity duration. A sample PERT analysis is shown in Figure 7.18. In contrast to the critical path method—which assigns a deterministic start and finish date for each activity—PERT uses a weighted average method. As shown in the figure, the most likely estimate is weighted by a factor of four, with the optimistic and pessimistic estimates having a weighting of 1. People frequently mistakenly refer to something called a PERT chart, which in reality is an activity on node network diagram (discussed in Chapter 6). However, as illustrated in Figure 7.18 PERT is

Figure 7.18 PERT analysis

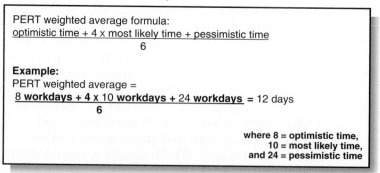

PERT weighted average formula:

$$\frac{\text{optimistic time} + 4 \times \text{most likely time} + \text{pessimistic time}}{6}$$

Example:

PERT weighted average =

$$\frac{8\ \textbf{workdays} + 4 \times 10\ \textbf{workdays} + 24\ \textbf{workdays}}{6} = 12\ \text{days}$$

where 8 = optimistic time,
10 = most likely time,
and 24 = pessimistic time

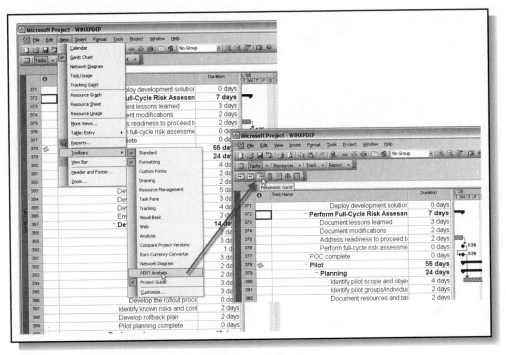

Figure 7.19 PERT analysis in Microsoft Project

not a chart, but rather a mathematical technique used to estimate task or project duration. Nonetheless, in many organizations the use of the term *PERT chart* to refer to an activity on node network diagram is common.

In Microsoft Project, a PERT analysis (see Figure 7.19) can be conducted by activating the PERT Analysis toolbar. This toolbar lets you view a PERT entry sheet for the optimistic, expected, and pessimistic durations, as well as a dialogue to modify the PERT weights for the individual estimates, in addition to other features. For most projects, CPM provides relatively accurate estimates, so project managers tend to rely less on PERT analyses.

Schedule compression involves the use of two mathematical techniques in an attempt to shorten the project schedule. These techniques are known as **crashing**, which looks at cost–schedule trade-offs, and **fast-tracking** (see Figure 7.20), which looks at the possibility of performing activities in parallel that would normally be done in sequence (these two techniques are also discussed in the *Tips from the Pros: When Things Go Wrong,* presented later in this chapter). An example of crashing might involve adding resources so that a data entry task scheduled to take two weeks could be accomplished in one week by hiring additional data entry personnel. Other types of crashing might involve the use of additional nonhuman resources, such as computer time, in order to shorten the time necessary to complete a task. Fast-tracking involves doing project tasks at the same time rather than in sequence. Fast-tracking requires, by necessity, that the task dependencies allow such parallel work.

What else can be done to shorten the critical path (and the duration of the project)? Here, you might need some creativity. You might want to see if some activities might be further broken down to allow fast-tracking. If dependencies between activities originally did not allow fast-tracking, breaking up these activities might open new possibilities to accomplish tasks in parallel. Maybe some activities do not have to be completely finished before a successor activity can be started. Thinking

Schedule compression
The use of mathematical techniques to shorten a project's duration.

Crashing
Dedicating extra resources to a particular activity in an attempt to finish the activity sooner than the scheduled completion date.

Fast-tracking
The performance of activities in parallel that would normally be performed in sequence, in an attempt to shorten the duration of a project.

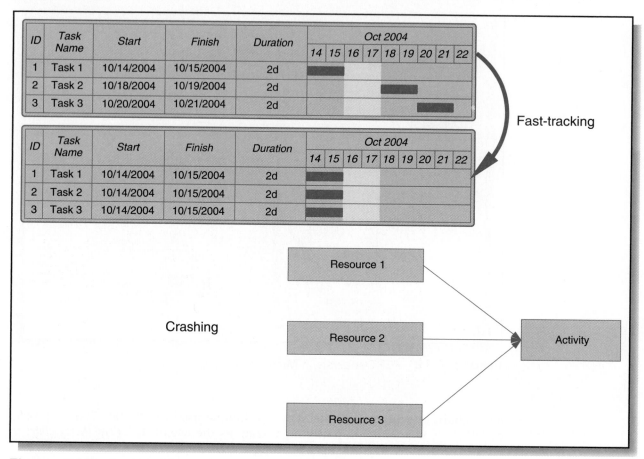

ID	Task Name	Start	Finish	Duration	Oct 2004								
					14	15	16	17	18	19	20	21	22
1	Task 1	10/14/2004	10/15/2004	2d									
2	Task 2	10/18/2004	10/19/2004	2d									
3	Task 3	10/20/2004	10/21/2004	2d									

Fast-tracking

ID	Task Name	Start	Finish	Duration	Oct 2004								
					14	15	16	17	18	19	20	21	22
1	Task 1	10/14/2004	10/15/2004	2d									
2	Task 2	10/14/2004	10/15/2004	2d									
3	Task 3	10/14/2004	10/15/2004	2d									

Crashing

Resource 1

Resource 2

Activity

Resource 3

Figure 7.20 Fast-tracking and crashing

creatively about the different activities on the critical path can help to possibly take them off the critical path, which helps to shorten the overall project schedule.

Another way to shorten the duration of the project might be to check the duration estimates of the critical activities—in Microsoft Project a simple double click on the task duration will open a Task Information dialog box (see Figure 7.21). Oftentimes, duration estimates are based on rules of thumb or include fudge factors. Breaking down the critical activities to a more detailed level lets you obtain more precise estimates because it can remove "noise" from the estimates. Doing so can often lead to a shorter critical path. Sometimes, such a detailed breakdown might adjust the durations upward. Although this does not help to shorten the critical path, it can save you from any surprises during the execution of the project, which can also be beneficial.

An additional tool for project schedule development is simulation. **Simulation** is the process of calculating project and activity durations using different assumptions, constraints, and resource allocations. Two commonly used types of simulation are Monte Carlo simulations and **what-if analyses**. You may recognize these two terms from your introductory statistics classes. Monte Carlo simulations are probabilistic analyses used to calculate a distribution of likely results (in our case likely project or task durations). What-if analyses take advantage of logic networks by simulating various scenarios, such as what if a major component for a system is delayed. Both these techniques allow additional insight into the duration of projects and project activities.

Simulation
A process of evaluating different scenarios and their effects on the project schedule.

What-if analyses
A process of evaluating alternative strategies by observing how changes to selected factors affect other factors and outcomes.

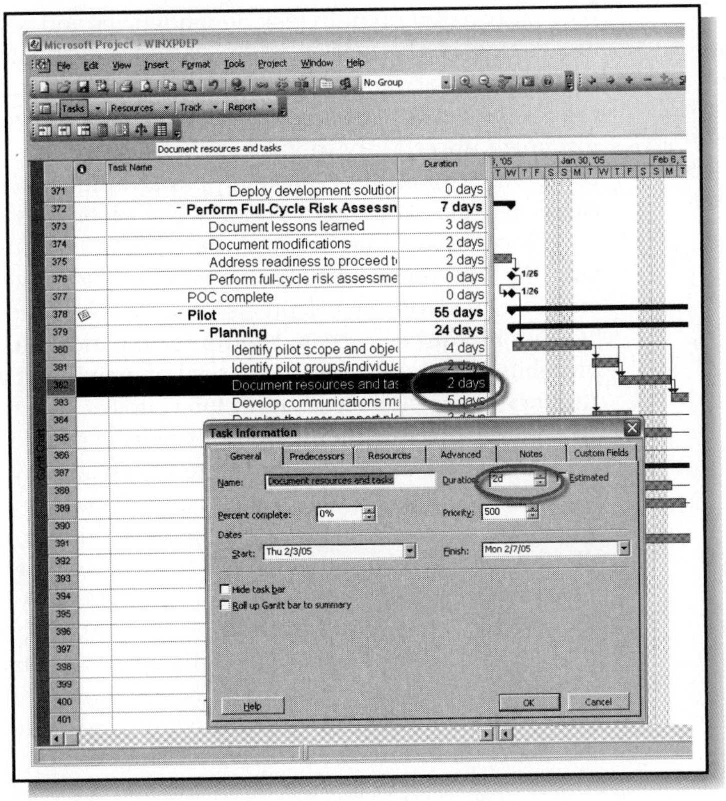

Figure 7.21 Task duration adjustments

Resource leveling
Any form of network analysis where resource management issues drive scheduling decisions.

Resource leveling heuristics
Rules of thumb used to allocate resources to project activities.

Resource leveling is any form of network analysis where resource management issues drive scheduling decisions. This process involves rescheduling activities so that resource requirements for any particular phase of a project do not exceed the availability of those resources. As an example, in a particular software development environment, there may be only one person who has the skill set or knowledge needed to accomplish particular aspects of the development process. If activities requiring that particular developer's skills were originally scheduled at the same time, resources leveling would be used to change the schedule so that they could be accomplished at different times. **Resource leveling heuristics** are rules of thumb used to allocate limited resources during a project. If conflicting needs for certain resources during the project must be resolved, the project manager can use such heuristics to allocate scarce resources to the activities most critical to the project. Resource leveling resulting from these types of resource constraints might lead to a suboptimal project schedule because one or more tasks might have to be delayed based on the availability of resources, delaying the entire schedule. Schedules based on resource leveling are referred to as resource-limited (or resource-constrained) schedules.

A final technique discussed in the PMBOK is the **critical chain method** (based on the theory of constraints by Eliyahu Goldratt). Similar to resource leveling, the critical chain method is used if activities contend for limited resources. When using the critical chain method, the critical path is first identified, independent of resource availability. Entering resource availability might then reveal conflicting activities, which were planned to be completed in parallel but draw upon the same (limited) resource. Based on resource availability, an alternative critical path is created. This

Critical chain
The longest path
through a network
diagram, considering
both task dependen-
cies and resource
dependencies.

new path, based on both task dependencies and resource dependencies, is referred to as a **critical chain**. If resources were unlimited, the critical path and the critical chain would be equal. So far, this process to some extent resembles resource leveling techniques. However, another advantage of the critical chain method is that it helps to minimize uncertainty in a project's schedule, therefore leading to a shorter overall completion time. The following paragraphs explain how critical chain scheduling can be used to influence a project's completion date.

People assigned to multiple concurrent tasks often resort to multitasking; that is, working a bit on one task, going on to the next, working a bit on a third task, and so on, before restarting work on task one. Unfortunately, this approach often wastes time because it requires repeated setup for the individual tasks. Critical chain scheduling prohibits multitasking with the goal of arriving at a shorter overall completion time. Another factor often leading to long project durations is the uncertainty inherent in any project. To cope with this uncertainty, a project's activities often contain duration buffers (i.e., additional time allocated to an activity to account for any unforeseen circumstances). Because this buffer is added to every activity, the entire project contains more reserve time than is usually needed. Further, there is often a tendency to fill the allotted time; in other words, if a certain amount of time is allotted for an activity, people tend to use it (this is known as Parkinson's law). If a buffer is added to an activity, people tend to use this buffer as well, no matter whether the additional time is needed or not. CCM thus suggests following aggressive target duration schedules to reduce overallocation of time, placing buffers at more strategic locations in the project timeline, avoiding multitasking because there are switching costs, emphasizing resources and the contention for resources when planning, and finally tracking the status of buffers managing both their depletion and replenishment.

COMMON PROBLEMS
Falling Prey to Critical Chain Assumptions

Consider two critical chain method assumptions regarding task duration estimation. The first is that when asked to estimate the duration of an activity the activity owner's estimate includes a "safety factor" that serves as a personal buffer. The second is that people will tend to use such buffers if they are available (Parkinson's law). Both of these assumptions are plausible (Raz, Barnes, and Dvir, 2003). After all, haven't we all taken the entire semester to complete a term paper even though we knew it would take only a week or two to complete it? The ultimate goal of CCM is to minimize or eliminate individual task-level buffers by incorporating them into feeding and project buffers (see the text that follows for feeding and project buffers). One difficulty that arises with these assumptions is that some preliminary evidence suggests that Parkinson's law is not *always* in effect. According to Hill, Thomas, and Allen's 2000 study of more than 500 tasks undertaken by the IS department

in an international financial services organization, 60 percent were completed in less time than their estimated duration, and 8 percent were completed within the original time estimate. Only 32 percent went longer than their original estimates.

Some possible problems arise when a project manager using CCM blindly makes these assumptions, regardless of the conflicting evidence on Parkinson's law (Raz et al., 2003). How does a project manager estimate the safety factor that the task owner has incorporated into his or her estimate to arrive at more aggressive but appropriate estimates? One popular method is to reduce the original estimate by 33 percent. However, how can you be sure that the percentage you've chosen is appropriate? Do all task owners estimate the same safety factor? Furthermore, if you could accurately estimate the safety factors task owners have incorporated, can you expect that those task owners will agree to shorten their estimates?

(continued)

Critical chain scheduling eliminates any buffers from individual activities; instead, a general project buffer is created. Eliminating individual buffers helps to decrease the entire duration of the project, whereas the project buffer protects the final due date. The removal of individual buffers serves the additional purpose of discouraging people from engaging in multitasking or other distractions. Because the duration estimates (without the individual buffers) are very aggressive, people focus on the task at hand in order to finish it in the allotted time.

In addition to the project buffer, critical chain scheduling uses feeding buffers to protect the activities on the critical path. Usually in complex projects, many noncritical activities feed into critical activities. Because critical chain scheduling eliminates the individual safety buffers, a change in duration of a noncritical activity feeding into a critical activity would influence the critical path and, thus, the duration of the entire project. To prevent this, a feeding buffer (i.e., additional time) is added to any noncritical activity feeding into a critical activity. The project manager can easily monitor the use of the feeding buffers and the project buffer to determine whether the project is on schedule. Project management software frequently employs third-party add-ons for critical chain scheduling.

When using any of these techniques, a project manager should always monitor the project calendars and resource calendars. In a large software development project of a multinational corporation, virtual teams located in different regions of the world might be working on completing a certain task; thus, teams could work in three continuous shifts. The resource calendar would specify these working times. On the other hand, the client organization might be available only during certain times, so that, for example, during requirements generation, the project team members cannot contact it. Such times would be specified in the project calendar.

Another factor to be considered during schedule network analysis is the use of leads and lags. In the activity sequencing stage, the leads and lags of the different activities have been established. To review, a lead is the time between the start of one activity and the start of an overlapping activity; a lag is the time between the finish of one activity and the start of a succeeding activity. As these leads and lags can significantly influence the schedule, their use should be carefully double-checked to minimize potential delays.

TIPS FROM THE PROS
Manual Critical Chain Method Analysis

Think of situations where you've had to delay some task because you didn't have access to your computer. You may end up in an impromptu meeting where some substantial progress might be made, but you have left your technological tools in your office or some other location. Or (gasp!) your technological tools are not in working order. So, how might you develop a critical path or critical chain diagram so

(continued)

that you can change the sequence or timing of tasks easily depending on resource availability and constraints? Lawrence Leach, founder of Advanced Projects Inc. (API), in his book *Critical Chain Project Management*, lays out an easy but fully functional manual method for developing a critical chain diagram that can easily be converted to an electronic version. In fact, in a team setting, this method might be more accessible to team members working together than a file on a computer no matter what the collaboration technology allows. Leach (2000) writes:

> The simplest and most commonly used method to manually create a plan is to create an activity on node network diagram (PERT chart) using sticky notes. The procedure follows:
>
> 1. Fill out a sticky note for each task, containing the task ID, title, duration, and controlling resources. (You may want to use color coding to identify the task duration controlling resource.) On the left of the note, indicate the tasks that provide needed input.
> 2. Lay the notes out on a board or table according to the task logic and following the rough time logic (this is called a time-phased PERT or a time-phased logic diagram).
> 3. Remove resource contentions.
> 4. Identify the critical chain.
> 5. Add sticky notes for the project and feeding buffers.
> 6. Size the feeding buffers.
> 7. Calculate the critical chain using a forward pass. Starting with the initial task, write the start times on the lower left of the note and the completion time (start time plus duration) on the lower right corner.
> 8. Calculate the feeding paths using a backward pass from where they enter the critical chain.
> 9. Remove any remaining resource contention and revise calculations.
>
> This process is not difficult for projects with fewer than about twenty tasks. It gets harder after that, as you need a lot of real estate to lay the project out. . . . Larger projects with more that 500 tasks have used this method successfully.

While we present several software supported options for accomplishing the concepts in this chapter, sometimes it is also useful to consider methods that do not rely on software. Doing so is frequently educational because it will reveal what is going on behind the scenes in software. Furthermore, this method can be easily converted to a Microsoft Project file for further collaboration.

Schedule model
Data and information that are complied and used in conjunction with manual methods or project management software to perform schedule network analysis to generate the project schedule.

Ultimately, all of the information that is generated through whatever schedule development techniques are used will be collected together and serve as the **schedule model**. The model, or tool, contains all of the logic, constraints, resources, and algorithms to do its calculation (Wilkens, 2004). The model may contain various electronic files, such as diagrams or documents generated during the estimating tasks. Microsoft Project contains many of these elements (see Figures 7.11, 7.13, 7.14, and 7.16) and can be thought of as a schedule modeling tool. By running the model, we generate an output, the project schedule. The next section describes the outputs of the schedule development process in further detail.

Schedule Development Outputs

Outputs from the schedule development process include a preliminary project schedule, schedule model data, and the schedule baseline. In addition, outputs should include updates to the resource requirements, activity attributes, the project calendar, or the project management plan and the schedule management plan, supporting detail, and resource requirement updates (refer back to Figure 7.12). The preliminary project schedule, at a minimum, should clearly show the start and finish dates of each activity. Additionally, the preliminary project schedule should contain schedule network diagrams with date information added, bar charts, and milestone charts.

This sort of information can be displayed in project management software. In the network diagram view of Microsoft Project, the individual activities are displayed, together with the duration and the start and finish dates, as well as the critical path (see Figure 7.22a). In Microsoft Project, a Gantt chart view is the default type of bar chart; activities are shown as a task list oriented vertically, with the durations of the tasks represented by horizontal bars. This same chart may also show dependencies of the different activities (Figure 7.22b). Finally, project milestones may also be shown (Figure 7.22c).

Schedule model data provide managers with additional information about resource requirements, alternative schedules (e.g., best-case or worst-case), and contingency plans. Once the schedule has been finalized and approved, it becomes the schedule baseline. This baseline, which shows the set of original start and finish dates, activity durations, as well as work and cost estimates, serves as a basis for comparison during project execution. In Microsoft Project, you can save a schedule baseline. While project baseline data can be shown in many views within Microsoft Project, the Gantt chart view will show a black bar for the baseline and a colored bar for the actual progress of the project.

Resource leveling techniques might require changes to resource requirements, which then have to be updated accordingly. Further, schedule development processes might necessitate updates to the activity attributes or the project calendar. Obviously, all changes have to follow the project's change control process. The schedule management plan, used to develop procedures for dealing with changes to the schedule as the project progresses, might have to be updated as well. If the schedule development process leads to the identification of any changes to these procedures, the schedule management plan has to be updated accordingly.

Schedule Control

Schedule control
The process of putting procedures and rules in place for controlling changes to the project schedules.

The last process within the Project Time Management knowledge area is **schedule control**, which establishes procedures and rules for controlling changes to the project schedule. Although control processes are covered in greater detail in the final chapter of this book, we will deal briefly with this topic here as it relates to Project Time

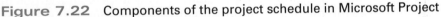

Figure 7.22 Components of the project schedule in Microsoft Project

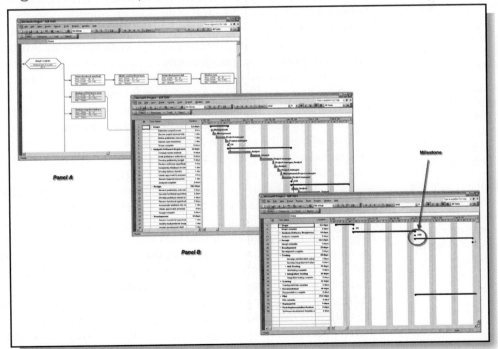

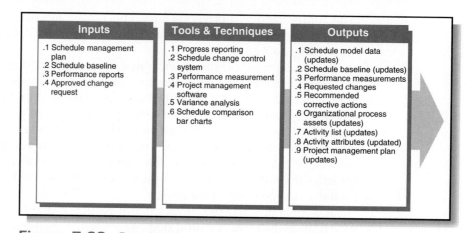

Inputs	Tools & Techniques	Outputs
.1 Schedule management plan .2 Schedule baseline .3 Performance reports .4 Approved change request	.1 Progress reporting .2 Schedule change control system .3 Performance measurement .4 Project management software .5 Variance analysis .6 Schedule comparison bar charts	.1 Schedule model data (updates) .2 Schedule baseline (updates) .3 Performance measurements .4 Requested changes .5 Recommended corrective actions .6 Organizational process assets (updates) .7 Activity list (updates) .8 Activity attributes (updated) .9 Project management plan (updates)

Figure 7.23 Required inputs, tools and techniques used, and resulting outputs during schedule control

Management. Inputs to the schedule control process include the project schedule, performance reports, change requests, and a schedule management plan (see Figure 7.23). The project schedule is the preliminary project schedule developed in the schedule development process. Performance reports are used to track the project at the activity level, such as tracking which activities have or have not been finished on time. Change requests are simply requests for changes in the project schedule. The schedule management plan is the plan developed during the schedule development process.

Tools and techniques used during the schedule control process are progress reporting, the schedule control system, performance measurement, variance analysis, and schedule comparison bar charts. Progress reporting refers to the continuous updates about the current status of the project. The **schedule change control system** determines the process for evaluating and implementing potential schedule changes, including change approval authorization hierarchies. **Performance measurement** determines the magnitude and criticality of schedule variations. For example, variations in a minor activity not on the critical path are typically much less disruptive than variance in the scheduled completion of a critical activity. Additional planning is often required as projects progress because some activities usually are not completed according to their scheduled estimates. Project management software is used to track project schedules and the effects, or forecast effects, of variations in activity completion dates. **Variance analysis** is used to evaluate potential and actual variance on the project schedule. Schedule comparison bar charts help to visualize any deviations of the current status from the baseline to see whether corrective actions need to be taken. If you have saved a baseline in Microsoft Project, you will see two bars for each activity: one for the baseline and one for the actual progress of the activity. If the updated progress information (e.g., start date, percent complete, or duration) is entered in the Gantt chart view, any deviation from the baseline is easily visualized.

Outputs from the schedule control process include updates to the schedule model data (i.e., documentation and notification procedures associated with schedule changes), the schedule baseline, the activity list, activity attributes, or the project management plan. Further, requested changes and recommended corrective actions result from the schedule control process. Corrective action is the procedure for addressing schedule performance problems. Finally, lessons learned include documentation of the causes of variance from the project schedule. Documenting lessons learned can prevent these problems from occurring in similar future projects. This documentation becomes part of the organizational process assets.

Schedule change control system
A control system developed to outline the process for the evaluation and implementation of schedule changes.

Performance measurement
A process used to determine the magnitude and criticality of schedule variations.

Variance analysis
An analysis used to evaluate the effects of variance on the schedule of project activities.

With all the possible contingencies organizations face during projects, it is no wonder that projects can go wrong. When things do go wrong, what techniques can project managers use to make them right again? Two specific techniques are fast-tracking and crashing. Fast-tracking involves performing in parallel activities that were originally planned to be performed in sequence. In some cases, during a software development project, a manager may choose to begin coding based only on a partial identification of user requirements. As we have already shown in previous discussions of the SDLC, these two activities normally would be performed in sequence. The primary advantage of fast-tracking is to shorten the duration of a project that is in danger of not being completed on schedule.

Crashing involves dedicating extra resources to a particular activity in an attempt to finish it sooner than its scheduled completion date. In particular, crashing can be seen as a trade-off between the dedication of resources and the project schedule. For example, a project manager may decide to use additional project resources (such as additional coders) to finish a particular task so that the schedule may be improved.

MANAGING PROJECT RESOURCES AND THE PMBOK

For Chapter 7, "Managing Project Resources," we have discussed the fundamentals, characteristics, and challenges related to allocating resources, estimating activity and project durations, and developing the final schedule with specific start and end dates. This information relates to PMBOK Knowledge Area 6, Project Time Management. In addition, we also identified types of resources and how they influence the estimation of task durations, which relates to Knowledge Area 9, Project Human Resource Management. Finally, we have also discussed the implications of the project schedule and resource assignments on Knowledge Area 8, Project Cost Management. Figure 7.24 identifies this coverage and illustrates the coverage of upcoming chapters, as well.

Figure 7.24 Chapter 7 and PMBOK coverage

Textbook Chapters →		1	2	3	4	5	6	7	8	9	10	11	12
PMBOK Knowledge Area													
1	**Introduction to Project Management**												
1.1	What is a Project?	●											
1.2	What is Project Management?	●											
1.3	Areas of Expertise		●										
1.4	Project Management Context	●											
2	**Project Life Cycle and Organization**												
2.1	The Project Life Cycle	●	●										
2.2	Project Stakeholders	●	●										
2.3	Organizational Influences		●	●	●			✓					

(continued)

Figure 7.24 (continued)

	Textbook Chapters ➡	1	2	3	4	5	6	7	8	9	10	11	12
	PMBOK Knowledge Area												
3	**Project Management Processes for a Project**												
3.1	Project Management Processes	●	●										
3.2	PM Process Groups	●	●										
3.3	Process Interactions		●										
3.4	Project Management Process Mapping		●										
4	**Project Integration Management**												
4.1	Develop Project Charter					●							
4.2	Develop Preliminary Project Scope Statement					●	●						
4.3	Develop Project Management Plan					●							
4.4	Direct and Manage Project Execution										○		
4.5	Monitor and Control Project Work												○
4.6	Integrated Change Control												○
4.7	Close Project												○
5	**Project Scope Management**												
5.1	Scope Planning					●							
5.2	Scope Definition					●							
5.3	Create WBS					●	●						
5.4	Scope Verification					●							
5.5	Scope Control					●							○
6	**Project Time Management**												
6.1	Activity Definition						●						
6.2	Activity Sequencing						●						
6.3	Activity Resource Estimating							✓					
6.4	Activity Duration Estimating							✓					
6.5	Schedule Development							✓					
6.6	Schedule Control							✓					○
7	**Project Cost Management**												
7.1	Cost Estimating							✓					
7.2	Cost Budgeting							✓					
7.3	Cost Control							✓					○
8	**Project Quality Management**												
8.1	Quality Planning								○				
8.2	Perform Quality Assurance								○				
8.3	Perform Quality Control								○				○

Figure 7.24 (continued)

	Textbook Chapters ➡	1	2	3	4	5	6	7	8	9	10	11	12
	PMBOK Knowledge Area												
9	**Project Human Resource Management**												
9.1	Human Resource Planning			●				✓					
9.2	Acquire Project Team			●				✓					
9.3	Develop Project Team			●				✓					
9.4	Manage Project Team			●				✓					
10	**Project Communications Management**												
10.1	Communications Planning				●							○	
10.2	Information Distribution				●							○	
10.3	Performance Reporting				●								○
10.4	Manage Stakeholders				●								○
11	**Project Risk Management**												
11.1	Risk Management Planning									○			
11.2	Risk Identification									○		○	
11.3	Qualitative Risk Analysis									○			
11.4	Quantitative Risk Analysis									○			
11.5	Risk Response Planning									○			
11.6	Risk Monitoring and Control									○			○
12	**Project Procurement Management**												
12.1	Plan Purchases and Acquisitions										○		
12.2	Plan Contracting										○		
12.3	Request Seller Responses										○		
12.4	Select Sellers										○		
12.5	Contract Administration										○		
12.6	Contract Closure										○		○

Key: ●-where material is covered in past chapters; ✓-current chapter coverage;
○-where material is covered in future chapters

RUNNING CASE

Managing Project Resources

Because it was Friday, Jim thought that most of his team members would be restless, so he started the meeting with a few minutes of informal chatting.

"Juanita, does Friday mean a lot more customers at the store?" Jim asked.

"It depends, Jim. Customer volume is based on the deals we have, and as soon as these deals are over, customer volume drops drastically. I think that's why this project is so important for this company."

(continued)

"I do most of my shopping on weekends," Sanjay said, "unless the store has an online presence."

"Yes, time is a constraint. I was thinking what other resources we might need to get this project completed," Jim said, trying to steer the conversation on to the main agenda of resource planning.

"Since the very first step is to understand different techniques to increase customer loyalty, we need to look at customer relations in depth," said Sally.

"Do we have anyone who has customer relations expertise?" Bob asked.

"I think there's a new grad working for the store who specializes in customer relations. It would be great if you could get that person on our team, Jim," Sally mentioned.

"OK, I'll talk to John as soon as possible about this," replied Jim.

"From the IT side, I think that smaller projects will have to be started. This would require a few more people for systems development and integration," Sanjay said.

"Hold on, now. Before we get into IT, I suggest we understand how much money we have at our disposal, so that we can understand the extent of this project," Bob replied.

"But since this is an important project for the company, I'm sure Ella will allocate as much as we want," Jim said smiling. "To get an estimate of how much we should ask for we need to know the extent of the project."

"That might require us to do a few iterations to get a good estimate. Would you guys excuse me for a moment? I have some new interns who need to be briefed before they start on Monday," said Juanita.

Over the next couple of hours, working individually and, at times, together, each team member determined the different resources that they would require from their area of expertise and how much they would cost. They revised their estimates a few times for each of their resources and aggregated the costs to obtain the overall project cost. The final resource allocations would be presented to Ella on Monday.

"This looks good. I think the cost would be fine with Ella. Now let's see how the resources are spread out from the resource graph," said Jim (see Figure 7.25).

"Oh, with this resource allocation, the new marketing expert will have to work 120 hours for 3 weeks in a row!" said Sanjay.

"I think we should share her a little more frugally," said Sally with a grin.

After a few more adjustments the team managed to keep everyone's workload under 45 hours a week, but it meant extending the overall project duration by 3 weeks. Jim looked slightly worried seeing this figure.

"I'm sure Ella would understand, with the 3-week extension. It's not like we've started the project. This is definitely a more realistic estimate of how quickly we can do this," said Bob, seeing Jim's apprehension.

"Yes, I think this is a frank estimate of the time required given the resources we have," said Jim. It was well past 6:00 P.M. by then. Jim closed the projector and his laptop and said, "Thanks, everyone for staying on late to complete the resource allocation and scheduling. See you guys on Monday!" He felt rather happy that he had a dedicated team to work with.

Figure 7.25 Petrie's resource allocation

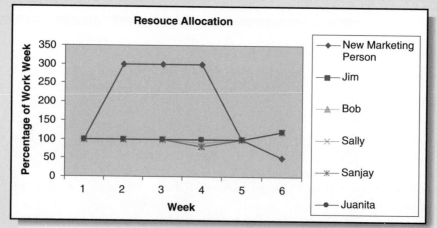

CHAPTER SUMMARY

Understand what resources are, and the types of resources that are typically available. As project managers transition from activity definition and activity sequencing into full-blown project schedule development, the main determinant in estimating activity and project duration is the availability of appropriate resources. While the resources needed to complete a given task may be clear, those resources may not be available at the most opportune time or for the length of time required. Considering this, activity duration estimating becomes much more complex than just assigning resources and assuming they will be available. Identifying the appropriate human and capital resources needed to complete the required project tasks, understanding their availability, and effectively managing these interactions can increase the project's likelihood of success immensely.

Appreciate the importance of managing project resources, and their effect on project duration. The efficient use of project resources should be a primary goal for every project manager because the allocation of resources can have a major influence on project schedules. Of specific concern are scarce resources because their allocation can easily scuttle the project schedule. Poor management of project resources can have a negative influence on things like project time, cost, quality, and risk. As described in the chapter, project durations can vary dependent upon the number of people assigned to the task, and their respective skill levels. Project resources also influence project cost management. Resources obviously have costs, and how they are allocated impacts the project's budget. The resources used to complete tasks may also influence the quality of project deliverables. Finally, if specific resources to be used during the project are new, project risk may be increased.

Apply project resource management tools and techniques for managing project time. When estimating the resources and duration needed to complete an activity, project managers rely on several tools and techniques. For estimating resources, these include expert judgment, alternatives analysis, published estimating data, and bottom-up estimating. For estimating activity durations, they include expert judgment, parametric estimating, reserve analysis, three-point estimating, and analogous estimating. Through the use of several estimating techniques for both resource and duration estimates, successful project managers are able to more accurately estimate resources and durations. After resources and durations have been estimated, the project manager is then ready to develop a full project schedule. By using several techniques, the successful project manager can develop an accurate schedule that can be used as a baseline to measure the progress of the project. Furthermore, the project manger can identify areas in the schedule with slack and float, should any unforeseen issues arise. These techniques include PERT analyses, the critical path method, and the critical chain method. By identifying areas of the schedule with slack and float, the project manager can use feeding buffers and project buffers to provide some insurance that the project can be completed in the allotted time. If these buffers are used up, the project manager may choose to fast-track or crash various activities in an attempt to complete some tasks faster than originally planned.

KEY TERMS REVIEW

- Activity duration estimation
- Activity resource requirements
- Alternatives analysis
- Analogous estimating
- Bottom-up estimating
- Capital resources
- Crashing
- Critical activities
- Critical chain
- Critical chain method

- Critical path
- Critical path method
- Duration
- Effort
- Expert judgment
- Fast tracking
- Free float
- Human resources
- Imposed dates
- Opportunity cost

- Parametric estimating
- Performance measurement
- Program Evaluation and Review Technique (PERT)
- Published estimating data
- Reserve analysis
- Resource
- Resource breakdown structure
- Resource calendar
- Resource leveling heuristics

- Resource leveling
- Schedule change control system
- Schedule compression
- Schedule control
- Schedule development
- Schedule network analysis
- Simulation
- Three-point estimates
- Total float
- Variance analysis
- What-if analyses

Match each of the key terms with the definition that best fits it.

1. _____ A source of supply or support, such as money, people, materials, technology and space.

2. _____ All project stakeholders, including customers, project team members, support staff, project suppliers, and end users.

3. _____ The tools and infrastructure used to produce other goods and services.

4. _____ The measure of the alternative opportunities forgone in the choice of one good or activity over others.

5. _____ Actual time spent working on an activity.

6. _____ Elapsed time between the start and finish of an activity.

7. _____ Estimation based on the experience of one or more experts on the particular activity or project.

8. _____ Hard data from specific activities carried out on previous projects that may be used to more accurately estimate resource needs.

9. _____ An estimating technique where trade-offs between the time needed, the resources invested, and the desired quality of the final deliverable are examined.

10. _____ An estimating technique where complex activities are further decomposed to a point where more accurate estimates can be made.

11. _____ A very detailed listing of the resource requirements for the individual activities.

12. _____ A hierarchical, graphical representation of all needed resources ordered by type or category.

13. _____ A specific type of project calendar used to track the hours when certain resources are available.

14. _____ The process of estimating the duration of project activities using both project scope and resource information.

15. _____ The estimation of activities' durations based upon the duration of similar activities.

16. _____ The estimation of activities' durations using some type of mathematical process.

17. _____ The estimation of activities' durations by averaging the optimistic, pessimistic, and most likely estimates.

18. _____ Technique used to establish contingency reserves during a project to guard against potential risk.

19. _____ The process of determining start and finish dates for project activities.

20. _____ Dates imposed to meet some type of development deadline.

21. _____ The process of calculating expected, early, and late start and finish dates of a project.

22. _____ A technique used for determining the sequence of task activities that directly affect the completion of a project.

23. _____ The longest path through a network diagram illustrating the shortest amount of time in which a project can be completed.

24. _____ Any activity on the critical path.

25. _____ The time an activity can be delayed without affecting the immediately following activity.

26. _____ The time an activity can be delayed without affecting the overall completion date of a project.

27. _____ A technique used to estimate project duration when there is uncertainty regarding individual activity duration estimates.

28. _____ The use of mathematical techniques to shorten a project's duration.

29. _____ Dedicating extra resources to a particular activity in an attempt to finish the activity sooner than the scheduled completion date.

30. _____ The performance of activities in parallel that would normally be performed in sequence, in an attempt to shorten the duration of a project.

31. _____ A process of evaluating different scenarios and their effects on the project schedule.

32. _____ A process of evaluating alternative strategies by observing how changes to selected factors affect other factors and outcomes.

33. _____ Rules of thumb used to allocate resources to project activities.

34. _____ A technique to develop a critical path using resource availability to determine activity sequences.

35. _____ The longest path through a network diagram, considering both task dependencies and resource dependencies.

36. _____ The process of setting procedures and rules in place for controlling changes to the project schedules.

37. _____ A control system developed to outline the process for the evaluation and implementation of schedule changes.

38. _____ A process used to determine the magnitude and criticality of schedule variations.

39. _____ An analysis used to evaluate the effects of variance on the schedule of project activities.

40. _____ Any form of network analysis where resource management issues drive scheduling decisions.

41. _____ A technique that uses optimistic, pessimistic, and realistic time estimates to calculate the expected time for a particular task.

REVIEW QUESTIONS

1. Define *resources*. Discuss the differences between human and capital resources and give three examples of each.

2. Discuss the differences between duration and effort with respect to estimating resources.

3. Should a project manager rely on only one technique for estimating resources? Why or why not?

4. Compare and contrast the four techniques presented for estimating resources.

5. List and briefly discuss the outputs to resource estimating.

6. Five activity duration estimating techniques were described; choose four and compare and contrast them.

7. What is a critical path? What is the difference between the critical path method and the critical chain method?

8. Which activities on a network diagram can have free float or total float? Which activities can't have free or total float, and why not?

9. Define *schedule compression*. Describe the two methods for compressing a schedule.

10. What are buffers? Define and discuss the differences between the two types of buffers presented.

11. Discuss the various techniques to exert schedule control.

1. You have been chosen as the project manager for a project to develop an e-commerce presence for your company, which has until now, been primarily a brick-and-mortar business. Upper management has arbitrarily chosen a launch date 6 months from now. You and your team have determined, through following the techniques described in this chapter, that completing the project in 6 months is possible, but unlikely. The project sponsor has asked you to tell him what day you expect the project to be complete. Explain why predicting the finish date down to the specific day is problematic. How might you explain this to reassure him that he has chosen the right project manager for the job.

2. Consider an organization that has a project management office. Discuss how this organization might have a strategic advantage over an organization that doesn't have a PMO. How might having a PMO be a disadvantage to an organization?

3. Consider a situation where you have enough money either to purchase textbooks for the term *or* to purchase a desktop PC (assuming you need one). Which purchase would you choose? Discuss your decision with respect to opportunity costs.

4. Consider a paper you need to complete for a current class or consider some project you're working on or anticipate working on. Identify four tasks needed to complete the paper or project, estimate the durations of each task, and discuss how effort relates to the task duration you've determined.

5. Develop a resource calendar for human resources for the month of December 2007, taking into consideration the following information:
   a. You can schedule four people, John, Sally, Pedro, and Eunice.
   b. The typical workweek for your company is 45 hours. Depending on the individual, schedules may include Saturdays and Sundays and can include graveyard or swing shifts.
   c. John's schedule is 6:00 A.M. to 4:00 P.M. with 1-hour lunches, Saturday through Wednesday.
   d. Sally works 3:00 P.M. to 3:00 A.M., with two 1-hour breaks, Monday through Thursday. Her remaining hours to reach 45 hours per week can be scheduled on Friday or Saturday in one block with no break for lunch.
   e. Pedro can be scheduled at any time except from 12:00 noon to 5:00 P.M. on Wednesdays. He must know his schedule by 12:00 noon on Wednesday the prior week.
   f. Eunice works 20 hours per week with John and 25 hours per week with Sally.
   g. Your company has declared December 24 and 25 as holidays.
   h. Eunice has scheduled her vacation for the week of Christmas.
   i. John has scheduled some personal time off for December 1 and 2.

6. Discuss a situation you've experienced when you made an inaccurate estimation for the duration of some activity. It doesn't necessarily need to be during a project, but discuss your reasoning for estimating the duration of the activity the way you did and the factors that caused your estimate to be inaccurate.

7. Describe a situation you've experienced where you had more time than needed to complete some task but took the entire time to complete it. Discuss the factors that influenced your filling up of the allotted time.

8. For the project described in Exercise 1 above, consider this situation. Your team has really performed well. The 6-month launch date is rapidly approaching, and you have figured out a way to meet the deadline. To meet the deadline, you will have to fast-track or crash the final four activities of the testing phase (deployment, training, and documentation still follow). Due to resource availability, you can only choose one method. What method would you choose? Why?

9. Now, based on Exercises 1 and 8, you discover that the final four activities of the testing phase have competing needs for the same resource. Discuss how this might change or reinforce your decision in Exercise 8, considering the concepts of resource leveling, free slack, and total slack.

10. Develop a three-point estimate for completing your degree. Discuss your reasoning for each of the three points.

11. Using the following weighting factors, conduct a PERT analysis on your estimate from Exercise 10. Optimistic × 1, most likely × 3, and pessimistic × 2.

CHAPTER CASE

Sedona Management Group and Managing Project Resources

Resource management is a fundamental part of project management and involves the allocation of resources to the different activities that need to be performed for the successful and timely completion of any project. These resources include human resources, equipment, space, and money. Each of them may be scarce, and for that reason, they have to be used effectively.

Poor resource allocation can have an adverse effect on project duration, cost, quality, and risk. In terms of project duration, if the required resources are not available when needed, it will be difficult to finish the project as targeted. Moreover, the time it takes to complete an activity depends on the number of people allocated to that activity. Resources also have associated costs, and consequently, resource allocation will impact the project's budget. Similarly, the quality of the resources used during a project affects the quality of the project deliverables. Finally, if the resources being used are new to a project, project risk will be affected. Consequently, it is very important to manage project resources effectively.

One important resource that has to be considered in any information systems project is human resources; that is, the trained professionals who assess users' needs, develop systems, and implement those systems. The success or failure of projects largely depends on the people who are working on them. At Sedona Management Group (SMG), given the small size of the organization, team composition remains largely the same as the company takes on new projects, such as

the Seattle Seahawks Web site development project. In addition, all members of the Sedona team typically have well-defined roles, which they repeat across projects, making efficient use of their individual skill sets (e.g., graphic design, database development, client communications, etc.). This approach may be different from other larger organizations, such as an IT consulting firm, where individuals are reassigned to new teams and roles as they take on new projects.

One challenge any project team takes on is multitasking, that is how to simultaneously manage a variety of different tasks. These diverse tasks may be related to one project (e.g., the interface designer may not only need to be working on continually gathering customer feedback but also may be involved in developing the interface itself), or in some instances on multiple projects, where a project member may be assigned to two or more projects (e.g., one project for the Seattle Seahawks and another for a small Seattle coffee shop). It is the job of Tim Turnpaugh to efficiently assign resources (in terms of personnel, equipment, etc.) so that the various projects the team is working on at a certain point in time are completed in a timely manner. He needs to watch for issues like committing a team member to too many tasks at one time or not having sufficient resources to accomplish a task when needed. To prevent such problems, SMG practices project techniques like resource leveling, which essentially involves spreading the work in a more balanced fashion.

CHAPTER 7 PROJECT ASSIGNMENT

You will need different resources to complete the entertainment Web site development project. In this assignment, you will identify the needed resources as well as update the Gantt chart you developed as part of the assignment for the previous chapter with this information.

1. Determine the types of resources you will need to complete this project. These resources should include human resources as well as any equipment, in terms of software, technology, and so on.

2. Discuss how the allocation of these different resources will affect project time, cost, quality, and risk.

3. In the previous chapter, you developed a work breakdown structure (WBS). Allocate the resources you determined in Exercise 1 to the different tasks in the WBS, and update the Gantt chart you developed in the previous chapter with this information.

4. Determine how the allocation of project resources can affect the critical path of your project.

5. Discuss some ways in which you and your team members will handle any overallocation of resources in the project.

REFERENCES

Battin, R. D., Crocker, R., Kreidler, J., and Subramanian, K. (2001). Leveraging Resources in Global Software Development. *IEEE Software* 18(2), 70–77.

Charette, R. N. (2005). Eyes Wide Open. *Cutter Consortium*. Retrieved November 6, 2005, from the CIO.com Web site: www2.cio.com/analyst/report 3837.html.

Edwards, H. K., and Swidhar, V. (2005). Analysis of Software Requirements Engineering Exercises in a Global Virtual Team Setup. *Journal of Global Information Management* 13(2), 21–41.

Harreld, H. (2001). Moving onto the Web. *InfoWorld*, 23(21), pg. 56.

Hill, J., Thomas, L. C., and Allen, D. E. (2000). Experts' Estimates of Task Durations in Software Development Projects. *International Journal of Project Management* 12(1), 13–24.

Johnson, J., and Horsey, D. C. (2001). The IT War Room. *Software Magazine* 21(3), 31.

Leach, L. P. (2000). *Critical Chain Project Management.* Boston: Artech House.

Raz, T., Barnes, R., and Dvir, D. (2003). A Critical Look at Critical Chain Project Management. *Project Management Journal* 34(4), 24–32.

Songini, M. (2004). Problems Bedevil EDS Case Management Project for U.K.'s Child Support Agency. *ComputerWorld* 38(36), 9.

Standish Group. (2001). *The Chaos Report: Extreme Chaos.* West Yarmouth, MA: The Standish Group, 2001.

Wilkens, T. (2004). The Definition Conundrum. Retrieved October 7, 2006 from the Project Management Institute College of Scheduling Web site: www.pmicos.org/topics/jul2004.pdf.

Chapter 8

Managing Project Quality

Opening Case: Quality: Is It a Mystery?

Gene Anderson, a senior IT project manager for a Web portal development company, was very disturbed by the inconsistent reports he was receiving about recent customer satisfaction. How could some customers be satisfied with the portal solutions being developed for their company while others were dissatisfied? Weren't all portals being developed according to the same quality standards? If not, what steps could he, as the company's senior IT project manager, take to ensure future projects were developed according to consistent quality standards?

LEARNING OBJECTIVES

After reading this chapter, you will be able to:

➤ Understand the concept of quality and why it is important.
➤ Discuss quality management pioneers and quality certifications and standards in industries today.
➤ Apply techniques for managing project quality, including quality planning, quality assurance, and quality control.

The problem Gene Anderson faced is not unique. In fact, project quality is often referred to as a fourth dimension of project management that must be considered along with the classic project constraints of cost, time, and scope. Project management experts argue that unless quality standards are realized, most projects should be considered failures even if the other constraints of cost, time, and scope have been met. In this chapter, we will learn about quality as it pertains to information systems (IS) projects (see Figure 8.1).

What Is Quality?

Project quality
The degree to which a set of inherent characteristics fulfill requirements.

Quality is about providing excellence in the products or services that an organization produces. The Project Management Institute defines **project quality** as "the degree to which a set of inherent characteristics fulfill requirements" (PMBOK Guide, 2004). Quality thus also depends somewhat upon whom the quality issue affects. For example, General Electric defines quality from different perspectives, including those of the customer, the process, and the employee (see Figure 8.2).

Why Is Project Quality Important?

Project quality is important because of its direct relationship to project success. Many examples of information system (IS) project success and failure can be attributed to project quality. In fact, many of the enterprise resource planning (ERP) systems

Figure 8.1 Information systems project team management focusing on managing project quality

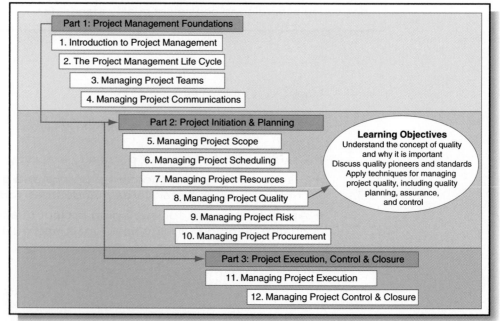

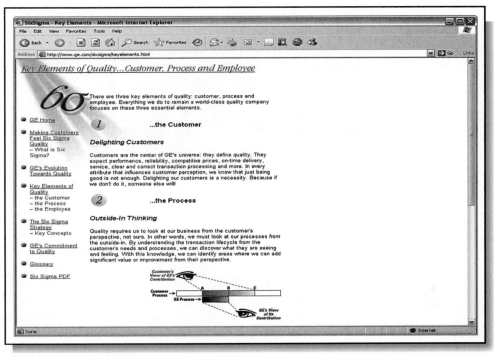

Figure 8.2 GE Web page on quality

Source: Reproduced with permission of General Electric Company www.ge.com

implementation failures discussed earlier in the text can be attributed to inattention to Project Quality Management.

Although quality is always an important concept, in some industries it can be critical. As an example, in the production of semiconductors, quality tolerances need to be quite tight to assure that the product works as expected. As a consequence, a vast infrastructure of quality planning, monitoring, and control surrounds the process of semiconductor production. As one part of this quality system, semiconductor manufacturers use clean rooms—sealed, highly sterile environments where semiconductor manufacturing occurs—in the manufacturing process (see Figure 8.3). In addition to monitoring air filtration, temperature, and humidity, workers in a clean room also follow strict procedures to avoid contaminating the workplace. The importance of such

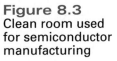

Figure 8.3
Clean room used
for semiconductor
manufacturing

Figure 8.4
Air traffic control
system

processes and the monitoring of the resulting manufactured product can be critical, considering where such semiconductors are used. As an example, they may be used in the health care industry in medical equipment, or in an industry like aerospace where they may be used to control flight functions of aircraft. Product quality in either environment can be a life or death matter.

While quality processes may be slightly different for developing information systems, quality planning, processes, and control are just as important in the software industry. As discussed earlier, systems may be used in contexts where there is little or no tolerance for error. One such example might include a program designed to support air traffic controllers—a system that controls the regulation and scheduling of incoming and outgoing flights at a major airport (see Figure 8.4). In such a situation, a glitch in the software might result in anything from a disruption of normal services to more disastrous results. Such was the case in 2002 when thousands of travelers were stranded at UK airports after a major air traffic control system stopped functioning (news.bbc.co.uk/1/hi/uk/1897885.stm). The quality errors resulted in a disruption to normal schedules, but more widespread system failure could have had much more serious consequences.

Frederick Reichheld, author of *The Loyalty Effect: The Hidden Force Behind Growth, Profits, and Lasting Value,* was recently quoted in *PM Network* regarding the importance of quality. Reichheld states that a simple 5 percent reduction in a company's customer defection rate can lead to a 25 to 85 percent increase in profits (Dimov and Alexandrova, 2003). Within the same article, Dimov and Alexandrova reference the results of research conducted by Xerox Corporation to determine the effect of customer satisfaction (one measure of quality) on purchase behavior. Xerox researchers found that customers who were "very satisfied" were 18 times more likely to repurchase from the company. Managing quality, therefore, is vital to a company's future success.

Managing Quality and the Project Life Cycle

Quality management processes are often considered during all the processes of project management, including initiation, planning, execution, control, and close-out. As teams initiate and choose projects, they need to understand what quality standards they must achieve. Quality perspectives also have to be practiced during the project planning process as project teams develop the quality control mechanisms they'll use throughout the project life cycle. During the execution and control processes, quality control mechanisms are put into practice, giving the project team constant feedback on their performance. Finally, quality management is also practiced in project closure when the team documents its experiences for future organizational projects.

There is an important relationship between project teams and quality. Teams are often used to help establish the development of company quality standards for future projects (in many instances these are former project teams). These quality standards can serve as a benchmark for future project efforts. In addition, once established, quality standards can be applied to how a team functions, what types of processes it uses to control quality, and how it can measure the success of its project management efforts.

Technology can facilitate the tracking and control of quality during IS projects. For instance, cost–benefit analyses are often performed using spreadsheet software. Project management software such as Microsoft Project can also help project teams manage project quality. Microsoft Project's Enterprise edition, in fact, includes common repositories for project documents. Using a repository allows for more consistent documentation because project team members share and reuse common documents. Further, project tracking features within Microsoft Project enable managers to quickly identify problem areas and take steps to eliminate them, ultimately resulting in improved quality.

QUALITY PIONEERS AND STANDARDS

The concept of quality has evolved over the years. In this section we briefly discuss some quality pioneers who have influenced how today's businesses think of quality. In addition, as a result of the concept's evolution, quality processes have become so important to modern corporations that many industries have adopted standards for quality to signal their attention to a company's quality processes, as well as to the quality of their product or service. We will also briefly discuss some of today's more common quality standards and certifications before transitioning to our discussion of specific quality management techniques.

Quality Management Pioneers

There have been many quality management pioneers throughout history. This section discusses some of the most well-known quality proponents.

W. Edwards Deming

W. Edwards Deming, who received a Ph.D. in mathematics from Yale University in 1928, is probably best known for his 14 points of quality, stated in his popular publication, *Out of Crisis*. Deming's 14 points are shown in Figure 8.5.

In addition to his academic appointments as a statistician and quality expert, as well as his numerous books, Deming achieved worldwide prominence and became known as the "prophet of quality." He played a significant role in the economic resurgence in Japan following World War II, where he served as a consultant to Japanese industry. This role is particularly noteworthy because Deming's management philosophies had a significant impact on Japanese business thinking and, as a result, on global trade as corporations competed on quality. A more complete background on Deming is available at www.deming.org.

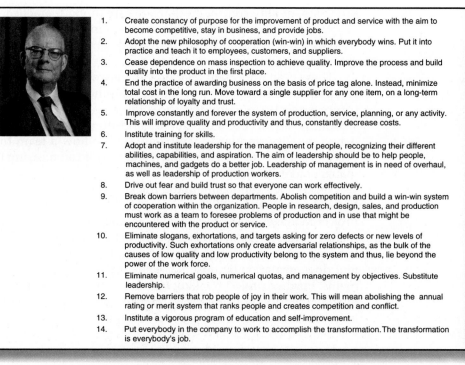

1. Create constancy of purpose for the improvement of product and service with the aim to become competitive, stay in business, and provide jobs.
2. Adopt the new philosophy of cooperation (win-win) in which everybody wins. Put it into practice and teach it to employees, customers, and suppliers.
3. Cease dependence on mass inspection to achieve quality. Improve the process and build quality into the product in the first place.
4. End the practice of awarding business on the basis of price tag alone. Instead, minimize total cost in the long run. Move toward a single supplier for any one item, on a long-term relationship of loyalty and trust.
5. Improve constantly and forever the system of production, service, planning, or any activity. This will improve quality and productivity and thus, constantly decrease costs.
6. Institute training for skills.
7. Adopt and institute leadership for the management of people, recognizing their different abilities, capabilities, and aspiration. The aim of leadership should be to help people, machines, and gadgets do a better job. Leadership of management is in need of overhaul, as well as leadership of production workers.
8. Drive out fear and build trust so that everyone can work effectively.
9. Break down barriers between departments. Abolish competition and build a win-win system of cooperation within the organization. People in research, design, sales, and production must work as a team to foresee problems of production and in use that might be encountered with the product or service.
10. Eliminate slogans, exhortations, and targets asking for zero defects or new levels of productivity. Such exhortations only create adversarial relationships, as the bulk of the causes of low quality and low productivity belong to the system and thus, lie beyond the power of the work force.
11. Eliminate numerical goals, numerical quotas, and management by objectives. Substitute leadership.
12. Remove barriers that rob people of joy in their work. This will mean abolishing the annual rating or merit system that ranks people and creates competition and conflict.
13. Institute a vigorous program of education and self-improvement.
14. Put everybody in the company to work to accomplish the transformation. The transformation is everybody's job.

Figure 8.5   W. Edwards Deming and his 14 points of quality

Joseph Juran

Dr. Joseph Juran is often credited with adding the human element to what was previously a statistical view of project quality. Dr. Juran is further credited with the Pareto Principle, or the 80/20 rule. The Pareto Principle is a rule of thumb used to indicate that a small number of issues typically create the most work in projects. This rule of thumb can be applied in a variety of ways. For example, 80 percent of a project's problems are likely caused by 20 percent of the defects, or 80 percent of a project manager's time is consumed by 20 percent of the problems in a project. The 80/20 Rule is typically used for project quality control, which we briefly introduce later in this chapter (see Figure 8.20), and then cover in more detail in Chapter 12. So influential was Juran that the American Society for Quality proposed changing the name of the Pareto Principle to the Juran Principle in 2003. Born in 1904, Juran worked as an engineer until deciding to devote the remainder of his life to the study of quality management in 1945. Juran authored both the *Quality Control Handbook* (first released in 1951) (see Figure 8.6), the standard reference work in this domain, and the *Juran Trilogy*. Published in 1986, the *Juran Trilogy* was accepted worldwide as a model for quality management; it focused on the three areas of quality planning, quality improvement, and quality control.

Philip B. Crosby

Philip B. Crosby (1926–2001), founder of Philip Crosby Associates, dedicated his career to convincing managers that preventing problems was cheaper than fixing them. Crosby published 14 best-selling books, the most recognized of which was *Quality Is Free* (1979). In his groundbreaking work, Crosby defined quality in an absolute way so that companies could readily see whether or not quality existed in the workplace.

Figure 8.6
Joseph Juran's
*Quality Control
Handbook*

Kaoru Ishikawa

Kaoru Ishikawa (1915–1989) is best known for his cause-and-effect diagram, also called a Ishikawa or **fishbone diagram** (see Figure 8.18 later in this chapter) a diagramming technique used to explore potential and real causes of problems. The fishbone diagram typically organizes problems into categories relevant to the industry. This diagramming technique will also be mentioned in Chapter 9's consideration of project risk and discussed more extensively in Chapter 12's treatment of project control. Ishikawa was also known for his insistence that quality could always be taken one step farther. Ishikawa expanded on Deming's plan-do-check-act model to create an actionable list of six items (see Figure 8.7).

1. Determine goals and target.
2. Determine methods of reaching goals.
3. Engage in education and training.
4. Implement work.
5. Check the effects of implementation.
6. Take appropriate action.

Fishbone diagram
A diagramming technique used to explore potential and real causes of problems.

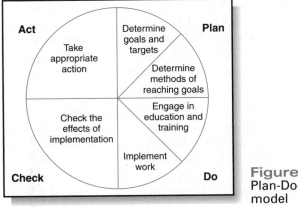

Figure 8.7
Plan-Do-Check-Act
model

Table 8.1 Well-Known Quality Management Pioneers and Their Achievements

Quality Proponents	Achievements
W. Edwards Deming	• Best known for his 14 points of quality
Joseph Juran	• Added the human element to project quality • Credited with the Pareto principle, or the 80/20 rule • Wrote a model for quality management based on quality planning, quality improvement, and quality control
Philip B. Crosby	• Convinced managers that preventing problems was cheaper than fixing them • Defined quality in an absolute way
Kaoru Ishikawa	• Best known for his cause-and-effect, or fishbone diagram • Also known for his insistence that quality could always be taken a step farther • Proposed an actionable list of six items to achieve quality

While many scholars and practitioners alike have focused on quality processes, these four individuals have certainly played a large role establishing the quality standards used in industry today. Table 8.1 lists these project management pioneers and their achievements. In many cases quality guidelines and metrics have been codified in quality standards, quality certifications, and quality awards. Among the more noteworthy are the ISO 9000 quality standard, the Six Sigma certification, and the Malcolm Baldrige Quality Award.

Robert Kaplan and David Norton

Balanced scorecard A tool for assessing organizational activity from perspectives beyond the typical financial analysis.

A new approach for managing and measuring business performance (including management and measurement related to quality) was developed in the early 1990s by Drs. Robert Kaplan and David Norton. They created a system named the balanced scorecard, which recognized some of the potential problems of previous management approaches. The balanced scorecard approach gives advice about what factors (or perspectives) companies should assess in addition to the traditional financial metrics that are typically used (Kaplan and Norton, 1992).

The balanced scorecard is a management system (as opposed to simply being a measurement system) that helps firms clarify and accomplish their corporate vision and strategy. The balanced scorecard is described as follows:

> The balanced scorecard retains traditional financial measures. But financial measures tell the story of past events, an adequate story for industrial age companies for which investments in long-term capabilities and customer relationships were not critical for success. These financial measures are inadequate, however, for guiding and evaluating the journey that information age companies must make to create future value through investment in customers, suppliers, employees, processes, technology, and innovation. (Arveson, 1998)

The balanced scorecard suggests viewing organizational activity from four perspectives: the learning and growth perspective, the business process perspective, the customer perspective, and the financial perspective. To use this method, metrics are developed and data are collected and analyzed to assess project performance relative to each of these perspectives. While the balanced scorecard was originally designed as a general management tool, it has been adapted to a wide variety of sectors and contexts, including the assessment of technology-focused projects. Given the inclusion of customer, business process, and learning perspective in this approach, this system has obvious implications for managing quality in organizations.

Quality Standards, Certifications, and Awards

In today's business environment companies pursue several quality management standards or goals not only to improve organizational quality but also to send competitive signals to the marketplace for the purpose of product or service differentiation. In many instances, organizations that have achieved certain levels of quality certification may require business partners and suppliers to achieve that same level of certification. This section provides an overview of several well-known quality certifications.

ISO 9000 Certification

ISO 9000
A generic management systems standard that any organization can follow to achieve ISO certification.

In 1987, the International Organization for Standardization instituted the voluntary ISO 9000 standard. **ISO 9000** is a generic management systems standard, which signifies that it is applicable to any industry or organization, including information systems focused enterprises. ISO 9000 is one of the most popular quality standards in the world. Thousands of organizations have adopted it and more continue to do so on a regular basis.

The ISO 9000 standard is primarily concerned with quality management, specifically the processes that the organization performs to satisfy customer quality requirements, to satisfy regulatory requirements, to enhance customer satisfaction, and finally to provide for continual improvement in performance of these objectives. ISO 9000 is based on quality management principles that focus on different aspects of an organization's purpose (see Figure 8.8).

As a family of standards, ISO 9000 can be customized and applied to various industries. One example specific to information systems development is the problem of software configuration management. In the process of building computer software, change frequently occurs during the development stage. Despite the intention to control factors like scope creep, user requirements frequently need to be modified as a project moves forward. Software configuration management is a set of activities designed to help manage or control such changes by assisting developers or project managers in identifying those work products that are most likely to change, establishing relationships among work products so that the developer can anticipate any associated changes that will also need to be made, defining ways to manage different versions of work products, and reporting on changes that have been made. ISO 9000 can provide guidance to help a firm establish documented procedures for controlling such changes.

Six Sigma Certification

While the statistical usage of the term *Six Sigma* can be traced back much farther in time, its application to quality management is attributed to a Motorola engineer named

---

ISO 9000 Principles

Principle 1 Customer focus
Principle 2 Leadership
Principle 3 Involvement of people
Principle 4 Process approach
Principle 5 System approach to management
Principle 6 Continual improvement
Principle 7 Factual approach to decision making
Principle 8 Mutually beneficial supplier relationships

Figure 8.8
ISO 9000 principles

Bill Smith. In fact, Six Sigma is a registered trademark of the Motorola Company. The purpose of the Six Sigma quality methodology is to reduce variation and, therefore, the number of product or service defects. Six Sigma has been embraced as a management philosophy that relies on factors such as company culture to enhance quality.

Six Sigma certification requires a company to embrace and learn a body of knowledge related to quality, to pass proficiency tests on the subject matter, and then to demonstrate appropriate levels of competency in real environments. The body of knowledge associated with Six Sigma includes understanding the basics of what Six Sigma is, as well as the processes that help an organization define, measure, analyze, improve, and control their activities. Six Sigma certification testing is done at different levels of proficiency—for example, green belt, black belt, master black belt, and champion. In addition to the knowledge associated with each level of proficiency, certification also requires organizational personnel to exhibit the quality standards through hands-on activities.

Six Sigma standards, like the ISO 9000 standards discussed previously, may be applied to information systems projects. In fact, the overlap between the information systems project management techniques discussed in this book and Six Sigma are evident if we compare the project life cycle of initiation, planning, execution, control, and closure discussed in this book to the objectives that companies try to meet in implementing the Six Sigma methodology:

- Defining the customer in terms of quality
- Measuring core business processes
- Analyzing the data collected
- Improving target processes
- Controlling improvements to ensure the processes remain in line with any changes

Six Sigma helps a company illustrate that they are adhering to processes that will improve both their product and service quality.

Baldrige National Quality Program

The Baldrige National Quality Program and the associated Malcolm Baldrige National Quality Award are focused on recognizing excellence and quality achievement. The award, established in 1987 and named after the former secretary of commerce, recognizes outstanding achievements in seven areas: leadership, strategic planning, customer and market focus, information and analysis, human resource focus, process management, and results.

Secretary Malcolm Baldrige was a firm believer that both quality and performance were crucial to the nation's long-term prosperity and economic health. The Malcolm Baldrige quality award program was established not only to recognize organizations operating in an exemplary fashion but also to provide a benchmark that can encourage other American companies to aggressively pursue a world-class commitment to excellence. While the award can be given to any type of firm, past award recipients have included technology-focused firms such as Xerox, AT&T, IBM, and Motorola. Award recipients are assessed by third-party examiners across a number of dimensions, with performance rated on both customer satisfaction and business processes. The Baldrige quality award also overlaps the concepts discussed in this book. Information systems project management is concerned with following rigorous process and procedures to enhance customer satisfaction as it relates to the information system being designed.

Total Quality Management

Total quality management (TQM) is a systematic approach to managing quality that originated in the 1950s and has grown in popularity since that time. Total Quality describes the culture, organization, and attitude of a company that works toward providing customers with products and services that truly satisfy their needs. Adopting such a culture necessitates quality in all aspects of a firm's operations. Processes are supposed to be done right the first time, with the goal of eliminating defects and waste from operations. TQM requires management and employees to become involved in the continuous improvement of the firm's goods and services. Companies that have implemented TQM include Ford Motor Company, Phillips Semiconductor, SGL Carbon, Motorola, and Toyota Motor Company.

TECHNIQUES FOR MANAGING PROJECT QUALITY

The Project Management Institute outlines three Project Quality Management processes within the PMBOK (PMBOK Guide, 2004). These processes are quality planning, quality assurance, and quality control. The inputs, tools and techniques, and outputs for each of these quality stages are summarized in Figure 8.9. The processes of quality planning and quality assurance will be detailed later in this chapter. Quality control will be summarized in this chapter and discussed more fully in Chapter 12, which focuses on control processes.

Figure 8.9 PMBOK Project Quality Management inputs, tools, and outputs

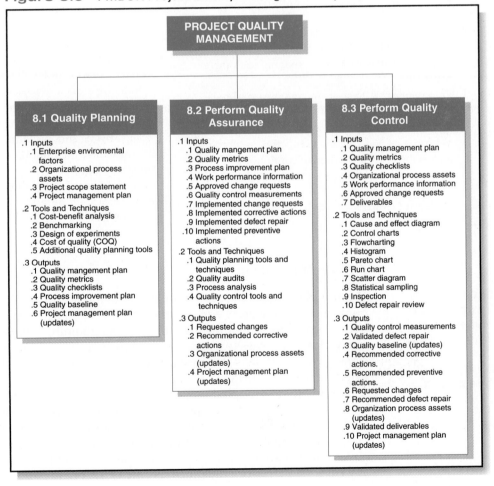

Information technologies (IT) and the information systems (IS) function have become very important to any organization. Organizations are taking advantage of IT to support business operations and increase the value of their products and services in an attempt to gain a competitive advantage in the marketplace. To attain these goals, it is essential for organizations to implement an IS quality system. Management of IS quality can be quite difficult because it includes many dimensions and is judged differently by different stakeholders involved in a particular project. Although project team members may be concerned about the daily operational details associated with controlling project quality, clients will typically be more concerned with the end product.

Several issues should be addressed when implementing an IS quality system. These include (Source: Stylianou and Kumar, 2000):

- *Customer focus.* The main goal of the IS department should be to provide products/services that add value and contribute to keeping customers satisfied.
- *Process approach.* Resources, activities, and outcomes of the IS function are interrelated, and therefore, these associations should be managed as processes. Viewing the IS function as a process makes the implementation of continuous improvement activities easier.
- *Leadership.* Most quality programs are successful because of strong leadership. Strong leaders are the ones who are willing to invest energy and resources to make the IS quality program a success.
- *Culture.* The cultural environment of an organization influences the success of a quality program. A culture where IS is treated as an important and integral function in organizational change should be promoted.
- *Broad participation.* IS quality management should be a joint effort, where all stakeholders participate in, and contribute to, the success of the quality program.
- *Motivating the troops.* For a quality program to succeed, committed and motivated personnel are very essential. IS personnel should be aware of the benefits of a quality program, in terms of work satisfaction and personal rewards.
- *Training.* Well-trained personnel are more likely to be leaders and will more vigorously work toward the success of a quality program.
- *Measurement and constructive feedback.* After the implementation of the IS quality program, results should be measured systematically in order to provide feedback for continuous improvement.
- *Accountability for results and rewarding achievements.* Teams and individual persons should be rewarded for their efforts in the success of the quality program.
- *Self-assessment.* The quality program should be evaluated continuously to provide critical feedback, which can be used to sustain it.

Quality Planning

Quality planning
The process of identifying relevant quality standards and developing a plan to ensure the project meets those standards.

Quality planning is the process of identifying relevant quality standards and developing a plan to ensure the project meets those standards. Quality planning is usually performed at the same time that other project planning issues are addressed because many planning issues (e.g., scheduling, resource allocation, etc.) have quality dimensions. Figure 8.10 lists the inputs required, the tools and techniques used, and the resulting outputs during the quality planning process.

Inputs to quality planning include enterprise environmental factors, organizational process assets, the project scope statement, and the project management plan. We have covered some of these inputs in other chapters (e.g., the project scope statement and project management plan). Enterprise environmental factors include the government regulations according to which the company must operate, as well as any rules standards or guidelines specific to the organization's products or services.

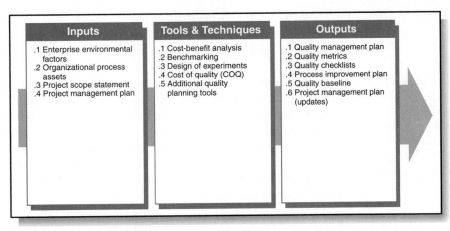

Inputs	Tools & Techniques	Outputs
.1 Enterprise environmental factors .2 Organizational process assets .3 Project scope statement .4 Project management plan	.1 Cost-benefit analysis .2 Benchmarking .3 Design of experiments .4 Cost of quality (COQ) .5 Additional quality planning tools	.1 Quality management plan .2 Quality metrics .3 Quality checklists .4 Process improvement plan .5 Quality baseline .6 Project management plan (updates)

Figure 8.10 PMBOK required inputs, tools and techniques used, and resulting outputs during quality planning

Quality policy
The overall intentions and direction of an organization with regard to quality, as formally expressed by top management.

Organizational process assets include factors like the organization's quality policies, quality-related procedures and guidelines, and finally, any documented lessons learned from prior projects. An example of a **quality policy** is illustrated in Figure 8.11. As can be seen from the ARM quality policy, this particular firm emphasizes customer-focused factors, as well as quality measures of products produced.

Figure 8.11 Web site on ARM quality policy

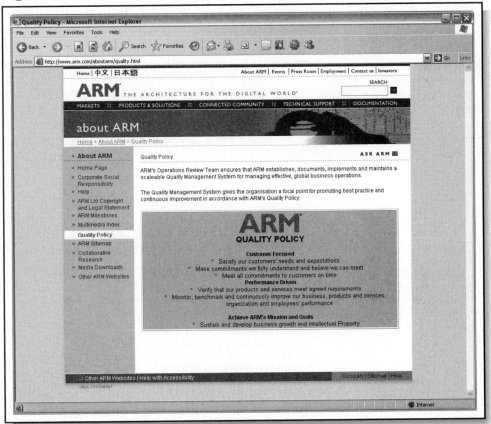

Quality Planning Techniques

Some tools and techniques available during the quality planning process include cost–benefit analysis, benchmarking, design of experiments, and cost of quality analysis.

Cost–benefit analysis
An evaluation of the costs and benefits of alternative approaches to a proposed activity to determine the best alternative.

A **cost–benefit analysis** can be used to determine the trade-off between the benefits of higher quality and the costs incurred by ensuring a particular product meets those higher quality standards. For example, certain products may experience a "quality threshold." In other words, a product may be of very high quality, yet if it does not fill a customer need, it will not be purchased regardless of its quality. In this case, it would not make sense to incur additional costs to improve the product's quality. While cost–benefit analyses originated as an analogy to investment decision-making where go or no-go decisions were frequently made, the technique is flexible enough to allow decision-makers to choose among a range of alternatives. Performing a cost-benefit analysis on alternative approaches to meeting project objectives might include calculating financial metrics, such as return on investment (ROI).

As an example of a cost–benefit analysis, consider an organization trying to decide whether to implement a new computer-based contact management system. Such a system presumably would allow the sales force to more efficiently and effectively maintain relationships with customers. The costs associated with such a system would include the computer equipment itself (such as PCs, servers, printers, and installation), as well as training and other associated expenses. The benefits of such a system might include increases in the ability to do mailings yielding a certain proportion of new customers, better management of telephone-based sales campaigns, improvement in customer retention, and more accurate customer information allowing improved contact with past customers regarding their needs. Dollar figures would be attached to both the costs and benefits resulting in a net cost or benefit value (see Figure 8.12) that could then be used in ROI or payback calculations. Given the typical effects of projects on multiple groups of stakeholders and the difficulty in quantifying such effects, however, cost–benefit analyses are sometimes criticized as being too simplistic or inaccurate because they reduce everything to monetary terms.

Benchmarking
The study of a competitor's product or business practices in order to improve the performance of one's own company.

Benchmarking is the study of a competitor's product or business practices for the purpose of improving a company's performance. In terms of IS project management, benchmarking may be used to compare a company's IS project management

Figure 8.12 Cost–benefit analysis

Cost Benefit Analysis Associated with a Contact Management System

Project Costs
- Personal Computers, $20,000
- Servers, $5,000
- Training, $10,000
- *Total costs = $35,000*

Project Benefits
- Increased Mailings, $5,000
- Improved Ability to Manage Telephone-Based Campaigns, $10,000
- Customer Retention, $25,000
- Improved Accuracy of Customer Information, $10,000
- *Total benefits = $50,000*

Net Benefits = $15,000

capabilities with those of other businesses. In this respect, benchmarking serves as an important tool for quality planning.

Serving a function similar to benchmarking are **capability maturity models (CMMs).** Capability maturity models are used to determine a company's capabilities with respect to best practices within a given industry. More specifically, CMM is a methodology used to develop and refine how an organization approaches its software development process. CMMs were originally developed by the Software Engineering Institute (SEI), a research and development center sponsored by the U.S. Department of Defense. CMM is a five-level evolutionary model of increasingly organized and systematically more mature processes for systems development. These five maturity levels for software processes are shown in Figure 8.13. The CMM is similar to ISO 9001, one of the ISO 9000 series of standards discussed earlier in this chapter. ISO 9001 focuses specifically on the development and maintenance of software and specifies minimally acceptable quality levels for the processes used to develop software. CMM goes beyond ISO 9001 in establishing a framework for continuous process improvements surrounding software development, and in providing more detail on how to achieve these new quality standards.

Design of experiments is another tool that can be used during project quality planning. Using statistical techniques, project personnel can test the efficiency of certain project management approaches by testing factors that might influence a specific variable. For example, managers might test the efficiency of teams made up of personnel with varying levels of expertise.

The design of experiments allows for a statistical framework to be used to systematically change factors that are important to the project rather than having to change these factors one at a time to determine their overall effect. The resulting experimental data should theoretically provide information that leads to optimal conditions for a particular product or process. Software or systems developers can use such a process to help design the most efficient system.

As a specific example, AT&T employees in 1992 designed a study to test an electronic-mail software solution over a PC-based local area network. In this study any number of factors (e.g., network loads, different types of system usage, etc.) were manipulated to examine possible faults in the software. While a full-blown testing scenario that involved changing one aspect of the system at a time would have required at least 8 weeks, the experimental study employed was able to identify

---

Capability maturity model
A technique used to determine a company's capabilities with respect to a set of procedures considered as best practices within a given industry.

Design of experiments
The use of statistical techniques to test the efficiency of certain project management approaches by testing factors that might influence a specific variable.

Figure 8.13 Capability Maturity Model levels

CMM's Five Maturity Levels of Software Processes

1. At the *initial* level, processes are disorganized, even chaotic. Success is likely to depend on individual efforts, and is not considered to be repeatable, because processes would not be sufficiently defined and documented to allow them to be replicated.

2. At the *repeatable* level, basic project management techniques are established, and successes could be repeated, because the requisite processes would have been made established, defined, and documented.

3. At the *defined* level, an organization has developed its own standard software process through greater attention to documentation, standardization, and integration.

4. At the *managed* level, an organization monitors and controls its own processes through data collection and analysis.

5. At the *optimizing* level, processes are constantly being improved through monitoring feedback from current processes and introducing innovative processes to better serve the organization's particular needs.

faults within 2 weeks. For additional details, see www.isixsigma.com/library/content/c030106a.asp.

One more tool that can be used during quality planning is the **cost of quality (COQ).** The cost of quality is comprised of both the costs to improve or ensure quality measures and the costs associated with a lack of quality. More specifically, the cost of quality might represent the amount of money a business could lose from products or services not being done well the first time around. These costs can include anything from rework to lawsuits resulting from poor quality. Estimates are that the cost of quality may run from 15 to 30 percent of total costs for most businesses (see www.isixsigma.com/dictionary/Cost_Of_Quality-497.htm).

As an extreme example of the cost of quality, one need only think back to the Y2K programming issue, where dates were stored in two-digit representations to save storage space in early information systems (e.g., 98 instead of 1998). It was anticipated that once the year 2000 came to pass, systems with the two-digit date representation scheme would not able to distinguish between the year 1998 and 2098, resulting in systems errors in any calculation involving time (such as interest calculations). The Gartner Group estimated the worldwide costs for the Y2K issue to range from $300 to $600 billion dollars (www.dmreview.com/article_sub.cfm?articleId=1949), including activities ranging from reprogramming efforts to the handling of lawsuits from angry clients. What was the cost of quality (i.e., the cost of not doing it right the first time) in this case? A high price tag indeed!

Quality Planning Outputs

The outputs from the quality planning stage include a quality management plan, quality metrics, quality checklists, a process improvement plan, a quality baseline,

COMMON PROBLEMS
The Costs of Software Quality

To maintain a competitive edge in the marketplace, software firms must deliver products of high quality on time and within budget. However, software managers may avoid quality inspections in an attempt to bring their products to the market faster because they feel such quality mechanisms only delay the software development process.

The costs of quality are divided into two major categories: conformance and nonconformance. The cost of conformance is the amount spent on achieving high-quality products. This category of quality costs is further divided into prevention and appraisal costs. Prevention costs are those associated with preventing any defects before they happen, whereas appraisal costs are those incurred in assuring conformance to quality standards. The cost of nonconformance includes all the expenses that result when things go wrong. This category of quality costs is also further divided into two subcategories, internal failure costs and external failure costs. Internal failure costs occur before the product is sent to the customer, whereas external failure costs arise from product failure at the customer's location. Table 8.2 lists the different types of quality costs, along with examples of each.

How can organizations decrease the costs associated with software quality? The best strategy involves:

• Avoiding any failure costs by driving defects to zero

• Investing in prevention activities to improve quality

• Reducing appraisal costs as quality improves

• Continuously evaluating and altering preventive efforts for more improvement

Quality improvements often result in cost savings that outweigh the money spent on quality efforts (Slaughter, Harter, and Krishnan, 1998). Which of the above strategies do you believe has the largest effect on controlling software quality?

Table 8.2 Types of Quality Costs

TYPES OF COST	EXAMPLES
COST OF CONFORMANCE	
Prevention costs	Costs of training staff in design methodologies
Appraisal costs	Code inspection and testing
COST OF NONCONFORMANCE	
Internal failure costs	Costs of rework in programming
External failure costs	Costs of support and maintenance

Quality management plan
A plan specifying how quality measures will be implemented during a project.

Quality metrics
Operational definitions of specific, processes, events, or products, as well as an explanation of how they will be measured in terms of quality.

Quality checklists
Tools used to ensure that a specific set of actions has been correctly performed.

Process improvement plan
A plan specifying how to identify wasteful and non–value-added activities.

Quality baseline
The basis for which project quality is measured and reported.

and updates to the project management plan. A **quality management plan** is a plan specifying how quality measures will be implemented during a project. Unlike the quality policy introduced previously the quality management plan lays out the specifics, rather than a philosophy of how quality will be managed during the project. The components of a quality plan (a rather substantial document) are shown in Figure 8.14. The quality plan serves the additional purpose of being an input into the overall project plan. **Quality metrics** are operational definitions of specific processes, events, or products and include an explanation of how they will be measured in terms of quality. **Quality checklists** are also produced as part of quality planning and are tools used to ensure that a specific set of actions has been correctly performed.

A **process improvement plan** is used to identify wasteful activities and non–value-added activities. A process improvement plan, a subcomponent of the project management plan discussed in Chapter 5, details the specific steps required to analyze processes to discover inefficiencies. These steps include:

- *Process boundaries.* Determine the specifics of each process, including when it starts and finishes, its purpose, its inputs and outputs, its major stakeholders, and its owner.
- *Process configuration.* Graphically represent the processes to examine how they interrelate and to help analyze them.
- *Process metrics.* Keep an eye on and maintain control over process status.
- *Targets for improved performance.* Targets give guidance to any process improvement activities.

A **quality baseline**, another quality planning output, is established in the quality planning stage to measure the project's quality performance. The quality baseline may be based on past performance metrics from other similar projects, or it may be

Components of a Quality Plan

A quality plan should ask

1. What needs to go through a quality check?
2. What is the most appropriate way to check the quality?
3. When should it be carried out?
4. Who should be involved?
5. What "Quality Materials" should be used?

Figure 8.14
Components of a quality plan

determined by experts in the domain. As an example, in an information systems project a quality baseline may be designed to compare current project performance with established values related to the number of hours necessary to complete project work package, output errors, system speed, or factors like system ease of use and user satisfaction.

As the quality planning stage is finalized, these quality planning outputs will serve as updates to the project management plan.

Quality Assurance

The **quality assurance** process is comprised of all the activities and actions required to ensure that the project meets the quality standards outlined during the quality planning phase. Quality assurance is typically overseen by a quality assurance department, a group responsible for making sure that a project satisfies all of the processes needed to meet stakeholder requirements. For a list of the inputs required, the tools and techniques used, and the resulting outputs during the quality assurance process, see Figure 8.15.

Global Implications: Quality Assurance Works Better Than Quality Control for Offshore Projects

Assume both a client company and an offshore vendor assign a project manager to an outsourcing project. The main role of the project manager at the client company is to work closely with the development team to ensure that the milestones and the project requirements are being met; thus, the home office project manager has to perform quality assurance rather than quality control. In an offshore project, managing quality is more difficult because, by the time the project results are verified, correcting mistakes could be quite costly. In such cases, quality assurance is useful because it focuses on the processes required to produce the results, and thus will help prevent problems before they occur. Here are some tips for managing project quality in offshore projects (Sources: Mochal, 2002; Tardugno, 2003):

1. A set of clear and comprehensive requirements should be developed for the project.
2. The project deliverables must be clearly described, and all stakeholders should agree to and approve this definition.
3. Project success should be clearly defined by developing the criteria for assessing the project deliverables in terms of completeness and correctness.
4. The project plan should clearly describe how the development team will do the work.
5. Milestones should be set for the major deliverables and there should be an approval and sign-off at each point to ensure quality.
6. All formal communication during the project life cycle should be addressed to the project managers. The project manager knows what is going on at every stage of the project and can, therefore, better manage everyone's expectations.
7. Any problems that arise during the life cycle of the project should be communicated and addressed as soon as possible.

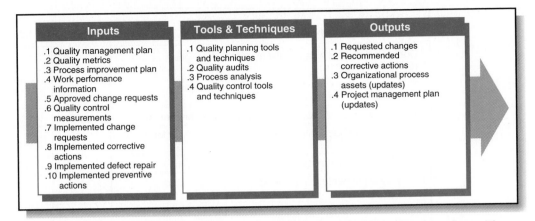

Inputs	Tools & Techniques	Outputs
.1 Quality management plan .2 Quality metrics .3 Process improvement plan .4 Work perfomance information .5 Approved change requests .6 Quality control measurements .7 Implemented change requests .8 Implemented corrective actions .9 Implemented defect repair .10 Implemented preventive actions	.1 Quality planning tools and techniques .2 Quality audits .3 Process analysis .4 Quality control tools and techniques	.1 Requested changes .2 Recommended corrective actions .3 Organizational process assets (updates) .4 Project management plan (updates)

Figure 8.15 PMBOK required inputs, tools and techniques used, and resulting outputs during quality assurance

As illustrated in Figure 8.15, the inputs to the quality assurance process include the quality management plan, quality metrics, process improvement plans, work performance information, approved change requests, quality control measurements, implemented change requests, implemented corrective actions, implemented defect repairs, and implemented preventive actions. The quality management plan and operational definitions were developed as part of the quality planning process outlined earlier. The quality management plan is used to outline the specifics of the quality measures that will be in place during the project. The results of the quality control measures are often based on quality testing procedures and should be formatted for further analyses.

Quality Assurance Tools and Techniques

The tools and techniques used as part of the quality planning process can also be used during quality assurance. Two new tools are also used in the quality assurance process, specifically quality audits and process analysis. **Quality audits** are activities designed to review other quality management procedures as well as to identify potential lessons learned. In a quality audit, the review is conducted in either scheduled or random fashion by trained personnel from within the organization or, in some cases, by qualified third-party auditors. Quality auditors typically examine a number of different project facets looking for ineffective or inefficient policies, processes, or procedures. Quality auditors may start with an established checklist and rate the various project facets evaluated. Such a checklist is shown in Figure 8.16.

Another tool used in the quality assurance process is a process analysis, which examines not what is done, but how it is done. A process analysis follows steps outlined in the process improvement plan, as discussed earlier.

Any lessons learned documented as part of the quality audit process are then used to improve performance during the current project or subsequent projects. Quality audits can be performed by in-house quality auditors or by outside auditors hired for a specific project.

Quality Assurance Outputs

Finally, the outputs from the quality assurance process are requested changes, recommended corrective actions, updates to organizational process assets, and updates to the project management plan. To create benefits for stakeholders and to properly assure

Quality audits
Structured and independent review activities designed to review quality management procedures and to identify potential lessons learned.

QUALITY ASSURANCE FUNCTIONS	YES	NO
Does the quality assurance unit or qualified designee do the following?		
1. approve or reject devices processed by another company		
2. approve or reject devices packaged by another company		
3. approve or reject devices held under contract by another company		
4. help provide solutions for quality system problems		
5. verify implementation of solutions for quality system problems		
6. assure that all quality system checks are appropriate and adequate		
7. assure that all quality system checks are performed correctly		

Figure 8.16   Sample quality audit checklist from the FDA's Center for Devices and Radiological Health

quality, requested changes should be recorded along with recommended corrective actions. As these quality assurance outputs are recorded, changes will be made to existing documents, resulting in updates to organizational process assets and the project management plan.

Quality Control

Quality control
The process of monitoring results to determine if the quality standards of the project are being met.

Quality control involves monitoring results to determine if the quality standards of the project are being met. The PMBOK inputs, tools and techniques, and outputs are presented briefly here; Chapter 12 will cover them in much more depth.

As you can see from Figure 8.9, the outputs of the quality planning and quality assurance stages serve as inputs into the quality control stage. Figure 8.17 shows the PMBOK inputs, tools, and outputs for quality control. Inputs discussed earlier include the quality management plan, quality metrics, quality checklists, organizational process assets, work performance information, approved change requests, and deliverables. **Work performance information** is a summary of the status of project

Work performance information
A summary of the status of project deliverables, any performance measures that have been collected, and any implemented changes from the original project management plan.

Figure 8.17   PMBOK required inputs, tools and techniques used, and resulting outputs during quality control

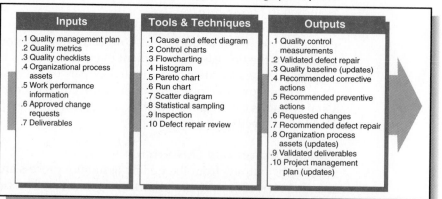

Inputs	Tools & Techniques	Outputs
.1 Quality management plan	.1 Cause and effect diagram	.1 Quality control measurements
.2 Quality metrics	.2 Control charts	.2 Validated defect repair
.3 Quality checklists	.3 Flowcharting	.3 Quality baseline (updates)
.4 Organizational process assets	.4 Histogram	.4 Recommended corrective actions
.5 Work performance information	.5 Pareto chart	.5 Recommended preventive actions
.6 Approved change requests	.6 Run chart	.6 Requested changes
.7 Deliverables	.7 Scatter diagram	.7 Recommended defect repair
	.8 Statistical sampling	.8 Organization process assets (updates)
	.9 Inspection	.9 Validated deliverables
	.10 Defect repair review	.10 Project management plan (updates)

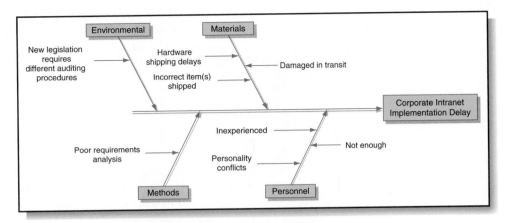

Figure 8.18 Cause-and-effect (fishbone) diagram sample

deliverables, any performance measures that have been collected, and any implemented changes from the original project management plan.

Several tools and techniques are available to convert these inputs into outputs. These include cause-and-effect (also called fishbone or Ishikawa) diagrams (Figure 8.18), **control charts** (Figure 8.19), **Pareto charts** (Figure 8.20), flowcharting (Figure 8.21), histograms, run charts, scatter diagrams, statistical sampling, inspection, and defect repair review. We depict a few of these tools graphically in this chapter but leave their explanation to Chapter 12.

Once you have utilized the various quality control tools and techniques to control the quality of the project, you will have produced a series of quality control outputs. These include quality control measurements, validated defect repair, updates to the quality baseline, recommended corrective actions, recommended preventive actions, requested changes, recommended defect repair, updates to organization process assets, validated deliverables, and updates to the project management plan. As with the inputs, and the tools and techniques for quality control, these outputs will be covered in more detail in Chapter 12.

Control charts
Graphical, time-based charts used to display process results.

Pareto charts
Histograms (or bar charts) where the values being plotted are arranged in descending order.

Figure 8.19 Control chart sample

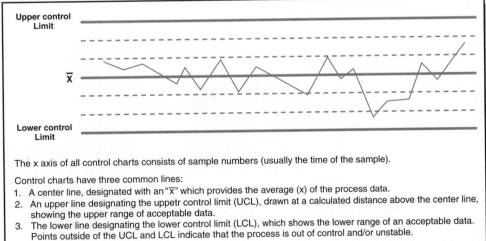

The x axis of all control charts consists of sample numbers (usually the time of the sample).

Control charts have three common lines:
1. A center line, designated with an "x̄" which provides the average (x) of the process data.
2. An upper line designating the uppetr control limit (UCL), drawn at a calculated distance above the center line, showing the upper range of acceptable data.
3. The lower line designating the lower control limit (LCL), which shows the lower range of an acceptable data. Points outside of the UCL and LCL indicate that the process is out of control and/or unstable.

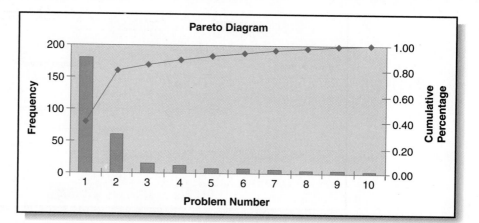

Figure 8.20 Pareto chart

Figure 8.21 Quality control flowchart

Source: Reproduced with permission of SmartDraw® from www.smartdraw.com

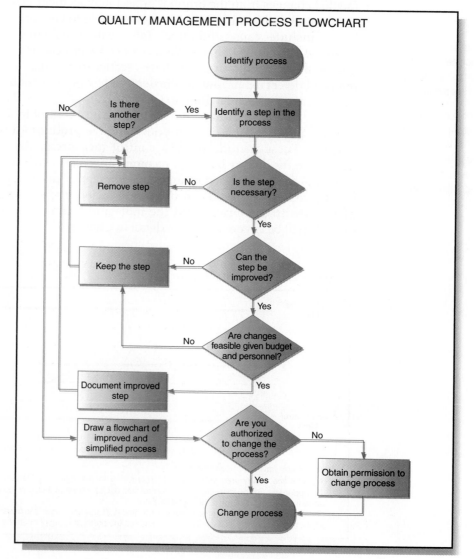

Table 8.3 Tools and Techniques Available for Project Quality Management

TOOLS AND TECHNIQUES	SHORT EXPLANATION
Cost–benefit analysis	An evaluation of the costs and benefits of alternative approaches to a proposed activity to determine the best alternative.
Inspection	Measurement and testing procedures to determine whether results conform to the particular project standards.
Statistical sampling	The process of selecting a random sample from a population in order to infer characteristics about that population.
Control charts	Graphical, time-based charts used to display process results.
Cause-and-effect (fishbone) diagrams	A diagramming technique used to explore potential and real causes of problems. The fishbone diagram typically organizes problems into categories relevant to the industry.
Pareto diagrams	Histograms ordered in terms of the number of occurrences of outline project problems that have been identified.

Table 8.3 lists the different tools and techniques available for Project Quality Management, as well as a short explanation of what they are.

Ethical Dilemma: Finding the Right Balance Between Speed and Quality

The mantra in many companies today is "do more with less." This expression is taking on a new meaning for IT project managers. Organizations are always focusing on costs. Consequently, IT projects, which used to take months, may have to be completed within weeks, while at the same time, the project deliverables are expected to be of the highest quality. Project managers are pressured to apply principles of rapid application development (RAD) and also maintain quality. The struggle for project managers is to find the right balance between quality and speed.

Kevin Heard, a project manager at Clarkston Consulting, says that this battle is hard. According to Mr. Heard, whereas sacrificing quality today can lead to additional expenses in the future, ensuring quality may likely result in longer project life cycles. The situation worsens because staff resources are frequently limited. As a result, the project manager needs to be adept at identifying available skills and making good use of limited resources.

Moreover, project managers are increasingly facing pressure from executives to take shortcuts on IT projects. For example, an IT manager at a midwestern manufacturer says that senior business leaders have been pressuring him to rush an enterprise resource planning (ERP) system by bypassing critical business processes. Ken McLennan, the senior vice-president of business solutions at Fujitsu Consulting, says that project managers not only must resist this pressure but also should inform executives of the risks associated with cutting corners during IT projects. One risk that should be communicated to executives is that if project failures are publicized the share price of the company will often be adversely affected (Source: Hoffman, 2004).

Discussion Questions
1. If faced with increasing pressure to get a project done ahead of time, what steps should a project manager take if he feels this will jeopardize project quality?
2. In addition to the effects that a rushed project might have on project quality, what kind of short-term and long-term effects might it have on project team members?

In this chapter, we have focused primarily on Knowledge Area 8, Project Quality Management, within the Project Management Body of Knowledge (PMBOK, 2004). One of the nine project management knowledge areas, Project Quality Management is often considered by some experts to be a fourth dimension that should be included in the cost-time-scope trade-off experienced during project management. An important topic, managing project quality should not be overlooked during any project and especially not during IS development. In this chapter, we have identified the various phases of Project Quality Management, including quality planning, quality assurance, and quality control. We have also identified the various tools and techniques that can be used in managing quality. Figure 8.22 identifies this coverage and illustrates the coverage of upcoming chapters as well.

Figure 8.22 Chapter 8 and PMBOK coverage

	Textbook Chapters ⟶	1	2	3	4	5	6	7	8	9	10	11	12
	PMBOK Knowledge Area												
1	**Introduction to Project Management**												
1.1	What is a Project?	●											
1.2	What is Project Management?	●											
1.3	Areas of Expertise		●										
1.4	Project Management Context	●											
2	**Project Life Cycle and Organization**												
2.1	The Project Life Cycle	●	●										
2.2	Project Stakeholders	●	●										
2.3	Organizational Influences		●	●	●			●					
3	**Project Management Processes for a Project**												
3.1	Project Management Processes	●	●										
3.2	PM Process Groups	●	●										
3.3	Process Interactions		●										
3.4	Project Management Process Mapping		●										
4	**Project Integration Management**												
4.1	Develop Project Charter					●							
4.2	Develop Preliminary Project Scope Statement					●	●						
4.3	Develop Project Management Plan					●							
4.4	Direct and Manage Project Execution										○		
4.5	Monitor and Control Project Work											○	
4.6	Integrated Change Control											○	
4.7	Close Project											○	

(continued)

Figure 8.22 (continued)

	Textbook Chapters ➡	1	2	3	4	5	6	7	8	9	10	11	12
	PMBOK Knowledge Area												
5	**Project Scope Management**												
5.1	Scope Planning					●							
5.2	Scope Definition					●							
5.3	Create WBS					●	●						
5.4	Scope Verification					●							
5.5	Scope Control					●							○
6	**Project Time Management**												
6.1	Activity Definition						●						
6.2	Activity Sequencing						●						
6.3	Activity Resource Estimating							●					
6.4	Activity Duration Estimating							●					
6.5	Schedule Development							●					
6.6	Schedule Control							●					○
7	**Project Cost Management**												
7.1	Cost Estimating							●					
7.2	Cost Budgeting							●					
7.3	Cost Control							●					○
8	**Project Quality Management**												
8.1	Quality Planning								✓				
8.2	Perform Quality Assurance								✓				
8.3	Perform Quality Control								✓				○
9	**Project Human Resource Management**												
9.1	Human Resource Planning				●			●					
9.2	Acquire Project Team				●			●					
9.3	Develop Project Team				●			●					
9.4	Manage Project Team				●			●					
10	**Project Communications Management**												
10.1	Communications Planning					●						○	
10.2	Information Distribution					●						○	
10.3	Performance Reporting					●							○
10.4	Manage Stakeholders					●							○

(continued)

Figure 8.22 (continued)

Textbook Chapters →	1	2	3	4	5	6	7	8	9	10	11	12
PMBOK Knowledge Area												
11 Project Risk Management												
11.1 Risk Management Planning									○			
11.2 Risk Identification									○		○	
11.3 Qualitative Risk Analysis									○			
11.4 Quantitative Risk Analysis									○			
11.5 Risk Response Planning									○			
11.6 Risk Monitoring and Control									○			○
12 Project Procurement Management												
12.1 Plan Purchases and Acquisitions										○		
12.2 Plan Contracting										○		
12.3 Request Seller Responses										○		
12.4 Select Sellers										○		
12.5 Contract Administration										○		
12.6 Contract Closure										○		○

Key: ●-where material is covered in past chapters; ✓-current chapter coverage;
○-where material is covered in future chapters

RUNNING CASE
Managing Project Quality

Sally reviewed the project charter, looking at the objectives of the system: track customer purchases, create a point system for customer to use toward redeeming merchandise, reward customer loyalty, and improve management information. Sally knew that the quality of this project needed to relate somehow to these objectives, but she wasn't quite sure how to approach the issue.

Certainly, a system to track customer purchases and then allocate points to those customers making purchases seemed to be rather straightforward. However, tracking whether they were adequately rewarding loyal customers and improving the information that management used—both being quality objectives—seemed a bit more vague.

The next day after the initial updates on project status, Sally presented her dilemma. "We need to figure out if this project is doing what management wants it to."

"Let's talk about customer loyalty for a second. Since we are measuring loyalty by the number of times a customer returns and makes a purchase, let's just track customer visits." said Bob.

"That's a good idea, but the problem is that we don't always know if they have visited. What if they pay cash?" said Sanjay.

"Ah, good point. How about if we track their use of the points? That's really the key point of the new system anyway, isn't it?" asked Bob.

"Well, yeah, but remember, while we want to reward customers for their loyalty, I think the real goal is to see how this loyalty impacts the bottom line," said Sanjay. "I think we need to somehow track the frequency of visits and maybe the size of the purchases. If these go up, the system is working. And then, let's not forget about the better information the system is supposed to provide to management. Is there a way to track information *quality*?"

"Wait," said Sally. "All this is related to whether the system is doing what we want at the end. What about managing the quality during the development of the system? How do we handle that?"

The meeting went on for some time as the team looked through materials for quality project management techniques and considered how they could apply to this project.

CHAPTER SUMMARY

Understand the concept of quality and why it is important. Project quality is defined by the Project Management Institute as "the degree to which a set of inherent characteristics fulfill requirements." Project quality is often defined by companies as both conformance to manufacturer specifications and fitness for use by the customer. Project quality is important because it has a direct relationship to project success. Many examples of information system project success and failure can be attributed to project quality. In many instances, information systems are used in contexts that have little or no tolerance for error. An example highlighted in the chapter was that of an air traffic control system—a system that controls the regulation and scheduling of incoming and outgoing flights at a major airport. A glitch in the software, caused by poor quality in designing or building such a system, could have disastrous results.

Discuss quality management pioneers and quality certifications and standards in industries today. There have been many quality management pioneers throughout history, including Deming, Juran, Crosby, and Ishikawa. Further, the need to manage quality has spurred the development of standards

and systems supporting quality management, including ISO 9000 and Six Sigma, as well as awards for quality, such as the Baldrige Award. Adopting the procedures associated with quality certification programs may help to improve the organization's bottom line.

Describe tools and techniques for managing including quality planning. quality assurance, and quality control. Managing project quality can be accomplished by following the major processes of quality planning, quality assurance, and quality control as specified by the PMBOK. Several tools and techniques were discussed in this chapter, including inspection, statistical control, control charts, cause and effect diagrams, and Pareto analysis. Each of these has specific uses within Project Quality Management. Technology plays a major role in Project Quality Management. Statistical analysis, document repositories, and project data tracking represent just a few of the ways in which technology can be used during quality management.

KEY TERMS REVIEW

- Balanced scorecard
- Benchmarking
- Capability maturity models
- Control charts
- Cost–benefit analysis
- Cost of quality
- Design of experiments

- Fishbone diagram
- Flowchart
- ISO 9000
- Pareto charts
- Process improvement plan
- Project quality
- Quality assurance

- Quality audits
- Quality baseline
- Quality control
- Quality management plan
- Quality metrics
- Quality policy

Match each of the key terms with the definition that best fits it.

1. _____ A technique used to determine a company's capabilities with respect to a set of procedures considered as best practices within a given industry.

2. _____ A tool for assessing organizational activity from perspectives beyond the typical financial analysis.

3. _____ The process of monitoring results to determine if the quality standards of the project are being met.

4. _____ A generic management systems standard that any organization can follow to achieve ISO certification.

5. _____ Definitions of specific, processes, events, or products, as well as an explanation of how they will be measured in terms of quality.

6. _____ The degree to which a set of inherent characteristics fulfill requirements.

7. _____ Graphical, time-based charts used to display process results.

8. _____ The study of a competitor's product or business practices in order to improve the performance of one's own company.

9. _____ Activities designed to review other quality management procedures and to identify potential lessons learned.

10. _____ The process of identifying relevant quality standards and developing a plan to ensure the project meets those standards.

11. _____ A diagramming technique used to explore potential and real causes of problems.

12. _____ The overall intentions and direction of an organization with regard to quality as formally expressed by top management.

13. _____ The process of ensuring that the project meets the quality standards outlined during the quality planning phase.

14. _____ An evaluation of the costs and benefits of alternative approaches to a proposed activity to determine the best alternative.

15. _____ Histograms (or bar charts) where the values being plotted are arranged in descending order.

16. _____ The use of statistical techniques to test the efficiency of certain project management approaches by testing factors that might influence a specific variable.

17. _____ The cost to improve or ensure quality measures, as well as the cost associated with a lack of quality.

18. _____ A plan specifying how quality measures will be implemented during a project.

19. _____ A plan specifying how to identify wasteful and non–value-added activities.

20. _____ The basis for which project quality is measured and reported.

REVIEW QUESTIONS

1. Define project quality.
2. Give two examples of quality during an ISD project.
3. List the processes of Project Quality Management.
4. List two inputs for each of the Project Quality Management processes.
5. List two tools or techniques for each of the Project Quality Management processes.
6. List two outputs for each of the Project Quality Management processes.
7. Describe the cost–benefit analysis.
8. What role does inspection play during Project Quality Management?
9. Describe the cause and effect (fishbone) diagram.
10. Describe the Pareto analysis. What is the 80/20 rule?
11. Describe the two well-known quality certifications.
12. Explain how technology can be used to manage quality.

1. What is project quality and why is it important?
2. Provide some examples of quality problems in information technology projects and discuss how these quality problems can be avoided.
3. Explain how cost–benefit analysis is used in the quality planning process.
4. Using the Internet, perform a search for benchmarking. Describe what it is and its usefulness. Also explain how this tool is important in managing quality.
5. Compare and contrast quality assurance and quality control.
6. Think of a recent project that you were involved in (or the project you are involved in as part of your current course). Identify a problem that you encountered. Next, determine potential categories for causes associated with the specific problem. Based on this information, develop a fishbone diagram.
7. Think of a recent project that you were involved in (or the project you are involved in as part of your current course). What were some of the problems you encountered? Were some of the causes of the problems more frequent than others? Using the 80/20 rule discussed in the chapter, construct a Pareto diagram illustrating the problems you encountered and the frequency of the causes.
8. Using the Internet or any other source, write a two-page report on quality management certification.
9. Using the Internet, perform a search for ISO 9000. What is involved in earning this certification? Is it important to have this certification? Why or why not?
10. Using the Internet, perform a search for ISO 14000. What is involved in earning this certification? Is it important to have this certification? Why or why not?
11. Using the Internet or any other source, write a two-page report on other quality management pioneers not mentioned in the chapter.
12. Discuss how a project team can know if their project delivers good quality.

CHAPTER CASES

Sedona Management Group and Managing Project Quality

Every project is affected in different ways by its scope, time, and cost goals. These three areas represent project management's triple constraint. However, lately there has been more and more agreement that quality should be included as a fourth dimension. Quality management is a very important topic in project management because it influences project success. The main goal of Project Quality Management is to ensure that the project satisfies the needs for which it was undertaken.

The Sedona Management Group (SMG) acknowledges the importance of managing project quality. Over the last ten years, the team has done a great job managing project quality by consistently delivering in a timely manner products that meet stakeholders' expectations. At SMG, project quality is illustrated by the amount of new work that Sedona does for repeat customers. In addition, due to the high quality of its work related to both interface design and underlying Web architecture, SMG has gained a reputation for being able to "clean up" Web sites built by other vendors. Satisfied customers spread the word about SMG's quality workmanship, so word-of-mouth advertising has been responsible for a substantial amount of Sedona's work over the last 10 years.

One of the first steps SMG follows in managing project quality is quality planning, which involves identifying the quality standards that are important to any given project, and then determining how to achieve these standards. In the case of the Seattle Seahawks project, it was important not only that the information conveyed on the Web site be accurate and easy to access but also that the system be highly reliable and secure. All of these factors were part of SMG's quality plan, part of which involved establishing the criteria that the Sedona team needed to meet to ensure project success.

While establishing quality objectives is important, part of managing project quality also involves establishing the quality management processes the team will practice as they develop the system. Such quality assurance and control processes include establishing sufficient communication with the clients to ensure that their needs are being met, scheduling regular project meetings to discuss issues, such as project problems and causes, and documenting problems so these lessons learned can be applied to future projects. Through regular meetings with the members of the project team, Turnpaugh ensures that these quality standards are being met throughout the life cycle of the project. The Sedona team also ensures quality by reusing software code that has proven reliable in past projects.

Mike Flood, vice president of community relations with the Seattle Seahawks, recognizes SMG's efforts at ensuring quality. He has been so satisfied that he regularly recommends SMG to other potential clients, and he has employed SMG for other Seahawks IT projects. Overall, the Sedona team has undertaken at least one project per year for the Seattle Seahawks since their original development of the Seahawks' Web site.

CHAPTER 8 PROJECT ASSIGNMENT

An activity associated with Project Quality Management is problem identification during a project. There are several techniques for doing this, one of which is the Pareto analysis. In this assignment, you will develop a quality plan for your project, and create a Pareto diagram that identifies problems you are encountering. You will have to:

1. Define quality as it relates to your project.
2. Determine the requirements of the Web site you will be developing.
3. The purpose of a quality plan is to define overall project quality guidelines that will be applied to the project. Develop a quality plan for your project. The project plan should contain information about:
   - How you will control changes to the project
   - How you will ensure that the developed Web site meets the requirements
   - How you will ensure that the Web site works properly
   - How you will plan for and execute testing, both when the Web site is being developed and when design is completed
   - How you will track and resolve defects
4. Identify and define the problems you are encountering during the project life cycle.
5. Determine the importance of these problems by assigning a weight to each of them. Note that the weights should sum to 1.0 or 100 percent. Generate a Pareto diagram based on these problems and write a small paragraph on what you learn from this diagram.

Special Case: Making it Work—Meeting Customer Expectations

Peter Dimov, a manager of software development at InterImage, and Petya Alexandrova, founder and president of Digital Enterprises Inc., recommend the following steps for meeting customer expectations, a critical component to quality (Dimov and Alexandrova, 2003).

Step 1: Build a communication channel and a trusting relationship. These managers recommend *using* a bilateral mode of communication to ensure that you understand the customer's needs. To earn trust, they state, managers must ensure the credibility of the information they provide to the client.

Step 2: Exchange relevant and meaningful information. Dimov and Alexandrova have found that to avoid

potential misunderstandings, managers must learn about clients' personalities, thought processes, background, and company lingo. Further, they state that both formal and informal lines of communication should be established.

Step 3: Establish a system to measure success. For this step, the authors recommend that managers and clients develop a mutual acceptance of what comprises project success.

Step 4: Conduct status meetings. As a final step, Dimov and Alexandrova stress the importance of status meetings to discuss and remedy any potential misunderstandings of misconceptions.

REFERENCES

Arveson, P. (1998). "What is the Balanced Scorecard?" Retrieved April 3, 2006, from: www.balancedscorecard. org/basics/bsc1.html.

BBC News. (2002). "Flights Halted by Computer Glitch." Acquired October 8, 2006 from news.bbc.co.uk/1/hi/ uk/1897885.stm.

Deming, W. E. (1986). *Out of Crisis.* Cambridge, MA: MIT.

Dimov, P. and Alexandrova. (2003). "Return Customers." *PM Network,* July, 48.

GE.com. "Key Elements of Quality. . . Customer, Process and Employee." Acquired October 8, 2006 from www.ge.com/sixsigma/keyelements.html.

Hoffman, T. (2004). "IT Project Management: Balancing Speed and Quality." *ComputerWorld,* Acquired October 8, 2006 from: http://www.computerworld. com/managementtopics/management/story/ 0,10801, 90199,00.html.

Ishikawa. K. (1985). *What is Total Quality Control?* (Lu, D. J., trans.) Upper Saddle River, NJ: Prentice Hall.

Kaplan, R. S., and Norton, D. P. (1992). "The Balanced Scorecard: Measures that Drive Performance." *Harvard Business Review* 70(1), 71–80.

Mochal, T. (2002). "Assume a Quality Assurance Role to 'Manage' an Outsourced Project." *TechRepublic.* Acquired October 22, 2002 from: techrepublic.com.com/ 5100–6330_11–1027918.html?tag=search.

PM Solutions company Web site: www.pmsolutions.com/ maturitymodel/whatismodel.htm.

Project Management Institute. (2004). *A Guide to the Project Management Body of Knowledge.* Newton Square, PA: PMI.

Reichheld, F. (1996). *The Loyalty Effect: The Hidden Force Behind Growth, Profits, and Lasting Value.* Cambridge, MA: Harvard Business School Press.

Slaughter, S. A., Harter, D. E., and Krishnan, M. S. (1998). "Evaluating the Cost of Software Quality." *Communications of the ACM* 41(8), 67–73.

Stylianou, A. C., and Kumar, R. L. (2000). "An Integrative Framework for IS Quality Management." *Communications of the ACM* 43(9), 99–104.

Tardugno, A. (2003). "Ten Keys to Successful Outsourcing." *TechRepublic.* Acquired April 2, 2003 from: techrepublic.com.com/5100–6298_11–5030382.html? tag=search.

Chapter 9

Managing Project Risk

Opening Case: Risk Mitigation and Transference Strategies Solve the Mystery of Nonfilers in California

Cathy Cleek, a PMP certified program director for the Franchise Tax Board in California, used a combination of risk mitigation and risk transference strategies during a recent database development project for the Franchise Tax Board of California. The new Web-based database system was designed to reduce the growing number of nonfilers in California. To mitigate risk associated with getting the right user requirements, Cleek used a series of customer focus groups consisting of taxpayers who failed to file their state tax forms, as well as tax attorneys and licensed tax preparers. As a result of these focus groups, Cleek and her team discovered that many of the nonfilers could not afford to pay their tax burden in one lump-sum payment. Based on this information, the team designed a Web site that included an installment payment function (see Figure 9.1). The risk transference strategy that Cleek used to help manage risk on this project involved a strong performance incentive for IBM, the primary technology supplier for the project (Essex, 2003). Such risk mitigation and risk transference strategies can vary substantially by project, but we discuss the underlying basic principles of these strategies in this chapter.

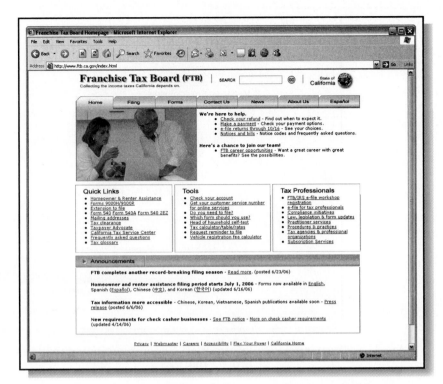

Figure 9.1　State of California Franchise Tax Board Web page

LEARNING OBJECTIVES

After reading this chapter, you will be able to:

➤ Understand the concept of risk and its relationship to project management.

➤ Identify categories of risk and their effect on information systems projects.

➤ Apply techniques for managing project risk, including risk management planning, risk identification, qualitative risk analysis, quantitative risk analysis, risk response planning, and risk monitoring and control.

INTRODUCTION

Organizations have to face risks virtually every day. Choices about which products to develop, which investments to make, which employees to hire, and which projects to undertake are all examples of organizational activities that involve risk. In this chapter, we will discuss the concept of risk and its relationship to project management, identify categories of risk and their effect on information systems projects, and apply techniques for managing project risk, including risk management planning, risk identification, qualitative risk analysis, quantitative risk analysis, risk response planning, and risk monitoring and control (see Figure 9.2).

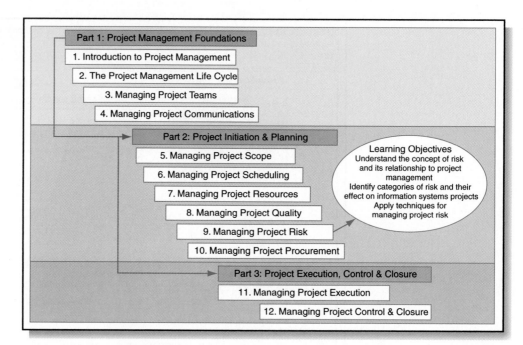

Figure 9.2 Information systems project management focusing on managing project risk

What is Risk?

Risk is generally viewed as threatening (see Figure 9.3). For example, the Merriam-Webster Online Dictionary (m-w.com/dictionary/risk) defines *risk* as: 1: possibility of loss or injury 2: someone or something that creates or suggests a hazard. A more accurate and sophisticated conceptualization of risk, however, involves an assessment of both the probability of a loss occurring and the size of the loss if it does occur. As an example, a company considering installing a new ERP will evaluate the risk associated with such an installation by assessing not just the likelihood of the system not doing what it is expected to do (i.e., the probability of failure), but also the resultant cost to the organization if such a failure occurs. Given that such ERPs are designed to affect a vast number of business functions, even if the likelihood of failure is small, the size of potential loss from such a failure may be quite large. As a result, such a system would normally be considered as highly risky. In contrast, a system focused on one functional area of a business or possibly on a less critical process (such as a parking permit system) may not be considered as risky even if the probability of system failure is high. In such a case, the size of the business loss may be low, and thus, the overall risk may be low.

Project risk
An uncertain event or condition that, if it occurs, has a positive or negative effect on a project objective.

But is risk always bad? PMI's definition of project risk would seem to indicate that risk may not always be something to be avoided: "**Project risk** is an uncertain event or condition that, if it occurs, has a *positive* or a negative effect on a project objective" (PMBOK 2004, page 8). This is a slightly different view of risk and takes into consideration that some uncertain events may enhance the project, although others may create problems.

The Costs of Project Failure

Power

Money   Market share

Competitive Advantage   Business Failure

Personnel Loss

Figure 9.3
Is this project
worth the risk?

Technology, Teams, and Managing Project Risk

The relationship between technology and project risk spans multiple dimensions. First, the volatile nature of technology (being subject to constant updates, sometimes in the middle of projects) creates special pressures in information systems projects. Technological changes need to be constantly monitored and considered as the information systems project develops. As a specific example, a manufacturing system may have originally been planned for the purpose of providing information internally to the manufacturing division within a company. However, a new software release may include features that allow the system to also have connectivity with suppliers. Realizing that such features may be desirable to project stakeholders, the project manager may need to discuss with a client the possibility of changing the project scope to include these new capabilities. Such a change would likely entail additional changes in the project cost and schedule, as well as changes in project risk.

Technology may also influence project risk by giving the project manager new tools to assess risk. Many technological aids now available are used by project managers in risk planning and risk identification, as well as in the analysis of risk. As an example, knowledge management systems may help project managers in the risk identification process. Similarly, statistical tools may also help the project manager to do quantitative risk analysis.

Although technology may help the project manager in assessing risks, it may also create risk. For example, project management software is only as good as the information that is put into it. Based on that information, scheduling updates, critical path information, and project status reports can easily be generated. This generated information can then be used by project managers for decision making. In many such cases, the sophisticated form in which information is presented may give this information an aura of accuracy. However, presentation does not guarantee accuracy. If any of the information entered into the system is unreliable or incorrect, the project manager's decision making may be adversely affected.

From a teamwork perspective, the entire project team may be involved in planning, assessing, measuring, or controlling risk. As a result, all of the teamwork and communication issues raised in Chapters 3 and 4 will come into play as risk is managed. Additionally, forming teams during projects incorporates risk. For example, how should managers assign organizational members to specific project teams? How should project team leaders be assigned? What technologies should project teams use to communicate? Should teams meet face-to-face, and if so, how often? These and many other questions must be addressed by project managers in charge of creating project teams, and the answer to each question may involve risk and ultimately affect project success.

Managing Risk and the Project Life Cycle

Risk may influence each of the project management process areas of initiation, planning, execution, closing, and control. During initiation, risk most often occurs in the project selection stage. During this process, top management must make project selection decisions based on the information provided to them. Project initiation decisions are usually based on multiple criteria. One important criterion often considered is the project's synergy with the direction and goals of the initiating organization. Sometimes, this may be a difficult decision. Based on its industry position, what strategies (and, thus, what projects) is the company pursuing? If the company is following a diversification strategy, project risks may increase as it pursues projects outside its core competency. Take, for instance, a recent technology focused project from the global coffee vendor, Starbucks. Facing the potential of a saturated retail coffee market, Starbucks has recently begun a series of projects designed to build locations where customers can use computer systems to download music and create personal CDs, all while enjoying a Starbucks drink (Overholt, 2004; see Figure 9.4). In pursuing such projects, Starbucks may need to build and manage a number of new technologies—an area where they may not have an adequate resource base, both in terms of skilled personnel and technology infrastructure. This serves to increase both corporate and project risks.

During project planning, other types of project risk may also be encountered. Risk associated with procurement planning is one example of potential risk during an IS development project. The instability of new technologies used during an IS project may result in unreliable estimated delivery dates from vendors trying to win

Figure 9.4
Starbucks' "Hear Music"

project contracts. Relying on these unrealistic delivery schedules can be very risky because the entire project can be delayed if the delivery of that technology is on the project's critical path. Another risk during project planning is associated with developing the project schedule. Project schedules built around the work breakdown structure are generally based on previous project information or on expert knowledge, as discussed in previous chapters. Neither of these techniques is completely foolproof. For example, if an IS development project schedule is based on archived project information, even slight differences between the previous and current projects can result in project delays. Further, basing schedule information on expert knowledge, although a valuable technique, nonetheless amounts to a risk taken by project managers because experts are only human and humans make mistakes. Thus, developing a project schedule and work breakdown structure during project planning is inherently risky.

During the execution of project activities, managers may find themselves faced with many decisions involving risk. For example, a vendor may inform a manager that a critical project component is in danger of not meeting the scheduled delivery date. In such a case, the project manager must decide whether to delay activities that are to be performed before and after the component's installation and focus on other project activities or to proceed with the schedule as planned and take a risk that the component will be delivered as scheduled. Another risk that may be taken by project managers involves technology upgrades, as discussed above. Managers may find that an upgraded version of a technology has become available during the execution process. Even if the upgraded version comes at no additional cost, managers must still risk problems associated with the new version's functionality.

During the closing process, managers may also face risk. One major risk involves the acceptance of the project as finished. This can be especially risky if major contracts are involved because the acceptance of the project may trigger significant closing payments to project contractors. Once the contracts have been signed off as met, it may become more difficult to get vendors to return and fix any problems without additional charges. Finally, control processes are used to monitor and react to project risk, a topic discussed more thoroughly in Chapter 12.

THE EFFECTS AND CATEGORIZATION OF PROJECT RISK

In this section we briefly discuss results of project-risk surveys administered to project managers, some examples of risk from both non-IS and IS related projects, and finally several categories of risks that may be specific to IS projects. After that, we will turn to a discussion of some project management techniques to help manage project risk.

Statistics about Project Risk

The results of a survey regarding project risk were published in a recent issue of *PM Network* (Foti, 2003). In that survey, project managers were asked how their respective organizations approached risk management. Thirty-eight percent of those responding stated that their organizations approached risk management in terms of the consequences and likelihood of their occurrence. This view is consistent with the risk

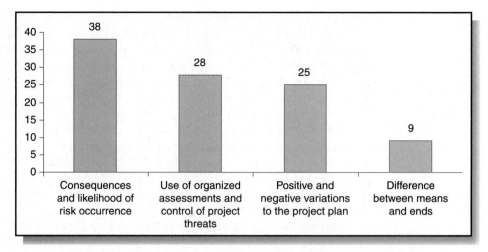

Figure 9.5 Different ways in which organizations approach risk management

management planning processes discussed in this chapter, specifically probability/impact analyses. Twenty-eight percent of those responding reported that their companies used systematic and organized assessments and control processes to deal with threats to projects and, therefore, to manage risk. Such techniques are part of the processes of risk identification, risk monitoring, and risk control. Twenty-five percent of those responding reported that their organizations approached risk management in terms of both positive and negative variations to the project plan. This view is consistent with our definition of project risk, which includes negative and positive effects on project outcomes. Finally, 9 percent of the project managers responding reported that their organizations approached risk management as the difference between means and ends. Figure 9.5 depicts these results.

In a separate survey conducted by Business Improvements Architects (BIA), managers were asked to identify the biggest challenges facing their organizations. Prominently noted among them was project risk. Thirty-six percent of the managers who were surveyed reported the biggest challenge facing their organizations was improper assessment or management of project risk (Silverstein, 2002).

Joan Knutson, contributing editor to *PM Network*, recently stated that several of the project management knowledge areas will continue to see dramatic change in the future. Among the areas she identified was Project Risk Management. Knutson states, "Risks are the holes in the dike. Too many holes in the dike can make it crumble. If risks are isolated and plugged, then the dike will stay together. The subdiscipline of risk has advanced in the areas of risk identification, analysis, planning, and management. Keep reading and exploring. New techniques are on the horizon" (Knutson, 2003, p. 60).

Examples of Risk

The experiences of Georgia Power during a recent transmission line installation project provide a clear example of how risks (in this case environmental risks) must be considered during projects (see Figure 9.6). In this case, even though the community recognized the need for power, the project still faced the potential risk of rejection by community members. To mitigate this risk, Georgia Power took

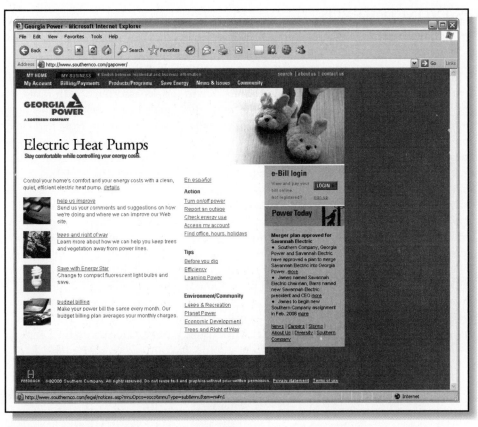

Figure 9.6 Georgia Power Web site

a proactive approach by personally meeting with the community and explaining that power needs had grown exponentially and that, unless the project was completed, power for life's basic needs might not be available. As an additional step toward gaining community acceptance, Georgia Power planted new shrubbery and trees throughout the right-of-way used for the new transmission line (Silverstein, 2002). This sort of interaction with users is common to IS projects as well, where many risk mitigation strategies involve creating a shared sense of project scope and buy-in.

An example of dealing with risk specific to information systems projects can occur in the context of extreme programming or rapid application development (RAD). Managers should be sure that critical steps are not skipped in the interest of time. The lack of detailed requirements specifications in this methodology adds an extra level of risk to the project and increases the need for effective communication between the developers and the users. Ron Thompson, product delivery director for govONE Solutions, discusses the problems associated with the use of RAD methodologies and the need for effective communication between users and developers: "Many of the rapid methods try to gain speed by isolating the development team. The problem is the definition of 'success.' If success means delivering a system in the allotted time, many teams are probably successful. If success means delivering a useful system, success is probably spotty at best" (Hall, 2003, p. 34). Different types of systems development methodologies may have different types of risks and consequently require different risk-management strategies.

Wilhelm Kross of Value & Risk in Bad Homburg, Germany, discusses the need for differing approaches to risk management depending on where in the world the project is being done. Kross states, "We are looking at the same obstacles that may decide on the likely failure or success of a project, but slightly different weightings—and a few self-induced obstacles." Kross further states that Europeans tend to factor in the potential for air and water pollution and the need to compensate for environmental damages more directly—"the polluter-pays principle" (see Figure 9.7). Reasons for this greater attention, Kross states, are denser populations and "the inherent scarcity of resources" (Silverstein, 2002).

Robert Lew, a software application development manager for the State of California, recommends resisting pressure to have developers work on the "easy parts" of an IS development project when using a rapid development methodology. To mitigate the risks associated with rapid development methodologies, Lew indicates, "our biggest lesson learned is to take the time upfront to develop the architectural specification so that when the system is subsequently partitioned, people are clear about the interaction among the parts" (Hall, 2003).

In both of these instances, different contexts call for different strategies to mitigate risk. Each situation may present special challenges. Information systems are developed in different cultures, in different organizations with different types of organizational politics, using different development methodologies and technologies, and drawing upon different human resources. Project managers need to be cognizant of all of these factors in order to control risk and bring projects to successful completion.

Figure 9.7 The environment

General Categories of IS Project Risk

At least four types of project risk are specifically associated with IS projects. These include risks associated with ongoing changes in technology, finding and assigning skilled personnel, gaining user acceptance, and choosing the correct development methodology (see Figure 9.8).

The first category of risk specifically associated with information systems projects relates to the constant flux of technology in today's business environment. Changing technology can have a variety of effects on project teams. First, in some cases software updates may enable changes in project scope. As an example, an enterprise system may be originally scoped to support multiple business units within a large corporation; however, in the middle of the development cycle for such an application, new capabilities may be released by the software vendor (e.g., SAP) that now enable better business-to-business integration, capabilities that are likely to be valued by the customer. Implementing these new capabilities, however, means that the project scope

Categories of IS Project Risk

- Constant flux of technology in today's business environment
- Locating, hiring, and retaining competent IS personnel
- User acceptance
- Numerous methodologies available during systems development

Figure 9.8
Different categories of risk pertaining to IS projects

needs to be redefined. Similarly, it is possible that in the middle of a development project, new development tools will become available, such as Microsoft's shift to the .NET development environment. Should the project team adopt this new development environment? The answer will depend on a large number of factors, including how far the project team has progressed, the project team's skill set, the estimated longevity of the project, and what sort of enhanced capabilities the change may provide for the development effort. A second major type of technology-related change that may affect risk is not software related but, rather, changes in the firm's information architecture. These include factors such as changes in hardware or in the networking infrastructure. Such changes may introduce new complexities, provide new opportunities, and alter design needs, all of which influence project risk.

A second category of risk that is specific to the unique nature of IS projects relates to the acquisition and use of skilled personnel. Locating, hiring, and retaining competent IS personnel not only is a monumental task for human resource managers during projects but also represents a specific category of risk. Getting the right people on an IS project can mean the difference between success and failure. If an experienced programmer familiar with the project chooses to leave for a better job during the implementation of an IS, replacing him or her with someone who is less familiar with the project will almost certainly result in project delays. This is particularly problematic when dealing with IS personnel, because background and skill sets in different development environments can vary widely. Further, related to the potential technology changes, project team members' skills will also dictate whether newly introduced technologies can be used during the project.

A third category of risk specific to IS projects involves the complications associated with user acceptance. Many IS projects are very large in scope and may need to be replicated across different parts of the organization, possibly in different parts of the world. Because of this, project managers must be sure that any new system will meet the needs of a diverse set of users, adding risk to the project. Further, end-users often think requests to change system requirements will be easier to implement than they really are. Small changes in scope—such as a request for an additional piece of information to be displayed on a customer support screen—may dramatically change the design of an underlying database, thus substantially changing project scope and potentially delaying system delivery. Project managers must constantly monitor and negotiate such project risks.

Finally, a fourth category of risk pertaining to the unique nature of IS projects is associated with the numerous methodologies that may be used during systems development. Not only is it difficult to fully understand and support the growing number of systems development methodologies and environments; it is also difficult to make the appropriate choice. Each methodology has its advantages and disadvantages, and the choice of methodology may change project risk. As an example, the use of rapid application development methodologies may introduce additional project risks related to effectively managing communication with the user.

Global Implications: Outsourcing and Project Risk

There have been conflicting arguments for and against outsourcing. Advocates of the practice argue that it results in significant cost reduction, given that it provides access to advanced capabilities, cheaper labor, and reduced requirements to support an additional organizational function outside of one's core competency. Opponents argue that outsourcing involves major risks. While certainly outsourcing does provide many opportunities, it is also important—particularly given the focus of this chapter—to understand the relationship between outsourcing and project risk.

One type of risk associated with outsourcing software development projects concerns internal resistance. Managers, project managers, developers, and other personnel in a company may feel threatened because they fear that there will be shifts in responsibilities and power or, possibly, layoffs. For those reasons, affected individuals may act to sabotage an offshore project throughout the life cycle of the project, adversely affecting project success. Rick Pfeiffer, former head of Asia-Pacific IT and operations at General Electric Co., says that 60 percent of offshore project failures can be attributed to internal opposition. Some of the ways to deal with internal resistance include ensuring strong support from upper management, picking the right people to be on the team, getting managers involved early in the outsourcing process, and appropriately reassuring employees regarding the goals of the outsourcing effort and how it will affect the company and project team members.

Another risk associated with outsourcing and offshoring is security and privacy. Some American companies fear that their data or proprietary processes might fall into the wrong hands. For example, recently, Jolly Technologies, which is a division of the U.S. company Jolly Inc., reported that portions of the source code and confidential design documents relating to one of its key products were stolen by an insider at its research and development center in Mumbai. Because of weak intellectual property laws and inefficient enforcement, the probability of intellectual property theft may be more pronounced in other countries. To ensure security and privacy, American countries have been demanding that these countries put security measures in place. These include physical security measures, such as electric fencing around buildings, the use of card keys and biometric authentication devices to gain access to facilities, and closed-circuit TVs for surveillance. Companies also want their data and information systems to be protected through the use of event logging and monitoring tools, intrusion-detection systems, firewalls, and encryption technologies.

TECHNIQUES FOR MANAGING PROJECT RISK

Risk is natural during IS development projects and is often magnified because new technologies and methodologies are used. However, using established project management processes can help to mitigate risk during IS projects. Specific risk management processes as identified by the PMBOK Guide (2004) include risk management planning, risk identification, qualitative risk analysis, quantitative risk analysis, risk response planning, and risk monitoring and control. The inputs, processes, and outputs for each of these project management processes related to risk are summarized in Figure 9.9. Each process, including specific examples applying the tools and techniques, is discussed in more detail in the following sections.

Figure 9.9 PMBOK Project Risk Management inputs, tools, and outputs

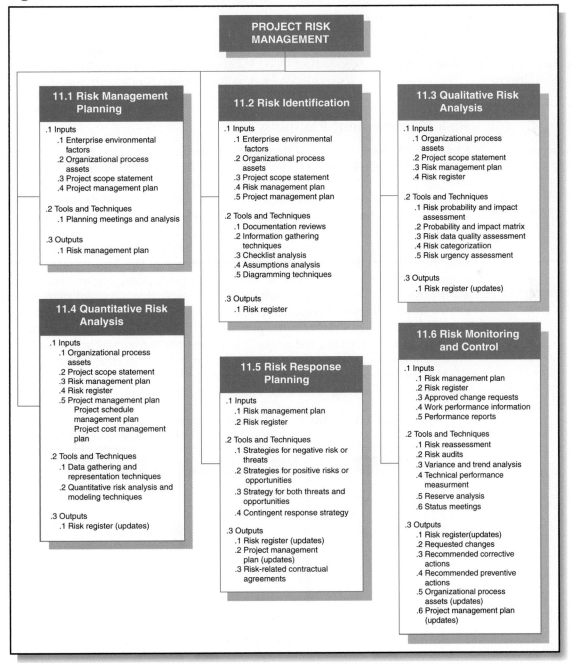

Software projects are notorious for being very difficult to manage with many ending in failure. These problems are common not only among U.S. firms, but also among organizations around the world. A survey of experienced software project managers from different countries (Finland, Hong Kong, and the United States) asked them to identify specific risk factors and then rank and rate those risks in terms of their importance. The respondents considered nearly a dozen factors to be important. In order of their relative importance they were (Keil et al., 1998; Wallace and Keil, 2004):

- Lack of top management commitment to the project
- Failure to gain user commitment
- Misunderstanding the requirements
- Lack of adequate user involvement
- Failure to manage end user expectations
- Changing scope/objectives
- Lack of required knowledge/skills in the project personnel
- Lack of frozen requirements
- Introduction of new technology
- Insufficient/inappropriate staffing
- Conflict between user departments

Risk Management Planning

Risk management planning
A systematic approach to planning the risk management activities of a given project.

Risk management planning involves a systematic approach to planning the risk management activities for a given project. It is important to plan a risk management strategy that matches the types of risk that may be encountered during the project and the importance of the project to an organization. Consider the development of a small-scale stand-alone IS; extensive project risk management planning may not be necessary in this case.

Figure 9.10 lists the inputs required, the tools and techniques used, and the resulting outputs during risk management planning. The four inputs of risk management planning are enterprise environmental factors, organizational process assets, the project scope statement, and the project management plan. Enterprise environmental factors (attitudes toward risk and risk tolerance), organizational process factors (the organizational processes put in place to handle risk), the project scope statement (defining the project), and the project management plan (summary document for the project) all serve as inputs for risk management planning.

Risk management planning meetings represent the main tool used during risk management planning. These meetings (see Figure 9.11) should be attended by

Figure 9.10 PMBOK required inputs, tools and techniques used, and resulting outputs during risk management planning

Inputs	Tools & Techniques	Outputs
.1 Enterprise environmental factors .2 Organizational process assets .3 Project scope statement .4 Project management plan	.1 Planning meetings and analysis	.1 Risk management plan

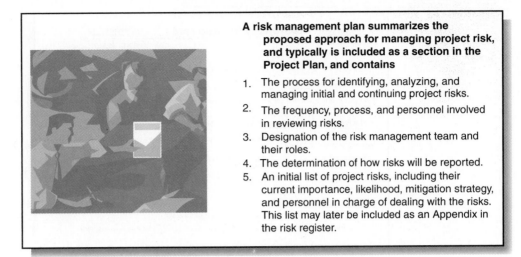

A risk management plan summarizes the proposed approach for managing project risk, and typically is included as a section in the Project Plan, and contains

1. The process for identifying, analyzing, and managing initial and continuing project risks.
2. The frequency, process, and personnel involved in reviewing risks.
3. Designation of the risk management team and their roles.
4. The determination of how risks will be reported.
5. An initial list of project risks, including their current importance, likelihood, mitigation strategy, and personnel in charge of dealing with the risks. This list may later be included as an Appendix in the risk register.

Figure 9.11 The risk management plan

senior managers, project team leaders, stakeholders, and project members who have decision-making responsibilities. During such meetings a variety of risk-related issues are discussed and decided, including determining the plans for conducting all risk management activities, as well as risk-related elements to be included in the budget and schedule. Further, responsibilities for dealing with risk are assigned. All of these factors are assembled into the output of the risk management planning process, specifically the risk management plan. The components of the risk management plan are summarized in Figure 9.11.

Risk management planning meetings also allow for the development of templates for defining and categorizing risk types, impacts, and probabilities (see Figure 9.12 for a risk management template). Serving the same purpose as templates in other areas of project management, risk management templates provide organizational standards for Project Risk Management. As with an organization's risk management policies, risk management templates may need to be modified to better fit a specific project.

Risk management plan
An overall plan used to outline risks and the strategies used to manage them.

The primary output from this process of risk management planning is a **risk management plan**. The Project Management Institute lists the following potential components of a risk management plan.

- *Methodology.* The methodology should discuss the approach to the management of risk during the project.
- *Roles and responsibilities.* This component of the risk management plan should establish project members' roles and responsibilities for the risk activities identified in the risk management plan.
- *Budgeting.* This is simply the preparation of a risk-management budget for the project.
- *Timing.* This section of the risk management plan should outline how the risk management activities will fit within the project life cycle.
- *Scoring and interpretation.* This section describes the scoring parameters and their associated interpretation from the qualitative and quantitative risk analyses to be performed during the project.
- *Thresholds.* This component of the risk management plan determines the criteria according to which risks will be acted upon. It is consistent with the tolerance-for-risk section that serves as an input to risk management planning.

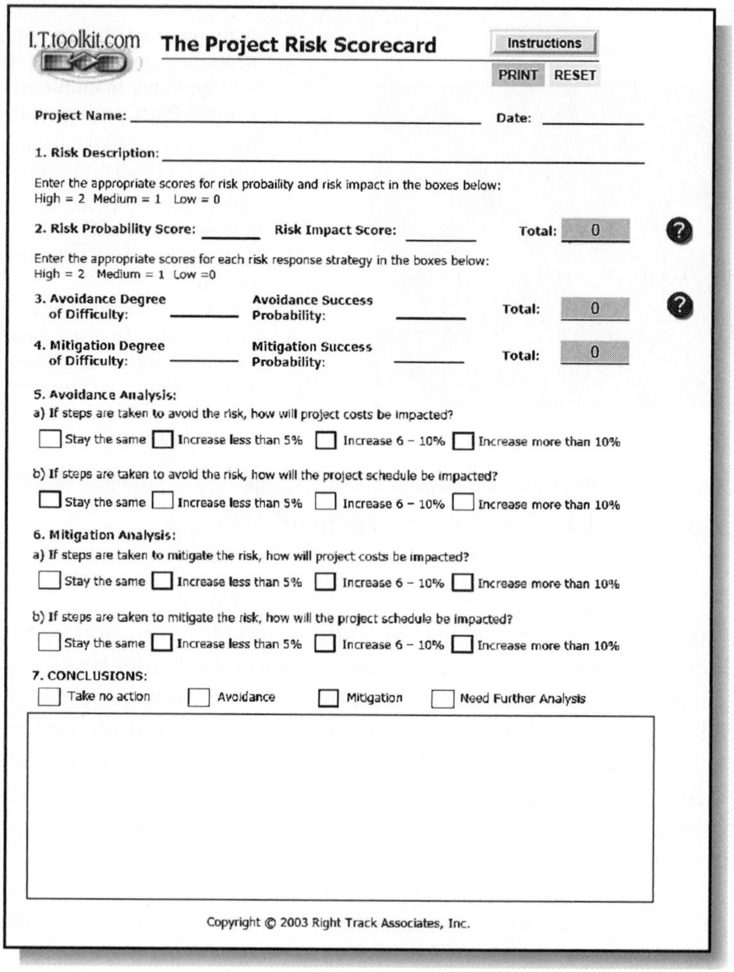

I.T.toolkit.com **The Project Risk Scorecard** Instructions PRINT RESET

Project Name: ______ **Date:** ______

1. Risk Description: ______

Enter the appropriate scores for risk probability and risk impact in the boxes below:
High = 2 Medium = 1 Low = 0

2. Risk Probability Score: ______ **Risk Impact Score:** ______ **Total:** 0

Enter the appropriate scores for each risk response strategy in the boxes below:
High = 2 Medium = 1 Low =0

3. Avoidance Degree of Difficulty: ______ **Avoidance Success Probability:** ______ **Total:** 0

4. Mitigation Degree of Difficulty: ______ **Mitigation Success Probability:** ______ **Total:** 0

5. Avoidance Analysis:
a) If steps are taken to avoid the risk, how will project costs be impacted?
☐ Stay the same ☐ Increase less than 5% ☐ Increase 6 – 10% ☐ Increase more than 10%

b) If steps are taken to avoid the risk, how will the project schedule be impacted?
☐ Stay the same ☐ Increase less than 5% ☐ Increase 6 – 10% ☐ Increase more than 10%

6. Mitigation Analysis:
a) If steps are taken to mitigate the risk, how will project costs be impacted?
☐ Stay the same ☐ Increase less than 5% ☐ Increase 6 – 10% ☐ Increase more than 10%

b) If steps are taken to mitigate the risk, how will the project schedule be impacted?
☐ Stay the same ☐ Increase less than 5% ☐ Increase 6 – 10% ☐ Increase more than 10%

7. CONCLUSIONS:
☐ Take no action ☐ Avoidance ☐ Mitigation ☐ Need Further Analysis

Figure 9.12 Risk management template

- *Reporting formats.* This section outlines the format for the risk response plan and describes how risk management processes will be documented and communicated during the project.
- *Tracking.* Project risk planning activities should be tracked, documented, and archived for use during future projects.

A template for a risk management plan is provided in Table 9.1.

Risk Identification

Risk identification
The process of identifying and documenting a project's potential risks.

Risk identification consists of identifying and documenting potential risks to the project. This process should be performed by project managers, project teams, the risk management team, experts, customers, end users, outside experts, and additional stakeholders. Figure 9.13 illustrates the inputs, tools, and outputs of risk identification.

Inputs include enterprise environment factors, organizational process outputs, the project scope statement, the risk management plan, and the project management plan. All inputs except the risk management plan were also inputs to the risk management planning process. The risk management plan is an output of the risk management planning process.

Table 9.1   Risk Management Plan Template

<**Project Name**>

Risk Management Plan

<Author>

<Date>

<Version>

1.0 REVISION HISTORY

NAME	DATE	REASON FOR CHANGES	VERSION
<author>		initial draft	1.0 draft1

2.0 STATEMENT OF PURPOSE

The purpose of this document is to describe and document the risk management procedures that are in place for <Project Name>. This document describes a) the methods that will be used to manage risks, b) the roles and responsibilities of those responsible for risk management, c) the budget and schedule for performing risk management activities, d) the main risk categories that need to be addressed, e) the probability and impact of various risk items, and f) how risk documentation will be conducted.

3.0 RISK MANAGEMENT STRATEGIES

PROCESS NAME	PROCESS DESCRIPTION
<ENTER PROCESS NAME HERE>	<DESCRIBE PROCESS HERE>
Example: Risk Identification	Example: The risk team will conduct a brainstorming session at the beginning of each project phase. A form will be available on the project Web site for team members to submit risk factors over the course of the project as well.
<Add more rows as necessary>	

3.1 RISK MANAGEMENT TOOLS

TOOL NAME	TOOL DESCRIPTION
<ENTER TOOL NAME HERE>	<DESCRIBE TOOL HERE>
Example: Risk Status Report	Example: Weekly report generated by the <Project Name> risk team to provide stakeholders with regular updates on risks and actions taken to mitigate risks.
<Add more rows as necessary>	

3.2 DATA SOURCES

DATA SOURCE NAME	DATA SOURCE DESCRIPTION
<ENTER DATA SOURCE NAME HERE>	<DESCRIBE DATA SOURCE HERE>
Example: Lessons Learned Database	Example: PMO maintained database with previous risk management documentation from earlier projects
<Add more rows as necessary>	

(continued)

Table 9.1 (continued)

4.0 ROLES AND RESPONSIBILITIES

Project Manager	The project manager will assign a risk officer to the project and identify this individual on the project's organization chart. The project manager and other members of the project management team <list names or roles> shall meet <state frequency; biweekly suggested> to review the status of all risk mitigation efforts, review the exposure assessments for any new risk items, and redefine the project's Top-Ten Risk List.
Risk Officer	The risk officer has the following responsibilities and authority: <describe what the risk officer will do; might include coordinating risk identification and analysis activities, maintaining the project's risk list, notifying project management of new risk items, reporting risk resolution status to management; the risk officer normally should not be the project manager.>
Project Members Assigned to Specific Risks	The risk officer will assign each newly identified risk to a project member, who will assess the exposure and probability for the risk factor and report the results of that analysis back to the risk officer. Assigned project members are also responsible for performing the steps of the mitigation plan and reporting progress to the risk officer biweekly.

5.0 RISK MANAGEMENT BUDGET AND SCHEDULE

BUDGET	$<ENTER FIGURE HERE>

RISK MANAGEMENT PROCESS SCHEDULE

<ENTER PROCESS NAME HERE>	<ENTER SCHEDULE DETAILS HERE>
Example: Risk Monitoring	Example: Risk officer will meet with project manager biweekly on <enter days here> to discuss project risk status.
	Probability and Impact figures are reexamined and modified if appropriate on <enter dates here>.
<Add more rows as necessary>	

6.0 RISK CATEGORIES

<List and describe the possible risk categories that may need to be considered during <Project Name>.

CATEGORIES	DESCRIPTION
<Add more rows as necessary>	

7.0 Risk Probability and Impact

<List each risk item and assign a probability and impact score; then compute the total risk score for each item.>

ITEM	PROBABILITY (P)	IMPACT (I)	TOTAL RISK SCORE
<List items here>	<Enter a value between 0.1 and 1.0>	<Enter a value between 1 and 10>	<Multiply P x I>
<Add more rows as necessary>			

Table 9.1 (continued)

8.0 DOCUMENTATION

Risk List	The risk factors identified and managed for this project will be accumulated in a risk list, which is located <state where risk list is located; could be an appendix to this plan, a separate document, or a database or tool somewhere>. The ten risk items that currently have the highest estimated risk exposure are referred to as the project's Top-Ten Risk List.
Risk Data Items	The following information will be stored for each project risk: <list and define risk data items. Some suggestions: risk ID, classification, description, probability, impact, risk exposure, first indicator that risk is becoming a problem, mitigation approaches, owner, date due, contingency plan, contingency plan trigger>
Closing Risks	A risk item can be considered closed when it meets the following criteria: <example: the planned mitigation actions have been completed and the estimated risk exposure of probability times impact is less than 2>

Risk register
A formal record listing all project risks, explaining the nature of the risk and management of the risk.

Risk categories can be helpful when developing the **risk register** (see Chapter 12 for an example), the primary output from the risk identification process. Risk categories specifically identified by the Project Management Institute (2004) include the following (also summarized in Figure 9.14).

- *Technical, quality, or performance risks.* The first of these, technical risk, is especially significant during IS development. As has been continually reiterated throughout the previous chapters, reliance on new, unproven or unreliable technology is one of the many challenges faced by IS development project managers. Quality and performance risk categories include performance goals that cannot easily be met and changing industry standards.
- *Project management risks.* This category includes risks associated with project management, including risks associated with poor project planning, and poor use of recognized project management processes.
- *Organizational risks.* This category includes risks that are organizationally driven; it can include inconsistent goals, lack of funding, and conflicting priorities, among others.

Figure 9.13 PMBOK required inputs, tools and techniques used, and resulting outputs during risk identification

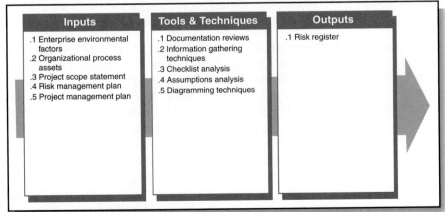

Inputs	Tools & Techniques	Outputs
.1 Enterprise environmental factors	.1 Documentation reviews	.1 Risk register
.2 Organizational process assets	.2 Information gathering techniques	
.3 Project scope statement	.3 Checklist analysis	
.4 Risk management plan	.4 Assumptions analysis	
.5 Project management plan	.5 Diagramming techniques	

Risk Categories	Examples
Technical risks	Reliance on new, unproven or unreliable technology
Quality and performance risks	Performance goals that cannot be easily met Changing industry standards
Project management risks	Risks associated with poor project planning and poor use of recognized project management processes
Organizational risks	Inconsistent goals Lack of funding Conflicting priorities
External risks	Legal events Environmental concerns Natural disasters, such as earthquakes and floods

Figure 9.14 Risk categories identified by PMI

- *External risks.* A category that can be easily overlooked, external risks include legal events, environmental concerns (see Table 9.1), and natural disasters such as earthquakes and floods.

Several tools and techniques are available to convert these inputs into outputs. These include documentation reviews, information gathering techniques, checklists, and diagramming techniques. **Documentation reviews** involve reviewing existing project documentation, which may include project plans and assumptions. Historical information is useful in developing the risk register and comprises any Project Risk Management information collected during the course of previous projects. Specific sources of historical information may include:

Documentation review
The review of organizational information to aid during risk identification.

- *Project files,* which include previous risk management plans, project reports, and lessons learned.
- *Published information,* which is often contained in public databases, published reports, academic studies, and through published benchmarking information.

Information gathering techniques are also used during risk identification. Some examples of information gathering techniques are:

Information gathering techniques
Techniques such as brainstorming, Delphi surveys, or SWOT analyses used to identify project risk.

- *Brainstorming.* Brainstorming is an often used technique for gathering information (see Chapter 3). In this case, brainstorming sessions are conducted to identify potential risks (see Figure 9.15 for an example of an electronic meeting room that groups can use to brainstorm). Once a list of potential risks has been generated, discussions are conducted to categorize them for further analysis.
- *Delphi technique.* The Delphi technique involves an iterative process of information gathering. This technique begins with the administration of an initial questionnaire to a group of experts designed to elicit a list of potential risks. These lists are then combined according to priority, as based upon the number of similar responses. This new list is then resubmitted to the original group of experts, who then rerank the identified risks. This process continues until a consensus is reached.

Figure 9.15
An electronic meeting facility at the University of Arizona can be used for brainstorming

- *Interviewing.* Experts and project managers can be interviewed as a means for identifying potential risks to the project. To facilitate this process, these individuals may be provided with relevant project information, such as the work breakdown structure and list of project assumptions.
- *Strengths, weaknesses, opportunities, and threats (SWOT).* You may recognize this term from your management or marketing courses. A commonly used technique, SWOT analysis can be used to increase the reach within which risks will be considered.

Checklists are valuable risk identification tools that enable risks for a project to be listed and checked off. They are especially useful for projects that are similar to past projects. Their limitation, however, is that it is often not feasible to develop a comprehensive list of potential project risks.

Diagramming techniques may also be used during risk identification. Specific diagramming techniques are:

Diagramming techniques
Diagramming tools, such as cause-and-effect diagrams, flow charts, or influence diagrams, used to help identify project risk.

- *Cause-and-effect diagrams.* Also known as fishbone diagrams, cause-and-effect diagrams were introduced in the chapter on managing project quality and will be discussed in more detail in the chapter on managing project control. These diagrams are useful during risk identification because they allow managers to identify potential risks and trace them back to their root causes.
- *System or process flow charts.* Flow charts depict the interrelations among project activities and can be used to help managers determine the risks associated with those interrelations.
- *Influence diagrams.* These diagrams graphically represent potential problems while accounting for causal influences, time, and other relationships between project activities and outcomes.

Triggers
Events that serve as early warnings of risk.

Qualitative risk analysis
The establishment of probabilities regarding both the impact and likelihood of specific risk occurrence.

The primary output of the risk identification process is the risk register, a key tool in managing project risk. The risk register includes a detailed list of identified risks and possible risk triggers (i.e., events that serve as early warnings of risk), potential responses to those risks, the root causes of the risk, and an updated list of risk categories (based on any new risks being identified that were not in the prior list of risk categories). A sample risk register is shown in Figure 9.16.

Qualitative Risk Analysis

Qualitative risk analysis involves the establishment of probabilities regarding both the impact and likelihood of specific risk occurrence. Qualitative risk analysis tools

Risk Register

Ref	The Risk *(What can happen and how it will it happen)*	The risk of the event happening uncontrolled		Initial Risk score	Risk Control Plan *(Strategies to eliminate or minimize risk)*	The risk of the event happening with controls		Final Risk Score
		Consequence	**Likelihood**			**Consequence**	**Likelihood**	
1	Exposure to hazardous substances in various operations including cleaning, research, educational. Risk of injury includes: • Chemical burns to eyes, skin, body. • Inhalation of vapors and fumes. • Explosion from potential ignition sources.	Major	The event could occur at some time	High	Implementation of Hazardous Substance Guidelines including: 1. Elimination of hazardous substance where possible; 2. Substitute of hazardous substance with less hazardous; 3. Isolation of hazardrous substance through engineering design; 4. Training requirements for users of hazardous substance; 5. Provision of personal protective equipment for users of hazardous substance.	Moderate	The event could occur, but only rarely	Medium

Figure 9.16   Sample risk register

are utilized to evaluate these dimensions. Figure 9.17 summarizes the required inputs, the tools and techniques used, and the resulting outputs for qualitative risk analysis.

Inputs to the qualitative risk analysis stage include the organizational process assets, the project scope statement, the risk management plan, and the risk register.

A variety of tools and techniques specified by the PMBOK guide can be utilized during the qualitative risk analysis stage. These include the risk probability and impact assessment, the probability/impact risk rating matrix, the risk data quality assessment, risk categorization, and risk urgency assessment. Risk probability and impact are important dimensions of qualitative risk analysis. Risk probability is concerned with the likelihood that a certain risk will occur and can be measured on a scale from very low to very high. Risk impact, or the consequences

Figure 9.17   PMBOK required inputs, tools and techniques used, and resulting outputs during qualitative risk analysis

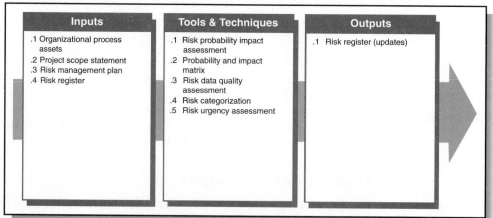

associated with the occurrence of a given risk, is concerned with the impact on project outcomes if the risk event occurs.

Probability/impact risk rating matrix
A technique used to analyze project risk in terms of its probability of occurrence and its impact on project outcomes.

A **probability/impact risk rating matrix** provides a valuable technique for analyzing project risk in terms of its probability of occurring and its impact on project outcomes. Probability scales are generally measured on a 0 to 1 scale, where 0 represents no chance that the event will occur and 1 represents the certainty of its occurrence. Probability scores are most often determined through expert judgment and are, therefore, susceptible to human error. Scores can be attributed on an ordinal scale, such as not at all likely to very likely, or by assigning specific values, such as 0.1, 0.2, 0.3, and so on. Impact scales represent the magnitude of the effect the risk occurrence may have on the project objective. Impact scores can be ordinal, as for probability scales, or cardinal, in which specific values are assigned to potential impacts. Importantly, both measures and their associated scales should be developed independently by organizations to reflect their risk analysis preferences. An example of a probability/impact matrix is shown in Figure 9.18. Such a matrix can be applied to a particular project (which could help assess a project's overall risk relative to other projects), or to particular components or tasks within a single project (which might help a project team prepare for project risks).

Project assumption testing
A technique used during qualitative risk analysis to test the assumptions made during risk identification.

The risk data quality assessment is simply an assessment of the quality of the data used to assess risk. This might include **project assumption testing,** a tool used to further test the assumptions embedded in risk identification. Data precision ranking can be used for risk data quality assessments. The following dimensions are considered in such a ranking:

- The extent to which a risk is understood
- Available risk data
- Data quality
- Data integrity and reliability

Risk categorization, as previously discussed, can help to determine which part of the project may be most susceptible to risk. For example, a risk breakdown structure (similar to a WBS) can be used to identify the risks organized by project component. A risk urgency assessment requires the project team to determine the priority of various risks (e.g., in terms of risk rating) to help decide which risks need to be dealt with on a priority basis.

The output from the a risk analysis is an update to the risk register (refer back to Figure 9.16).

Quantitative Risk Analysis

Quantitative risk analysis
The analysis of the probability of occurrence and the impact of risk on project objectives using numerical techniques.

Similar to qualitative risk analysis, **quantitative risk analysis** is used to analyze the probability of occurrence and the impact of risk on project objectives. However, during quantitative risk analysis, more quantitative numerical analyses are conducted.

Figure 9.18 Probability/impact risk rating matrix

Impact/Probability	Very High	High	Medium	Low	Very Low
Catastrophic	High	High	Moderate	Moderate	Low
Critical	High	High	Moderate	Low	None
Marginal	Moderate	Moderate	Low	None	None
Negligible	Moderate	Low	Low	None	None

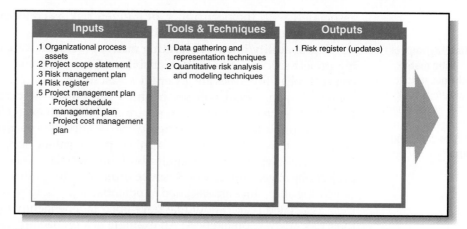

Inputs	Tools & Techniques	Outputs

.1 Organizational process assets
.2 Project scope statement
.3 Risk management plan
.4 Risk register
.5 Project management plan
  . Project schedule management plan
  . Project cost management plan
	.1 Data gathering and representation techniques
	.2 Quantitative risk analysis and modeling techniques
		.1 Risk register (updates)

Figure 9.19 Required inputs, tools and techniques used, and resulting outputs during quantitative risk analysis

Figure 9.19 lists the required inputs, the tools and techniques used, and the resulting outputs during quantitative risk analysis. Decision techniques are used to provide the following information to project managers:

- The likelihood of realizing a specific project objective
- Risk quantification in terms of additional scheduling and cost needs
- Identifying the most salient risks in terms of the project
- Setting realistic targets in terms of scope, cost, and schedule

Quantitative risk analysis can be performed separately or with qualitative analysis. Decisions whether to use one or the other or both should be made on an individual project basis.

Inputs for this stage comprise outputs from the previous risk management processes, including organization process assets, project scope statement, the risk management plan, the risk register, and the project management plan. Tools and techniques used during the quantitative risk analysis process include data gathering and representation techniques, as well as quantitative risk analysis and modeling techniques. Data gathering and representation techniques include interviewing, sensitivity analysis, decision-tree analysis, and simulation. We will introduce some of the key techniques in this section.

Interviewing techniques are instrumental during the quantitative risk analysis process because interviews with project experts and other stakeholders can assist in quantifying risk probabilities and consequences. Probability distributions can be applied to represent data gathered during interviews or through other data gathering techniques. Such probability distributions can illustrate the probability of something's occurring or, in some cases, more general results such as optimistic, most likely, and pessimistic scenarios.

Quantitative and risk analysis techniques include the use of **sensitivity analysis, decision tree analysis, expected monetary value analysis (EMV),** and **simulation**. Sensitivity analysis is used to determine which risks have the largest potential impact on a project. One example of a sensitivity analysis is the **tornado analysis**, which graphically shows, in descending order, which risks can cause the greatest variability in some outcome. The risks at the top can cause the greatest variability, and the risks at the bottom cause the least variability. A tornado analysis is illustrated in Figure 9.20; it shows how different risks can cause variability in the base value of an information system. In this case, changes in the discount rate, the ability to avoid costs, and the changing nature of hardware costs are the top three risk factors and could have a very

Sensitivity analysis
A technique used to examine the potential impact of specific risks to a project.

Decision tree analysis
A diagramming technique used to evaluate courses of action in terms of their potential cost and benefits relative to other courses of action.

Expected monetary value analysis (EMV)
A statistical technique that captures the average value of potential projects by analyzing the likelihood of possible project outcomes as well as each outcome's financial consequences.

Simulation
A technique, such as Monte Carlo analysis, used to perform what-if analyses to determine the impact of a given situation on a project objective.

Tornado analysis
A diagramming technique that graphically shows, in descending order, which risks can cause the greatest variability on some outcome.

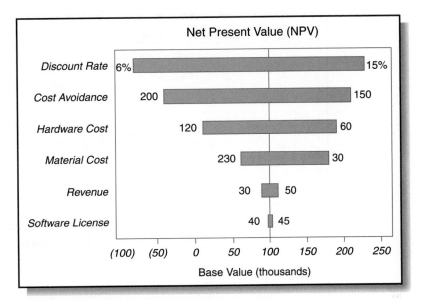

Figure 9.20 Tornado analysis

Source: Reproduced with permission from Odellion Research Corporation.
All Rights Reserved. www.odellion.com

large effect on the base value of this system. Conversely, uncertainty about the system's ultimate revenue generating capability and about the costs associated with software licenses are likely to have much smaller effects on the base value.

Expected monetary value analysis is a statistical technique that captures the average value of potential projects by analyzing the likelihood of possible project outcomes as well as each outcome's financial consequences. A graphical depiction of EMV can be captured in a decision tree analysis. A decision tree analysis is a diagramming technique used to evaluate a given course of action in terms of its costs and benefits relative to other courses of action. Figure 9.21 depicts a decision tree; the right-hand column shows the net path values.

As illustrated in the figure, the choice to build a new plant or upgrade the existing plant was conducted using the EMV approach following these steps. First, the various *project options* are depicted (in this case building a new plant or upgrading an existing plant). Next, the possible *project consequences* of pursuing those projects are illustrated (shown in the diagram as scenarios of strong and weak demand) along with their probability of occurrence and financial results. The *net path value* represents the value associated with a particular path (e.g., the first path in the diagram is valued at $200) minus the costs of pursuing that option ($120). To arrive at the EMV for each *project option* you simply multiply the probability times the expected financial result for each *project consequence;* then sum those values for each *project option;* finally, subtract the *initial estimated project cost* of each *project option.* Thus, the EMV calculations as illustrated for Project 1 (new plant) would be:

$$EMV = [(65\% \times \$200) + (35\% \times \$90)] - 120 = \$41.5$$

For Project 2 (upgrade) the EMV calculations would be:

$$EMV = [(65\% \times \$120) + (35\% \times \$60)] - 50 = \$49.0$$

Using the EMV technique, a project selection committee would rate Project 2 as more desirable because of its higher EMV. In a decision tree diagram, the designation

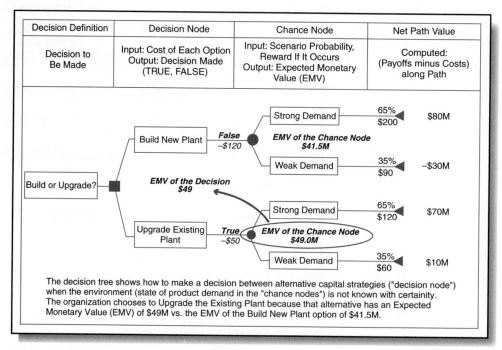

Decision Definition	Decision Node	Chance Node	Net Path Value
Decision to Be Made	Input: Cost of Each Option Output: Decision Made (TRUE, FALSE)	Input: Scenario Probability, Reward If It Occurs Output: Expected Monetary Value (EMV)	Computed: (Payoffs minus Costs) along Path

The decision tree shows how to make a decision between alternative capital strategies ("decision node") when the environment (state of product demand in the "chance nodes") is not known with certainity. The organization chooses to Upgrade the Existing Plant because that alternative has an Expected Monetary Value (EMV) of $49M vs. the EMV of the Build New Plant option of $41.5M.

Figure 9.21   Decision tree and EMV analysis

"True" indicates the selected project, whereas "False" indicates the rejected option. While this particular decision making scenario focuses on a capital strategy (upgrading an existent plant or building a new plant), this technique could just as easily be applied to a make, buy, or upgrade decision related to an information system.

Finally, simulation is a technique that allows managers to run what-if analyses to determine the effect of a given situation (differing input variables) on a project objective. Simulations typically refer to an analytical method that imitates some sort of real-life system. Without using simulations, spreadsheet based what-if models typically only examine the effect of changes in input variables to one outcome at a time. In contrast, simulations vary input variables and examine multiple possible outcomes.

Monte Carlo analysis is probably the most recognized form of simulation analysis. In the case of a Monte Carlo simulation, values for uncertain input variables (such as changes in resource availability or time to complete particular project tasks) are randomly generated over and over to achieve a distribution of possible project outcomes.

Outputs from this stage again include updates to the risk register.

Risk Response Planning

Risk response planning
The process of developing methods for responding to project risks.

During the **risk response planning** process, methods for responding to project risks are developed. Responses are developed based on anticipated adverse effects of risk, as well as any opportunities that may be present as a result of a specific risk. Risk response planning should consider the severity of the risk, the type of project, and cost-benefit information. This process is focused at developing suitable risk management strategies as well as determining who is responsible for dealing with the risk. All project stakeholders should agree upon any risk planning actions to be implemented.

Ethical Dilemma: The Difficult Job of Managing Project Risk

Managers often face ethical dilemmas related to risk. Consider the following example of a project manager's ethical dilemma during software testing. Software testing can be done in many ways, with differing levels of comprehensiveness. Although a more comprehensive test may require substantial downtime, simpler tests can be done, possibly employing fewer sample values or runs. In many cases, a project manager is faced with the following dilemma. Should he or she do robust testing, risking project implementation delays and cost increases but delivering the system on time and on budget or implement the system without such comprehensive testing, getting the system delivered to the client without delay. Usually, the answer depends on the context and critical nature of the system being developed.

Discussion Questions

1. Under what situation(s) should a system be more robustly tested?
2. If you were a project manager facing pressure to reduce testing time when you believed more robust testing was needed, what tactic would you use to try to convince the manager to follow your advice?

Risk owners
Project members responsible for specific risk activity decisions.

Risk avoidance
A risk response strategy designed to avoid potential project risks.

Figure 9.22 shows the required inputs, tools and techniques used, and resulting outputs during risk response planning. Inputs to the risk response planning process include the *risk management plan* and *risk register*. The risk management plan (see the risk management plan template at the end of the chapter) and risk register are outputs from preceding risk processes. Both are influenced by the risk threshold of the organization, a list of potential responses, risk owners, common risk causes, trends identified during the qualitative and quantitative risk analysis processes, the list of prioritized risks, the risk ranking of the project, the prioritized list of quantified risks, probabilistic analysis of the project, and the probability of achieving the cost and time objectives. **Risk owners** or project members who are responsible for specific risk activity decisions should be involved during risk response planning.

Many techniques and strategies are available for risk response planning. They include avoidance, transference, mitigation, and acceptance. **Risk avoidance** is

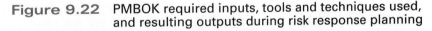

Figure 9.22 PMBOK required inputs, tools and techniques used, and resulting outputs during risk response planning

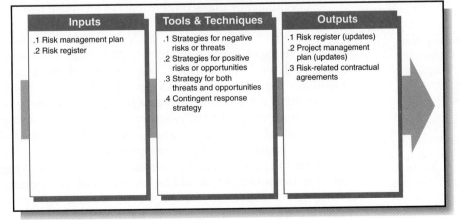

Inputs	Tools & Techniques	Outputs
.1 Risk management plan .2 Risk register	.1 Strategies for negative risks or threats .2 Strategies for positive risks or opportunities .3 Strategy for both threats and opportunities .4 Contingent response strategy	.1 Risk register (updates) .2 Project management plan (updates) .3 Risk-related contractual agreements

designed to avoid any identified risks to the project. Within an IS development project, this may include avoiding the use of an untested technology or avoiding changes to the scope of the system.

Risk transference involves the transfer of risk to another party. Risk transference is often facilitated through the use of contracts in which the risk associated with a given activity is transferred to another party. Depending on the type of contract being used, risk may be transferred from the seller to the buyer or from the buyer to the seller. For a detailed discussion of contracts, see Chapter 10, the procurement management chapter.

Risk mitigation is used to reduce, eliminate, or transfer the chances of risk occurrence or to reduce the impact of the risk on project objectives. An example of risk mitigation during an IS development project is the use of a known technology provider rather than reliance on a less established vendor.

Risk acceptance occurs when managers simply decide that an effective response cannot be developed for a specific risk. In such a circumstance, the project team may decide to not alter the project management plan to deal with this particular risk, given the lack of a suitable response strategy. For example, an IS development project team may accept the risk that a new version of a particular software released during the execution phase of a project may not function as intended.

Outputs from the risk response planning process include updates to the risk register, project management plan updates, and risk related contractual agreements. The project management plan contains the risk management plan, a subcomponent of which is a **risk response plan**. According to the Project Management Institute (PMI, 2004) the risk response plan should include some or all of the following components:

- Any risks that have been identified along with a description and the areas and objectives the identified risk may affect
- The roles and responsibilities of any risk owners
- Qualitative and quantitative risk analysis results as well as any trends identified during either of these processes
- A description of the risk response strategies including avoidance, transference, mitigation, and acceptance, and the specific risks to which the various strategies will be applied
- An acknowledgement of any residual risk projected to remain after any risk response strategies have been applied
- A list of actions to be used to implement the risk response strategies
- Budget and schedule information for any risk response
- Any contingency plans used as part of an active response to accept risks

Some other terms are also useful to understand in risk response planning. **Residual risks,** or those risks that remain after avoidance, transfer, or mitigation strategies have been applied, are identified during risk response planning. **Secondary risks** are those risks resulting from the application of a risk response strategy. **Risk-related contractual agreements** for the purpose of risk transfer are another important output of risk response planning. During an IS development project, they could include a transfer of responsibility for systems implementation or some other phase of systems development. Contingency reserve (a provision held in reserve by the project sponsor to meet unanticipated changes in factors like project scope) amounts needed should be estimated based upon risk information generated during risk management. Inputs to other processes, as with other risk management activities, represent another important output to be considered during response

---

Risk transference
A risk response strategy designed to transfer risk to another party often through the use of contracts.

Risk mitigation
A risk response strategy in which steps are taken to mitigate project risk.

Risk acceptance
A risk response strategy in which risks are simply accepted and contingency strategies are planned.

Risk response plan
A documented plan for risk response.

Residual risks
Any risks remaining after risk response strategies have been applied.

Secondary risks
Any risks resulting from the application of a risk response strategy.

Risk-related contractual agreements
Any contracts for the purpose of risk transference during the project.

Inputs	Tools & Techniques	Outputs
.1 Risk management plan .2 Risk register .3 Approved change requests .4 Work performance information .5 Performance reports	.1 Risk reassessment .2 Risk audits .3 Variance and trend analysis .4 Technical performance measurement .5 Reserve analysis .6 Status meetings	.1 Risk register (updates) .2 Requested changes .3 Recommended corrective actions .4 Recommended preventive actions .5 Organizational process assets (updates) .6 Project management plan (updates)

Figure 9.23 PMBOK required inputs, tools and techniques used, and resulting outputs during risk monitoring and control

Risk monitoring and control
The process of monitoring identified risks for change and controlling those changes.

Project risk response audits
Audits designed to evaluate the effectiveness of risk response strategies and risk owners.

Periodic project risk reviews
Reviews designed to review existing risk activities and to monitor any changes to the project.

Technical performance measurement
An important tool used to determine whether important technical milestones are being met.

planning. For example, identified risks and their assigned response strategies may provide information for other project management processes. These risk response planning outputs serve as inputs to the project plan so that the risk response activities can be incorporated into the project schedule.

Risk Monitoring and Control

Consistent with the process of project management control, identified risks must be monitored for change and controlled. **Risk monitoring and control** generally takes place over the entire life of the project. Although risk monitoring and control will be covered in depth in Chapter 12, we introduce the topic here. The purpose of risk monitoring and control is to identify, analyze, and plan for newly arising risks; to watch existent risks (on the watch list); to monitor conditions that would trigger risk responses; and finally, to determine if such responses are working. Risk monitoring and control employs such tools as variance or trend analysis using performance data, **project risk response audits, periodic project risk reviews, technical performance measurements**, and others to update the risk register and project management plan and other outputs. Again, a more complete treatment of this topic is reserved for Chapter 12.

Figure 9.23 shows a list of the required inputs, tools and techniques used, and resulting outputs during risk monitoring and control.

MANAGING PROJECT RISK AND THE PMBOK

In this chapter, we have focused primarily on Knowledge Area 11, Project Risk Management, within the Project Management Body of Knowledge (PMBOK, 2004). In this chapter, we have identified the various phases of Project Risk Management, including risk management planning, risk identification, qualitative risk analysis, quantitative risk analysis, risk response planning, and risk monitoring and control. We have also identified the various tools and techniques that can be used in managing risk. Figure 9.24 identifies this coverage, and illustrates the coverage of upcoming chapters as well.

Figure 9.24 Chapter 9 and PMBOK coverage

	Textbook Chapters →	1	2	3	4	5	6	7	8	9	10	11	12
	PMBOK Knowledge Area												
1	**Introduction to Project Management**												
1.1	What Is a Project?	●											
1.2	What Is Project Management?	●											
1.3	Areas of Expertise		●										
1.4	Project Management Context	●											
2	**Project Life Cycle and Organization**												
2.1	The Project Life Cycle	●	●										
2.2	Project Stakeholders	●	●										
2.3	Organizational Influences		●	●	●			●					
3	**Project Management Processes for a Project**												
3.1	Project Management Processes	●	●										
3.2	PM Process Groups	●	●										
3.3	Process Interactions		●										
3.4	Project Management Process Mapping		●										
4	**Project Integration Management**												
4.1	Develop Project Charter					●							
4.2	Develop Preliminary Project Scope Statement					●	●						
4.3	Develop Project Management Plan					●							
4.4	Direct and Manage Project Execution											○	
4.5	Monitor and Control Project Work												○
4.6	Integrated Change Control												○
4.7	Close Project												○
5	**Project Scope Management**												
5.1	Scope Planning					●							
5.2	Scope Definition					●							
5.3	Create WBS					●	●						
5.4	Scope Verification					●							
5.5	Scope Control					●							○
6	**Project Time Management**												
6.1	Activity Definition						●						
6.2	Activity Sequencing						●						
6.3	Activity Resource Estimating							●					
6.4	Activity Duration Estimating							●					
6.5	Schedule Development							●					
6.6	Schedule Control							●					○

(continued)

Figure 9.24 (continued)

	Textbook Chapters →	1	2	3	4	5	6	7	8	9	10	11	12
	PMBOK Knowledge Area												
7	**Project Cost Management**												
7.1	Cost Estimating							●					
7.2	Cost Budgeting							●					
7.3	Cost Control							●					○
8	**Project Quality Management**												
8.1	Quality Planning								●				
8.2	Perform Quality Assurance								●				
8.3	Perform Quality Control								●				○
9	**Project Human Resource Management**												
9.1	Human Resource Planning			●				●					
9.2	Acquire Project Team			●				●					
9.3	Develop Project Team			●				●					
9.4	Manage Project Team			●				●					
10	**Project Communications Management**												
10.1	Communications Planning				●							○	
10.2	Information Distribution				●							○	
10.3	Performance Reporting				●								○
10.4	Manage Stakeholders				●								○
11	**Project Risk Management**												
11.1	Risk Management Planning									✓			
11.2	Risk Identification									✓	○		
11.3	Qualitative Risk Analysis									✓			
11.4	Quantitative Risk Analysis									✓			
11.5	Risk Response Planning									✓			
11.6	Risk Monitoring and Control									✓			○
12	**Project Procurement Management**												
12.1	Plan Purchases and Acquisitions										○		
12.2	Plan Contracting										○		
12.3	Request Seller Responses										○		
12.4	Select Sellers										○		
12.5	Contract Administration										○		
12.6	Contract Closure										○		○

Key: ●-where material is covered in past chapters; ✓-current chapter coverage;
○-where material is covered in future chapters

RUNNING CASE
Managing Project Risk

"I received the official notice of Juanita's promotion to Minneapolis. It's too bad that we lost our only contact on the floor," says Jim.

"I'm sure Juanita will be willing to spend some time for the project from Minneapolis. At least for the transition phase while we find someone else to replace her on the project," said Sally.

"I'm not sure," said Jim. "Bob has talked to her and said that she would require a few months to settle into her new environment before she can contribute to the project."

"Looks like we'll just have to work without her till the next person comes in!" Sally exclaimed.

"That's fine," said Jim as he turned to Sanjay and Bob. "Would you both find out the tasks that Juanita was assigned and the resources that she had planned for those tasks? I'd like to see how much is done and how much is left. Depending on this, I'd like to see how much can be held off till the new person comes in."

"Sure," said Sanjay while Bob nodded his head. Both of them walked out of conference room chatting about Juanita.

Jim takes a brief call, and after getting off the phone says, "We got a new person from the store in Irvine, California! His name is Rick Piccoli. He should be on the phone with us in a few minutes."

Just then, Bob stormed into the room and said, "Angela McKenzie has given her two-months' notice because she received an offer from BestBuy. I'm sure we've lost her, too."

"That's okay. Forget about Juanita's part; I think we've got her replacement. Would you both see the status of Angela's part in the project? By the way, Juanita's replacement is Rick Piccoli from the Irvine, California store," said Jim.

Bob nodded his head in his characteristic manner and left.

"One after the other," Jim exclaimed. "This really had the potential to throw off the project. Managing project risk would not have been so easy without such explicit scheduling and resource allocation."

"I can take on most of Angela's work," offered Sally, "I've done a little bit of customer relations quite some time back."

"Thanks, I'll need all the help I can get if I want to keep this project on schedule!"

CHAPTER SUMMARY

Understand the concept of risk and its relationship to project management. Risk is frequently defined in terms of potential losses, but as we have seen from this chapter, the Project Management Institute thinks of risk as "an uncertain event or condition that, if it occurs, has a *positive* or a negative effect on a project objective," accordingly risks can offer opportunities as well as threats. Further, risk should be considered to be a combination of both the probability of occurrence and the overall effect of the occurrence. Risk may be associated with the project management processes of initiation, planning, execution, closing, and control. Teams may be formed to manage risk during projects, and the forming of teams may be risky as well.

Identify categories of risk and their effect on information systems projects. Risk is natural during IS development projects. Specific risk categories were discussed as they pertain to the unique nature of IS projects. Among these categories were risks as a result of the rapid technological change associated with today's businesses, the difficulty of hiring and retaining key IS personnel, acceptance by diverse users, and the numerous systems development methodologies available. Using established project management processes can help to mitigate risk during IS projects.

Apply techniques for managing project risk, including risk management planning, risk identification, qualitative risk analysis, quantitative risk analysis, risk response planning, and risk monitoring and control. Specific risk management processes include risk management planning, risk identification, qualitative risk analysis, quantitative risk

342 Part II Project Initiation and Planning

analysis, risk response planning, and risk monitoring and control. Many tools and techniques used during risk management were discussed in this chapter. Among them were information gathering techniques such as brainstorming and Delphi analysis. Risk response strategies such as avoidance, mitigation, transference, and acceptance were also discussed. Finally qualitative and quantitative analysis tools such as probability/impact matrices were discussed.

KEY TERMS REVIEW

- Risk-related contractual agreements
- Decision tree analysis
- Diagramming techniques
- Documentation review
- Expected monetary value analysis
- Information gathering techniques
- Periodic project risk reviews
- Probability/impact risk rating matrix
- Project assumption testing

- Project risk
- Project risk response audits
- Qualitative risk analysis
- Quantitative risk analysis
- Residual risks
- Risk acceptance
- Risk avoidance
- Risk identification
- Risk management plan
- Risk management planning
- Risk mitigation
- Risk monitoring and control
- Risk owners

- Risk register
- Risk response plan
- Risk response planning
- Risk transference
- Secondary risks
- Sensitivity analysis
- Simulation
- Technical performance measurement
- Tornado analysis
- Triggers

Match each of the key terms with the definition that best fits it.

1. _____ The process of identifying and documenting a project's potential.

2. _____ Events that serve as early warnings of risk.

3. _____ A technique used during qualitative risk analysis to test the assumptions made during risk identification.

4. _____ A systematic approach to planning the risk management activities of a given project.

5. _____ The establishment of probabilities regarding both the impact and likelihood of specific risk occurrence.

6. _____ A diagramming technique used to evaluate courses of action in terms of their potential cost and benefits relative to other courses of action.

7. _____ An uncertain event or condition that, if it occurs, has a positive or negative effect on a project objective.

8. _____ Project members responsible for specific risk activity decisions.

9. _____ Diagramming tools, such as cause-and-effect diagrams, flow charts, or influence diagrams, used to help identify project risk.

10. _____ A risk response strategy designed to avoid potential project risks.

11. _____ A technique used to analyze project risk in terms of its probability of occurrence and its impact on project outcomes.

12. _____ An important tool used to determine whether important technical milestones are being met.

13. _____ The analysis of the probability of occurrence and the impact of risk on project objectives using numerical techniques.

14. _____ A diagramming technique that graphically shows, in descending order, which risks can cause the greatest variability on some outcome.

15. _____ A technique, such as Monte Carlo analysis, used to perform what-if analyses to determine the impact of a given situation on a project objective.

16. _____ Techniques such as brainstorming, Delphi surveys, or SWOT analysis used to identify project risk.

17. _____ A risk response strategy in which steps are taken to mitigate project risk.

18. _____ Any risks resulting from the application of a risk response strategy.

19. _____ An overall plan used to outline risks and the strategies used to manage them.

20. _____ A risk response strategy designed to transfer risk to another party, often through the use of contracts.

21. _____ The process of monitoring identified risks for change and controlling those changes.

22. _____ The review of organizational information to aid during risk identification.

23. _____ A statistical technique that captures the average value of potential projects by analyzing the likelihood of possible project outcomes as well as each outcome's financial consequence.

24. _____ A risk response strategy in which risks are simply accepted and contingency strategies are planned.

25. _____ Any risks remaining after risk response strategies have been applied.

26. _____ A technique used to examine the potential impact of specific risks to a project.

27. _____ The process of developing methods for responding to project risks.

28. _____ Audits designed to evaluate the effectiveness of risk response strategies and risk owners.

29. _____ A documented plan for risk response.

30. _____ Any contracts for the purpose of risk transference during the project.

31. _____ A formal record listing all project risks, explaining the nature of the risk and management of the risk.

32. _____ Reviews designed to review existing risk activities and to monitor any changes to the project.

REVIEW QUESTIONS

1. Define *risk.*
2. Define *project risk.*
3. Give two examples of risk during an ISD project.
4. List the processes of Project Risk Management.
5. List two inputs for each of the Project Risk Management processes.
6. List two tools or techniques for each of the Project Risk Management processes.
7. List two outputs for each of the Project Risk Management processes.
8. Describe probability/impact risk analysis.
9. Discuss qualitative risk analysis.
10. Discuss quantitative risk analysis.
11. List the common elements of a risk response plan.
12. List some general categories of risk faced during IS development projects.

CHAPTER EXERCISES

1. Explain how project risk can have both a positive and a negative effect on a project objective.
2. Describe how risk can affect each of the five project management process areas.
3. What are the different risk management processes? Provide a brief description of each
4. Identify the common sources of risks in information technology projects. Provide suggestions for managing them.

5. Find an example of a risk management plan on the Internet or any other source. What are the elements of this plan?
6. Using the Internet or any other source, write a two-page report on information gathering techniques. Be sure to discuss the information gathering techniques discussed in the chapter.
7. Think of a recent project that you were involved in (or the project you are involved in as part of your current course). What were some of the risks you faced? Were some of the risks more likely to occur than others? What was the potential impact of the risks you faced? Using this information, construct a probability/impact matrix as outlined in this chapter.
8. Using the Internet or any other source, write a two-page report on qualitative and quantitative risk analysis. Be sure to discuss the analyses discussed in the chapter.
9. Discuss the various techniques for quantitative risk analysis.
10. Compare and contrast risk avoidance, risk transference, risk mitigation, and risk acceptance.
11. Find an example of a risk response plan on the Internet or any other source. What are the elements of this plan?
12. Explain the different categories of risk pertaining to the uniqueness of IS projects.

CHAPTER CASE

Sedona Management Group and Managing Project Risk

All projects involve a certain level of risk. Project risk is any uncertain event that may have a positive or negative effect on a project objective. Project Risk Management, therefore, involves understanding the possible problems that might occur during the project life cycle and how they will affect the success of the project. Significant improvements in project outcomes result from effectively managing project risk. Organizations need to understand that Project Risk Management processes are an investment—these processes cost money but can also yield benefits.

Sedona Management Group (SMG) typically associates different categories of risks with the information systems projects they pursue. The first category includes risks associated with the constant flux of technology in today's business environment. The team at SMG has mitigated—or reduced—this type of risk by constantly scanning for new technologies that will reduce development time, reduce the costs of maintenance, and stimulate the reuse of code in an efficient manner for new projects. The second category includes risks associated with locating, hiring, and retaining competent personnel. As mentioned in an earlier case, SMG strives to provide a work environment that has a fun organizational culture and that is also

professionally and financially rewarding. Providing such a work environment has been a critical element in SMG's ability to hire and retain valued employees and in its success in today's high-technology business environment. The third category involves risks associated with the user's acceptance of the system. The Sedona team mitigates this type of risk by keeping the customer constantly involved throughout the life cycle of the project. Consequently, SMG's customers know what to expect, and there are no surprises.

Risk occurs at every stage of the project life cycle. In the initiation phase, risk occurs in the project selection process. In any company, the selection of the wrong project, whether in terms of profitability or complexity, may harm the company. In the case of SMG's commercial Web site development business, the result might be that the company could no longer sustain itself. As a result, SMG employs a detailed process for selecting projects, and as mentioned earlier, projects that don't meet SMG's criteria are rejected.

In the planning stage, other types of risks may be encountered. Tim Turnpaugh recognizes that the probability of project success increases with good planning. The company's experience with successful projects over the last ten years helps the Sedona team define the scope, time, and cost of any project quite accurately. By using processes that accurately identify project scope, the team can determine the budget and time it would take to complete the project. All of these standardized processes are used to manage project risk. The contract that SMG uses for its clients also minimizes the risks associated with the development process by explicitly describing the customers' expectations, the technology used in the development of the system, the capabilities of the final system, the customer's availability for project related communication, and finally the costs associated with any changes in project scope.

In the execution phase, other types of risks will be encountered. Despite a thorough plan developed with the client, there is still the risk that the project somehow won't meet client expectations. To mitigate this risk, SMG involves the customer throughout the development process, so that any potential issues can be identified early. In the case of the Seattle Seahawks, the Sedona team produced several different potential designs based on the initial requirements set forth by the Seahawks. Mike Flood, the Seahawks' manager in charge of the development effort, was able to assess these prototypes in connection with potential Web site users and chose to continue the development process with the version that seemed to best meet their needs.

Another area where risk can be managed is in project control and closure. Project control involves measuring the progress of the project in terms of the project objectives, monitoring any deviation from the project plan, and taking any corrective action required to match the progress with the plan. Turnpaugh has rigid rules about change requests. If the customer requests any substantial changes during the project life cycle, these change requests will result in a modified project budget and schedule. The purpose of project closure involves ensuring that the project deliverables have been completed and delivering the final product to the customer. The Sedona team ensures the customer understands how to adequately maintain the delivered system, which prevents downstream maintenance risks, as well as risks to Sedona's reputation. At the closure stage, SMG also documents any lessons learned during the project to reduce the risks of future efforts.

CHAPTER 9 PROJECT ASSIGNMENT

During the life cycle of a project, it is important to manage risk because it can have an impact on the project scope, schedule, and budget. In this exercise, you will have to identify the potential risks that might occur when you are developing the entertainment Web site.

1. Define risk as it relates to your project.
2. Identify sources of risks that will occur at different stages of your project.
3. Referring to the quality management chapter (Chapter 8), develop a cause-and-effect, or fishbone, diagram to trace the root causes of the risks you identified for Question 2.
4. Discuss the different techniques (e.g., risk avoidance, risk transference, risk mitigation, or risk acceptance) that you will use to address these risks.
5. Develop a risk response plan, which is a documented plan for risk response. The document should contain:
   - The identified risks
   - The project areas or objectives the risk may affect
   - The roles and responsibilities of any risk owners
   - A description of the risk response strategies, including avoidance, transference, mitigation, and acceptance that will be used to address the identified risks
   - An acknowledgement of any residual risks projected to remain after any risk response strategies have been applied
   - A list of actions to be used to implement the risk response strategies.

REFERENCES

www.buckterrellathletics.com/Risk%20Minimization%20in%20Pole%20Vaulting.htm

www.ittoolkit.com/workbooks/chk_risk.pdf

staff.uow.edu.au/ohs/managingrisk/OHS148-Risk Register.pdf

www.odellion.com/assets/financialmodels/tornado.gif

Essex, D. (2003). "A Matter of Public Record." *PM Network,* August, 22–26.

Foti, R. (2003). "What the Doctor Ordered." *PM Network.* September, 26–32.

Hall, P. (2003). "Make Haste Slowly." *PM Network,* August, 32–35.

Keil, M., Cule, P. E., Lyytinen, K., and Schmidt, R. (1998). "A Framework for Identifying Software Project Risks." *Communications of the ACM* 41(11), 76–83.

Knutson, J. (2003). "A Project Management Renaissance: The Future Is Already Here." *PM Network,* July, 60–61.

Overholt, A. (2004). "Listening to Starbucks." *Fast Company,* July.

Project Management Institute. (2004). *A Guide to the Project Management Body of Knowledge.* Newton Square, PA: PMI.

Rao, H. R., Nam, K., and Chaudhury, A. (1996). "Information Systems Outsourcing." *Communications of the ACM* 39(7), 27–28.

Ribeiro, J. (2004). "Source Code Stolen from U.S. Software Company in India." *ComputerWorld,* August 5. Retrieved from: www.computerworld.com/governmenttopics/government/legalissues/story/0,10801,95045,00.html.

Silverstein, K. (2002). "Closing the Circuit." *PM Network,* August, 40–44.

Thibodeau, P. (2004). "Internal Resistance Can Doom Offshore Projects." *ComputerWorld,* January 26. Retrieved from: www.computerworld.com/managementtopics/outsourcing/story/0,10801,89364,00.html.

Vijayan, J. (2204). "Security Expectations, Response Rise in India." *ComputerWorld,* August 30. Retrieved from: www.computerworld.com/managementtopics/outsourcing/story/0,10801,95533,00.html.

Wallace, L., and Keil, M. (2004). "Software Project Risks and Their Effect on Outcomes." *Communications of the ACM* 47(4), 68–73.

Chapter 10

Managing Project Procurement

Opening Case: Outsourcing Is Big Business

When an organization decides to outsource its information technology (IT) development and management, it typically looks to a few familiar firms. One of the best known names in IT, IBM is the leader in the global information IT outsourcing market. In 2002, the global IT outsourcing market was valued at $68.5 billion, and IBM controlled 22 percent of that market, with $15.3 billion in revenues. EDS, Computer Sciences Corporation, and Fujitsu held the second, third, and fourth spots, with $11.1, $3.8, and $3.3 billion in revenues, respectively. Hewlett-Packard (HP) is fifth, with 1.8 percent of the market. The global IT outsourcing market is expected to reach $100 billion in revenues by 2007.

IT outsourcing varies in scope and range of services provided, but outsourcing contracts typically involve a company's handing over to an IT service provider such major tasks as data center management, software development, call center operations, and desktop and network support.

In 2003, beverage maker Diageo signed over management of its worldwide IT infrastructure to IBM. Diageo is known for its many widely recognized brands, such as Cuervo tequila (Figure 10.1), Guinness beer, and Smirnoff vodka. Analysts estimate the deal to be worth $400–500 million over seven years. Diageo was formed through the merger of beverage makers Guinness and Grand Met, along with subsequent acquisitions, so another part of the outsourcing agreement involved the integration of several disparate systems the company had acquired through that mergers and acquisition process. Diageo previously had a long-term agreement with HP for the management of its IT infrastructure (Sources: Gilbert, 2003; Hines, 2003)

Figure 10.1
Diageo, maker
of Cuervo tequila,
signed a 7-year,
$500 million
outsourcing deal
with IBM in 2002

Sources: Gilbert, 2003;
Hines, 2003.

LEARNING OBJECTIVES

After reading this chapter, you will be able to:

➤ Describe the various sources of systems and software components.
➤ Understand the appeal of outsourcing.
➤ Explain Project Procurement Management.
➤ Describe how to plan purchases and acquisitions.
➤ Explain how to plan contracting.
➤ Understand how to request seller responses.
➤ Describe how to select sellers.
➤ Explain contract administration.
➤ Understand contract closure.

INTRODUCTION

As the opening case illustrates, outsourcing the management of a company's information technology infrastructure is big business. Just how big outsourcing has become in the past 20 years illustrates how much procurement of information technology and information systems has changed. Almost no serious systems development is done from scratch by in-house information systems personnel anymore. Instead, entire systems or various system components are purchased from outside the organization and then integrated with existing systems. In some cases, development and management of systems is completely handed over to another company, as is the case with the outsourcing example in the opening case. Whether a company is procuring an entire information infrastructure and its management or simply the software components needed for its internal systems development efforts, procurement, the subject of this chapter, becomes a key project management activity.

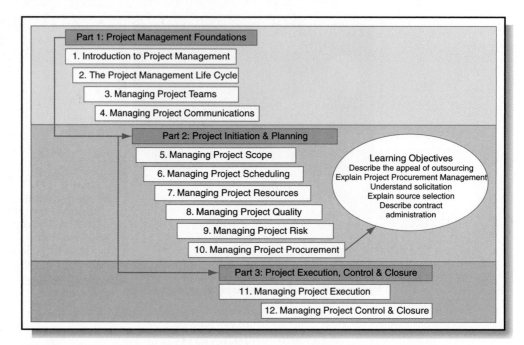

Figure 10.2 Information systems project management focusing on managing project procurement

This chapter has two main parts. The first part is about the many current choices available today for systems development. This section of the chapter is organized according to the types of organizations from which software or its components can be procured. These include: 1) information technology services firms, 2) packaged software providers, 3) vendors of enterprise-wide solution software, 4) on-demand computing providers, and 5) open-source software. The next topic in this section on sources of software is outsourcing. The second part of the chapter is about the procurement process and the various steps that are a part of it. These project procurement processes include: planning purchases and acquisitions, planning contracting, requesting seller responses, selecting sellers, contract administration, and contract closure (Figure 10.2).

ALTERNATIVES TO INTERNAL SYSTEMS DEVELOPMENT

In the first wave of systems development for organizational application software, development was done in-house, and the software was written from scratch. Systems development was an art practiced by a talented few who often left few clues of how they worked their magic for the bewildered maintenance programmers who followed them. In the second wave of systems development, the effort was made to convert the craft of development into a more regulated, planned, engineering-oriented process. There was a heavy emphasis on the process of systems development and on creating proper documentation of what had been done and why. Computer-assisted software engineering (CASE) tools helped considerably with this new perspective because they were based on specific development processes and simply using them created useful documentation. The third, and current, wave, the use of agile methodologies, is a reaction to the focus on planning and documentation in the second wave. It also grew out of experience with development using object-oriented techniques.

The first wave of systems development, developing systems in-house was the only alternative. The off-the-shelf software industry did not exist until the late-1960s, so organizations that needed software built it themselves. For the second wave, externally developed software was available, but developers typically suffered from the "not built here" syndrome. They believed the only way to ensure the proper operability and quality of software was to build it themselves. Although the engineering approach was an improvement over the craft approach, the reliance on planning and documentation tended to slow the overall development process, just when the pace of business generally was quickening and expanding to become a rapid, global process. As the business world acquired Internet speed in the mid-1990s, the not built here syndrome was no longer acceptable. Software had to be developed quickly to meet rapidly changing business needs. More and more, software development relies on obtaining software from an outside provider. Why reinvent the wheel internally when someone else has already built and tested that wheel and is willing to sell it to you for a good price?

Procurement, then, has become an important part of information systems development. Internal corporate IS shops now spend a smaller and smaller proportion of their time and effort developing systems from scratch. In 1998, corporate IS groups reported spending 33 percent less time and money on traditional software development and maintenance than they did in 1997 (King and Cole-Gomolski, 1999). Instead, they increased work on packaged applications by a factor of three, and they increased outsourcing by 42 percent. Where in-house development occurred, it was related to Internet technology. In-house development can lead to a larger maintenance burden than other development methods, such as packaged applications, according to a recent study (Banker, Davis, and Slaughter, 1998). The study found that using a code generator as the basis for in-house development was associated with an increase in maintenance hours, while using packaged applications was associated with a decrease.

What, then, are the possible sources from which systems and software components can be procured? In this chapter, you will learn about the various sources of software for organizations. First you will read about the five types of organizations that provide software. Next you will read about outsourcing, where all or part of an organization's information systems, their development, and their maintenance are given over to another organization. In all of these situations, **external acquisition** occurs where systems or software components are procured from outside vendors, so the project procurement processes you will read about later in the chapter all apply.

External acquisition
The procurement of products and/or services from an outside vendor.

External Acquisition

We can group organizations that produce software into five major categories: 1) information technology services firms, 2) packaged software providers, 3) vendors of enterprise-wide solution software, 4) on-demand computing providers, and 5) open-source software (Figure 10.3).

Information Technology Services Firms

If a company needs an information system but does not have the expertise or the personnel to develop the system in-house and a suitable off-the-shelf system is not available, the company will likely consult an information technology (IT) services firm. **IT services firms** help companies develop custom information systems for

IT Service firms
Firms that help companies develop custom information systems for internal use, or develop, host, and run applications for customers.

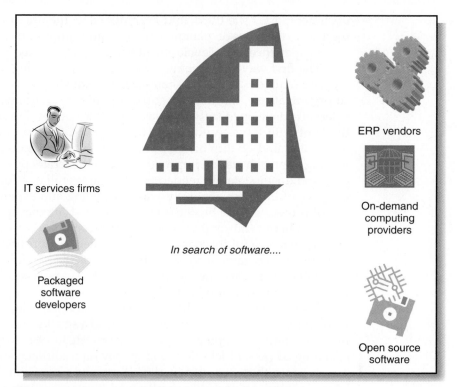

Figure 10.3 Sources of application software

internal use; they develop, host, and run applications for customers; or they provide other services. Note that in Table 10.1, a list of the top ten global software firms, five out of ten specialize in services, which includes custom systems development. These firms employ people with expertise in the development of information systems. Their consultants may also have expertise in a given business area. For example, consultants who work with banks understand financial institutions as well as

Table 10.1 The Top 10 Global Software Companies

Rank	Company	2005 Software/Services Revenue (million USD)	Software Business Sector
1	IBM	$61,307	Middleware/application server/Web server/ systems integration services/IT consulting
2	Microsoft	$33,969	Operating systems
3	EDS	$20,669	IT sourcing
4	Computer Sciences Corp.	$15,188	Systems integration services/ IT consulting
5	Accenture	$15,114	Systems integration services/IT consulting
6	Hewlett Packard	$13,778	Systems integration services/IT consulting
7	Oracle	$10,156	Database/business process management
8	Hitachi	$9,491	Telecommunication services
9	SAP America	$9,313	Business process management
10	Capgemini	$8,581	Systems integration services/IT consulting

Note: All figures are in U.S. dollars.

Source: From *Software* magazine's Web site, www.softwaremag.com/L.cfm?Doc=2005–09/2005–09 editorial.

information systems. Consultants use many of the same methodologies, techniques, and tools that companies use to develop systems in-house.

It may surprise you to see IBM listed as the top global software producer. You may think of IBM as primarily a hardware company, despite what you read in the opening case about IBM being the leader in the IT global outsourcing market. Yet IBM has been moving away from a reliance on hardware development for many years. Its purchase of the IT consulting arm of PricewaterhouseCoopers in 2002 solidified its move into services and consulting. IBM is also well known for its development of Web server and middleware software. Other leading IT services firms include traditional consulting firms, such as Computer Sciences Corp., Accenture, and Capgemini. The list also includes HP, another company formerly focused on hardware that has made the transition to being an IT services firm.

Packaged Software Producers

The growth of the software industry has been phenomenal since its beginnings in the mid-1960s. Some of the largest computer companies in the world produce software exclusively. A good example is Microsoft, number 2 in the top 10 list. Almost 98 percent of Microsoft's revenue comes from its software sales, mostly from its Windows operating systems and its personal productivity software, Office. Number 7 on the list, Oracle, is exclusively a software company, known primarily for its database software, but it also makes enterprise systems. The third top-10 company that is primarily in the business of developing and selling off-the-shelf software solutions is number 9, SAP. SAP develops enterprisewide system solutions.

Packaged software producers
Companies in the business of developing and selling off-the-shelf software.

Packaged software producers develop what are sometimes called prepackaged, off-the-shelf, or shrink-wrapped systems. Microsoft's Project and Intuit's Quicken, QuickPay, and QuickBooks are popular examples of such software. The packaged software development industry serves many market segments. Their offerings range from general, broad-based packages, such as general ledger, to very narrow, niche packages, such as software to help manage a day care center. Software companies develop software to run on many different computer platforms, from microcomputers to large mainframes. They range in size from just a few people to thousands of employees. Software companies consult with system users after the initial software design has been completed and an early version of the system has been built. The systems are then tested in actual organizations, by beta-testers, to find any problems or learn if any improvements can be made. Until testing is completed, the system is not offered for sale to the public.

Turnkey systems
Off-the-shelf software that cannot be modified to meet the specific, individual needs of an organization.

Some off-the-shelf software systems cannot be modified to meet the specific, individual needs of a particular organization. Such application systems are sometimes called **turnkey systems.** The producer of a turnkey system will only make changes to the software when a substantial number of users ask for a specific change. Other off-the-shelf application software products can be modified or extended, however, by the producer or by the user to more closely fit the needs of the organization. Even though many organizations perform similar functions, no two organizations do the same thing in exactly the same way. A turnkey system may be good enough for a certain level of performance, but it will never perfectly match the way a given organization does business. A reasonable estimate is that off-the-shelf software can at best meet 70 percent of an organization's needs. Thus, even in the best case, 30 percent of the software system does not match the organization's specifications.

Enterprise resource planning (ERP) system
A system that integrates individual traditional business functions into a series of modules so that a single transaction occurs seamlessly within a single information system rather than over several separate systems.

Enterprise Solutions Software

More and more organizations are choosing complete software solutions, called enterprise solutions or **enterprise resource planning systems (ERP),** to support their operations and business processes. These ERP software solutions consist of a series of integrated modules. Each module supports an individual, traditional business function, such as accounting, distribution, manufacturing, and human resources. The difference between the modules and traditional approaches is that the modules are integrated to focus on business processes rather than on business functional areas. For example, a series of modules will support the entire order entry process, from receiving an order to adjusting inventory, shipping, billing, and on to after-the-sale service. The traditional approach would use different systems in different functional areas of the business, such as a billing system in accounting and an inventory system in the warehouse. Using enterprise software solutions, a firm can integrate all parts of a business process in a unified information system. All aspects of a single transaction occur seamlessly within a single information system rather than in a series of disjointed, separate systems focused on business functional areas.

The benefits of the enterprise solutions approach include a single repository of data for all aspects of a business process and the flexibility of the modules. A single repository ensures more consistent and accurate data, as well as less maintenance. The modules are very flexible because additional modules can be added as needed once the basic system is in place. Added modules are immediately integrated into the existing system.

There are also disadvantages to enterprise solutions software. The systems are very complex, so implementation can take a long time to complete. Organizations typically do not have the necessary expertise in-house to implement the systems, so they must rely on consultants or employees of the software vendor, which can be very expensive. In some cases, organizations must change how they do business in order to benefit from a migration to enterprise solutions.

There are few major vendors of enterprise solution software. The best known is probably SAP AG, the German firm mentioned earlier, known for its flagship product, R/3. SAP stands for Systems, Applications, and Products in Data Processing. SAP AG was founded in 1972, but most of its growth has occurred since 1992. In 2005, SAP AG was the ninth largest software company in the world. The number-two supplier of enterprise solution software is Oracle, a company more often associated with its database products. In 2004, Oracle extended its market share in the ERP software segment by purchasing PeopleSoft Inc., a U.S. firm founded in 1987. PeopleSoft had been the third leading ERP firm and was best known for its human resources management systems. Just before being purchased by Oracle, PeopleSoft had boosted its corporate strength in 2003 through acquiring another ERP vendor, J. D. Edwards. Together, SAP and Oracle control about 60 percent of the ERP market, which was estimated at around $24 billion in revenues for 2005. The market for ERP is predicted to grow in the range of 6 to 7 percent per year through 2009 (Woodie, 2005). Because the higher end of the market has become saturated with ERP systems, most ERP vendors are looking to medium and small businesses for growth.

Although the general trend has been for a firm to deal exclusively with a single vendor for a single enterprise-wide implementation of ERP products, some firms have instead followed a best-of-breed strategy. Such a strategy typically entails using different products from different ERP vendors, as well as specialized products from non-ERP vendors, and developing other software in-house to fill in the gaps and ease cross-product integration. The key advantage of a **best-of-breed strategy** is that it capitalizes on the strengths of individual vendors' products. For example, a firm might use SAP's order entry modules and Oracle's financial and human resources products. For the increased system functionality offered in such a scheme, however, the firm gives up the single architecture, single interface, and single vendor advantages that come with adopting one ERP vendor's products to support all functions throughout the firm.

Best-of-breed strategy
A strategy of using different software products from different sources (including in house development) to capitalize on the strengths of different products.

On-Demand Computing Providers

Another method for organizations to obtain computerized applications is to rent them or license them from third-party providers who run the applications at remote sites. Companies pay on a usage basis. IBM calls this service **on-demand computing,** and HP calls it **utility computing,** but the idea is the same: Customers pay for IT services only as needed, much like they pay for utilities such as electricity (Dignan, 2002). One company purchases server time or processing power from another company that takes care of maintenance and other concerns. This way, companies do not have to buy their own servers and the personnel to run and maintain them. On-demand providers charge for usage the same way utilities do: When service spikes, so do costs. The goal is for IT bills to look a lot like electricity bills, where a standard rate has been set for services, with itemized bills for bandwidth, data center usage, and so on.

On-demand, or utility, computing is in its infancy. It will take some time for large providers like IBM and HP to tie together all of the infrastructure and monitoring controls needed to provide computing services in the same way utilities provide electricity. In some ways, utility computing resembles the application service provision movement, which promised users would be able to obtain applications from third-party providers who run the applications at remote sites, whenever and wherever they needed them. Unlike application service provision, which focused on application usage, on-demand computing is larger, focusing on the provision of total computing services. The idea of on-demand computing is not expected to appeal to all industries equally. Industries that invest heavily in IT and have standard business practices, such as financial services and telecommunications firms, are expected to be the most likely customers (Dignan, 2002).

Open-Source Software

Open-source software is unlike the other types of software you have read about so far. **Open-source software** is different because it is freely available, not just the final product but the source code itself. It is also different because it is developed by a community of interested people instead of by employees of a particular company. Open-source software performs the same functions as commercial software, such as operating systems, e-mail, database systems, and Web browsers. Some of the most well-known and popular open-source software names are Linux, the operating system; mySQL, a database system; and Firefox, a Web browser. Open-source also applies to software components and objects. Open-source is developed and maintained by communities of people, and sometimes these communities can be very large. Developers often use common Web resources, such as SourceForge.net, to organize their activities. In March 2006, SourceForge.net hosted about 117,000 projects and had almost 1.3 million registered users. There is no question that the open-source movement would not be having the success it enjoys without the availability of the Internet for providing access and organizing development activities.

If open-source software is free, you might wonder how anybody makes any money by developing it. There are two primary ways companies and individuals can make money with open-source: 1) by providing maintenance and other services, or 2) by providing one version of the software for free and selling a more fully featured version. Some open-source solutions have more impact on the software industry than others. Linux, for example, has been very successful in the server software market, where it is estimated to have 24 percent of the market share, a number projected to grow to 33 percent by 2007 (Hamm, 2005). Of desktop operating systems, Linux now has a 3 percent market share, projected to double to 6 percent by 2007. These market shares together translate into a market value of $11 billion for Linux currently, with the potential of the market value to grow to $35.7 billion by 2008. Other open-source

On-demand computing
Use of computing resources on the basis of users' needs, often on a pay-per-use basis. Also called utility computing.

Utility computing
Use of computing resources on the basis of users' needs, often on a pay-per-use basis. Also called on-demand computing.

Open-source software
Systems software, applications, and programming languages of which the source code is freely available for use and/or modification.

Table 10.2 Comparison of Five Different Sources of Software Components

PRODUCERS	WHEN TO GO TO THIS TYPE OF ORGANIZATION FOR SOFTWARE	INTERNAL STAFFING REQUIREMENTS
IT services firms	When task requires custom support and the system can't be built internally	Internal staff may be needed, depending on application
Packaged software producers	When supported task is generic	Some IS and user staff to define requirements and evaluate packages
Enterprise-wide solutions	For complete systems that cross functional boundaries	Some internal staff necessary, but mostly consultants
On-demand computing providers	When the company already invests heavily in IT and has standard business processes	Ideally, none
Open-source software	When the supported task is generic but cost is an issue	Some IS and user staff to define requirements and evaluate packages

software products, such as mySQL, have also been successful, and open-source's share of the software industry seems destined to continue to grow.

Table 10.2 compares the five different sources for systems and software components. Choosing between a package or an external supplier will be determined by your needs, not by what the supplier has to sell. The results of your procurement planning analysis will define the type of product you want to buy and will make working with an external supplier much easier, productive, and worthwhile.

Outsourcing

Outsourcing
The practice of turning over responsibility for some or all of an organization's information systems applications and operations to an outside firm.

As you learned in the opening case, the practice of one organization's developing or running a computer application for another organization is called **outsourcing.** Outsourcing includes a spectrum of working arrangements. At one extreme is having a firm develop and run your application on their computers—all you do is supply input and take output. A common example of such an arrangement is a company that runs payroll applications for clients so that clients don't have to develop an independent in-house payroll system. Instead, the clients simply provide employee payroll information and, for a fee, the service provider returns completed paychecks, payroll accounting reports, and tax and other statements for employees. For many organizations, payroll outsourcing is very cost-effective. In another example of outsourcing, you might hire a company to run your applications at your site on your computers. In some cases, an organization employing such an arrangement will dissolve some or all of its information systems unit and transfer most or all of those employees to the company brought in to run the computing operations.

Outsourcing is a large and growing segment of the IS industry, with a global market of $68.5 billion in 2002 and projected growth to $100 billion by 2007 (Gilbert, 2003). The market is expected to continue to grow rapidly over the next decade. More than 80 percent of all large corporations are expected to use some form of global IS outsourcing in 2004 (King, 2003). Outsourcing provides a way for firms to leapfrog their current position in IS and to turn over development and operations to staff with skills not found internally.

Why would an organization outsource its information systems operations? As we saw in the payroll example, outsourcing may be cost effective. If a company specializes in running payroll for other companies, it can leverage the economies of scale it achieves from running one very stable computer application for many organizations into very low prices. Outsourcing also allows access to increased knowledge and expertise that may not be available internally, and it enables companies to take advantage of the availability and quality of vendors who provide outsourcing services (Ketler and Willems, 1999). Other reasons for outsourcing include:

- Freeing up internal resources
- Increasing the revenue potential of the organization
- Reducing time to market
- Increasing process efficiencies
- Outsourcing non-core activities

TIPS FROM THE PROS
Assuring Offshore Project Success

As you have read, procurement many times reaches offshore. Although offshore providers are often sought for their lower costs, they frequently do not have the necessary management and organizational skills to deliver all of the anticipated business benefits. Here are some tips on how to assure that offshore procurement is successful, from Craig Rintoul, a consultant who specializes in outsourcing and IT management and who works with PA Consulting Group in Cambridge, Massachusetts.

1. *Onshore team*: The onshore business leadership team must take a hands-on approach. They must ensure that the offshore team delivers business benefits. The onshore team has to ensure that the offshore team delivers both technical and business benefits.

2. *Program management*: Offshore projects are very susceptible to changes in budget, timing, and deliverables. The program management team needs to be able to redeploy resources as needed and to anticipate change before it happens.

3. *Delivery of benefits*: Early benefit delivery from offshore projects is very important in proving feasibility and sustainability of service. Specific benefits need to be aligned with each requirement and linked to implementation milestones. It is important to plainly map dependencies so that it

is clear what needs to be done to deliver a particular milestone.

4. *Change and project management*: The geographic separation and mix of cultures inherent in an offshore project increase risk, worsen that arise, and lengthen time to resolution. A back-to-basics approach in project and change management will increase the chances of success. The offshore vendor's and the client's responsibilities need to be clearly defined and understood by both parties.

5. *Geographic and cultural differences*. One of the greatest challenges is overcoming differences in language, culture, and geography. While good communication is important to any project, it is crucial to offshore projects. The onshore company has to be aware of cultural differences and their effect on how directions are received, problems resolved, and responsibility delegated. When agreeing on schedules or reviewing specifications, onshore project managers should ensure that everyone correctly understands the details. Scheduling is also made difficult by differences in the number and timing of local holidays and vacation practices across countries. In some countries, for example, workers may typically get four to six weeks of paid vacation per year (Source: Rintoul, 2004).

Global Implications of Outsourcing: Managing Security

The key motivation for procuring development services offshore is to save money and improve productivity. In the process, however, security may suffer. The issue is not so much that firms in India and China do not observe standard security measures such as firewalls and data backup—they do. The real issue is that differences in culture result in differences in how corporate data are treated. In close-knit cultures such as India, the attitude toward personal privacy is more relaxed than in the United States and Europe. Workers may not think twice about sharing what could be sensitive corporate and client data, according to Gartner India research vice president Partha Iyengar.

What can a company do to ensure that security is not overlooked in the procurement of services offshore? Suggestions from Iyengar and others include:

- Document corporate processes and get vendors to sign off on them
- Have vendors perform background checks on their staff
- In some countries, such as India, ask vendors to hire only applicants who have Indian passports, which can be acquired only after passing vigorous security checks by Indian law enforcement
- Have vendors increase security awareness through employee training
- Write security and regulatory compliance concerns into the procurement contract
- Visit offshore outsourcing facilities and check them out personally
- Investigate and understand local laws regarding Internet access and restrictions

Source: Pruitt, S. "When Outsourcing, don't forget security, experts say." 9/21/04. © 2004 ComputerWorld, Inc. Computerworld and Computerworld.com and the respective logos are trademarks of International Data Group Inc.

STEPS IN THE PROCUREMENT PROCESS

Once the decision has been made to outsource products or services or both, the project team begins the project procurement process. According to the PMBOK (2004), there are six management processes in the Project Procurement Management knowledge area. These are planning purchases and acquisitions, planning contracting, requesting seller responses, selecting sellers, contract administration, and contract closure. As with all other management processes in the PMBOK, each of the procurement processes can be understood in terms of its inputs, internal tools and techniques, and outputs. Figure 10.4, from the 2004 PMBOK, shows all six processes and their inputs, tools and techniques, and outputs.

A quick look at Figure 2.21 will show which process group each of the six procurement processes belongs in. Planning purchases and acquisitions and planning contracting are both part of planning; requesting seller responses and selecting sellers belong to the executing process group; contract administration is part of the monitoring and controlling process group; and contract closure is a closing process. There are no procurement processes in the initiating process group.

Planning purchases and acquisitions is the process of determining which of your projects needs can best be met by obtaining services or products from outside the project organization. Typically, this implies vendors from outside of the overall organization, although it is possible for some services and products to be obtained from other units within the organization. Once the decision has been made to procure externally, planning contracting can begin. The main task of planning contracting is to create the documents needed to support the processes of requesting seller responses and selecting sellers. These documents are used to seek proposals from prospective vendors. They describe what is to be purchased and ask for offers from vendors who are interested in providing it. Common

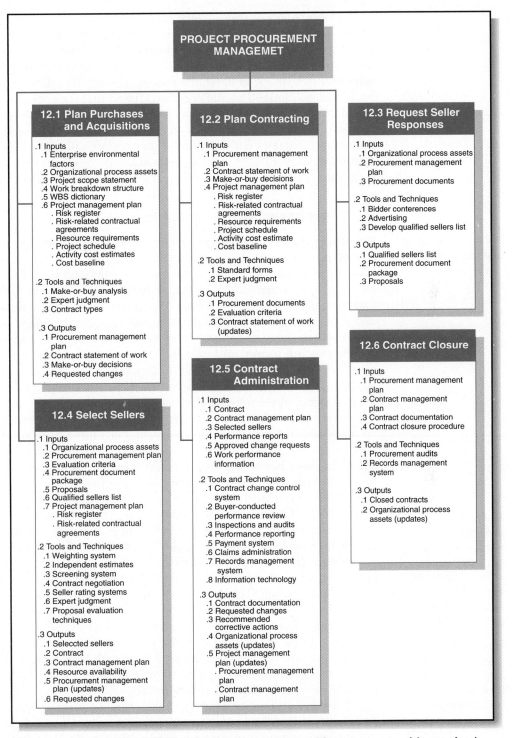

PROJECT PROCUREMENT MANAGEMET

12.1 Plan Purchases and Acquisitions

.1 Inputs
  .1 Enterprise environmental factors
  .2 Organizational process assets
  .3 Project scope statement
  .4 Work breakdown structure
  .5 WBS dictionary
  .6 Project management plan
   . Risk register
   . Risk-related contractual agreements
   . Resource requirements
   . Project schedule
   . Activity cost estimates
   . Cost baseline

.2 Tools and Techniques
  .1 Make-or-buy analysis
  .2 Expert judgment
  .3 Contract types

.3 Outputs
  .1 Procurement management plan
  .2 Contract statement of work
  .3 Make-or-buy decisions
  .4 Requested changes

12.4 Select Sellers

.1 Inputs
  .1 Organizational process assets
  .2 Procurement management plan
  .3 Evaluation criteria
  .4 Procurement document package
  .5 Proposals
  .6 Qualified sellers list
  .7 Project management plan
   . Risk register
   . Risk-related contractual agreements

.2 Tools and Techniques
  .1 Weighting system
  .2 Independent estimates
  .3 Screening system
  .4 Contract negotiation
  .5 Seller rating systems
  .6 Expert judgment
  .7 Proposal evaluation techniques

.3 Outputs
  .1 Seleccted sellers
  .2 Contract
  .3 Contract management plan
  .4 Resource availability
  .5 Procurement management plan (updates)
  .6 Requested changes

12.2 Plan Contracting

.1 Inputs
  .1 Procurement management plan
  .2 Contract statement of work
  .3 Make-or-buy decisions
  .4 Project management plan
   . Risk register
   . Risk-related contractual agreements
   . Resource requirements
   . Project schedule
   . Activity cost estimate
   . Cost baseline

.2 Tools and Techniques
  .1 Standard forms
  .2 Expert judgment

.3 Outputs
  .1 Procurement documents
  .2 Evaluation criteria
  .3 Contract statement of work (updates)

12.5 Contract Administration

.1 Inputs
  .1 Contract
  .2 Contract management plan
  .3 Selected sellers
  .4 Performance reports
  .5 Approved change requests
  .6 Work performance information

.2 Tools and Techniques
  .1 Contract change control system
  .2 Buyer-conducted performance review
  .3 Inspections and audits
  .4 Performance reporting
  .5 Payment system
  .6 Claims administration
  .7 Records management system
  .8 Information technology

.3 Outputs
  .1 Contract documentation
  .2 Requested changes
  .3 Recommended corrective actions
  .4 Organizational process assets (updates)
  .5 Project management plan (updates)
   . Procurement management plan
   . Contract management plan

12.3 Request Seller Responses

.1 Inputs
  .1 Organizational process assets
  .2 Procurement management plan
  .3 Procurement documents

.2 Tools and Techniques
  .1 Bidder conferences
  .2 Advertising
  .3 Develop qualified sellers list

.3 Outputs
  .1 Qualified sellers list
  .2 Procurement document package
  .3 Proposals

12.6 Contract Closure

.1 Inputs
  .1 Procurement management plan
  .2 Contract management plan
  .3 Contract documentation
  .4 Contract closure procedure

.2 Tools and Techniques
  .1 Procurement audits
  .2 Records management system

.3 Outputs
  .1 Closed contracts
  .2 Organizational process assets (updates)

Figure 10.4 2004 PMBOK Project Procurement Management, with required inputs, tools and techniques used, and resulting outputs

names for these documents include invitation for bid, request for proposal (RFP), request for quotation, tender notice, invitation for negotiation, and contractor initial response. In this chapter, we will refer to these procurement documents primarily as RFPs. The main task of requesting seller responses is to obtain bids that respond to the RFP. Once responses or bids are in hand, the process of selecting sellers begins. Here the bids are compared and judged by the selection criteria that the project organization has established. A vendor is chosen, and a contract is prepared. Contract administration is the process through which the project organization works with the vendor for the duration of the contract. Finally, once the terms of the contract have been satisfactorily met, contract closure begins. Both sides of the agreement accept the work performed, and the contract is completed. In the next sections, you will read more about each of these six processes.

Plan Purchases and Acquisitions

Planning purchases and acquisitions involves determining which project needs can best be met by outsourcing. As detailed in Figure 10.4, the inputs for planning purchases and acquisitions are enterprise environmental factors, organizational process assets, project scope statement, work breakdown structure (WBS), WBS dictionary, and the project management plan. Enterprise environmental factors are the services and products available in the marketplace, the key providers, and the circumstances under which the services or products are available. Organizational process assets are the existing formal and informal policies, procedures, guidelines, and management systems that are considered in developing the procurement management plan. Some organizational process assets include lists of prequalified vendors, which limit the number of direct sellers to the organization. The project scope statement provides the current boundaries of the project, including requirements, constraints, and assumptions. The most common constraint is limited funding. The work breakdown structure is the hierarchical decomposition of the work to be performed by the project team (see Chapter 6). The *WBS dictionary* provides detailed statements of work that include descriptions of the work and resulting deliverables. The project management plan provides the overall plan for managing the project and includes subsidiary plans that can provide guidance for procurement (see Chapter 5).

The key technique used in procurement planning is a **make-or-buy analysis.** For information systems projects, "make" used to be the routine determination, but now the routine decision is more likely to be "buy." Another useful technique is expert judgment, which can be used to develop criteria for evaluating proposals submitted by vendors. Planning purchasing and acquisitions is also characterized by the determination of the type of contract to be offered to vendors. Three types of possible contracts are fixed-price, cost-reimbursable, and time-and-material contracts.

For a **fixed price contract,** the project requirements have been sufficiently detailed for suppliers to feel comfortable in establishing a fixed price. The supplier or vendor is bound to the price provided in the contract. A fixed-price contract is less problematic when the product or service is well-defined.

A **cost-reimbursable contract** involves the reimbursement of the vendor's actual costs in providing the product or service plus, typically, a fee that represents the vendor's profits. Costs are considered to be either direct or indirect. Direct costs are those incurred by the vendor in providing the product or service. Indirect costs, also called overhead costs, are part of the vendor's cost of doing business and involve such things as the salaries of managing executives. Indirect costs are typically billed as a percentage of direct costs. For example, many sponsored research contracts between universities and government sources involve cost-reimbursable contracts, and indirect cost rates set by universities are as high as 50 percent or more.

Time-and-material contract
A type of contract where vendors provide an hourly rate and estimate the amount of time and materials required.

Procurement management plan
A plan that addresses such issues as who will prepare the evaluation criteria, how multiple vendors will be managed, where standardized procurement documents can be obtained, and how procurement will be coordinated with other project tasks.

Statement of work (SOW)
Document prepared for potential vendors that describes the service or product being sought.

Under **time and materials (T&M) contracts,** vendors state an hourly rate and estimate the amount of time and materials required. It is possible to cap a T&M contract by asking the vendor to provide a not-to-exceed price. Otherwise, the price is open. For a T&M contract, it is often recommended that contract requirements specify review points and progress assessments. The contractor may also want to tie payment to deliverables (Porter-Roth, 2002).

As with all types of planning, planning purchasing and acquisitions attempts to anticipate all of the resources and processes necessary to make the overall effort a success. One of the key outputs for this process, then, is a **procurement management plan.** The plan addresses such issues as who will prepare the evaluation criteria, how multiple vendors will be managed, where standardized procurement documents can be obtained, and how procurement will be coordinated with other project tasks.

Another key output is a statement of work. The **statement of work (SOW)** is a document prepared for potential vendors that describes the service or product being sought in enough detail that potential vendors can determine if they can supply it. The SOW assures a common understanding of the project needs and is a very useful communication tool. Figure 10.5 shows the outline for SOWs required by the U.S. Federal Aviation Administration. This outline gives you an idea of the scope of information required in a typical SOW. Statements of work are not necessarily static documents. Instead they tend to be revised and refined as they move through the procurement process. For example, an SOW may change after a prospective vendor has suggested a cheaper or more efficient way to provide the desired product or service.

There are two other outputs from the process of planning purchases and acquisitions: make-or-buy decisions and requested changes. "Make-or-buy decisions" is a list

Figure 10.5 Outline of statement of work required by the U.S. Federal Aviation Administration

Source: www2.faa.gov/ara/asu/bits/BITS%20II/sow.htm. Used with permission.

```
1. Introduction and Overview
   1.1 Background
   1.2 Scope of Work
   1.3 Objectives
2. References
3. Requirements
3.1 Tasks
   • Desired Methodology
   • Illustrations/Drawings/Diagrams, if any
   • Specifications
   • Data/Property/Facilities
   • Level-of-Effort
   • Place/Travel
3.2 End Results/Deliverables
   3.2.1 List of Deliverables by Task
3.3 Schedules/Milestones
   3.3.1 Who Does What When Report
3.4 Other Considerations
4. Progress/Compliance
   The Government requires the following to monitor progress and ensure compliance:
   • Weekly Status Report
   • Weekly Meetings
   • Monthly Progress Report
   • Project Management Team (PMT) Meetings
   • Program Reviews
   • Outlines and Drafts
5. Transmittal/Delivery/Accessibility
6. Notes
```

A big part of procuring IT services is obtaining product support for your organization from the vendor of the services. Two key types of service contracts are available: 1) incident-based support models, and 2) subscription-oriented models. Incident-based models provide for the vendor to charge the client organization for each support related call the vendor handles. A subscription-oriented model involves unlimited support from the vendor.

According to Billy Marshall, vice president of enterprise sales at Red Hat, the Linux provider, incident-based support contracts are a bad idea for any organization. He cites two main reasons. The first is that a contract based on payment per support call provides an incentive for the vendor to sell bad or broken technology to clients. If the amount of revenue a vendor receives is tied to the volume of service calls received, then the natural result, according to Marshall, is "poor technology, poor documentation, and poor service such that the customer is required to call repeatedly." The second reason that incident-based support contracts are a bad idea is that they promote "incident hoarding." Given that they are penalized for each call they make (i.e., they have to pay for each call with real money), customers search for other ways to take care of their problems rather than waste a support call. They may try to solve the problems themselves or engage in extensive searches on the Internet for solutions. Such behavior may in the long run be even more expensive than support calls because customers waste time looking for solutions instead of doing the jobs they are paid to do and because the solutions they find may actually cost the organization additional money if they are so bad that they cause their own costly problems.

Marshall recommends subscription-based support contracts that give customers the opportunity for unlimited contact with the vendor's technical support staff. The emphasis in such contracts is on maximizing the value the customer derives from the technology the vendor delivers. Marshall says such contracts "allow customers to build better infrastructures by building more worthwhile customer–vendor relationships. Customers are allowed—even encouraged—to freely collaborate with their chosen vendors to create better technology and solutions"

Source: © 2004 ComputerWorld, Inc. Computerworld and Computerworld.com and the respective logos are trademarks of Internati362onal Data Group Inc. Marshall, B., "Support Contracts can Encourage Lousy Products." Computerworld, 6/1/04.

of project products and services that the project team will either purchase or develop. This includes products and services needed to do the work of the project, as well as for operating the project's ultimate product. Requested changes to the project management plan could result from planning purchases and acquisitions, and these changes are processed through the integrated change control process (see Chapter 12).

Plan Contracting

Plan contracting
The process of creating documents used to solicit proposals from vendors.

Procurement documents
Documents used to solicit proposals from vendors.

Request for proposal (RFP)
A document provided to vendors to ask them to propose a solution to a specific problem related to your project.

The procurement management plan, the statement of work, and the make-or-buy decisions that were outputs of planning purchases and acquisitions become inputs for plan contracting. These and any other relevant planning documents, such as the project management plan itself, are used along with the tools of standard forms and expert judgment to generate the outputs of **plan contracting**: procurement documents such as a request for proposal (RFP), evaluation criteria, and SOW updates. Updates to the SOW are simply revisions that are made as the result of plan contracting. Procurement documents and evaluation criteria require more explanation.

Procurement Documents

Procurement documents are used to solicit proposals from vendors. The most common procurement document is the **request for proposal (RFP)**. According to Porter-Roth (2002), an RFP is "a standard tool used by governments and businesses to purchase equipment and services by promoting competitive proposals among

Table 10.3 Eight Parts of a Request for Proposal

1) Project overview and administrative information section
2) Technical requirements section
3) Management requirements section
4) Supplier qualifications and references section
5) Suppliers' section
6) Pricing section
7) Contract and license agreement section
8) Appendices

Source: Porter-Roth, 2002; used with permission.

suppliers." An RFP allows buyer and supplier to communicate using the same rules, requirements, schedule, and information. It is more than just a presentation of a problem that needs a solution: Once a vendor responds to the request, the RFP becomes a foundation for the future working relationship between the buyer and the vendor (or supplier). In fact, the proposal prepared by the vendor often becomes a part of the final contract, as an addendum or exhibit, between the supplier and the vendor.

Although the format and content of RFPs differ by industry, individual company, and the product or service sought, there is a standard outline for the contents of a typical RFP. Table 10.3 lists the eight basic parts of an RFP. The project overview and administrative information section contains an overview of the company and a statement of the problem the RFP is designed to solve. The administrative information part of this section lists all of the requirements for an acceptable proposal. These include where and when to submit the proposal, if and when a bidders' conference will be held, the relevant dates for procurement, specific requirements for preparing proposals, how proposals will be evaluated, RFP staff contact names and addresses, and other information required for a supplier to be judged responsive. The technical requirements section includes an overview of the relevant technical information so that potential vendors can determine if they can provide the solution that is being sought. This section will include technical factors critical to the success of the project, functional specifications, performance specifications, and so on. The management requirements section contains information about the project's needs for implementation, installation, training, maintenance, and related matters, such as staffing requirements, installation schedule, and acceptance test requirements.

The fourth part of the RFP, the supplier qualifications and references section, is a request for information about the potential vendor. Its purpose is to help the buyer determine if the vendor is really qualified to supply the needed product or service. Information requested includes the vendor's financial status, the number of its currently installed systems or components, and the names of customers who can provide references for the vendor. The next section, the suppliers' section, asks for any additional information the potential vendor thinks may be relevant. For example, the vendor here may explain a unique solution to the problem that the buyer had not previously thought about. The sixth section, the pricing section, provides a detailed format for vendors to follow to prepare their price proposals. Pricing can be broken down into separate items for such things as maintenance, licensing, and documentation. If the RFP is for a complete system, then the price proposal should include separate items for software, hardware, installation, systems integration, and so on. In any proposal, the vendor should also distinguish between one-time and recurring costs. The next section, the contract and license agreement section, provides guidance to potential vendors on how to respond to contracts and agreements, and also provides contracts used by the buyer so suppliers can study them. The last section is the appendices. Appendices provide additional information that supplements the rest of the RFP or that was too technical or detailed to be included in the main body of the document. At the very least, an RFP must contain four of these eight sections: project overview and administrative information, technical requirements, management requirements, and pricing (Porter-Roth, 2002).

Creating and evaluating an RFP is often a project in itself and can take up to six months or longer. Often an RFP team is created to manage the process, and the RFP team has a project leader. Like any other project, creating and evaluating an RFP requires following many different steps, typically in a specific order. A sample list of activities to be followed for an RFP is included in Table 10.4. Note that many activities

Table 10.4   Sample Project Schedule for a Request for Proposal

Pre-RFP Activities:
> Identify need.
> Perform initial study.
> Write project justification.
> Estimate budget for project.
> Approve RFP project.

RFP Activities:
> Identify RFP team.
> Identify project schedule and key dates.
> Identify high-level requirements.
> Start vendor and/or technology education.
> Identify and interview users.
> Develop technical requirements.
>> Review requirements with users.
>> Review requirements against corporate standards & constraints.
>> Finalize technical requirements.
> Develop management requirements.
>> Review requirements with users.
>> Review against corporate standards.
>> Finalize management requirements.
> Write RFP.
> Develop evaluation criteria.
> Develop RFP schedule.
> Review finished RFP.
> Send RFP to suppliers.

Post-RFP Activities:
> Allow question and answer period.
> Receive proposals.
> Evaluate proposals.
> Ask suppliers questions if needed.
> Hold supplier presentations, site visits, demonstrations & reference checks.
> Select winning supplier.
> Negotiate contract.
> Provide supplier debriefings for losing proposals.
> Review, clean up and store losing proposals.
> Start project implementation.

Source: Porter-Roth, 2002; used with permission.

occur before the main work on the RFP begins and that many other activities take place after the RFP has been written and sent to potential vendors. Most of the activities listed in Table 10.4 under post-RFP activities are covered in the next two sections on the project management processes of solicitation and source selection.

Evaluation Criteria

Evaluation criteria are used to rate proposals that are received in response to a request for proposals. The criteria can be objective or subjective, and they are often included in the RFP. Typically, the most important evaluation criterion is price, but that alone may not be enough to determine the best proposal. Other criteria include how well the vendor understands the problem, whether or not the vendor has the technical ability to perform appropriately, and whether the vendor has or can obtain the financial resources necessary to deliver what is promised in the proposal. Buyers may also want to consider how long the vendor has been in business, how many employees the vendor has, whether an established vendor may be about to change business lines or emphases, and the number of other comparable projects the vendor has completed or is currently engaged in.

Request Seller Responses

The process of **requesting seller responses** involves obtaining responses to the procurement documents produced during plan contracting. The procurement documents serve as input to requesting seller responses, as do lists of qualified sellers that come from organizational process assets. As you read earlier, in some organizations, lists are kept of qualified vendors and their past relationship with the organization. Procurement documents can be sent to these vendors and any others that the project team has identified as potential bidders. A third input is the procurement management plan. Potential vendors can also be identified through advertising in newspapers or trade magazines or professional journals. Another way to attract potential bidders is through vendor conferences (also called contractor or bidder conferences), where members of the project team can meet with prospective bidders. At these conferences, project team members can explain the procurement process and goals, and potential bidders can ask questions. The answers to some of the questions asked at these conferences may even become part of the revised procurement document. The project team can also develop its own list of qualified vendors from the Internet, relevant local sources, or library directories. The output from requesting seller responses includes a list of qualified vendors who are asked to submit a proposal, formal procurement documents (called procurement document packages in the PMBOK), and the proposals themselves. Proposals may be supplemented with oral presentations if desired.

Ethical Dilemma: When Relations Between Procurement Managers and Vendors Are Too Close

A big part of procurement is working with vendors. Procurement officials work with vendors to get the best deal for their companies. The relationship between procurement and outside vendors is supposed to be neutral, with each side out to get the best deal for the organizations they represent. Sometimes, however, the relationship turns cozy. Procurement managers and vendors become too close, especially in industries where few vendors can supply what a company needs. In these situations, vendors have considerable power over procurement and over the managers who are in charge of buying. Vendors in such situations have more influence over the terms of the deal than would be the case if lots of vendors were available, a situation that favors the buying organization. Where there are few vendors, the buying organization is at a disadvantage. To make it easier for a procurement manager to go along with a deal that is disadvantageous to his or her company, a powerful vendor may offer kickbacks or other inducements, such as a job at the vendor's at some point down the road or other personal favors.

The ethical issues involved in procurement are well illustrated by a case that involved Boeing Co., the airplane manufacturer, and the U.S. Air Force. For more than a decade as the Air Force's second-highest contracting officer, Darleen Drunyun systematically steered various contracts to Boeing, as she admitted during her trial in October 2004. She left the Air Force and went to work as a vice president for Boeing in December 2002, but she was fired in 2003 when it was revealed that she had negotiated her $250,000 per year job at Boeing while overseeing the company's contracts with the Air Force. She was found guilty of conspiracy to violate conflict-of-interest laws and was sentenced to nine months in prison.

Among the things she admitted to doing, Ms. Drunyun confessed to handing Boeing a $4 billion project to upgrade C-130 transport planes even though Boeing rival Lockheed Martin Corp. manufactured the planes and was in a better position to modernize them. One of the reasons Ms. Drunyun gave for awarding the contract to Boeing was that the company had hired and retained her daughter and son-in-law as employees. In her trial, Ms. Drunyun also confessed to negotiating "sweetheart" deals with Boeing for two other aircraft programs: 1) maintenance of C-17 cargo planes, and 2) a restructuring of plans to buy early-warning aircraft for the North Atlantic Treaty Organization. Ms. Drunyun admitted at trial that both deals were overpriced in Boeing's favor. Her biggest deal favoring Boeing, however, was a proposed $23 billion deal to lease aerial-tankers for refueling aircraft from Boeing as a way to provide "a parting gift to Boeing" before leaving the Air Force.

On its part, after the trial, Boeing issued a statement pledging to "work with any and all government agencies that have concerns about the actions of Ms. Drunyun." Chief Executive Officer Harry Stonecipher said Ms. Druyun's admissions of wrongdoing during her trial came "as a total surprise" (Source: Pacztor, 2004).

Discussion Questions:
1. What is the proper role for a procurement officer in relation to his or her company's major vendors? Justify your answer.
2. How might a procurement officer resist the temptations offered by a powerful vendor to steer business their way? What are the ethical implications of such a situation? What do you think Ms. Drunyun should have done in her role in U.S. Air Force procurement?

Select Sellers

Selecting sellers
The process of selecting a seller to supply the desired product or service.

The goal of **selecting sellers** is a contract with a vendor to supply the desired product or service. A contract is a legal relationship between parties, and it is subject to remedy in the court system. Most organizations have policies governing who can sign a procurement contract on behalf of the organization. Because contracts are legal documents, they are typically subject to lengthy internal reviews by an organization's legal representatives. To determine which bidder may win the procurement contract, the bids are all evaluated according to the criteria that have been established as part of the procurement process. Although the key output from selecting sellers is the contract, other outputs include a list of selected sellers (if there is more than one), a contract management plan, a statement of resource availability, updates to the procurement management plan, and requested changes to the project management plan. A contract management plan is exactly what it sounds like—an outline that guides the oversight of the contract during its lifetime. Resource availability refers to the quantity and availability of resources and when they will be needed. You are familiar with updates to the procurement management plan and requested changes from reading about outputs from other procurement management processes.

There are several inputs to selecting sellers, all of which have been discussed earlier: organizational process assets, the procurement management plan, evaluation criteria, the procurement document package, proposals, qualified sellers list, and the project management plan. The tools and techniques used to select sellers are designed to discriminate among the bids, so that a winner can be chosen. These tools and techniques include a weighting system, independent estimates, a screening system, contract negotiations, seller rating systems, and expert judgment. These are discussed in more detail in the following sections.

Weighting System

A **weighting system** is a method to quantitatively compare the proposals that are received from prospective vendors. Each of the proposals is seen as an alternative solution, and each of the evaluation criteria are converted to attributes. A value is assigned to each attribute of each alternative. The attributes themselves are then weighted to reflect their relative importance. Attribute values are then multiplied by the weights to generate scores, and the scores are totaled across attributes to give sum totals for each alternative. The alternative with the highest score should then be the best one, and as such, it should be the best alternative in the set. The vendor with the best alternative should be chosen for the contract.

An example of how this technique works in included in Table 10.5. On the left, we have listed six different evaluation criteria. These criteria were all derived from the evaluation criteria section above, and for simplicity, we have kept them at a fairly high level. The criteria are weighted in terms of what is most important to the project team. In this case, price is considered the most important criterion, with 40 percent of the total weight. Solution functionality and the vendor's financial resources carry the most weight after price, with 15 percent each. The remaining three criteria, vendor technical ability, vendor experience, and whether the vendor team has a PMI certified project manager, all carry 10 percent of the total weight. Notice that all of the weights add up to 100. Weights are arrived at in discussions among the project team and others who

Table 10.5 Weighted Evaluation of Three Proposals

		Company Alpha		Company Beta		Company Gamma	
	Weight	Rating	Score	Rating	Score	Rating	Score
Price	40	3	120	3	120	2	80
Vendor technical ability	10	4	40	4	40	4	40
Solution functionality	15	4	60	3	45	2	30
Vendor experience	10	3	30	3	30	4	40
Vendor financial resources	15	4	60	3	45	4	60
PMI certified project manager	10	5	50	1	10	1	10
TOTAL	100		360		290		260

possess key knowledge or have a stake in the effort. Weights tend to be fairly subjective and, for that reason, should be determined through a process of open discussion to reveal underlying assumptions, followed by an attempt to reach consensus.

In this example, we have received three proposals in response to our RFP. Each one is listed across the top of Table 10.5. We have simply named the potential suppliers Company Alpha, Company Beta, and Company Gamma. Under each company name, there are two columns. The first is for the ratings given to each evaluation criterion for that proposal. The second is for the score for each criterion for that proposal. Scores are computed by multiplying the weight for a criterion by the proposal's rating for that criterion. The ratings are on a scale of 1 to 5. A rating of 1 indicates that the proposal does not meet the evaluation criterion very well. A rating of 5 indicates that the proposal meets or exceeds the criterion. Ratings are even more subjective than weights and should also be determined through ample open discussion among the members of the evaluation team. The final step is to add the weighted scores for each proposal. We have included totals for the weights and for each proposal. Note that the proposal from Company Alpha is the best because it scored a total of 360 points. The proposal from Company Beta is second best with 290 points, and the proposal from Company Gamma, with 260 points, is last. The proposal from Company Alpha should win.

Independent Estimates

Sometimes the organization issuing the RFP may prepare its own **independent estimates** of price for whatever is being procured. These estimates act as a check against the prices offered in the proposals. Major differences in these estimates and the prices in a proposal indicate the vendor did not adequately understand what was being asked for or did not respond fully. Sometimes these independent estimates are called should-cost estimates.

Screening System

A different way to select a winning proposal is to use a **screening system.** Under a screening system, the project team establishes minimum values for one or more of the performance criteria. Any proposal that does not meet the minimum values is eliminated. To see how this works, look again at Table 10.5. Let's assume that the project team has decided that any proposal that did not score at least a 3 on price would be eliminated. Because 1 is the worst rating for a criterion, a 1 on price would mean that the proposal's price was very high and out of range. A rating of 5 would mean that the proposal's price would be considered good. A 3 would be in the middle—neither too high nor too low—and, therefore, a 3 would be a reasonable minimum. Looking at Table 10.5, the proposal from Company Gamma has been given a rating of 2 on price, so it would be eliminated from further consideration. That still leaves the proposals from Companies Alpha and Beta. Both have ratings of 3 on price. We would then move to another criterion to distinguish between the two remaining proposals. Let's choose whether or not the proposal features a PMI certified project manager. The proposal from Company Alpha has a rating of 5 on this criterion, meaning it does have a PMI certified project manager. The proposal from Company Beta has a rating of 1, meaning the proposal does not mention a PMI certified project manager. The proposal from Company Beta would be eliminated, and in this case, the proposal from Company Alpha would once again be chosen as the winner.

Contract Negotiation

In **contract negotiation,** representatives from the buyer and the vendor chosen for the contract engage in discussions to clarify and reach agreement on the structure and the requirements of the contract prior to its being signed. All agreements reached to date should be reflected in the contract. Topics to be covered include responsibilities, authority, applicable terms and law, contracting financing, and price. Typically, the buying organization will have personnel who are in charge of negotiating contracts. If this is the case, it is very important that the people in charge of contracts have access to any documents that were generated during the proposal process, as well as to the individuals who were involved. Personnel from purchasing also may play a role in contract negotiations.

Seller Rating Systems

Seller rating system
A system used to select vendors based on factors such as past performance, quality ratings, delivery performance, and contractual compliance.

Seller rating systems have been developed by some companies as an additional way to select vendors. These systems use information about vendors, such as their past performance, quality ratings, delivery performance, and contractual compliance. Companies may have such information on vendors because they have dealt with them before and collected this information as part of the contract administration process.

Expert Judgment

As you read earlier, expert judgment can be called upon to develop the criteria used to evaluate proposals, and it can also be used to evaluate proposals directly. Proposals can be circulated to domain experts from universities or the government or other organizations, and these experts can provide their own evaluations and rankings of the proposals, independent of the procuring organization. The expertise can also come from within the organization but from outside the project team and can include legal, financial, accounting, manufacturing, engineering, and other experts.

Contract Administration

Contract administration
The process of comparing what was contracted for with what is being done or has been done to ensure that both parties perform according to the contract.

The contract resulting from selecting sellers is the most obvious input into the contract administration process. Because **contract administration** involves comparing what was contracted for with what has been done, other key inputs are the contract management plan, the list of selected sellers (if there is more than one), performance reports, and work performance information. However, remember that projects and the work they involve are rarely static. Instead, approved change requests, asked for by the project organization, are also inputs to contract administration. Change requests may include changes to the terms of the contract or to descriptions of the work to be performed.

The tools and techniques used in contract administration are contract change control, buyer-conducted performance reviews, inspections and audits, performance reporting, a payment system, claims administration, records management systems, and information technology. Contract change control is a very important process and is covered in more detail in Chapter 12. Essentially, a contract change control system embodies the process, agreed on by all parties to the contract, through which the contract can be modified. Change requests, tracking mechanisms, processes for resolving disputes, and a process for approving changes are all key parts of the change control process. **Buyer-conducted performance reviews** are structured reviews of the vendor's progress in fulfilling the terms of the contract. They focus on how well the vendor has been able to adhere to the project's standards for quality and to the project's budget and schedule. Inspections and audits are conducted by the procuring organization, with the assistance of the vendor, to determine if there are any weaknesses in the vendor's work processes or deliverables. Performance reporting is a process through which the vendor or supplier reports to the procuring

Buyer-conducted performance reviews
Structured reviews of the vendor's progress in fulfilling the terms of the contract.

Payment system
A system set up by the buying organization to pay the vendor for work performed.

Claims administration
The management of claims or disputes related to whether required work was done or what the submitted work is worth.

Record management system
An automated record-keeping system that helps the project manager to keep track of contract documentation and results.

organization about the progress it is making in fulfilling its contractual obligations. A **payment system** is set up for the buying organization to pay the vendor for work performed, and payments are usually handled by the buyer's accounts payable system. **Claims administration** refers to the process through which claims, or disputes, are managed. Claims can come from the buyer or the vendor and contest whether required work was done or what the submitted work is worth. The contract establishes the way in which claims are documented and managed. A **record management system** is simply an automated record-keeping system and the processes governing its creation and operation; its purpose is to help the project manager keep track of contract documentation and results. Information technology supports the record management system and many other aspects of contract administration, including the payment system, claims administration, and so on.

The primary output of contract administration is contract documentation. Other outputs include organizational process asset updates and recommended corrective actions. Updates to organization process assets include correspondence between the buyer and the vendor, payment schedules and requests, and seller performance evaluation documentation. This documentation is the result of buyer-conducted performance reviews, vendor performance reporting, and inspections and audits. Corrective actions consist of anything needed to bring the vendor into compliance with the contract. The remaining outputs are familiar to you by now: requested changes and project management updates.

Contract Closure

Contract closure
The process of verifying that all products and services contracted are acceptable.

Procurement audit
A structured review of the procurement process from the plan purchases and acquisition process through the contract administration process.

Contract closure supports the process of closing the project (see Chapter 4) and involves verification that all products and services contracted for are acceptable. Its inputs are the procurement management plan, the contract management plan, contract documentation of work performed, and the contract closure procedure. The techniques used for contract closure are the **procurement audit**—a structured review of the procurement process beginning with the process of planning purchases and acquisitions process and continuing through the contract administration process—and the records management system. Outputs from contract closure are the closed contract, by which the buyer provides notice to the vendor that the contract has been completed, and updates to organizational process assets. These updates include the contract file, which is a complete set of indexed contract records, deliverable acceptance, and lessons learned documentation. Deliverable acceptance is a formal written notice from the buyer that the deliverables have been accepted or rejected. Lessons learned documentation results from an analysis of the contract and the vendor used. It can provide very useful information for future procurement planning.

PROJECT PROCUREMENT AND THE PMBOK

As Figure 10.6 demonstrates, you have covered almost all of the Project Management Body of Knowledge after reading this chapter. We have only two chapters left in the book, Chapters 11 and 12. The primary topic of Chapter 10 is project procurement, and as you can see from Figure 10.6, this material corresponds to Chapter 12 in the PMBOK, which covers Project Procurement Management. All six areas of the PMBOK that relate to procurement were covered in Chapter 10.

Figure 10.6   Chapter 10 and PMBOK coverage

Textbook Chapters →	1	2	3	4	5	6	7	8	9	10	11	12
PMBOK Knowledge Area												
1 Introduction to Project Management												
1.1 What Is a Project?	●											
1.2 What Is Project Management?	●											
1.3 Areas of Expertise		●										
1.4 Project Management Context	●											
2 Project Life Cycle and Organization												
2.1 The Project Life Cycle	●	●										
2.2 Project Stakeholders	●	●										
2.3 Organizational Influences		●	●	●			●					
3 Project Management Processes for a Project												
3.1 Project Management Processes	●	●										
3.2 PM Process Groups	●	●										
3.3 Process Interactions		●										
3.4 Project Management Process Mapping		●										
4 Project Integration Management												
4.1 Develop Project Charter					●							
4.2 Develop Preliminary Project Scope Statement					●	●						
4.3 Develop Project Management Plan					●							
4.4 Direct and Manage Project Execution										○		
4.5 Monitor and Control Project Work												○
4.6 Integrated Change Control												○
4.7 Close Project												○
5 Project Scope Management												
5.1 Scope Planning					●							
5.2 Scope Definition					●							
5.3 Create WBS					●	●						
5.4 Scope Verification					●							
5.5 Scope Control					●							○
6 Project Time Management												
6.1 Activity Definition						●						
6.2 Activity Sequencing						●						
6.3 Activity Resource Estimating							●					
6.4 Activity Duration Estimating							●					
6.5 Schedule Development							●					
6.6 Schedule Control							●					○

(continued)

Figure 10.6 (continued)

	Textbook Chapters →	1	2	3	4	5	6	7	8	9	10	11	12
	PMBOK Knowledge Area												
7	**Project Cost Management**												
7.1	Cost Estimating							●					
7.2	Cost Budgeting							●					
7.3	Cost Control							●					○
8	**Project Quality Management**												
8.1	Quality Planning								●				
8.2	Perform Quality Assurance								●				
8.3	Perform Quality Control								●				○
9	**Project Human Resource Management**												
9.1	Human Resource Planning			●				●					
9.2	Acquire Project Team			●				●					
9.3	Develop Project Team			●				●					
9.4	Manage Project Team			●				●					
10	**Project Communications Management**												
10.1	Communications Planning				●						○		
10.2	Information Distribution				●						○		
10.3	Performance Reporting				●								○
10.4	Manage Stakeholders				●								○
11	**Project Risk Management**												
11.1	Risk Management Planning									●			
11.2	Risk Identification									●	○		
11.3	Qualitative Risk Analysis									●			
11.4	Quantitative Risk Analysis									●			
11.5	Risk Response Planning									●			
11.6	Risk Monitoring and Control									●			○
12	**Project Procurement Management**												
12.1	Plan Purchases and Acquisitions										✓		
12.2	Plan Contracting										✓		
12.3	Request Seller Responses										✓		
12.4	Select Sellers										✓		
12.5	Contract Administration										✓		
12.6	Contract Closure										✓		○

Key: ●-where material is covered in past chapters; ✓-current chapter coverage;
○-where material is covered in future chapters

Although the customer loyalty project at Petrie's Electronics had gone slowly at first, the past few weeks were fast-paced and busy, project manager Jim Woo thought to himself. The weeks it took to finish the request for proposals (RFP), to line up potential vendors to submit bids, and to receive the bids, all seemed to have zipped right by. Jim was on his way to meet with Ella Whinston, the company's COO, to discuss the remaining bids and the one he thought should win.

"Hi, Ella," Jim said, as he walked into her office and sat down at her desk.

"Hi, Jim," Ella said. "I'll be right with you." Ella finished replying to an e-mail message and then turned around and faced Jim. "I have been reviewing the three remaining bids. Even though I opposed it originally, I think your strategy of having a panel of IT and marketing professionals rate the bids and eliminate the inappropriate ones turned out to be a good one. I think we can succeed with any one of these proposals. Do you have a favorite?"

"Well, actually, I have already compared the remaining proposals, and I do have one that I think we should choose," Jim replied. "Just for review, here is a copy of the memo I sent you, with the requirements and constraints, and with the three competing systems summarized" (Table 10.6).

Table 10.6 Requirements, Constraints, and Alternatives for Petrie's Customer Loyalty Project

Requirements:

Effective customer incentives—System should be able to effectively store customer activity and convert to rewards and other incentives.

Easy for customers to use—Interface should be intuitive for customer use.

Proven performance—System as proposed should have been used successfully by other clients.

Easy to implement—Implementation should not require outside consultants or extraordinary skills on the part of our staff or require specialized hardware.

Scalable—System should be easily expandable as number of participating customers grows.

Vendor support—Vendor should have proven track record of reliable support and infrastructure in place to provide it.

Constraints:

Cost to buy—Licenses for one year should be under $500,000.

Cost to operate—Total operating costs should be no more than $1 million per year.

Time to implement—Duration of implementation should not exceed three months.

Staff to implement—Implementation should be successful with the staff we have and with the skills they already possess.

Alternatives:

Alternative A: Data warehousing-centered system designed and licensed by Standard Basic Systems Inc. (SBSI). The data warehousing tools at the heart of the system were designed and developed by SBSI and work with standard relational DBMS and relational/OO hybrid DBMS. The SBSI tools and approach have been used for many years and are well-known in the industry, but SBSI-certified staff are essential for implementation, operation, and maintenance. The license is relatively expensive. The customer loyalty application using the SBSI data warehousing tools is an established application, used by many retail businesses in other industries.

Alternative B: Customer relationship management-centered system designed and licensed by XRA Corporation. XRA is a pioneer in CRM systems, so its CRM is widely recognized as an industry leader. The system includes tools that support customer loyalty programs. The CRM system itself is large and complex, but pricing in this proposal is based only on modules used for the customer loyalty application.

(continued)

Alternative C: Proprietary system designed and licensed by Nova Innovation Group Inc. The system is relatively new and leading edge, so it has only been implemented in a few sites. The vendor is truly innovative but small and inexperienced. The customer interface, designed for a standard Web browser, is stunning in its design and is extremely easy for customers to use to check on their loyalty program status.

"Thanks," Ella said, "This keeps me from having to dig through all my stuff to find my copy. Did you also bring me a copy of your evaluation matrix?"

"Yes, here it is." (Table 10.7)

"So, your matrix favors the XRA CRM system," Ella noticed. "Looks like their proposal meets our requirements the best, but the Nova group's proposal does the best job with the constraints."

"Yes, but just barely. There is only a five point difference between XRA and Nova, so they are pretty comparable when it comes to constraints. But I think the XRA system has a pretty clear advantage in meeting our requirements."

"We've never worked with XRA, but they seem to be pretty highly rated in your matrix in terms of all of the requirements. You have them ranked better than the other two proposals for implementation, scalability, and vendor support. The 5 you gave them for proven performance is one of the few 5s you have in your whole matrix."

"They are one of the best companies in the industry to work with," Jim responded. "Their reputation is stellar."

"OK, then," Ella said. "Your numbers convince me. But I don't have the authority to approve this choice alone. Let me get started on the approval process. Meanwhile, I think you better set up a meeting with Legal to get started on a contract." Ella smiled.

"Will do," Jim said, and he sighed with relief.

Table 10.7 Evaluation Matrix for Customer Loyalty Proposals

CRITERIA	WEIGHT	ALT A		ALT B		ALT C	
		RATING	SCORE	RATING	SCORE	RATING	SCORE
REQUIREMENTS							
Effective customer incentives	15	5	75	4	60	4	60
Easy for customers to use	10	3	30	4	40	5	50
Proven performance	10	4	40	5	50	3	30
Easy to implement	5	3	15	4	20	3	15
Scalable	10	3	30	4	40	3	30
Vendor support	10	3	30	4	40	3	30
	60		220		250		215
CONSTRAINTS							
Cost to buy	15	3	45	4	60	5	75
Cost to operate	10	3	30	4	40	4	40
Time to implement	5	3	15	3	15	3	15
Staff to implement	10	3	30	4	40	3	30
	40		120		155		160
TOTAL	100		340		405		375

CHAPTER SUMMARY

Describe the various sources of systems and software components. Systems are hardly ever developed from scratch, in-house these days. Instead, systems, software, and software components are procured from various other organizations. These organizations include information technology services firms, packaged software producers, enterprise-wide solutions, providers of on-demand computing, and open-source software. Each different source of systems and software has its own advantages and disadvantages, and making the proper choice among them depends on knowing their strengths and weaknesses.

Understand the appeal of outsourcing. Global information technology outsourcing is projected to grow to a $100 billion per year business by 2007. More and more large business organizations have either outsourced large pieces of their IT infrastructure and systems management or are moving in that direction. Although outsourcing has its disadvantages, it appeals to companies that feel their IT operations are outside of their core competency and can best be managed by someone else.

Explain Project Procurement Management. Project Procurement Management is the part of a project that covers the acquisition of resources, whether products or services or both, from outside the project's home organization. Project Procurement Management, according to the PMBOK, has six steps: plan purchasing and acquisitions, plan contracting, request seller responses, select sellers, contract administration, and contract closure.

Describe how to plan purchases and acquisitions. Planning purchases and acquisitions is the process of determining which project needs can best be met by obtaining services or products from outside the project organization. One of the key processes at the heart of planning purchases and acquisitions is the make-or-buy decision. A major output of the process is a statement of work, a document that describes the product or service being sought.

Explain how to plan contracting. Once the decision has been made to procure externally, the process of planning contracting can begin. The main task of planning contracting is to create a document that describes what is to be procured and asks for offers from vendors who are interested in providing it. Such a document has many names but is referred to here primarily as a request for proposal, or RFP. Another important output of planning contracting is the set of evaluation criteria used to judge the proposals that vendors write in response to the RFP.

Understand how to request seller responses. The main task of requesting seller responses is obtaining bids that respond to the RFP. An important part of this process is an attempt to find the potential vendors who are the best equipped to respond to the RFP. The primary output from requesting seller responses is a set of vendor proposals.

Describe how to select sellers. Once responses or bids are in hand, the process of selecting sellers begins. Here the bids are compared to each other and are judged by the selection criteria that the project organization has established. One vendor is chosen, and a contract is prepared. One way to help determine the best proposal is use of a weighted system; another way is use of a screening system.

Explain contract administration. Contract administration is the process through which the project organization works with the vendor for the duration of the contract.

Understand contract closure. Once the terms of the contract have been satisfactorily met, contract closure begins. Both sides of the agreement accept the work performed, and the contract is completed.

KEY TERMS REVIEW

- Best-of-breed strategy
- Buyer-conducted performance reviews
- Claims administration
- Contract closure
- Contract administration
- Contract negotiation
- Cost-reimbursable contract
- Enterprise resource planning (ERP) systems
- Evaluation criteria
- External acquisition
- Fixed-price contract
- Independent estimates
- IT Service firms
- Make-or-buy analysis
- On-demand computing
- Open-source software

- Outsourcing
- Packaged software producers
- Payment system
- Plan contracting
- Planning purchases and acquisitions
- Procurement audit

- Procurement documents
- Procurement management plan
- Record management system
- Request for proposal (RFP)
- Requesting seller responses
- Screening system
- Selecting sellers

- Seller rating system
- Statement of work (SOW)
- Time-and-material contract
- Turnkey systems
- Utility computing
- Weighting system

Match each of the key terms with the definition that best fits it.

1. _____ The practice of turning over responsibility for some or all of an organization's information systems applications and operations to an outside firm.

2. _____ A system that integrates individual traditional business functions into a series of modules so that a single transaction occurs seamlessly within a single information system rather than over several separate systems.

3. _____ A document provided to vendors to ask them to propose a solution to a specific problem related to your project.

4. _____ Document prepared for potential vendors that describes the service or product being sought.

5. _____ Firms that help companies develop custom information systems for internal use, or develop, host, and run applications for customers.

6. _____ The procurement of products and/or services from an outside vendor.

7. _____ Companies in the business of developing and selling off-the-shelf software.

8. _____ Off-the-shelf software that cannot be modified to meet the specific, individual needs of an organization.

9. _____ A strategy of using different software products from different sources (including in house development) to capitalize on the strengths of different products.

10. _____ Use of computing resources on the basis of users' needs, often on a pay-per-use basis. Also called utility computing.

11. _____ Use of computing resources on the basis of users' needs, often on a pay-per-use basis. Also called on-demand computing.

12. _____ Systems software, applications, and programming languages of which the source code is freely available for use and/or modification.

13. _____ The process of determining which project needs can best be met by going outside the project organization to obtain them.

14. _____ A technique to determine whether a product or service should be produced inhouse, or procured from an outside vendor.

15. _____ A type of contract specifying a fixed price for a product/service.

16. _____ A type of contract that involves payment for the actual cost of the product plus a fee that represents the vendor's profits.

17. _____ A type of contract where vendors provide an hourly rate and estimate the amount of time and materials required.

18. _____ A plan that addresses such issues as who will prepare the evaluation criteria, how multiple vendors will be managed, where standardized procurement documents can be obtained, and how procurement will be coordinated with other project tasks.

19. _____ The process of creating documents used to solicit proposals from vendors.

20. _____ Documents used to solicit proposals from vendors.

21. _____ Criteria used to rate proposals that are received in response to a request for proposals.

22. _____ The process of obtaining responses to the procurement documents produced during plan contracting.

23. _____ The process of selecting a seller to supply the desired product or service.

24. _____ A method used to quantitatively compare proposals that are received from potential vendors.

25. _____ Estimates prepared independently of proposals which act as a check against the prices offered in proposals.

26. _____ A system using minimum values for one or more performance criteria to eliminate proposals that do not meet the minimum values.

27. _____ Discussions between the buyer and seller to clarify and reach agreement on the structure and the requirements of contract.

28. _____ A system used to select vendors based on factors such as past performance, quality ratings, delivery performance, and contractual compliance.

29. _____ The process of comparing what was contracted for with what is being done or has been done to ensure that both parties perform according to the contract.

30. _____ Structured reviews of the vendor's progress in fulfilling the terms of the contract.

31. _____ A system set up by the buying organization to pay the vendor for work performed.

32. _____ The management of claims or disputes related to whether required work was done or what the submitted work is worth.

33. _____ An automated record-keeping system that helps the project manager to keep track of contract documentation and results.

34. _____ The process of verifying that all products and services contracted are acceptable.

35. _____ A structured review of the procurement process from the plan purchases and acquisition process through the contract administration process.

REVIEW QUESTIONS

1. What is outsourcing?
2. Describe the types of software and systems that IT services firms produce.
3. What is an ERP system?
4. What is on-demand, or utility, computing?
5. What is open-source software and what are its benefits?
6. Explain the process of planning purchases and acquisitions, including its inputs, processes, and outputs.
7. What is a statement of work? Why is it important to procurement?
8. Explain how to plan contracting, including its inputs, processes, and outputs.
9. What is an RFP? What is it good for?
10. What are the basic contents recommended for any RFP?
11. Explain the process of requesting seller responses, including its inputs, processes, and outputs.
12. Explain the process of selecting sellers, including its inputs, processes, and outputs.
13. Explain how a weighting system is used for comparing proposals from an RFP.
14. Explain how a screening system is used for comparing proposals from an RFP.
15. Explain contract administration, including its inputs, processes, and outputs.
16. Why is a contract a special document? How is it treated differently from other documents?
17. Explain contract closure, including its inputs, processes, and outputs.

1. Compare and contrast the various organizations that supply systems and systems components. What are their relative strengths and weaknesses? For each source, describe a situation where that particular source would be the best choice.

2. Write a short essay on outsourcing comparing its benefits to its disadvantages. When would you never want to use outsourcing? When would you always want to use it?

3. Draw a new variation of Figure 10.4 that shows how the different project management processes for procurement are related to each other. Be creative.

4. Create a statement for work for a job that you know well.

5. Locate an RFP from someone you know (e.g., a parent, an employer, a professor). Analyze it carefully, comparing its structure and content to the guidelines provided in the chapter, and write a two-page essay about what you find.

6. Explain how project procurement fits within the larger picture of project management. When would you ever be involved in a project that did not involve procurement of products and services from outside your organization?

7. Bob's project team is working on developing a Web store. As part of their project, the team has decided it makes little sense to develop their own shopping cart system, given that so many complete shopping cart systems are available on the market. Bob's team needs to write an RFP for a shopping cart system. Do some research on shopping cart systems for Web stores, and using the outline in this chapter for the contents of an RFP, write a short version of the RFP Bob's group would need.

8. Bob's team, described in Exercise 7, has issued its RFP and has received three responses. The team has developed the following evaluation criteria. Price is the most important criterion; the second most important is the extent to which the shopping cart system can be modified; the third most important is the number of features available in the system; fourth is the number of years the vendor has been in business; and fifth is the number of employees the vendor has. For price, the lowest price is best. For modification, more is better, and the same is true of the number of features. The longer the vendor has been in business, and the more people the vendor employs, the better.

   The first proposal, from Three Guys Who Are Programmers Inc., had a licensing cost of $1,500 per year with unlimited clients and charged $400 per year for technical assistance. Bob's team judged the system from Three Guys to be moderately modifiable, but it had very few features. Three Guys has been in business for two years and currently employs 12 people.

   The second proposal, from Global Domination Software Inc. (GDSI) cost $5,000 per year for a license with unlimited clients, and technical assistance was offered for free as long as there were fewer than 12 requests for assistance. After that, each request cost $100. Bob's team found the software to be very limited in terms of the number of modifications that could be made, but it had an incredibly high number of features. GDSI has been in business for 25 years and has 20,000 employees worldwide.

   The last proposal was from E-Commerce Associates Inc. (ECA). A one-year license for unlimited clients with free technical assistance cost $3,000. The software was moderately modifiable and had an average number of e-commerce features. ECA has been in business for 10 years and currently has 50 employees.

   Which proposal should Bob's team choose? Which proposal should win? Create a weighting system like the one described in this chapter (use a spreadsheet if you want), and demonstrate which proposal should be chosen.

9. Using the information supplied in Exercise 8, develop a screening system that will help you choose among the alternative proposals. First, use price as your filter. Next, try aspects of the software, such as the number of features. Which proposal wins under these schemes? Is it the same as the proposal that won in Exercise 8? If you had a different winner, explain why.

CHAPTER CASE

Sedona Management Group and Managing Project Procurement

Many companies do not have the required personnel or expertise to develop the systems that they need. Consequently, when these companies need new systems, they elect to outsource such projects to other companies that specialize in systems development. This process is known as procurement and involves the acquisition of goods or services from an outside source. The advantages associated with outsourcing include the availability of knowledge and expertise that might not be available internally, an increase in the revenue potential of the acquiring organization, and a reduction of time to market the final product.

The Seattle Seahawks' core competency is running a professional sports organization, not Web site development. When they realized they needed a Web site for the reasons mentioned in previous chapter cases, they decided to outsource the project. To make sure that it was completed successfully, the Seahawks went through several of the processes related to Project Procurement Management, including the processes to plan purchases and acquisitions, plan contracting, request seller responses, and select sellers and of contract administration. The main purpose of Project Procurement Management is to manage the acquisition of resources from an outside source.

One of the first steps the Seattle Seahawks followed in managing procurement was to plan purchases and acquisitions. During this process, the Seahawks focused on identifying project needs and which of those needs would be best met by using services outside the organization. The Seattle Seahawks wanted a reliable and secure Web site that conveyed accurate information and was easy to access. An initial statement of work (SOW) was developed, which allowed prospective outsourcing partners to determine whether they were capable of providing the service or the product required as well as to determine an appropriate price for the project.

In the next stage of procurement management, the focus is on identifying the evaluation criteria that will be used to determine which vendor will be awarded the contract. Writing a request for proposal (RFP) is typically a part of the solicitation planning phase. The RFP is a document that is used to solicit proposals from prospective sellers. The RFP issued by the Seattle

Seahawks contained, among other features, a statement of purpose of the RFP, background information on the company, the statement of work, and schedule constraints. Once an RFP is available, it is issued to the prospective sellers.

During the process to request seller responses, proposals or bids are obtained from the prospective sellers. After receiving these proposals, the Seattle Seahawks went through the process of selecting sellers, where they evaluated the bidders' proposals to choose the best one. The evaluation criteria identified in the process of planning contracting are used to make this choice. During this stage of procurement management, the Seattle Seahawks chose Sedona Management Group (SMG) to work on their Web site development project. The Seahawks' key criteria were project quality and the ability of the outsourcing partner to deliver its products on time and on budget. On both dimensions, SMG excelled.

Once the Sedona team was informed that they would be working on the Web site development project, Mike Flood from the Seattle Seahawks met with the project team several times to further communicate the project needs. After the project requirements were clearly determined, the next step was to work on the contract. SMG uses a fixed price contract, which involves a fixed total price for a well-defined product or service. In such a contract, the Seattle Seahawks were exposed to a low level of risk because the risk associated with cost overruns was assumed by the developer—in this case SMG. However, given SMG's well delineated project management processes, the Sedona team was confident that they could deliver the project on time and within budget.

The Seahawks-SMG contract consisted of several sections. The first section laid out the assumptions the team used to develop the contract. These assumptions included information about the technology to be used to develop the system and which server would be used to host the system, as well as the contact information of the individual from SMG who would be available for immediate information during business hours throughout the development process. The second section included the scope of work, which included a detailed description of all the activities the Sedona team would perform to complete the project. In the next section, the terms of the contract were explained regarding project cost and the delivery date. In a section entitled Other Considerations, SMG explained that the Seattle Seahawks would own the final code, the database, and the Web site once the project was completed. The Sedona team began working on the project the next business day after both parties agreed to the clauses of the contract.

CHAPTER 10 PROJECT ASSIGNMENT

An important part of an entertainment Web site is the availability of a shopping cart for fans to buy the products being promoted by the entertainer. The success of your Web site requires this feature, but you realize that it is beyond your and your team members' expertise. So you decide to outsource this feature to an outside source. In this exercise, you will work on the documents you require for the outsourcing process.

1. Conduct a make-or-buy analysis. This analysis involves identifying the pros and cons of developing this feature yourself or outsourcing.
2. Develop a statement of work (SOW) for the shopping cart development project. The SOW is a document prepared for the vendors that describes thoroughly the product being sought. The SOW should contain:

- An introduction and overview section, which includes some background information about your project, the scope of work, and the objectives of the project being outsourced
- A requirements section for the shopping cart feature
- The list of deliverables
- A list of milestones
- Any other considerations

3. Develop a request for proposal (RFP) for this outsourcing project. The RFP is a document that will be submitted to potential vendors, asking them to propose a solution to the shopping cart problem. The RFP should contain:
- A project overview
- An administrative section, which contains contact information
- Technical requirements
- Management requirements
- Suppliers' section
- Any appendices
4. Determine the evaluation criteria you and your team will use to rate the received proposals.
5. Compare and contrast the different types of contracts that are available. Indicate which one of these you will use for this outsourcing project. Provide justification for your answer.

REFERENCES

Banker, R. D., Davis, G. B., and Slaughter, S. A. (1998). "Software Development Practices, Software Complexity, and Software Maintenance Performance: A Field Study." *Management Science* 44(4), 433–450.

Desmond, J. P. (2005). "The 2005 Software 500 Points to a Bright Future." *SoftwareMag.com*, Retrieved March 29, 2006, from: www.softwaremag.com/L.cfm?Doc= 2005-09/2005-09editorial.

Dignan, L. (2002). "IT's Exercise in Utilities." CNET News.com. Retrieved January 15, 2004, from: zdnet. com.com/2100-1106-962663.html?tag=nl.

Gilbert, A. (2003). "Report: Big Blue Still Biggest in IT Outsourcing." CNET News.com. Retrieved January 15, 2004, from: zdnet.com.com/2100-1104_2-5085055.html.

Hamm, S. (2005). "Linux Inc." *BusinessWeek*, January 31.

Hines, M. (2003). "IBM Spirits Diageo Away from HP." CNET News.com. Retrieved January 15, 2004, from: zdnet.com.com/2100-1103-5067132.html?tag=nl.

Ketler, K., and Willems, J. R. (1999). "A Study of the Outsourcing Decision: Preliminary Results." *Proceedings of SIGCPR '99*, New Orleans, LA, 182–189.

King, J. (2003). "IT's Global Itinerary: Offshore Outsourcing Is Inevitable." Retrieved October 12, 2006, from: www.computerworld.com/managementtopics/ outsourcing/story/0,10801,84861,00.html.

King, J., and Cole-Gomolski, B. (1999). "IT Doing Less Development, More Installation, Outsourcing." *ComputerWorld*, January 25, 4+.

Marshall, B. (2004). "Support Contracts Can Encourage Lousy Products." *ComputerWorld*, June 1. Retrieved November 12, 2004, from: www.computerworld.com/ managementtopics/management/story/0,10801,93568, 00.html.

Pacztor, A. (2004). "Air Force Ex-Official's Dealings Put Pentagon Under Spotlight." *Wall Street Journal*, October 4, 2004, A2.

Porter-Roth, B. (2002). *Request for Proposal: A Guide to Effective RFP Development.* Boston: Addison-Wesley.

Project Management Institute. (2000). *A Guide to the Project Management Body of Knowledge.* Newton Square, PA: PMI.

Project Management Institute. (2004). *A Guide to the Project Management Body of Knowledge.* 3rd ed. Newton Square, PA: PMI.

Pruitt, S. (2004). "When Outsourcing, Don't Forget Security, Experts Say." *ComputerWorld.* Retrieved December 20, 2004, from: www.computerworld.com/management-topics/outsourcing/story/0,10801,96074,00.html.

Rintoul, C. (2004). "Ten Tips for Assuring Offshore Project Success." *ComputerWorld.* Retrieved October 4, 2006, from: www.computerworld.com/management-topics/outsourcing/story/0,10801,89742,00.html.

Woodie, A. (2005). "ERP Market Grew Solidly in 2004, AMR Research Says." *The Windows Observer* 2(25). Retrieved October 25, 2005, from: www.itjungle.com/two/twp062205-story04.html.

Chapter

Managing Project Execution

Opening Case: REJ

In 1938, a group of mountain climbers formed a consumer cooperative to supply themselves with high-quality ice axes and climbing gear. This cooperative—Recreational Equipment Inc. (REI)—has grown into a national retail supplier of specialty outdoor products in the United States (Figure 11.1). The REI Gear and Apparel Division—the product research and development organization within REI—creates products that bear the REI brand and bicycles in the Novara line. In this division, employees work tirelessly on more than 600 projects each year. Even with this tremendous workload, the division consistently brings high-quality products to market.

In the past, project managers in this division used effective, but disparate, tools to perform a few project management tasks mainly related to planning. They loosely managed project documents on personal hard drives and servers, lacked the tools to manage entire product portfolios, and had limited ways of prioritizing resources division-wide and across product seasons.

The division used traditional methods of collaboration: face-to-face meetings, conference calls, faxes, and e-mail. Team members didn't always collaborate and manage projects from the same central source, so they often worked on overlapping tasks, didn't always use best practices, and sometimes wasted precious time.

The Gear and Apparel Division recognized that to increase the efficiency of its processes and employees it needed to take a more integrated, analytical approach to process and project management. It needed a single business solution it could use to visualize, diagram, and optimize product development processes. It also needed to generate project plans from process diagrams that it could use to manage and execute projects. Then it needed to analyze the plans and measure how effective they would be. Finally, the division needed to integrate and align all process and project management tools, tasks, documents, and data so it could more efficiently manage projects across the division.

Apprentice Systems Inc.—a Microsoft Office Visio Solution Provider—and PM Solutions—a Microsoft Office Enterprise Project Management (EPM) Partner—worked with REI's Gear and Apparel Division to remodel and improve their process and project management. With Apprentice Process Modeler, a solution developed using Microsoft Office Visio 2003 drawing and diagramming software, REI domain process experts can visually map as-is business processes, experiment with what-if scenarios, optimize the processes, and then generate project plans from them. With the Microsoft Office Enterprise Project Management (EPM) Solution—Microsoft Office Project Server 2003, Microsoft Office Project Professional 2003, and Microsoft Project Web Access—and the project configuration assistance of PM Solutions, REI project managers can manage project portfolios and division resources online. With Microsoft Windows SharePoint Services and the Microsoft Office Outlook messaging and collaboration client, REI team members can communicate, collaborate, and manage documents.

Using the new approach, members of the Gear and Apparel Division report increased productivity, efficiency, and consistency when compared with the old ad hoc approach. Improved collaboration has allowed the staff to become more aware of quality assurance issues and proper process execution. Most importantly, the new approach allows REI to get their same high-quality products to market faster (Source: Microsoft Office System Customer Solution Case Study, "REI Improves Its Product Development Processes by Integrating Process and Project Management Tasks." Copyright 2003, Microsoft Corp. Used with permission).

LEARNING OBJECTIVES

After reading this chapter, you will be able to:

➤ Describe the seven project management processes that are part of project execution.
➤ Discuss the activities project managers engage in during project execution.
➤ Explain some of the key problems in IT projects that occur during project execution.
➤ Describe the importance of communication to project execution.

Figure 11.1
Outdoor products
available at REI

Figure 11.2 Information systems project management focusing
on managing project execution

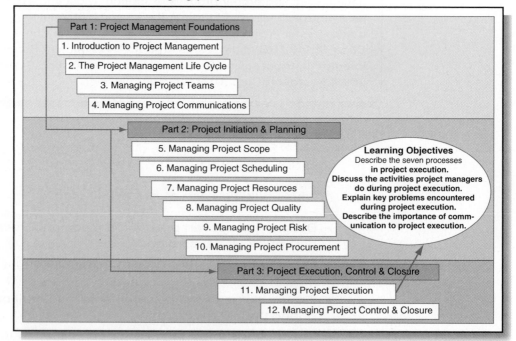

INTRODUCTION

Project execution
The process of carrying out the project plan to accomplish the required work.

In Chapter 2, you read about the five different major processes in project management: initiating, planning, executing, monitoring and controlling, and closing. Planning is easily the most extensive and involved process in project management. In Chapters 5 through 10, we discussed many different aspects of project planning, from planning for scope, schedule, human resources, quality, risk, and procurement. Once planning is completed, it is time to carry out the plan. **Project execution** is where the project plan is carried out; it is where the product of the project is created. For information technology (IT) projects, execution is where the system is developed and released.

In Chapter 1, we discussed the large number of IT projects that fail because they are either late, over budget, or do not meet specifications. Such project failures waste thousands of work hours and millions of dollars each year. We also discussed the causes of project failure, including failed communication within the project, poor planning, poor quality control, poor project management, lack of attention to human and organizational factors, and so on. Some of these causes of project failure, most notably failed communication, poor management, and lack of attention to detail, occur as part of the project execution process. Learning about project execution involves learning how to avoid these problems and thus be better able to ensure a successful project outcome.

In PMI's Project Management Body of Knowledge (PMBOK), project execution is part of Project Integration Management. Project Integration Management comprises seven major processes: 1) develop project charter, 2) develop preliminary project scope statement, 3) develop project management plan, 4) direct and manage project execution, 5) monitor and control project work, 6) integrated change control, and 7) close project. The first three processes, all of which deal with planning, were featured in Chapter 5, while the last three processes are the focus of Chapter 12. This chapter is exclusively about the fourth process in Project Integration Management, project execution.

The chapter is organized as follows. The next section introduces the different project management processes that make up project execution in the PMBOK. The inputs, tools and techniques, and outputs of project execution are all discussed. The section after that deals with key duties for project managers during execution, namely monitoring progress and managing change. There we will discuss the various activities project managers engage in during execution, such as the kickoff meeting, as well as the problems that are common to the execution of IT projects. In the next section, we discuss an area that is central to successful project execution: managing communication and documentation. The last section in the chapter focuses on project execution and the PMBOK. Figure 11.2 illustrates these chapter learning objectives.

PROJECT PLAN EXECUTION

According to the PMBOK, seven project management processes are part of project execution. Figure 2.21 lists all seven, and Figure 11.3 shows how the processes are related to each other. The seven processes are: 1) direct and manage project execution, 2) perform quality assurance, 3) acquire project team, 4) develop project

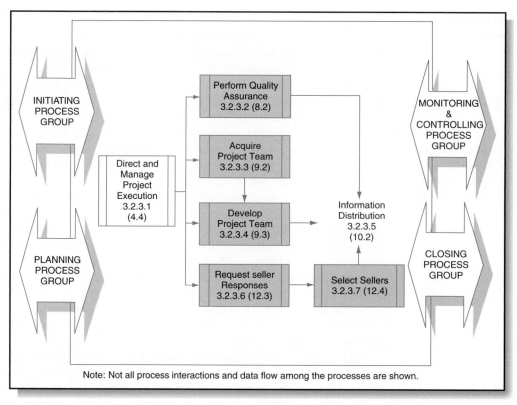

Figure 11.3 Relationships among the PMBOK executing processes
Source: PMBOK third edition, used with permission.

team, 5) information distribution, 6) request seller responses, and 7) select sellers. Directing and managing project execution involves managing the technical and organizational processes and interfaces that are necessary for completing the project work identified in the project management plan. Completing the work envisioned in the plan results in producing the deliverables defined there. The next process, performing quality assurance, is part of the Project Quality Management knowledge area discussed in Chapter 8. Performing quality assurance, you will recall, involves evaluating project progress on a regular basis in order to determine if the project will satisfy established quality standards. The next two processes, acquiring the project team and developing the project team, are part of the Human Resources Management knowledge area of the PMBOK and were discussed in Chapters 3 and 7. Acquiring a team involves getting the people needed to complete the project, whereas team development involves improving project performance through improving individual and group competencies and interactions. Information distribution is part of the Project Communications Management knowledge area and was introduced in Chapter 4. Information distribution means making needed information available to project stakeholders in a timely manner. The final two processes, requesting seller responses and selecting sellers, are both part of project procurement and were discussed in Chapter 10. Remember that requesting seller responses involves obtaining bids and proposals for performing project plan activities. Selecting sellers involves choosing from among the proposals that have been received.

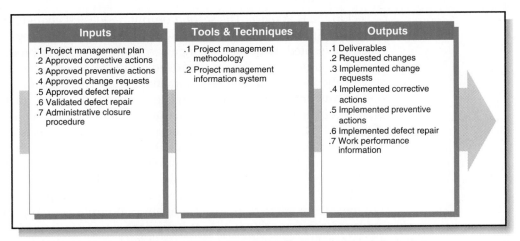

Inputs	Tools & Techniques	Outputs
.1 Project management plan .2 Approved corrective actions .3 Approved preventive actions .4 Approved change requests .5 Approved defect repair .6 Validated defect repair .7 Administrative closure procedure	.1 Project management methodology .2 Project management information system	.1 Deliverables .2 Requested changes .3 Implemented change requests .4 Implemented corrective actions .5 Implemented preventive actions .6 Implemented defect repair .7 Work performance information

Figure 11.4 PMBOK required inputs, tools and techniques used, and resulting outputs of project plan execution

Source: PMBOK third edition, used with permission.

Project plan execution, like the other key knowledge areas in the PMBOK, requires inputs, tools, and techniques to get the job done, and it produces outputs (Figure 11.4). Execution has seven main inputs: 1) the project management plan, 2) approved corrective actions, 3) approved preventive actions, 4) approved change requests, 5) approved defect repair, 6) validated defect repair, and 7) the administrative closure procedure. The most obvious input is the project management plan itself. Approved corrective actions are anything that can be done to bring project performance back in line with the plan. For example, corrective action will need to be taken when the project manager realizes that activities on the critical path will not be completed on time. Preventive actions are any actions that minimize the probability of negative consequences associated with project risks. Approved change requests are documented and authorized changes to the project scope, either to reduce it or to enlarge it. Approved defect repairs occur when defects are found in products during an audit and the authorization is sought to fix them. These products are created as part of the project's work. Validated defect repairs are notifications that the repairs have either been approved or have been denied approval. Finally, closure procedures are all those administrative activities and interactions needed to close out the project.

These seven inputs go into the two tools and techniques used in project execution, the project management methodology and the project management information system. The methodology defines a process for the project team to use to execute the project management plan. In other words, the methodology provides the approach the team will use to turn the plan into reality. The information system can be anything that helps the team perform the work described in the plan, whether bought off-the-shelf or built in-house.

Just as there were seven inputs to project execution, there are also seven outputs. These are: 1) deliverables, 2) requested changes, 3) implemented change requests, 4) implemented corrective actions, 5) implemented preventive actions, 6) implemented defect repair, and 7) work performance information. The deliverables are simply the products and services identified in the project plan that must be made or provided in order to complete the project. The deliverables are the reason for the project in the first place. The second output, requested changes, reflects the fact that projects are not static and that product requirements change even as the project plan is being executed. Requested changes typically result from processing the approved change request inputs, one of the seven inputs to project plan execution mentioned previously. These changing requirements may involve resources and scheduling as well as functional requirements and features. Successfully tracking and managing change requests is an essential part of any project, but this is especially true for IT projects. Many of the problems encountered in IT projects are related to unsuccessful change management, which will be discussed in more detail in the next section. The next four outputs are the implemented counterparts of four of the inputs: 1) Implemented change requests are approved change requests that have been executed; 2) implemented corrective actions are approved corrective actions that have been successfully implemented; 3) implemented preventive actions are approved preventive actions that have been successfully performed; and 4) implemented defect repairs are approved defect repairs that have been successfully carried out.

The final output is work performance information. This information reflects the status of project activities recorded in the project plan. When a project task has been completed, that information has to be communicated to the project manager and documented in the project information system, along with the resources that were used to complete the task. The extent to which quality standards have been met must also be recorded. In addition to information about schedule, resources, and quality, work performance information also can include information about cost, the status of deliverables, and documented lessons learned. You will recall reading in more detail about performance reporting in Chapter 4. It is important to remember that performance reporting also involves reporting on work that has not yet been completed, especially if that work is behind schedule.

MONITORING PROGRESS AND MANAGING CHANGE

Executing the project plan means that all the preparations are done, and now it is time to do the job. If the plan has been put together well, and if it is written at the necessary level of detail, then all the project manager has to do is follow directions. What could be simpler? Actually, execution is anything but simple. Things rarely go as planned. The assurance, "Everything is going according to plan," may be common in the movies and on TV, but it's not one that most project managers use often. Instead, it sometimes seems that nothing goes according to plan. A big part of a project manager's job during execution is to monitor everything to understand what is not going according to plan and what the implications are for missing expectations. Monitoring progress and the activities a project manager engages in during execution are the topics of the next two subsections. Then, we discuss the problems common to IT project execution and about managing change.

New managers face a tough challenge. They have to manage the work of others while learning how to be a manager at the same time. Here are some guidelines for becoming a good manager when starting out. Although these tips apply to all aspects of managing a project, most of them are especially applicable to the execution phase.

1. *Don't make promises you can't or won't keep.* This is one of the worst things a new manager can do. Not keeping promises erodes trust and leads to a lack of respect on the part of the employee.

2. *Don't offer inappropriate awards.* Rewards should match performance. A coffee mug is appropriate for cutting a couple of days off the schedule, not for saving the project millions of dollars.

3. *Reward ambitious workers* with important tasks.

4. *Set aside time to meet with workers* to talk about things from both your perspective and theirs.

5. *Ask workers about their career goals* and how you can help them achieve their objectives.

6. *Offer your top performers* opportunities for training.

7. *Ask workers about their outside interests* and offer them rewards that match those interests, such as gift certificates and event tickets.

8. *Comment on good or bad work right away.* Don't save feedback for regularly scheduled employee performance evaluations.

9. *Don't assume good workers know how much they are valued.* People don't always know how good they are and how much they are appreciated. Don't ignore good workers, as that is a sure way to get them to stop doing so well.

10. *Take your role as manager seriously.* Don't put off rewards and feedback, and don't downplay the importance of regularly scheduled performance evaluations.

Source: Solomon, M., 2001.

Monitoring Progress

Monitoring progress
The process of keeping track of all project tasks and the details surrounding each one.

Once the project plan has been approved, then all of the tasks have been identified, along with who is responsible for each task, the resources that are necessary to complete them, the deliverables for each task, the milestones for the deliverables to be delivered, and the relationship of each task to all of the other tasks. The project manager's job in **monitoring progress** is to keep track of all tasks and all of the details surrounding each one. The more well-defined the schedule and the deliverables, the easier it is to check progress. It is easier to compare reality to expectations when expectations are explicitly defined. To measure reality accurately, however, requires open, two-way communication. Even medium sized projects would soon overwhelm managers if there were not ways to keep track of all the details. You have read about different techniques that have been developed to keep track of those details, such as PERT and Gantt charts. A more powerful method is a project information system, but the basic idea of an organized system for project management is the same.

For an example of how a project manager might use a monitoring system, refer to Figure 11.5. The figure shows two weeks in the life of a project. Five related activities are to be performed during this time: 1) Write a request for proposals (RFP); 2) create a list of potential vendors to receive the RFP; 3) prepare an information

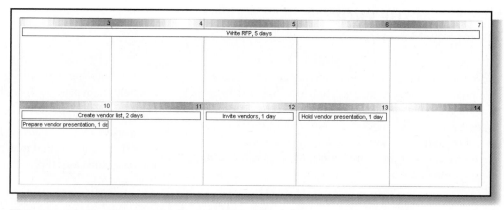

Figure 11.5   Two weeks in a project schedule

presentation for the potential vendors; 4) invite the vendors to the presentation; and 5) hold the presentation. You can see from the calendar in Figure 11.5 that writing the RFP takes five days, creating the list of vendors to invite takes two days, and the other three tasks all take one day each. You can't really tell from the calendar how the activities are related; for that, you need to look at a network diagram that represents these two weeks of the project (Figure 11.6).

Figure 11.6 shows that writing the RFP is the starting activity in this network and holding the presentation for vendors is the ending activity. The RFP must be completed before anything else can start, and all of the other activities have to be completed before the presentation can take place. The critical path for this network goes from writing the RFP, through creating the vendor list, through inviting the vendors, to the final presentation. The actual creation of the presentation is off the critical path, so whoever has that responsibility has two days of slack time.

Suppose at a regularly scheduled staff meeting, the person in charge of creating the presentation announces that she suddenly has to leave town immediately on family business. Luckily there is a staff member available who can put together the presentation, but because he is new to the project and to the organization, it will take him three days instead of one to prepare the same quality presentation. With this change, there are now two critical paths through the network. Nothing can go wrong if the presentation is to be held on March 11, as planned, and the auditorium is already booked for that day. The booking can't be changed without losing a hefty deposit. Just as the project manager begins to think about the current situation and how she can't afford any more problems, another staff member says he has determined he can put together a complete list of potential vendors in only one day. He can save time by starting with another list of potential vendors that fits their needs and was used by another project team. Now the critical path changes again (Figure 11.7), going through the presentation preparation. Neither creating

Figure 11.6   Original project network diagram

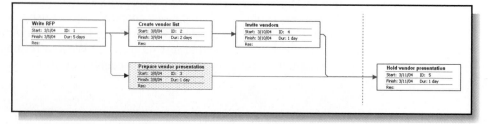

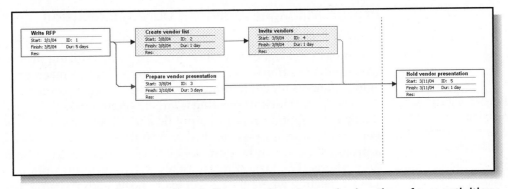

Figure 11.7   Project network diagram after change in duration of two activities

the vendor list nor inviting the vendors is on the critical path. The project manager has just won another day of slack.

This example has been kept simple to make a point. Most project managers probably wish their lives were that easy. Just to give you an idea of how difficult and demanding project execution can be, here is a list of all the things project managers must do simultaneously for each project they manage:

- Allocate and distribute work to team members at the right time while also managing task dependencies
- Update progress of each task
- Determine consequences and predict their effects on future tasks and milestones
- Manage changing team membership
- Manage roles of third parties, such as vendors and suppliers
- Enforce ownership of tasks

Notice that the first three activities in this list involve monitoring. Project managers can't allocate work during execution unless they know the status of all the tasks being worked on at a particular point in time and who is assigned to work on each task. The progress on a task can't be updated unless the project manager knows the status of the task. The effects of the present on the future can't be determined unless the project manager understands the present. In other words, you can't figure out where you want to go and how to get there until you know where you are. Project managers have to continually monitor project activities in order to get the needed information to manage the project effectively. Regular staff meetings are one way to get this information, but there are others, and we will have more to say about them later in the chapter. The last three activities in the list have more to do with managing personnel than with monitoring. Team membership is not static, and people leaving and joining a project can have significant impacts. Tasks left unfinished through a team member's departure have to be reassigned to someone else, and new people have to be brought up to speed on the project and how they can contribute. The project manager also has to deal with people outside the project team, such as vendors, who also contribute to the project. The more procurement a project involves, the more effort the project manager will have to expend on managing third-party relationships through contract administration. Finally, the project manager has to make sure that the people assigned to different tasks, whether inside the project organization or working for a third party, continue to take responsibility for those tasks.

Project Manager Activities During Execution

From the list of project manager responsibilities in the previous section, you can see that project managers do many different things during project execution. Here we will briefly describe three: holding the project kickoff meeting, establishing and managing channels for communication, and managing procurement activities.

Project kickoff meeting
A ceremonial meeting marking the beginning of a project in a very public and memorable way.

The **project kickoff meeting** is largely ceremonial. It is important because it marks the beginning of a project in a public and memorable way. The project team in the Petrie's Electronics case held their kickoff meeting at the end of Chapter 4. Sometimes a project kickoff can be quite an elaborate affair, with food, live music, gifts, and decorations. The kickoff does not always have to be a big party. Sometimes it is a simple meeting where the project team meets with the project sponsor, who explains what is involved and what is expected for the project. Who attends the kickoff sends a strong signal to the project team and the company as a whole as to how important the project is. For example, if the chief executive officer and the company president both attend the kickoff, everyone knows this project is important to the entire organization. Whatever form the kickoff takes, it should be something special and out of the ordinary that signifies the start of a dedicated group effort. Just how elaborate the kickoff is depends on the style of the project manager and the budget for the project.

Once the project has begun, it is vital to the project's success that the team establish open, two-way communication channels. Creating and monitoring these channels is also part of the project manager's role. There are many different ways for teams to communicate during project execution, including project information systems, regular meetings, all types of electronic communication, written reports, and Web-based systems that run on the organization's intranet. All of these communication channels will be explored in more depth later in the chapter.

As you saw in Chapter 10, procurement can be a prominent part of any project. Three key procurement activities occur during project execution. The first is soliciting bids and quotes and proposals from potential vendors; the second is deciding among vendors; and the third is administering the contract with the winning vendor. For medium and large projects, many different procurement activities will be going on simultaneously, with more than one solicitation and with more than one contract to administer. Keeping on top of all of these simultaneous activities is another responsibility the project manager must manage successfully.

Common System Development Project Problems

People related mistakes
System development mistakes arising from adding people too late to a project, lack of necessary skills, or unrealistic expectations.

Process related mistakes
System development mistakes arising from insufficient planning, overly optimistic schedules, or planning to catch up later.

Product related mistakes
System development mistakes arising from feature creep and requirements gold-plating.

Technology related mistakes
System development mistakes arising from overestimating savings from new tools or methods or the silver bullet syndrome.

Despite the best efforts of the best project manager, things can still go wrong during project execution. IT projects are notorious for being problematic. Steve McConnell lists 36 different classic development mistakes in systems development projects, 10 of which are included in Table 11.1. Most of the **people-related mistakes, process-related mistakes, product-related mistakes,** and **technology-related mistakes** listed in Table 11.1 are easily understood from their brief descriptions, such as unrealistic expectations, insufficient planning, and overestimated savings from new tools or methods. Some of the others need additional explanation.

Under people-related mistakes, weak personnel refers to employees who are not adequately trained in the skills necessary to a particular project. Personnel who do not have the necessary technical skills for a specific project will struggle, and the project will suffer. The second type of mistake in this category, adding people late to a project, may not seem like a mistake. In fact, common sense would dictate that additional

COMMON PROBLEMS

Anticipating Problems During Execution

During execution, the project team is focused on the job at hand, which is successfully implementing the project plan. With the focus on execution, the project team often does not spend the time and energy it should on anticipating and finding problems. The State of California's Department of Finance has prepared a list of potential problems that may arise during project execution. They include:

1. Lack of good data on activity progress.
2. Inadequate definition of requirements.
3. Frequent and uncontrolled changes to the baseline requirements.
4. Poor time and cost estimates.
5. Difficulties in concluding the project because of a lack of completion criteria.
6. Frequent replacement of developmental personnel.
7. Inadequate tracking and directing of project activities.

Many of these problems will not arise if careful planning takes place. Planning, however, is not perfect, and one of the jobs of the project manager and project team is to make sure that inadequate planning is not translated into inadequate deliverables during execution. Once a problem is suspected, it is very important that the project team act immediately to take care of it, regardless of the cause.

Source: www.dof.ca.gov/otros/statewideit/simm/SIMM200/PM5.1% 20Project% 20Execution%20Introduction.pdf. Retrieved October 12, 2006.

---

people should add to productivity because the remaining work can now be divided among more people, leaving each person with less to do in the same amount of time. But as Brooks (1995) convincingly argued, adding more people also adds more need for coordination among all the people on the project, new and old. Adding more people actually ends up reducing productivity on a project. Brooks also identified the problem called the silver-bullet syndrome. The **silver-bullet syndrome** occurs when developers believe a new and usually untried technology is all that is needed to cure the ills of any development project. In application development, however, there is no silver bullet. No one technology can solve every problem, and those who believe there is, are likely to disappointed.

Two other mistakes from the list that need additional explanation are both product-related: feature creep and requirements gold-plating. **Feature creep** refers to the tendency of system requirements to change over the lifetime of the development project. It is called feature creep because more and more features that were not in the original specifications for the application "creep in" during the development process. The average project may see a 25 percent change in requirements, all of

Silver bullet syndrome
A problem occurring when developers believe a new and usually untried technology is all that is needed to cure the ills of any development project.

Feature creep
The tendency of systems requirements to change over the lifetime of the development project.

Table 11.1 Ten of Steve McConnell's 36 Classic Development Mistakes

PEOPLE-RELATED	PROCESS-RELATED	PRODUCT-RELATED	TECHNOLOGY-RELATED
Weak personnel	Insufficient planning	Feature creep	Silver-bullet syndrome
Adding people to a project late	Overly optimistic schedules	Requirements gold-plating	Overestimated savings from new tools or methods
Unrealistic expectations	Planning to catch up later		

Requirements gold-plating
Adding more requirements than necessary to an application, even before the beginning of a project.

which can delay the project and add costs. Changes to an application typically cost 50 to 200 times less if they are made during requirements determination rather than during the physical design process. **Requirements gold-plating** means an application may have more requirements than it needs, even before the development project begins. In addition to being unnecessary, many of these requirements can be extreme and complex.

Managing Change

Managing change
The process of dealing with change requests during project execution.

Given the pressure to change system requirements during project execution, it is almost certain that a project team will be **managing change** related to the project, dealing with change requests during project execution. So, how does a project manager deal with changing requirements? First, it is important to note that every request for change does not result in a change to the requirements. Every request should be documented. Processes should be set up to review each request to determine if it can or should be accepted. Every change that is accepted will affect the project deliverables, the schedule, and the budget, so changes have to be considered very seriously. Each project organization will typically have in place organizational processes and procedures for change evaluation and implementation.

Another key area of project change is change in team membership. Contrary to popular views of teams and teamwork, teams are almost never static. Projects add people when needed. Similarly, they lose people when team members are relocated within the organization or quit to take new jobs or for some other reason. This ebb and flow of people on and off a project can be disruptive, and it is rarely anticipated in the project plan. Experienced project managers who have developed the management skills discussed in Chapter 2 have learned how to deal with the disruptions caused by the flow of people in and out of projects. Less experienced project managers will develop these skills over time. In either case, it is important to recognize that project team membership is fluid and dynamic, and project managers should anticipate and plan for changes in personnel to whatever extent they can.

COMMUNICATION AND DOCUMENTATION

We have already mentioned the need for open, two-way communication in any successful project. Communication serves to facilitate the exchange of information and can take many forms. The staff of REI's Gear and Apparel Division relied on such traditional communication modes as meetings, conference calls, faxes, and e-mail. Here we briefly discuss five methods to support team communication: meetings, written reports, a project management information system, electronic communication, and Web-based solutions (Figure 11.8). We follow this discussion on communication with a discussion of documentation.

Meetings

Meetings have been around for a long time. If they can be short, well-run, and focused, meetings can be very effective for exchanging information. (See Chapter 4, especially Table 4.4, for more about how to run a project meeting effectively.) If the purpose of a regularly scheduled staff meeting is for everyone to report on their progress and their

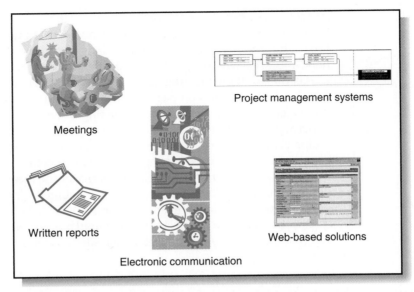

Figure 11.8 Communication for project management

problems and for the project manager to provide information on the larger project status, then meetings can work well. You know from your own experience that meetings do not always work well, however. Sometimes meetings are not well run, and the discussion is allowed to drift. Sometimes people seem unwilling or unable to exchange necessary information. Getting everyone involved to come to the same place at the same time on a given day, giving up time they would rather be using to do their "real work," can also be an issue. Although meetings are familiar and potentially useful, they have enough problems that project team communication can successfully occur in other ways.

Written Reports

One of the other ways that project team communication can occur is the preparation and distribution of written reports about the project and its progress. The emphasis here is on written, rather than oral, and regular, rather than ad hoc. We should also emphasize that the reports need to be timely and accurate. Reports that do not reflect the current status of project tasks are practically worthless. The point of regular written reporting is to let the project manager know the status of all of the various tasks that are part of the project. Having regular written reports generates a discipline for providing up-to-date information that the project manager can use to put together an overall picture of the project's status.

Project Management Information Systems

Once project managers have status information, they can use it to update the status of the overall project and determine just where things are and how far things are from where they want them to be. As you have seen, project management information systems (e.g., Microsoft Project) make the project manager's job in this regard much easier. A host of information systems are available to support project management, from shareware to commercial systems that run on every conceivable platform.

Electronic Communication

We have already talked about meetings and written reports as ways to communicate project information. The types of meetings we implied in our discussions were traditional meetings where people come together in one place and time for a certain duration to accomplish their meeting goals. The types of reports we implied were also traditional: written, printed on paper, distributed manually to those concerned. Today, it is no longer necessary to hold every meeting in one place and at one time, and printed paper reports that are centrally distributed are becoming more and more rare. Due to online chat, audioconferencing, and videoconferencing, meeting participants can be geographically dispersed during a same-time meeting. People who are far away from the meeting place can still participate. Similarly, the meeting can be asynchronous, with people contributing over time, so that the meeting itself might span a week, giving people the opportunity to log in and contribute over that entire period. As for reports, they can be transmitted in the body of e-mail messages or they can be attachments. Alternatively, they can be posted to Web sites created to support project management.

Global Implications: Project Execution After Outsourcing

Whether development project work is outsourced overseas or to another firm in the same country, in many instances this means that some employees within the company have lost their jobs. Project managers in an outsourcing situation have to manage everyone on the team, whether they are part of the outsourced work team or part of the local team. What project managers may not realize is that local survivors of the outsourcing effort may not all react the same way. Determining how different individuals react and how their reactions affect the project execution effort is one more burden project managers have to bear.

Survivors of outsourcing can react in many different ways. While you would expect them all to be happy they have kept their jobs, basic reactions will vary. Some employees will be outraged that outsourcing occurred in the first place; others will be afraid they might be next. Some will work even harder to make sure they survive the next outsourcing efforts; others may become incapacitated by guilt caused by their surviving while other employees they knew and worked with lost their jobs.

How can project managers deal with such a wide range of reactions? Ignoring the ways different employees react to outsourcing is the wrong thing to do, says Eileen Strider, an organizational effectiveness consultant. One approach is to let employees vent their concerns and fears. It is also important for executives to be honest with employees about why outsourcing occurred and to provide them with some semblance of stability. In extreme cases, employees may be encouraged to seek counseling, or the company itself may need to bring in counselors if feelings of fear and betrayal are widespread. The important point is that employee reactions need to be recognized and dealt with because employee reactions to outsourcing affect their work, which in turn affects the complete project
(Source: © 2004 ComputerWorld, Inc. Computerworld and Computerworld.com the respective and logos are trademarks of International Data Group Inc. Hamblen, M., "Sidebar: After the Outsourcing." Computerworld.)

Web-Based Solutions

One of the main objectives of communication during a project is the exchange of status information. Project managers need to be able to react to problems and to proactively prevent problems during project execution, but they can only do these things effectively if they know the current status of all of the constituent parts of the project. Instead of having each team member or each third-party vendor report progress and delays to the project manager, who then has to use that information to update the project, why not allow team members and third parties to update the project information system directly? Such direct updating is supported with Web-based access to the project information system. Users can access the system through their Web browsers and report on the status of their tasks. Web accessible project management systems are becoming more widely available. An example of a commercial system especially relevant to project execution is ProAct International's Project Management Execution (PME) Web-based solution (Figure 11.9).

ProAct's PME and other Web-based tools like it offer many communication related capabilities. Team members and third parties can access the system from anywhere they have access to a Web browser. All team members can update the status of their tasks, and the overall project software is immediately updated. Team members can notify each other of when their tasks will be completed (which is useful for those who are downstream of and dependent on these tasks), and their availability for new work. Project managers will then be able to monitor the project in real time, provided team members and vendors update their task status in a timely and accurate manner. With current information, managers should be able to better anticipate and deal with problems as they arise.

Figure 11.9 ProAct International's Project Management Execution Web-based tool

Source: ProAct International, used with permission.

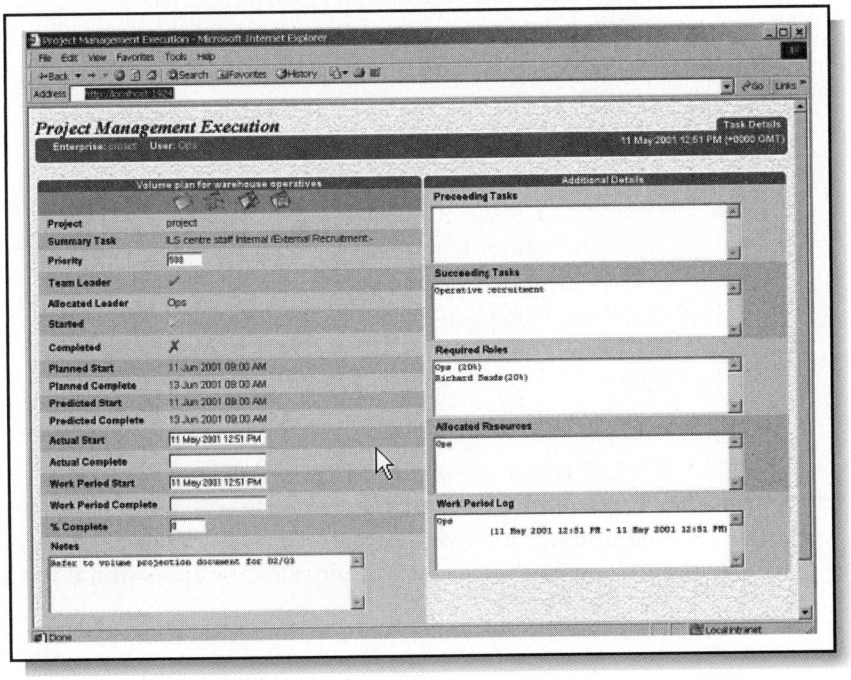

Documentation

Communication is usually accompanied by documentation. Ordinarily someone takes minutes in a meeting. People often log phone calls and make notes about their contents. Electronic communication media, such as e-mail, are their own documentation because electronic messages are stored on computer servers for later retrieval. Documentation, which creates a record of how the project proceeds over time, is important for many reasons. First, a record of the process is valuable for the project team in case they need to trace how a decision was made or how a product specification has changed during the project. Second, documentation provides a record that can be audited or that can be used as part of a legal defense in case of disputes between buyers and suppliers. Third, documentation from an outstandingly successful project may be used as the source of best practices to improve processes in other projects.

Ethical Dilemma: Relying on a Professional Code of Ethics

During project execution, you may run into ethical dilemmas and you may want to review a professional code of ethics from the project management profession for guidance. Where do you find a professional code of ethics for project management?

The Project Management Institute's ideas on projects and their management have become standards in the industry. PMI has established a detailed member code of ethics that is available on their Web site (www.pmi.org/prod/groups/public/documents/info/ap_memethstandards.pdf).

Although PMI is the predominant professional institute for project management, it is not the only one. Another professional association for project management is the International Association of Project and Program Management (IAPPM). It also has a code of professional ethics. It is available at www.iappm.org/code.htm. It is useful to visit the IAPPM site and compare its code of ethics with the PMI code.

Discussion Questions

1. Compare the PMI and IAPPM codes of ethics. What is contained in both codes?
2. Why do you think the PMI code is so much longer than the IAPPM code? Does it make a difference? Why?
3. What's the point of a professional code of ethics? Why are they needed?

Source: Pacztor, A. "Air Force Ex-Official's Dealings Put Penatgon under Spotlight, *Wall Street Jounal*, October 4, 2004, p. A2. *Wall Street Journal: Eastern Edition.* Copyright 2004 by Dow Jones & Company, Inc. Reproduced with permission of Dow Jones & Company, Inc. in the format Textbook via Copyright Clerance Center.

PROJECT EXECUTION AND THE PMBOK

The primary topic of Chapter 11 has been project plan execution, but as Figure 11.10 shows we have covered other relevant areas in the PMBOK, such as project phases and processes.

Figure 11.10 Chapter 11 and PMBOK coverage

	Textbook Chapters ——→	1	2	3	4	5	6	7	8	9	10	11	12
	PMBOK Knowledge Area												
1	**Introduction to Project Management**												
1.1	What Is a Project?	●											
1.2	What Is Project Management?	●											
1.3	Areas of Expertise		●										
1.4	Project Management Context	●											
2	**Project Life Cycle and Organization**												
2.1	The Project Life Cycle	●	●										
2.2	Project Stakeholders	●	●										
2.3	Organizational Influences		●	●	●			●					
3	**Project Management Processes for a Project**												
3.1	Project Management Processes	●	●										
3.2	PM Process Groups	●	●										
3.3	Process Interactions		●										
3.4	Project Management Process Mapping		●										
4	**Project Integration Management**												
4.1	Develop Project Charter					●							
4.2	Develop Preliminary Project Scope Statement					●	●						
4.3	Develop Project Management Plan					●							
4.4	Direct and Manage Project Execution											✓	
4.5	Monitor and Control Project Work												○
4.6	Integrated Change Control												○
4.7	Close Project												○
5	**Project Scope Management**												
5.1	Scope Planning					●							
5.2	Scope Definition					●							
5.3	Create WBS					●	●						
5.4	Scope Verification					●							
5.5	Scope Control					●							○
6	**Project Time Management**												
6.1	Activity Definition						●						
6.2	Activity Sequencing						●						
6.3	Activity Resource Estimating							●					
6.4	Activity Duration Estimating							●					
6.5	Schedule Development							●					
6.6	Schedule Control							●					○

(continued)

Figure 11.10   (continued)

	Textbook Chapters →	1	2	3	4	5	6	7	8	9	10	11	12
	PMBOK Knowledge Area												
7	**Project Cost Management**												
7.1	Cost Estimating							●					
7.2	Cost Budgeting							●					
7.3	Cost Control							●					○
8	**Project Quality Management**												
8.1	Quality Planning								●				
8.2	Perform Quality Assurance								●				
8.3	Perform Quality Control								●				○
9	**Project Human Resource Management**												
9.1	Human Resource Planning			●				●					
9.2	Acquire Project Team			●				●					
9.3	Develop Project Team			●				●					
9.4	Manage Project Team			●				●					
10	**Project Communications Management**												
10.1	Communications Planning				●							✓	
10.2	Information Distribution				●							✓	
10.3	Performance Reporting				●								○
10.4	Manage Stakeholders				●								○
11	**Project Risk Management**												
11.1	Risk Management Planning									●			
11.2	Risk Identification									●		✓	
11.3	Qualitative Risk Analysis									●			
11.4	Quantitative Risk Analysis									●			
11.5	Risk Response Planning									●			
11.6	Risk Monitoring and Control									●			○
12	**Project Procurement Management**												
12.1	Plan Purchases and Acquisitions										●		
12.2	Plan Contracting										●		
12.3	Request Seller Responses										●		
12.4	Select Sellers										●		
12.5	Contract Administration										●		
12.6	Contract Closure										●		○

Key: ●-where material is covered in past chapters; ✓-current chapter coverage;
○-where material is covered in future chapters

RUNNING CASE
Managing Project Execution

Jim Woo was in his new car, driving down I-5, on his way to work. He dreaded the phone call he knew he was going to have to make.

The original go-live date for a pilot implementation of Petrie's Electronics' new customer relationship management (CRM) system was July 31. That was only six weeks away, and Jim knew there was no way they were going to be ready. The XRA CRM they were licensing turned out to be a lot more complex than they had thought. They were behind schedule in implementing it. Sanjay Agarwal, who was a member of Jim's team and who was in charge of systems integration for Petrie's, wanted Jim to hire some consultants with XRA experience to help with implementation. So far, Jim had been able to stay under budget, but missing his deadlines and hiring consultants would push him over his budget limit.

It didn't help that John Smith, the head of marketing, kept submitting requests for changes to the original specifications for the customer loyalty program. As specified in the project charter, the new system was supposed to track customer purchases, assign points for cumulative purchases, and allow points to be redeemed for "rewards" at local stores. The team had determined that those rewards would take the form of dollars-off coupons. Customers who enrolled in the program would be given accounts that they could access from Petrie's Web site. When they signed on, they could check their account activity to see how many points they had accumulated. If they had earned enough points, they were rewarded with a coupon. If they wanted to use the coupon, they would have to print it out on their home printer and bring it to a store to use on a purchase. The team had decided long ago that keeping everything electronic saved Petrie's the considerable costs of printing and mailing coupons to customers.

But now marketing had put in a change request that would give customers a choice of having coupons mailed to them automatically or printing them at home from the Web site. This option, while nice for customers, added complexity to the XRA system implementation, and it added to the costs of operation. Jim had also learned yesterday from the marketing representative on his team, Sally Fukuyama, that Smith wanted another change. Now he wanted customers to be able to use the coupons for on-line purchases from Petrie's Web site. This added a whole new layer of complexity, affecting Petrie's existing systems for ordering on-line, in addition to altering yet again the implementation of the XRA CRM.

As if that weren't enough, Rick Piccoli was now telling Jim that he would not be ready to let the team pilot the system in his Irvine store. Rick was saying his store would not be ready by the end of July. Maybe that wouldn't matter because they were going to miss the go-live date for the pilot. But Rick was hinting he would not be ready for months after that. It seemed as if he didn't want his store to be used for the pilot at all. Jim didn't understand it. But maybe he could talk Juanita Lopez into letting them use her Minneapolis store as the pilot site. Juanita used to be on their team before she was transferred to Minneapolis. Jim thought she would be willing to help.

Jim was almost at his exit. Soon he would be at the office, and he would have to call Ella Whinston and tell her the status of the project. He would have to tell her that they would miss the go-live date but in a way it didn't matter because he didn't have a pilot location to go live at. In addition to going over schedule, he was going to have to go over budget, too. He didn't see any way they would be ready for the pilot anywhere close to when they had scheduled unless he hired the consultants Sanjay wanted. And he would have to stop the latest change request filed by marketing. Even more important, he would have to keep the rumored change request to use coupons for on-line purchases from being submitted in the first place.

Maybe, just maybe, if he could hire the consultants, fight off the change requests, and get Juanita to cooperate, they might be ready to go live with a pilot in Minneapolis on October 15. That gave him four months to complete the project. He and the team were going to have to work hard to make that happen.

Jim realized he had missed his exit. Great, he thought, I hope it gets better from here.

Describe the seven project management processes that are part of project execution. According to the PMBOK, seven project management processes are part of project execution: project plan execution, solicitation, source selection, contract administration, quality assurance, team development, and information distribution. Project plan execution is the process where the project plan is carried out. Solicitation involves obtaining bids and proposals for performing some number of project plan activities. Source selection involves choosing from among the proposals that have been received, and contract administration involves managing the relationship between the project organization and the selected vendor. Quality assurance involves evaluating project progress on a regular basis in order to determine if the project will satisfy established quality standards. Team development involves improving project performance through improving individual and group competencies. Information distribution means making needed information available to project stakeholders in a timely manner.

Discuss the activities project managers engage in during project execution. A big part of a project manager's job during execution is to monitor everything in order to understand what is not going according to plan and what the implications are for missing expectations. Another big part of the job is managing change, in both project requirements and project personnel. Other activities a project manager engages in during execution include organizing the project kickoff meeting, establishing and managing channels for communication, and managing procurement activities.

Explain some of the key problems in IT projects that occur during project execution. Many different types of problems can occur during project execution. Some of the problems discussed in this chapter include having to deal with weak personnel, adding people late to a project, feature creep, and requirements gold-plating.

Describe the importance of communication to project execution. The quality of communication among project team members can be the difference between a successful and an unsuccessful project. Some useful channels for communication discussed in this chapter include regular team meetings, regular written reports, project management information systems, electronic communications, and Web-based project plan execution systems.

KEY TERMS REVIEW

- Feature creep
- Managing change
- Monitoring progress
- People related mistakes
- Process related mistakes
- Product related mistakes
- Project execution
- Project kickoff meeting
- Requirements gold-plating
- Silver bullet syndrome
- Technology related mistakes

Match each of the key terms above with the definition that best fits it.

1. _____ The process of keeping track of all project tasks and the details surrounding each one.

2. _____ System development mistakes arising from feature creep and requirements gold-plating.

3. _____ The process of carrying out the project plan to accomplish the required work.

4. _____ A ceremonial meeting marking the beginning of a project in a very public and memorable way.

5. _____ A problem occurring when developers believe a new and usually untried technology is all that is needed to cure the ills of any development project.

6. _____ System development mistakes arising from adding people too late to a project, lack of necessary skills, or unrealistic expectations.

7. _____ System development mistakes arising from overestimating savings from new tools or methods or the silver bullet syndrome.

8. _____ System development mistakes arising from insufficient planning, overly optimistic schedules, or planning to catch up later.

9. _____ The tendency of systems requirements to change over the lifetime of the development project.

10. _____ The process of dealing with change requests during project execution.

11. _____ Adding more requirements than necessary to an application, even before the beginning of a project.

REVIEW QUESTIONS

1. What is project plan execution?
2. According to the PMBOK, what are the seven management processes that make up project plan execution? Where else in the book have you studied some of them?
3. Explain the inputs to project plan execution.
4. Explain the tools and techniques that are used in project plan execution.
5. Explain the outputs from project plan execution.
6. Describe some of the activities that project managers perform during project plan execution.

7. What four problems encountered during project plan execution are described in this chapter?
8. What are two types of change that project managers have to deal with during execution?
9. Name and describe five different ways that project teams can communicate during project plan execution.
10. Explain how project plan execution can be documented.

CHAPTER EXERCISES

1. Note that two of the seven management processes in project plan execution are part of procurement. Why is procurement such a major part of execution?
2. Why is monitoring project progress so important to project plan execution? What can project managers do to help themselves monitor project status?
3. Using the Web and other resources, research information systems for project plan execution. Write a report that describes each system you found and that compares and contrasts the features of each system.
4. Suppose you are the project manager for the following project:

Task	Duration	Predecessor(s)
1	1 day	—
2	3 days	1
3	2 days	1
4	3 days	2
5	5 days	3
6	3 days	4, 5
7	1 day	6

First, draw a network diagram for the project. Determine the critical path and slack times for all of the tasks. This completes your plan for the project schedule. During project plan execution, you become aware of the need to change the duration of Task 4 to five days.

Meanwhile, Task 3 has been finished one day early, so it only took one day to do. What, if any, effect do these changes have on your project? What would have happened if you had not been monitoring the status of the project?

5. Find and interview project managers about how they communicate with team members concerning their projects during project plan execution. Which methods work best for them? How do they incorporate communication into their execution activities? Write a report explaining what you found.

6. Everyone has managed projects, whether in the workplace, in school, or at home. Describe the activities you undertook during execution. What type of system did you use to manage the project (e.g., computer-based or manual)? How well did the system work for you? What kinds of problems did you encounter and how did you deal with them?

CHAPTER CASE

Sedona Management Group and Managing Project Execution

Project execution is the phase of the project in which the activities necessary for project completion are undertaken. The execution processes include coordinating the project resources to carry out the project plans developed in the planning stage. The products or deliverables of the project are produced during the project execution phase. Seven project management processes form part of the execution phase of the project, one of which is the core process entitled project plan execution. The other six facilitating processes are directing and managing project execution, performing quality assurance, acquiring the project team, developing the project team, information distribution, requesting seller responses, and selecting sellers.

Project execution comprises several key activities, including providing project leadership, monitoring progress, assuring quality, managing change, and managing channels for communication. Positive leadership contributes to project success. A positive leader is one who is a good team builder and communicator, has high self-esteem, focuses on results, demonstrates trust and respect, and sets realistic goals. Tim Turnpaugh takes his role as Sedona Management Group's (SMG's) leader very seriously. Over the years, the practices that have worked best for him as a project leader include the establishment of clear goals, strict adherence to the project schedule, and keeping project team members motivated. For any project, Turnpaugh has to ensure that he clearly understands the customer's needs and, at the same

time, that every project team member has that same level of understanding.

Another best practice Turnpaugh employs as a project leader is to establish milestones for any project SMG takes on and then assess those milestones over the life cycle of the project. By doing detailed planning during earlier project phases—including identifying tasks, allocating resources for tasks, and identifying the outputs from each task—the Sedona team can create a good baseline for use in comparing their actual progress with the project's planned progress.

In the case of the Seattle Seahawks, Turnpaugh and his team created a detailed plan for building the Seahawks' Web site. Mike Flood of the Seahawks identified several key characteristics the Seahawks needed in their Web site. Flood wanted a Web site that was secure, reliable, conveyed accurate information, and was easy to access. Based on these requirements and through the experience gained with working for other clients, Turnpaugh determined the system that would work best for the Seahawks, and a contract was drafted. The contract had a very detailed scope of work that stated clearly what the Sedona team would accomplish for the Seattle Seahawks. In the event that, after signing the contract, the customer asked for some significant change to the project scope during project execution, Turnpaugh would only undertake the change if the project's budget and the delivery date for the final product were changed. Change control is essential for ensuring time project execution.

Communication is also a key factor influencing successful project execution. In addition to the considerable amount of time SMG spends with each client during the initiation and planning stages, during the project execution phase SMG has regular meetings with the customer to ensure that the project is going according to the customer's expectations. As mentioned earlier, during the execution phase Turnpaugh ensures that both someone from his team and from the customer's organization are always accessible for exchanging information.

CHAPTER 11 PROJECT ASSIGNMENT

In the execution phase, you will perform the activities necessary to ensure project completion. Some of the important activities include monitoring progress and managing change. In this exercise, you will learn about each of these different activities.

1. Describe project execution as it relates to your project. In other words, explain what you will do to ensure project completion.
2. You developed a Gantt chart for the project assignment in Chapter 6 and updated it with resource information in Chapter 7. Determine how many of the activities you have completed so far, and update the Gantt chart from Chapter 7 with this new information.
3. Describe any changes to the project plan that have been needed so far. Were all these change requests approved?
4. Develop a progress report that describes what you and your team members have accomplished so far for the entertainment Web site development project. The progress report should include:
   - Your accomplishments so far, related to the tracking Gantt chart you developed above
   - Your plans, which include what remains to be accomplished for project completion
   - Any issues that have surfaced during the project life cycle
   - A list of any approved changes made to the project
5. Describe how you and your team members keep each other updated on the status of your project. In particular, indicate the different forms of communication you are using (e.g., e-mail, face-to-face meetings, collaborative tools, and so on).

REFERENCES

Brooks, F. P., Jr. (1995). *The Mythical Man-Month.* Anniversary ed. Reading, MA: Addison-Wesley.

Hamblen, M. (2004). "Sidebar: After the Outsourcing." *ComputerWorld*, November 11. Retrieved December 20, 2004 from: www.computerworld.com/management-topics/outsourcing/story/0,10801,97223,00.html.

McConnell, S. (1996). *Rapid Development.* Redmond, WA: Microsoft Press.

Project Management Institute. 2000. *A Guide to the Project Management Body of Knowledge.* Newton Square, PA: PMI.

Project Management Institute. (2004). *A Guide to the Project Management Body of Knowledge.* 3rd ed. Newton Square, PA: PMI.

Solomon, M. (2001). "Tips for New Managers." *ComputerWorld*, October 29. Retrieved October 4, 2004, from: www.computerworld.com/careertopics/careers/story/0,10801,65079,00.html.

Managing Project Control and Closure

Opening Case: Poor Project Control Leads to CONFIRM Failure

In 1988, Hilton Hotels, Marriott, Budget Rent-A-Car, and American Airlines Information Services (AMRIS), a subsidiary of American Airlines (AMR), teamed up to form Intrico, the International Reservations and Information Consortium. The aim of this consortium was to develop and market a new information system called CONFIRM, which was intended to become the industry's most advanced, comprehensive travel reservation system by combining airline, rental car, and hotel information. This new system would offer consumers information about flight, room, and car availability, as well as details of any special offers, while also providing an efficient way to book flights, rooms, and cars.

AMRIS was to play two different roles in this project, acting both as a partner and as the primary developer of the CONFIRM system. The project was budgeted at $55.7 million and had a three-year timetable for completion. From 1988, work on the project progressed, though there were very few external signs of activity. In May 1990, the Intrico group held a conference to inform the press that the project was in the programming stage and still on course for the scheduled delivery date. In early 1992, part of the CONFIRM system was available for live testing by Hilton Hotels. However, the beta test revealed several major problems with the CONFIRM system. It was estimated that resolving these problems would take an additional 18 months of work before the system would be ready. This meant that the system would be delivered in 1993 instead of 1992 as originally planned. By the middle of 1992, the Intrico consortium dismantled, as Hilton, Marriott and Budget Rent-A-Car announced that they were dropping the project. Eventually, after a few weeks of work, AMRIS indicated that the project was cancelled.

One of the main reasons the CONFIRM project failed was the lack of control during execution. This system required teamwork for its successful completion, but because the lines of authority and responsibility for project activities were not clear, members of Intrico blamed each other for any problems. As a result, corrective actions were not taken when needed. Several unforeseen technical difficulties were evident throughout the execution phase. However, because no status meetings were scheduled, these technical issues, as well as any other performance issues, could not be addressed. Consequently, these small, unresolved problems worsened over time and eventually contributed to the cancellation of the project (Sources: Ewusi-Mensah, 1997; Oz, 1994).

LEARNING OBJECTIVES

After reading this chapter, you will be able to:

➤ Define project control and closure.
➤ Understand the importance of, and general philosophies behind, project control and closure.
➤ Apply techniques for managing project control and closure.

INTRODUCTION

Throughout this textbook, we have discussed most of the concepts and techniques for initiating, planning, and executing a project successfully. Possibly the most important issue to consider for ensuring project management success is project control, as indicated in the opening case. After all, how successful can a project be if once the planning is finished you sit back and wait for the tasks to be completed? What happens if a critical task takes two weeks longer to complete than planned? How do you know if costs are running unexpectedly high? Could issues arise that affect the quality of the product you are producing or the risks associated with the project? Are you even aware of these potential problems? Project control is an important element in the overall success of a project because it allows managers to identify and deal with problems and promotes flexibility within the plan to allow for inevitable difficulties.

Given the overarching role that project control plays in project management, project control techniques span all preceding project life cycle phases and overlap many of the project management knowledge areas already discussed in this book. We will explore how control can be exerted over the various project phases, and describe specific techniques and tools that successful project managers use to control projects and ensure their successful completion (see Figure 12.1).

In addition to project control, another important concept that successful project managers embrace is project closure. Think back to your freshman year. After completing your first classes, you undoubtedly had learned some lessons that you continue to use today in your academic career. Once your finals were over, that wasn't technically

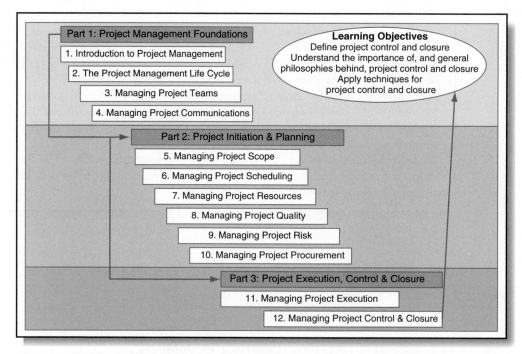

Figure 12.1 Information systems project management focusing on managing project control and closure

the end of your classes. Your instructors "signed off" on your completion of the courses by giving you a final grade. Just as you learned lessons and received confirmation that your efforts were sufficient to pass those classes, successful project managers seek verification from the project stakeholders that they have successfully completed all the deliverables. If problems arise, project managers document them to enable the project team to reflect on them and apply any lessons learned to reduce the likelihood of project failures in the future. We will present the elements and techniques of project closure that help ensure the success of the current project and provide valuable information for future projects.

What Is Project Control?

Project control
The process of monitoring and measuring project progress and influencing the plan to account for any discrepancies between planned progress and actual progress.

Project control is the process of monitoring and measuring project progress and influencing the project plan to account for any discrepancies between planned progress and actual progress. Project control allows a project manager to keep tabs on the progress of the various tasks, identify problems, solve problems, and make changes to the plan based on any problems and their solutions.

For instance, consider a project manager who requires a series of weekly status reports from each project team member. In the course of reviewing these reports, the project manager realizes that one of the more critical project team members is repeatedly late with deliverables. Considering the importance of that team member's role in the project, the project manager now has valuable information for making decisions about this unproductive team member. Does the person need a different form of incentive or perhaps more task support? Should the person be replaced? Armed with sufficient information, the successful project manager can now make an appropriate decision.

What Is Project Closure?

Project closure
Final implementation and training related to the project, acceptance and signoff on the project, and archiving of the project's results.

Project closure involves the final implementation and training related to the project, getting acceptance and signoff on it, and finally archiving the results of the project and lessons learned. For instance, your client has commissioned a new customer relationship management (CRM) software package from you, and you have developed the package to meet your client's specifications. Now you must install the new package at your client's location and train their personnel to use it. Next, you must gain approval from the stakeholders and clients that the delivered product meets their requirements and fulfills the contract. Finally, you archive the materials generated over the course of the project and write an end report that summarizes the project management methods used. This report allows you to document any lessons learned over the course of the project and to record any unresolved issues.

Global Implications: Managing Project Control

One of the realities of offshoring is that you cannot just outsource a software development project. The company doing the outsourcing cannot assume that an offshore development team will do better work than its in-house programmers. Software development is a creative and dynamic process that requires constant attention. Throughout the project life cycle, growth plans, changing technology requirements, and differing customer requirements can alter project plans, and therefore, such changes must be managed and controlled properly. There has to be constant engagement between the outsourcing company and the offshore team.

Recently, far more tools have become available for managing offshore projects. The outsourcing company and the offshore company can use these tools for interpersonal collaboration and for sharing software artifacts. At the same time, these tools provide a measure of command and control to the outsourcing company. Most current groupware tools were designed primarily for in-house use, but now new tools are available to the open-source software community that allow developers to coordinate and manage their disparate needs, making them particularly suitable for use in offshore software development projects. These tools can be Web-based or can be hosted by one of the parties in the outsourcing relationship.

Software-configuration management tools are also very useful in managing offshore projects. These tools keep track of software assets, such as source code, compiled binaries, documentation, and test results. They are very suitable for offshore software development because members of the development team can be widely dispersed and still receive the information, which can be accessed over the Web or hosted by either the onshore company or the offshore team. Such tools run on Windows, Mac OS, and Linux workstations.

The final category of tools that is particularly suitable for managing offshore projects includes quality assurance tools. These include static-analysis, load testing, and runtime debugging tools that the onshore company can use to verify all externally developed codes. Also, the offshore team can use new automated error prevention tools when developing codes. Such tools allow error-free codes by enforcing coding standards and building testing into the development process (*Source:* Zeichick, 2004).

THE IMPORTANCE AND PHILOSOPHIES OF PROJECT CONTROL AND CLOSURE

This section provides an overview of both project control and project closure. We first discuss the importance of project control and provide an example of project control issues. We follow this with a discussion of the philosophies of project control and the levers for exerting control over projects. We then discuss the importance of project closure and provide an example of successful project closure.

Why Is Project Control Important?

Controlling processes (PMBOK, 2004) are important factors in six of the nine project management knowledge areas: integration, scope, time, cost, quality, and risk. In addition, project control also overlaps in more subtle ways with project communications management and human resource management. Considering that control processes occur at every stage of a successful project's life cycle, it is easy to see how important project control is. Again, think back over your college career up to this point. Surely you or a classmate has run into a situation where a course required in your major was already full or unavailable when you tried to register. To keep the status of your project (your degree) on track, you didn't just allow the unavailability of that class to push back the attainment of your goals. Hopefully, you exerted control over your project by enrolling in an alternate class (to keep your number of credits above a certain level), or you approached the instructor of that course to arrange for enrollment under special circumstances, or you even made changes to your existing plan by deciding to take the class during the summer session. As you can see, successful outcomes of any project require control at every stage of the project.

Example of Project Control Problems

One specific example of a project that had problems as a result of ineffective control was the Denver International Airport (DIA) Computerized Baggage Handling System (CBHS). In 1989, the construction of DIA had been through almost a decade of planning and was finally transitioning into the execution stage. During the construction of the airport, each airline was responsible for developing and building its own baggage-handling system. United Airlines had planned on making DIA its major hub, so it commissioned construction of a complex, technologically advanced baggage-handling system. Recognizing the utility of such an advanced baggage-handling system, the DIA project managers decided to mirror this effort and develop an airport-wide system similar to United's. The problem was that when DIA made this decision the other airlines had already begun to plan their own individual baggage-handling systems. In a sense, a change request had occurred at two levels. First, each airline was requested to change the specifics of its own baggage-handling project. In addition, DIA as a whole was now implementing a change for the baggage-handling capabilities of the entire airport. Both changes endangered the timely completion of the airport.

After developing specifications for an airport-wide CBHS and requesting bids from several companies for the new system, airport planners were surprised to find that only three bids were submitted and all three were insufficient. Even the company commissioned by United (BAE Automated Systems Inc.) decided not to bid on the new airport-wide CBHS. Following the unsuccessful request for bids, airport planners and management pressured BAE to develop the airport-wide CBHS despite overwhelming evidence of the difficulties involved. In essence, these new plans were a dramatic change in project scope, and DIA's change management and scope control processes were now threatening the potential success of the system.

Considering the difficulty of developing the system under such time pressure, BAE tried to implement its own scope-control processes. One of these was the use of freeze dates, meaning that changes could not be made to certain components of the baggage-handling system after a specified date. These control techniques, had they been followed, might have allowed BAE to complete the airport-wide CBHS, but several events over the next several months ensured the project's failure. The chief airport engineer and main champion for the airport-wide system, Walter Slinger, died six months after the contract to build the system had been awarded to BAE. Prior to Slinger's death, reasonably tight controls were being enforced to try to make the project a success. However, soon after Slinger's passing, airlines began requesting changes to the system design, and these changes, which were frequently approved, caused delays that mounted until the opening of the airport was delayed: Rather than opening in October 1993, as originally planned, the airport finally opened in late February 1995, a delay of 16 months. Worse, the airport was close to $2 billion over budget. While many other factors contributed to the DIA CBHS failure, lack of project control on the part of both DIA and BAE can be seen as a major contributor to the cost overruns and delays.

A graphic example of problems with this project happened in April 1994. The City of Denver invited the press to observe BAE's test of the system. The press watched as baggage was thrown from the telecars transporting the baggage. Reporters saw clothing and personal items from some of the 7,000 bags lying on the ground under the telecar tracks. Clearly, initial tests conducted prior to the press event should have been part of the project control process.

BAE's original contract with United Airlines had been frozen to allow BAE to work for DIA rather than only for United. The failure of the airport-wide system meant that United's originally planned CBHS had been sacrificed as well. To this day, United uses a very scaled-down version of the CBHS and only for outgoing baggage. The remaining airlines went back to the labor-intensive motorized carts seen at most other airports (Mähring, Holmström, Keil, and Montealegre, 2004). All in all, changes to the DIA project were not managed effectively.

Philosophies of Controlling Projects

Just as management styles differ, project managers also subscribe to different philosophies of project control. A **philosophy of project control** refers, in a sense, to the management style the manager employs in following a plan and dealing with problems or changes that arise. Two distinctly different approaches are the **dogmatic philosophy** and the **laid-back philosophy**. As the names imply, a manager who subscribes to a dogmatic philosophy has little or no tolerance for deviation from the original plan and may manage autocratically to maintain adherence to the plan. At the other end of the spectrum, a manager who subscribes to the laid-back philosophy may simply embrace the multiple changes or problems that arise. A more likely scenario is for a manager to embrace a

Philosophy of project control
The management style the manager employs in following a plan and dealing with problems or changes in the plan.

Dogmatic philosophy
A philosophy of project control that emphasizes strict adherence to the project plan, with little tolerance for deviations.

Laid-back philosophy
A philosophy of project control that allows for project problems or change issues to be dealt with as they arise, on an ad hoc basis.

Pragmatic philosophy
A compromise between the dogmatic and laid-back philosophies that sticks to a plan but is flexible enough to allow for changes.

philosophy somewhere between these two extremes, which might be thought of as a **pragmatic philosophy**.

Each of these philosophies might be appropriate in a given situation. One common determinant for the most appropriate project control philosophy is the size of the project. At the extreme end, consider the student who is studying for a pop quiz. It is likely that little formalized planning is done, such as developing a work breakdown structure, producing a network diagram that sequences the tasks, and the like; rather, the student probably will look over the course notes and skim through the textbook. Deviations from this very informal plan are probably not tracked, documented, and identified as potential problem areas. Finally, formal documents related to the closure of this project are not likely produced. This does not mean that this type of planning is inappropriate for this type of project. In this case, the team is small (one person), the project has very limited scope (reviewing one chapter), and the downside risks of not optimizing on the project may be limited (because the pop quiz is worth only a few points). For this relatively small project, the laid-back philosophy taken by the student is more than adequate—in fact, preferred—because it allows the student to focus on reviewing the material rather than *planning* how to review the material and so forth.

Contrast the student reviewing for the quiz with the DIA CBHS project. This was a very large project with high stakes, involving many large airlines and national stakeholders. From the beginning, the chief engineer adopted a dogmatic philosophy, and while he was sometimes controversial, he was also known as a project manager who ensured that projects were well controlled and successful. After his death, his replacement, Gail Edmond, managed in a more laid-back style. Whether a function of the authority vested in her by the City of Denver or of her personal style, following Slinger's death the airlines began requesting significant changes to the system that, under the original plan, should not have been allowed after the specified freeze dates (Mähring et al., 2004).

Levers for Controlling Projects

In addition to the philosophy of project control employed, the project manager also needs to exert control. Before we discuss specific formalized project control techniques, let's first examine several levers that successful managers use to exert control over projects, including communication, participation, analysis and action, and commitment.

Communication

Perhaps the most important aspect of successful project management is the efficient flow of information. In this respect, successful communication is *required* to successfully control a project. Consider the difficulty of controlling a project if you don't implement your control techniques because your ability to communicate with team members is hampered or nonexistent. How will your software engineers know that they need to crash a task if you don't have effective ways for communicating with them? Conversely, how will you know whether a task is on track or needs to be crashed if the team members responsible for that task do not communicate with you?

Another communication issue is the quality of the communication. Even if project team members do communicate to you, what happens if their communications are ambiguous or are not focused on the appropriate issues? Communication for communication's sake is not effective. Project communication must be timely, focused, directed at the correct person, and thorough enough to effectively accomplish its goal.

Ethical Dilemma: To Blow the Whistle or Not

Performance reporting is an important tool in project control. It involves collecting and reviewing information about project status to take any corrective actions that might be needed to bring the project in conformance to the plan. However, evidence suggests that both employees and outside contractors sometimes withhold unwelcome but important information concerning projects and their status. Consequently, information about problems may never reach the higher levels of the organizational hierarchy, and decision makers who have the necessary authority cannot take any corrective actions to change the direction of the project.

Communicating bad news up the hierarchy, or "blowing the whistle," can be extremely difficult in organizations. Employees often choose not to blow the whistle because of the personal risks involved. In most organizations, whistle blowing is seen as an "illegitimate" behavior, so these employees face the fear of being fired because they will be blamed for the negative consequences of unwelcome information. Consequently, they withhold the information, a situation known as the mum effect. Sometimes when employees do choose to blow the whistle, upper management ignores the information. This is known as the deaf effect, where there is reluctance to hear the whistle.

The conditions for effective whistle blowing vary across different organizations. Organizations should strive to become "healthy" by creating an environment where employees are not afraid to communicate bad news. At the same time, the feedback gathered from these employees should be used effectively to change the direction of the project, if necessary. Large organizations with established and legitimate audit staffs typically have a healthy climate for whistle blowing. Another way to promote a healthy climate is to outsource **project audits**, essentially having a third-party from outside the organization responsible for reporting on a project's status—reducing the political consequences of whistle blowing (Source: Keil and Robey, 2001).

Discussion Questions

1. What type of organizational culture might "inhibit" whistle blowing?
2. What should a project manager do to encourage his project team's willingness to report project problems?

Project audit
A systematic and formal inquiry into a project's expenditures, schedule, and quality of work.

Participation

Obviously, you expect participation from your team members, and in some cases, you will encounter team members who excel and participate with energy and enthusiasm. However, you will also encounter team members who prefer to go with the flow and not offer suggestions or participate beyond the most basic requirements. These team members need to be encouraged to participate, to offer opinions, and to take responsibility when problems arise. The importance of project team participation, as well as the participation of all project stakeholders, is emphasized in the introductory chapters of this textbook, which are focused on managing project communications and managing project teams. Critical topics in these chapters related to the relationship between participation and project control include project team selection, motivation, and conflict management, to name a few.

Analysis and Action

The ability to analyze situations is also an important lever for exerting control. After all, how effective will your controlling process be if you haven't properly analyzed the problem you happen to be dealing with? Analysis is important for taking the most appropriate course of action to resolve the problem or, at the very least, for understanding the situation in such a way as to minimize further problems that may arise. If action is required, taking that action in a timely and decisive fashion is crucial. In fact, the longer a problem persists, the more costly and difficult it will be to resolve. For this reason, leadership—as well as the topics related to project-related decision-making—are also critically important. In a project where communication is encouraged and effective, participation is required and embraced, and analysis is conducted regularly and accurately, appropriate actions leading to project success should occur naturally.

TIPS FROM THE PROS
Some Managerial and Financial Tools to Help in Project Control

Project control ensures that all stakeholders work together to achieve the project objectives and that the project progresses in line with the plan established in the planning stage. The steps in project control include setting performance standards, monitoring current performance, and taking any corrective actions necessary when there are any deviations. This is known as the checks-and-balances approach. Several managerial and financial tools are available to help in this process. Managerial tools include:

1. *Feasibility analysis.* This analysis helps to determine whether the project is feasible from organizational, financial, political, and technological perspectives. More importantly, it establishes how the project should be done.

2. *Schedule monitoring.* Activities can be classified as critical and noncritical. A critical activity must be completed on schedule, whereas a noncritical activity has some slack, which means that it can be delayed. During schedule monitoring, the project manager ensures that the critical activities are completed as scheduled while still keeping an eye on the noncritical activities.

3. *The establishment of a steering committee.* This committee includes senior managers who represent users and general management, as well as the director of the IT function or the CIO. The purpose of this committee is to monitor the project's performance and ensure that the project deliverables are according to standards. In addition, this committee can also help resolve conflicts, for example in disputes of resources or project scope.

4. *System development life cycle (SDLC) standards.* The project is broken into phases, with people assigned to document each phase and authorize transition to the next phase. The life cycle can,

therefore, be used as a checklist, enabling top management to trace progress on a project at any given time.

5. *Quality assurance.* General management and the project steering committee should evaluate the project management process and the system being developed in terms of quality measurements.

6. *Project management and CASE tools.* These tools help in the schedule, control, and communication of project activities.

7. *The liaison officer.* This person acts as the liaison between the users and the various functions in the IT department, coordinating all project-related activities, communicating requests from end users to IT, and reporting the project status to the end users. With the help of the liaison officer, the project manager can improve control over the project because the liaison officer gives a clear and reliable account of the project's status.

Financial tools include:

1. *Continuous cost/benefit analysis.* The investments in the project should be financially justifiable. Performing a cost/benefit analysis periodically ensures that the benefits the project will produce outweigh its cost.

2. *Project budgeting.* A detailed project budget should be developed, including expenses for components such as human resources, hardware, and software at various stages.

3. *Budget deviation analysis.* By comparing the actual performance with the budget, general management and the project manager can detect any major deviations from the planned budget and correct them before such deviations cause any major consequences (Source: Ahituv, Zviran, and Glezer, 1999).

Commitment

A final lever that project managers use to help in project control relates to gaining commitment from project stakeholders, including other project team members. By encouraging commitment to the goals of the project, schedule, and project management concepts, team members will feel more responsible for meeting such goals, following and keeping up with the schedule, and following project management concepts. Team members who are committed should feel a greater responsibility and accountability for their role in the project. The project manager's ability to get the commitment of team members and other stakeholders is related to leadership ability and communication style, and to the ability to influence project team members, topics covered in Chapters 3 and 4.

Now that we have discussed the importance of project control, project control philosophies, and levers for exerting project control, let us turn to the importance of project closure before we begin examining techniques for controlling and closing projects.

Why Is Project Closure Important?

Project closure may seem to be a noncritical step, but successful project managers fully embrace the closure process when finishing a project. It may seem obvious that the handover of the project needs to occur for the project to end, but what might happen if the handover is inadequate? Part of the handover procedure includes training the end users and other organizational members on the use of the new product. If that step is glossed over, all of the project team's hard work may be worthless. Hence, proper training and adequate installation and support for an appropriate period of time following the handover are required to ensure that the client organization can adequately implement its new system or product. In addition, formal signed-off closure helps prevent a project from going on and on without ever truly being finished.

Another issue to consider during the closure process is the documentation and archiving of the project management methods used. As a project team member or manager, you can expect to take part in future projects. It is likely that in these future projects, you will encounter issues and problems similar to those you encountered during the current project. Two years from now, you might face a problem like one you faced on the current project, but after two years, it may be difficult to remember how you dealt with the problem originally. Furthermore, your approach to the problem might have been ineffective, and in this case, the lesson you learned was not to address that problem in the same manner if it came up again. While we all think that we'll surely remember the details of such problems, the reality is that most project managers are constantly juggling many balls; thus, keeping documentation on lessons learned helps prevent you from repeating mistakes, allows you to concentrate on other issues, and finally, provides your organization with knowledge transfer on how to approach such issues in the future. By not following through with these closure procedures, you set yourself up to repeat mistakes and produce products that are insufficient for the needs of the client. Further, good project closure activities allow you to better assess whether you met client needs and then document how to enhance your success with clients in the future.

Example of Successful Project Closure

We have seen what can happen when project management principles are not followed, as at the Denver International Airport. Now let's consider what can happen when project management principles are followed. In this case, we will explore an e-mail system compatibility project in a New England–based medical company.

This medical company was actually a division of a larger global conglomerate, and had recently acquired another medical firm. One of the requirements necessary to successfully merge the operations of these two companies was the successful integration of their e-mail systems. A consulting company was hired, successfully merged these systems, and (related to our topic of project closure) provided an excellent example of closure techniques. Not only did the consulting company formally close the entire project, but they also employed techniques that closed each phase of the project. At the end of each phase, the consulting company drafted lessons-learned documents that helped the clients understand the capabilities of the new system. In closing the entire project, the consulting firm "trained the end users to properly use the new e-mail system" and trained system administrators to maintain the servers (Kloppenborg and Petrick, 2004). Using such procedures helps the project team keep the client happy and documents ways to enhance project management in the future.

In the next section, we present techniques that can be used to control projects with specific examples for implementing these techniques. Following this, the final section will conclude with techniques for managing project closure.

TECHNIQUES FOR MANAGING PROJECT CONTROL

We've discussed project control philosophies and various levers for exerting project control. Now we will discuss the techniques that you will use to control projects. Project control spans many of the knowledge areas of project management, and therefore, this section of the chapter is rather extensive in order to adequately address all of the control topics identified by the PMBOK. First, we will introduce some overarching project control techniques that are applicable to the entire project life cycle, specifically the use of standard operating procedures. Then, we will briefly review those techniques listed in the PMBOK's Project Integration Management section under the titles Monitor and Control Project Work and Integrated Change Control (see Figure 12.2). Following this, we will turn to a more detailed discussion of control techniques associated with the different project management core areas of knowledge listed in the PMBOK Guide (2004). These include scope control, schedule control, cost control, perform quality control, and risk monitoring and control.

Standard operating procedures
Activities and reporting methods instituted during the course of the project to monitor its progress and to provide reports for project managers and stakeholders.

Project log
A technique for controlling a project that involves recording information such as changes requested by the client, completion dates of deliverables, and so on.

Standard Operating Procedures

Standard operating procedures are activities and reporting methods instituted during the course of the project to monitor its progress and to provide reports for project managers and stakeholders. These may include regularly scheduled meetings, logs that are maintained as records of the progress being made, and regularly distributed reports so that managers and stakeholders can keep track of the progress being made. Chapter 4 provided important concepts to keep in mind as you plan for meetings. A **project log** contains information such as meeting times and outcomes, changes requested by the client, completion dates of project deliverables, and issues related to deliverables not completed on time. Many successful project managers also keep personal project logs in the form of notes, voice recordings, or even a journal or diary. Figure 12.3 shows an example of a project log. Regular reporting is another key technique for controlling a project. Stakeholders like to be kept informed on the status of various parts of the project,

Figure 12.2 PMBOK project integration management overview

Monitoring and controlling project work
The process of collecting, measuring, and disseminating information related to performance, as well as assessing measurements and trends in order to make any improvements.

project managers like to stay well informed of any problems or issues that come along, and individual team members like to see how their contributions are influencing the status of the entire project. Figure 12.4 shows a progress report template.

Monitor and Control Project Work

Monitoring and controlling project work includes techniques that project teams should use to monitor and control the various project processes, including initiation, planning, execution, and closure. As detailed in Figure 12.5, the inputs for this

Table of contents

1.0 Statement of Purpose

The purpose of this document is to keep an ongoing record of the progress on the project. This document includes (a) the date when progress on the project was monitored and (b) a list of the different events that happened on that date.

2.0 Project Log

Date	Event(s)
<Enter date here>	<Enter events(s) here>
.....	
June 3, 2007	Meeting held between client (HR Department) and IS Department. An initial project scope statement was devised, which was to be expanded on by the project manager.
June 6, 2007	Project team members selected.
June 7, 2007	Project team members met and went over project scope, developing the scope statement in more detail for client approval.
June 14, 2007	Meeting between project manager and client on the amended scope statement.
June 15, 2007	Stakeholder list and communication plan generated
<Add rows as necessary>	

Figure 12.3 Sample project log

process include the project management plan, work performance information, and rejected change requests. The project management plan is a document that defines how the project will be executed, monitored and controlled, and closed. Work performance information indicates the status of the different project activities that need to be completed. Finally, rejected change requests include the change requests, any supporting documentation, and justification of why they were rejected.

The techniques that can be used for monitoring and controlling project work include the use of project management methodologies, project management information systems, earned value technique, and expert judgment. A **project management methodology** is a defined process that helps the project team

Project management methodology
The process that helps the project team monitor and control the work being performed in accordance to the project management plan.

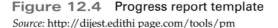

Project Progress Report

Period: Start date thru end date (Week Number)
Project Manager: Project Manager's Name

Accomplishments this Period:
• List accomplishments this period as bullets.

Scheduled Items Not Completed:
• List items/targets missed in this reporting period as bullets.

Activities Next Period:
• List proposed activities for next period as bullets.

Issues:
• Reference any new issues identified this period from the Project Issues Log.
• Reference any resolved issues this period from the Project Issues Log.

Changes to Stage Schedule:
• Identify any predicted slippage to the schedule end of stage date.
• List causes of slippage.
• Specify corrective action.

Figure 12.4   Progress report template
Source: http://dijest.edithi page.com/tools/pm

monitor and control the work being performed in accordance with the project management plan. Figure 12.6 shows a diagram illustrating the project management methodology used by Michigan state government agencies (although Michigan's project management processes are very similar to those discussed in this text, the processes used by other businesses or agencies may differ). The objective of this project management methodology is to establish clear guidelines and methods to ensure that projects are being conducted in a consistent manner, such that quality is promoted and the project deliverables are delivered on time and within budget.

Project information systems, such as Microsoft Project, help the team monitor and control the different activities being performed. The **earned value management (EVM)** technique is a very powerful cost-control method that provides estimates of the likelihood the project will meet schedule and budget requirements. It will be discussed in

Earned value management (EVM)
A technique that measures project performance over time, and provides a way to forecast future performance based on past performance.

Figure 12.5   PMBOK monitor and control project work inputs, tools and techniques, and outputs

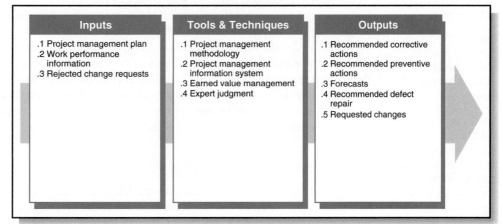

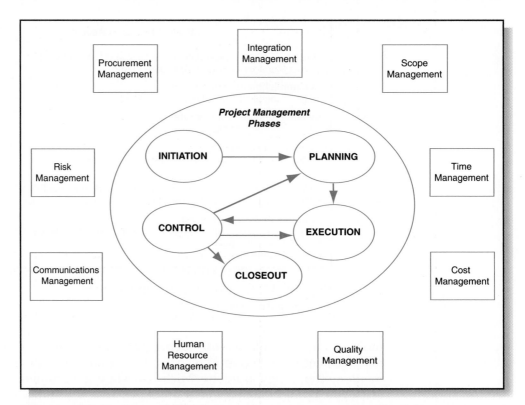

Figure 12.6 State of Michigan project management methodology

more detail later in this chapter as a specific technique associated with project cost control. Expert judgment, which has been discussed in prior chapters, relies on skilled and experienced personnel to make recommendations related to monitoring and controlling project work.

Finally, the outputs from the techniques listed in Monitor and Control Project Work include recommended corrective actions, recommended preventive actions, forecasts, recommended defect repair, and requested changes. **Recommended corrective actions** are documented recommendations needed to bring future project performance into conformance with the project management plan. **Recommended preventive actions** are documented recommendations that minimize the probability of negative consequences to the project. For example, in September 2005, the Government Accountability Office (GAO) reported to Congress their study of an ERP project in the Department of Defense (DOD). The GAO listed several corrective actions that should be taken to make sure the project stayed on target (see Figure 12.7). **Forecasts** are estimates or predictions of conditions or events in the project's future; they are determined from information and knowledge available at the time of the forecast. Any defects found in the product must be repaired. While the project is being executed, changes may be requested to reduce the project scope, modify the project cost, revise the project schedule, and so on.

Integrated Change Control

Integrated Change Control involves the identification, evaluation, and management of changes that occur from project initiation through project closure. Figure 12.8 provides a summary of the inputs, tools and techniques, and outputs associated with

Figure 12.7
Recommended preventive actions for the Navy's ERP implementation

Source: Adapted from http://ww.gao.gov/new.items/d05858.pdf.

integrated change control. Important inputs to this process include the project management plan, requested changes, work performance information, recommended preventive actions, recommended corrective actions, recommended defect repair, and deliverables. The project management plan (introduced as the baseline project plan in Chapter 5) provides the baseline necessary to identify and control changes. Requested changes are often identified when the project is executed, and these need to be documented. As discussed previously, work performance information is an indication of the status of the different activities required to complete the project. Recommended preventive actions, corrective actions, and defect repair have been discussed previously as the outputs of the monitor and control project work process. A deliverable is any unique and verifiable product of a process that is defined in the project management plan.

The techniques used to process these inputs into outputs include project management methodology, project management information systems, and expert judgment, all of which were discussed earlier in this chapter.

Outputs from the integrated change control process are approved change requests, rejected change requests, updates to the project management plan, updates to the scope statement, approved corrective actions, approved preventive actions, approved defect repair, validated defect repair, and deliverables. **Approved change requests** are the

Approved change requests
Documented and authorized changes that are scheduled for implementation by the project team.

Figure 12.8 PMBOK integrated change control inputs, tools and techniques, and outputs

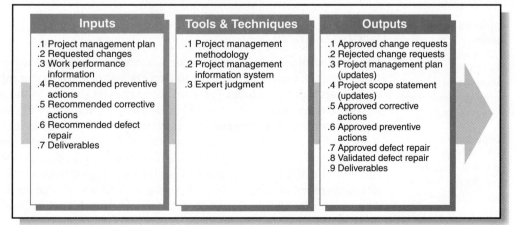

Inputs	Tools & Techniques	Outputs
.1 Project management plan .2 Requested changes .3 Work performance information .4 Recommended preventive actions .5 Recommended corrective actions .6 Recommended defect repair .7 Deliverables	.1 Project management methodology .2 Project management information system .3 Expert judgment	.1 Approved change requests .2 Rejected change requests .3 Project management plan (updates) .4 Project scope statement (updates) .5 Approved corrective actions .6 Approved preventive actions .7 Approved defect repair .8 Validated defect repair .9 Deliverables

2.0 Change Request Log: HR Intranet Project									
No	Description	Requestor Name	Request Date	Request type	Urgency	Assigned To	Assigned Date	Status	Close Date
1	Change regarding project scope— additional linkages to employee salary information with appropriate levels of security	John Allen	8/15/07	Scope	High	Bob Doe	8/16/07	In-Progress	\<pending\>
2	New layout of homepage requested by client to include additional menu items on top of screen	Sue King	8/28/07	Scope	Moderate	Lynn Talbot	8/30/07	In-Progress	\<pending\>
	....								
	\<add rows as necessary\>								

Figure 12.9 Approved change request form for 3GPP

Rejected change requests
Requested changes that were not chosen for implementation.

Approved corrective actions
Documented and authorized guidelines necessary to bring future project performance in conformance with the project management plan.

Approved defect repair
Approved and authorized actions that are recommended to correct defects in the project deliverables.

Scope control
The process of assuring that only agreed-upon changes are made to the project's scope.

documented and authorized changes that are scheduled for implementation by the project team (see Figure 12.9). **Rejected change requests** are those changes that have not been scheduled for implementation. The project management plan and the scope statement must be updated if changes are made during project execution. **Approved corrective actions** are documented and authorized guidelines necessary to bring future project performance in conformance to the project management plan. **Approved preventive actions** are those that are intended to reduce the probability of negative consequences to the project due to identified risks. An **approved defect repair** is any approved and authorized action that is recommended to correct defects in project deliverables. As discussed earlier, a deliverable is a product that is produced as part of the project.

We now turn our attention to those project control techniques that are specific to the different project management core areas of knowledge. These include the PMBOK (2004) areas of scope control, schedule control, cost control, perform quality control, and risk monitoring and control.

Scope Control

Scope Control is a formal process for assuring that only agreed-upon changes are made to the project's scope. Figure 12.10 depicts a summary of the inputs, tools and techniques, and outputs associated with scope control. Inputs to the scope control process include the scope statement, work breakdown structure (WBS), WBS dictionary, scope management plan, performance reports, approved change requests, and work performance information. The scope statement provides the current boundaries of the project, as described in Chapter 5. The WBS, covered in Chapter 6, is the list that results from the process of dividing the entire project into manageable tasks or work packages. The detailed content of the work packages in a WBS are described in the WBS dictionary. The scope management plan is a document that describes how the project scope is defined, documented, verified, managed, and controlled during the project life cycle.

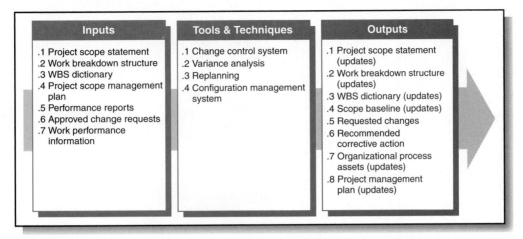

Inputs	Tools & Techniques	Outputs
.1 Project scope statement .2 Work breakdown structure .3 WBS dictionary .4 Project scope management plan .5 Performance reports .6 Approved change requests .7 Work performance information	.1 Change control system .2 Variance analysis .3 Replanning .4 Configuration management system	.1 Project scope statement (updates) .2 Work breakdown structure (updates) .3 WBS dictionary (updates) .4 Scope baseline (updates) .5 Requested changes .6 Recommended corrective action .7 Organizational process assets (updates) .8 Project management plan (updates)

Figure 12.10 PMBOK scope control inputs, tools and techniques, and outputs

Performance reports describe what the project team has accomplished so far in terms of the deliverables that have been completed. An approved change request (as discussed earlier and illustrated in Figure 12.9) impacts the project scope because it is a modification to the agreed-upon project scope baseline, which is defined by the scope statement, WBS, and WBS dictionary. Work performance information is an indication of the status of the different activities required to complete the project.

To transform these inputs into outputs, specific tools and techniques may be used during the scope control process, including a project scope change control system, variance analysis, replanning, and a configuration management system. A **change control system** is a formal, documented process that describes the procedures for changing the project scope and product scope. Although we have introduced the concept of a change control system here in the scope control section, the term *change control system* is a generic term that includes a systematic process or system that the project team uses to handle changes to a variety of project aspects. Additional examples include change control systems focused on controlling schedules or costs. These change control systems can be implemented as flow charts, as in Figure 12.11, or they can be a checklist of items that must be addressed or satisfied before the change can be instituted. Figure 12.11 provides an example of a change control system proposed by *Project Magazine* (www.projectmagazine.com/jan02/scope4.html).

Variance analysis is an umbrella term referring to a set of techniques that can be used to determine the status of the various project management areas in order to evaluate the difference between the planned baselines and the actual results and to identify and correct any problems causing unacceptable variances. Within each control process, a variety of techniques can be utilized to conduct variance analyses (see Figure 12.12). As an example, scope variance analysis involves identifying the cause of variance relative to the project baseline and determining whether any corrective action is needed. Scope variance analysis draws upon variance analyses done in other core project areas, such as project quality, costs, and schedule. Scope reporting specifically refers to the process of periodically ascertaining and documenting the status of cost, schedule, and technical (quality) performance.

In the next section, we will learn how features within Microsoft Project can be used to aid in variance analysis. Any approved change requests will affect the project scope, and consequently, the project scope management plan will need to be updated. A **configuration management system** provides guidelines that ensure that

Change control system
A formal, documented process that describes the procedures by which the project and product scope can be changed.

Variance analysis
The process of identifying the cause of variance relative to the project baseline and determining whether any corrective action is needed.

Configuration management system
A scope control technique that ensures that the requested changes to the project and product scope are thoroughly considered and documented before being implemented.

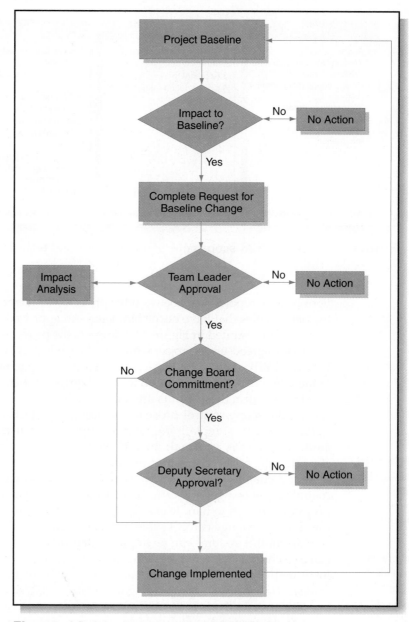

Figure 12.11 Change control system sample

Source: http://www.deprep.org/2004/Attachedfile/tb04d239-enc2.htm

the requested changes to the project and product scope are thoroughly considered and documented before being implemented. Similar to the change control system illustrated in Figure 12.11, a configuration management system can be represented in the form of a flowchart.

Finally, outputs from the scope control process include updates to the project scope statement, updates to the WBS, updates to the WBS dictionary, updates to the scope baseline, requested changes, recommended corrective action, updates to the organizational process assets, and updates to the project management plan. If approved change requests (which come through the change control system) have an effect on the project scope, then the scope statement, the WBS, the WBS dictionary,

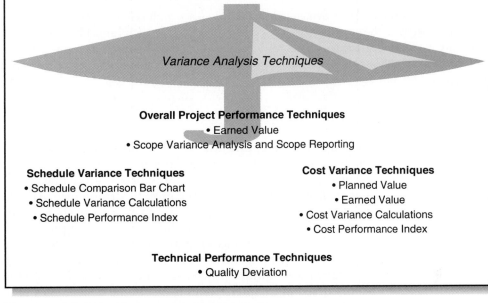

Figure 12.12 Variance analysis techniques

COMMON PROBLEMS
Recovering Troubled Projects

Variances are likely to occur on any project. In a successful project, variances are acceptable. In contrast, a troubled project is one in which the variances are beyond acceptable tolerances. It is identified by poor performance in terms of time, cost, and quality. The task of the project team is to recover the troubled project and take corrective actions to bring it back in line with the plan.

The first step in the recovery process is to recognize that the project is in trouble. Fortunately, some warning signs help in this process:

- None of the project team members knows when the project will be completed.
- The project deliverables do not meet the set quality standards.
- Team members have to work overtime to complete their parts of the work.
- The project requirements are not stable.
- The stakeholders have lost interest in the project because they believe that it will never be completed.
- The morale of the team is low and conflicts among team members are rampant.
- The customer is planning to sue the performing organization for not delivering the project.

(Source:http://builder.com.com/5100-6315-1058679.html. Accesssed October 16, 2006.)

The next step is to get a detailed assessment regarding the status of the project. The project manager should determine the status of each of the work packages in the work breakdown structure (WBS). This assessment can help the project manager determine whether the project can be recovered or should be terminated.

If the project can be recovered, the final step is to develop the recovery plan. The project manager should determine what corrective actions should be taken to regain control of the project. This involves identifying any repair work needed, any issues to be resolved, and any other outstanding items. Here are some general guidelines that can be used to recover troubled projects (Source: Sifri, 2003):

- When trying to resolve project issues, the project team should focus on analyzing the findings to develop the recovery plan instead of focusing on what happened or who is to blame.
- There are no ready-made recipes or silver-bullet solutions. The project team should work together to develop the recovery plan.

- The project should be recovered to bring it in conformance with the objectives.
- Any work activity listed as "done" or "completed" should only be so categorized if all aspects of the activity are fully completed.

- It is important to be realistic in determining what can or cannot be fixed.
- The project team members should be open-minded and ready to accept any changes.

the scope baseline, and the project management plan need to be updated. The results of scope control can lead to new change requests. Recommended corrective actions are any documented and authorized guidelines (refer back to Figure 12.7) that are necessary to bring future project performance in conformance to the project management plan. If the approved change requests have an effect on the project scope, the historical database of the organizational process assets must be updated with the causes of variances identified during variance analysis, the justification for any corrective action, and any lessons learned during the scope control process.

Many scope control processes can be done with project management software. As discussed in Chapters 5 and 6, one of the deliverables of the scope management process that is extremely valuable for large projects with many tasks is the work breakdown structure (WBS), which can be created in products such as Microsoft Project (see Figure 12.13). Further, if any of the change requests are approved

Figure 12.13 WBS created in Microsoft Project

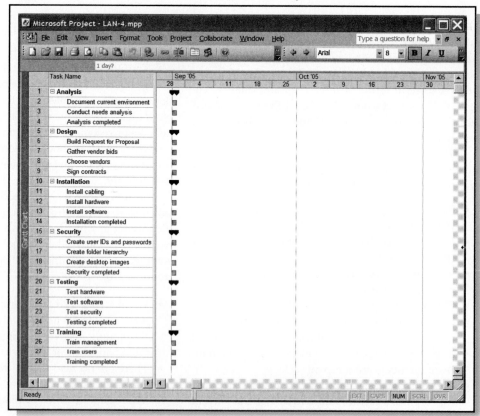

through the scope control process, it is easy to modify the WBS because it only involves moving, or copying and pasting tasks within the already created document.

Schedule Control

Schedule Control
The process of putting in place procedures and rules for controlling changes to the project schedule.

Schedule Control is the process of putting in place procedures and rules for controlling changes to the project schedule. Inputs to the schedule control process include the schedule management plan, schedule baseline, performance reports, and approved change requests. The schedule management plan indicates how the project schedule will be managed and controlled. The approved project schedule, also referred to as the schedule baseline, is used in measuring and reporting scheduling performance. Performance reports describe what the project team has accomplished so far in terms of the planned dates that have been met and those that have not. An approved change request impacts the project schedule because it is a modification to the agreed upon schedule baseline.

As detailed in Figure 12.14, the tools and techniques that can be used to convert these inputs into outputs include progress reporting, schedule change control systems, performance measurements, project management software, variance analysis, and schedule comparison bar charts. Progress reporting involves describing what the project team has accomplished during a certain period of time. The schedule change control system is used to determine the process for evaluating and implementing potential schedule changes, including change approval authorization hierarchies. Similar to change control systems, the schedule control system may be either a flow chart documenting the process by which changes can be made to the schedule or a list of items that must be satisfied before the change can be implemented. Performance measurement is used to determine the magnitude and criticality of schedule variations. Project management software is used to track project schedules or forecast the effects of variations in activity completion dates. Variance analysis is used to evaluate potential and actual variance on the project schedule. A schedule comparison bar chart (Figure 12.15) displays two bars, one that shows the status of an activity based on the schedule baseline, and another that depicts the current status of the same activity. This type

Figure 12.14 PMBOK schedule control inputs, tools and techniques, and outputs

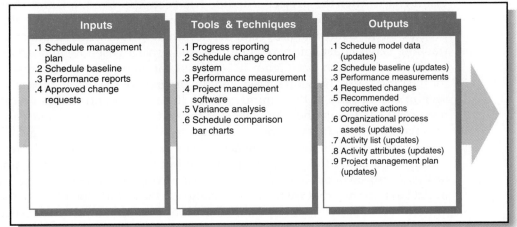

Inputs	Tools & Techniques	Outputs
.1 Schedule management plan .2 Schedule baseline .3 Performance reports .4 Approved change requests	.1 Progress reporting .2 Schedule change control system .3 Performance measurement .4 Project management software .5 Variance analysis .6 Schedule comparison bar charts	.1 Schedule model data (updates) .2 Schedule baseline (updates) .3 Performance measurements .4 Requested changes .5 Recommended corrective actions .6 Organizational process assets (updates) .7 Activity list (updates) .8 Activity attributes (updates) .9 Project management plan (updates)

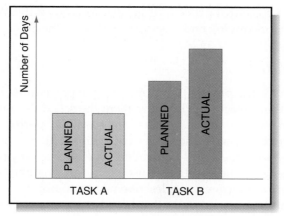

Figure 12.15
Schedule comparison
bar chart

of bar chart provides a graphical representation of whether the schedule is progressing as planned. A quick look at such a chart allows a project manager to quickly determine that task A is on schedule, whereas task B is not.

Outputs from the schedule control process (refer back to Figure 12.14) include schedule updates, performance measurements, requested changes, recommended corrective actions, updates to organizational process assets, updates to the activity list, updates to activity attributes, and updates to the project management plan (all of which have been introduced in prior chapters). The approved change requests will impact the project schedule, and as a result, the schedule baseline, the activity list, and any affected activity will need to be updated. The stakeholders will need to be notified of the performance measurements. The results of schedule variance analysis can lead to new change requests. Recommended corrective actions are the procedures initiated to address schedule performance problems. If the approved change requests have an effect on the project schedule, the historical database of the organizational process assets must be updated with the causes of variances identified during variance analysis, the justification for any corrective action, and any lessons learned during the schedule control process. The schedule component of the project management plan will need to be updated to reflect any approved changes that result from the schedule control process.

A feature of Microsoft Project that is helpful in schedule control is the tracking Gantt chart. After the project schedule has been approved, a Gantt chart can be created based on the information in the approved schedule. As the project progresses, the Gantt chart can be updated with the actual schedule information. The tracking Gantt chart compares planned (the project baseline) and actual project schedule information (see Figure 12.16). This chart allows the project team to monitor the progress of individual tasks and the progress of the whole project. As can be seen in Figure 12.16 at the summary level, the analysis and design modules have been completed (note the 100% labels at the ends of the analysis and design bars). The installation module is 52 percent complete, with varying percentages of completion for its individual tasks. If the actual date were, say, May 1, 2005, we might be feeling good about the progress on this project because we're getting portions of tasks done ahead of our baseline schedule. However, if the date were June 3, 2005, we might be concerned that we have yet to complete the installation phase of the project. We can see from the tracking Gantt chart that we are behind with respect to our approved schedule.

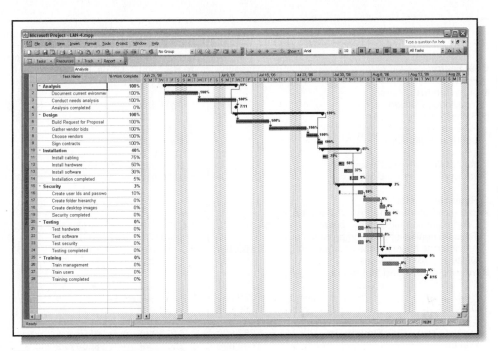

Figure 12.16 Tracking Gantt chart

Cost Control

Cost Control is the process of monitoring cost performance to ensure that only appropriate changes are included in the modified cost baseline. As shown in Figure 12.17, the inputs to the cost control process include the cost baseline, project funding requirements, performance reports, work performance information, approved change requests, and the project management plan. The cost baseline is a time-phased budget that is used to measure and monitor cost performance. An example is presented in Figure 12.18, where the cost baselines for four possible alternatives to migrate the U.S. House of Representatives' eight mainframe-based applications to new technology are presented. Funding requirements are determined from the cost baseline, but it is common for funding requirements to exceed the cost baseline by a margin to account

Figure 12.17 PMBOK cost control: inputs, tools and techniques, and outputs

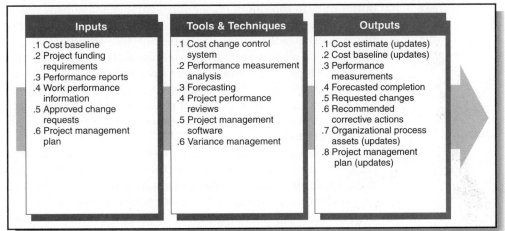

Inputs	Tools & Techniques	Outputs
.1 Cost baseline	.1 Cost change control system	.1 Cost estimate (updates)
.2 Project funding requirements	.2 Performance measurement analysis	.2 Cost baseline (updates)
.3 Performance reports	.3 Forecasting	.3 Performance measurements
.4 Work performance information	.4 Project performance reviews	.4 Forecasted completion
.5 Approved change requests	.5 Project management software	.5 Requested changes
.6 Project management plan	.6 Variance management	.6 Recommended corrective actions
		.7 Organizational process assets (updates)
		.8 Project management plan (updates)

Cost Factor	FY 99 Baseline	System-Wide Alternatives			
		Re-Platform to RS/6000	Relocation to Legis. Branch	Replacement withC/S COTS	Top-Ranked Alternative
1. Non-Recurring Costs					
Installation/Conversion	$5,500	$301,458	$252,458	$380,708	$266,458
Software Customization	$0	$0	$0	$1,127,500	$11,000
Hardware Purchase	$0	$1,010,480	$215,000	$161,391	$255,300
Software Purchase	$0	$349,480	$0	$513,230	$103,000
Training	$0	$24,000	$7,000	$71,000	$22,000
Year 2000 Software Renovation	$573,000	$573,000	$573,000	$423,000	$463,000
Total Non-Recurring Costs	**$578,500**	**$2,258,418**	**$1,047,458**	**$2,676,829**	**$1,120,758**
2. Recurring Costs					
Personnel Salaries and Fringe Benefits					
Computer Operations (Enterprise)	$4,108,213	$4,108,213	$2,212,114	$2,212,114	$2,212,114
Telecommunications (Communications)	$316,016	$316,016	$316,016	$316,016	$316,016
Applications Maintenance (Integration)	$3,160,164	$3,160,164	$3,160,164	$2,844,147	$3,160,164
Office of Mailing Services	$0	$0	$632,033	$632,033	$632,033
Hardware (Lease and Maintenance)					
Mainframe Processor Costs	$1,258,761	$0	$0	$0	$0
RAID	$279,097	$0	$0	$0	$0
DASD	$59,863	$0	$0	$0	$0
STK Tape Silos	$487,923	$0	$0	$0	$0
FileNet Optical Disk Storage Unit	$253,938	$253,938	$253,938	$0	$253,938
Printers	$609,699	$609,699	$609,699	$609,699	$609,699
Printer Usage	$60,519	$60,519	$60,519	$60,519	$60,519
New Hardware (Maintenance)	$0	$479,819	$102,091	$76,635	$121,227
Software (License and Maintenance)					
Mainframe Operating system	$974,063	$0	$0	$0	$0
Utility software	$1,446,923	$866,888	$0	$0	$0
COTS Applications	$805,864	$805,864	$256,438	$246,383	$352,386
External Vendor Services					
Inter-Agency Timesharing (Legis. Branch)	$0	$0	$1,093,113	$943,045	$1,080,812
Disaster Recovery/Back-Up	$82,004	$82,004	$82,004	$82,004	$82,004
NCOA Services (Gov't or Comm. Vendor)	$0	$0	$680,694	$0	$0
Total Recurring Costs	**$13,903,047**	**$10,743,124**	**$9,458,823**	**$8,022,595**	**$8,880,912**
Total Estimated Costs	**$14,481,547**	**$13,001,542**	**$10,506,281**	**$10,699,424**	**$10,001,670**

Figure 12.18 Cost baselines for U.S. House of Representatives mainframe migration

Source: http://www.house.gov/IG/98hoc03/Image99.gif

for cost overruns. Budgetary estimates for the cost baseline can be done top-down or bottom-up. In top-down budgeting, senior management sets spending limits, which allows for greater control over expenses. In bottom-up budgeting, expected costs have the potential to be more accurate, but less incentive is provided to economize. Performance reports provide information related to cost and resource performance as the project is executed. Work performance information is an indication of the status and cost of the different activities required to complete the project. An approved change request impacts the project budget because it incurs a modification of the cost baseline. The project management plan developed in the planning stage of the project is used in the Cost Control process.

The PMBOK Guide recognizes several tools and techniques to assist in cost control. These include a cost control change system, performance measurement analysis, forecasting, project performance reviews, project management software, and variance management. The cost control change system provides the procedures by which changes can be made to the cost baseline, just as the schedule change control system is used to provide procedures for making changes to the schedule. Such a system might be represented in flowchart form (as in Figure 12.11), which will stimulate certain activities such as filling out change request forms. In many cases, this may be the same system used to outline the steps necessary to make changes to the scope and schedule.

Performance measurement analysis helps the project team in assessing the magnitude of any variance that may occur during project execution. A very powerful tool used for performance measurement analysis is the earned value technique, which will be discussed in detail in the next section of this chapter. Forecasts are estimates or predictions of conditions or events in the project's future that are determined from information and knowledge available at the time they are made. An example might include forecasted changes in pricing or availability of resources needed by the project team.

Performance reviews are meetings held to assess cost performance over time, the activities that are running over or under budget, and milestones that have been met and those that remain to be met. These reviews are typically used in conjunction with performance reporting techniques, which include variance analysis, trend analysis, and the earned value technique. Large deviations from the planned cost performance should be carefully investigated, and corrective actions should be taken to bring the future cost performance in conformance to the budgeted project cost. Trend analysis is a cost control method for examining project cost performance over time to determine whether performance is improving or deteriorating. Figure 12.19 shows one method for evaluating cost performance over time by graphing the percentage over or under budget across time. As in many of the control techniques listed throughout this chapter, project management software can assist the project team to track actual performance against planned performance and to forecast the effects of any changes on the planned project cost. Variance management, the last tool mentioned in Figure 12.17 involves determining how changes to the cost baseline will be managed.

Finally, the outputs of the cost control process (refer back to Figure 12.17) include updates to the cost estimates, updates to the cost baseline, performance measurements, forecasted completion, requested changes, recommended corrective actions, organizational process assets updates, and updates to the project management plan. If any of the change requests are approved, they will affect the cost baseline. Consequently, the cost estimates, the cost baseline, and the project management plan need to be updated to reflect the approved changes. Based on the earned value technique, the

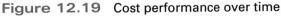

Figure 12.19 Cost performance over time

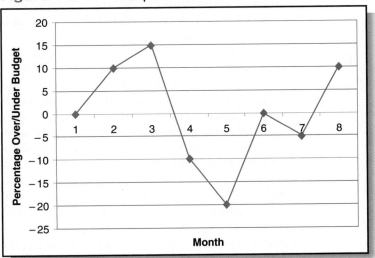

performance measurements will be reported to the key stakeholders. Similarly, the earned value technique will provide a forecasted completion date as well as the cost at completion. The process of cost control itself can lead to the need for change requests, and recommended corrective actions are done to address any cost performance problems. If the approved change requests affect the project cost baseline, the historical database of the organizational process assets must be updated with the causes of variances identified, the justification for any corrective action, and any lessons learned during the schedule control process.

Earned Value Management

The earned value technique is one tool for doing variance analysis. It incorporates scope, time, and cost data. Given a cost baseline, the project team can determine how well the project is meeting scope, time, and cost goals by entering actual information and then comparing it to the baseline.

The easiest way to get started with the earned value technique is to break the project into discrete time periods, usually by activities or summary activities from the WBS. Key values are then calculated for each activity. The key terms and their formulas are:

- *Planned value* (PV) is the budgeted cost for the work scheduled to be completed on an activity up to a given point in time. Because it is part of the established budget, its value should be known. Planned value is also known as the Budgeted Cost of Work Scheduled (BCWS).
- *Earned value* (EV) involves the budgeted amount for the work actually completed on the activity during a given time period. This is the product of the planned value and the percentage of work completed on the activity during that time period ($EV = PV \times \%\ completed$). Earned value is also known as the Budgeted Cost of Work Performed (BCWP).
- *Actual cost* (AC) refers to the actual costs associated with work on an activity during a particular time period. It is not calculated but drawn from invoices and other financial records. Actual cost is also known as the Actual Cost of Work Performed (ACWP).
- *Cost variance* (CV) is the difference between the earned value (EV) and the actual cost (AC), ($CV = EV - AC$). Cost variance is thus a monetary indicator of whether the project has cost more than it should have up to a particular point in time. If EV is greater than the AC, this means the organization has "earned" more value on the project than it has actually cost, and thus the project is currently coming in under budget. If EV is less than AC, the project is costing more than it should.
- *Schedule variance* (SV) is the difference between the scheduled completion of the activity and the actual completion. This is the difference between EV and PV ($SV = EV - PV$). Schedule variance is thus a monetary indicator of whether the project is on time. If EV (a monetary measure of the amount of work that has been completed at this point in the project) is greater than the PV (a monetary measure of the amount of work that *should* have been competed at this point in the project), then SV is positive, indicating that the project is ahead of schedule.
- *Cost performance index* (CPI) is the ratio of EV to AC and is expressed as a percentage, $CPI = (EV/AC) \times 100$. Similar to cost variance, CPI looks at EV and AC—but this time as a ratio—to calculate how efficiently the project is being accomplished from a cost standpoint. A CPI value of 100 percent means the project is progressing as expected in relation to project costs. A CPI value of less than 100 percent (e.g., 80 percent) means that the project is costing more than expected and has been only about 80 percent efficient from a cost perspective.

A CPI of greater than 100 percent means the project team is being more efficient than anticipated in relationship to project costs.

- *Schedule performance index* (SPI) is the ratio of EV to PV and is also expressed as a percentage, $SPI = (EV/PV) \times 100$. Similar to schedule variance, SPI looks at EV and PV—but this time as a ratio—to calculate how efficiently the project is being accomplished from a schedule standpoint. A SPI value of 100 percent means the project is progressing as expected in relation to the project schedule. If the SPI is below 100 percent (e.g., 80 percent), the indication is that the activity (or project as a whole) is behind schedule 20 percent. If the SPI is above 100 percent, the indication is that the activity is ahead of schedule.

Table 12.1 provides an example of earned value calculations. Suppose a project included an activity A that took a week to be completed and would cost a total of $10,000. The planned value of PV is $10,000. The percentage of work completed on activity A during week 1 is 100 percent. Therefore, the earned value (EV) is $10,000 (100% × $10,000). From Table 12.1 we can see that during week 1, $12,000 was spent on activity A, when the budget had allotted $10,000 for this activity. The actual cost (AC) is therefore $12,000.

Using these values, we can now calculate the other key values. The cost variance is the difference between the earned value (EV) and the actual cost (AC), or –$2,000. A negative CV means that it cost more than planned to perform the work. The schedule variance is the difference between the earned value (EV) and the planned value (PV), which is 0. The cost performance index (CPI) is the ratio of the EV to the AC, expressed as a percentage, which is 83 percent. The CPI indicates that the activity is over budget. The schedule performance index is the ratio of the EV to the PV expressed as a percentage, which is 100 percent. This indicates that the activity is on schedule. Therefore, from a quick glance at Table 12.1, an experienced project manager could see that after the first week activity A was on track to meet its scheduled completion time (SPI) but was over budget for the first week (CPI). The key to understanding the variances and indexes described is that for variances, negative values indicate possible problems, while for indexes, values below 100 percent indicate possible problems.

To use the earned value technique to determine the status of the entire project (as opposed to just one activity), all project activities that have been fully or partially completed must be analyzed. Depending on the size and scope of the project, the time periods under examination may be days, weeks, or months. Performing a project-level EVM allows you to gauge the overall health of the entire project. Table 12.2 shows an EVM for a 10-week project. From this example, we can see that after 6 weeks this particular project is over budget and behind schedule. Knowing that the project is currently behind schedule and over budget allows you to make changes or arrangements to the remaining activities to bring it back to the planned schedule and budget.

Table 12.1 Earned Value Calculations for Activity A Over Two Weeks

Activity A	Week 1	Week 2
Earned Value (EV)	10,000	10,000
Planned Value (PV)	10,000	10,000
Actual Cost (AC)	12,000	8,000
Cost Variance (CV)	–2,000	2,000
Schedule Variance (SV)	0	0
Cost Performance Index (CPI)	83%	125%
Schedule Performance Index (SPI)	100%	100%

Table 12.2 Project Level EVM for a 10-Week Project

	Wk 1	Wk 2	Wk 3	Wk 4	Wk 5	Wk 6	Wk 7	Wk 8	Wk 9	Wk 10	Plan	%	EV
Initial meeting with sponsor	16,000										16,000	100	16,000
Draft project requirements		24,000	8,000								32,000	100	32,000
Review with stakeholders			4,000	8,000							12,000	100	12,000
Develop and approve project charter				9,000							9,000	100	9,000
Develop WBS				12,000							12,000	100	12,000
Estimate durations					13,000						13,000	100	13,000
Assign resources					8,000	8,000					16,000	75	12,000
Determine task relationships					8,000						8,000	50	4,000
Enter cost information					16,000						16,000	25	4,000
Review plan with stakeholders							8,000				8,000		
Review off-the-shelf training materials								23,000			23,000		
Negotiate contract for materials								24,000	16,000		40,000		
Develop communications about new training									18,000		18,000		
Create survey to determine needs										24,000	24,000		
Administer survey										12,000	12,000		
Develop list of instructors										6,000	6,000		
Coordinate with facilities to setup classrooms							30,000	30,000			60,000		
Schedule courses										4,000	4,000		
Develop system for signing up for classes										16,000	16,000		
Develop course evaluation form										20,000	20,000		
Weekly PV	16,000	24,000	12,000	29,000	45,000	8,000	38,000	77,000	34,000	82,000	365,000		114,000
PV or cumulative plan	16,000	40,000	52,000	81,000	126,000	134,000	172,000	249,000	283,000	365,000			
Weekly AC	17,000	25,000	13,000	30,000	46,000	9,000							
AC or cumulative actual	17,000	42,000	55,000	85,000	131,000	140,000							
Weekly EV	16,000	24,000	12,000	29,000	27,000	6,000							
EV or cumulative EV	16,000	40,000	52,000	81,000	108,000	114,000							
Project EV as of Week 6	114,000												
Project PV as of Week 6	134,000												
Project AC as of Week 6	140,000												
CV = EV – AC	–$26,000												
SV = EV – PV	–$20,000												
CPI = EV/AC	81.43%												
SVI = EV/PV	85.07%												
Estimated cost at completion	$448,246												
Estimated time to complete	12												

Two additional pieces of information available in this EV analysis allow managers to determine how critical it is to make changes in an effort to bring schedules and budgets back under control. Estimated cost at completion and estimated time to complete (the bottom two rows in Table 12.2) give estimates for how much the completed project will cost and how long it will take if the status quo is maintained. In other words, if no changes are made and the remaining tasks end up being similar to previous tasks in terms of budget and schedule, these two estimates will give you an idea of when the project will be completed and how much it will cost.

To compute the estimated cost at completion, the additional piece of information required is the budget at completion (BAC), or the total budgeted cost of the project. To compute the estimated cost at completion (EAC), the budget at completion (BAC) is divided by the cost performance index (CPI) for the current project status ($EAC = BAC \div CPI$). As an example, if the originally anticipated cost (BAC) is \$100,000 and the project CPI is .80, then the EAC is \$125,000 (i.e., the cost is running over budget). To compute the estimated time to complete (ETC), the additional piece of information required is the original time estimate for completion of the project. The estimated time to completion is calculated by dividing the estimate for completion by the schedule performance index (SPI), ($ETC = Original\ Time\ Estimate \div SPI$).

Microsoft Project has built-in variance analysis tools that allow the project manager to determine whether there have been any deviations from the baseline. As the tasks are updated with the actual information as the project progresses, Microsoft Project automatically calculates the variance. The project manager can refer to this information to determine whether there are any variances to budget or schedule so that corrective actions can be taken to bring the project in conformance to the plans. Figure 12.20 shows how this feature of Microsoft Project can be used to determine the variance in a project schedule.

Figure 12.20 Variance analysis

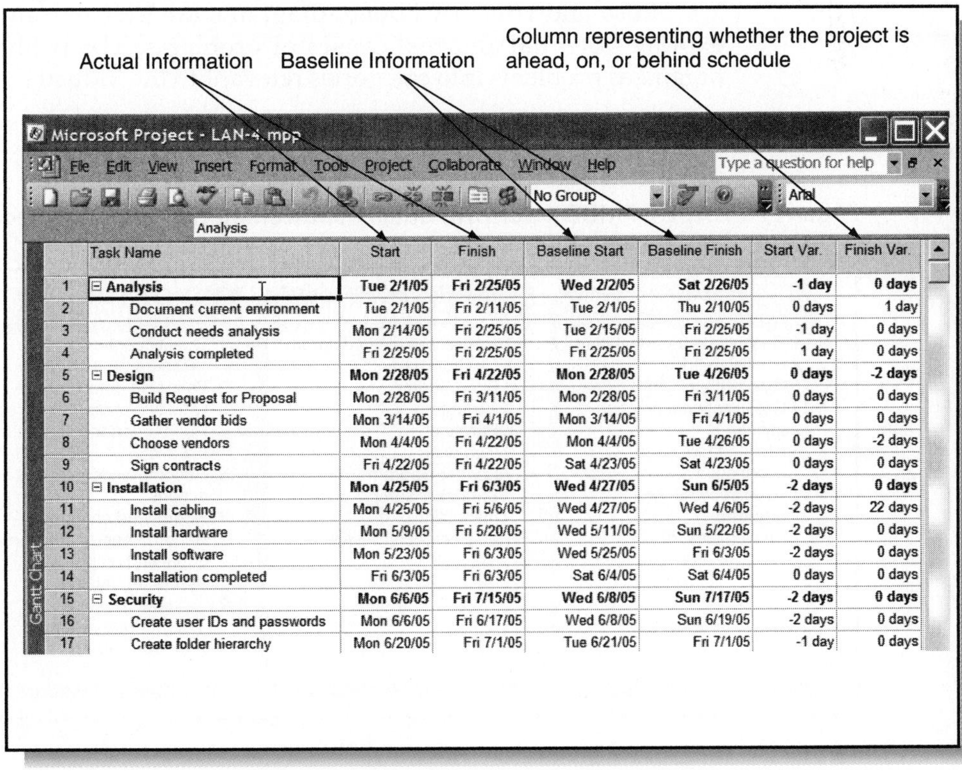

	Task Name	Start	Finish	Baseline Start	Baseline Finish	Start Var.	Finish Var.
1	**⊟ Analysis**	**Tue 2/1/05**	**Fri 2/25/05**	**Wed 2/2/05**	**Sat 2/26/05**	**-1 day**	**0 days**
2	Document current environment	Tue 2/1/05	Fri 2/11/05	Tue 2/1/05	Thu 2/10/05	0 days	1 day
3	Conduct needs analysis	Mon 2/14/05	Fri 2/25/05	Tue 2/15/05	Fri 2/25/05	-1 day	0 days
4	Analysis completed	Fri 2/25/05	Fri 2/25/05	Fri 2/25/05	Fri 2/25/05	1 day	0 days
5	**⊟ Design**	**Mon 2/28/05**	**Fri 4/22/05**	**Mon 2/28/05**	**Tue 4/26/05**	**0 days**	**-2 days**
6	Build Request for Proposal	Mon 2/28/05	Fri 3/11/05	Mon 2/28/05	Fri 3/11/05	0 days	0 days
7	Gather vendor bids	Mon 3/14/05	Fri 4/1/05	Mon 3/14/05	Fri 4/1/05	0 days	0 days
8	Choose vendors	Mon 4/4/05	Fri 4/22/05	Mon 4/4/05	Tue 4/26/05	0 days	-2 days
9	Sign contracts	Fri 4/22/05	Fri 4/22/05	Sat 4/23/05	Sat 4/23/05	0 days	0 days
10	**⊟ Installation**	**Mon 4/25/05**	**Fri 6/3/05**	**Wed 4/27/05**	**Sun 6/5/05**	**-2 days**	**0 days**
11	Install cabling	Mon 4/25/05	Fri 5/6/05	Wed 4/27/05	Wed 4/6/05	-2 days	22 days
12	Install hardware	Mon 5/9/05	Fri 5/20/05	Wed 5/11/05	Sun 5/22/05	-2 days	0 days
13	Install software	Mon 5/23/05	Fri 6/3/05	Wed 5/25/05	Fri 6/3/05	-2 days	0 days
14	Installation completed	Fri 6/3/05	Fri 6/3/05	Sat 6/4/05	Sat 6/4/05	0 days	0 days
15	**⊟ Security**	**Mon 6/6/05**	**Fri 7/15/05**	**Wed 6/8/05**	**Sun 7/17/05**	**-2 days**	**0 days**
16	Create user IDs and passwords	Mon 6/6/05	Fri 6/17/05	Wed 6/8/05	Sun 6/19/05	-2 days	0 days
17	Create folder hierarchy	Mon 6/20/05	Fri 7/1/05	Tue 6/21/05	Fri 7/1/05	-1 day	0 days

Quality Control

Perform Quality Control is the process of screening project results to determine whether they conform to relevant quality standards and then identifying means to eliminate causes of unsatisfactory results. As shown in Figure 12.21, the inputs required for accomplishing quality control include the quality management plan, quality metrics, quality checklists, organizational process assets, work performance information, approved change requests, and deliverables. A quality management plan specifies how quality measures will be implemented during a project (see Figure 12.22). Quality metrics—such as response time for a software application—define specific processes, events, or products and include an explanation of how their quality will be measured.

Quality checklists, another input for performing quality control, are produced as part of quality planning and are tools used to ensure that a specific set of actions necessary for quality control has been correctly performed (see Figure 12.23 for an abbreviated example of items that might be found on a quality checklist). Organizational process assets represent the organization's learning and knowledge from previous projects. Work performance information includes technical performance measures, project deliverables completion status, and the implementation of the required corrective actions. An approved change request impacts project quality because it requires a modification of the quality management plan. A deliverable is any unique and verifiable product of a process that is defined in the project management plan.

The tools and techniques recommended for the PMBOK's perform quality control (as process shown in Figure 12.21) includes the cause-and-effect diagram, control charts, flowcharting, histograms, Pareto charts, run charts, scatter diagrams, statistical sampling, inspection, and defect repair reviews. These tools and techniques were also introduced in Chapter 8, but we discuss them in some detail here as well.

Cause and effect (fishbone) diagrams are a diagramming technique used to explore potential and real causes of problems. The fishbone diagram typically organizes problems into categories relevant to the industry and allows project team

Figure 12.21 PMBOK perform quality control: inputs, tools and techniques, and outputs

Inputs	Tools & Techniques	Outputs
.1 Quality management plan .2 Quality metrics .3 Quality checklists .4 Organizational process assets .5 Work performance information .6 Approved change requests .7 Deliverables	.1 Cause and effect diagram .2 Control charts .3 Flowcharting .4 Histogram .5 Pareto chart .6 Run chart .7 Scatter diagram .8 Statistical sampling .9 Inspection .10 Defect repair review	.1 Quality control measurements .2 Validated defect repair .3 Quality baseline (updates) .4 Recommended corrective actions .5 Recommended preventive actions .6 Requested changes .7 Recommended defect repair .8 Organization process assets (updates) .9 Validated deliverables .10 Project Management Plan (Updates)

Figure 12.22 Quality management plan table of contents

members to work backward from major problems (outputs) to identify potential causes (inputs) (see Figure 12.24). As illustrated in the figure, a delay in a corporate intranet implementation could be traced back to a variety of potential problem areas, including personnel, materials, methods, and environmental factors. Each of these main factors could in turn be the result of several different issues. Personnel problems might include inexperienced programmers, too few people working on the project, or personality conflicts among those working on the project. Similarly, materials related issues causing project delays might include delays in hardware shipments, incorrect shipments, or materials damaged in transit. Fishbone diagrams are a tool for structuring the project team's thinking about potential problem areas and then uncovering the specific causes of problems in those areas. While we discuss fishbone diagrams as a control technique in this chapter, it is also useful in managing project quality (see Chapter 8) and managing project risk (see Chapter 9) as a method to anticipate potential project problems and risk factors.

Control charts are graphical, time-based charts used to display process results. As shown in Figure 12.25, these charts can be used to determine whether process deviations are the result of random or systematic causes. Normally fluctuations around the mean, or target value, on such a chart will be random (see the solid line on Figure 12.25). Control charts provide a visual tool for the project team to examine these fluctuations. Sudden systematic results on one side of the target value might require an investigation by the target team. A more concrete example in the information systems domain might be search time in a corporate intranet. If, during systems testing, search time suddenly and inexplicably started to take longer than expected (see the dashed line on

Quality Checklist				
Requirement	Yes	No	N/A	Comments/Remarks
Is there a well-developed set of procedures and metrics that have been identified and agreed upon for the project?				
Is there is an established and accessible knowledge base for the acceptable procedures and metrics (for example, project plan, test plan and training plan)				
Have the project team members been trained (according to the training plan) so as to adhere to the quality requirements mentioned in the above knowledge base?				
Is there an individual who is entrusted with the authority of verifying and enforcing the project quality?				
Are the procedures and metrics mentioned in the plans being followed?				
Are proper measurement techniques being used to gauge the quality of the project?				
Do the deliverables meet the project requirements?				
Are any problems recognized in the testing phase being properly documented?				
Are corrective actions being taken for identified problems in the testing phase?				
Are any changes to the test plan and the project plan (as identified in the testing phase) being properly incorporated?				

Figure 12.23   Quality checklist sample

Figure 12.25), an investigation might be launched to determine the cause and possible solutions (e.g., a larger server or better networking technology).

A flowchart is a graphical representation of a process (see Figure 12.26). Flowcharting helps to analyze how problems occur so that approaches can be developed to deal with them. A histogram is a bar chart showing a distribution of

Figure 12.24   Cause-and-effect diagram

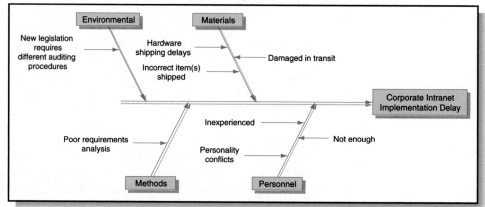

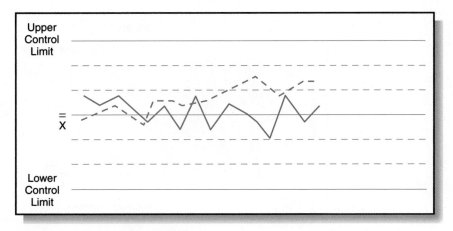

Figure 12.25 Control chart
Source: PMBOK 2000.

variables, with the height of each column representing the relative frequency of a quality problem. As an example, a histogram could be used to show categories of objects along with the frequency of their occurrence. One such application of a histogram is a Pareto diagram, which shows the various types of problems being encountered in a project, along with each problem's frequency (see Figure 12.27). Pareto diagrams were named based on Pareto's law, or the 80/20 rule, which states that 80 percent of problems are the result of 20 percent of the causes. By helping

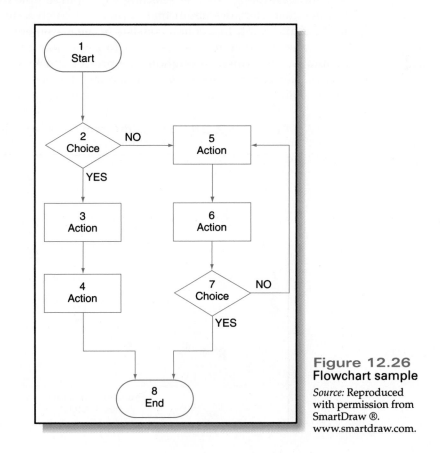

**Figure 12.26
Flowchart sample**

Source: Reproduced with permission from SmartDraw ®. www.smartdraw.com.

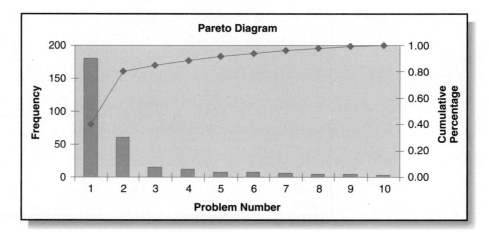

Figure 12.27   Pareto diagram

identify those problems occurring most frequently, the Pareto diagram gives the project team guidance on what problems are most critical to solve.

Run charts show trends in a process over time, variation over time, or declines or improvements in a process over time. These charts are used for trend analysis. A scatter diagram (see Figure 12.28) represents the pattern of relationship between two variables. The quality team can use this tool to study and identify the possible relationship between changes observed in the variables. This particular figure illustrates an exponentially increasing number of errors as the program grows in complexity. Statistical sampling involves selecting a random sample from a population in order to infer characteristics about that population. Such sampling might be integrated into a scatter plot. Inspection consists of measurement and testing procedures to determine whether results conform to particular project standards. Inspection should be performed throughout the project and throughout each of the project phases. Defect repair review is an action taken to ensure that the project defects are repaired and brought into compliance with standards.

Figure 12.28   Scatter diagram showing software errors by system size

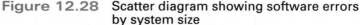

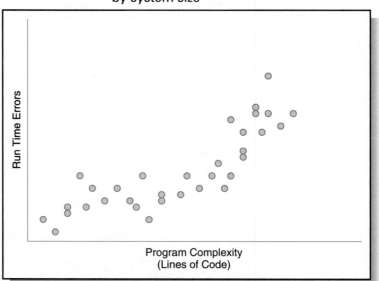

The outputs from the perform quality control (refer back to Figure 12.21) include quality control measurements, validated defect repair, updates to the quality baseline, recommended corrective actions, recommended preventive actions, requested changes, recommended defect repair, updates to the organization process assets, validated deliverables, and updates to the project management plan. As discussed in Chapter 8 the quality baseline may be based on past performance metrics from other similar projects or it may be determined by experts in the domain. Approved corrective actions are the documented and authorized guidelines necessary to bring the quality of project deliverables in conformance to the standards. Approved preventive actions are those that are intended to reduce the probability of nonconformance to the standards.

The results of the perform quality control process can also lead to new change requests. Defects in the project deliverables must be identified and recommended for repair. The historical database of organizational process assets is updated with the causes of variances, the justification for any corrective action, and any lessons learned during the process. The quality of project deliverables is compared to the standards, and only those that conform to the standards are accepted. The project management plan is updated to reflect the approved changes to the quality management plan.

Risk Monitoring and Control

The last topic discussed under project control is the **Risk Monitoring and Control** process, which involves identifying, analyzing, and planning for new risks, keeping track of identified risks, re-analyzing existing risks, monitoring trigger conditions for contingency plans, monitoring residual risks, and reviewing the execution of risk responses (see Figure 12.29). The inputs to the risk monitoring and control process include the risk management plan, risk register, approved change requests, work performance information, and performance reports. The risk management plan, developed during the risk management planning process, includes information such as the assignment of people (including the risk owners), time, and other resources to project risk management. The risk register (Figure 12.30) provides valuable information, including identified risks and risk owners, agreed-upon risk responses, specific implementation actions, warning signs of risk, residual and secondary risks, and the time and cost contingency reserves. An approved change request impacts project risk because it incurs a modification of the risk management plan developed in the risk management planning process. Work performance information includes project deliverables status, corrective

Figure 12.29 PMBOK risk monitoring and control inputs, tools and techniques, and outputs

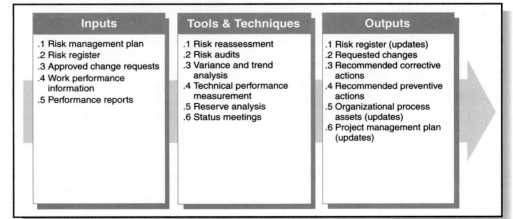

Inputs	Tools & Techniques	Outputs
.1 Risk management plan	.1 Risk reassessment	.1 Risk register (updates)
.2 Risk register	.2 Risk audits	.2 Requested changes
.3 Approved change requests	.3 Variance and trend analysis	.3 Recommended corrective actions
.4 Work performance information	.4 Technical performance measurement	.4 Recommended preventive actions
.5 Performance reports	.5 Reserve analysis	.5 Organizational process assets (updates)
	.6 Status meetings	.6 Project management plan (updates)

actions, and performance reports. Performance reports provide information on work performance, such as an analysis that may influence the risk management processes.

Figure 12.30 Sample risk register

<Project Name>
Risk Register

<Author>

<Date>

1.0 Statement of Purpose

The purpose of this document is to document and track identified risks to ensure that appropriate personnel are assigned and strategies are applied to address the risks. This document contains: a) a description of the Project's scope, b) the risk rating scheme for <project name>, c) recommended response for each rating, and d) the register itself.

2.0 Project Scope

<Describe <project name>'s scope here>

_____

_____

_____

3.0 Risk Rating Scheme

CONSEQUENCES		LIKELIHOOD	
Rating	**Consequence**	**Rating**	**Likelihood**
1	Major	A	Will occur in most cases.
2	Moderate	B	Could occur at some time.
3	Minor	C	Could occur, but rarely.
4	Insignificant	D	May occur, but probably never will

		CONSEQUENCES			
		1	**2**	**3**	**4**
Likelihood	A	E	E	H	M
	B	E	H	M	M
	C	H	M	M	L
	D	M	M	L	N

Recommended Mitigation Actions

Grade	Description	Mitigation Action
E	Extreme Risk	Mitigation actions to reduce the likelihood and seriousness of risk to be identified and implemented as soon as the project commences.
H	High Risk	Mitigation actions to reduce the likelihood and seriousness of risk to be identified and appropriate actions implemented during project planning and/or during project execution.
M	Medium Risk	Mitigation actions to reduce the likelihood and seriousness of risk to be identified and appropriate actions implemented during project execution.

(continued)

Figure 12.30 (continued)

L	Low Risk	Mitigation actions to reduce the likelihood and seriousness of risk to be identified and evaluated for possible action if funds permit.
N	Negligible Risk	To be noted; no action is needed unless grading increases over time.

CHANGE SINCE LAST ASSESSMENT

New	New risk item
—	No Change
↓	Grade decrease
↑	Grade increase

4.0 Risk Register

ID#	Description of Risk	Likelihood	Consequence	Grade	Change	Actions Taken	Responsible Party	$
1.1	Inadequate Funding	B	2	H	New	Re-scope Project	Project Manager	n/a
1.2								
<Add more rows as necessary>								

To transform these inputs into outputs, the PMBOK Guide specifies certain tools and techniques that may be used during risk monitoring and control; they include risk reassessment, risk audits, variance and trend analysis, technical performance measurement, reserve analysis, and status meetings. Risk reassessment involves evaluating new risks as the project progresses because new risks may emerge and additional response planning may be required to deal with them. Risk reassessment may be part of a regularly planned project team meeting, where team members are asked if existing risks have changed or if there are new risks that need to be dealt with.

Designed to evaluate the effectiveness of risk strategies as well as risk owners, project risk response audits are often conducted during different phases of the project life cycle to examine and document the effectiveness of risk responses. Variance analysis, as discussed earlier, allows the project team to identify deviations from the baseline plan. Large deviations should be carefully investigated, and corrective actions should be taken to bring performance in conformance to the plan. Trend analysis is done by having the project team examine performance data over time to determine whether performance is ameliorating or deteriorating. Technical performance measurement is a particularly important tool in IS development projects. If performance metrics—such as the accuracy of inventory updates when implementing a new corporate-wide inventory system—do not meet the goals associated with a specific project milestone, risks to the schedule may be indicated. Reserve analysis is a comparison of the amount of contingency reserves remaining to the amount of risk remaining at any time in the project. As an example, a large information systems project done for a major petroleum company may literally have financial contingency reserves in the millions of dollars; however, if risk is high (which might be revealed through a tool such as trend analysis, discussed earlier) these contingency reserves may still not be sufficient.

Reserve analysis allows the project team to determine whether the remaining reserve is adequate. Status meetings are an important part of communicating, monitoring, and controlling projects. Project risk management should be discussed at these meetings because risk management becomes easier the more it is practiced and because talking more about risks becomes easier and more accurate with frequent discussions.

The outputs from the Risk Monitoring and Control process include updates to the risk register, requested changes, recommended corrective actions, recommended preventive actions, updates to the organizational process assets, and updates to the project management plan. The risk register—which details all project risks identified at the beginning and during the life of a project, an assessment of their likelihood of occurrence, the seriousness of their potential impact, and initial plans for mitigating the risks—must be updated with the outcomes of risk assessments, risk audits, and periodic risk reviews. This includes updating the probability, impact, priority, response plans, ownership, and other elements of the risk register (Figure 12.30).

The implementation of contingency plans or work-arounds leads to the need for changes to the risk management plan. Recommended corrective actions include contingency and work-around plans, which are both responses that were not initially planned but are needed to deal with emerging risks as the project progresses. Recommended preventive actions are necessary to bring the project into compliance with the project management plan. The historical database of organizational process assets is updated with the causes of variances, the justification for any corrective action, and any lessons learned during the risk monitoring and control process. If the approved change requests have an impact on the risk management processes, then the corresponding components of the project management plan related to risk management must be revised and reissued to reflect the approved changes. Figure 12.29 depicts a summary of the inputs, tools and techniques, and outputs associated with integrated change control.

Microsoft Project has many built-in reports, views, and filters to assist in project control. For example, for schedule control, the project manager can quickly run a report to list all the tasks that have been completed (see Figure 12.31). Corrective actions can be taken to make sure that those tasks that have not yet been completed as planned are finished as soon as possible. This information can be included in the performance reports, too. These reports can also be used for cost control. Figure 12.32 shows a report of tasks that are over budget. After looking at this report, the project manager can determine the appropriate corrective actions to bring these tasks back to budget.

Figure 12.31 Report of completed tasks

\multicolumn{7}{c}{Completed Tasks as of Mon 10/16/06 LAN-4.mpp}						
ID	Task Name	Duration	Start	Finish	% Comp.	Cost
September 2006						
2	Document current environment	4 days	Mon 8/18/06	Thu 9/21/06	100%	$0.00
3	Conduct needs analysis	1 wk	Thu 9/21/06	Wed 9/27/06	100%	$0.00
6	Build Request for Proposal	4 days	Wed 9/27/06	Mon 10/2/06	100%	$0.00
October 2006						
6	Build Request for Proposal	4 days	Wed 9/27/06	Mon 10/2/06	100%	$0.00
7	Gather vendor bids	1 wk	Mon 10/6/06	Fri 10/6/06	100%	$0.00
8	Choose vendors	2 days	Fri 10/6/06	Mon 10/9/06	100%	
9	Sign contracts	1 day	Mon 10/9/06	Mon 10/9/06	100%	$0.00

		Over-Budget Tasks as of Mon 10/16/06 LAN-4.mpp					
ID	Task Name	Fixed Cost	Fixed Cost Accrual	Total Cost	Baseline	Variance
2	Document current environment	$ 50,000.00	Prorated	$ 51,120.00	$ 46,000.00	$ 5,120.00
3	Conduct needs analysis	$ 2,000.00	Prorated	$ 2,000.00	$ 1,000.00	$ 3,000.00
4	Analysis completed	$ 2,000.00	Prorated	$ 2,000.00	$ 1,000.00	$ 1,000.00
		$ 54,000.00		$ 57,120.00	$ 48,000.00	$ 9,120.00

Figure 12.32   Report of over-budget tasks

Techniques for Managing Project Closure

Now that your project has been executed, you've exercised control to keep it on track, and its final deliverables are ready for implementation, what's next? In this section, we discuss techniques successful project managers use to close a project.

While the size of the project may determine the intensity of the closure processes, project closure at any level is very important to clients, stakeholders, team members, and project managers for future projects. Three elements are critical to successful project closure: production of an end report, project handover, and a postimplementation review.

End Report

Two primary closure documents are created when a project is completed. The first is the **end report**, also called a project closure report, which addresses the project management methods and techniques followed over the project life cycle. Suggested content of the end report is shown in Figure 12.33.

Other items to include in the end report might be a list of outstanding items. Outstanding items are items or activities that remain to be addressed but, because of their nature, may have to be taken care of by the clients themselves or assigned to a team member to attend to after the official project handover. Finally, the end report can also document the lessons learned during the project.

Figure 12.33   Sample table of contents for an end report
Source: http://www.ogc.gov.uk/sdtoolkit/reference/documentation/p32_endproj.html

End Report Contents

1) Achievement of the project's objectives, summarizing whether the project was successful or not

2) Performance against the planned target time and cost

3) The effect on the original project plan and business case of any changes that were approved

4) Final analysis on change issues received during the project

5) The total impact of approved changes

6) Analysis for all quality work carried out

7) Post-Project Review date and plan

Project closure typically involves both the aforementioned end report, as well as a second document entitled the post implementation review. We will discuss the postimplementation review document following the next section on project handover.

Project Handover

Handover
The process of delivering the project to the client and training personnel to use it.

Post implementation review
A document that is usually completed 6 to 12 months after implementation as a check on whether the outcomes of the project were as expected, whether ongoing costs are as expected, and whether implementing the product yields net benefits.

This is the step you've been waiting for. You now get to hand over your hard work to the client. The question is whether the client is actually prepared to take over the project you are ready to deliver. The **handover** is the process by which the appropriate personnel are brought up to speed on the new product or system. This includes training the client's personnel on the new artifact and debriefing project team members.

Post Implementation Review

Finally, you've completed your project (hopefully on time and on budget). How successful was it? While your project's performance with respect to the planned schedule and budget are important measuring sticks for the success of the project, how did the client organization perceive the success of its investment in you? Did the product meet the client's requirements? The **post implementation review**—also sometimes called the post project review—is a document that is usually completed 6 to 12 months after implementation as a check on whether the outcomes of the project were as expected, whether ongoing costs are as expected, and whether implementing the product yields net benefits (see Figure 12.34).

Figure 12.34 Sample post implementation review table of contents
Source: Retrieved from http://www.deakin.edu.au/its/methodology/spice/pm431.php

Table of Contents

1	**EXECUTIVE SUMMARY**		**6**
2	**PROJECT HISTORY**		**6**
	2.1	DETAILS	7
	2.2	OBJECTIVES	7
	2.3	SCOPE	7
	2.4	CURRENT STATUS	8
3	**REVIEW METHODOLOGY**		**8**
	3.1	INTERVIEWS	9
	3.2	QUESTIONNAIRES AND SURVEYS	10
	3.3	HARDWARE & NETWORK PERFORMANCE	10
	3.4	SUPPORT ANALYSIS	11
	3.5	<OTHER>	11
4	**REVIEW OUTCOMES (FINDINGS ?)**		**11**
	4.1	COST ASSESSMENT	12
	4.2	VENDOR ASSESSMENT	12
	4.3	BENEFITS ASSESSMENT	12
	4.4	SUPPORT ASSESSMENT	13
	4.5	COMPLIANCE WITH SERVICE LEVEL AGREEMENTS	14
	4.6	SOFTWARE EVALUATION	15
	4.7	<OTHER>	15
5	**RECOMMENDATIONS**		**16**
	5.1	STRENGTHS & WEAKNESSES	16
	5.1.1	Strengths	17
	5.1.2	Weaknesses	18
	5.1.3	Opportunities	18
	5.1.4	Threats	18
	5.2	LESSONS LEARNED	19
	5.3	FUTURE PROJECT OBJECTIVES	21

Project Control and Closure and the PMBOK

This chapter has discussed the fundamentals, characteristics, and challenges of managing various controlling and closure processes over the course of a project. We have defined control, identified the major philosophies of control, and discussed how control can be achieved. We have also discussed how closure is important in the context of a project and discussed several documents that can help the closure process occur. Figure 12.35 identifies this coverage.

Figure 12.35   Chapter 12 and PMBOK coverage

Textbook Chapters ⟶	1	2	3	4	5	6	7	8	9	10	11	12
PMBOK Knowledge Area												
1 Introduction to Project Management												
1.1 What Is a Project?	●											
1.2 What Is Project Management?	●											
1.3 Areas of Expertise		●										
1.4 Project Management Context	●											
2 Project Life Cycle and Organization												
2.1 The Project Life Cycle	●	●										
2.2 Project Stakeholders	●	●										
2.3 Organizational Influences		●	●	●			●					
3 Project Management Processes for a Project												
3.1 Project Management Processes	●	●										
3.2 PM Process Groups	●	●										
3.3 Process Interactions		●										
3.4 Project Management Process Mapping		●										
4 Project Integration Management												
4.1 Develop Project Charter					●							
4.2 Develop Preliminary Project Scope Statement					●	●						
4.3 Develop Project Management Plan					●							
4.4 Direct and Manage Project Execution											●	
4.5 Monitor and Control Project Work												✓
4.6 Integrated Change Control												✓
4.7 Close Project												✓
5 Project Scope Management												
5.1 Scope Planning					●							
5.2 Scope Definition					●							
5.3 Create WBS					●	●						
5.4 Scope Verification					●							
5.5 Scope Control					●							✓

(continued)

Figure 12.35 (continued)

	Textbook Chapters →	1	2	3	4	5	6	7	8	9	10	11	12
	PMBOK Knowledge Area												
6	**Project Time Management**												
6.1	Activity Definition						●						
6.2	Activity Sequencing						●						
6.3	Activity Resource Estimating							●					
6.4	Activity Duration Estimating							●					
6.5	Schedule Development							●					
6.6	Schedule Control							●					✓
7	**Project Cost Management**												
7.1	Cost Estimating							●					
7.2	Cost Budgeting							●					
7.3	Cost Control							●					✓
8	**Project Quality Management**												
8.1	Quality Planning								●				
8.2	Perform Quality Assurance								●				
8.3	Perform Quality Control								●				✓
9	**Project Human Resource Management**												
9.1	Human Resource Planning			●				●					
9.2	Acquire Project Team			●				●					
9.3	Develop Project Team			●				●					
9.4	Manage Project Team			●				●					
10	**Project Communications Management**												
10.1	Communications Planning				●							●	
10.2	Information Distribution				●							●	
10.3	Performance Reporting				●								✓
10.4	Manage Stakeholders				●								✓
11	**Project Risk Management**												
11.1	Risk Management Planning									●			
11.2	Risk Identification									●	●		
11.3	Qualitative Risk Analysis									●			
11.4	Quantitative Risk Analysis									●			
11.5	Risk Response Planning									●			
11.6	Risk Monitoring and Control									●			✓

(continued)

Figure 12.35 (continued)

Textbook Chapters →	1	2	3	4	5	6	7	8	9	10	11	12
PMBOK Knowledge Area												
12 **Project Procurement Management**												
12.1 Plan Purchases and Acquisitions										●		
12.2 Plan Contracting										●		
12.3 Request Seller Responses										●		
12.4 Select Sellers										●		
12.5 Contract Administration										●		
12.6 Contract Closure										●		✓

Key: ●-where material is covered in past chapters; ✓-current chapter coverage;
○-where material is covered in future chapters

RUNNING CASE
Managing Project Control and Closure

"How long did they say they'd give us on-site support at no extra cost?" asked Jim.

"Six months," Sanjay answered.

"Are they on schedule for the last kiosks at Piccoli's store?"

"Yep!"

"Wow, that's great!"

"They also completed half of Juanita's store too."

"I'm quite sure we are going to pull this project off well before schedule! I think the documentation is coming along well, too."

Sally showed a "thumbs-up."

"There is one last component that needs to be completed before we start winding down this project. We need to show the metrics for the pilots to Ella," said Jim.

"I'll do that," said Bob. "I have nearly all the performance metrics that we ran last week at Piccoli's store. I'll just update it one more time before I send it in to Ella."

"Well," said, Jim, "I think, with that, we are at our last stage of the project. I've got T-shirts for all you guys!"

"Actually, Jim, I don't think we are done," said Sally.

"Oh?" Jim wondered.

"Yeah, remember all that 'there are great benefits to following a fairly formal project management process when designing a new system,' and 'moving forward with care' stuff you taught me at the beginning?"

"Ah, you're talking about lessons learned aren't you?" Jim realized.

Sally replied, "Yes, and realizing that we were getting close to the end, I searched around and found some information about closing a project. The stuff I read talked about a document called lessons learned. I don't know about the rest of you, but I know I learned a lot that I'll need to know when I work on projects in the future. If I could refer back to some file that contains information about what went well, what didn't, and how we dealt with the stuff that didn't, it would make future projects go more smoothly."

"So, with all that extra time you had to search around to find information on finishing up the project, I don't suppose you wrote this lessons learned document up, did you?" Jim asked hopefully.

"Well, no. But, I didn't get the feeling it should be a one-person job. I found this template that I think we can modify a little to fit with the Petrie's structure and culture a little better" (see Figure 12.36). "A big part of it is one last project meeting to discuss the particulars because each one of us probably learned something a little different than everyone else. By doing it together in a meeting, we'll make sure we don't leave anything out."

"All right," Jim said. "In addition to the T-shirt, Sally gets the 'Keeping us all on track' award."

Everybody laughed while Sally sighed and shook her head.

The team closed down the project by submitting the metric reports and documentation to Ella and conducting a final meeting to compose the lessons-learned document.

Figure 12.36 Sample lessons learned document template

<Project Name>
Lessons Learned

<Author>

<Date>

1.0 Statement of Purpose

The purpose of this template is to provide a repository of knowledge gained from experience so that future projects and the organization may benefit. This document contains a) a project journal, b) the close-out discussion of lessons learned, and c) acknowledgement signatures from project team members.

2.0 Project Journal

At each project status meeting, discuss and record areas of success and areas that need improvement. Discuss the processes that led to success, and suggest ways to improve deficient areas.

AREAS OF SUCCESS

Meeting Date	Description
<Enter Date Here>	<Enter Description Here>
<Add more rows as necessary>	

AREAS FOR IMPROVEMENT

Meeting Date	Description
<Enter Date Here>	<Enter Description Here>
<Add more rows as necessary	

CONCLUSIONS

<Enter conclusions drawn from the above items here>

3.0 Close-Out Discussion of Lessons Learned

Conduct a meeting with relevant stakeholders to fill out the following sections on Lessons Learned from <Project Name>.

LIST THIS PROJECT'S TOP THREE SUCCESSES

Description	Factors Influential in Success
<Add rows as necessary>	

LIST THIS PROJECT'S TOP THREE FAILURES.

Description	Factors Influential in Failure
<Add rows as necessary>	

(continued)

Figure 12.36 (continued)

LIST AND DESCRIBE POTENTIAL STRATEGIES TO ADDRESS FAILURES OR AREAS NEEDING IMPROVEMENT

Description	Strategies to Improve
<Add rows as necessary>	

4.0 Acknowledgement Signatures
Project Manager:

As project manager on <project name>, I hereby acknowledge and agree with the information contained in this document

Name	Position	Signature	Date

The signatures above represent stakeholders' agreement and acknowledgement of the information contained in this document. Those signing this document agree that this is the formal Lessons Learned document for <project name> to be filed with <enter location of project documentation here>.

CHAPTER SUMMARY

Define project control and closure. Project control can be thought of as the processes that allow monitoring and measurement of project progress and directing influence over the plan to account for any discrepancies between the actual progress and the planned progress made up to that point. Project closure involves both the final implementation and training related to the project, getting acceptance and signoff on the project, and finally archiving the results of the project and lessons learned from the project.

Understand the importance of and general philosophies behind project control and closure. Project control is important because it allows a project manager to keep tabs on the progress of the various tasks, identify problems, solve problems, and make changes to the plan based on any problems and their solutions. Project closure is important because it ensures that handover of the project is successful and documentation occurs such that future projects can be improved from lessons learned from previous projects. Producing an end report, handover, and conducting a postimplementation review ensures proper project closure. General philosophies underlying project control include the dogmatic philosophy (where the established plan is followed to the letter, no ifs, ands, or buts) and the laid-back philosophy (where little or no control is exerted and the project can take on a life of its own). A pragmatic philosophy is a compromise between the two; the plan is followed, but flexibility exists to deal with problems as they arise. Communication, participation, analysis, action, and commitment all give a project manager the necessary tools for exerting control over the project.

Apply techniques for managing project control and closure. There are many techniques for controlling projects. Typically, these techniques can be applied to the project as a whole—as in the PMBOK's topic of Project Integration Management—or in the individual areas of scope control, schedule control, cost control, quality control, and risk control. This chapter discusses and provides examples of control exercised across all these areas. In addition, we discuss the importance of good project closure, as well as some techniques for accomplishing this. Organizations that embrace formalized processes related to control and closure can head off problems before they occur and more actively manage costs and schedules over the course of the project.

- Change control system
- Configuration management system
- Cost control
- Dogmatic philosophy
- Earned value management
- End report
- Forecasts
- Handover
- Integrated change control

- Laid-back philosophy
- Monitoring and controlling project work
- Performing quality control
- Philosophy of project control
- Postimplementation review
- Pragmatic philosophy
- Project audit
- Project closure
- Project control

- Project log
- Project management methodology
- Recommended corrective actions
- Recommended preventive actions
- Risk monitoring and control
- Schedule control
- Scope control
- Standard operating procedures
- Variance analysis

Match each of the key terms above with the definition that best fits it.

1. _____ Activities and reporting methods instituted during the course of the project to monitor the progress of the project and provide reports, both for project managers and for project stakeholders.

2. _____ The process of identifying the cause of variance relative to the scope baseline and determining whether any corrective action is needed.

3. _____ Documented recommendations needed to bring future project performance into conformance with the project management plan.

4. _____ The management style that the manager employs with respect to following the plan and dealing with problems or changes in the plan.

5. _____ The process of assuring that only agreed upon changes are made to the project's scope.

6. _____ The process of delivering the project to the client and training personnel to use it.

7. _____ A technique that measures project performance over time, and provides a way to forecast future performance based on past performance.

8. _____ Estimates or predictions of conditions or events in the project's future.

9. _____ The process of ensuring that only appropriate changes are included in the modified cost baseline.

10. _____ A philosophy of project control that emphasizes strict adherence to the project plan, with little tolerance for deviations.

11. _____ A document that is usually completed 6 to 12 months after implementation as a check on whether the outcomes of the project were as expected, whether ongoing costs are as expected, and whether there are net benefits from implementation of the product.

12. _____ The process of identifying, analyzing, and planning for new risks, keeping track of identified risks, reanalyzing existing risks, monitoring trigger conditions for contingency plans, monitoring residual risks, and reviewing the execution of risk responses.

13. _____ A formal, documented process that describes the procedures by which the project scope and product scope can be changed.

14. _____ The process of identifying, evaluating, and managing changes that occur from project initiation through project closure.

15. _____ A technique for controlling a project that involves recording information such as changes requested by the client, completion dates of deliverables, and so on.

16. _____ The process that helps the project team monitor and control the work being performed in accordance to the project management plan.

17. _____ Documented recommendations that minimize the probability of negative consequences to the project.

18. _____ The process of collecting, measuring, and disseminating information related to performance, as well as assessing measurements and trends in order to make any improvements.

19. _____ Final implementation and training related to the project, acceptance and signoff on the project, and archiving of the project's results and lessons learned.

20. _____ A scope control technique that ensures that the requested changes to the project and product scope are thoroughly considered and documented before being implemented.

21. _____ The process of monitoring and measuring project progress and influencing the plan to account for any discrepancies between planned progress and actual progress.

22. _____ A philosophy of project control that allows for project problems or change issues to be dealt with as they arise, on an ad hoc basis.

23. _____ A compromise between the dogmatic and laid-back philosophies that sticks to a plan but is flexible enough to allow for changes.

24. _____ The process of screening the project results to determine whether they conform to relevant quality standards and identifying means to eliminate causes of unsatisfactory results.

25. _____ Document that contains a record of the project management techniques that were employed over the course of the project, surveys, and outstanding items that still need to be resolved.

26. _____ A systematic and formal inquiry into a project's expenditures, schedule, and quality of work.

27. _____ The process of putting in place procedures and rules for controlling changes to the project schedule.

REVIEW QUESTIONS

1. Define project control.
2. Explain what a project control philosophy is.
3. Discuss the different types of project control philosophies with respect to the kinds of projects that might be appropriate for each type.
4. List and briefly describe the various levers that can be used to exert control over a project.
5. List and briefly describe the various project control techniques.
6. Describe the components of standard operating procedures techniques.
7. List and provide the formulas (if required) for the components of an earned value management (EVM) analysis.
8. Explain how cost performance indexes and schedule performance indexes provide estimates on the budget and schedule performance of the project.
9. Define project closure.
10. Describe what is involved in project handover.
11. Compare and contrast an end report with a postimplementation review.

CHAPTER EXERCISES

1. Explain how controlling processes can affect project integration, scope, time, cost, quality, and risk.
2. Discuss how the computerized baggage handling system (CBHS) project at Denver International Airport (DIA) could have been a success with proper control.
3. Compare and contrast the three different philosophies of controlling projects. Which one do you believe is the best?
4. List and explain the different levers that project managers use to exert control over projects. Give an example of how each lever can be used in project control.
5. The planned value for a project is $17,800, the earned value is $19,450, and the actual cost is $21,870. Based on this information, calculate the cost performance index and the

schedule performance index. What do these indices tell you about the status of the project in terms of cost and schedule?

6. The budget at completion of this project was estimated at $20,000, and the estimated time to complete was 13 months. Use the information from Exercise 5 to compute the estimated cost at completion and the estimated time to complete. Is the project on budget and schedule?

7. Use the Internet or any other source to search "variance analysis." Define what it is and explain its usefulness in project control.

8. Review Chapter 8 for the different tools and techniques that can be used in performing quality control. Explain how each of them can be used to control quality.

9. "Once a project is completed, the project team members should forget about it and move to the next project." Do you agree with this statement? Explain why.

10. Compare and contrast the different reports produced in the project closure phase.

11. Explain the importance of project handover.

12. How can the performing organization assess whether the project is a success at the client's organization?

CHAPTER CASE

Sedona Management Group and Managing Project Control and Closure

Project control is the process of ensuring that project objectives are being met. It is the project team's job to measure progress toward the project objectives, monitor any divergence from the plan developed in the initiation and planning phase, and take any corrective actions necessary to match progress to the plan. Controlling processes are performed at all of the other phases of the project life cycle. Once the project objectives have been met, the final phase in the project life cycle is project closure, which involves formalizing the acceptance of the project and bringing the project to an orderly end.

Tim Turnpaugh recognizes the importance of control during the life cycle of a project. There are many project control techniques, but at Sedona Management Group, two project control techniques have been particularly helpful to consistent project success. The first technique is the use of standard operating procedures. SMG has established a well-defined process of assessing what the customer needs, and this type of project control occurs in both the initiation and planning phases of a project. By using standardized requirements-gathering techniques, as well as having established planning templates that have proven successful in the past, SMG reduces project risk as well as variance in the quality or timing of project outcomes.

A second control technique SMG employees rely on is prevention. Turnpaugh tells members of his team to "inspect what they expect." In other words, project team members are charged with preventing problems by ensuring that the various requirements of the project are met. In many cases, given the variety of projects that any project team may be concurrently managing, a team may become lax in ensuring that each feature of a system works as expected. This is particularly important in situations where an IS project team may be using reusable code. Turnpaugh believes it is critical to never assume that the application will behave the same way it has in the past, and that the only way to ensure performance is through testing of all features during development.

In project closure, the team prepares to deliver the project to the customer by ensuring the project is functioning correctly, making sure the personnel responsible for managing the new system are appropriately trained, obtaining customer acceptance, and finally documenting—for the project team's own purposes—any problems or issues that they may want to attend to in future projects. Closing activities include administrative closure, personnel transition, and the discussion of lessons learned. Administrative closure involves verifying and documenting the project results to formalize the stakeholders' acceptance of the project deliverables.

CHAPTER 12 PROJECT ASSIGNMENT

Throughout the project life cycle, control processes are important to ensure that the project objectives are being met. Once all these project objectives have been met, the project should be brought to formal closure. In this assignment, you will discuss the control and closing processes that will be used for your project.

1. Prevention is better than cure. Discuss this statement as it applies to your project. In other words, explain what preventive measures will be used to ensure project success.

2. Explain the importance of an earned value analysis. Also define BCWP, ACWP, BCWS, CPI, and SPI.

3. Conduct an earned value analysis, using BCWP, ACWP, and BCWS to calculate CPI and SPI. You will need to estimate your own values for your project for the BCWP, ACWP, and BCWS in order to come up with your CPI and SPI. Costs can be calculated by assuming that each individual on your team works for $35/hour.

4. Create a project closure document, which includes:
   - A statement indicating whether the project objectives were met
   - What requirements of the project were not met
   - A tracking Gantt chart
   - An explanation of whether the project schedule and budget were met, based on the earned value analysis

5. Write a list of lessons learned in the project process. Explain what you did effectively, what you did ineffectively, and what you will do differently next time.

REFERENCES

Ahituv, N., Zviran, M., and Glezer, C. (1999). "Top Management Toolbox for Managing Corporate IT." *Communications of the ACM* 42(4), 93–99.

Ewusi-Mensah, K. (1997). "Critical Issues in Abandoned Information Systems Development Projects." *Communications of the ACM* 40(9), 74–80.

Keil, M., and Robey, D. (2001). "Blowing the Whistle on Troubled Software Projects." *Communications of the ACM* 44(4), 87–93.

Kloppenborg, T. J., and Petrick, J. A. (2004). "Managing Project Quality." *Quality Progress* 27(9), 63–69.

Mähring, M, Holmström, J., Keil, M., and Montealegre, R. (2004). "Trojan-Actor Networks and Swift Translation: Bringing Actor-Network Theory to IT Project Escalation Studies." *Information Technology and People* 17(2), 210–238.

Oz, E. (1994). "When Professional Standards Are Lax: The CONFIRM Failure and Its Lessons." *Communications of the ACM* 37(10), 9–36.

PMBOK (2004). *A Guide to the Project Management Body of Knowledge*. 3rd ed. Newtown Square, PA: Project Management Institute.

Sifri, G. (2003). "Getting Detailed Projects Back on Track." *TechRepublic*, March 19.

Zeichick, A. (2004). "Tools Foster Engagement with Offshore Developers." *ComputerWorld*. Retrieved March 9, 2004, from: www.computerworld.com/developmenttopics/development/story/0,10801,90927,00.html

Appendix A

Microsoft Project Tutorial

LEARNING OBJECTIVES

After reading this appendix, you will be able to:

➤ Become familiar with Microsoft Project
➤ Enter tasks, estimate task durations, and sequence tasks in Microsoft Project.
➤ Enter resources and assign resources.
➤ Track project progress.
➤ Report project status.

Introduction

In keeping with the technological focus of this textbook, this appendix will provide you with a basic introduction to Microsoft Project, a powerful project management software package that can help project staff manage schedules and resources and to track project progress. Although several vendors provide project management software (see Chapter 1) across a variety of price points and a variety of specific industries, Microsoft Project is one of the most widely used project management software applications available. Considering its widespread use and its familiar Microsoft Office user interface, we chose Microsoft Project to illustrate how project management software in general can support and facilitate information systems project management.

While the use of project management software can enhance and support the project management function, project management software should not be used in lieu of becoming familiar with the project management concepts presented in this textbook. This appendix is written with the expectation that the reader possesses some basic knowledge of the IS project management concepts presented in Chapters 1 through 12.

Microsoft Project Basics

If you do not already have Microsoft Project 2003, a trial version can be downloaded from Microsoft at: www.microsoft.com/office/project/prodinfo/trial.mspx.

Follow the directions on the Web site to install Microsoft Project on your computer. During the installation process, you will be asked whether you prefer the "typical" installation, or whether you want a "complete" or "custom" installation. The typical installation includes the most commonly used features of Microsoft Project; however, if you would prefer some additional features (e.g., PERT analysis), choose the complete installation.

Microsoft Project 2003 is a Microsoft Office application, so it has many elements similar to other Office titles such as Word, Excel, and PowerPoint. To begin using Microsoft Project, first start the application by clicking on the Start menu, All Programs, and select Microsoft Project, which is located in the Microsoft Office folder by default. Alternatively, if there is a program icon for Project on the desktop, double-click the icon to open Microsoft Project. The application will open with the screen shown in Figure A.1.

As you can see, elements of the user interface should be familiar to you if you've used Word or Excel. Specifically, the menu bar, the toolbar, and (in Office 2003 and later) the getting started pane (see Figure A.2). Depending on settings specific to your computer, your opening screen may not appear exactly as shown, but the differences will be minor.

Before getting started with specific project management activities, we will first explore the help menu and some interface characteristics that will help you configure Project to your preferences. Unless you are opening an existing project, you may wish to close the Getting Started pane. To do so, click on the X at the top

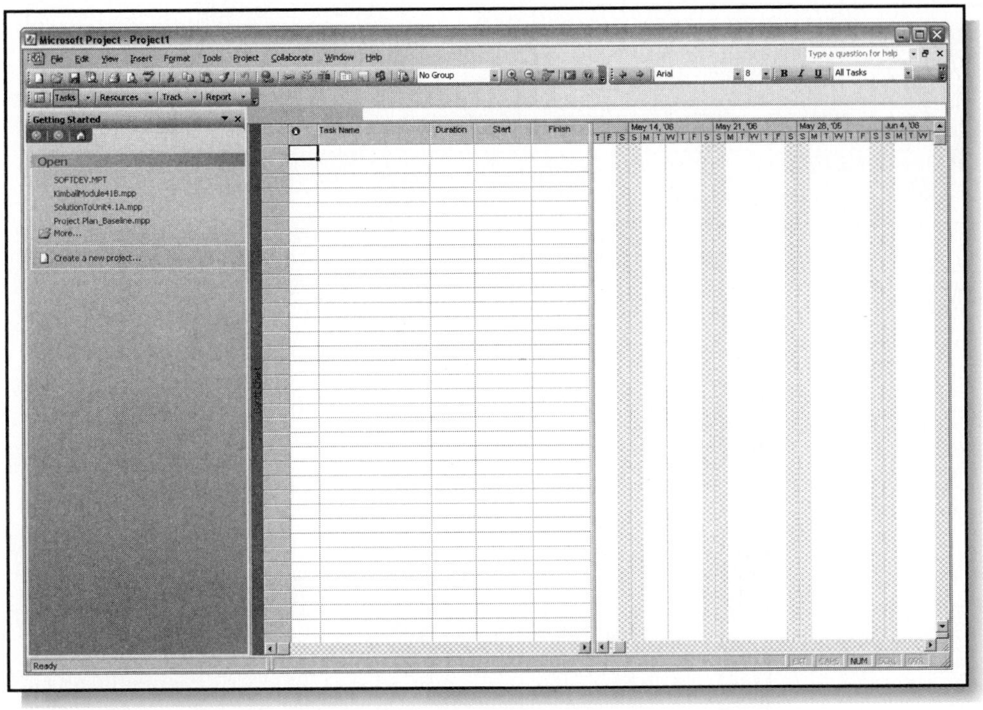

Figure A.1 Microsoft Project opening screen

right of the Getting Started pane. Notice the Getting Started pane is replaced by the Tasks pane (see Figure A.3). The function of the Tasks pane will be discussed later.

Microsoft Project Help

One of the most important (and underused) features of Microsoft Project is the Help menu. To get help in Microsoft Project, click on the Help menu in the menu bar, and click on "Microsoft Project Help" (see Figure A.4), or hit the F1 key.

Figure A.2 Microsoft Project screen elements

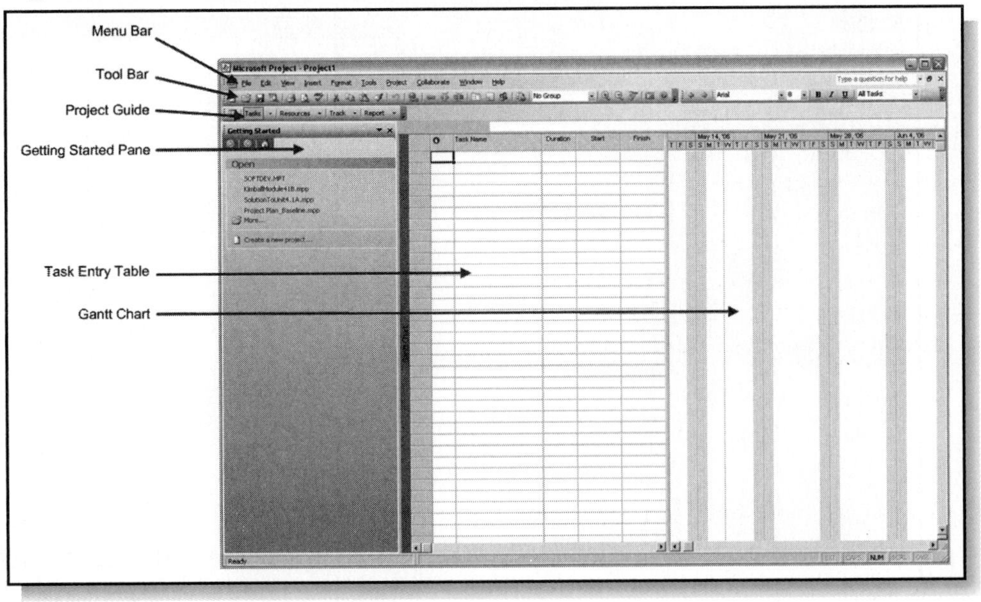

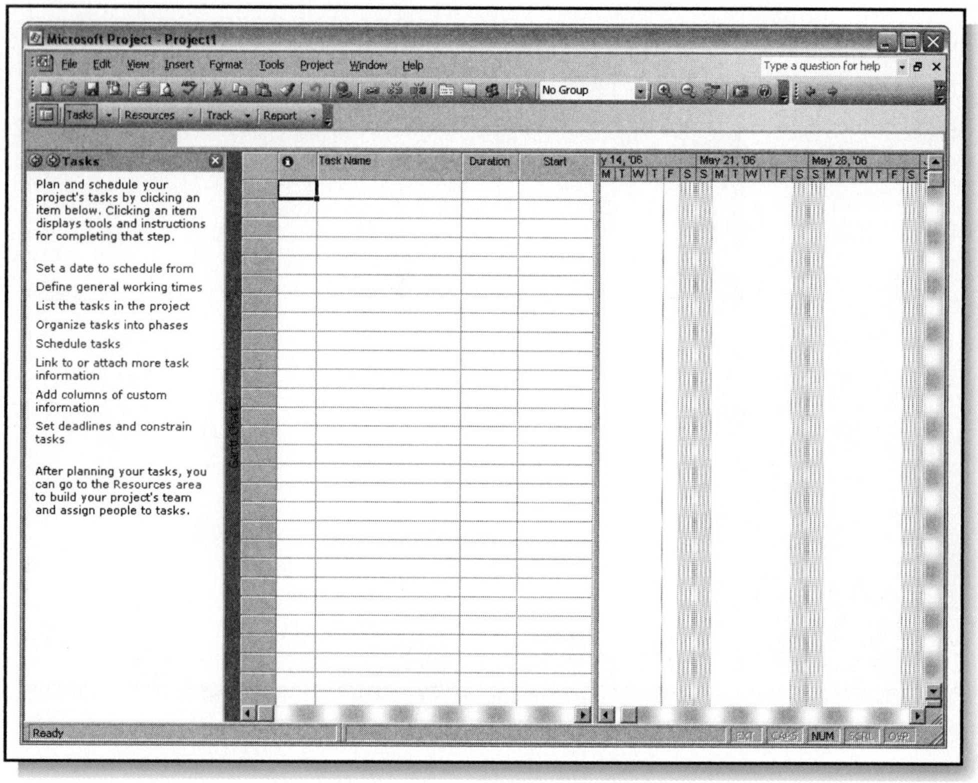

Figure A.3 Project with Getting Started pane closed

Figure A.4 Help menu

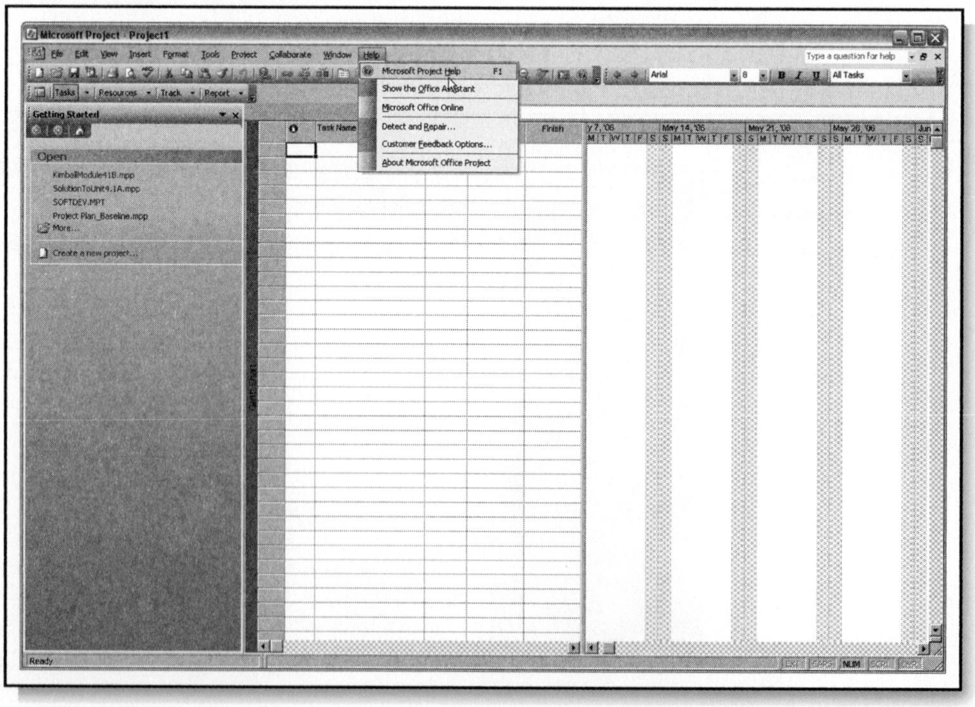

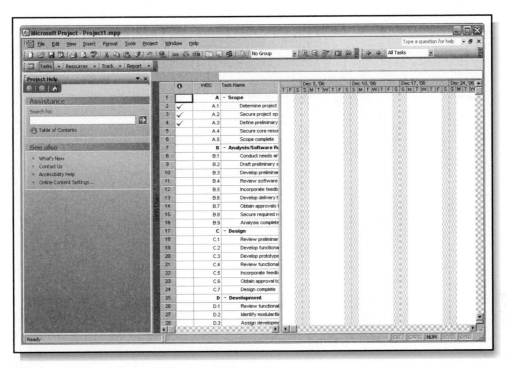

Figure A.5 Microsoft Project Help pane

After clicking on "Microsoft Project Help," the leftmost pane will become the Help pane (see Figure A.5). The Help pane opens with a field to type keywords or questions into. It also includes a link to open the Help table of contents. Additionally, the Help pane includes a link for Online Content Settings. Clicking on the Online Content Settings link will allow you to choose between settings that will allow Microsoft Project to draw from Microsoft's Office Online content (see Figure A.6).

If you choose to include online content in the help search, click the checkbox for "Show content and links from Microsoft Office Online"; then choose the option or options that you prefer. Notice in Figure A.6, when making changes to the Online Content settings, you must restart the application for the changes to take effect. With the Online Content included in the Help pane, several other options are available, such as Assistance, Training, Communities, and Downloads (see Figure A.7). Each of these options opens a browser window to the relevant topic on Microsoft's Web site.

As noted above, the Help menu can be a valuable resource for assistance with common, and not-so-common issues. The Help menu should become the first stop for answers to questions that may be beyond the scope of this introductory appendix.

For the following section, and many others throughout this appendix, the project being shown in the screenshots is adapted from the SOFTDEV.mpt file, which is a Microsoft Project Template. It can be loaded by clicking on the File menu, then choosing "New." The Getting Started pane is replaced by the New Project pane (see Figure A.8). Click on the "On My Computer" link under the Template heading. The Templates dialog box will appear (see Figure A.9), then click on the Project Template tab to see the templates included in the Microsoft Project software. Scroll down to find the Software Development template (which we will refer to as the SOFTDEV template for the remainder of this appendix). To illustrate how Microsoft Project helps support project activities, the SOFTDEV template will be used to show some of the features of this software. It may be useful for you to open the SOFTDEV template to follow along.

Views in Microsoft Project

When Microsoft Project is opened, it opens by default into the Gantt chart view. Other views of a project also exist, such as a Network Diagram view. These other views (as well as other options) are available using the View menu (see Figure A.10).

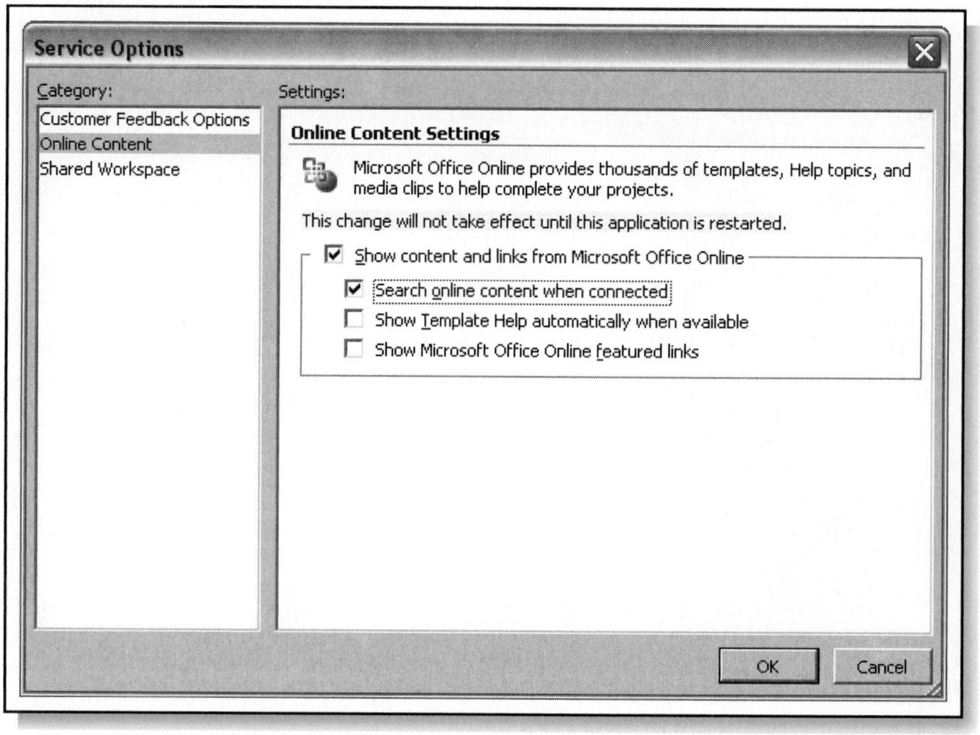

Figure A.6 Online Content settings

Figure A.7 More Online Content options

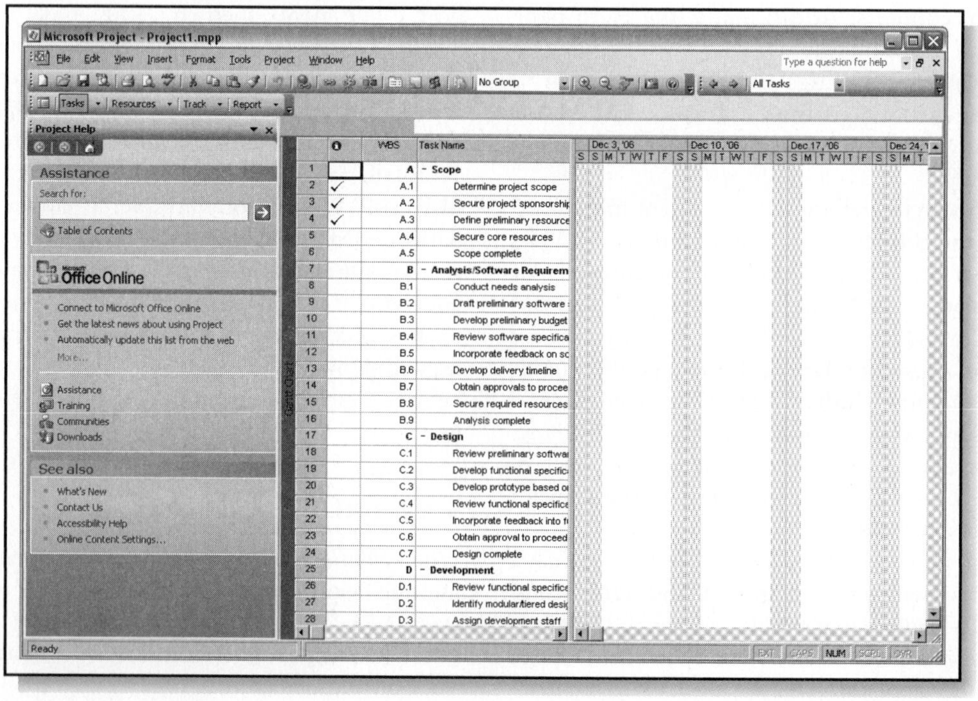

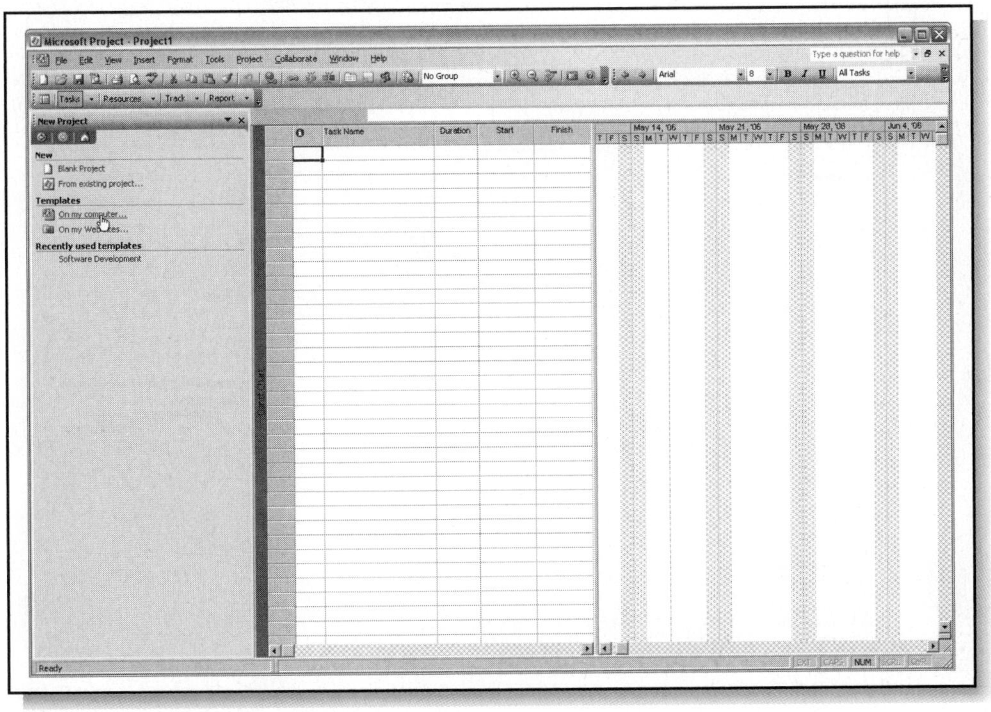

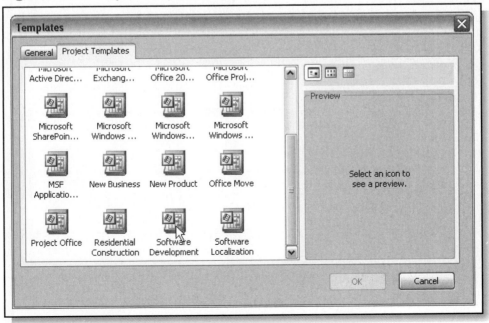

Figure A.8 New Project pane

The View menu includes the most commonly used views, such as the Calendar view (see Figure A.11), or the Network Diagram view (see Figure A.12). If you can't find the view you're looking for on the main View menu, click on the More Views option for a dialog box with all possible view choices and options for editing views (see Figure A.13).

For the remaining sections of this appendix, make sure your Project Guide toolbar is visible in Microsoft Project. To verify that it is open, click on

Figure A.9 Project Template dialog box

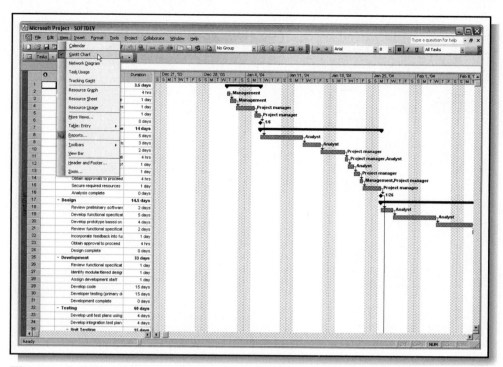

Figure A.10 Microsoft Project View menu

Figure A.11 Calendar View

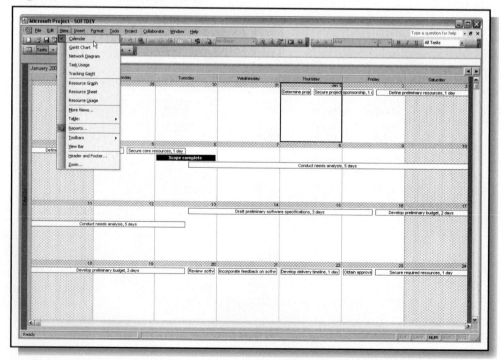

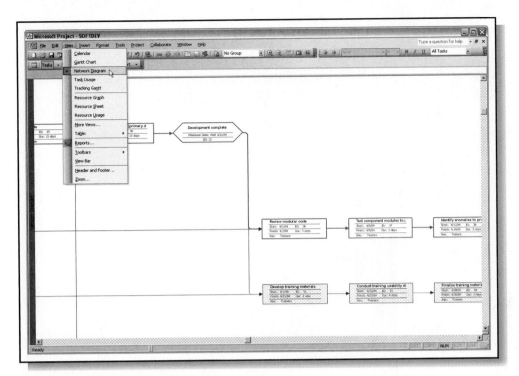

Figure A.12 Network Diagram view

Figure A.13 More views

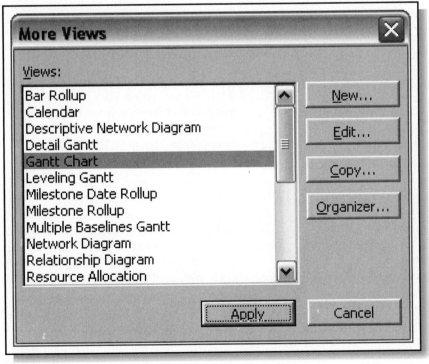

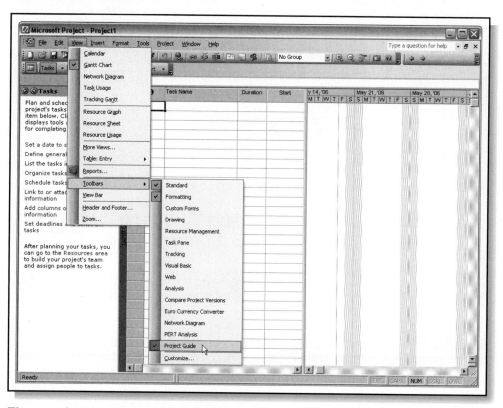

Figure A.14 Project Guide Toolbar view

the View menu, move your mouse down to the Toolbars option to open the Toolbar menu, and then verify the Project Guide option is checked (see Figure A.14).

Microsoft Project Guide

To help you get started using Microsoft Project to manage your project, the software has an embedded step-by-step guide to define the project, enter and schedule tasks, identify, assign, and manage resources, track project status, manage changes, and generate reports. The Microsoft Project Guide (see Figure A.2) is a toolbar that includes the most often used tools in Microsoft Project. To begin using the project guide, click on the Tasks button on the Project Guide (see Figure A.15). Note that while we will use the Project Guide to help you become familiar with the functionality of Microsoft Project, in reality all the activities discussed later may be done outside of the Project Guide, and in a different order than specified later.

The Task Pane

After clicking on the Tasks button in the Project Guide, your screen should resemble that in Figure A.3, a new project with the Task Pane open on the left side of the screen. To get started, click on the "Set a date to schedule from" link in the Task pane. Set the estimated start date for your project in the dropdown menu for the date. For example, in Figure A.16, the estimated start date is January 1, 2007.

Working Time

After choosing the estimated start date of your project, click on the "Done" link at the bottom of the Task pane. This will return you to the Task pane. The next step is to define the working time for the project. Defining the project's working time is a five-step process that walks you through setting up the general project working times (specific resources may be scheduled differently later). First, click on the "Define general working times" link in the Task pane to start the five-step process. The first screen (see Figure A.17) offers three calendar templates

Figure A.15　Opening the Task pane

Figure A.16　Set date to schedule from

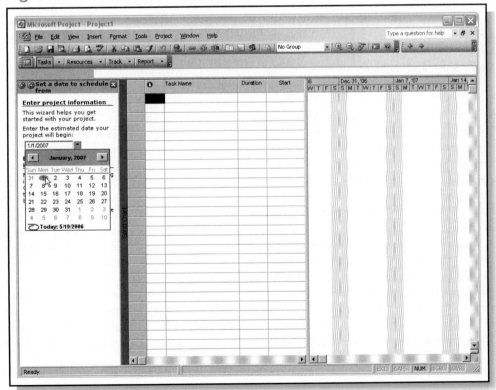

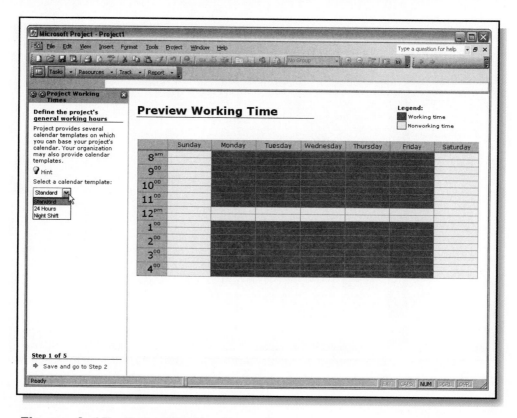

Figure A.17 Project Working Times, Step 1

to choose from for the basic working time for the project. Default is the standard 40 hours a week, Monday through Friday schedule with weekends off. The other options are Night Shift, and 24 Hour. To illustrate the next steps in this example, we will choose the Standard schedule.

After you have made the general working time choice, click on the "Save and go to Step 2" link at the bottom of the Task pane. Step 2 allows you to manipulate the days of the week, and if requested, the daily working times (see Figure A.18).

After making any needed changes, click on the "Save and go to Step 3" link at the bottom of the Task pane. Step 3 allows you to specify nonworking time, such as holidays, or to specify hours during a given day that are not working hours. For instance, January 15, 2007, is the U.S. national holiday to celebrate Martin Luther King, Jr.'s, birthday. To specify that day as nonworking time, click on the "Change Working Time" link in the Task pane to bring up the Change Working Time dialog box (see Figure A.19). Next, click on Monday, January 15, to select it. Notice the working time is filled in on the right side of the dialog box (see Figure A.20).

To specify January 15, 2007, as nonworking time, click on the radio button for "Nonworking time" to select the entire day as nonworking time. If your organization does work on that day but only works a half-day, as an example, choose the "Nondefault working time" radio button, and then specify the working time for that day in the fields provided. Figure A.21 shows the dialog box with a morning half-day specified for January 15; notice the date is bold and underlined, indicating that the working time for that day has been edited.

After specifying all nonworking time during the estimated time of the project, click the "Save and go to Step 4" link at the bottom of the Task pane. Step 4 allows you to specify the number of hours per day, the number of hours per week, and the number of days per month (see Figure A.22). Notice the instructions in the Task pane suggest making sure these values match those specified in earlier steps. This is important because Project calculates schedules based on hours. So, if you schedule the duration of a task as 2 days and the setting for work days is 8 hours, then Project will specify 16 hours for that task.

You may wish to make changes here if you have selected the Standard schedule but have made changes

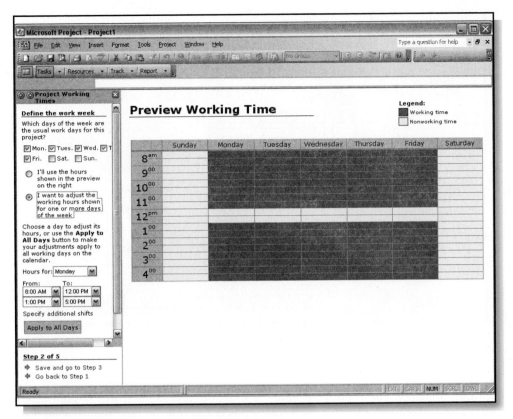

Figure A.18 Project Working Times, Step 2

Figure A.19 Project Working Times, Step 3

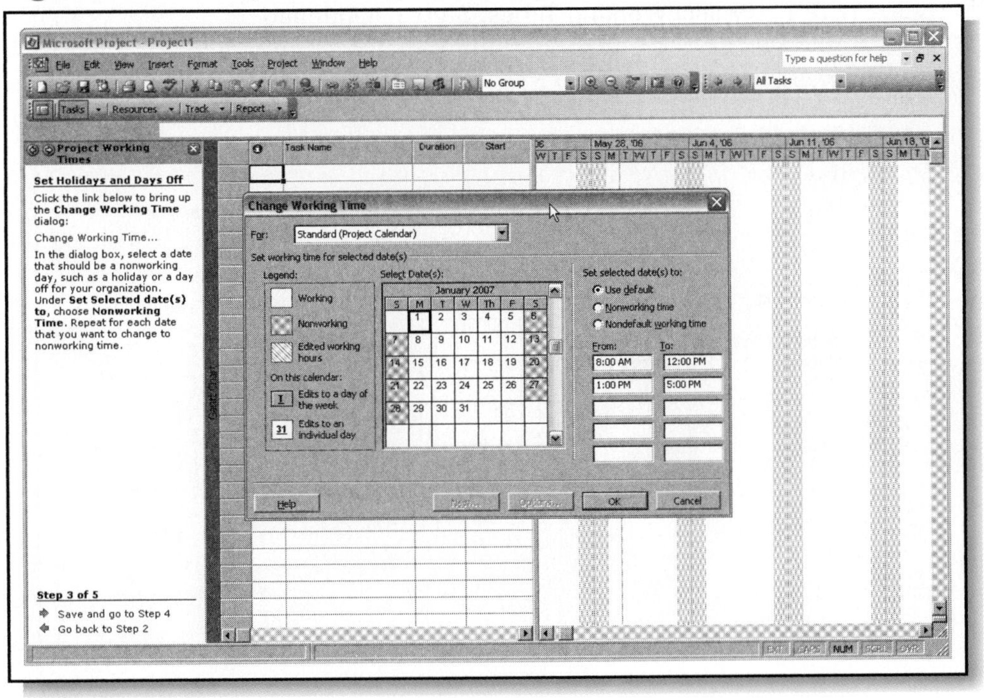

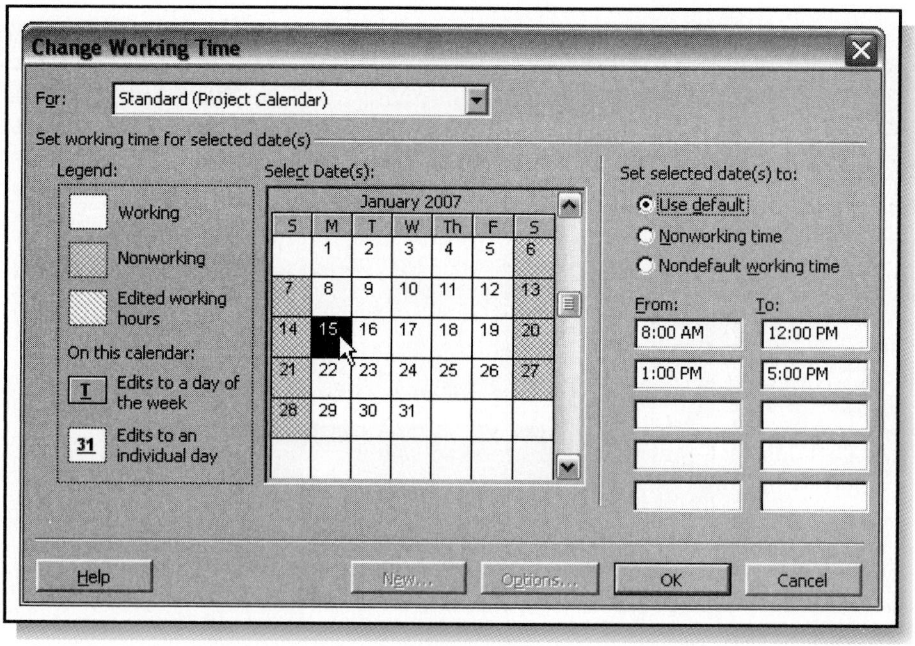

Figure A.20   Project Working Times, Step 3, continued

to the working times in Step 2. For example, if your organization works on compressed schedules, 4 days per week at 10 hours a day, making changes here will ensure that if you specify a task to take 2 days, it will be a 20-hour task rather than a 16-hour task. Once the values in this step are finalized, click on the "Save and go to Step 5" link at the bottom of the Task pane. The final step in the Project Working Times process is verification

Figure A.21   Project Working Times, Step 3, continued

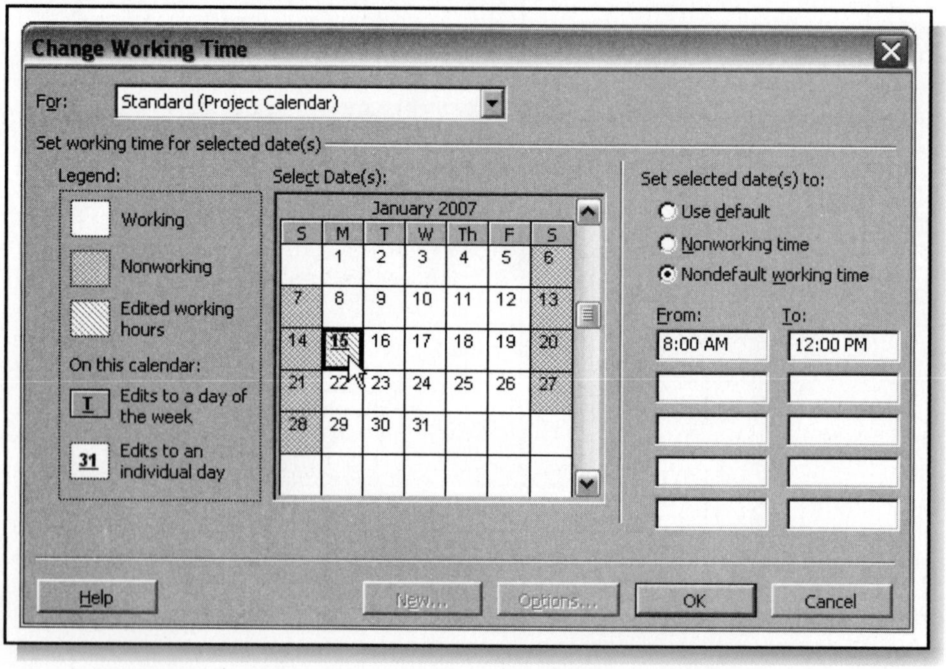

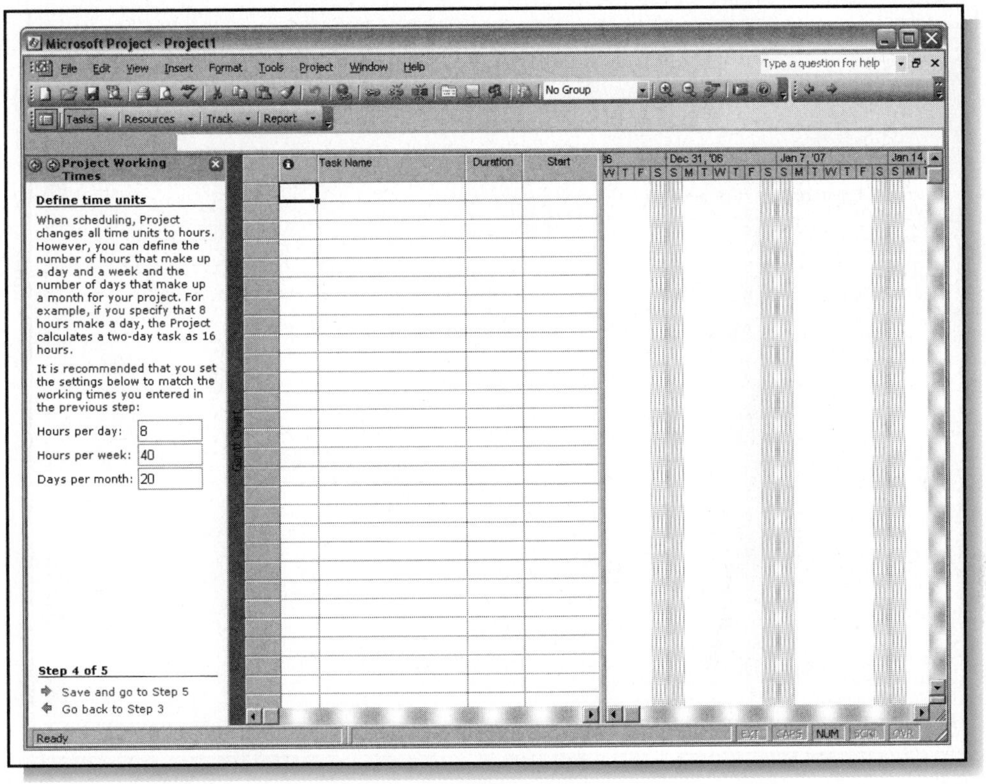

Figure A.22 Project Working Times, Step 4

that the project's calendar has been set and that resources will be scheduled based on the calendar that has been specified during these steps (see Figure A.23). There is an option at this step to define a different calendar for a different set of resources. This might be useful if your organization utilizes a pool of part-time workers, for example. If you are satisfied with the calendar, click on the "Save and Finish" link at the bottom of the Task pane.

Task Entry

Now that the calendar has been set and saved, the next step is to enter the tasks to develop a Work Breakdown Structure (WBS). First, click on the "List the tasks in the project" link in the Task pane to bring up the List Tasks pane (see Figure A.24). There are two additional options to consider here as well. First, there is an Import wizard if there is another file with tasks already listed, such as an Excel spreadsheet. Second, there is the option to specify a task as a milestone.

Notice that Project suggests in this pane specifying durations for the tasks. You may wish to enter dura-

tions at this stage; however, if your goal is to develop a WBS (as shown in Chapter 6), you may wish to wait until a later step to specify durations. Figure A.25 shows the beginnings of a task list with no durations specified, that is, a WBS. Notice at this point, that no durations and no start or finish dates have been specified for any tasks.

Once all of the tasks have been entered into the Task entry table, click on the "Done" link in the List Tasks pane to return to the Task pane. The next step is to create summary tasks that represent phases of the project. Click on the "Organize tasks into phases" link in the Task pane to bring up the Organize Tasks pane. Notice in the task list, the first five tasks listed involve issues related to scope. Considering that these tasks are all related, and the fifth task is a milestone referred to as "Scope complete," we may wish to group these five tasks into a larger summary task. To do this, select the first task in the list, and then click on the button to insert a new row (see Figure A.26). For this example, we'll enter the summary task's name as "Scope" (see Figure A.27).

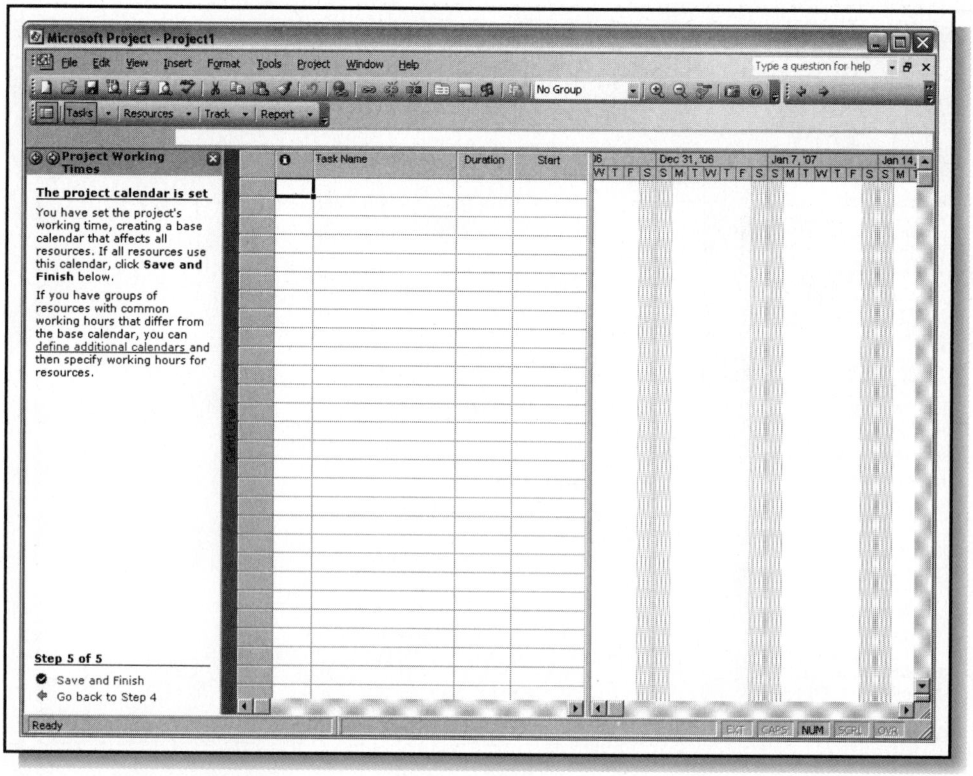

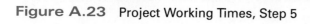

Figure A.23 Project Working Times, Step 5

Figure A.24 Enter Tasks

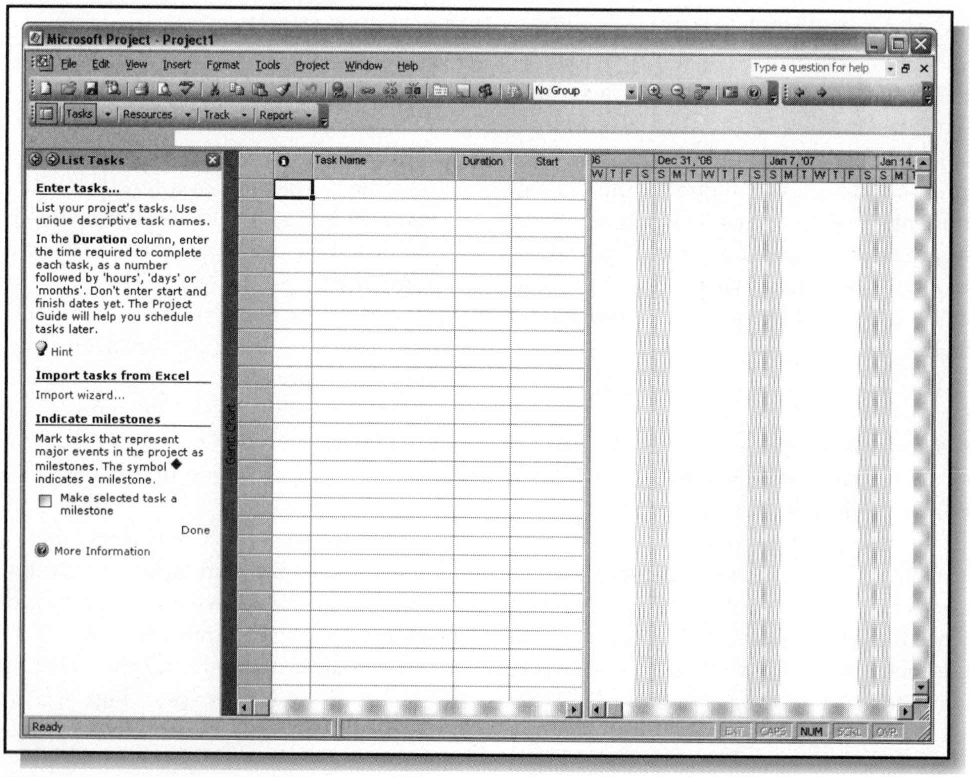

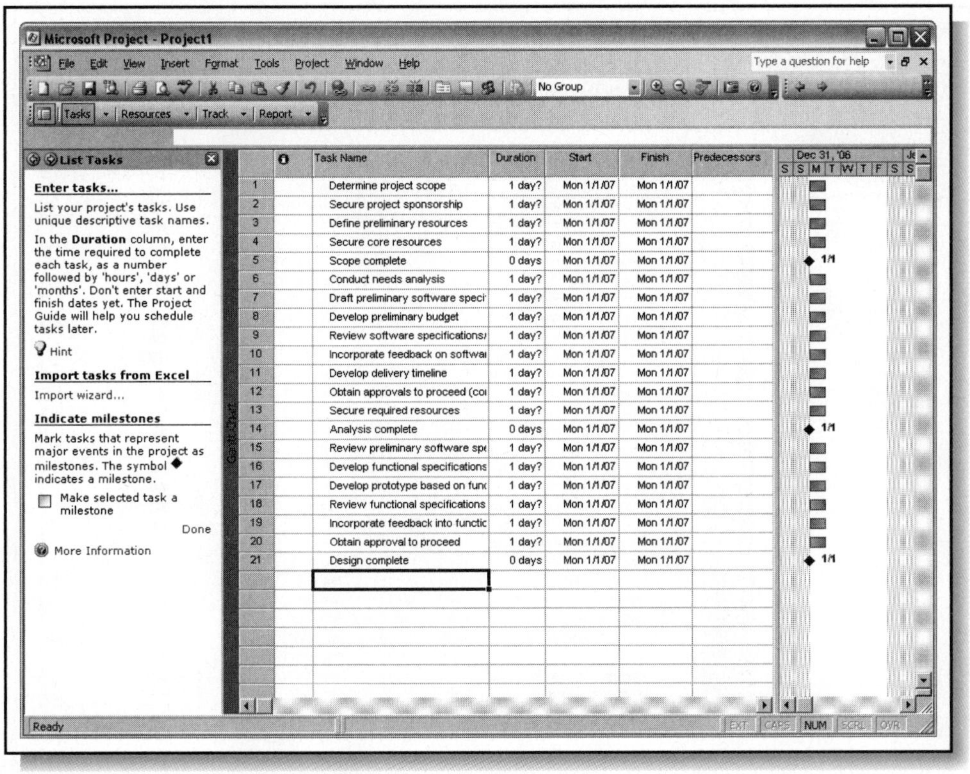

Figure A.25 Starting a WBS

Figure A.26 Inserting a row for a summary task

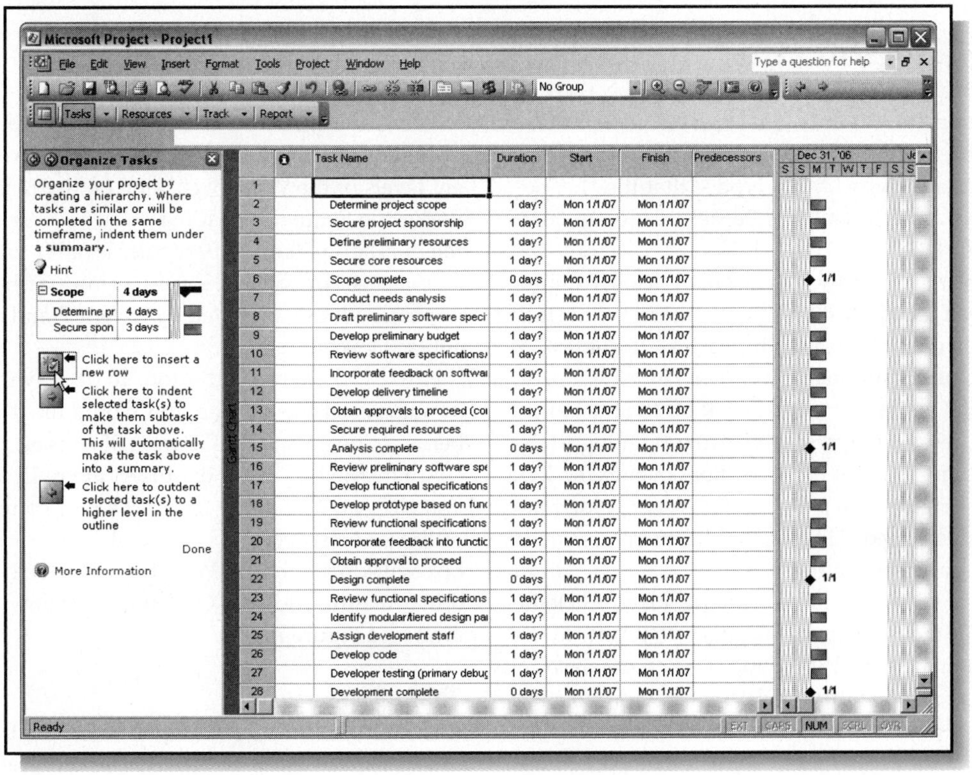

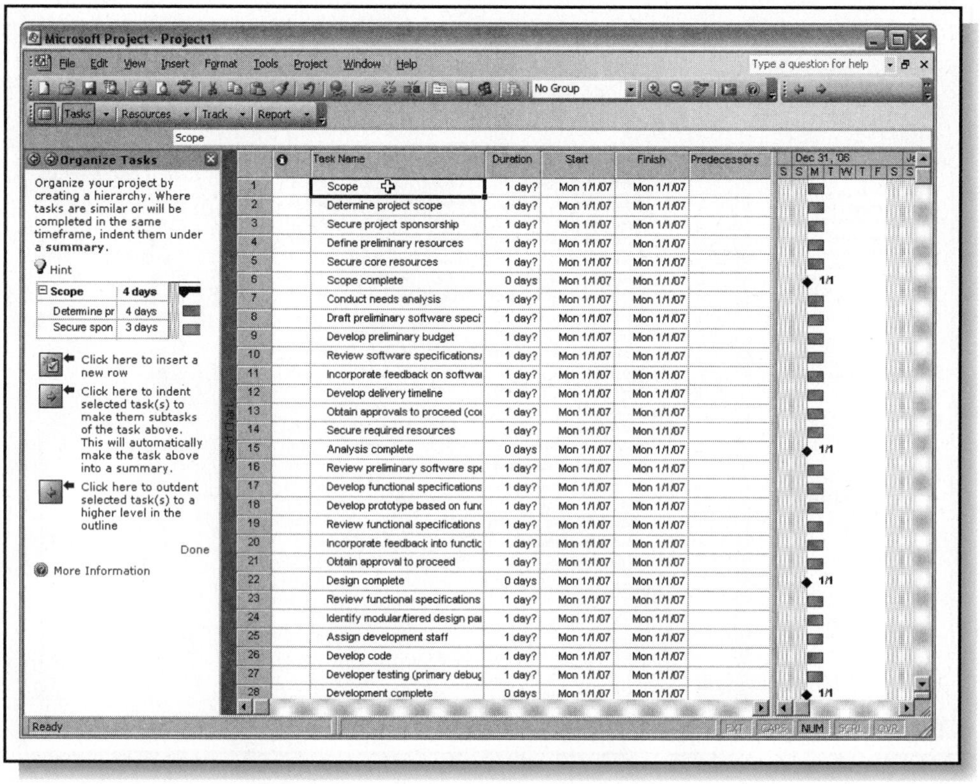

Figure A.27 Entering the summary task name

Now, to set the "Scope" task as a summary task, select the five following tasks ("Determine project scope" through "Scope complete"), and then click the button with the arrow pointing to the right to indent the selected tasks (see Figure A.28). Notice that the "Scope" task is now bold and has a black, rather than blue, duration indicator.

In Figure A.29, a row has been inserted to enter a summary task called "Testing," but just entering the task into the row makes it appear as though it is a subtask of the "Development" summary task (see Figure A.30). To make "Testing" a summary task, click on the button (in the Organize Tasks pane) with the arrow pointing to the left. This outdents (moves the indention level to the left) "Testing" (see Figure A.31). Once subtasks to testing are identified and indented, "Testing" will then be displayed as a summary task (see Figure A.32).

Once all of your tasks have been organized, click the "Done" link in the Organize Tasks pane to return to the Task pane. To finalize the WBS, Project can generate WBS numbering codes to identify the levels of decomposition for each task level. To generate the WBS codes for your project, click on the Project menu in the menu bar, mouse

over the WBS option, then click on Define code (see Figure A.33).

Depending on the complexity of your project, and the level of decomposition of the tasks, you can display different levels of the WBS by clicking on the dropdown menu under the Sequence heading and choosing the format of the numbering for that particular level. In Figure A.34, the formatting for the WBS numbering has been set to an uppercase letter, followed by a period and a number for subtask levels.

Next, click the OK button. To display the WBS numbering, select the column you would like the WBS numbering to be next to; in Figure A.35, this is the Task Name column. Next, click on the Insert menu in the menu bar, and click on "Column" to insert a new column to the left of the selected column. The Column Definition dialog box will open; choose WBS from the Field Name dropdown menu. Click the OK button to show the WBS column (see Figure A.36).

Task Scheduling

At this stage, we have a completed WBS in Project that we can use as we estimate activity durations and determine

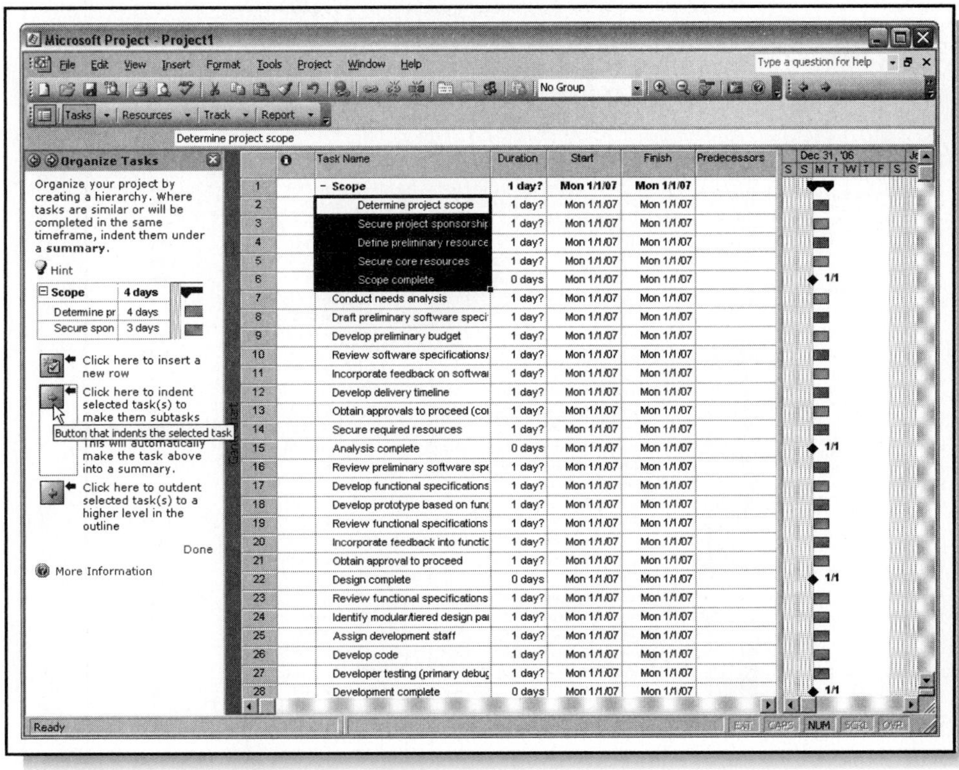

Figure A.28 Indenting subtasks

Figure A.29 Continuing summary tasks

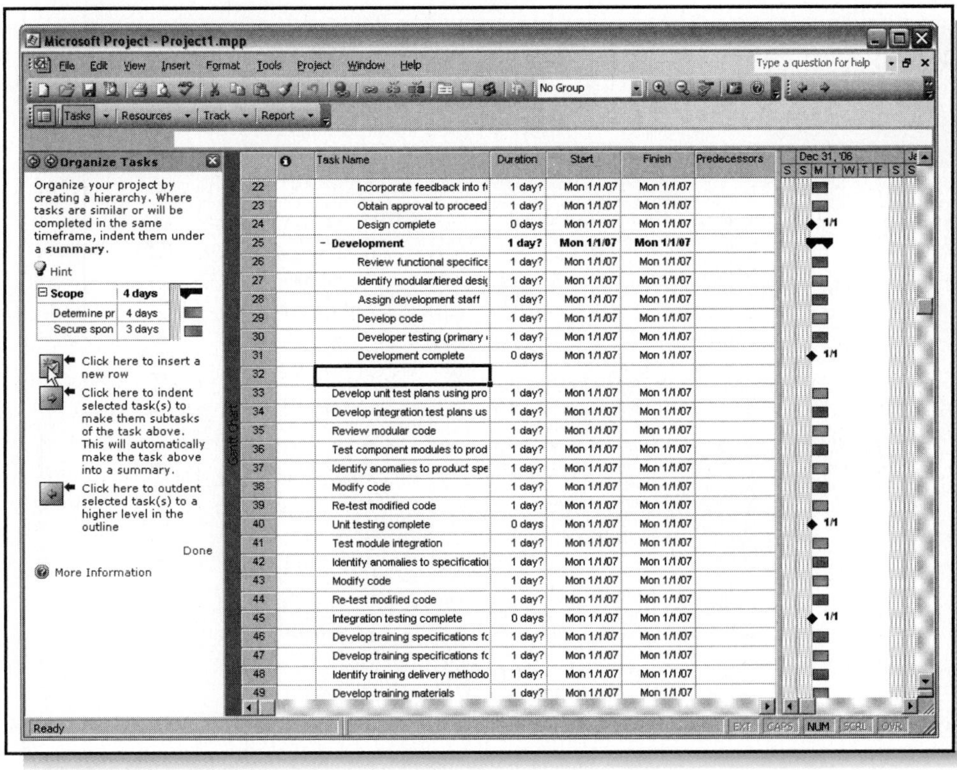

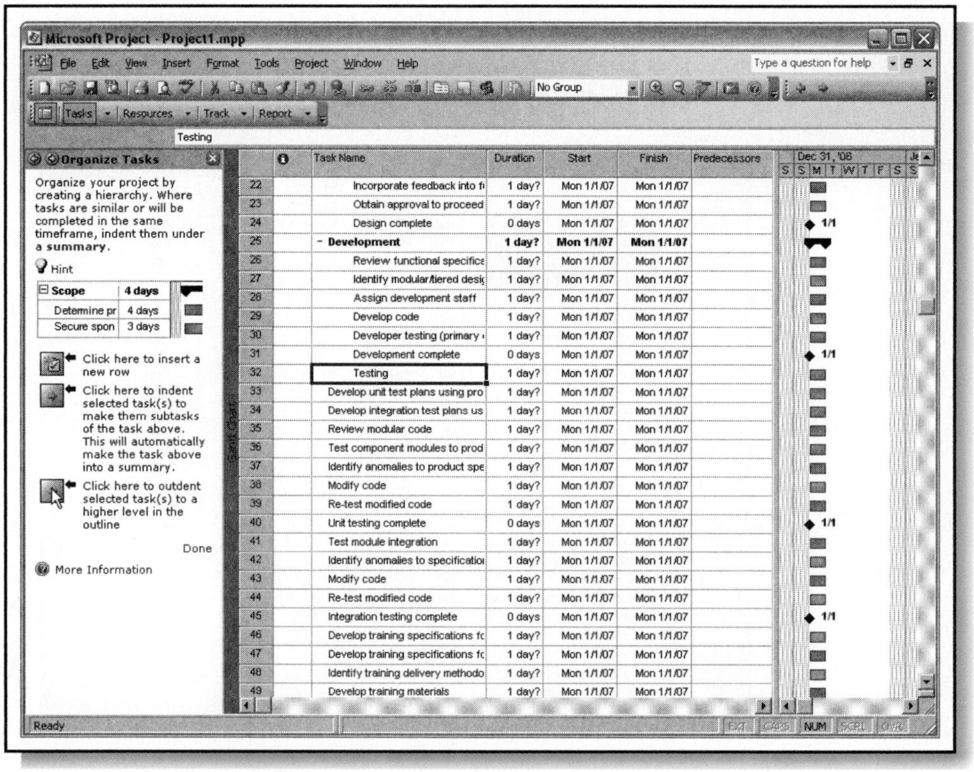

Figure A.30   Indented summary task

Figure A.31   Outdented summary task

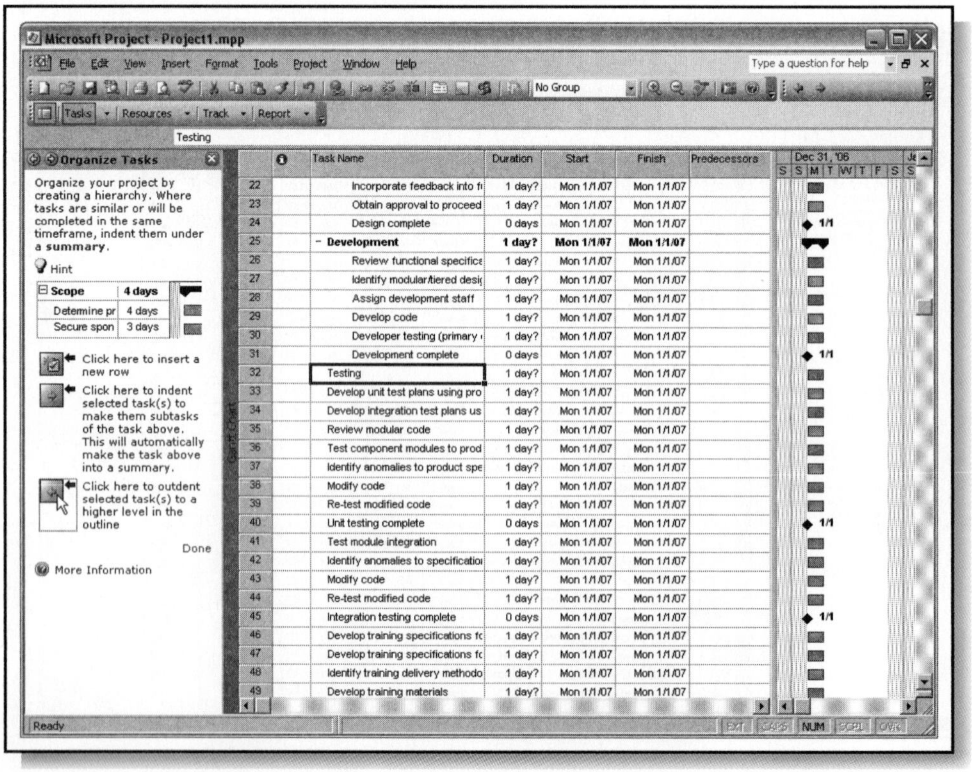

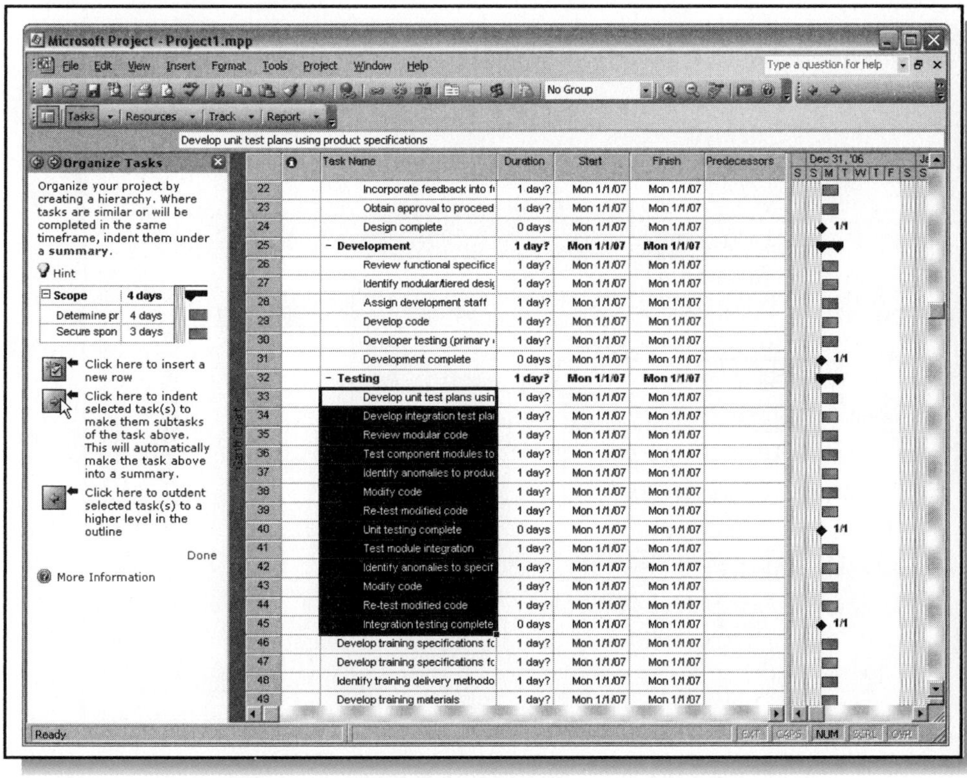

Figure A.32   Indenting "Testing" subtasks

Figure A.33   WBS Code definition dialog

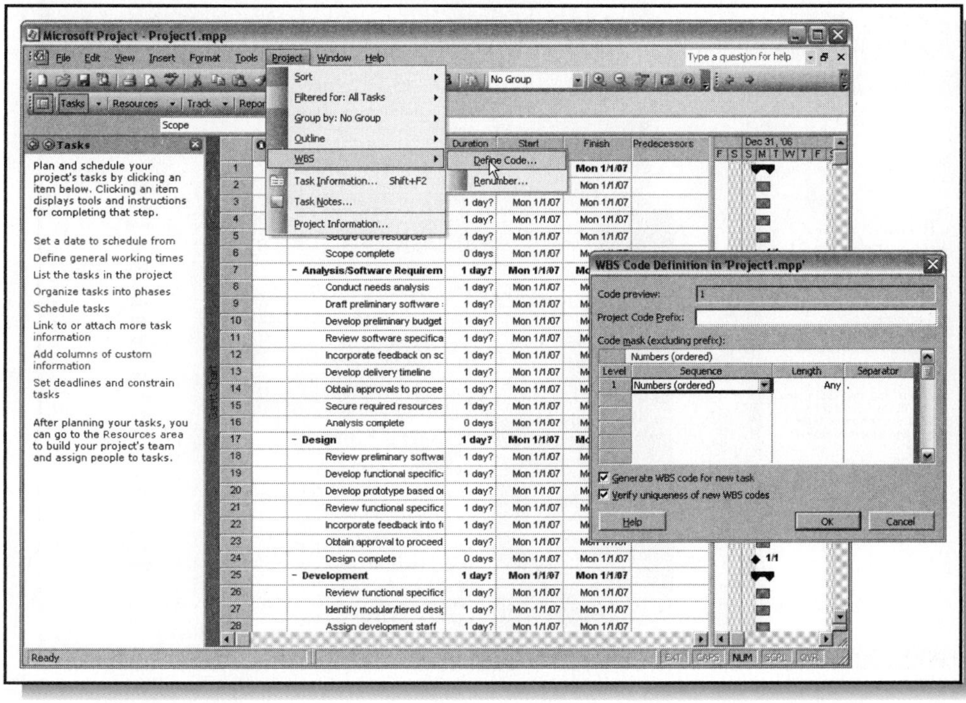

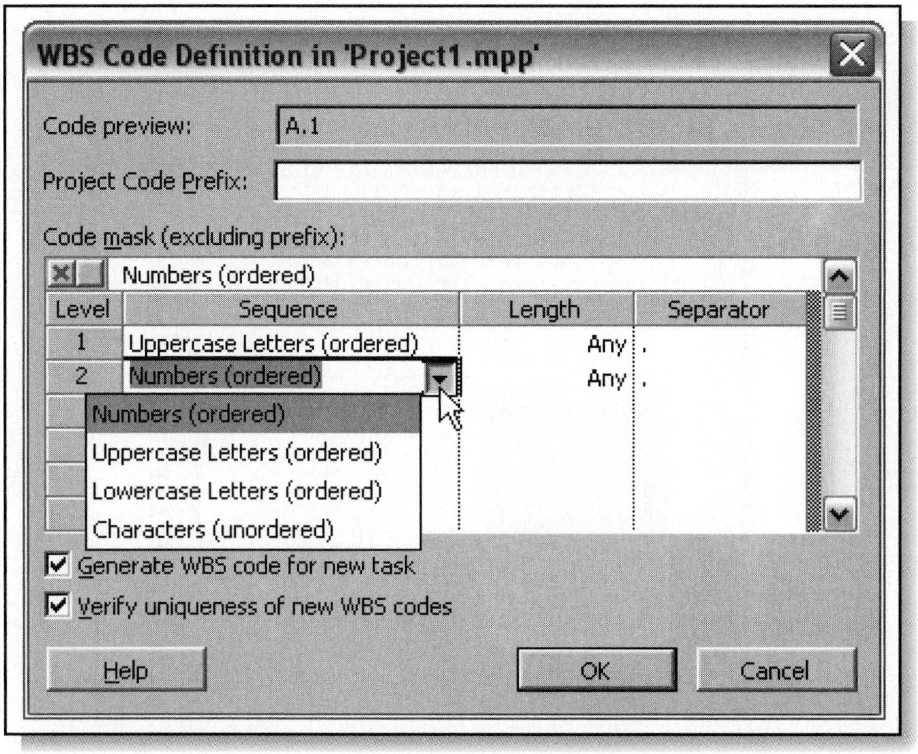

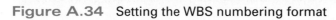

Figure A.34 Setting the WBS numbering format

Figure A.35 Insert WBS column

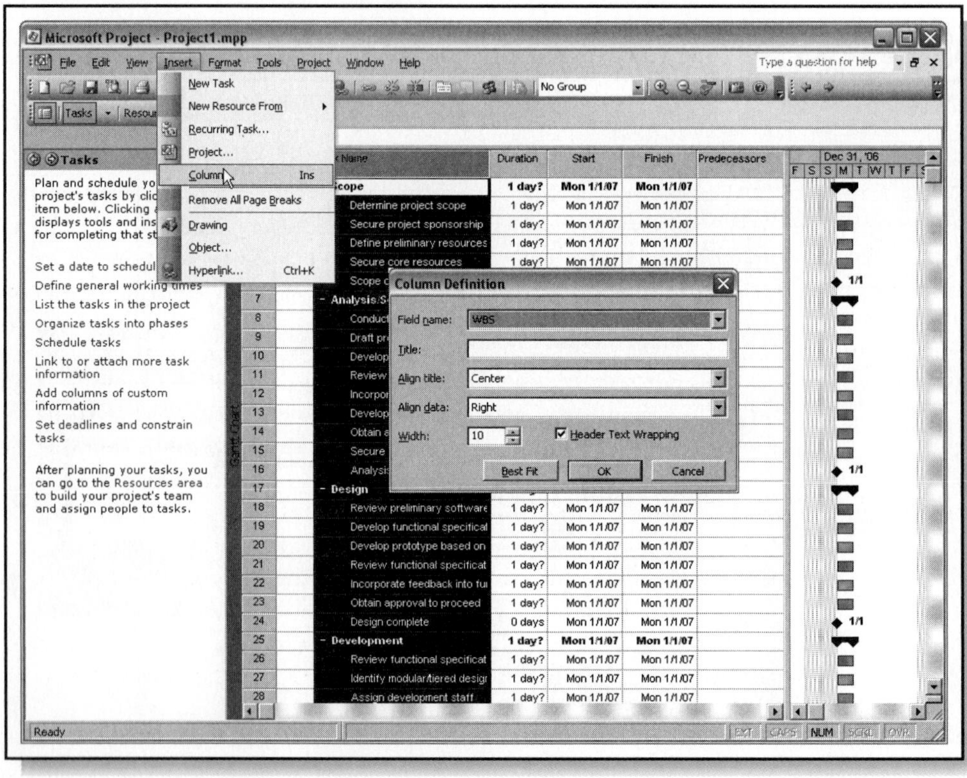

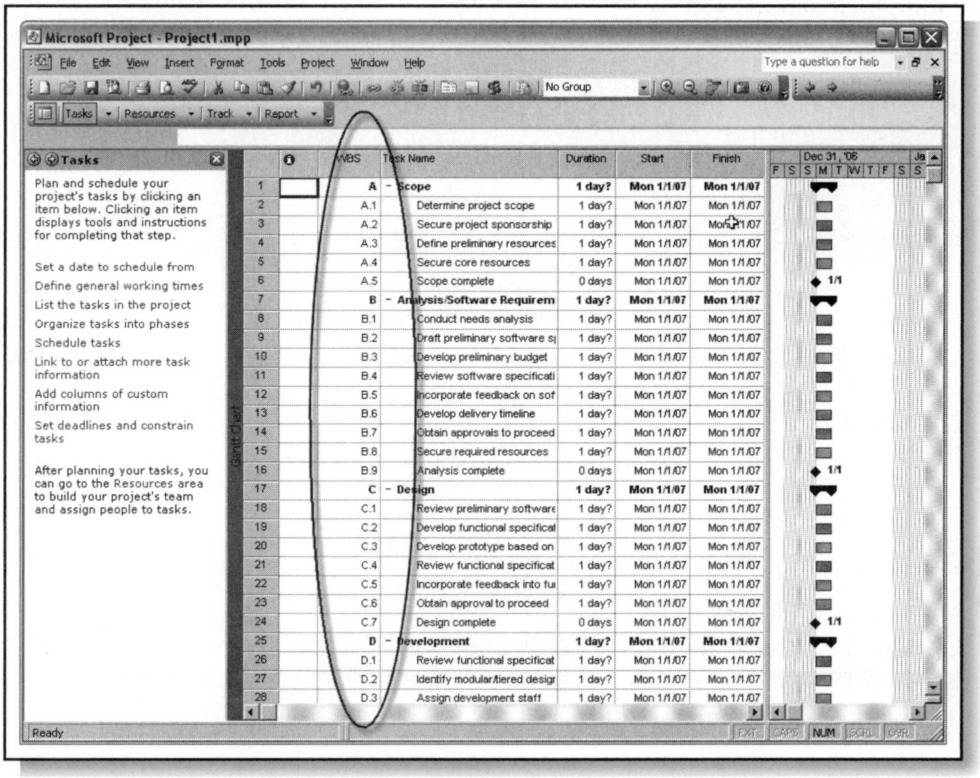

Figure A.36 WBS with codes showing

task dependencies. To set the durations of each task, use the menus in the Duration column, or you can enter any number followed by "days," "hours," or "months." The default is "days," so if you know the task will not take a full day, you may wish to enter the time in hours (see Figure A.37). Do not set start or finish times; Project will calculate these automatically. If you need to constrain a task to begin or end at a specific time, that will be done in a later step. Figure A.38 shows the Tasks with durations set. Notice that Project will not allow you to set a duration for the summary tasks because Project will compute these automatically. Thus, you only need to set the durations for tasks that are not summary tasks.

Once you have set the durations for all of your tasks (milestones remain with 0 durations), it is time to schedule the tasks by setting their dependencies. From the main Task pane, click on the "Schedule tasks" link to bring up the Schedule Tasks pane (see Figure A.39). Three options are available in this pane for setting task dependencies—finish to start, start to start, and finish to finish. To set a dependency between two tasks, select the tasks in the Task entry table, then click on the dependency you would like

to specify. Figure A.39 shows a finish to start dependency for tasks A.1 and A.2.

While the Schedule Tasks pane only gives three available dependencies to choose from, you may change the relationship to start to finish by double clicking on the dependency arrow on the Gantt chart to bring up the Task Dependency dialog box (see Figure A.40). Click on the dropdown menu to choose from the four dependency types. Use this dialog to set lag times for tasks as well.

For the purposes of this running example, we will specify all dependencies as finish to start. If several tasks are sequential, you can select all of the sequential tasks at once and then click the finish to start dependency button to set the dependencies for those tasks.

Now with all of the task dependencies set, notice that Project has determined the start and finish dates and times for each task based on the project's estimated start date, working and nonworking times, and task parameters (see Figure A.41). Additionally, after setting task dependencies, the Predecessor column in the Task entry table is now completed.

Finally, in project scheduling, tasks may sometimes have specific deadlines or may not be able to begin until

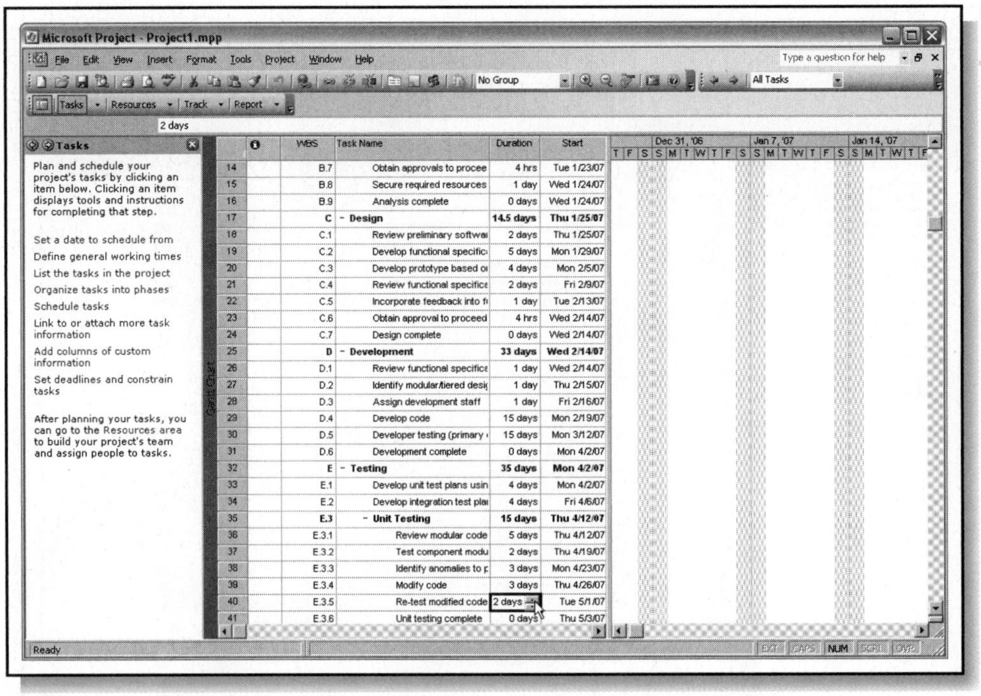

Figure A.37 Setting task durations

Figure A.38 WBS with task durations set

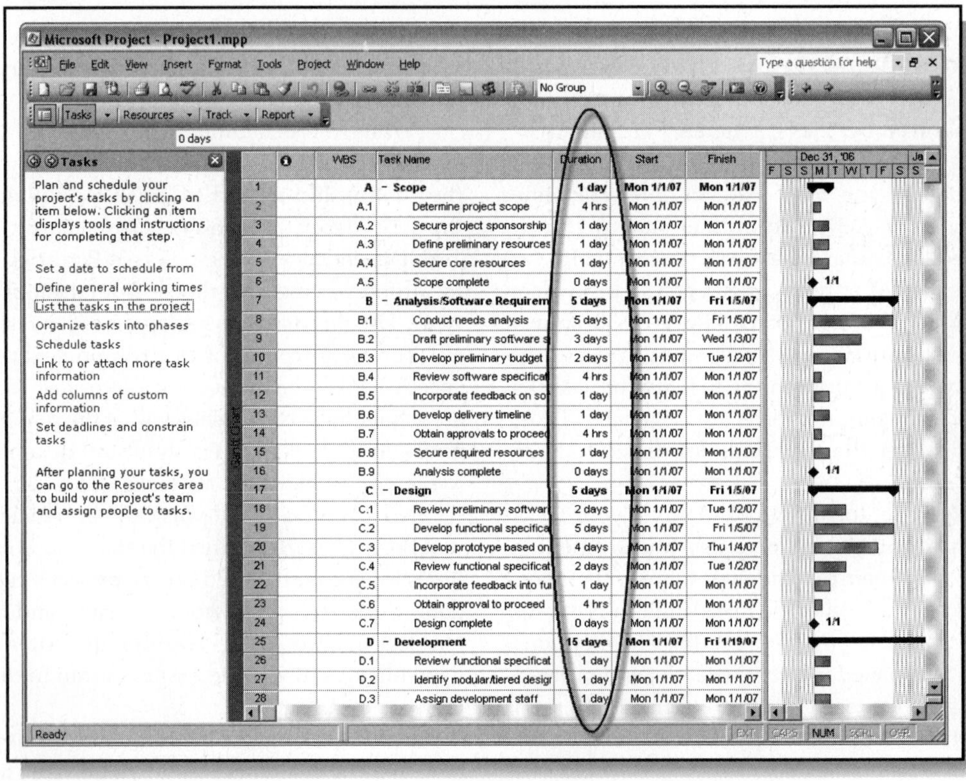

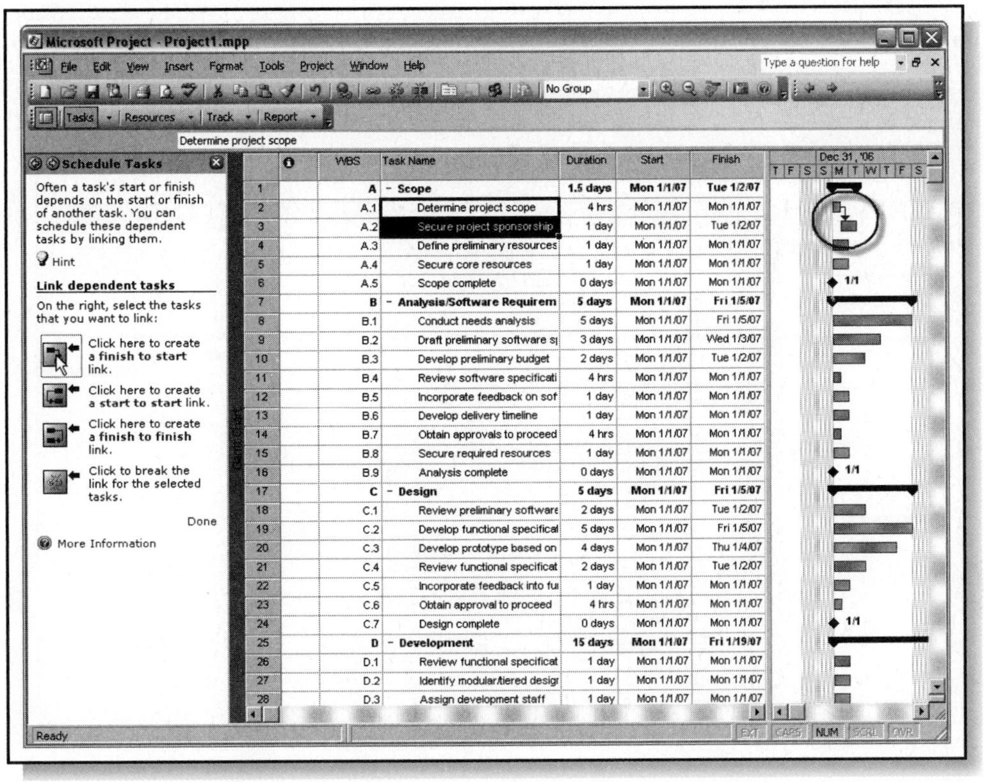

Figure A.39 Setting task dependencies

Figure A.40 More dependencies

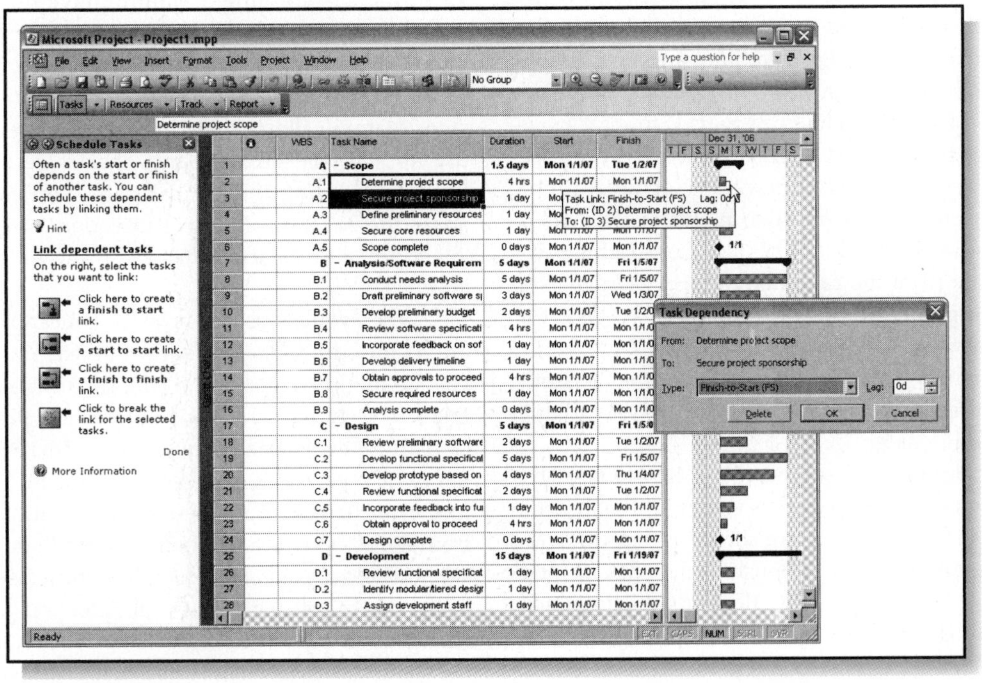

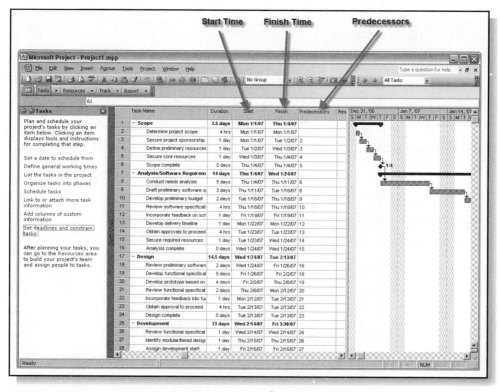

Figure A.41 Task dependencies set

a certain date. In these cases, you may wish to set a deadline for (or constrain) those tasks. To set a deadline click on the "Set deadlines and constrain tasks" link in the Task pane. This will open the Deadlines and Constraints pane. The top half of the pane can be used to set a deadline for a task. The bottom half can be used to set various types of constraints on the task. If you need to set a deadline for a task, select the task you wish to set the deadline for and then click the dropdown menu in the "Set a deadline" portion of the Deadlines and Constraints pane to select a date from the calendar. Figure A.42 shows a deadline being set for the Scope summary task for Friday, January 5, 2007. It might be useful to set such a deadline if there is slack in the schedule for that task but the task requires some resource that is only available until the deadline date.

Another option is to set a constraint on a task. By default, every task is set to start as soon as possible. The other options for constraints are shown in Figure A.43. For instance, you may wish to push back a task as long as possible, particularly one with float or slack, in which case you would set the constraint to start "As late as possible."

Displaying the Critical Path

At this stage, you might want to have the critical path shown in the Gantt chart. To display the critical path on your Gantt chart, from the Format menu choose "Gantt Chart Wizard." The wizard will lead you through several steps that will allow you to make a number of changes to the appearance of the Gantt chart (see Figure A.44). Besides showing the critical path, you can choose to show the baseline, and on subsequent screens you can specify resources and dates to be shown on the Gantt chart as well.

When you choose to show the critical path, tasks that are on the critical path are shown in red. You may wish to change the font color of the critical path tasks in the task entry table as well. To change the critical path tasks' font color, from the Format menu, choose "Text Styles" to open the Text Styles dialog box (see Figure A.45). From the Item to Change dropdown menu, choose Critical Tasks; then from the color dropdown menu, choose Red. You also may wish to bold and/or underline the critical tasks, which can be done in this dialog box as well. After you have made the changes you wish to make, click the OK button to return to the Gantt chart view (see Figure A.46).

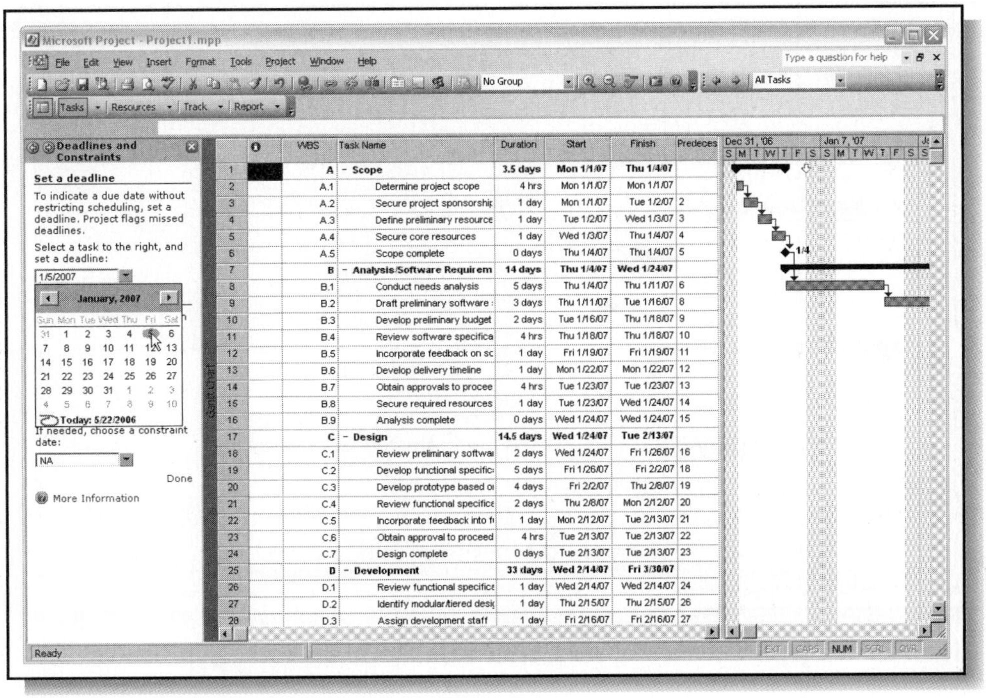

Figure A.42 Deadline set for summary task

Figure A.43 Constraints

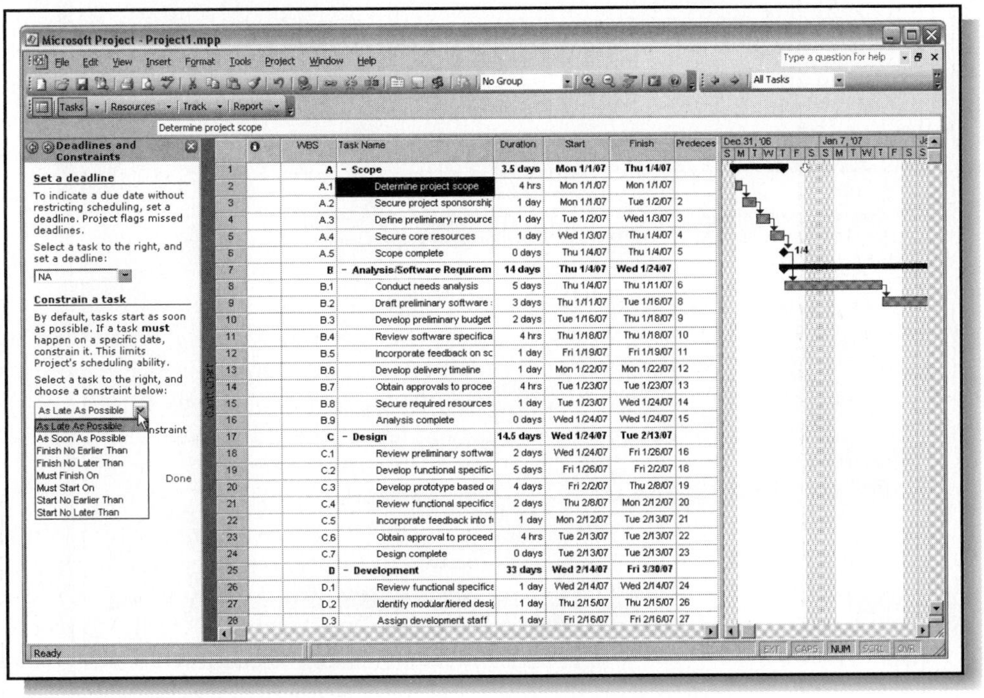

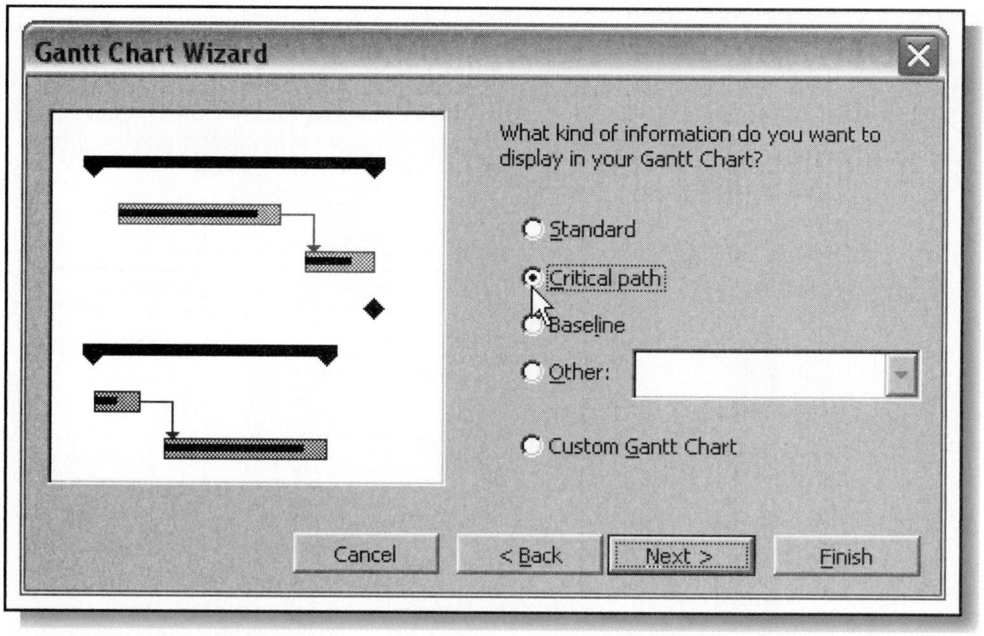

Figure A.44 Gantt chart wizard, critical path

Figure A.45 Critical path tasks font color

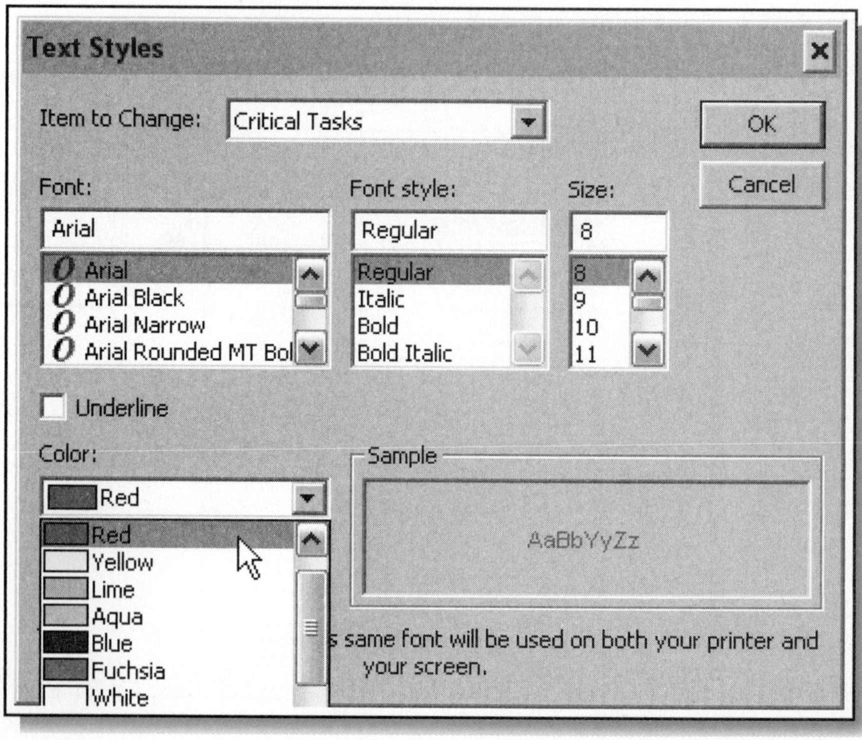

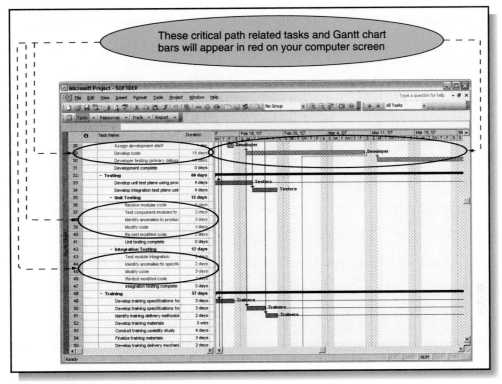

These critical path related tasks and Gantt chart bars will appear in red on your computer screen

Figure A.46 Critical path

The Resources Pane

Now that the project has been decomposed and tasks have been identified, their durations estimated, and scheduled, it is time to identify and assign resources. To begin working with resources, click on the Resources button on the Project Guide toolbar. The Resources pane will open on the left side of the Task entry table (see Figure A.47).

Enter Resources

The first step is to identify the people and equipment that will comprise the resources for your project. Click on the "Specify people and equipment for the project" link in the Resources pane to open the Specify Resources pane (see Figure A.48). The screen now shows the Resource entry table and the Specify Resources pane gives three options for identifying resources for your project. If your organization maintains a company-wide address book (e.g., Outlook Exchange Server), or a company directory, click on the radio button next to the relevant choice to bring up the dialog box to choose the resources to assign to the project.

For the purposes of this appendix, the following examples will be based on manually entering resources. Click on the radio button next to "Enter resources man-

ually" and begin entering your human resources into the Resource entry table (see Figure A.49). The columns allow you to enter the resource's name, e-mail address, hourly rate, and overtime rate of pay. Other columns, such as material resources, are available and will be covered below.

Notice the "Entering Material Resources" link in the Specify Resources pane. If you click that link, detailed instructions will be shown in the pane on how to enter material resources. Several steps should be taken to enter material resources. First, we need to add two columns to the Resource entry table. Select the E-mail address column by clicking on the column heading. Next, select "Column" from the Insert menu to open the Column Definition dialog box. From the "Field name" dropdown menu, choose "Type" and click OK to insert the Type column (see Figure A.50).

The next column to add is the Material Label column. You can follow the steps above or, after selecting the e-mail address column, right click on the column heading and select "Insert Column" to bring up the Column Definition dialog box. Select "Material Label" from the "Field name" dropdown menu and click OK to insert the Material Label column (see Figure A.51).

Once these columns have been added, enter any material resources needed for the project. These may

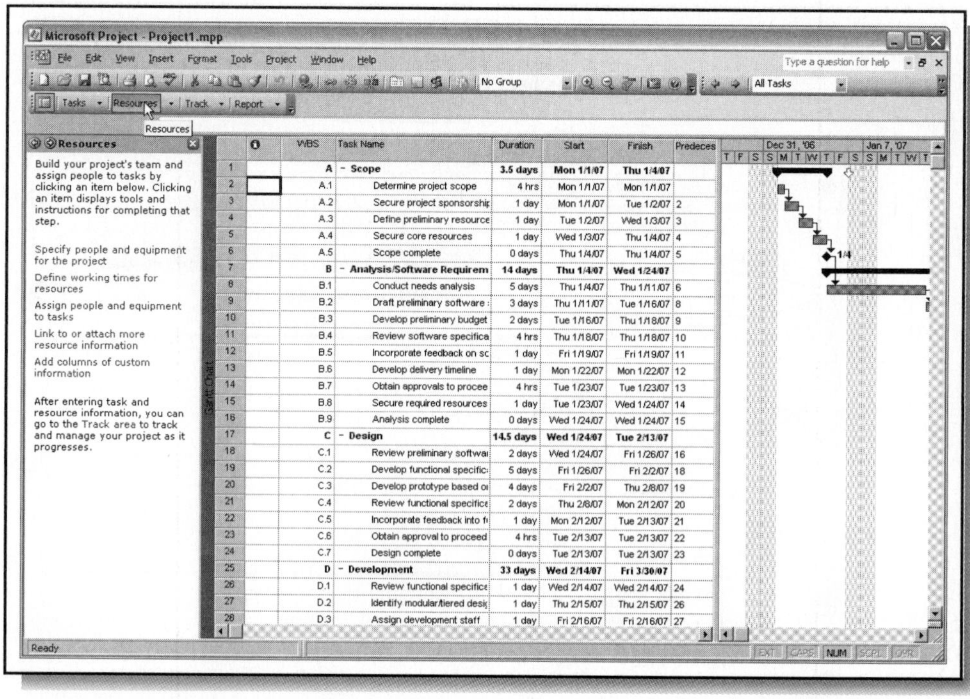

Figure A.47 Resources pane

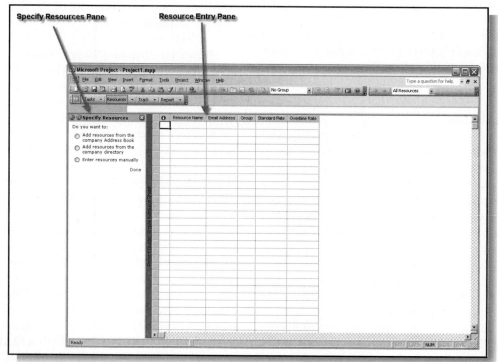

Figure A.48 Specify Resources screen

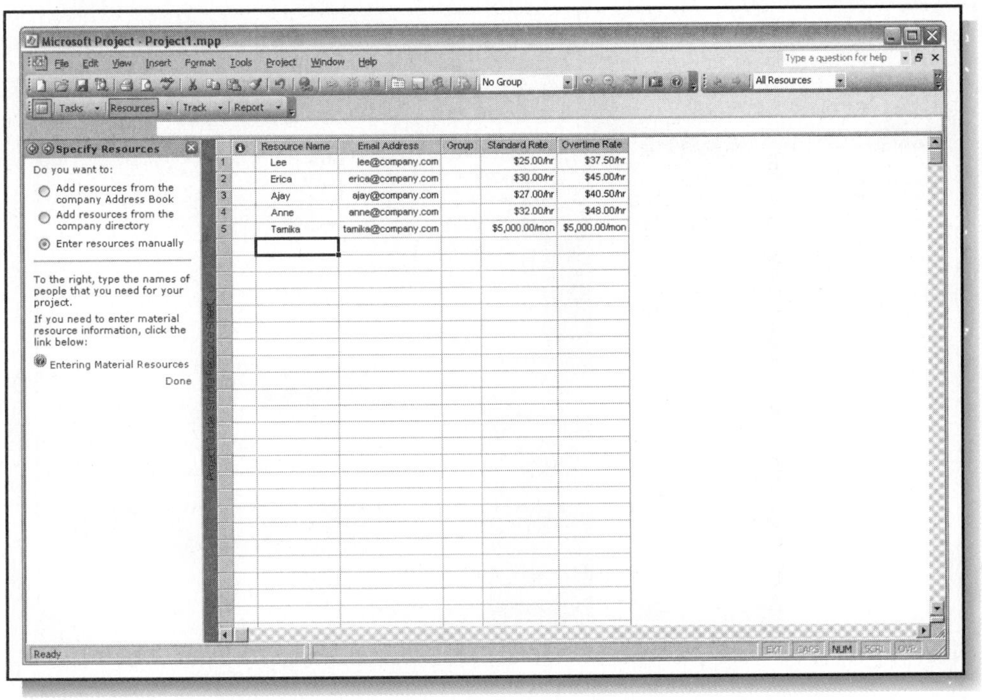

Figure A.49 Adding resources

Figure A.50 Adding the Type column

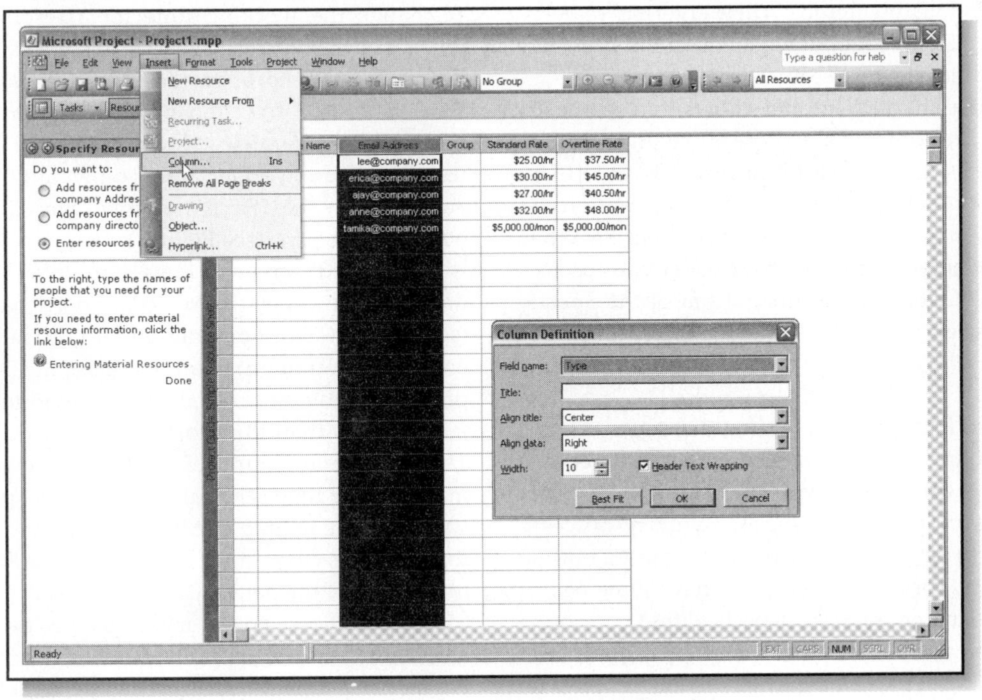

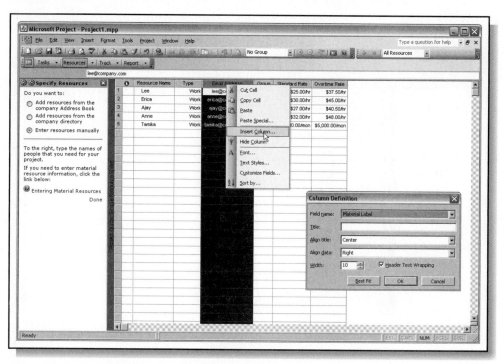

Figure A.51 Adding the Material Label column

include software and equipment, even transportation to and from the job site. Notice that when you added the Type column to the Resource entry table, the column was already filled in with "Work" for the human resources you had previously entered. When entering material resources, click on the dropdown menu in the Type field to select Material for that resource (see Figure A.52).

The Material Label column allows you to specify the cost per unit of the material resource. In the example in Figure A.52, the project is logging costs of $10 for 100 CD-R discs, $15 per hour of laptop computer use, and $.05 per page printed by the laser printer. When you are done entering all the resources for your project, click on the "Done" link at the bottom of the Specify Resources pane.

Define Working Time for Resources

Once the resources have been identified and entered into the Resource entry table, you may wish to identify individual working times associated with resources—particularly those that differ from the project's normal working times. For instance, you may have some people who are working on multiple projects within your organization and can be allocated to work on your project only on certain days. Or, you may have some people who

have scheduled vacation time that needs to be accounted for in their working time. Microsoft Project allows you to specify working time for individual resources that are different from the project's normal working time. To change the working time for a resource, click on the "Define working times for resources" link in the Resources pane to open the Resource Working Times pane. This is a five-step process very much like the process to set the project's working time. First select the resource whose working time you would like to change and click on the "Save and go to Step 2" link at the bottom of the pane (see Figure A.53).

The next screen allows you to select a calendar template specific to that particular resource (see Figure A.54). For example, if you had a flex-time employee, you might want to choose the 24 hours template to be able to schedule that individual during different hours than the project's normal working times. The example in Figure A.54 will keep Anne on the normal working time schedule, but we will specify Anne's vacation time in Step 4. After choosing the template for this resource, click on the "Save and go to Step 3" link at the bottom of the pane.

Step 3 allows you to make changes to specific days and hours within the template you have chosen (see Figure A.55). If you are satisfied with the default settings

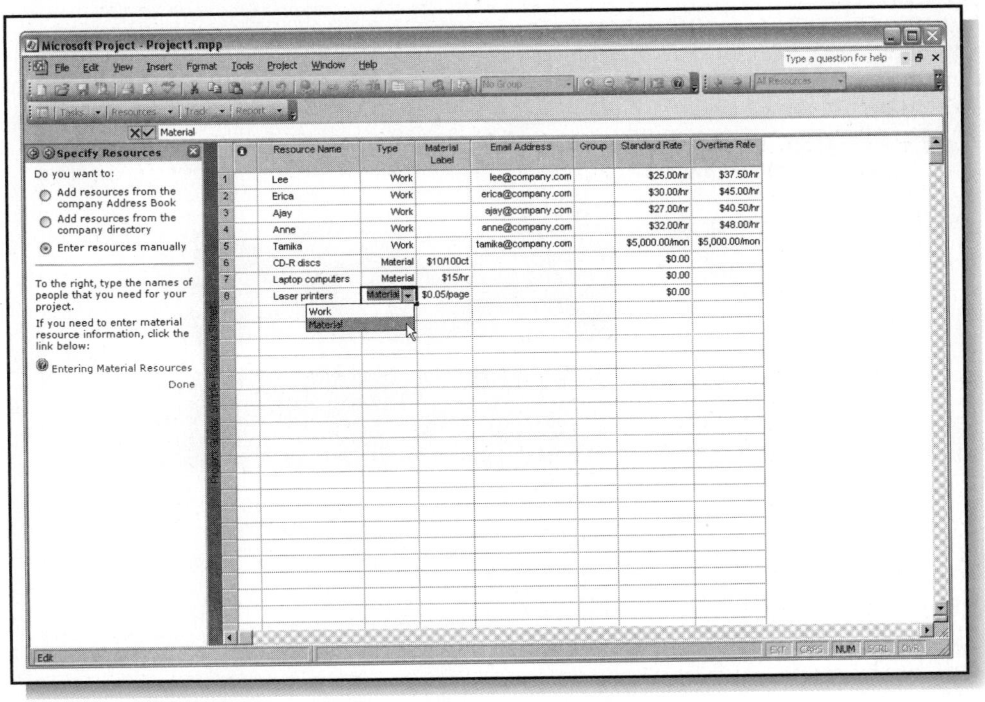

Figure A.52   Changing Resource type

Figure A.53   Resource Working Time, Step 1

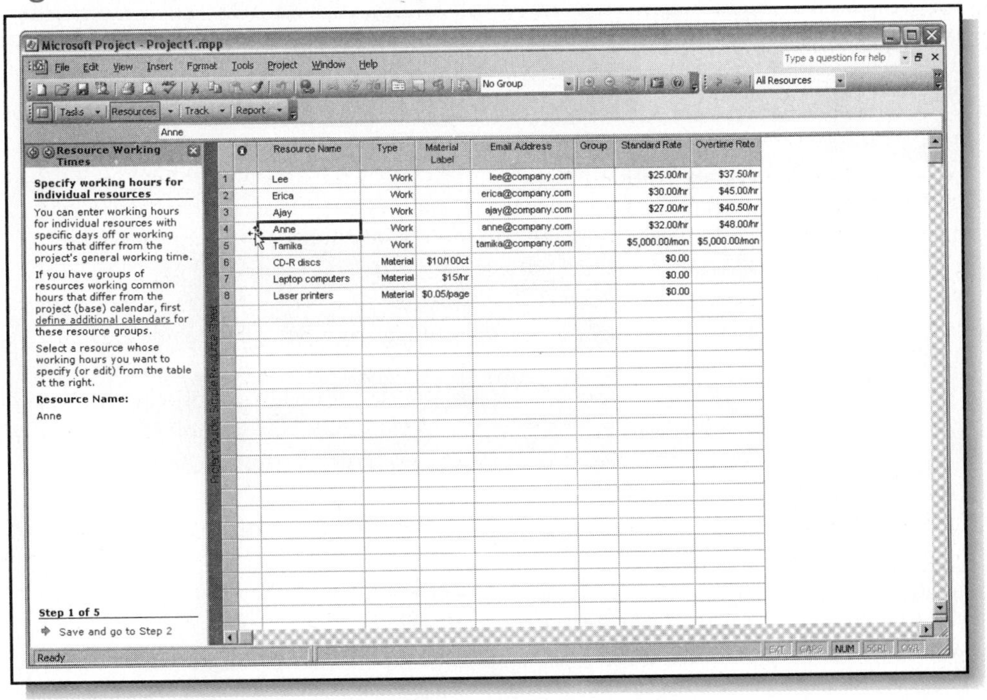

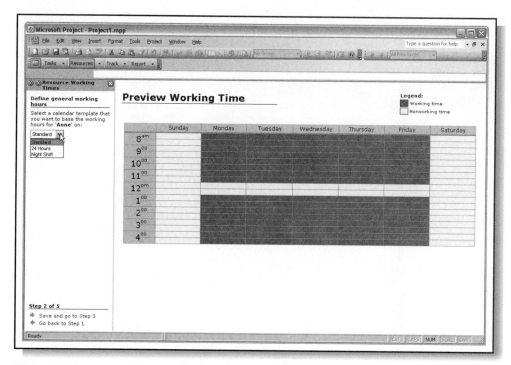

Figure A.54 Resource Working Time, Step 2

Figure A.55 Resource Working Time, Step 3

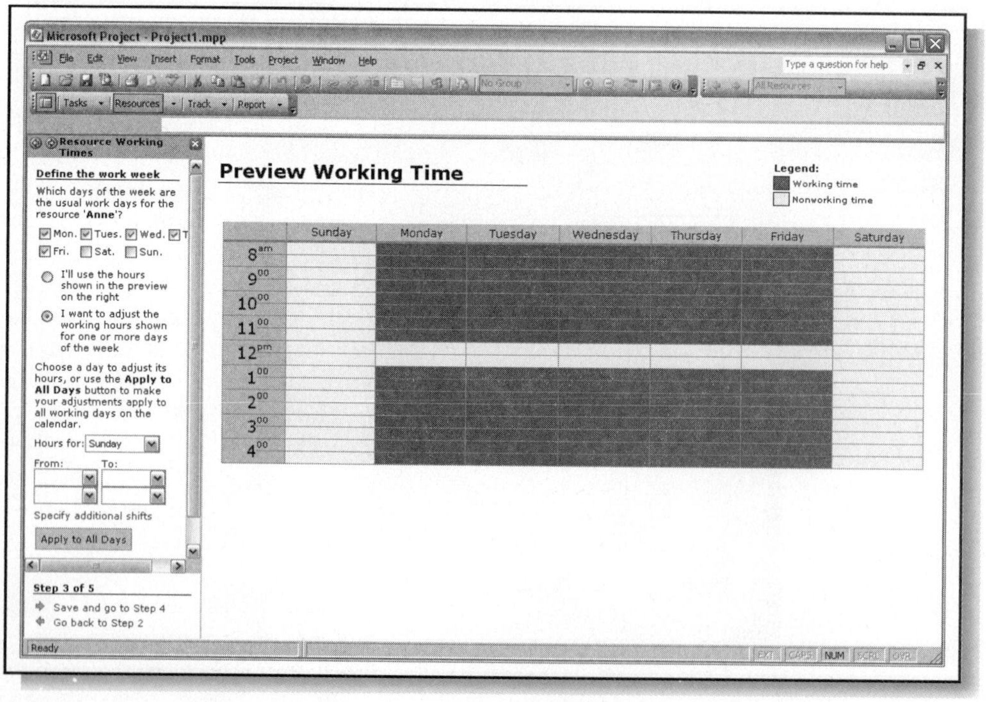

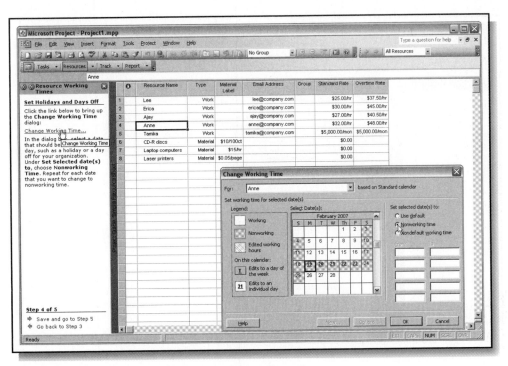

Figure A.56 Resource Working Time, Step 4

or when you have made changes that you are satisfied with, click on the "Save and go to Step 4" link at the bottom of the pane.

Step 4 allows you to specify nonworking time for the resource. In the example in Figure A.56, we have specified Anne's vacation time, February 19–23, by selecting those dates and clicking the radio button next to "Nonworking time." After you have specified any nonworking time for this resource, click on the "Save and go to Step 5" link at the bottom of the pane.

Step 5 is a verification screen that the resource's calendar is now defined and gives you the opportunity to specify the working times of additional resources (see Figure A.57). You can click on the "specify working hours for another resource" link to do so, or click on the "Save and Finish" link to return to the Resources pane.

Assign Resources

Now that all the resources have been specified and working times have been determined, the next step is to assign resources to tasks. From the Resources pane, click on the "Assign people and equipment to tasks" link to open the Assign Resources pane. The Assign Resources pane lists four steps to assign resources to each task. The first step is to click on the "Assign resources" link to open the Assign Resources dialog box. The second step is

to select the task to assign resources to in the Task entry table. The third step is to assign specific resources to that task. To assign resources, select the resource to assign and click the Assign button in the Assign Resources dialog box (see Figure A.58).

The first time you assign resources to a task, Project calculates the work required to complete the task by multiplying the duration of the task by the percentage of work units. For example, the "Determine project scope" task has originally been estimated to take 4 hours, so when we assign both Ajay and Anne to this task at 100%, Project keeps the duration of the task at 4 hours, but calculates that it takes 8 hours of actual work to complete the task— 4 hours × 200% assignment units (Ajay at 100% and Anne at 100%) = 8 hours work (notice the circled area of Figure A.58). Once resources for a task have been finalized, any subsequent resource additions or subtractions will cause Project to prompt you to make a decision. In Figure A.59, after assigning Ajay and Anne to the "Determine project scope" task, we've decided to add Erica to that task as well. Notice the warning diamond that appears next to the Task Name field when Erica is added to the task. Mouse over the warning diamond to get the option for the dropdown menu. Within the dropdown menu, there are three options for assigning the extra resource to the task. You can 1) reduce the duration to keep the work the same, now

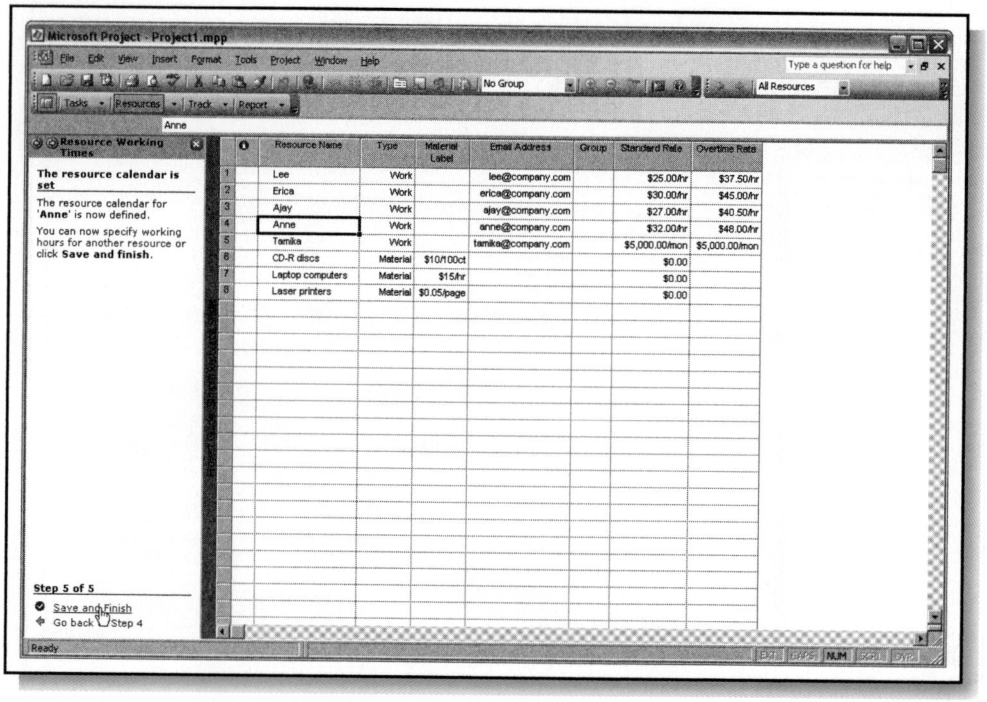

Figure A.57 Resource Working Time, Step 5

Figure A.58 Assigning resources

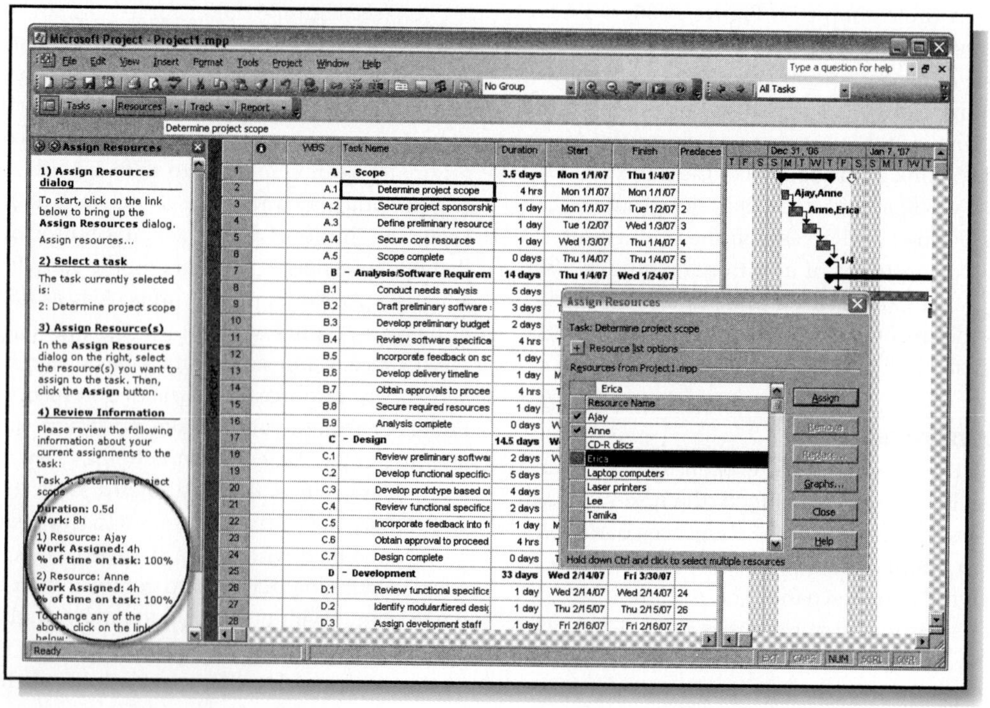

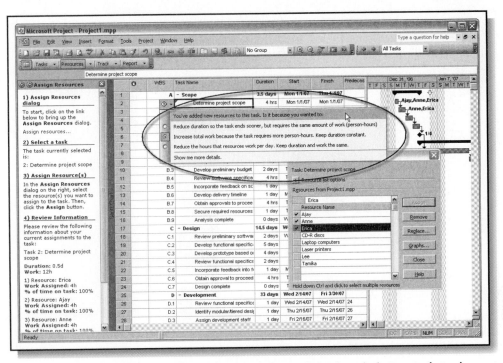

Figure A.59 Adding resources to a task that has already been assigned

across three people instead of two; 2) increase the work required for the task to keep the duration constant, in this case, all three people now assigned 4 hours of work for 12 total hours instead of 8; or 3) keep both the hours of work *and* the duration constant, reducing the number of hours that the resources work per day.

These decisions should not be made lightly. While it might be tempting—and in some cases advisable—to assign additional resources to a task to shorten its duration (effort-driven scheduling), having too many people assigned to a task can sometimes cause more problems than it solves, both administratively and financially.

Resource Views

After assigning resources to tasks, you may wish to explore different views of the resources that Project provides. From the View menu in the Menu toolbar, click on Resource Graph to view a graph of the resources and their percentage of allocation (see Figure A.60).

The middle pane of this view indicates which resource the graph represents. Use the horizontal scroll bar at the bottom of the pane to view other resources. The graph view shows the percent of allocation for that resource on the dates shown. Depending on how you have assigned resources, you can end up with resources being over-allocated. This view provides an intuitive, easy-to-understand representation of such overallocation

by indicating overallocation with a red bar in the bar graph.

Another valuable resource view is the Resource Usage view. Open the Resource Usage view by choosing Resource Usage from the View menu. The middle pane of this view lists each resource and each task that is assigned to the resources (see Figure A.61). The usage view shows the number of hours each resource is working on each task on a given day.

More Information and Columns

The two remaining options in the Resources pane allow you to attach notes or hyperlinks to the resources and add additional columns to the resource entry table. To perform these tasks, click on the appropriate link in the Resources pane, "Link or attach more resource information" or "Add columns of custom information." Follow the instructions in the corresponding panes to perform these steps.

After you have completed identifying, assigning, and managing the project's resources, it is time to start tracking the progress of the project.

The Track Pane

Now that tasks have been scheduled and resources have been assigned, it is time to utilize Project to help you manage the progress of your project. First, click on the "Track

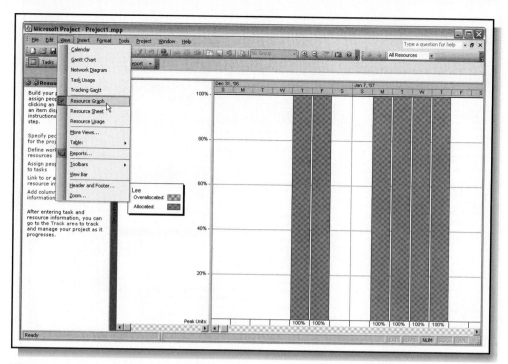

Figure A.60   Resource graph view

Figure A.61   Resource usage view

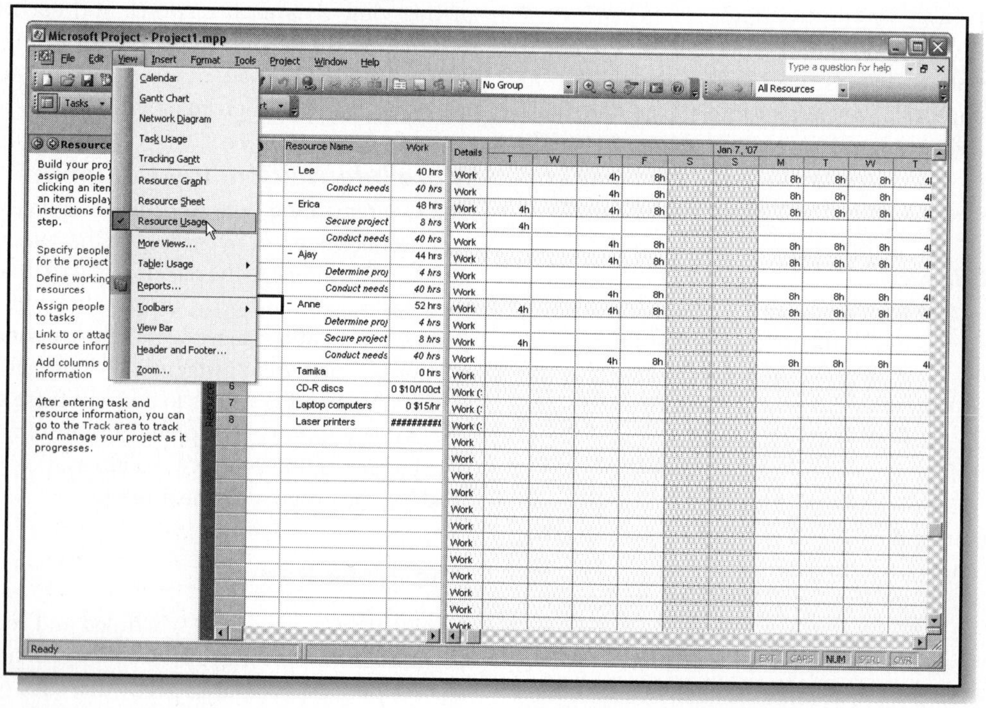

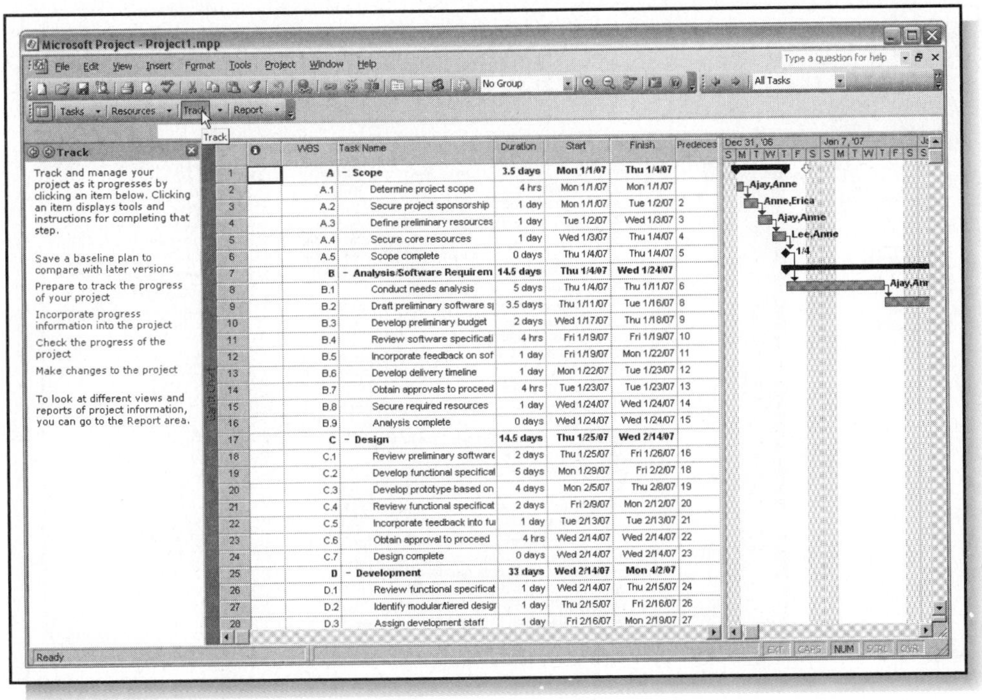

Figure A.62   The Track pane

area" link in the paragraph at the bottom of the Resources pane or click on the Track button in the Project Guide toolbar to begin tracking your project (see Figure A.62).

Save the Baseline Plan

The first step in the Track pane is to save a baseline plan to compare with later versions. If you have saved your project at any time up to this point by clicking on the Save icon in the toolbar or by choosing Save from the File menu, Project by default saves it normally, not as a baseline plan. This is important because once the project is saved as a baseline plan, all subsequent changes will be shown in relation to that baseline plan. First, click on the "Save a baseline plan to compare with later versions" link in the Track pane to open the Save Baseline pane. If you have not already saved a baseline plan, the screen will resemble the one in Figure A.63. Click on the Save Baseline button to save the project as a baseline plan. If you have already saved a baseline plan, when you click on the "Save a baseline plan to compare with later versions" link in the Track pane, the Save Baseline pane will appear as in Figure A.64.

Notice in Figure A.64, that you can save a new baseline or update the existing baseline, and you can choose to update specific tasks or the entire project. Once the baseline plan has been saved, the next step is to specify how progress on the tasks has been completed. To make

this specification, click on the "Prepare to track the progress of your project" link in the Track pane to open the Setup Tracking pane.

Setup Tracking

There are three options for setting up how progress is tracked throughout the project (see Figure A.65). These three choices relate to the level of accuracy for each method. According to the instructions for each option in the Setup Tracking pane, each option should be considered understanding its limitations.

OPTION	LEVEL OF ACCURACY AND TIME CONSUMPTION
Always track by entering the Percent of Work Complete	The least accurate, but fastest, method of tracking. Your resources will specify the percentage of work complete, between 0 (no work has been performed on the task) and 100 (all the work has been completed on the task).
Always track by entering the Actual Work Done and Work Remaining	A moderately accurate and moderately time-consuming method of tracking. Your resources will specify how much work has been on each task, and how much work is left to do.
Always track by entering the hours of work done per time period	The most accurate though time-consuming method of tracking. Your resources will specify the hours worked on each task during each time period.

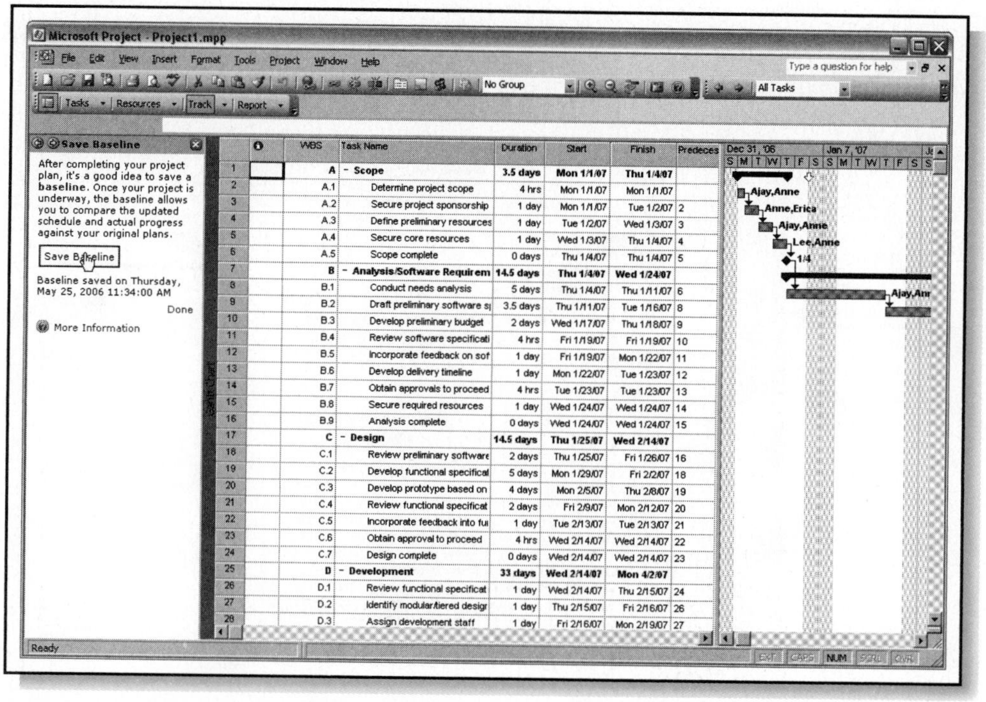

Figure A.63 Saving the baseline plan

Figure A.64 Other options for saving the baseline plan

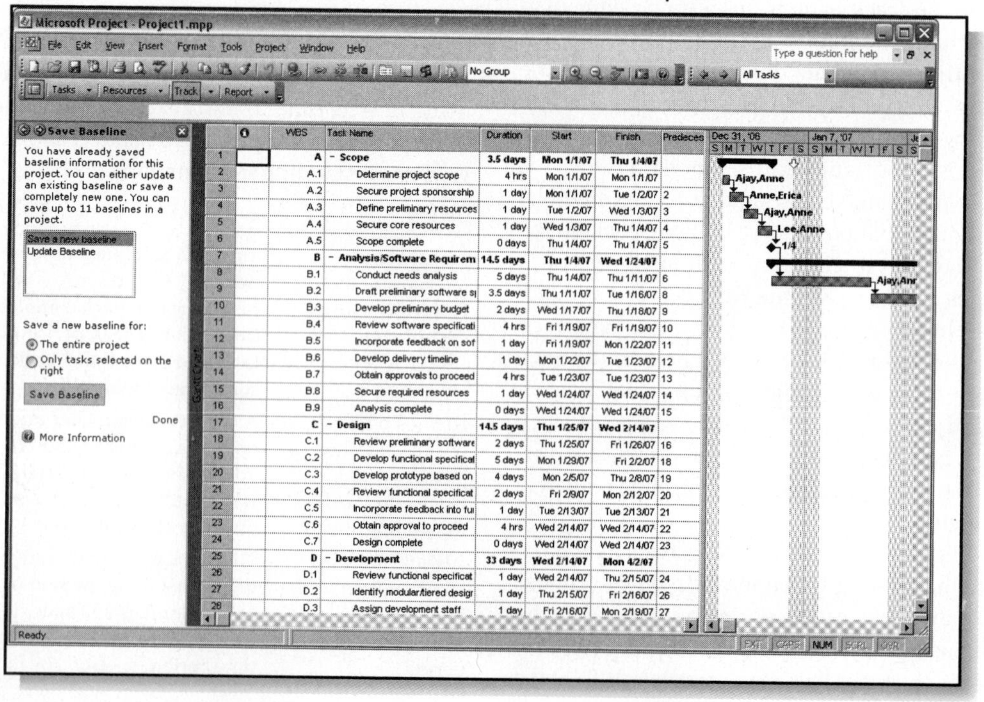

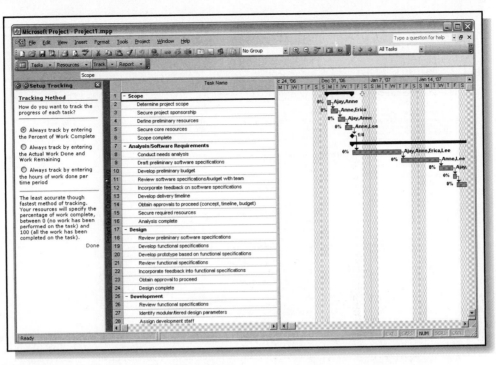

Figure A.65 Setup Tracking pane

Now that Project is set up to track your project's progress, it is time to incorporate the progress that has been made on the project into the project plan.

Incorporating Progress

Depending on how you chose to track progress, there are three possibilities for entering progress. From the Track pane, click on the "Incorporate progress information into the project" link to open the Incorporate Progress pane. You must first set a status date, which Project will use when tracking progress. In the example in Figure A.66, the status date is set to January 2, 2007. This sets Project to track task completion relative to January 2. The ability to change the status date can be useful when comparing phases of a project, especially when comparing phases that have already been completed to phases that are still in progress. In such a case, you might set the status date for the completed phase to be consistent with the current stage of the incomplete phase to make an informed comparison. After setting the status date, begin entering the percentage of work complete for each task by entering the percentage in the "% Work Complete" column of the task entry table.

If you have chosen to track the progress of your project by entering the actual work done and work remaining, you will still set the status date but will then enter the amount of work done and/or the amount of work

left to complete each task. Project provides two new columns—"Actual Work" and "Remaining Work"—in the task entry table to enter this type of progress. If you enter the amount of actual work done, Project will compute the amount of remaining work to be done based on the task duration you have specified for that task. You can also enter the amount of work remaining, and Project will compute the amount of work completed in the same manner. However, you may wish to enter the amount of actual work done *and* the amount of work remaining. This can cause the task's duration to change but may be necessary depending on the circumstances. Notice that in Figure A.67, 6 hours have been completed for the "Determine project scope" task, but we have determined that it will take 4 more hours to complete the task. This brings the total work for the task to 10 hours, where before it was 8 hours (4 hours duration × 2 resources = 8 hours work). Because two people are assigned to this task (Anne and Ajay), Project makes changes to the work needed to complete the task (10 hours) and changes to the duration of the task (5 hours) based on the progress information entered and the number of resources assigned to the task.

If you have chosen to track the progress of your project by entering the hours of work done per time period, you will still set the status date, but the task entry pane will be replaced with a calendar view listing each task

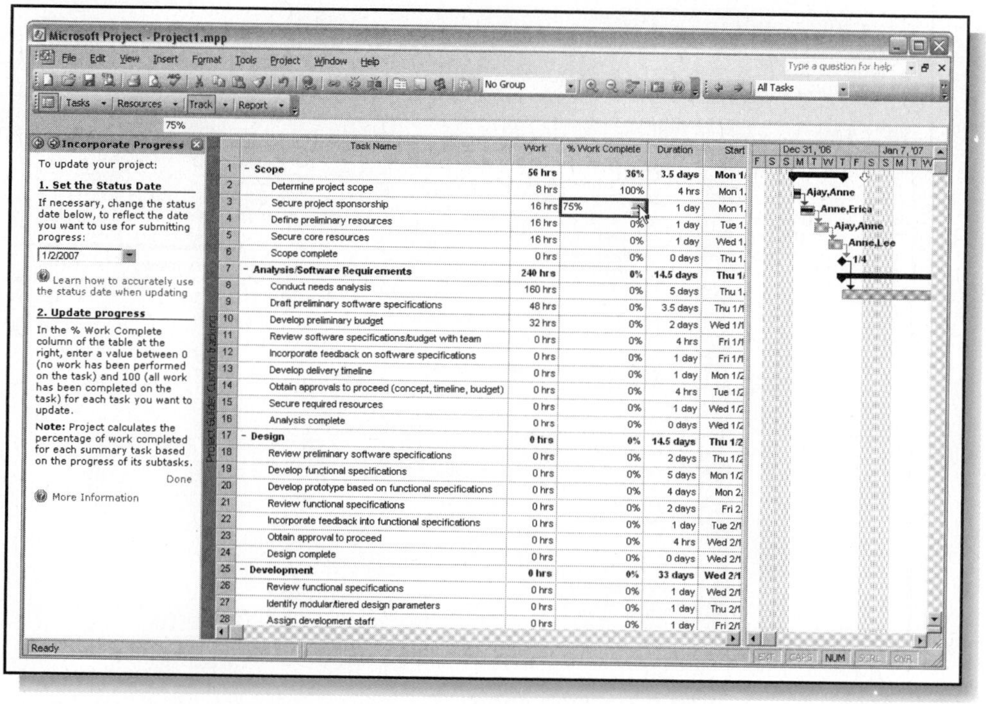

Figure A.66 Tracking progress by percentage of work complete

Figure A.67 Tracking progress by entering actual work done

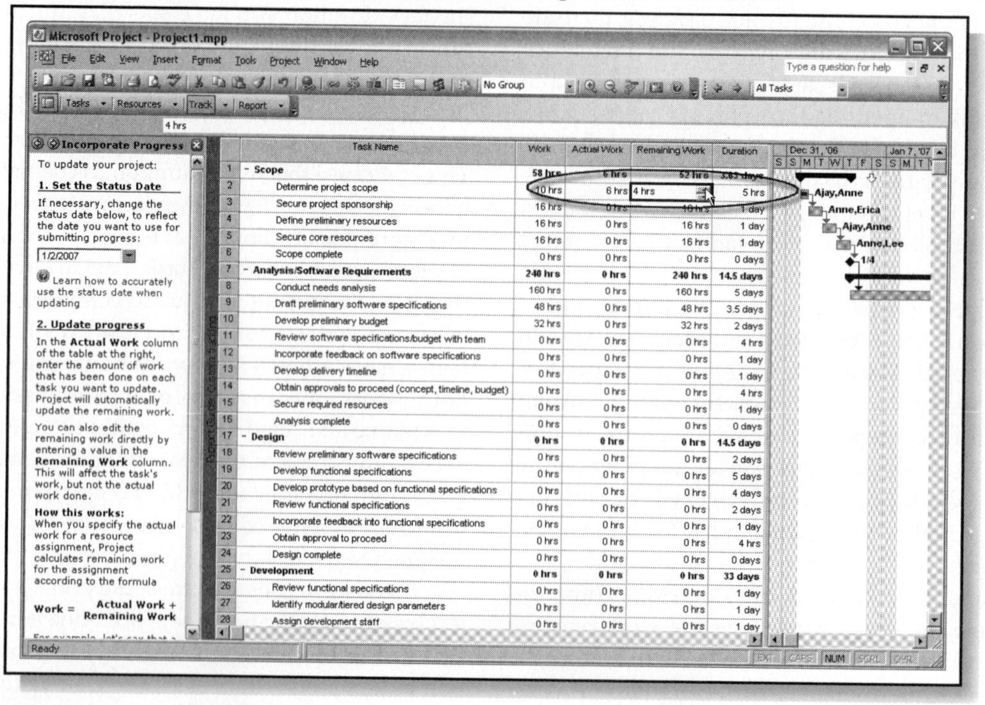

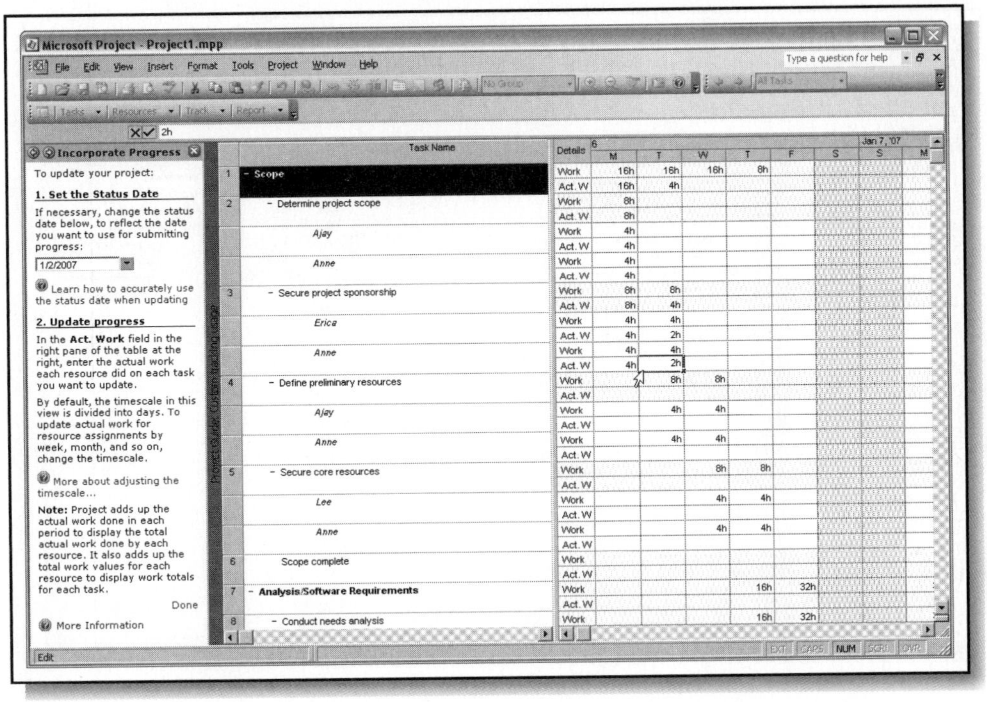

Figure A.68   Tracking progress by entering number of hours worked

and each resource under each task (see Figure A.68). In the calendar pane at the right, each resource will have the estimated work to be done entered in each "Work" row for each task. To incorporate progress information, enter actual hours worked for each resource in the "Act. W" row of each resource for each task. In the example in Figure A.68, on Monday, each task has been completed in the number of hours estimated. Notice, however, that on Tuesday Erica and Anne have only completed 2 hours each on the Secure Project Sponsorship task.

Checking Progress

Now that you have begun entering progress information, Project can indicate which tasks are on schedule, which are not, and which have already been completed. To check the progress of your project, click on the "Check the progress of the project" link from the Track pane to open the Check Progress pane (see Figure A.69). As with entering tracking information, you will select a status date for which to check the progress of the project. Depending on the tracking information you entered in the previous steps and the status date you have chosen, Project will indicate which tasks have been completed, which are on schedule, and which are

behind schedule, or late, with icons in the Status Indicator column.

Making Changes

Once you have begun tracking the progress of your project, you may find situations where you need to make changes to the project plan. Microsoft Project allows you to make task duration, work, and resource assignment changes in one central place. To make any changes, click on the "Make changes to the project" link in the Track pane to open the Change Project pane (see Figure A.70). Because task duration, work, and resource assignments are all interrelated, changes made to one may impact the others, so be aware of the possible impacts that any change you make can have on other aspects of the project (see the Controlling Changes instructions in Figure A.70).

Now that you have begun to enter in project progress information and have begun to track the status of your project, you might find that the Tracking Gantt Chart view allows you to see at a glance how your project is progressing. In Figure A.71 we can easily see that the Scope summary task is almost complete by noticing the hash marks beneath the summary task indicator. We can also easily see which tasks have been

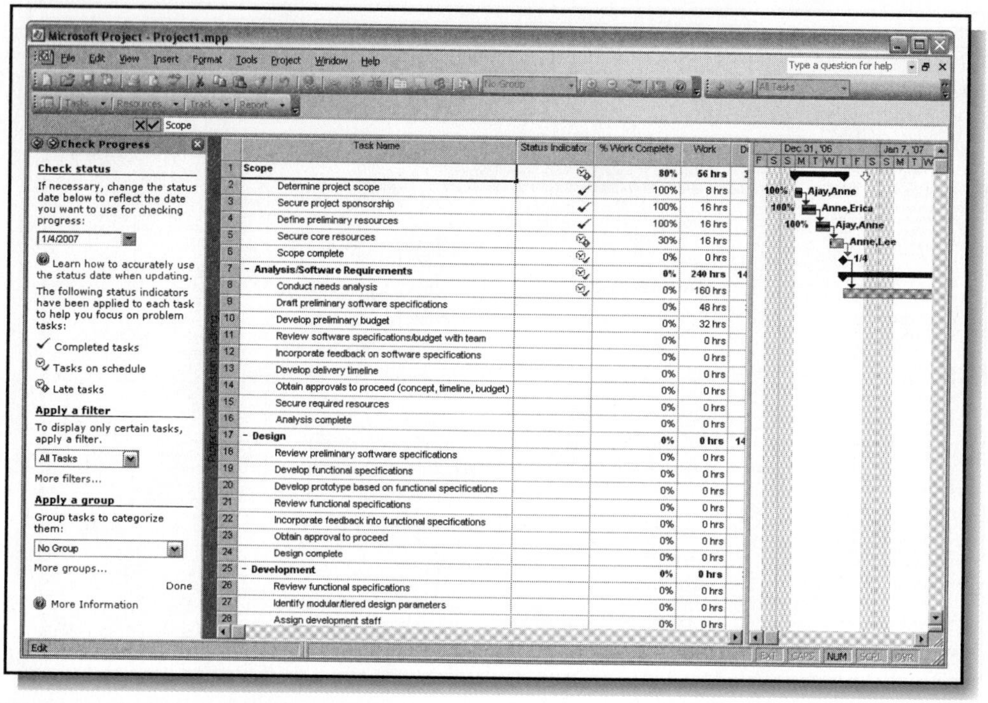

Figure A.69 Checking progress

Figure A.70 Making changes

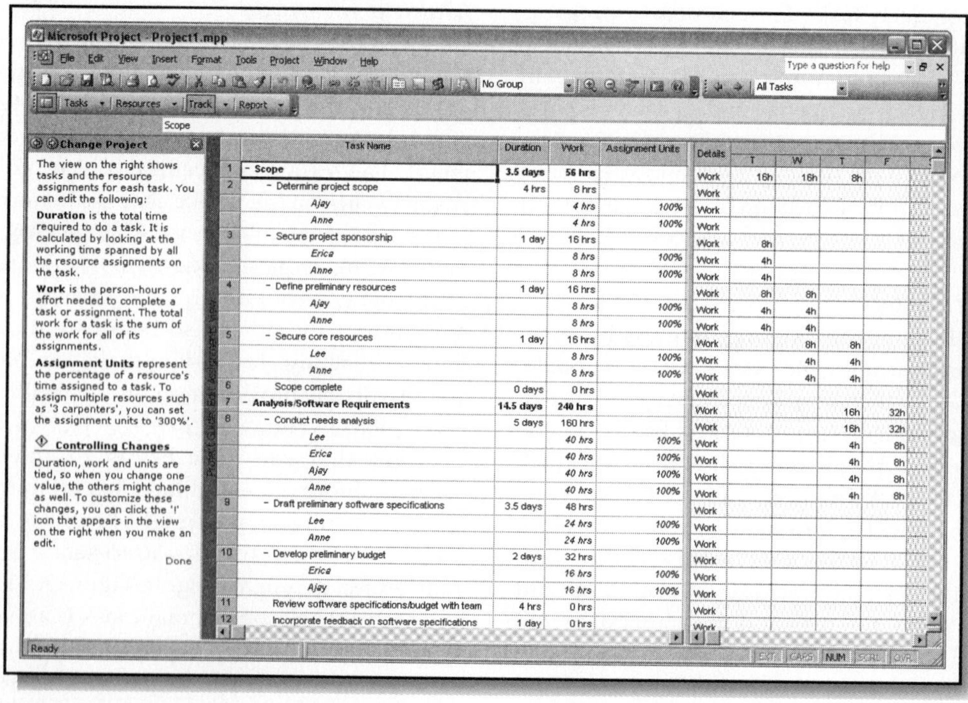

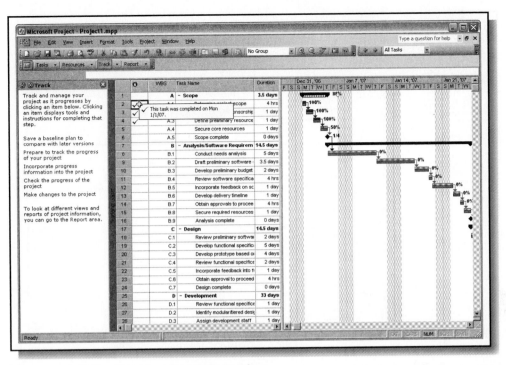

Figure A.71 Tracking Gantt chart view

completed by the check marks located in the first column of the task entry table. Notice that the bar for each task is split horizontally with the black bar on the bottom and a colored bar on top. The black bar indicates the baseline plan, and the colored bar indicates the actual progress made for the project. In the example in Figure A.71, no changes have been made yet to the project plan relative to the baseline plan. Also notice that once a task has been completed, it is no longer considered a critical path task and reverts to a blue bar on the Gantt chart.

The Report Pane

With the incorporation of tracking information into your Project file, you are now in a position to begin reporting your project's progress to stakeholders regarding a number of project criteria. To begin analyzing and reporting project information using the Project Guide, click on the Report button in the Project Guide toolbar to open the Report pane. Many of the choices in the Report pane we have addressed above, such as "Change the look or content of the Gantt chart" link. If you click on this link, you will be prompted to use the Gantt chart wizard, which we used to show the critical path. Clicking on the "Print current view as a report"

link allows you to print the view that you have active on the screen. The options in the Print Current View pane allow you to shrink your entire project to fit onto one page or to change the settings to allow it to print across multiple pages. The "Compare progress against baseline work" link changes the current view to the Tracking Gantt chart view, and the "See the project's critical tasks" link changes the Gantt chart to show the critical path.

The key feature in the Report pane is the "Select a view or report" link. Click on that link to open the Views and Reports pane. Two options are available, either to change the view (which was covered with the View Menu discussion earlier), or to print a report (see Figure A.72).

To select a report to print out, click on the radio button next to the "Print a project report" option in the Views and Reports pane to open the Reports dialog box (see Figure A.73).

From the Reports dialog box, you can choose from 22 or more types of reports to print. Each choice in the Reports dialog box opens another dialog box with up to 6 reports to choose from (see Figure A.74).

The Custom reports option gives you the opportunity to make minor changes to any of the report options in the five previous choices. For example, if you wanted

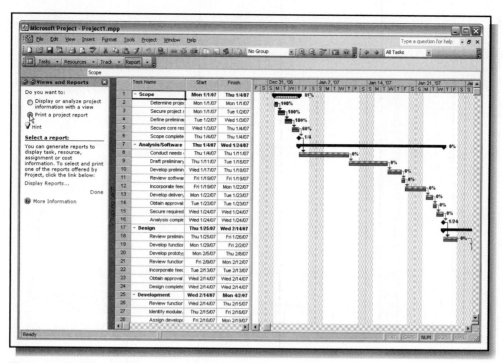

Figure A.72 Options in the Views and Reports pane

to show the resources associated with each task in the Earned Value report, you could make those changes in the Custom reports dialog box. To see the Earned Value report as Project prints it, from the Costs option in the Reports dialog box, click on the Earned Value choice and then click on the Select button to open the Print Preview dialog box (see Figure A.75).

Notice that Microsoft Project uses labels for the key values in an Earned Value report that might be slightly different than those sometimes employed in

Figure A.73 Reports dialog box

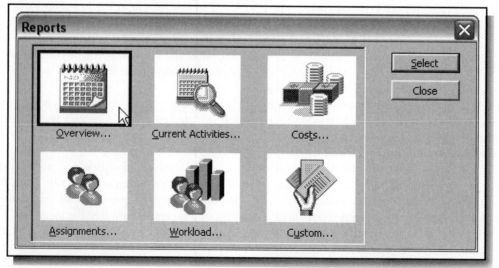

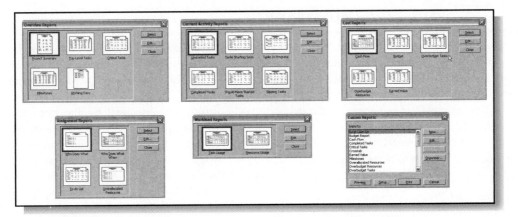

Figure A.74 Reports to choose from

![Microsoft Project - Project1.mpp]

Earned Value as of Tue 5/30/06
Project1.mpp

ID	Task Name	BCWS	BCWP	ACWP	SV	CV	EAC
2	Determine project scope	$236.00	$236.00	$236.00	$0.00	$0.00	$236.00
3	Secure project sponsorship	$496.00	$496.00	$496.00	$0.00	$0.00	$496.00
4	Define preliminary resources	$472.00	$472.00	$472.00	$0.00	$0.00	$472.00
5	Secure core resources	$456.00	$273.60	$273.60	($182.40)	$0.00	$456.00
6	Scope complete	$0.00	$0.00	$0.00	$0.00	$0.00	$0.00
8	Conduct needs analysis	$456.00	$0.00	$0.00	($456.00)	$0.00	$4,560.00
9	Draft preliminary software specification	$0.00	$0.00	$0.00	$0.00	$0.00	$1,368.00
10	Develop preliminary budget	$0.00	$0.00	$0.00	$0.00	$0.00	$912.00
11	Review software specifications/budget	$0.00	$0.00	$0.00	$0.00	$0.00	$0.00
12	Incorporate feedback on software spec	$0.00	$0.00	$0.00	$0.00	$0.00	$0.00
13	Develop delivery timeline	$0.00	$0.00	$0.00	$0.00	$0.00	$0.00
14	Obtain approvals to proceed (concept,	$0.00	$0.00	$0.00	$0.00	$0.00	$0.00
15	Secure required resources	$0.00	$0.00	$0.00	$0.00	$0.00	$0.00
16	Analysis complete	$0.00	$0.00	$0.00	$0.00	$0.00	$0.00
18	Review preliminary software specificati	$0.00	$0.00	$0.00	$0.00	$0.00	$0.00
19	Develop functional specifications	$0.00	$0.00	$0.00	$0.00	$0.00	$0.00
20	Develop prototype based on functional	$0.00	$0.00	$0.00	$0.00	$0.00	$0.00
21	Review functional specifications	$0.00	$0.00	$0.00	$0.00	$0.00	$0.00
22	Incorporate feedback into functional sp	$0.00	$0.00	$0.00	$0.00	$0.00	$0.00
23	Obtain approval to proceed	$0.00	$0.00	$0.00	$0.00	$0.00	$0.00
24	Design complete	$0.00	$0.00	$0.00	$0.00	$0.00	$0.00
26	Review functional specifications	$0.00	$0.00	$0.00	$0.00	$0.00	$0.00
27	Identify modular/tiered design paramet	$0.00	$0.00	$0.00	$0.00	$0.00	$0.00
28	Assign development staff	$0.00	$0.00	$0.00	$0.00	$0.00	$0.00
29	Develop code	$0.00	$0.00	$0.00	$0.00	$0.00	$0.00
30	Developer testing (primary debugging)	$0.00	$0.00	$0.00	$0.00	$0.00	$0.00
31	Development complete	$0.00	$0.00	$0.00	$0.00	$0.00	$0.00
33	Develop unit test plans using product s	$0.00	$0.00	$0.00	$0.00	$0.00	$0.00
34	Develop integration test plans using pr	$0.00	$0.00	$0.00	$0.00	$0.00	$0.00
36	Review modular code	$0.00	$0.00	$0.00	$0.00	$0.00	$0.00
37	Test component modules to product sp	$0.00	$0.00	$0.00	$0.00	$0.00	$0.00
38	Identify anomalies to product specifica	$0.00	$0.00	$0.00	$0.00	$0.00	$0.00
39	Modify code	$0.00	$0.00	$0.00	$0.00	$0.00	$0.00
40	Re-test modified code	$0.00	$0.00	$0.00	$0.00	$0.00	$0.00
41	Unit testing complete	$0.00	$0.00	$0.00	$0.00	$0.00	$0.00
43	Test module integration	$0.00	$0.00	$0.00	$0.00	$0.00	$0.00
44	Identify anomalies to specifications	$0.00	$0.00	$0.00	$0.00	$0.00	$0.00

Page: 1 of 4   Size: 2 rows by 2 columns

Figure A.75 Earned Value report

other project documentation. Both types of labels were also identified and explained in the textbook. The following table gives their equivalents.

COMMONLY USED NOTATIONS		MICROSOFT PROJECT LABEL
PV	=	BCWS
EV	=	BCWP
AC	=	ACWP
CV	=	CV
SV	=	SV
EAC	=	EAC
BAC	=	BAC
BAC − EAC	=	VAC

Also notice that the report spans several pages. The bar at the bottom of the window notes, "Page 1 of 4; Size: 2 rows by 2 columns." Also notice the arrow buttons at the top left of the window. These buttons allow you to switch to adjacent pages in the report.

We have presented the Earned Value report here as an example of the many reports available in Microsoft Project. Later, you can explore and become familiar with the many other available reports.

APPENDIX SUMMARY

Become familiar with Microsoft Project. Microsoft Project shares some common elements with other Microsoft Office titles, so it should be somewhat familiar. Major screen elements were noted and explained. The various Help options were discussed, along with additional Online content settings. Project also provides several view options with which to see various aspects of the project.

Enter tasks, estimate task durations, and sequence tasks in Microsoft Project. The Project Guide feature of Microsoft Project makes entering tasks to develop a WBS simple. Once some of the project's parameters, such as the estimated start date and project working times, are set, you can enter tasks directly into the task entry pane. After entering the tasks, you can have Microsoft Project number each of the tasks based on your organization's WBS numbering convention. Once your WBS is set, you can begin entering the estimated durations of the tasks and you can schedule the tasks relative to each other by setting their dependencies. After the tasks have been scheduled, you can also set constraints on the tasks and change the Gantt chart view to show the critical path.

Enter resources and assign resources. Now that the tasks have been scheduled, it is time to specify the resources for the project. This involves identifying each resource, and for human resources, specifying their working rates and working times. Material resources are also identified and entered with two additional columns; the Type column that identifies them as "Work" or "Material" resources, and the material label column. Once all the resources have

been specified for the project, it is time to assign resources to tasks. Microsoft Project computes the number of hours of work needed to complete the task in the task's scheduled duration by multiplying the duration of the task by the percentage of work assigned to the task. After the first assignment of resources to the tasks, if any subsequent resource assignments occur, Microsoft Project prompts you to decide whether to shorten the duration of the task, increase the amount of work to complete the task, or keep both the duration and work constant by decreasing the number of hours worked by the resources assigned. Microsoft Project provides several views with which to see and manage resources during a project.

Track project progress. Microsoft Project provides many options for tracking the progress of your project. Once your plan is entered (tasks scheduled and resources assigned), you can save the plan as a baseline plan against which all progress is compared. You must decide how to enter progress, and then progress can be incorporated into the plan. If changes need to be made, Project provides a central place for making them to the schedule and/or resources.

Report project status. Microsoft Project contains a wide variety of reporting options to facilitate communication with stakeholders. The various reports are grouped into six main options—Overview, Current Activities, Costs, Assignments, Workload, and Custom. Each main grouping contains a variety of reports to choose from that can easily be printed directly from Microsoft Project.

INDEX